Corrections

Corrections: Foundations for the Future

Second Edition

by Jeanne B. Stinchcomb
Florida Atlantic University

THE AUTHOR'S PURPOSE

"This book was written for one purpose only . . . to be read. That may sound extremely basic, even superficial. But in today's world of video games, text-messaging, television, and countless other forms of electronic stimulation, reading seems to be a vanishing practice.

Motivating contemporary generations to read a 600-page textbook has thus become a creative challenge. It demands engaging dialogue, controversial positions, stimulating graphics, real-life stories, and meaningful photos. These, however, are only the beginning blocks for writing a book that will engage readers and hold their interest.

When readers are engaged, they are continually learning, which is best facilitated by a comprehensive, organized approach. Narrative must therefore be combined with supporting materials into a well-integrated overall product. In other words, learning goals motivate, narrative enlightens, photos and graphics illustrate, close-up stories entertain, and discussion questions enliven. Each has a closely connected functional purpose, designed to blend into a seamlessly unified learning experience. And ultimately, the test questions I have prepared link directly with each learning goal, measuring the extent to which expected outcomes have actually been achieved.

But that is just the structure. It is the content that is most enticing. Few subjects are more fascinating—but also more frustrating—than corrections. And in the end, there is no one with a greater stake in its success or failure than each and every one of us. Enjoy this journey through the correctional conglomerate. Sit back and do some old-fashioned reading."

Jeanne B. Stinchcomb
Florida Atlantic University

5 WAYS THIS BOOK IS ORIGINAL AND OUTSTANDING

1. Written by a master teacher with over a decade of experience in federal, state, and local justice agencies, this is the most comprehensive, yet affordable corrections text on the market. Students will like everything about it—from the reasonable cost to the user-friendly narrative that keeps them engaged.

2. Uses measurable learning goals that are placed strategically throughout all chapters and which are easy to locate and reference (see, for example, pp. 22, 24, 31, 40, but also throughout the text).

3. Provides objective discussions of widely-varying points of view so that students can analyze facts and make informed decisions. See, for example, the coverage of:

   - the necessity for treatment as well as custody (pp. 14, 18–19, 40–43, 94–95, 114–116)
   - the details of restorative as well as retributive justice (pp. 14–19, 32–34, 485–487)
   - the development of private as well as public correctional facilities (pp. 137–166, 466–475)
   - the challenges of jails as well as prisons (pp. 124–135, 475–483)
   - the use of community-based alternatives along with custodial confinement (pp. 77–102)
   - the rights as well as restrictions of those behind bars (pp. 424–460)
   - the needs of mainstream as well as special offender populations (pp. 167–198, 359–395)
   - the support for and opposition to capital punishment (pp. 449–456).

4. Devotes an entire chapter to the correctional workforce (pp. 396–423) which gives students insights into the challenges as well as rewards of such employment.

5. **Companion Website:** Unique to authors of texts in corrections, Jeanne B. Stinchcomb has written all her own instructor support material, including more than 500 superb objective and essay test questions (keyed to the text's learning goals), PowerPoint lectures, as well as annotated web links and teaching tips for *every* chapter of her book, all based on her extensive teaching career, previous correctional experience, and ongoing research. The Companion Website can be accessed at www.routledge.com/textbooks/9780415873338

   For more information on this title go to www.routledge.com/books/details/9780415873338/

ALSO AVAILABLE

Customizable Content: *Any* portion of this text may be *custom selected* by instructors, ordering only that amount of text specified (in digital, or print, or both versions) *regardless of student enrollment size*, with pricing *proportionate* to the number of pages selected. This service is available from the publisher's partner University Readers. To learn more, go to http://routledge.customgateway.com/routledge-criminal-justice/corrections.html

Criminology and Justice Studies Series

Edited by **Chester Britt**, *Northeastern University*, **Shaun L. Gabbidon**, *Penn State Harrisburg*, and **Nancy Rodriguez**, *Arizona State University*

Criminology and Justice Studies offers works that make both intellectual and stylistic innovations in the study of crime and criminal justice. The goal of the series is to publish works that model the best scholarship and thinking in the criminology and criminal justice field today, but in a style that connects that scholarship to a wider audience including advanced undergraduates, graduate students, and the general public. The works in this series help fill the gap between academic monographs and ·encyclopedic textbooks by making innovative scholarship accessible to a large audience without the superficiality of many texts.

Books in the Series

Published:

Biosocial Criminology: New Directions in Theory and Research edited by Anthony Walsh and Kevin M. Beaver
Community Policing in America by Jeremy M. Wilson
Criminal Justice Theory: Explaining the Nature and Behavior of Criminal Justice edited by David E. Duffee and Edward R. Maguire
Lifers: Seeking Redemption in Prison by John Irwin
Race, Law and American Society: 1607 to Present by Gloria J. Browne-Marshall
Today's White Collar Crime by Hank J. Brightman
White Collar Crime: Opportunity Perspectives by Michael Benson and Sally Simpson
The New Criminal Justice: American Communities and the Changing World of Crime Control by John Klofas, Natalie Hipple, and Edmund McGarrell
The Policing of Terrorism: Organizational and Global Perspectives by Mathieu Deflem
Criminological Perspectives in Race and Crime, 2/e by Shaun Gabbidon

Forthcoming:

Crime and the Lifecourse by Michael Benson
Crime Emergence: Reducing Uncertainty in Theory and Research by Christopher Sullivan, Jean McGloin, and Les Kennedy
Criminal Justice Research by Brian Withrow
Experiencing Criminal Justice: Practitioners' and Outsiders' Perspectives of Policing, Courts, and Corrections edited by Heith Copes and Mark Pogrebin
Race, Racism, and Crime: A Theory of African American Offending by Shaun Gabbidon and James Unnever

Titles of Related Interest

Published:

Regression Analysis for the Social Sciences by Rachel Gordon
GIS and Spatial Analysis for the Social Sciences by Robert Parker and Emily Asencio
Social Statistics: The Basics and Beyond by Thomas Linneman·

Forthcoming:

Graduate Social Statistics by Rachel Gordon
Crime and Terrorism Risk: Studies in Criminology and Criminal Justice by Les Kennedy and Edmund McGarrell

Corrections

Foundations for the Future

Second Edition

Jeanne B. Stinchcomb
Florida Atlantic University

Routledge
Taylor & Francis Group

NEW YORK AND LONDON

First edition published 2005
by American Correctional Association
This edition published 2011
by Routledge
270 Madison Avenue, New York, NY 10016

Simultaneously published in the UK
by Routledge
2 Park Square, Milton Park, Abingdon, Oxon OX14 4RN

Routledge is an imprint of the Taylor & Francis Group, an informa business

Typeset in ITC Stone Serif by RefineCatch Limited, Bungay, Suffolk
Printed and bound in the United States of America on acid-free paper by
Edwards Brothers, Inc.

Library of Congress Cataloging in Publication Data
Stinchcomb, Jeanne B.
  Corrections : foundations for the future / Jeanne B. Stinchcomb.
    p. cm.—(Criminology and justice studies series)
  1. Corrections—United States.   2. Corrections—United States—History.   I. Title.
  HV9471.S834 2011
  365'.973—dc22   2010032539

ISBN 13: 978–0–415–87333–8 (pbk)
ISBN 13: 978–0–203–83158–8 (ebk)

Reflecting the past . . . Reporting the present . . . Rebuilding the future . . .

To everyone who has offered inspiration to someone without a dream, guidance to someone without direction, encouragement to someone without hope. For without you there would be no change. And without change there can be no correction.

Jeanne B. Stinchcomb

Brief Contents

Detailed Contents

PART 3
CORRECTIONAL INSTITUTIONS: CUSTODY, TREATMENT,
CONFINEMENT, AND RELEASE

Preface

As this book was headed to press, virtually every economic indicator in the U.S. was scraping rock bottom. The news was becoming dimmer each day: skyrocketing unemployment rates, widespread mortgage foreclosures, massive investment losses, and record numbers of personal bankruptcies. Suddenly, hundreds of thousands of Americans were no longer basking in the former security of full-time work. Even retirees who had counted on hard-earned "nest eggs" often found themselves back in the marketplace, desperately competing with younger applicants in search of scarce jobs. Many others postponed the luxury of retirement in the face of needs ranging from health insurance to pin money. Some prisons even closed their doors—and not for lack of inmates. For everyone who had been taking economic security for granted, it was a very loud wake-up call.

In times like these, we are all reminded that most of us are just a few paychecks away from financial destitution. But it is those who are at the brink of desperation who are affected the most. Many of them are already clients of the "correctional conglomerate," personally experiencing the devastating impact of this country's "out of sight, out of mind" approach to social problems.

In our intensity to remove anyone who offends us from free society, we have created overcrowded correctional facilities, confronted legal impediments, and encountered fiscal dilemmas. As a result, prisons and jails have suffered from the repercussions of unplanned releases, "no frills" policies, and scaled-back programming. Since it is one of the largest components of most state budgets, corrections is always a visible target when tax revenues nosedive. As the director of corrections in a state with a deficit in the billions of dollars put it, "You don't save that kind of money by cutting back on toilet paper!" But how much are we really saving by curtailing everything from drug treatment to vocational training? Surely this is a prime example of how short-term cutbacks incur long-term costs.

Nevertheless, a textbook is not the place for taking sides. Whatever the topic, readers deserve to have an objective discussion of all points of view in order to analyze the facts and make informed decisions. Thus, in these upcoming chapters, you will find comprehensive coverage of the:

- necessity for treatment as well as custody;

- details of restorative as well as retributive justice;

- development of private as well as public correctional facilities;

- challenges of jails as well as prisons;

- use of community-based alternatives along with custodial confinement;

- rights as well as restrictions of those behind bars;

- needs of mainstream as well as special offender populations;

- support for and opposition to capital punishment;

- current trends as well as future challenges facing the correctional conglomerate.

Balancing the pros and cons, controversial issues are tackled—from pretrial release to three strikes legislation, inmate amenities, truth in sentencing, speculative prisons, electronic monitoring, boot camps, home furloughs, and even the use of condoms behind bars. Additionally, contemporary challenges that are transforming the field today are discussed, including:

- high-tech innovations—from ground-penetrating radar to telemedicine, smart cards, retinal image scanning, satellite surveillance, and variable threat lasers;

- proactive approaches for reducing crowding, controlling inmates, eliminating prison rape, and managing officer stress;

- what works in correctional treatment—from cognitive restructuring to therapeutic communities;

- current trends in staff certification, workforce development, vicarious liability, correctional administration, and visionary leadership.

Beyond its wide-ranging contents, this book is written with a style that combines passion, insight, and objective analysis of both sides of every issue. It also incorporates proven concepts of instructional design, with such unique features as:

- measurable learning outcomes that are placed strategically throughout the chapters;

- presentation of material in a "building-block" method designed to sequentially enhance learning;

- "Close-up on Corrections" boxes that reinforce narrative content with real-life stories (often written by or about inmates and staff);

- realistic insights into virtually every aspect of the correctional conglomerate—from the impact of sentencing policies to the effects of institutional life, difficulties of reentry, and challenges of working in correctional institutions.

As one reviewer said, "this is an exceptional book that captures the contemporary issues driving the field of corrections, the relevant research important to informing policy, and the real life experiences of both the keepers and the kept as they live the reality of our corrections system." To make it widely accessible, electronic versions are available for online and hybrid courses, and the book is customizable in inexpensive paperback form. Additionally, the instructor's manual features numerous extra resources, including annotated websites, teaching tips, PowerPoint slides, and hundreds of high-quality test items all written by the author. This is available on the book's Companion Website, which can be accessed at www. routledge.com/textbooks/9780415873338

As the title of this book reflects, it seeks to establish a firm foundation for the future of corrections by comprehensively reflecting the past, analyzing the present, and projecting the future. In that regard, it is marked by an upbeat optimism that is not generally characteristic of corrections. In a field that society often identifies with past failures, it can become difficult to stay focused on a more promising future, especially when the future is so uncertain.

Like a teetering economy, corrections likewise seems to exist in a state of perpetual imbalance, shifting dramatically between retributive demands and rehabilitative dreams, hopscotching down a meandering path of politically charged minefields. Every so often, one of those mines explodes, policy-makers react, and corrections is left to pick up the pieces. Needless to say, such knee-jerk responses—devoid of either practice-based insights or research-based outcomes—do not represent the best way to advance public policies or refine operational practices. Nevertheless, correctional paradigms in this country have largely been planted in the shifting sands of personal emotion, outspoken opinion, and political backlash. Community-based corrections goes out. Intermediate sanctions come in. Rehabilitation goes out. Incapacitation comes in. Soft-on-crime goes out. Zero tolerance comes in. That is where we have been. The real question remaining, however, is where we are going.

Unlike the victims of oil spills, earthquakes, hurricanes, or other natural disasters, the human disasters that land on correctional doorsteps do not often become front-page headlines. They do not rate presidential visits. They do not qualify for federal assistance. They do not arouse heartfelt public compassion. To the contrary, they are more likely to harden a public already convinced that corrections itself is a misnomer—a public more concerned with how long offenders can be segregated than how well they can be reassimilated. Yet where the challenges are deepest, the rewards are greatest.

Working in such an environment, correctional staff face the monumental challenge of maintaining a positive outlook in the face of overwhelming odds against them. In that respect, they share a lot in common with their clients. Both have a long-term stake in the direction that public policy is heading throughout the remainder of the twenty-first century. But then, so do we all.

Acknowledgments

Writing a book is never a solitary venture, and this one is no exception. From brief insights to boundless efforts, many people contributed to the final product. At the risk of overlooking some, special appreciation is extended to:

- staff of the American Correctional Association, the Bureau of Justice Statistics, and the National Institute of Corrections' Information Center, whose resourceful assistance, timely responses, and ongoing willingness to help were invaluable;

- the American Jail Association—particularly Gwyn Smith-Ingley, executive director, and retired staff member Ken Kerle, for always "being there" whenever dependable advice, capable assistance, or networking contacts were needed;

- Brittany Goldberg, former graduate student in Florida Atlantic University's Criminology and Criminal Justice master's program, whose comprehensive online research capabilities contributed significantly, especially to development of annotated websites in the instructor's guide;

- Susan McCampbell and the many practitioners throughout the country involved with initiatives conducted by the Center for Innovative Public Policy, who provided me with a solid foundation of operational insights and research opportunities that both enriched and enlivened the narrative;

- Leah Babb-Rosenfeld and Steve Rutter at Routledge for their ongoing advice, responsiveness, and patience with me as the manuscript painstakingly emerged;

- the many manuscript reviewers whose positive feedback provided encouraging support, and whose constructive criticism offered guiding visions for improvement, including:

  - Bill Collins, legal trainer and national consultant
  - Michael Coyle, California State University, Chico
  - Susan Craig, University of Central Florida (along with her graduate corrections students)
  - Kathleen Dennehy, Suffolk University

○ Faith Lutze, Washington State University
○ Ken McCreedy, Ferum College
○ Marilyn McShane, University of Houston Downtown
○ Charles Seeley, Portland Community College
○ William Sondervan, University of Maryland, University College
○ Christine Tartaro, Richard Stockton College of New Jersey.

• and, most importantly, Jim Stinchcomb—my professional mentor, personal partner, and perpetual supporter.

While responsibility for the content of this book is mine, recognition of everything from the confidence to write it to the ability to research it belongs to those listed above. Without the assistance of some, it would not have evolved as well. Without the inspiration of one—my husband—it would not have emerged at all.

With sincere admiration for all of your capabilities, and deepest appreciation for applying them to this project.

Jeanne B. Stinchcomb

About the Author

Jeanne B. Stinchcomb is Professor of Criminology and Criminal Justice at Florida Atlantic University in Ft. Lauderdale. With a combination of over 30 years of administrative, educational, and training experience in corrections, she is well-equipped to write on this topic. In fact, her teaching has spanned virtually every adult classroom setting—from universities and community colleges to police and correctional training academies (including the National Institute of Corrections and the California Department of Corrections). Topics she has taught likewise range from introductory corrections courses to graduate-level leadership development, as well as advanced instructional techniques and test design and construction.

Her background additionally includes more than a decade of administrative experience on the staffs of federal, state, and local criminal justice agencies—ranging from the FBI in Washington, DC, to the Miami-Dade Department of Corrections and Rehabilitation. She has also been active in the American Correctional Association, where she chaired the national Commission on Correctional Certification. In partnership with the American Jail Association and the Center for Innovative Public Policies, Dr. Stinchcomb has recently spearheaded national research projects designed to help jails more effectively recruit, retain, and develop the twenty-first-century correctional workforce.

As a result of her significant research contributions to the field of corrections, Dr. Stinchcomb was honored with the Peter Lejins Research Award in 2002. In addition to her two-volume publication on *Stress Management: Performing under Pressure*, her research appears in such publications as *Justice Quarterly, Crime and Delinquency, Journal of Offender Rehabilitation, Criminal Justice Policy Review, American Journal of Criminal Justice, Federal Probation, Public Organization Review, Corrections Today, Corrections Compendium, American Jails*, and *Drug Education, Prevention and Policy*. Overall, her work has been devoted to bringing researchers and practitioners closer together in mutually-beneficial collaboration.

She invites you to send any inquiries, comments, or feedback on *Corrections: Foundations for the Future* to her e-mail address: stinchco@fau.edu.

PART 1

The Nature, Scope, and Function of Corrections

Justice in a democracy demands fair treatment of all citizens, neither ignoring victims nor degrading prisoners.[1]

American Correctional Association

CORRECTIONS IS BOTH FASCINATING AND FRUSTRATING. Changing the direction of an offender's life can be a fulfilling challenge. Helping a juvenile get back on the right track, linking an ex-offender with community resources, getting an alcoholic into treatment, or simply making time in a facility more tolerable for an inmate can all be very personally rewarding experiences. Corrections offers unlimited opportunities for such meaningful contributions—for work that has a purpose and makes a difference.

At the same time, when corrections is ineffective, it can be a frustrating experience. When the same offenders keep reappearing, when budgets are overwhelmed, when no one agrees about what corrections should be doing, when the public is unconcerned and unsupportive, much of the fascination is diminished. Facing such obstacles can create confusion and conflict. It can also provide the potential for change—if obstacles are seen as opportunities.

Certainly, there is considerable opportunity for change in corrections. But before exploring where corrections might be tomorrow, it is essential to determine where this field is today and how it got there. Only with an understanding of the past and the present can we begin to shape the future. Thus Part 1 of this book focuses on an overview of the nature, scope, and function of corrections.

The framework is set in Chapter 1 with a description of what is included in this vast collection of facilities, programs, and services collectively called "corrections." With a better understanding of the correctional conglomerate, Chapter 1 then addresses the public's role in shaping correctional practices. Through conflicting models of policy-making, we realize how correctional practices have changed over time as social opinion has fluctuated.

With this foundation, Chapter 2 explores the impact of sentencing policies on corrections. As sentencing practices have shifted from indeterminate to determinate, we see how the nature of structured sentencing guidelines, truth in sentencing, and similar approaches fulfill crime-related public policies and generate correctional caseloads as well as institutional populations. Since it is society's response to crime that is of greatest concern to corrections, Chapter 2 concludes with a review of the various perspectives that have guided public opinion—from retribution, deterrence, and incapacitation to rehabilitation and reintegration.

Chapter 3 then takes a step back in time to see how corrections evolved over the years. Although we would find it difficult to imagine living in a society without prisons or jails, these have been relatively recent "inventions." The harshness of past punishment practices is described in vivid detail—in contrast to the more humanitarian forces that eventually resulted in the evolution of correctional institutions, the reform movement, and the rehabilitative era. Historical developments conclude with a consideration of how the past has shaped the present, along with a challenge for the future—accommodating demands for punishment without abandoning directions toward positive change. In corrections, it is easy to resign oneself to the frustrations. The challenge is to rekindle the fascinations.

CHAPTER 1

The Correctional Conglomerate

Corrections remains a world almost unknown to law-abiding citizens, and even those within it often know only their own particular corner.[1]
President's Commission on Law Enforcement and Administration of Justice

CHAPTER OVERVIEW

Much of the confusion surrounding corrections and what it should be accomplishing is related to the wide variety of institutions, programs, and services provided within what is broadly viewed as "corrections." This chapter therefore begins by considering just what is included within this vast correctional conglomerate. But even understanding its nature reveals only part of its complexity, for corrections does not operate in isolation. As a component of the criminal justice system, corrections interacts with—and is affected by—both law enforcement and the courts. The criminal justice system, in turn, reflects social policy—as anchored in the executive, legislative, and judicial functions of government.

Policy, in turn, is influenced by the values, opinions, and interests of society. As a public service ultimately responsive to the community, corrections is also subject to various political and social pressures. At times, these have created conflicting expectations, and when society demands public policies that emphasize goals ranging from retribution and punishment to treatment and rehabilitation, it is sometimes difficult to determine exactly what corrections is supposed to be accomplishing. The question therefore becomes not just what corrections is but, more importantly, what it is expected to do. As a member of society, you have not only a personal stake in the answers, but also a role in shaping them.

LEARNING GOALS

Do you know:
1. why corrections can be considered a "conglomerate"?
2. the levels of government at which corrections functions?
3. the differences between prisons and jails, as well as probation and parole?
4. the percentage of inmates under correctional supervision who are confined in custodial institutions, as compared with those under community supervision?
5. the definition of "corrections"?

THE CORRECTIONAL CONGLOMERATE

conglomerate: a complex organization composed of numerous diverse functions.

In private enterprise, a massive business corporation with far-reaching markets, numerous customers, and a vast array of products and services would be called a **conglomerate**. Similarly, a government service composed of as many employees, clients, and diverse activities as corrections can also be considered a conglomerate. The difference between a business conglomerate and corrections is that you have a personal stake in the "profits" or "losses" of corrections—it is *your* tax dollars that support it, citizens in *your* community who are its "customers," and *your* safety that is involved in its success or failure. Moreover, it is through your elected and appointed government officials that the policies, procedures, and future directions of corrections are established. It is therefore in your interest to take a closer look at the correctional conglomerate.

As with any conglomerate, operating the correctional system requires massive fiscal and human resources.

- *What does all of that cost?* Well over $60 billion annually,[2] which is on a par with the national budget of Austria, Taiwan, or Poland.[3] As indicated in Exhibit 1.1, corrections has been receiving a steadily increasing share of total criminal justice resources. In fact, its rate of growth from 1982 to 2003 (423 percent) outpaced both police and the courts. As a result, the correctional conglomerate has been consuming an increasing share of tax dollars—far outpacing the growth of other public services in many states. Second only to Medicaid, corrections has become the fastest-growing general fund expenditure in the U.S.[4] Between 1987 and 2007, for example, total state expenditures on corrections more than doubled.[5] In fact, one state recently made deep cuts in the budget for such essential services

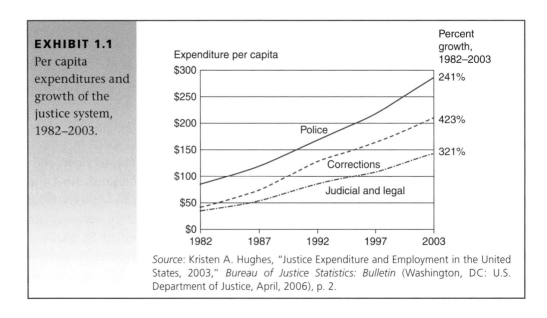

EXHIBIT 1.1
Per capita expenditures and growth of the justice system, 1982–2003.

Source: Kristen A. Hughes, "Justice Expenditure and Employment in the United States, 2003," *Bureau of Justice Statistics: Bulletin* (Washington, DC: U.S. Department of Justice, April, 2006), p. 2.

as mental health and education, while at the same time funding an extra $6 million for its prisons.[6] Experts have been expressing concern that this spending pattern may continue until it hits "critical mass"—the point at which there may be few resources available for anything else.[7]

- *How many people does all of that money employ?* The nearly 750,000 correctional employees throughout the U.S.[8] would populate a large city with people in positions ranging from correctional officers to administrators, social workers, psychologists, psychiatrists, doctors, nurses, lawyers, teachers, counselors, office staff, and maintenance personnel. In fact, just about every professional and support occupation you can name is probably employed somewhere in the correctional conglomerate.

- *Where do all of these employees work?* In the federal government (5 percent), the 50 states (62 percent), and the thousands of municipalities and counties (33 percent) throughout the United States.[9]

- *How many clients does this conglomerate serve?* Picture the combined populations of Baltimore, Dallas, and San Diego. On any given day, an estimated 7.3 million adults are under some form of correctional supervision,[10] which is actually larger than the population of 45 countries.[11] Statistically, of every 31 adults you encounter, one is currently a correctional **client**. Of course, you would need to visit a prison or jail to encounter many of them. But do not mistakenly assume that the majority are confined to secure institutions. Most are not.

client: someone under the care, custody, or control of a correctional agency.

Custodial Institutions

Corrections is easily stereotyped by its most visible physical structures—custodial institutions. For adults, these are **prisons** and **jails**. For juveniles, they are training schools, detention centers, and boot camps. In fact, what do you picture when you hear the word "corrections"? Often, our first thought is of a forbidding-looking gray fortress surrounded by thick concrete walls with rifles protruding from guard towers, where expressionless inmates move in dull routines under the constant supervision of uniformed officers. That is generally the image of corrections portrayed in movies and on television.

prisons: state or federal correctional institutions that confine those serving sentences of longer than one year.

But, of all adult inmates housed in correctional institutions throughout the U.S., only about one-third are serving time in such *maximum-security* prisons.[12] Far more inmates are confined to *medium-security* institutions—where wire fencing replaces concrete walls, armed towers are nonexistent, and inmate supervision is less intense. The lowest-risk offenders, who can be trusted with more freedom, are serving their sentences or preparing for parole in *minimum-security* facilities such as halfway houses, which bear no more resemblance to a prison than a dormitory or an apartment building.

jails: local correctional institutions that primarily confine those awaiting trial or serving sentences of less than one year.

In addition to being distinguished by their level of security, correctional facilities function within all three levels of government: *local, state*, and *federal*. The private sector also provides correctional services and now operates a sizeable number of custodial institutions. But corrections is primarily a function of state government. States are responsible for the operation of *prisons*, where inmates serving time in excess of one year are generally confined. Those convicted of federal crimes who are sentenced to a year or more serve their time in federal prisons. However, there are far fewer federal (102) than state (1,719) prisons in the United States.[13]

In contrast to prisons, *local jails* traditionally hold those serving sentences of less than one year, as well as unconvicted arrestees awaiting trial. These are generally suspects who either cannot make bail or are determined to be a potential threat to the community if released. Those who are denied some type of pretrial release—while still innocent in the eyes of the law—remain confined pending trial.

Such unconvicted offenders make up about 63 percent of the population of local jails.[14] This means that nearly half a million technically innocent people are incarcerated throughout the country, and the longer their trials are delayed, the longer they remain incarcerated. Although many such inmates are of sufficient danger to the community to justify their confinement, it does point out that a sizeable number of inmates enter local correctional systems before a formal finding of guilt or innocence by the courts. (While the federal government also incarcerates those awaiting trial or serving short sentences, federal jails are usually called either federal detention centers or metropolitan correctional centers.)

There are considerably more local jails (3,168)[15] than state and federal prisons combined (1,821). But ironically there are fewer inmates confined in local jails (785,556) than in state and federal prisons (1,610,584).[16] Although jails are more numerous, they are smaller facilities designed to hold fewer offenders.

Noncustodial Alternatives

To find most clients of the correctional conglomerate, however, you would not look behind bars. Of all adults who are under some form of correctional supervision, almost *three out of four are not confined in prison or jail*.[17] As Exhibit 1.2 illustrates, the

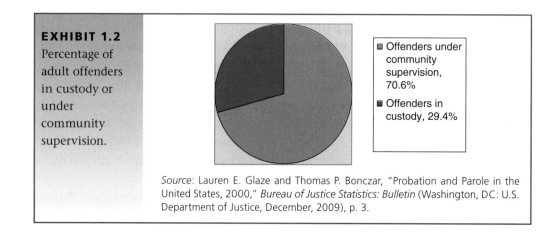

EXHIBIT 1.2
Percentage of adult offenders in custody or under community supervision.

- Offenders under community supervision, 70.6%
- Offenders in custody, 29.4%

Source: Lauren E. Glaze and Thomas P. Bonczar, "Probation and Parole in the United States, 2000," *Bureau of Justice Statistics: Bulletin* (Washington, DC: U.S. Department of Justice, December, 2009), p. 3.

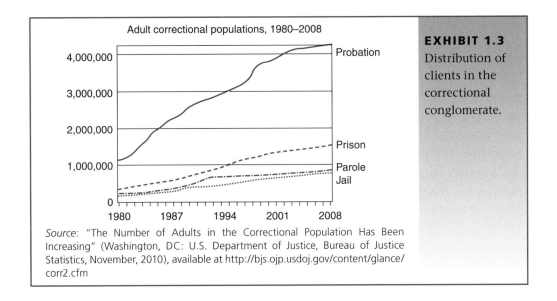

EXHIBIT 1.3
Distribution of clients in the correctional conglomerate.

Adult correctional populations, 1980–2008

Source: "The Number of Adults in the Correctional Population Has Been Increasing" (Washington, DC: U.S. Department of Justice, Bureau of Justice Statistics, November, 2010), available at http://bjs.ojp.usdoj.gov/content/glance/corr2.cfm

vast majority (over 70 percent) are actually serving their sentence in the community through such noncustodial alternatives as probation or parole. This certainly dispels any notion that corrections is limited to those serving time in secure confinement.

Offenders under **community supervision** are predominately either on probation or on parole. As the largest providers of correctional services, probation is a sentence offered as an alternative to going *to* an institution, whereas parole is early release offered as an alternative to remaining *in* an institution. Both enable the offender to serve time in the community rather than in a correctional facility. But probation is a sentencing option used by the courts, whereas parole is an administrative decision to conditionally release an inmate from prison following a period of confinement.

community supervision: services, programs, or facilities provided within the community to offenders who are not incarcerated.

Despite the fact that such noncustodial alternatives as probation and parole are not the most visible part of corrections, they represent the majority of the correctional conglomerate. Probationers are by far the largest population served by corrections, as shown in Exhibit 1.3. And, even though several states have abolished it, over 800,000 adults are still on parole.[18] Moreover, noncustodial alternatives are not limited to probation and parole. Other offenders are paying fines, making **restitution**, or performing community service in lieu of incarceration.

Corrections also encompasses criminal suspects who are released from jail after arrest on their formal promise to appear at trial. Growing numbers of these pretrial releasees are being electronically monitored while under "house arrest" during specified curfew hours. Nor are such noncustodial alternatives limited to adults.

restitution: monetary payment or the rendering of services by a convicted offender to compensate for criminal behavior.

Juvenile Programs and Facilities

The correctional conglomerate likewise includes juveniles released prior to adjudication, housed in detention, or participating in many residential and nonresidential treatment programs. Juvenile correctional services are provided at the local and state levels of government, along with considerable involvement of the private sector.

Like their adult counterparts, most youths are not confined primarily in secure institutions. There are far fewer juveniles in locked-down custodial institutions and detention centers than there are on probation or in alternative community-based programs and facilities.[19]

This does not mean that many children are not dealt with as severely as adults, and in some cases perhaps more severely. Unlike its adult counterpart, the juvenile correctional system embraces a wider clientele. It includes both *delinquents* (whose offenses would be considered crimes if they were older) and *status offenders* (whose activities are considered illegal only because of their age), as well as children voluntarily admitted by their parents, and in some cases can even extend to those who are dependent or neglected. Although corrections does not have jurisdiction over court dispositions, there have been trends in recent years toward dealing more harshly with serious delinquents involved in violent crime, while removing from secure confinement those whose behavior poses no obvious threat to society.

Corrections Defined

Although the specific functions of the correctional conglomerate vary in different parts of the country, in general corrections encompasses the following custodial institutions and noncustodial, community-based alternatives:

- *Custodial institutions:*

  - *jails:* local correctional institutions for those awaiting trial or serving short sentences (usually medium-security);

  - *prisons:* state or federal correctional institutions for those serving sentences longer than one year (usually medium- or maximum-/close-security);

  - *other (less secure) facilities:* local, state, or federal facilities for low-risk offenders serving sentences or preparing for parole, such as halfway houses;

  - *juvenile detention centers:* local or state facilities confining juvenile defendants prior to adjudication;

  - *training schools and secure institutions:* local, state, or private custodial facilities confining adjudicated juvenile offenders.

- *Noncustodial alternatives:*

  - *pretrial release programs:* alternatives to incarceration for those awaiting trial;

  - *probation:* a conditional sentence that is served under supervision in the community;

- *parole (or mandatory supervised release):* conditional release after serving time in prison;

- *other community-based programs:* restitution, community service, community treatment programs, electronic monitoring, and similar noncustodial alternatives;

- *group homes and juvenile treatment programs:* residential and nonresidential alternatives to secure confinement for juveniles.

As this listing illustrates, responsibilities of the correctional conglomerate extend from violent criminals in maximum security to far less serious offenders serving time in community-based facilities, from unconvicted suspects awaiting trial in jail to convicted offenders on probation or home confinement, and from adult offenders on parole to children in juvenile detention. Given these diverse, wide-ranging

EXHIBIT 1.4
Although we tend to envision the stark reality of prisons and jails when we think of corrections, most clients of the correctional conglomerate are actually beyond the barbed wire, under some form of supervision in the community.

functions, it becomes apparent that corrections is accountable for the care, custody, and control of offenders through either confinement or noninstitutional alternatives. In this context, control encompasses not only incapacitation, but also the multitude of treatment activities directed toward changing behavior and, ultimately, replacing *correctional* control with *self*-control.

Thus corrections can be defined as *the combination of public and private services with legal authority to provide for the care, custody, and control of those accused or convicted of a crime or status offense.* How effectively is that authority used? How well are care, custody, and control provided? Who are those accused or convicted of an offense? As in any human endeavor, there are no simple answers, but all of these topics will be addressed as we explore the correctional conglomerate in greater detail, discovering its fascinations as well as its frustrations.

GOVERNMENT, SOCIETY, AND CORRECTIONS

The workload of corrections is determined by other components of the justice system, as well as government practices and social values in general. The police can decide whether or not to make an arrest. Judges can decide whether or not to incarcerate an offender and, if so, for what period of time. But corrections cannot decide which clients to accept and has limited influence over how long they will remain under correctional supervision.

The policies, procedures, and practices of the entire justice system have a significant impact on corrections. As with the assembly line that produces an inferior product when something goes wrong along the way, much of the success or failure of corrections is dependent on the entire criminal justice system, as well as the governmental structure within which it operates and the citizens who determine its policies.

To assure that no one branch becomes so powerful as to endanger the rights and freedoms guaranteed by the Constitution, government in the United States is divided into legislative, judicial, and executive functions. Corrections is part of the executive branch of government. Just as an executive in private enterprise manages the operations of a company, correctional officials manage the day-to-day operations of government that are related to implementing the sanctions decreed by the courts (although jails also confine suspects prior to trial).

The executive branch is further divided into local, state, and federal levels of government, which means that correctional facilities operate only within specific jurisdictions. For example, jails represent the local branch of corrections; prisons operate at the state level; and the federal government maintains both detention centers and prisons for federal offenders.

Jurisdictional Separation and Functional Fragmentation

As might be expected, these divisions of government by function and jurisdiction have both benefits and drawbacks. On the one hand, they bring government closer to the people and provide checks and balances to assure that no one agency becomes too powerful. But, on the other hand, they foster **jurisdictional separation** and **functional fragmentation**—that is, lack of cooperation, insufficient coordination, and even territorial rivalries. Like the loyal employee of one company who views outside firms and competitors in other territories as rivals, employees of criminal justice agencies may tend to view others in the system with suspicion and mistrust.

Fragmentation of the criminal justice system is not unlike the fragmentation that can occur within a family as parents and children pursue conflicting activities—when everyone is operating on different schedules, when no one takes time to listen, when everyone believes that their own interests are most important, or when no one works to keep everyone together as a unit. Similarly, a system becomes fragmented when its parts function independently, becoming isolated from each other. In criminal justice, each component serves different clients, performs different functions, and pursues different directions, often working at cross-purposes. Yet, as with a dysfunctional family, the actions of each affect those of the others.

In large part, this lack of coordination results from the autonomy that was purposely built into each component of the justice system. The police, courts, and corrections have separate and distinct missions, which are at times almost contradictory. Each has separate budgets, personnel, physical facilities, missions, and policies. They often compete with each other for scarce resources. Yet the actions of each have ripple effects throughout the "system," as illustrated in the "Close-up on Corrections" that follows. Although Pleasantville is a fictitious community, the scenario in this "Close-up" illustrates the all-too-real domino effect of one component of the system on the others.

jurisdictional separation: the division of criminal justice responsibilities by local, state, and federal levels of government.

functional fragmentation: lack of coordination resulting from the constitutional separation of powers creating independent functions for each component of the justice system.

CLOSE-UP ON CORRECTIONS
Unanticipated Consequences

The citizens of Pleasantville were concerned about rising crime rates and no longer felt safe in their community. Demands for more police protection resulted in the city commission authorizing additional funds to hire more police officers. Dissatisfaction with what the public felt was lenient sentencing resulted in the election of judges who campaigned on the promise to "get tough" with criminals. To the public's surprise, crime did not decline, but in fact increased, and convicted offenders actually spent less time incarcerated. Why?

Perhaps more crime was being committed. More likely, more crimes were being detected by the new recruits. Although their average arrest rate remained about the same, the total number of arrests increased with the additional officers.

No extra funds were authorized for jail personnel. But bookings and admissions increased proportionately with the added arrests. Nor were more funds allocated for the prosecutor's office or public defender, both of whom worked under the burden of increasing caseloads. Everyone had less time to prepare for more cases, and prosecutors felt pressured to negotiate pleas to avoid further trial delays.

Judges kept their promise to increase the length of sentences. But the state prison, operating under a court-mandated population limit, simply could not admit any more offenders. Those sentenced to prison therefore backed up in the already crowded jail, where exhausted staff—burned out, overworked, and seeing no end in sight—began resigning. To make room for more inmates, prison officials were authorized by the state legislature to initiate an early release program. Previously, offenders served an average of two-thirds of their court-imposed sentence before being eligible for release. The average dropped to one-third with early release measures.

One of the offenders released through the program returned to Pleasantville and engaged in a spree of robberies that resulted in the death of a prominent citizen. The community was outraged and once again called for more police protection and stiffer sentences.

Criminal Justice Impact Assessment

When plans are made to construct a public building, it is mandatory to conduct an impact study to assess the potential damage to the environment. But few states require a similar *system impact assessment* to determine the potential systemwide disruption of new public policies.

Whenever police departments are expanded, new laws are created, sentencing practices are altered, or any other crime-related action is taken, the change will create a ripple effect throughout the criminal justice system. In many cases, the impact can be so severe that unanticipated consequences will result. In fact, as described in the "Close-up" above, the long-term outcome may be completely contradictory to the initial intent. If no one anticipates how crowded jails and prisons will become with more punitive sentences, and if no one provides the resources to expand the capacity of corrections to deal with more offenders, then no one will be satisfied when "longer" sentences actually translate into less time served.

The legislative branch of government has a tendency to increase prison sentences with great public fanfare. But when it becomes apparent that correctional facilities cannot accommodate the influx, lawmakers much more quietly authorize speeded-up formulas whereby inmates can amass credits toward early release. Such measures are short-term, shortsighted reactions to crisis conditions. If we truly wish to change and improve corrections, it must be done in a proactive, long-term manner.

Using statistical projection techniques, decision-makers can estimate the impact of new policies on future correctional populations and associated costs. Some might argue that prison capacity or financial limitations should not determine criminal justice practices. But criminal justice policy does not operate in a vacuum and "must be held accountable for its effect on the allocation of human and fiscal resources. At some point we must ask whether we can afford to lock up everyone who offends us."[20]

In that respect, the American Bar Association's Criminal Justice Committee has for almost 20 years called for a "rational sentencing policy" in response to the nation's drug crisis, which, among other things, recommends that "all legislative actions affecting sentencing should be accompanied by a prison impact statement."[21] Likewise, a National Institute of Justice report has long suggested that a funding plan be included in mandatory sentencing legislation in order to "ensure awareness of and responsibility for long-term costs."[22]

With the foresight of a funding plan or systemwide impact assessment, new policies and programs could be implemented more sensibly. Citizens and elected officials would know in advance what effect would be created on the system, what staffing and physical facilities would be needed for effective implementation, and what the ultimate cost would be. The quick-fix, shortsighted fads that have characterized so much of the management of criminal justice agencies could be replaced by long-term analysis. Independent decisions could be replaced by systemwide planning. Emotionally based reactive change could be replaced by proactively addressing challenges through evidence-based research. Otherwise, criminal justice agencies will continue to compete for limited resources, trying to do more with less, but in fact doing more less effectively.

CONFLICTING CORRECTIONAL GOALS

Systemwide planning through an impact assessment of criminal justice policy would better coordinate the efforts of police, courts, and corrections. It is not, however, a panacea for resolving their differences. To function effectively, a system requires goals upon which all stakeholders mutually agree.

Even within criminal justice agencies themselves, goals can be contradictory. Some police administrators, for example, place greater emphasis on crime prevention and community relations; others focus on "by-the-book" enforcement and criminal apprehension. Some judges stress holding offenders fully accountable for their crimes; others are more likely to consider extenuating circumstances. Some correctional officials see their mission as incapacitation; others believe that corrections has a responsibility to promote behavioral change. In fact, within the correctional system itself, there is a wide variety of opinions about what constitutes "success," ranging from lack of escapes to lack of recidivism. But criminal justice decision-makers do not function in isolation. They are

LEARNING GOALS

Do you know:
8. the difference between the medical model, the justice model, and the balanced and restorative model of public policy?
9. how corrections has been affected by society's change from the medical model to the justice model?

responsible to elected officials, who in turn are responsible to the public. The difficulty for corrections is trying to operate efficiently in the midst of the resulting political pressures and public policy changes.

Changing Public Policies

From time to time, the public changes its perspective about what causes people to commit crime, what types of sentences offenders should receive, and what corrections should be accomplishing. Such changes are reflected in what has come to be known as the **medical model** and the **justice model** of policy-making.

medical model:
the concept of rehabilitating offenders through diagnosis and treatment, reflected in public policy from the 1930s to the mid-1970s.

justice model: the concept of achieving greater sentencing equity and holding offenders more accountable through determinate sentences, reflected in public policy since the 1980s.

Before exploring these policy models in greater detail, however, it is important to note that they do not necessarily represent clearly defined, distinct phases or an overnight transition from one to the other. Rather, each emerged gradually over time and, in fact, the "medical" and "justice" labels attached to them were coined in retrospect. It is only through the analysis of hindsight that their philosophies and resulting practices appear to be so unique and even contradictory today.

The Medical Model.   When you are ill, you see a doctor. You trust the doctor to diagnose your problem and prescribe medication to cure your illness. You do not expect the doctor to punish you for being sick. Similarly, the medical model of criminal justice (prevalent from the 1930s through the mid-1970s) views offenders as engaging in crime because of forces beyond their control. The forces shaping criminal behavior might be psychological (e.g., mental illness), sociological (e.g., disruptive family environment), economic (e.g., unemployment), or even physiological (e.g., improper diet). The point is that offenders are not held strictly accountable for their actions any more than a patient suffering from an illness would be.

Because much of the burden for crime causation is placed on society in this line of reasoning, it is society that the medical model holds responsible for "diagnosing" the offender's "illness" and prescribing a "cure." This view translated into corrections being accountable for converting clients into law-abiding citizens and successfully returning them to the community—that is, rehabilitating and reintegrating.

It is not surprising that the medical model emerged in the 1930s, when exciting advances in psychology, psychiatry, and social work were demonstrating the potential for successful treatment of personal and social problems. It was also during this era that a worldwide economic depression changed our outlook. Many who had previously believed that success and stability were solely the products of one's own initiative began to realize that external factors we cannot control also shape our destiny. The principles of the medical model clearly reflected public opinion at the time.

If offenders were to be effectively treated according to the medical model, it was essential that sentencing address their individual needs. Yet social and psychological sciences are somewhat imprecise, making it difficult to determine how long a client would require treatment before being "cured," which translated into **indeterminate sentences**.

Under indeterminate sentencing practices, convicted offenders receive flexible terms, which can range anywhere from one year (or less) to life. Indeterminate sentencing was designed to enable a specific treatment plan to be prepared in which the offender participated for an indefinite period of time until rehabilitated. When correctional officials, in conjunction with treatment personnel, determined that rehabilitation had occurred, the inmate was released on parole.

But, while the medical model was so named because of its resemblance to the medical profession, it did not apply quite so precisely to corrections. Criminals convicted of the same offenses ended up serving widely differing lengths of time in correctional institutions, creating **sentencing disparities**.

Some inmates learned to manipulate the system to their advantage, essentially faking behavioral changes. Others were able to adjust their behavior while confined, but—unable to cope with freedom—reverted to criminal activities (in other words, recidivated) upon release. Nor did taxpayers provide the full array of resources needed to adequately address the wide-ranging needs of correctional clientele (even assuming that their needs could be accurately identified).

Corrections may have been faced with an impossible mandate. But few took this into consideration as escalating crime rates, more conservative public attitudes, and high rates of recidivism created "get-tough-on-crime" demands by the mid-1970s. Perhaps the most devastating blow to the medical model came with the 1974 Martinson report,[23] which has often been cited to demonstrate the ineffectiveness of various forms of treatment programs: "Although the report merely confirmed the reality which correctional workers had been facing for years—namely, that some approaches work with some offenders under certain conditions and that nothing works with all offenders under all conditions—it had profound political and policy effects on corrections."[24]

Combined with other social forces, the Martinson report was interpreted as evidence that the medical model was not working. As public confidence eroded in the ability of corrections to truly "rehabilitate," people's faith in the model also diminished.

The Justice Model. By the mid-1970s, society had become increasingly frustrated with the system's inability to deal effectively with crime. No longer were people as eager to "excuse" criminal behavior as the product of forces outside of the offender's control. A renewed emphasis on personal responsibility emerged, which eventually became known as the justice (or crime control) model, since its focus was on controlling crime and seeing justice served.

Under this new philosophy, people are viewed as capable of making rational choices—of deciding through their own free will whether or not to engage in

indeterminate sentence: flexible, with a low-to-high range (in contrast to the fixed nature of determinate sentences).

sentencing disparity: inequity created when the severity of sentencing or time served differs for similar offenses committed under similar circumstances.

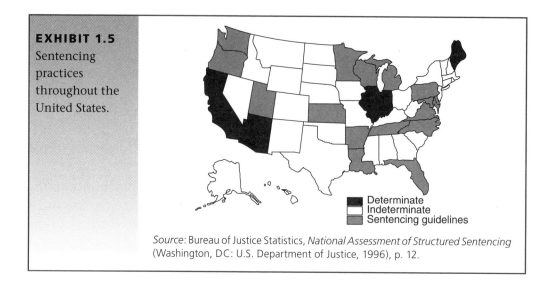

EXHIBIT 1.5
Sentencing practices throughout the United States.

Determinate
Indeterminate
Sentencing guidelines

Source: Bureau of Justice Statistics, *National Assessment of Structured Sentencing* (Washington, DC: U.S. Department of Justice, 1996), p. 12.

crime. It therefore stands to reason that, if one freely elects to commit a crime, punishment should follow to deter other potential criminals, achieve justice, and hold the person accountable for his or her actions.

Unlike the indeterminate sentencing practices of the medical model, determinate sentences of "flat" or "fixed" length are the hallmark of the justice model. States embracing the justice model often employ sentencing guidelines to assure more uniformity, as shown in Exhibit 1.5.

With such guidelines, sanctions are designed to be clear and predictable. The theory is that, this way, criminals know what punishment will be imposed for their actions, and similar crimes will receive similar sentences. With sentences that are proportional to the seriousness of the crime, the justice model maintains that offenders receive their "just deserts," society obtains retribution for their criminal acts, and the community is protected during the period of their incarceration. Since this model is not based on the goal of rehabilitation, the length of the sentence is not determined by treatment effectiveness.

In fact, the justice model incorporates treatment only on a voluntary basis, in keeping with the belief that changing one's behavior cannot be forced but, rather, requires voluntary consent. As with the commission of crime, it holds that one must freely elect whether or not to seek personal change. Under the medical model, involvement in treatment was virtually required to become eligible for parole. However, the justice model would advocate the abolishment of parole discretion to assure more uniformity in sentencing.

Implications for Corrections

As every correctional administrator knows all too well, theory does not necessarily reflect reality. While a conservative society enthusiastically embraced the punitive sentencing, free will, and just-deserts principles of the justice model, corrections has not escaped blame for the failures of its clients. When ex-offenders recidivate, the public still wants to know why corrections is not doing its job, while many correctional employees wonder just what that job is supposed to be.

Whether implicitly or explicitly, corrections often becomes the scapegoat when the crimes of ex-offenders are not prevented. Public policies notwithstanding, it is corrections that remains accountable for its former clients. The fact that this situation is not officially recognized and endorsed by society only makes the mission of corrections all the more difficult and ambiguous. It is like telling a football coach to win games, and then restricting the game plan and the equipment (not to mention draft choices). Corrections was never well equipped to fulfill its rehabilitative function, and, when that function became submerged with the justice model, it created a situation of accountability without authority. Although corrections remains inherently "responsible" for its clients, it has neither the scope of authority nor sufficient resources to fulfill that responsibility successfully.

In contrast to the rehabilitation and reintegration goals of the medical model, the mission of corrections changed to a greater emphasis on incapacitation under the justice model. As citizens became increasingly frustrated with the crime problem, states adopted mandatory sentencing laws covering everything from the use of a firearm during the commission of a crime to drunk driving and drug-related offenses. Moreover, as rhetoric took on fever pitch during the 1990s, states virtually jockeyed to surpass each other's punitive responses to crime. Thus entered the era of "three strikes" laws that mandate lengthy (sometimes life) terms for a third felony conviction.

In part, the logic behind such legislation was to selectively incapacitate those identified as a danger to the community because of the seriousness of their crimes and their potential for recidivism. However, at least one study has found that over one-third of all federal prisoners incarcerated under mandatory laws for drug offenses "were considered low-level offenders."[25] Other research has reported little or no deterrent effects of mandatory sentencing laws.[26]

Nevertheless, with mandatory treatment no longer required, the justice model defines the role of corrections as legally and humanely controlling the offender, through either community supervision or incarceration. As a result, the focus of institutional corrections has shifted to risk assessment and inmate management,[27] as opposed to reform and rehabilitation. In fact, the very terms we use to describe such facilities have likewise shifted from "correctional institutions" to "state prisons."[28] In theory, corrections is therefore not accountable for changing behavior, but only for safe and secure oversight while the offender is under correctional supervision. (See Exhibit 1.6 for a summary of the differences between the medical model and the justice model.)

EXHIBIT 1.6
Comparison of the medical, justice, and balanced and restorative justice models.

		Medical Model	Justice Model	Balanced and Restorative Justice Model
	Crime is a result of...	Forces in society over which the offender has little or no control	The free will of the offender, who elects to engage in crime over law-abiding alternatives	Interpersonal conflict involving one person's violation of another
	Crime is best prevented by...	Changing the motivations that shape one's behavior	The deterrent effect of swift and certain punishment	Changing the offender's perspective to accept accountability for harmful actions and building positive social relationships
	Sentencing should be designed to...	Cure the offender through treatment, rehabilitation, and reintegration into the community	Punish the offender, protect society, and hold criminals accountable for their behavior through incarceration	Repair the harm caused by crime, with sentencing input by victim and community and minimal use of incarceration
	The sentence should be...	Indeterminate (flexible)	Determinate (fixed)	A balanced response addressing the victim, offender, and community needs
	Inmates should be released from confinement...	Through parole, when they are rehabilitated	Through mandatory release, after they have served their full term	After being provided with opportunities to make reparation

Balanced and Restorative Justice

In the meantime, an alternative to both the medical model and the justice model has emerged. Known as the *balanced and restorative justice model*, this approach attempts to balance the interests of offender, victim, and community. Under this perspective, the justice process focuses on:

• *offender accountability:* restoring victim losses;

• *community protection:* matching risk with intervention strategy;

• *competency development:* improving the offender's ability to function in a productive way.[29]

Since this model is becoming the framework for shaping new directions in the juvenile justice system, it is explained in greater detail in Chapter 12, "Juvenile Corrections." But its potential for application to the adult criminal justice system may well begin to capture the attention of policy-makers anxious for an alternative with meaningful consequences that hold offenders responsible for their behavior without overreliance on costly incarceration. In that regard, balanced and restorative justice can provide a more productive option for both victim and offender as well as protection for the community.[30] (For an overview of how this new paradigm compares to the traditional medical and justice models, see Exhibit 1.6.) If for no other reason than economic self-interest, the burgeoning prison and jail population may stimulate such rethinking in terms of society's response to crime.

More recently, with the economy plummeting to levels of unemployment, mortgage foreclosures, and personal bankruptcy not seen since the Great Depression, public policy is shifting yet again as the political pendulum swings in new directions. Whether such financial disarray will yet again prompt a renewed interest in more treatment-oriented initiatives remains to be seen. What is clear, however, is that public opinion will continue to influence public policy—which, in turn, will continue to shape correctional operations. In any event, as long as there is crime, there will be a need for corrections—regardless of what specific ideologies guide its practices.

SUMMARY

Developing a framework for the study of corrections is no easy task, given the complexity of its services, the nature of its relationships within the criminal justice system, and the impact of public policies on its operations. At a cost of over $60 billion, nearly 750,000 workers service the needs of 7.3 million people. This conglomerate includes both custodial institutions and community-based alternatives. It assists adults as well as juveniles. It operates maximum-, medium-, and minimum-security facilities and programs. It functions at the federal, state, and local level of government, and even within the private sector. In short, it provides care, custody, and control to those accused or convicted of a criminal offense. But it does not do so in a vacuum.

Every action taken, every policy formulated, and every priority established by those within the criminal justice system has a potential impact on corrections. It is the product of a system burdened by functional fragmentation and jurisdictional separation. It is affected by the laws created by the legislature, appointments made by elected officials, and decisions rendered by the judiciary. But, perhaps above all, it is a reflection of the changing values, beliefs, and attitudes of society, which have variously directed corrections to treat, rehabilitate, and reintegrate offenders through the medical model and, more recently, simply to incapacitate and control those confined under the justice model. It is a complex, diverse, and often frustrating field of endeavor—which is exactly what makes it such a challenging, dynamic, and fascinating subject of study.

FOR FURTHER DISCUSSION

1. Explain why corrections could be considered a "conglomerate," including what implications that has for you as a taxpayer.

2. Describe what negative impact both jurisdictional separation and functional fragmentation have had for the field of corrections. Despite this, explain why both are necessary in a democracy by exploring the potential negative repercussions that would result if they were abolished.

3. Argue in support of accompanying new justice-related public policies with a criminal justice impact assessment, but, from a political perspective, determine why this is unlikely.

4. Explain how prevailing historical conditions have influenced the two primary paradigms that have shaped criminal justice policy in recent years, and discuss how they have affected corrections.

5. Using prevalent social, political, and/or economic trends to justify your answer, discuss whether public policy in the U.S. will continue to embrace the justice model, return more toward the medical model, or move in a different direction, such as balanced and restorative justice.

CHAPTER 2

The Impact of Sentencing Policies on Corrections

Right now, we think that the imposition of a sentence is our way of saying to the offender, "We're done with you." In the future, we should look at this moment as an opportunity to say, "We're just beginning to deal with you."[1]

Jeremy Travis

CHAPTER OVERVIEW

Criminal activity is portrayed in fiction as a violent, often exciting lifestyle. But, in reality, many "criminals" are rather inconspicuous people whose involvement in crime is more an inability to cope with life than a search for excitement—the alcoholics, drug addicts, and social "misfits" who often can be more harmful to themselves than to others.

The primary offenders arrested are not murderers, armed robbers, or rapists. They are drunk drivers (1.4 million), thieves (1.1 million), and drug violators (1.8 million).[2] Perhaps you know some of them as friends, co-workers, classmates, neighbors, or even family members. Typical criminals are ordinary people. Some of them do very extraordinary things, but most do not. Anyone who has ever driven home after having too much to drink, taken something of value from a store or office, or used illegal drugs has committed a crime for which many Americans are arrested every day.

It is such ordinary people who compose a large portion of the correctional clientele. They have violated the criminal law and have therefore damaged the social order by their failure to conform to expected behavior. In addition, of course, they are the ones who got caught.

Ultimately, it is the manner in which society responds to criminal behavior that determines the essence of corrections. That response is initiated by legislative action which designates certain behaviors as "criminal" and therefore punishable by law. It is then guided by police officers on the street as they make day-to-day decisions about what laws to enforce, against whom, and under what circumstances. It is additionally shaped by prosecutorial and judicial discretion as selected cases proceed further into the justice system. All of these activities and decisions are influenced by the public opinions and political pressures that formulate social policy choices. As we saw in Chapter 1, such policies during recent years have fluctuated between a rehabilitative (medical model) and a retributive (justice model) orientation toward crime. But it is in the nature of sentencing that the impact of such policy choices is even more evident in shaping correctional practices.

CORRECTIONS AND THE CRIMINAL JUSTICE SYSTEM

The crime statistics generated by police intervention are of concern to corrections for two reasons. First, they influence social policy. Crime data often fuel the fear and outrage that result in public demands for more punitive responses to criminal behavior. The public's perception of crime influences voting behavior—and subsequently justice system policies and practices. Secondly, crime statistics concern corrections because they generate the correctional caseload. This does not mean that those represented in crime data immediately become correctional clients. Many crimes are not solved and, even when arrests are made, hundreds of thousands of cases are settled or dropped before penetrating further into the system. Offenders will have been through a long screening process by the time they arrive on a caseload or in a correctional institution.

As the justice process moves from arrest to arraignment and, potentially, adjudication, prosecutors and judges—who are either elected or politically appointed officials—enter the picture. Thus, they are also well grounded in decision-making that is responsive to prevailing public opinion. Prosecutors play a key role in deciding whether to press charges, how vigorously to pursue a case, and what penalty to advocate. But it is the sentencing judge who most clearly and directly reflects the mandates of the public, as well as affects the functions of the correctional system. For it is judges who determine what form of punishment the offender will receive and how long it will endure. Although we will see how judicial decision-making has been curtailed by legislative mandates in recent years, judges nevertheless are critical gatekeepers.

The definition of corrections in Chapter 1 noted that responsibility for correctional care, custody, and control extends to adult criminals and juvenile delinquents who are either *accused* or *convicted* of violating the law. Corrections does not have the authority to intervene until a person is at least formally charged with a crime by the police, although in practice most correctional services are provided after the accused offender is convicted and sentenced by the courts. As cases penetrate further and further into the criminal justice system, the number of offenders who remain in the system diminishes. As a result, corrections in general—and custodial institutions in particular—becomes the repository for those who were not able to "escape" at any prior stage. It is primarily those who pass through this ultimate screening process who become clients of the correctional conglomerate—and it is the sanctions imposed upon that clientele which largely shape the nature of correctional practices.

Sentencing Options

Some would point out that sentencing is not the business of corrections—that corrections is responsible only for the implementation of sanctions imposed by the courts. Technically, that is true. But, as a former official of the American Correctional Association has noted, "Sentencing defines the very nature of our work. To the extent that sentences are unjust, we who must carry them out become agents of injustice."[3] It is, of course, the decisions of judges that ultimately determine how just or unjust the sentencing process is. As shown in Exhibit 2.1, they can elect to impose sentences ranging from a fine, restitution or community service to probation, electronic monitoring, incarceration, or even capital punishment. Sentences which fall in the mid-range of severity—between probation and incarceration—are known as *intermediate sanctions*, and include options such as intensive supervision probation, house arrest, or electronic monitoring.

As we have seen in terms of the number of offenders who are under community supervision rather than institutional confinement, judges often select *noncustodial* sentencing alternatives, especially in less serious property or misdemeanor cases. Although probation, fines, and other community-based programs are sometimes viewed as being too lenient by "letting offenders off" without "real punishment," they do impose conditions and intrusions on a person's life that can appear quite

---

PRISONS
AND JAILS

BOOT CAMP

HALFWAY HOUSE

HOUSE ARREST AND
ELECTRONIC MONITORING

DAY REPORTING

COMMUNITY SERVICE

RESTITUTION AND FINES

INTENSIVE SUPERVISION
PROBATION

PROBATION

EXHIBIT 2.1
Range of sentencing options.

Source: William M. DiMascio, *Seeking Justice: Crime and Punishment in America* (New York: The Edna McConnell Clark Foundation, 1997), pp. 32–33. Reprinted by permission of The Edna McConnell Clark Foundation.

punishing from the perspective of the offender. In fact, it is not unheard of for someone to opt for incarceration in the face of a highly restrictive community alternative. However, community-based correctional approaches are generally preferable for both the public and the nondangerous offender, since they offer a number of advantages by:

- allowing the offender to remain employed, thereby enabling family support, payment of fines, or victim compensation;

- avoiding the negative and stigmatizing effects of imprisonment;

- providing supervision without breaking ties to the community;

- reducing costs to the public, since community-based approaches are far less expensive than incarceration.

In deciding what disposition to impose, judges often rely on probation officers to prepare a *presentence investigation* (PSI). This report outlines the offender's prior record (if any), family stability, employment, education, problems in such areas as substance abuse, and other relevant factors, along with a sentencing recommendation. While the PSI report has been very influential over the years in determining case disposition, its influence is more restricted today in states with restrictive sentencing guidelines. That is because, in a number of jurisdictions, what sanction the offender receives is no longer primarily a function of judicial discretion.[4]

LEARNING GOALS

Do you know:

4. how determinate and indeterminate sentences differ?

5. what was the intent as well as the impact of sentencing guidelines?

6. how mandatory minimum provisions have affected judicial discretion, correctional budgets, and minority populations?

Indeterminate and Determinate (Structured) Sentencing

The sentencing options available to the judge are actually established by legal statutes. This means that judicial discretion is bound by limits imposed by the law. Such boundaries have traditionally been quite flexible. From the 1930s to the mid-1970s, virtually every jurisdiction in the U.S. maintained *indeterminate sentencing* practices.[5] Under this approach to sentencing, the intent was to tailor dispositions to the specific needs of individual offenders, along with the safety risks they posed. Thus judges had extensive discretion, and an offender's prison term could range widely (for example, 10 to 20 years). Moreover, two offenders convicted of similar crimes could be sentenced to significantly different terms, and release from confinement was determined by the state's parole board.

About half of the U.S. states still retain systems primarily based on an indeterminate sentencing model.[6] But dissatisfaction with unequal punishment for similar offenses—as well as public demands to "toughen up" on serious crime—had begun to stimulate a significant change by the mid-1970s, when Maine and

California became the first states to enact determinate sentencing. Also called *structured* sentencing because it more closely limits and controls judicial discretion, determinate sentencing is based on legislatively established sentencing guidelines.

Sentencing Guidelines

In some states, **sentencing guidelines** are legislatively mandated, while in others they are considered "advisory," and compliance with them is voluntary. In some jurisdictions, they are accompanied by the abolishment of parole, but in others early supervised release from a correctional institution is still an option.

Contrary to popular belief, sentencing guidelines were not necessarily designed to be more punitive by imposing longer prison terms. In fact, only half of the states that have implemented sentencing guidelines report that their primary reason was a desire for harsher penalties.[7] Nor were they designed to create strict uniformity in sentencing by, for example, imposing the same sentence for all armed robberies. Given differences in the nature of the offense, the level of harm inflicted, and the offender's past criminal record, that would be just as unfair as more subjective sentencing. Rather, the majority of states indicate that their guidelines were enacted to achieve greater equity in sentencing.[8] In other words, objective guidelines were meant to produce a more rational approach to arriving at a sentence—one that would allow for some variation within a consistently applied framework. As the matrix in Exhibit 2.2 shows, the guidelines generally take into account both the severity of the offense and the offender's prior criminal record.

sentencing guidelines: formulas for calculating sentences, which judges are required to use in many jurisdictions.

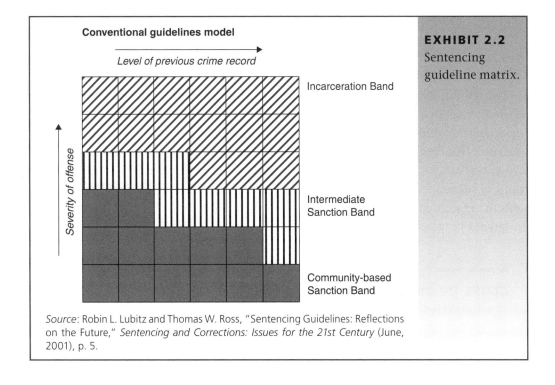

EXHIBIT 2.2
Sentencing guideline matrix.

Source: Robin L. Lubitz and Thomas W. Ross, "Sentencing Guidelines: Reflections on the Future," *Sentencing and Corrections: Issues for the 21st Century* (June, 2001), p. 5.

In most states, judges still have some discretion to deviate from sentencing guidelines through "upward" or "downward" departures, particularly when aggravating or mitigating circumstances are involved. Aggravating circumstances—such as an especially heinous crime or complete lack of remorse by the offender—could justify a more severe penalty. On the other hand, mitigating circumstances—youthfulness or prior abuse of the offender—might call for a less serious penalty, resulting in a downward departure from the guidelines. Even where exceptions are permitted, however, such decisions must be justified in writing, with the judge's rationale subject to review in order to prevent abuse of judicial discretion. Moreover, both guideline departures and judicial discretion become obsolete concepts when minimum terms are specified by law.

Mandated Minimums

Perhaps the most prevalent form of mandatory minimum legislation in recent years has been *"three strikes"* statutes that require substantial sentences—up to life imprisonment without parole—for a third felony offense. Because these statutes direct judges to impose fixed sentences in a "cookie-cutter" approach, sentencing authority actually emerges from the legislature.

Beyond the issue of properly balancing power between the legislative and judicial branches of government, concerns have also been expressed about the equity of such sentences. After studying mandatory minimum sentences for drug-related crimes, the American Bar Association criticized these penalties as being unfair and distorted, as well as requiring expenditures that are "disproportionate to any deterrent or rehabilitative effect they might have."[9]

Since such mandates essentially "tie the hands" of the sentencing judge, they have been denounced by members of the judiciary themselves. In a protest very uncharacteristic of federal judges, all 12 federal judicial circuits issued statements opposing mandatory sentencing, and several prominent judges either resigned or refused to hear cases involving mandatory drug charges.[10] Some of the reasons for these drastic actions are illustrated in the next "Close-up on Corrections," which describes bizarre but true examples of the unjust and disproportionate sentences that can result from the rigid uniformity of three strikes sentencing practices. As a result of subsequent legal challenges, the Supreme Court has now ruled that, while sentencing guidelines must still be taken into consideration, they are "not binding on federal judges, but merely advisory."[11]

CLOSE-UP ON CORRECTIONS
The Realities of Mandatory Minimum Sentencing

- A man with no criminal record accepted $5 to give an acquaintance a lift to a fast food restaurant, where the acquaintance was arrested for selling 100 grams of crack to an undercover drug agent. The judge who imposed the mandatory ten-year sentence on the driver was moved to tears and called the sentence "a grave miscarriage of justice."

- A man convicted of first-offense simple possession of a pound and a half of cocaine was sentenced to mandatory life imprisonment. When arrested, he voluntarily surrendered a concealed, registered handgun, perhaps not realizing that this would make the penalty for his drug offense the same as the penalty for murdering a police officer.
- A secretary was sentenced to a five-year mandatory minimum term because her drug-dealing son hid 120 grams of crack in her attic.

Source: Henry Scott Wallace, "Mandatory Minimums and the Betrayal of Sentencing Reform: A Legislative Dr. Jekyll and Mr. Hyde," *Federal Probation,* Vol. 57, No. 3 (September, 1993), p. 13.

Rose Medina is locked up in a Colorado prison. She is about forty years old. Her sentence: life without parole. Unless the courts overturn her sentence or the governor commutes her sentence, she will die in prison. Her last offense of conviction: forgery. Her offense of conviction before that one: forgery. Her offense before that one: forgery. Rose was caught, charged, and convicted under a habitual offender law.

Source: R.J. Lauen, *Positive Approaches to Corrections: Research, Policy, and Practice* (Lanham, MD: American Correctional Association, 1997), p. 9.

For additional cases, see the website of Families against Mandatory Minimums, http://famm.org.

Fiscal Impact of Structured Sentencing

In addition to dramatically reducing judicial discretion, minimum sentencing statutes have had a tremendous impact on corrections. As they have been applied to drug offenses, for example, these mandates have had two primary effects: first, an increase in the proportion of arrested drug offenders who are sentenced to prison; and, second, an increase in the length of time that these offenders serve.[12] With more offenses drawing longer and more compulsory prison terms, much of the prison growth in recent years has been attributed to drug-related offenses, at a significant cost to taxpayers.[13]

Overcrowded correctional institutions have become a burdensome by-product of such sentencing practices, along with diminishing returns for the resources expended. In terms of cost-effectiveness, for instance, analysts report that spending tax dollars on reducing drug consumption through treatment would reduce serious crimes 15 times more effectively than incapacitating offenders by funding mandatory prison terms.[14] Likewise, another study concludes that interventions with high-risk families have considerably greater long-term benefit than three strikes policies.[15] But, as high-cost cellblocks take priority over proactive social programs on the fiscal agenda, society experiences significant "lost opportunity costs." In other words, opportunities for early intervention are forsaken, thereby reinforcing a reactive cycle that continually heightens the cost of crime at the expense of preventive efforts that could begin to break the cycle.

EXHIBIT 2.3
Determinate sentencing policies such as "three strikes" and "mandatory minimums" have resulted in the need to expand prison capacity to accommodate increasing numbers of offenders sentenced for longer periods of time.

Source: Courtesy of the Federal Bureau of Prisons, Butner, North Carolina, Medical Center.

Racial Impact of Structured Sentencing

Even more troublesome than lost fiscal opportunities is the potential for racial discrimination in the process of implementing mandatory minimum sanctions. It has already been noted that much of the sentencing enhancements and mandates accompanying the justice model have been directed toward drug-related offenses. In practical terms, this means that such policies have disproportionately affected minority groups, particularly African Americans.

Moreover, reports have surfaced of racial disparities in the implementation of mandatory minimum sanctions—such as how charges are pursued, prior records are calculated, plea bargains are negotiated, and so on.[16] While some may question these findings, the overall picture is clear—almost one of every three black males between 20 and 29 years of age is either incarcerated or on probation or parole.[17] Nor is this dismal reality expected to improve. As shown in Exhibit 2.4, projection of the lifetime likelihood of imprisonment for black males is almost double that of Hispanics and over five times the percentage for white males. (See Exhibit 2.5 for female comparisons.) At current rates of incarceration, nearly one in three black males in America are likely to go to prison. Worse yet, the devastating impact of their imprisonment has ripple effects on families throughout minority communities—where, by age 14, over half of black children born in 1990 to high school dropouts had a father imprisoned.[18]

In response to these figures, it might be argued that the African American population is more likely to engage in crime. However, contrary evidence shows that over half (51.4 percent) of the increase in the number of inmates between 1980

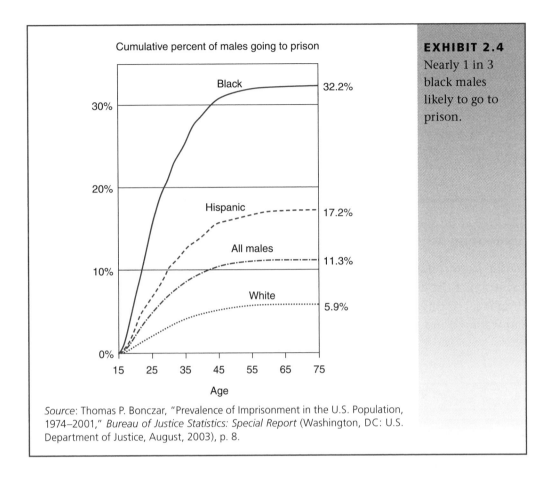

Cumulative percent of males going to prison

EXHIBIT 2.4
Nearly 1 in 3 black males likely to go to prison.

Source: Thomas P. Bonczar, "Prevalence of Imprisonment in the U.S. Population, 1974–2001," *Bureau of Justice Statistics: Special Report* (Washington, DC: U.S. Department of Justice, August, 2003), p. 8.

and 1996 can be explained by the greater likelihood of receiving a prison sentence (with only 11.5 percent attributable to higher offense rates).[19] Why have minorities been so disproportionately affected by justice model sentencing practices? The next "Close-up on Corrections" provides some insights into this troubling question.

CLOSE-UP ON CORRECTIONS
Two Fronts in the "War on Drugs"

The parents of one seventeen-year-old boy, already concerned about possible drug use, examine their son's bedroom while he is at school. They discover what appears to be some drug residue and a substantial amount of cash hidden in a drawer. Confronting their son when he comes home, he admits he has been using cocaine and occasionally selling to some friends.

How do the parents respond? Do they call the police, demand that their son be arrested for using and selling drugs, and receive a five-year mandatory minimum sentence for his behavior? The question is ludicrous, of course.

Instead, the parents do what any good middle-class family would do: they consult with their insurance provider and secure the best treatment program they can find. The criminal justice system never even becomes an issue for them.

A few miles away, picture another family in a low-income section of the city. Their son, too, appears to be getting involved with drugs. Unfortunately for him, his parents have no health insurance, and there are few drug treatment programs available in the neighborhood. Finally, he is picked up one night on a street corner and charged with drug possession with the intent to sell.

Two families with substance abuse problems, two different responses. What does this tell us?. . . Since 1980, no policy has contributed more to the incarceration of African Americans than the "war on drugs.". . . As a national policy, the drug war has exacerbated racial disparities in incarceration while failing to have any sustained impact on the drug problem.

Source: Marc Mauer, *Race to Incarcerate* (New York: The New Press, 2006), pp. 157–158.

Sentencing Alternatives

By the beginning of the twenty-first century, however, several states were starting to recognize the devastating economic, social, and humanistic impact of mandatory drug laws. As one commentator put it, "by now, one thing should be obvious about our war on drugs. Drugs won."[20] Just as California was in the forefront of the "three

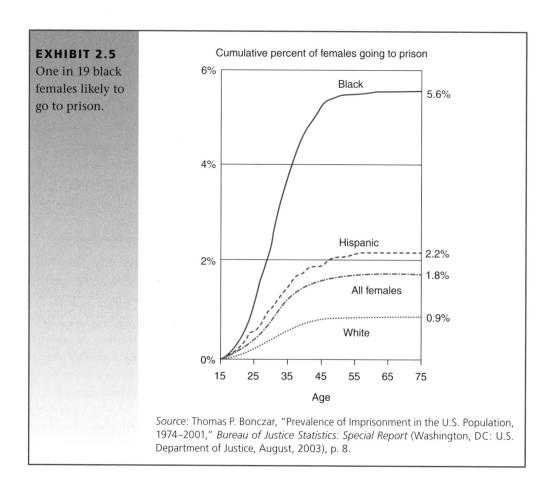

EXHIBIT 2.5
One in 19 black females likely to go to prison.

Cumulative percent of females going to prison

Source: Thomas P. Bonczar, "Prevalence of Imprisonment in the U.S. Population, 1974–2001," *Bureau of Justice Statistics: Special Report* (Washington, DC: U.S. Department of Justice, August, 2003), p. 8.

strikes" movement, it again took the lead in sentencing reform. With the approval in November, 2000 of Proposition 36, the Substance Abuse and Crime Prevention Act, California voters dramatically changed the battle plan in the "war on drugs." Now certain nonviolent adult offenders who use or possess illegal drugs receive treatment in the community rather than incarceration, in an effort to:

- preserve jail and prison space for serious violent offenders;

- enhance public safety by reducing drug-related crime;

- improve public health by reducing drug abuse through treatment.

Since California's pioneering effort, a number of states have passed similar reforms, with more appearing on ballots throughout the country each year. In states that have advanced such public policy alternatives, the challenge now is to assure that adequate resources are available to meet additional treatment demands.[21]

Truth in Sentencing

Historically, adequate resources have not been associated with public policy transitions. This is the primary reason that, even with the greater certainty of being incarcerated for a longer time under determinate policies, the sentence received has not always been the one that is served. It is one thing to sentence an offender to a particular amount of time behind bars. But assuring that the sentence imposed actually matches the time served can be quite a different matter.

LEARNING GOALS

Do you know:
7. what is meant by truth in sentencing?
8. how restorative justice differs from current sentencing trends?

As harsher sentencing practices produced widespread prison crowding, a number of states began to discover that the pace of new construction could not keep up with the demand for more bedspace. Facing court-imposed mandates to reduce crowding, states resorted to measures ranging from sentence reductions through generous "good-time" credits to wholesale release of large groups of offenders to make room for incoming inmates. Whatever the remedy, the result was the early release of many offenders who had originally been sentenced to considerably longer terms. Inevitably, some of them continued a life of crime, and their involvement in several high-profile incidents generated a public outcry for "truth in sentencing."

Congress responded to the crowding crisis in 1994 by making hundreds of millions of dollars in grants available to help states build or expand prisons—with one major catch. To be eligible for these federal funds, states had to pass laws or adopt guidelines that required violent offenders to serve at least 85 percent of the sentence imposed. Thus parole eligibility and good-time credits had to be restricted or eliminated. By 1997, all 50 states had received funding under this program by documenting that violent offenders were serving a substantial portion of their sentences.[22] Eventually, however, states expressed concerns that the truth-in-sentencing grants were too small to offset the construction and operating costs that would be required to comply with the 85 percent requirement. Vermont, for example, estimated that it would cost several million dollars to comply with the federal requirements in order to be eligible for $80,000 in grant funding.[23]

Restorative Sentencing

While various forms of indeterminate and determinate sentencing tend to characterize the criminal justice process in most states, there is yet another alternative on the horizon that has been developing for the past several decades in the juvenile justice system—that is, restorative justice. Also called the "balanced approach," it differs from traditional sentencing practices by involving the interests of all relevant stakeholders in the sentencing process—the victim, the offender, and the community (as illustrated in Exhibit 2.6).

balanced and restorative justice: a model that attempts to balance community protection with offender accountability and competency development.

Rather than simply punishing the offender, **balanced and restorative justice** seeks to repair the harm that occurred and "restore" community well-being. It therefore assumes a broad-based, problem-solving approach that attempts to individualize justice by emphasizing accountability, while at the same time providing help to the offender, protecting the community, and compensating the victim's losses. But doing so calls for an unstructured, unstandardized approach that is based on the unique circumstances of each case—quite the opposite of the uniformity required under structured sentencing guidelines. As a result, restorative goals of achieving relevant, individualized dispositions come into conflict with contemporary trends toward certainty and consistency in sentencing.[24] Until this discrepancy is resolved—or the public opinion that fuels it changes direction—it is

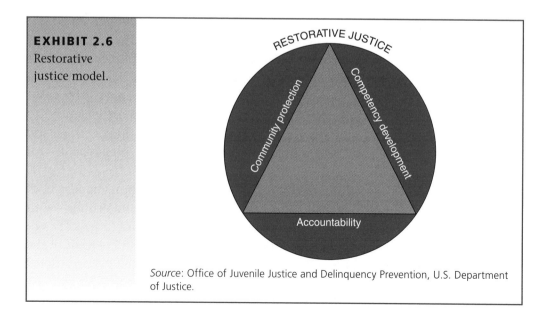

EXHIBIT 2.6
Restorative justice model.

Source: Office of Juvenile Justice and Delinquency Prevention, U.S. Department of Justice.

uncertain whether the balanced and restorative approach will ever exert as much influence on adult sentencing as it has within the juvenile justice system.

CRIME-RELATED PUBLIC POLICY

Despite the current popularity of a more punitive approach to criminal punishment, there are those who question why their tax dollars have to support "criminals" at all. The answer involves public policy, which is often a trade-off between economic goals and social values—a balance between what is economically feasible and what is humanely desirable.

Public policy is a reflection of the prevailing views of society, which can differ widely when it comes to dealing with criminal behavior. Public opinion concerning the appropriate response to crime forms the basis for identifying the purpose of corrections—that is, what corrections is supposed to be accomplishing. Although public policy sets the broad parameters within which corrections functions, as we will see shortly, it does not always provide very clear-cut guidance or direction for correctional operations. As a result, sentencing practices have at various times reflected demands for retribution, deterrence, incapacitation, or rehabilitation—as illustrated in the next "Close-up on Corrections."

LEARNING GOALS

Do you know:
9. how punishment is justified under retribution and what forms of retribution are used today?
10. the difference between specific and general deterrence?
11. what selective incapacitation is and what issues it raises with regard to moral justice?
12. what impact collective incapacitation has had on crime and incarceration rates?

CLOSE-UP ON CORRECTIONS
Just What Are We Trying to Achieve?

An example is the sentencing of persistent petty thieves. In a court where a prison sentence of a year, for example, is routine for such cases, the year will be imposed in one case by a judge who believes it will dissuade other thieves, in a second case by a judge who hopes it will dissuade this particular thief, in a third case by a judge who is concerned only with punishing theft because theft is bad, and in a fourth case by a judge who is content to put a dent in thievery by incapacitating for a year someone known to have committed theft on a regular basis.

Source: Michael E. Smith and Walter J. Dickey, "Reforming Sentencing and Corrections for Just Punishment and Public Safety," *Sentencing and Corrections: Issues for the 21st Century* (Washington, DC: National Institute of Justice, U.S. Department of Justice, September, 1999), p. 4.

Retribution

The belief that criminals deserve to be punished as repayment for their misdeeds is one of the oldest reactions to wrongdoing. The "law of retaliation" (*lex talionis*) traces its origins to the Code of Hammurabi as well as the Law of Moses and the Old and New Testaments. In seeking retaliation, ancient and medieval punishments were violent and bloody—completely out of proportion to the seriousness of offenses. Common penalties were flogging, public boiling, mutilation, stocks and pillories, blinding, disemboweling (alive), drawing and quartering, cutting out tongues, and similar tortures.[25]

retribution: achieving justice for a criminal act by responding in kind with punishment.

The modern-day concept of **retribution** is considerably more civilized than its early origins, although some still denounce it because it sounds punitive and vindictive. In that regard, it has been noted that retribution differs from revenge in that it is impersonally administered by "disinterested parties" through due process of law, which is designed to "balance the wrong done to the victim" rather than "incite retaliation."[26]

As the public has become increasingly fearful of violent crime, frustrated over inability to control it, and concerned that criminals are not receiving their "just deserts," retribution has again gained in popularity. Proponents of this view maintain that offenders freely elect to engage in criminal activities and should therefore be punished in order to "pay their debt" to society.

Punishment according to the modern view of retribution is generally in the form of some type of compensation or imprisonment. Fines, restitution, community service, and other methods of "paying back" society have always been frequently used forms of punishment, although incarceration is more highly publicized. In retributionist fervor, there are those who would argue for less humane conditions of confinement, even advocating a return to corporal punishment, and in fact the death penalty—the ultimate retribution—remains an option in 37 states (and the federal government).[27]

While there is no valid evidence that the fear of punishment prevents crime, that is not technically the objective of retribution. Rather, the focus of retribution is on the satisfaction achieved by society in general and the victim in particular when criminals are required to "pay for their crimes"—whether in the form of economic compensation, loss of freedom, or even death.

Deterrence

deterrence: proactively discouraging future criminal behavior through fear of punishment.

Unlike retribution, which reacts to past events, **deterrence** aims to prevent (in other words, to deter) future criminal behavior. But, despite the proactive emphasis of deterrence, it is not entirely unrelated to retribution. Both believe in holding offenders accountable for their behavior. Both see a relationship between increasing penalties and decreasing crime. In fact, it could be said that retribution promotes deterrence or, put another way, that deterrence theory provides a "politically correct" rationale for vengeance. While some would feel morally uncomfortable with demanding revenge, seeking to deter criminal behavior is more socially acceptable, even if the outcome is essentially the same for the offender.

In any event, deterrence focuses on two approaches, specific and general:[28]

• *Specific deterrence* is based on the belief that, if the punishment is made sufficiently unpleasant, the offender will be discouraged from committing violations in the future. Just as a child is disciplined for inappropriate behavior to prevent its repetition, the idea is that criminals will avoid recidivism if punished properly. But people are motivated by different things, and what is a deterrent to one person is not necessarily equally productive with others. Beyond that inherent drawback, deterrence theory's assumption of offender rational choice is based on shaky premises:

> There are doubtless some criminals who carefully calculate the possible gains and risks. But much crime is committed on impulse, given the opportunity presented by an open window or unlocked door, and it is committed by offenders who live from moment to moment. . . . [I]t is unrealistic to construct sentencing on the assumption that most offenders will weigh the possibilities in advance and base their conduct on rational calculation.[29]

• *General deterrence* is designed to use the offender to "set an example" for those who might otherwise consider engaging in similar criminal activities. Thus it requires punishment that is severe enough to have an impact, assurance that the sanction will be carried out, and enough examples so that people are well aware of what will happen if they violate the law. Thus, both *certainty* and *severity* of punishment are essential ingredients in general deterrence. This approach has been praised as necessary to "send a message" that crime will not be tolerated and that those involved in such activities will be dealt with firmly.

  On the other hand, however, general deterrence has been criticized because making an example of an offender demands punishment for what others might do, which may be disproportionate to the current offense. Such generalized penalties raise the question of equity, particularly when the punishment is out of proportion to the seriousness of the offense or the actual harm caused to society.

Whether deterrence is general or specific, the overall logic of deterrence theory is based on assumptions that:

1. law violators believe they will be apprehended (which most do not);

2. criminals rationally plan their activities—in other words, that "burglars think like district attorneys";

3. the "crime rate will diminish as the penalty scale increases."[30]

But many crimes are acts of passion or spontaneous responses, or committed under the influence of alcohol or drugs, and many criminals are repeat offenders who have already experienced the presumably "deterrent" effect of punishment. For a look at why deterrence theory has failed when applied to drug-related crime, see the next "Close-up on Corrections."

CLOSE-UP ON CORRECTIONS
The Theory and Reality of Deterrence

Standard deterrence theory tells us that people calculate the pain and pleasure of their actions, and that if we make the pain of the disfavored conduct great enough, the frequency of that behavior will decline. Few people doubt that this theoretical assumption is the driving force behind current national drug policy, as courts and lawmakers have made it increasingly easy to detect, arrest, convict, and punish those who possess the contraband. Some of this movement may be inspired by retributive or incapacitative goals, but overwhelmingly, the political assumption seems to be that the current problems are the result of inadequate brute force, and that if we punish people severely enough, they will change their ways. . . .

One difficulty with using the criminal law as the main response to the drug problem is that it necessarily treats all drug users the same . . . as though they had the ability to conform their conduct to the standards the law requires. . . . Many who buy drugs are recreational users who presumably can and would stop if they perceived the risks of detection to be too great. . . . On the other hand, perhaps no realistic penal sanction can deter those who are addicts. . . . One of the problems with the criminal law model is its failure to distinguish those who can be deterred from those whose reasoning has been sufficiently compromised by drug use that deterrence is ineffective.

Source: Andrew D. Leipold, "The War on Drugs and the Puzzle of Deterrence," *Journal of Gender, Race and Justice* (Spring/Summer, 2002), pp. 111–129.

Ultimately, whether justice should be individualized to address specific deterrence or generalized to serve as a warning to others is not really the issue. In both cases, the extent to which convicted or potential law violators are deterred by severe punishment is based on uncertain theoretical assumptions, and in practice is virtually impossible to determine accurately, because only those who are not deterred become clients of the criminal justice system.

Incapacitation

incapacitation: constraining offenders by depriving them of liberty.

If retribution is viewed as reactive and deterrence as proactive, **incapacitation** could be characterized as something in between, or perhaps a combination of both. In its reactive sense, being restrained in a correctional institution is punishment for past behavior. In a proactive sense, it is designed to prevent criminal activities—not so much in the future, as with deterrence but, more realistically, during the period when an offender is actually incarcerated.

As a result, incapacitation is probably the most pragmatic sentencing goal. It does not specifically seek to prevent future crime, deter potential criminals, or change behavior. It simply focuses on constraining offenders in an effort to curtail their opportunities to commit additional crimes. That is not to say that criminal acts do not occur behind bars, although they are not usually committed against those in free society.

Such constraint is traditionally accomplished through isolation from society in secure correctional facilities. While the definition of incapacitation could be extended to include the community-based controls imposed through home confinement or electronic monitoring, it is incarceration that most closely reflects the fundamental intent of incapacitation—rendering an offender incapable of preying further upon the public. Like deterrence, incapacitation can be divided into two categories—selective and collective. **Selective incapacitation** is reflected in habitual offender ("three strikes") laws, which mandate specified sentences for those convicted of a certain number of prior offenses. Often it is employed in response to the overuse of incarceration, or what has become known as *collective incarceration*.

selective incapacitation: targeting habitual or chronic offenders for more extensive incarceration.

Selective Incapacitation.   To maximize the benefit of incapacitation, those who are most likely to be repeat offenders would represent the logical target for such isolation. Research has long demonstrated that, among both juvenile delinquents and adult criminals, a relatively small number of "chronic offenders" are disproportionately responsible for a large amount of crime.[31] The idea is that, if these chronic recidivists could be selectively incapacitated, the overall crime rate would be reduced.

While research points to the theoretical validity of selective incapacitation, it also raises several operational and ethical difficulties. Foremost is how to accurately determine who should be confined extensively because of their potential threat to the community. Although detailed "prediction tables" have been formulated,[32] anticipating future behavior is never an exact science, creating the potential for selectively incapacitating some who would not actually pose any further threat to the community (or vice versa—overlooking those who would). In fact, it has been estimated that, "for every offender correctly labeled dangerous, at least one offender will be erroneously labeled dangerous."[33]

Then there is the issue of the moral justice involved in sentencing on the basis of possible future actions. In a democratic system of due process, where defendants are innocent until proven guilty and punishment is presumably related to the offense *committed*, this presents a serious dilemma. Ethically, morally, and legally, can we extend incarceration to a longer term on the basis of what someone might do if released? Even if the answer is affirmative, on a more practical level selective incapacitation of habitual offenders can be expected to further increase an already overburdened prison population.

Collective Incapacitation.   Strong advocates of incapacitation would have society accede to a "lock-'em up" philosophy, resigned to the belief that no other option will work as well. But a significant drawback to such collective incapacitation is its shortsighted perspective. Although crime may be curtailed during the period of confinement, what happens upon release? With the exception of the relatively few inmates who die behind bars, all others will eventually return to the community. If "incapacitation" is synonymous with "warehousing," and nothing productive is accomplished during the time they serve, little can be expected in terms of long-range effectiveness.

Moreover, the impact of incarceration on crime is not completely clear. Overall, there is no simple correlation between incarceration and crime rates. In the words of one authority on the subject, "As imprisonment increased steadily for ten years, trends in crime rates were inconsistent. This certainly suggests that the relationship between these factors is far more complex than political rhetoric would make it appear."[34]

In a summary of major published research projects addressing collective incapacitation, the most striking finding was that, despite popular belief, incapacitation does not appear to achieve the large reductions in crime that might have been expected from a "lock-'em-up" strategy. To the contrary, America's "love affair with prisons" has been criticized as using incarceration for reasons not directly linked with crime reduction, or even punishment for criminal behavior, but rather to deal with social problems and to control "marginalized and impoverished groups in society."[35]

While the impact of collective incapacitation on crime reduction has been limited, however, the effects on the prison population have been dramatic.[36] The obvious question, then, is why incapacitation is not producing more beneficial results. Some of the potential answers are contained in the next "Close-up on Corrections."

EXHIBIT 2.7
America's "love affair with prisons" reflects a crime control strategy that relies on collective incapacitation, despite contradictory research evidence.

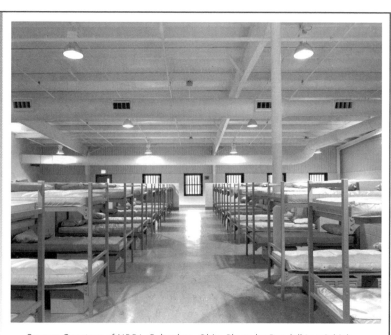

Source: Courtesy of NBBJ, Columbus, Ohio. Photo by Randall Lee Schieber.

CLOSE-UP ON CORRECTIONS
Why Building More Prison Cells Won't Make a Safer Society

Why don't prisons do more to lower the crime rate?... It is one thing to say that a person will not commit a crime while incarcerated and quite another to say that society's overall crime rate will be affected. Put another way, more prison cells.... won't reduce crime. Here's why.

- A lot of predatory crime is committed by juveniles too young to be eligible for prison, or by young adults unlikely to be sent to prison for most first felony convictions. . . .
- Prison terms are usually imposed late in an offender's criminal career when criminal activity, on average, is tapering off. . . .
- Because the justice system only deals with an insignificant proportion of [total] crime, its ability to affect crime levels is minimal. . . . [Many crimes are] either unreported or unsolved.
- Studies have shown that much individual crime (particularly violent crime) is an impulsive response to an immediate stressful situation, often under the influence of drugs or alcohol. Rational-choice models require an offender to think clearly about the costs and benefits of committing crime, weigh those costs, and determine that the costs outweigh the benefits. Yet more than half of all violent offenders are under the influence of drugs or alcohol at the time of their crime, a state of mind with little affinity for rational judgment.
- For imprisonment to deter offenders and potential offenders, it must be stigmatic and punishing. . . . But many of an offender's peers and relatives also have done time . . . so the stigma attached to having a prison record in these neighborhoods may not be as great as it was when prison terms were relatively uncommon.
- Imprisonment may increase post-release criminal activity. RAND analysts recently studied a "matched sample" of California offenders convicted of similar crimes and with similar criminal records. The two groups differed only in their sentence—members of one group went to prison, the others received probation. After tracking the groups for three years, researchers found consistently higher re-arrest rates for offenders sentenced to prison. . . .
- Most important, for imprisonment to reduce crime, inmates must not be immediately replaced by new recruits. . . .

Prisons, to be sure, are an important and necessary component of the criminal justice system. . . . But drug clinics do more to rehabilitate drug addicts than prison, job training does more to reduce recidivism than jails, and early childhood prevention programs do more than any other factor to reduce a propensity to crime. . . . Every additional corrections officer may mean one fewer teacher, and every prison cell constructed may mean a gang-prevention program unfunded.

Source: Joan Petersilia, "Building More Prison Cells Won't Make a Safer Society," *Corrections Today*, Vol. 54, No. 8 (December, 1992), pp. 168–170. Reprinted with permission of the American Correctional Association, Alexandria, VA.

LEARNING GOALS

Do you know:

13. how determinate and indeterminate sentences differ?

14. why rehabilitation has suffered from ineffectiveness?

15. how the Martinson Report affected corrections?

16. why reintegration is necessary following release from correctional custody?

17. which correctional goals are reflected in the justice model and which are represented by the medical model?

rehabilitation: the process of redirecting an offender's behavior toward conduct that is law-abiding and socially-acceptable.

Rehabilitation

It is the belief that something positive should be accomplished during incarceration (or community supervision) that forms the basis of the rehabilitative approach. **Rehabilitation** advocates maintain that criminal sanctions should be used as an opportunity to make some type of positive change in the offender. As George Bernard Shaw once pointed out, "if you are going to punish a man retributively, you must injure him. If you are to reform him, you must improve him. And men are not improved by injuries."[37]

Since rehabilitation literally means "to *restore* to good condition," some would maintain that the term is more properly "habilitation," as the condition of many offenders is not one to which corrections would wish to restore them. Regardless of semantics, the objective is to help offenders change their behavior so that they can reenter society as contributing citizens, or at least not dangerous ones.

Just as retribution, deterrence, and incapacitation form the foundation of the justice model described earlier, rehabilitation is the hallmark of the medical model. Like incapacitation, it seeks to reduce crime, but through "radically different means"—that is, by changing the "need or desire to commit crimes," not simply preventing the offender from "having an opportunity to do so."[38] Thus the goals of rehabilitation are the most ambitious, and therefore perhaps the most elusive, of the various responses to crime. Moreover, the rehabilitative approach has been plagued by numerous operational difficulties, ranging from ineffective implementation techniques to discouraging evaluation results.

Implementation Techniques.   Rehabilitative efforts can take many forms—from education and vocational training to detoxification and acupuncture. But most traditional approaches have centered on individual and group counseling, psychotherapy, and other clinical treatment procedures. Although these terms may imply individualized treatment, the rehabilitative routine is more likely to take the generic form of "counseling for everyone." As a result, it has been far from uniformly effective.

It is somewhat ironic that the rehabilitative approach has been denounced for its "rubber stamp" procedures, since it was originally designed to address specific needs of the individual. The intent was to assess the offender's problems, develop a personalized treatment plan, and provide an indeterminate (flexible) sentence whereby the length of confinement would largely be determined by the person's progress toward rehabilitation. That was the theory. In reality, those incarcerated for similar offenses ended up serving widely different amounts of time, which raised the issue of sentencing equity. Additionally, the correctional officials, treatment personnel, and parole board members charged with determining when sufficient "rehabilitation" had occurred to justify release were not infallible. Since human nature cannot be precisely predicted, some offenders were inevitably released before it was appropriate, while others were held longer than necessary.

Beyond these operational difficulties, to some extent the rehabilitative concept was almost destined to flounder from the start because of the manner in which it was implemented. Given the long-term nature of clinical treatment approaches, they have been offered primarily in institutional settings. As a result, offenders must experience the negative impact of incarceration in order to receive the treatment necessary for their rehabilitation. The coercive nature of high-security correctional facilities is hardly the ideal environment for obtaining treatment and achieving rehabilitation. Nor are institutions equally well staffed and equipped to provide such services.

Empirical Results.   Even among more valid rehabilitative programs, results have been far from encouraging. In his comprehensive report of studies assessing attempts at rehabilitation from 1945 through 1967, Robert Martinson concluded that, "with few and isolated exceptions, the rehabilitative efforts that have been reported so far have had no appreciable effect on recidivism."[39] The Martinson report has been widely cited as offering proof of the ineffectiveness of treatment. Its empirical evidence that "nothing" supposedly works has been used to justify moving from the medical model to the justice model, despite subsequent questions about his methodology[40] and more recent attempts to revitalize interest in rehabilitative concepts.[41] In fact, evidence today indicates that, when treatment is appropriately applied to the right target population, when it is delivered properly by qualified staff, and when it is focused on offender risk and criminogenic needs, it does, indeed, tend to "work."[42]

Nevertheless, issues of sentencing inequities, untimely releases, and ineffective procedures have always plagued the rehabilitative approach. By the 1980s, these concerns were combined with a more conservative political climate, rising crime rates, increasing recidivism, and the indictment of empirical research. Society seemed to have reached the limits of its tolerance for the unfulfilled promise of the rehabilitative ideal.

As a result of this combination of forces, public policies began to be directed toward determinate (fixed) sentences, elimination of parole, and voluntary (versus mandatory) participation in rehabilitative programs. However, not everyone agrees that society is actually as opposed to rehabilitation as legislators and policy-makers would like to think. Empirical evidence has been offered demonstrating "the myth of the punitive public," which indicates that, even during the conservative 1980s, there was still considerable belief in rehabilitation as a legitimate correctional goal.[43] In that regard, it may not be surprising that, when Americans were asked in a 1968 Harris poll to choose between protection of society, punishment, and rehabilitation in terms of what the main goals of imprisonment should be, more than 70 percent selected rehabilitation as the most important. Yet a 1996 study using that same question revealed that, while those choosing rehabilitation as their top priority dropped to 41 percent, it nevertheless still ranked as the most frequently selected prison goal.[44]

Reintegration.   Regardless of either evaluation results or public opinions, the demise of rehabilitation also may be related to the difficulty of reintegrating ex-offenders back into the community after long-term confinement. It has already been noted that much of what was pursued in the name of rehabilitation occurred within the isolated institutional environment of secure correctional facilities. In prison, every movement is under scrutiny. Strict compliance with rules is enforced. Established routines regulate everything. In response to this "total institutional" climate,[45] an inmate subculture develops to socialize the population. The negative effects of this regulation, routinization, and socialization into prison life can be intensive and long lasting.

It is one thing to achieve behavioral change among those under such close supervision. It is quite another to assure that any improvements continue upon release—when ex-offenders are again faced with making their own decisions, regulating their own lives, and replacing institutional control with self-control. Reestablishing ties with the community is an essential ingredient in this process, and it is the focus of **reintegration**. If ex-offenders feel estranged from society, the chances are much greater that they will fall into old patterns of behavior and return to corrections as recidivists. Thus reintegration efforts such as parole are not simply a privilege for the offender but also a protection for the community.

Yet successful reintegration can be difficult for all but the most motivated to achieve. Once convicted and incarcerated, offenders lose a number of privileges, such as eligibility to apply for certain types of employment. They are also stigmatized or "labeled" as high risks for personal relationships and business transactions. Former friends and even family members may distance themselves. Potential employers may be reluctant to "take a chance" by hiring someone with a record. Apartment managers may find excuses to avoid renting. Banks may deny a car loan. The overwhelming sense of frustration from experiencing such rejections can make the ex-offender a prime target for returning to crime.

While parole was in part designed to assist with such community reintegration, parole has a dual mandate of providing both support and continued supervision. When caseloads are high and public pressure is strong to detect recidivism, it is not surprising to find parole officers' supervisory functions taking precedence over their supportive role. In addition, offenders serving full mandatory sentences without the possibility of parole can leave the institution without either supervision or support.

reintegration: to restore ties with the community following custodial confinement.

Public Policy Transition

During the 1980s, both rehabilitation and reintegration were deemphasized in favor of retribution, deterrence, and incapacitation, as public policies shifted from the medical model to the justice model. Yet there are those who continue to argue against abandoning rehabilitation, if for no other reason than because of its humanizing influence on the correctional system.[46] Rehabilitation has played an important role in reforming not only the individual offender, but the system as well—perhaps not as effectively as its lofty goals intended, but not as ineffectively as its abolishment would justify. It is true that nothing works all the time with every inmate. Yet that is not to say that we should reject all hope that anything ever works with anyone.

Nevertheless, the focus in more recent years has transitioned toward either deterring criminal behavior or, when prevention is unsuccessful, holding violators accountable for their actions. To the extent that "holding accountable" translates into lengthy prison sentences, there remains a need to address reintegration. The question is whether that need will again be officially recognized, or whether ex-offenders will be left to reestablish socially acceptable lifestyles as best they can. Those who can will disappear with the rest of us into the anonymity of law-abiding society. Those who cannot will continue to provide media headlines and correctional clientele.

SUMMARY

Correctional clients are those against whom society has taken official action because their behavior is in violation of the criminal law. What is considered to be a crime will therefore determine who are identified as "criminals." Even in those cases where the offense is reported, a suspect is apprehended, and official action is taken, however, a lengthy screening process eliminates many of the accused long before they reach the correctional system.

Many of the decisions, practices, and policies of the justice system are based on public opinions and political pressures. But that does not mean that society is in widespread agreement about how to respond to crime. As a result, we retain a broad range of sentencing options. While indeterminate sentencing practices still exist in most states, recent trends have embraced more determinate sentencing structures, often implemented through sentencing guidelines, mandatory minimums, and truth-in-sentencing provisions. As a result, U.S. sentencing practices have become fragmented, reflecting a wide variety of correctional goals.

Seeking repayment for the wrongdoing of criminal offenders, retribution guided the community's response to criminal behavior for centuries. As society accepted some responsibility for crime, experiments with rehabilitation surfaced. Treatment programs were introduced to change one's motivation to commit crime, as well as to reintegrate the ex-offender more effectively into the community. But, when the desired results were not forthcoming, the public became increasingly disenchanted with the ability of corrections to achieve lasting change. Thus the popularity of retribution reemerged. Efforts were directed toward assuring that criminals receive their "just deserts." Offenders were incapacitated in correctional facilities—both to deter them specifically and to send a general deterrence message to the community. But apparently not everyone has received the message. In upcoming chapters we explore some of the reasons why.

FOR FURTHER DISCUSSION

1. Argue in support of determinate, guideline-based sentencing; then play the role of a trial court judge and refute each of your arguments.

2. Using a controversial case that has recently been in the news, explain why the resulting sentence does not appear to be rational and equitable. Provide recommendations for how the system could be improved when similar cases are addressed in the future.

3. Determine what your state is spending on institutional corrections, compared to other social services (e.g., health care, transportation, education, etc.). Then calculate how many college scholarships could be funded with a 10 percent reduction in the prison population.

4. Based on your age, sex, race, and ethnicity, calculate the approximate chances that you will go to prison within your lifetime.

5. Explain how restorative justice and guideline-based sentencing conflict, and offer creative solutions for how they might operate collaboratively.

6. Using a sentence that has recently been handed down for a high-profile crime in your area, discuss how it fits (or does not fit) within retributive, deterrence, and rehabilitative theories. Then critique both the potential cost and the effectiveness of this sentence.

7. Select a high-profile domestic violence crime that has recently been committed in your community and, in terms of the circumstances surrounding the offense, discuss the relevance of deterrence theory to possibly having prevented it. If deterrence theory does not seem to apply effectively, make the case for another theory that you think would have had more preventive impact.

8. Provide several reasons why relying on strategies of collective incapacitation is not likely to have the expected impact on crime reduction, especially in terms of lost opportunity costs.

9. Explain how rehabilitation and reintegration are related, using insufficient attention to the latter to explain why there has been limited success with the former.

The Development of Corrections

In the years to come, it is hoped that . . . citizens will direct a new generation of correctional workers to create more positive chapters in corrections' history. For the harm done through their wrongdoings, offenders are responsible. But for using inappropriate methods for treating offenders, when better methods are known, we are all guilty.[1]

American Correctional Association

CHAPTER OVERVIEW

If it is true that society is judged by how it treats its prisoners, the methods employed in the past are harsh indictments indeed. For those of us living today, it may be difficult to envision the savage treatment of offenders in the past. Life without prisons and jails, or even courts and trials, may be incomprehensible to us—yet these have been relatively recent "inventions." But, while there have not always been correctional institutions and justice as we know it today, there has always been criminal behavior—and our predecessors were rather ingenious at devising brutal methods of responding to it. It was not without reason that America's forefathers established a constitutional guarantee against "cruel and unusual punishment."

Over time, our concept of what is "cruel and unusual" has changed, and along with it our correctional practices. The tortures, floggings, and public humiliations that characterized "corrections" of the past conflict with today's concept of the worth of life and human dignity. Although there are still countries where severe physical punishment is the preferred response to criminal behavior, the humanitarian values upon which democracy in the United States is based preclude such practices.

Undoubtedly, there are times when, in extreme frustration with our inability to deal with crime, demands arise for a return to the "good old days" when offenders were more likely than not assumed to be guilty, and harsh punishment could be meted out by the victim. (In fact, it is in part for this reason that you will occasionally find graphic descriptions of those times in this chapter—to enable you to view them in the light of rationality rather than with the emotion of nostalgia.) With every social advancement come trade-offs. Just as we tolerate some amount of crime for the right to be free of overly restrictive government intrusions, we have traded the barbarity of vengeance for the civilization of due process and respect for human rights.

LEARNING GOALS

Do you know:

1. what the role of the victim was in achieving justice during primitive times?
2. what is meant by the concept of *lex talionis*?
3. how "benefit of clergy" and "right of sanctuary" influenced early developments in this field?
4. how jails were first used and funded, in contrast to modern jails today?
5. how the fee system worked in early jails?

lex talionis: the law of retribution; retaliating in like manner.

ANCIENT AND MEDIEVAL PRACTICES

Every society has had methods of social control—ranging from public disapproval to death—that hold its members to expected standards of behavior. As primitive people formed tribes, group living created certain customs that everyone was expected to observe. "Justice" was a very personal matter. It was also a brutal process. If a person stole game from his neighbor's traps, he could expect to pay for the crime in a pot of boiling oil or a cage of wild beasts.[2]

Ancient cultures developed the idea of justice based on vengeance, retribution, and compensation. When a crime was committed, punishment was carried out by the victim personally, along with help provided by family members. On a practical basis, personal retribution by the victim was still the dominant method of control. In fact, the law of retaliation (**lex talionis**) against the offender was reflected in the Code of Hammurabi, as well as the Old Testament: "Breach for breach, eye for eye, tooth for tooth, as he has caused a blemish in a man, so shall it be done to him again" (Leviticus 24:20, 570 B.C.). However, the New Testament spoke in opposition to retribution: "Ye have heard that it hath been said, An eye for an eye, and a tooth for a tooth: But I say unto you, That ye resist not evil: but whosoever shall smite thee on thy right cheek, turn to him the other also" (Matthew 5:38, 39, A.D. 65).

Despite this constraint in the New Testament, retribution remained the primary form of social control. The influence of Christian teachings on everyday practice was not to occur for many years. In fact, in a somewhat ironic development, punishments became even more severe with the rise of the major religions. It was believed that sin and crime were offenses against God, and thus became infractions of divine law and God's will, as well as being damaging to society.

The many references to "prison" in the Old and New Testaments and other religious books were there long before the modern concept of prison evolved. At that time, they referred to confinement in rooms and facilities not originally designed for punishment—such as old cellars, dens for animals, and other makeshift resources. They were used in a manner not unlike sending an errant child to his or her room for detention. The concept of jails and prisons in the modern sense was still centuries away.

By the medieval period, influence of the Roman Catholic Church was unmistakable. Benefit of clergy provided a reprieve to members of the clergy because of their ability to read and write. Later it was expanded to include those who could prove their literacy by reading a "test" verse in Psalms 51 (appropriately, the passage that begins with the words "Have mercy on me"). However, as those who were illiterate began to memorize this psalm, the practice gradually ended.[3] The right of sanctuary was also recognized, through which certain locations (often churches or holy places) were designated as places where an offender might go, at least temporarily, to escape punishment.

Medieval Punishments

For those who could not escape, medieval punishments were very brutal. Knives, axes, whips, barnacles, collars, and cuffs were commonly used to inflict pain, along with confinement in cold, dark, damp, vermin-infested dungeons. "Man's primitive fear of being confined in the darkness" was used "as both torture and punishment."[4]

The death penalty was invoked frequently—not in the quick, almost sterile manner in which it is carried out today, but through methods designed to extract as much pain and suffering as possible. Several ingenious devices were designed for this purpose. Among the most grotesque was the "iron maiden"—a boxlike device with the front half hinged like a door so that a person could be placed inside. When the door was shut, protruding spikes, both back and front, entered the body of the victim. Equally barbaric was the "rack"—a device for dragging apart the joints by the feet and hands.

Executions by burning, beheading, and hanging were also employed liberally. These were public events, attended by crowds of gleeful onlookers. Perhaps most reprehensible was the "widespread practice of taking children to see hangings and gibbetted corpses and whipping them soundly on the site."[5]

Those fortunate enough to escape the gallows or the tortures inflicted in castles and dungeons might find themselves confined to the galleys of convict ships that sailed the seas aimlessly with a cargo of felons. These vessels may have been offshoots of the "hulks" or non-seaworthy vessels that had been anchored in the River Thames in London and elsewhere as places of confinement. As in the slave galleys of ancient Rome and Greece, floggings were common and conditions were extremely harsh: "chained to their crowded benches, often for six months at a time and perhaps for longer . . . [t]he rowers were exposed to all weathers and were fed on hard fare, and frequently much stinted in water-supply."[6] In addition, many of these vessels also contained their own torture devices.

Confinement Practices

Originally, incarceration was used only until a confession was obtained or the death penalty was imposed. It was the Roman Catholic Church that first made use of long-term confinement of offenders by locking them into the gatehouse of the abbey during the Middle Ages as a humane gesture to replace execution. In the twelfth century, some private prisons were constructed by wealthy landowners. This enabled those with sufficient power and influence to build their own prisons and incarcerate anyone who interfered with their political ambitions.[7]

Following the signing of Magna Carta by King John in 1215, the crown could no longer imprison or execute subjects unless they were first tried by a jury of fellow citizens. The Magna Carta also reduced much of the king's power and returned it to the local community. A growing philosophy of government by the consent of the governed was evolving. It included provisions for courts, free elections, and greater local control. During this period, the origins of civil and constitutional rights as we know them were emerging. However, these were very rudimentary beginnings, and in reality "justice" was still largely determined by social class.

Early English Jails

With the development of trials, a place was needed to confine offenders until the king's court could be convened in the county where the crime occurred. That place became the *gaol* (or, as it is now spelled, "jail"), which comes from the Latin *gaviola*, meaning cage or hole[8]—probably quite descriptive of the earliest facilities. In contrast to its use today, offenders did not serve time as punishment in jail. Rather, the jail was used to confine those awaiting either trial or the imposition of punishment (functions that are still performed by modern jails). However, during this period of time, the punishment being awaited was more often than not death.

The crown provided no funds for jail operations. As a result, sheriffs contracted with "keepers" to assure that inmates did not escape. Although the keeper was paid no salary, such contracts were actually quite lucrative. They generated income from fees charged to inmates, since prisoners were required "to pay for every service and good provided by the keeper."[9] For example, fees were charged to be booked, to eat, to sleep on a mattress, to obtain a bed, and to be released (even with a judicial order). Because the physical structures were so insecure and prone to easy escape, prisoners were often weighted down by "manacles, shackles, and iron collars, which they also paid the keeper a fee for the privilege of wearing."[10] To pay for their keep, inmates could beg or accept charitable donations, and profit was also made by selling inmate labor. Essentially, offenders were required to "pay for the privilege of being in jail"[11] through a system that basically amounted to extortion. For a vivid account of physical conditions and the fee system in a famous London gaol, see the next "Close-up on Corrections."

Wealthy offenders could pay for the privilege of living in plush quarters. But others "faced virtually intolerable living conditions. Everyone was literally dumped together. Children and adults, men and women, felons and debtors, healthy and sick (including lepers)—all were forced to live communally."[12] Given the extreme crowding, the filthy, rat-infested environment, and the lack of proper nutrition, it was not surprising that the strong preyed on the weak. Rape was common. Illnesses abounded. Many died of starvation or disease. The hopelessness of people confined in such conditions is well illustrated in the words scrawled on a cell wall by one desperate inmate:

> To the builders of this nitemare though you may never get to read these words. I pity you; for the cruelity [*sic*] of your minds have designed this hell; if men's buildings are a reflection of what they are, this one portraits the ugliness of all humanity. IF ONLY YOU HAD SOME COMPASSION.[13]

CLOSE-UP ON CORRECTIONS
London's Famous Newgate Gaol

The outside had a nice appearance, but the inside was another matter. The dark and gloomy cells were poorly ventilated, the water supply inadequate, and the stench appalling. These conditions gave rise to outbreaks of gaol fever, which was a form of typhus. The gaol fumes help spread the disease to many prisoners. . . .

There seems to have been very little, if any, segregation of the Newgaters, with the exception of those cast into the lower dungeons. . . . According to an inmate placed there in 1724, it was "a terrible stinking dark and dismal place situated underground into which no daylight can come. It was paved with stone; the prisoners had no beds and lay on the pavement whereby they endured great misery and hardship."

Those prisoners who could afford to do so had their food and clothing sent to them from the outside. The alternative was to purchase such items from the keeper and his turnkeys, which resulted in tidy profits. . . . The gaol workers also made sums of money from the sale of spirits, candles, food, and even water. Gaolers also charged for the privilege of being released from irons and for allowing prisoners to approach the warming fire.

Source: J.M. Moynahan and Troy R. Bunke, "London's Famous Newgate Gaol (1188–1902)," *American Jails*, Vol. 5, No. 2 (May/June, 1991), pp. 76–77.

Breakdown of the Feudal System

As long as people were tied to the land and obliged to landowners through serfdom and tithings, they were relatively easy to control. But with the breakdown of the feudal system and the decline of craft guilds came mass unemployment and poverty. People moved about from county to city, dissolving their ties to neighbors, family, and the land that had held them in bounds for centuries. The hungry and jobless migrated from rural areas to the cities, bringing with them a rise in crime that society was ill equipped to cope with.

To deal with social outcasts, debtors' prisons were established in addition to jails and workhouses.[14] In fact, it was the poor and the insane who were first confined for purposes other than awaiting death or corporal punishment. With the scarcity of laborers following the Black Death,

LEARNING GOALS

Do you know:
6. what impact the breakdown of the feudal system had on the development of debtors' prisons and workhouses?
7. why banishment and exile were used extensively following the Industrial Revolution, and what brought an end to the transportation of offenders to the U.S.?

workhouses were used as sources of cheap, forced labor. One of the first was established in London at St. Brigit's Well—called Bridewell—in 1557. The use of workhouses became widespread throughout Europe to house the insane and to "reform" minor offenders (such as beggars and pickpockets) by hard work and discipline. Debtors' prisons housed the indigent, who were incarcerated until family, friends, or charitable sources paid their monetary obligations—or until death.

Banishment and Exile

banishment or exile: forms of punishment whereby offenders were transported to distant lands, often to work at hard labor, with no hope of return.

Serious offenders were transported to **banishment or exile**. Banishment was considered an appropriate response to misbehavior, a means of ridding civilized society of nuisances through a sentence to the wilds of the unknown, as reflected in the following decree:

> I sentence you . . . but to what I know not—perhaps to storm and shipwreck, perhaps to infectious disorders, perhaps to famine, perhaps to be massacred by savages, perhaps to be devoured by wild beasts. Anyway, take your chance, perish or prosper, suffer or enjoy; I rid myself of the sight of you. . . . I shall give myself no more trouble over you.[15]

Banishment was also a reflection of the economic conditions of the time. Replacement of the feudal system with a developing capitalistic economy occurred with the Industrial Revolution in the mid-eighteenth century. The mechanization provided by the Industrial Revolution made slavery no longer profitable. Consequently, criminals had to be exported. Russia sent its criminals to Siberia. Spain and Portugal sent theirs to Africa. France sent its to South America. England sent its criminals to Australia and America. As one historian has noted, "wilderness was the first penal colony."[16]

Because the exiled prisoners provided a free source of labor in the developing colonies, there was a considerable economic advantage to this practice. At the beginning of the American Revolution in 1776, however, America was closed to British prisoners because the government did not want to risk shipping more able-bodied Englishmen who would take up arms against the mother country. Subsequently, some offenders were confined in "hulks" (old ships anchored in rivers and harbors),[17] while others were sent to Australia until 1879, when that practice was terminated. Prisons eventually substituted for banishment.

LEARNING GOALS

Do you know:
8. what types of punishments were first employed in the American colonies?
9. when and where the first U.S. prison was established?

EARLY AMERICAN CORRECTIONS

Corrections in America had a harsh beginning. Most of the early development of the United States centered on the northeastern sea-board, where the English came in search of freedom from religious persecution. The Puritans who settled

EXHIBIT 3.1
During colonial times, even relatively minor offenders could find themselves in a revolving pillory, subjected to public humiliation in the town square.

Source: Courtesy of the Federal Bureau of Prisons.

there, however, were equally intolerant of religious views that conflicted with their own.

The colonists brought with them extremely severe criminal codes from England, which, combined with the Puritans' strict concepts of sin, created a rigid system of social control. The famous witchcraft trials in 1692 were prompted by this religious fervor. Even the celebration of Christmas was considered sacrilegious and was outlawed in 1659, and the Connecticut Code of 1650 "stipulated the death penalty for children who disobeyed their parents."[18]

Colonial Punishments

Infractions were dealt with severely. Reflecting the colonists' British heritage, corporal and capital punishment were used frequently and carried out publicly. Branding and various forms of mutilation were also employed, both as punishment and to mark the lawbreaker with identification, since it would then be nearly impossible to find honest employment. Minor offenders such as gossips might find themselves subjected to public humiliation through the ducking stool (submerged in water until near drowning), similar to what is known as "water-boarding" today.

Stocks and pillories secured the offender's head and hands within wooden frames that were located in the town square. These devices were not just passive measures. In addition to provoking verbal ridicule, they enabled passers-by to pelt the constrained offender with stones and various other missiles. "The victim might also be whipped or branded while in the stocks or pillory" and, when released, "compelled either to tear his ears loose from the nails or have them cut away carelessly by the officer in charge."[19] For more serious crimes, capital punishment was imposed—by hanging, burning at the stake, or breaking on the rack.[20]

Colonial Correctional Institutions

Along with England's laws and punishments, early settlers brought with them the English system of jails, which became the first correctional institutions in this country. Like British gaols, early American jails housed defendants waiting trial or convicted offenders waiting the imposition of their sentence. The concept of "serving time" in jail was still unknown. Also like their British counterparts, Americans adopted the *fee system* for operating jails, along with the resulting abuses and corruption. The first U.S. jails, established in Virginia during the early seventeenth century, charged "two pounds of tobacco" as the fee for admission or release.[21]

Despite the democratic ideals on which this country was founded, the British practice of enabling the rich to avoid jail or live in comfortable quarters was adopted. In contrast to the privileges afforded the wealthy, the poor were confined in gruesome conditions of hunger, filth, and disease spread by communal living. Food was minimal, sanitary conditions deplorable, and discipline nonexistent. Similarly to their jailed English counterparts, "it was not uncommon for individuals with no resources to die of starvation."[22]

The first institution intended for long-term punishment rather than pretrial detention was Newgate Prison, established in Simsbury, Connecticut, just prior to the American Revolution (1773). Actually, Newgate was an abandoned copper mine, with administrative buildings constructed over the mine's shaft. Three excavated caverns with one pool of fresh water constituted the prison. Offenders were confined underground, in the dripping water, foul air, and horrid gloom of what has been described as essentially a dungeon. Men and women, adults and children, sick and well, criminals and political prisoners (Tory sympathizers) were all placed together. Escapes were frequent, since "existence in the dungeon was so unbearable that getting out was the one incentive that kept its inmates alive."[23]

Enlightenment: the Age of Reasoning that followed the Middle Ages, reflecting a period of expanded knowledge and search for truth.

FROM VENGEANCE TO JUSTICE

By the mid-eighteenth century, conditions were ripe for major changes in both Europe and the United States. Punishments had become excessively violent and bloody, totally out of proportion to the seriousness of the offense. At the same time, Europe was experiencing the impact of the **Enlightenment** (also known as the "Age of Reason"). Traditional assumptions were challenged, greater emphasis was placed on individual equality, and the barbarity of punishment practices was called into question.

John Howard's Prison Reforms

Among the pioneers insisting on changes in penal practices was the sheriff of Bedfordshire, John Howard, a former prisoner himself. The next "Close-up on

Corrections" features an account of Howard's personal experiences, which inspired his demands for change.

CLOSE-UP ON CORRECTIONS
John Howard (1726–1790)

John Howard's interest in prisons began when he was on his way to Portugal in 1754. His ship was captured by a French privateer, and those on board were treated with great severity. While confined, he gained sufficient evidence to show that hundreds of English prisoners had perished because of poor treatment. He was permitted to return to England on parole to negotiate an exchange, and in 1773, he became the high sheriff of Bedfordshire. In that capacity, he visited the jail which he was in charge of and found people detained for months until they paid fees for their own release. His first act was to apply for a salary for the jailer in order to reduce the reliance on fees. From that time on, he devoted himself to penal reform.

Source: D.L. Howard, *John Howard: Prison Reformer* (London: Christopher Johnson, 1958).

Struck by the deplorable conditions that he found when he became responsible for the local gaol, Howard embarked on visits to prisons throughout both Britain and Europe, documenting what he found and pressing for reform. His blistering essay on *The State of the Prisons in England and Wales* (1777) for the first time called public attention to the plight of incarcerated offenders. Among the improvements that he advocated were:[24]

- segregation of prisoners by age, sex, and severity of their offense;
- cells for prisoners, to reduce moral and physical contamination;
- salaried staff to prevent the extortion of prisoners;
- appointment of chaplains and medical officers to address the spiritual and physical needs of inmates;
- prohibitions against the sale of liquor to prisoners;
- provision of adequate clothing and food to ensure continued good health.

It was, in fact, Howard who coined the term "penitentiary" to indicate that such institutions should be designed according to the Quaker philosophy of penance and contrition by reflecting on one's sins. The impact of his legacy lives on even today through prison reform groups that commemorate his name—the John Howard societies.

The U.S. Constitution

Rejecting Europe's class-based aristocracy and monarchy rule, American colonists embraced equality and a democratic system of government. Moreover, the

Constitution of the United States was developed during the period of the Enlightenment, reflecting many of its humanitarian principles.

The Constitution is critical to corrections, because it provides the framework for the American system of administering justice. Citizens (including criminal offenders) may lose some of their civil rights but never their constitutional guarantees. While the Constitution itself establishes our democratic system of government, it is the first ten Amendments that are of particular importance—the Bill of Rights. (See the next "Close-up on Corrections" for a look at how those amendments pertain to corrections.) This emphasis on the worth of human life, along with the liberty to enjoy it, was in stark contrast to the arbitrary and inhumane practices of the past.

CLOSE-UP ON CORRECTIONS
Constitutional Rights Related to Corrections

Amendment 1

The First Amendment establishes our right to freedom of religion, freedom of speech, and freedom of the press, along with the right to peaceably assemble and "petition government for a redress of grievances." Prisoners have used their First Amendment privileges to challenge the conditions of their confinement.

Amendment 5

Among other provisions, the Fifth Amendment requires "due process of law" before anyone can be deprived of "life, liberty, or property." This has implications for such correctional procedures as the revocation of probation or parole.

Amendment 6

The Sixth Amendment protects citizens against arbitrary practices of government, and therefore can be invoked in conjunction with disciplinary actions in correctional facilities.

Amendment 8

It is this provision that is often cited by inmates challenging the constitutionality of their confinement, since it prohibits the infliction of "cruel and unusual punishment" as well as "excessive bail."

Amendment 14

Further applying constitutional guarantees to the states, the Fourteenth Amendment assures all citizens that no state shall "deprive any person of life, liberty, or property without due process of law; nor deny to any person . . . the equal protection of the laws."

THE PENITENTIARY EMERGES

Even before such protections were established in the Constitution, Pennsylvania had a reform-minded governor, William Penn. He replaced existing regulations governing conduct in that colony with the Quaker criminal code. Quite humane in comparison to the extremely severe laws in effect at the time, it called for:

- abolishing capital punishment for crimes other than homicide;

- substituting imprisonment at hard labor for bloody punishments;

- providing free food and lodging to inmates;

- replacing the pillory and stocks with houses of detention.[25]

Penn's humanitarian principles were repealed at the time of his death in 1718, but they were later revived. With both capital punishment and excessive displays of harsh public reprisals denounced as serving only to harden criminals, the nature of punishment began to shift from physical to psychological.

The Walnut Street Jail

If the widespread use of corporal and capital punishments was to be abandoned, it was necessary to develop an alternative sanction. It was for this purpose that the Quakers established the first penitentiary in 1790 at Philadelphia's **Walnut Street Jail**. "Unlike the workhouses, prisons, and jails already in existence, the Walnut Street Jail was used exclusively for the correction of convicted felons."[26] In stark contrast to Newgate, it was the first institution designed for reform—that is, to make the offender penitent (hence the term "penitentiary").

Walnut Street Jail: actually a prison, established by the Quakers in 1790, with emphasis on penitence instead of harsh punishment.

Following many of the concepts advocated by John Howard, men and women were housed in separate facilities. Liquor was prohibited. Inmates were classified by the seriousness of their offense. During the day, they worked on handicrafts in their cells under strict rules of silence. A small exercise yard was attached to each cell. Cells were constructed to provide solitary confinement in order to eliminate moral contamination from other prisoners. This also served to encourage inmates to meditate at night on the evils of their ways.

The Quakers' religious orientation created a more humane prison aimed at treatment by solitary confinement, hard work, religious instruction, and Bible reading. With no distractions, the intent was to focus exclusively on pursuing penitence and reformation. Despite its relative progressiveness, however, imposed silence and lack of personal contact over extended periods of time took a toll on the inmates' psychological health—in terms of both suicides and mental illness.

EXHIBIT 3.2
In 1790, the Walnut Street Jail in Philadelphia became the birthplace of the first penal facility directed toward the correction of convicted felons.

The Walnut Street Jail served as the model for what became known as the **Pennsylvania system**. It was adopted at Eastern State Penitentiary (Philadelphia), the Western State Penitentiary in Pittsburgh, and in prisons throughout a number of other northeastern states. While we will see that the Pennsylvania system did not survive in this country, it did make a permanent impact on the public's response to criminal behavior and the nature of correctional practices.

Pennsylvania system: the approach developed by the Quakers that advocated achieving repentance through solitary confinement, reading the Bible, and reflecting on one's sins.

The Auburn System

It is somewhat ironic that the major competition to the Pennsylvania system came from the **Auburn system**, since the facility constructed at Auburn, New York in 1815 was originally based on many of the principles of the Walnut Street Jail. In fact, both systems included solitary confinement in separate cells and enforced silence at all times to prevent inmates from communicating. But, while prisoners at Auburn were locked in their cells at night, during the day they participated together in congregate work. Although the mental distraction of work may appear to create a more humane system, Auburn was far from a humanitarian environment. As described in the next "Close-up on Corrections," inside accounts reveal rigid routines and harsh discipline to control inmate behavior. Adding further to their humiliation, although inmates were not permitted to receive visitors, "citizens who paid admission could come into the prison and look them over," as if they were in a zoo.[27]

Auburn system: the approach focused on production through congregate work and harsh discipline, initiated in Auburn, NY.

Unlike the Auburn system, the Pennsylvania system provided work within one's cell only as a limited diversion from its major emphasis on seeking penance through required Bible reading and reflection on one's sins. Complete solitary confinement was considered essential at all times in order to maintain discipline, prevent contamination, and more effectively manipulate the inmate's will. In contrast, the Auburn system could confine inmates in smaller units—since they did not need cell space in which to work, and discipline could be assured with on-the-spot lashings for rule violations. But more importantly, because Auburn could generate productive labor, the goal of reformation was dropped in favor of efficiency and economy.[28] Thus, it became a more profitable system to operate.

CLOSE-UP ON CORRECTIONS
Discipline in the Auburn System

The prisoners are obliged to obey instantly all orders issued by the foremen, to work quickly and efficiently without pause, in silence, and with downcast eyes. . . . They may not speak to one another except when ordered to do so by their supervisors. . . . They are expressly forbidden to converse with visitors. . . . The least breach of these rules is punished immediately and sternly. Any misdeed shall be penalized instantly and without mercy by flogging with a whip or a cane on the shoulders or the naked back. Every supervisor has the right to mete out punishment, and there is no fixed limit to the number of stripes that may be given.

Source: Torsten Eriksson, *The Reformers: An Historical Survey of Pioneer Experiments in the Treatment of Criminals* (New York: Elsevier, 1976), pp. 56–57.

For a number of years, intense debate raged in both the United States and Europe over the merits of each system. While Europeans eventually opted for the more treatment-oriented philosophy of the Pennsylvania system, most American states adopted the economical Auburn plan. The Pennsylvania system was geared toward small crafts that were rapidly becoming outdated, whereas Auburn's procedures were adaptable to the emerging factory-oriented methods of industrial production. In fact, vestiges of the Auburn system can still be seen in large penitentiaries, and the degrading "prison stripes" uniforms introduced there more than 170 years ago briefly made a comeback in some places during recent years.

U.S. PRISON DEVELOPMENTS

Along with Auburn's philosophy of congregate work, U.S. prisons adopted its stern discipline and degrading practices. Emphasizing strict rules and obedient compliance, infractions were dealt with swiftly and harshly. Staff were relatively free to respond to misbehavior and "disrespect" as they saw fit. This promoted efficiency in terms of administrative operations, but it did little in terms of constructive change for the offenders. Prisons were judged by their "production record and number

LEARNING GOALS

Do you know:
14. how Alexander Maconochie and Walter Crofton influenced correctional developments?
15. what caused the downfall of the industrial era of corrections?
16. the types of prison labor still in use today?

of escapes, not by the number of inmates rehabilitated," and during much of the nineteenth century "silence characterized not only prisoners, but the public" as well.[29]

Most of the prisons in populated areas during this period were large, industrial, gothic-style "fortresses," designed to hold as many as 4,000 to 6,000 inmates in conditions of tight security. In less settled places, territorial jails eventually developed into prisons, and even a few floating hulks emerged in California during the gold rush.[30]

Southern states developed in a different pattern. The agricultural economy there was based on a semifeudal system in which the plantation owners maintained hired help and slaves on large tracts of land. As a result, there was little need for large, central prisons. It was the occupation armies from the North who established the first real prisons in most southern states following the Civil War.

In the postwar South, there were not enough tax funds to support adequate schools, so it is not surprising that correctional institutions received low priority. Arrangements were made in most southern states for a **lease system**, where prisoners were leased to the highest bidder. The bidders were generally large landowners, railroad companies, or contractors. Unfortunately, such enterprises were more concerned with making profits than with providing humane conditions for their laborers. The abuses, exploitation, and atrocities that resulted from this system have created a sordid chapter in correctional history, and in the overall saga of man's inhumanity to man.[31] "In retrospect, the most that can be said for this period of American prison history is that . . . it was better than a return to the barbarities of capital and corporal punishment."[32]

lease system: the practice of contracting with large landowners or companies to hire-out prisoners to work for the highest bidder.

The Reform Era

With attention no longer diverted by war, the sorry plight of American prisons had finally recaptured public notice by 1870. Reform-minded prison administrators, members of Congress, and prominent citizens gathered in Cincinnati that year to form the **National Prison Association**, conducting the first meeting of what has now become the American Correctional Association (ACA). The tradition of ACA as a national corrections advocate was firmly established by the foresighted principles adopted at the 1870 meeting, described in the next "Close-up on Corrections."

National Prison Association: now the American Correctional Association, a group of reform-minded leaders who first met in 1870 to improve correctional practices.

CLOSE-UP ON CORRECTIONS
Principles of the 1870 National Prison Association

1. Reformation, not the vindictive infliction of suffering, should be the purpose of penal treatment.
2. Prisoners should be classified on the basis of a mark system patterned after the Irish system.

3. Rewards should be provided for good conduct.

4. Prisoners should be made to realize that their futures rest in their own hands.

5. Indeterminate sentences should be substituted for fixed sentences, and disparities in sentences removed.

6. Religion and education are the most important agencies of reformation.

7. Discipline should be administered so that it gains the cooperation of the inmate and maintains his self-respect.

8. The goal of the prison should be to make industrious free citizens, not orderly and obedient prisoners.

9. Industrial training should be fully provided.

10. Prisons should be small; separate institutions should be provided for different types of offenders.

11. The social training of prisoners should be facilitated; silence rules should be abolished.

12. Society at large must realize that it is responsible for the conditions that breed crime.

Source: Enoch C. Wines, ed., *Transactions of the National Congress on Penitentiary and Reformatory Discipline* (Albany, NY: Argus, 1871).

Among the leaders influencing deliberations in Cincinnati and, later, developments throughout the country were:

- *Rutherford B. Hayes*, former president of the United States, who was elected as the first president of the National Prison Association, serving until his death in 1893. A progressive social reformer, Hayes pressed for jail reform, separation of offenders by age, indeterminate sentences, and improved academic and vocational education for inmates.[33]

- *Captain Alexander Maconochie*, a Scot in charge of the British penal colony on Norfolk Island in the South Pacific. When Maconochie arrived at his post in 1840, conditions were so bad that "men reprieved from the death penalty wept, and those who were to die thanked God."[34] While he did not totally abandon punishment, he maintained that an attempt should also be made to reform offenders by providing incentives to encourage good behavior and hope for early release. Since determinate sentencing offered no chance for release until the full term was served, Maconochie implemented the first form of indeterminate sentencing—a "mark system," whereby freedom could be earned through hard work and proper behavior. An elaborate process of earning "marks" through labor and good conduct was developed, with discipline gradually diminished as inmates progressed through the system and earned early release. But Maconochie's practices were not well received among the British business enterprises dependent on inmate labor, and he was eventually removed from office. His visionary concepts, however, lived on.[35]

- *Sir Walter Crofton*, chairman of the board of directors of the Irish Convicts Prisons. Influenced by Maconochie's efforts, Crofton also believed that the amount of time served should be related to the prisoner's reformation. Based on that theory, in 1854 he established the Irish ticket-of-leave system, essentially the first form of parole. Offenders could earn their release by progression through a series of stages from solitary labor to congregate work. As offenders moved through various later stages, both discipline and the length of their sentences were reduced. During the final stage, they worked outside without supervision, moving freely between the prison and the community. Those who proceeded successfully through all stages were awarded a conditional "ticket of leave," which could be revoked any time before the original sentence expired if the offender violated established standards—in much the same manner as parole can be revoked today.

• *Zebulon Brockway*, superintendent of the Elmira Reformatory in New York, which opened in 1876 for young offenders. In the United States, it was Brockway who first experimented with these new approaches. With approval of the legislature to permit indeterminate sentencing, release was earned through a modified version of the mark system, combined with the Irish ticket of leave. But, although Brockway has been acclaimed for introducing such reforms as education and vocational training at Elmira, he did so with an iron fist. History portrays him as a cruel administrator whose harsh and degrading physical punishments ultimately resulted in serious charges culminating in an investigation which concluded that "the brutality practiced at the reformatory has no parallel in any modern penal institution in our country."[36] For a disturbing description of conditions at Elmira, see the next "Close-up on Corrections."

CLOSE-UP ON CORRECTIONS
Elmira—Reform or Repression?

The nation's model correctional institution was overcrowded, understaffed, and grossly mismanaged. Key treatment programs did not fulfill their stated goals and objectives. Violence, escapes, smuggling, theft, homosexuality, revolts, arson, and other forms of inmate resistance were serious problems. Inmates suffered extraordinarily harsh punishments—including severe whippings and months of solitary confinement in dark, cold dungeons—and deliberate psychological torture. In the words of one inmate [who was removed from his cell with prodding from a hot poker in order to be punished for failure to complete his work]: "A hook was fastened into my shackles, and I was hoisted off the floor. I got a half dozen blows with the paddle right across the kidneys. The pain was so agonizing that I fainted. They revived me, and when I begged for mercy, Brockway struck me on the head with a strap, knocking me insensible. . . . I stayed in the dungeon that night and the next day, shackled, and received only bread and water. The following day I was again hoisted up and beaten, returned to the dungeon, and after one day's rest, beaten again. . . . I remained for twenty-one days on bread and water."

Elmira was, quite simply, a brutal prison . . . [where] beatings caused discolored faces, bloody noses, and swollen eyes . . . medical care was inadequate, and inmates had been whipped, punched, and chained in solitary confinement on bread and water. Balancing the conflicting aims of repression and reform proved to be a difficult, if not impossible, task.

Source: Alexander W. Pisciotta, *Benevolent Repression: Social Control and the American Reformatory-Prison Movement* (New York: New York University Press, 1994), pp. 33, 36–37, 57–59, citing the 1884 *Report and Proceedings of the New York State Board of Charities.*

The promise of original intentions was also diminished by the introduction of probation (which diverted the most promising offenders from reformatories), as well as the lack of qualified staff (who were better prepared to promote discipline than provide education). That is not to say that the visions of early reformers were entirely fruitless, for they did stimulate faith in the potential for positive change.

The Industrial Era

Inmate labor has been central to the development of prisons since the first workhouses in the sixteenth century. Even in the penitence-minded Walnut Street Jail, private contractors furnished raw material that prisoners turned into finished products in their cells for an agreed price. More profitable industrial production has been a feature of corrections since the Auburn Penitentiary and, as we have seen, played a major role in the Auburn versus Pennsylvania debate. Self-supporting prisons have always been popular with taxpayers. As early as 1828, prisons at Auburn and Sing Sing were paying for themselves.

Not until the twentieth century, however, did inmate industries flourish on a large scale. Although leasing inmates outside of the prison continued, at this time, a new system of **contract labor** emerged. Prison factories were constructed

contract labor: the practice of using prisoners to work under contract to private industry.

EXHIBIT 3.3 Industrial production has always been an integral feature of American prisons, originally to enable prisons to be self-sufficient and, more recently, to reduce idleness and teach vocational trades.

Source: Courtesy of the California Department of Corrections.

within the walls of the institution, and administrators contracted with firms either for wages or for the sale of finished products. In rural areas, offenders worked at manual labor on prison-owned farms. Many of these operations were justified under the guise of achieving reform through disciplined work, but the underlying motive was profit or, more explicitly, achieving the greatest return for the least investment.

Inmates were often virtual slaves of the state, working long hours under harsh conditions with minimal subsistence. A stinging indictment of such practices was issued as early as 1875 in the attorney general's vivid description of prevalent abuses: "[T]he prisoners work for cruel taskmasters . . . are improperly fed and clothed, overworked, sometimes severely beaten for slight offenses, and are made a source of large profit to those who avail themselves of this kind of forced labor."[37]

Other accounts further attested to the barbarity of conditions, noting that "a sentence to such imprisonment was, in effect, a life sentence," as most men could not survive the brutal conditions for more than ten years.[38]

Chain Gangs

Perhaps the most notoriously abusive practices were the infamous chain gangs of this era—intentionally used to repress and humiliate prisoners.[39] Chained together, offenders swung sledgehammers in monotonous unison under the watchful eye of shotgun-toting supervisors who administered lashes to those who could not keep up with the line. Nor did they hesitate to shoot anyone attempting to escape. In one grisly expression of the pent-up anger induced by such treatment, inmates in a labor camp who were breaking up rocks took the sledgehammers and actually used them to break their own legs during an uprising.[40] As one historian put it, the exploitation of inmate labor during this shameful period "embittered the hearts of prisoners to the extent that they came out more vindictive and more ready to injure society than they were when first placed within prison walls."[41]

The chain gangs continued working on road projects and prison construction in some states for many years. However, the late 1920s marked the beginning of the end for large-scale prison industries. This time it was not the progressive views of humanitarian reformers that altered prison practices, but rather, the political realities of the labor market. As organized labor emerged in the industrial northeast, paid workers complained about competing with free inmate labor, which dramatically reduced the price at which their goods could be sold. In response to these concerns, Congress passed the **Hawes–Cooper Act** of 1929, which reduced the competitive advantage of prison goods and subjected them to the laws of the state to which they were shipped. This was the first of a number of restrictions on inmate products.

Hawes–Cooper Act: the first federal legislation placing restrictions on prison industries.

Production Restrictions

With the severe unemployment of the Great Depression in the 1930s, there was even more pressure to prohibit the interference of inmate labor with free markets. Additional legislation was passed to limit prison industries by requiring a "prison-made" label and, ultimately, prohibiting the shipment of prison goods across state lines. By 1940, every state had passed similar restrictions on prison-made products as the power and influence of organized labor increased. Some of these restrictions remain in force today.

Such developments have curtailed the profit motive and dramatically altered the shape of prison industry, but they have not abolished it completely. There are generally three types of prison labor currently in use by various correctional departments throughout the country:

1. *State account system.* Goods are produced in prison and sold on a restricted market within the state.

2. *State use system.* Goods produced are restricted to items that can be used by other state agencies (such as schools) and mental health institutions.

3. *Public works system.* Inmates provide labor for construction and maintenance of roads, parks, conservation projects, and other public facilities.

Industrial Renewal

Certainly, the widespread abuse and exploitation of inmate labor prevalent during the industrial era called for change, but unfortunately change came in the form of political restrictions rather than practical reforms. For years, corrections struggled to cope with the complete reversal from forced labor to forced leisure. Although inmate idleness is a problem that still faces correctional administrators, there have been renewed efforts to provide offenders with meaningful labor.

EXHIBIT 3.4
While inmates actively contributed to the war effort, prison industries declined dramatically in the years following World War II.

Source: Courtesy of the Federal Bureau of Prisons.

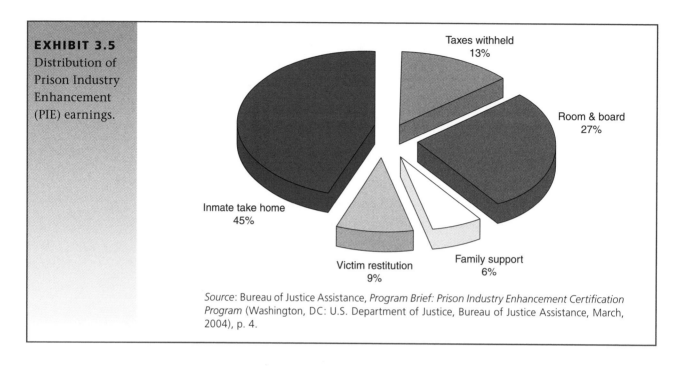

EXHIBIT 3.5
Distribution of Prison Industry Enhancement (PIE) earnings.

Taxes withheld
13%

Room & board
27%

Inmate take home
45%

Victim restitution
9%

Family support
6%

Source: Bureau of Justice Assistance, *Program Brief: Prison Industry Enhancement Certification Program* (Washington, DC: U.S. Department of Justice, Bureau of Justice Assistance, March, 2004), p. 4.

By the mid-1970s, a resurgence of support for prison industries emerged. This reemphasis gained an advocate in 1983 when former Chief Justice Warren Burger called for prisons to become "factories with fences,"[42] to provide relief from the boredom of prison life, equip inmates with marketable skills, and create a prison environment more reflective of the real world. Since then, progressive leaders have been undertaking renewed efforts to promote the merits of correctional industries to the public. As described in the next "Close-up on Corrections," joint-venture projects between prisons and the private sector have formed a number of successful partnerships that have contributed millions of dollars in taxes, room and board, family support, and victim compensation (as illustrated in Exhibit 3.5).

CLOSE-UP ON CORRECTIONS
Developments in Prison Industries

In 1979 Congress lifted the ban on interstate transportation and sale of prison-made goods—but only under certain conditions. Participants must meet the requirements of the Private Sector/Prison Industry Enhancement Certification Program (commonly known as PIE), which specifies that:

- inmate workers are paid the prevailing wage in the local area;
- local unions are consulted before the program starts;
- inmate employment does not displace free-society workers or occur in occupations for which there is a labor surplus in the community.

PIE programs not only enhance job skills and reduce prison idleness, but also make significant contributions; for example:

- If you attended a high school or college commencement ceremony wearing a graduation gown—or if you buy leisure clothes from a major department store—they may have been made by inmates in the South Carolina Department of Corrections.
- If you want your furniture reupholstered for a good price, contact the Arizona Department of Corrections.
- If you wear a baseball cap featuring the emblem of your favorite team, it may have been produced by inmates working at the Connecticut Department of Corrections.
- If you are fishing with a top-of-the-line, handmade rod, it may have been produced by inmates working at the Colorado Department of Corrections.
- If you need a wild horse tamed, get in touch with the Utah Department of Corrections.

Sources: Compiled from George Sexton, "Work in American Prisons: Joint Ventures with the Private Sector," *National Institute of Justice: Program Focus* (Washington, DC: U.S. Department of Justice, 1995), p. 12; the website of the National Correctional Industries Association, www.nationalcia.org; and Bureau of Justice Assistance, *Program Brief: Prison Industry Enhancement Certification Program* (Washington, DC: U.S. Department of Justice, Bureau of Justice Assistance, July, 2002).

Despite such overall economic benefits, however, the public is not always supportive of prison industries. As one company manager said when driven out of business after a federal prison industry won a lucrative contract, "It's hard for me to accept that the government would put the welfare and benefit of convicted felons above the interests of taxpayers."[43] Throughout correctional history, this tension between improving prisoner productivity and interfering with private enterprise has played an ongoing tug-of-war that intensifies with every economic downturn.

CORRECTIONS TODAY

As punitive punishments became less and less acceptable, a new emphasis on treatment and rehabilitation had emerged by the late 1930s. Concerns were raised about the negative effects of imprisonment. Sentencing options other than incarceration became more attractive alternatives. Society began to display a greater interest in what was happening behind prison walls. Institutions became more open to public scrutiny. In general, there was excitement and optimism about the possibility of salvaging offenders through treatment—of accomplishing what the term "corrections" is meant to imply.

LEARNING GOALS

Do you know:

17. what factors stimulated the rehabilitative era of corrections?
18. what basic constitutional rights of inmates the Supreme Court recognized during the 1960s?
19. what social forces during the 1980s generated the move to determinate sentencing, what major correctional problem resulted, and what has been done in response?

But improvements did not occur quickly or uniformly. In retrospect, it is apparent that corrections overall was never well equipped to achieve rehabilitative ideals. Nor was the extensive idleness imposed by drastic reductions in prison industries offset by therapeutic, educational, or training programs. Through it all, administrators were forced to accommodate greater numbers of inmates in often antiquated facilities. At the same time, the courts were beginning to recognize the rights of inmates to challenge conditions and procedures that violated constitutional protections. All of these events—positive and negative—have had an impact on the nature of corrections today.

The Rehabilitative Era

With the stock market crash and resulting Great Depression of the 1930s came economic disaster. The security previously enjoyed by society was destroyed. Savings were wiped out virtually overnight. Unemployment skyrocketed to all-time record highs. Hunger reduced distinctions between social classes. Many who had been economically comfortable—even wealthy—were living in poverty. The most desperate committed suicide. Others turned to crime for survival. All of this was due to events they had no ability to influence. The long-held explanations of crime as "sins" or personal weaknesses of the offender no longer seemed as valid. Society began to realize that perhaps it was through no fault of their own that some people engage in crime, but rather, that it may be a reaction to forces so far beyond their control as worldwide economic markets.

At the same time, the psychological and social sciences were making major advances. Freud's theories of psychoanalytic treatment offered potential for "curing" criminal behavior. The field of social work gave legitimate recognition to attending to the needs of the underprivileged. With these developments, more attention was focused on corrections, and a new role was created for offenders as psychiatric and social work clients.

Along with changing perspectives on crime and renewed hope for dealing with it came a new philosophy of corrections—the medical model. Emphasis moved from retribution through incapacitation to improvement through rehabilitation. Chain gangs, lockstep marching, and striped uniforms gave way to psychological diagnosis, individual counseling, and group therapy. Determining inmates' needs began to take priority over punishing their deeds. By the 1950s, indeterminate sentences and the widespread use of parole held out the possibility of early release for progress in treatment programs.

That does not mean that all abuses had vanished. Although shifts in ideology pointed the field in a new direction, progress was relative to the dismal conditions of the past. Eventually, it would take the outside attention demanded by inmate riots and court intervention to improve the substandard physical conditions and dehumanizing supervisory techniques to which prisoners were still subjected.

Impact of the 1960s

The medical model reached its height in the midst of the turbulent 1960s—a period marked by liberal social attitudes, extensive federal funding, wars on poverty and crime, and massive civil rights demonstrations. The nation was swept up in vocal and sometimes violent protests against the status quo. Pressure mounted for change. The authority of social institutions was challenged on a widespread, nationwide basis, and corrections was no exception.

In keeping with the euphoria of the 1960s and its advocacy on behalf of the powerless in society, the Supreme Court intervened in the previously sacrosanct world of correctional administrators. Prior to that time, the courts had generally maintained a hands-off approach toward corrections.

That perspective changed dramatically as inmates gained powerful advocacy in the Supreme Court. By the mid-1960s, the Court had recognized the constitutional right of those incarcerated to maintain access to the judicial process and, specifically, to challenge the conditions under which they were confined.[44] Even more important, the Court later prohibited correctional administrators from denying or obstructing that fundamental right.[45] It became the duty of correctional officials to assure that the constitutional protections of inmates under their charge were not violated—opening a floodgate of litigation that held correctional personnel accountable for their actions.

It was also at this point that the public was becoming increasingly concerned about crime and the ability of the criminal justice system to deal with it. Thus, in 1965, President Lyndon Johnson convened the President's Commission on Law Enforcement and Administration of Justice, a prestigious group of national experts, to address the nation's crime problem and make recommendations for improving the police, courts, and corrections. The Commission's *Task Force Report: Corrections* represented the first comprehensive analysis of correctional practices in this country.

The task force firmly believed that "above all else" the effectiveness of corrections relies on "a sufficient number of qualified staff."[46] Many of its recommendations therefore called for major improvements in the selection, training, supervision, and accountability of correctional personnel. Moreover, the task force established correctional standards for operating institutions and programs. Concern for the proper treatment and well-being of inmates is illustrated in the standards for custodial supervision and discipline, which called for elimination of bread-and-water diets, corporal punishment, and useless "make-work" for purposes of humiliation.[47]

At the same time, the federal government was also becoming active in providing funds to support new correctional philosophies and innovative approaches. For example, the federal Prisoner Rehabilitation Act of 1965 offered grants to stimulate model projects. Many of these focused on alternatives to institutionalization—for the first time giving official recognition and status to community-based corrections.

Even though national studies, presidentially appointed commissions, and federally funded projects could not change conditions overnight, their impact was certainly felt. By the 1970s, the public had become much more aware of and concerned about the state of corrections. Minimum-security community-based approaches were used far more commonly. Within institutions, inmates were classified and separated by age, offense, and special needs. Specialized treatment facilities emerged. The Commission on Accreditation for Corrections was established to set and monitor standards for everything from cell size to health care. "Guards" were becoming "correctional officers," with job descriptions that focused as much on relating to offenders as on restricting their behavior. In places that were slow to adapt, reforms were stimulated by the courts. But, despite improvements, crime was still increasing, much of it committed by repeat offenders who had presumably been rehabilitated.

The Past as Prologue

Belief that "the past is prologue to the future" is perhaps nowhere better illustrated than in the retreat from rehabilitation toward a renewed emphasis on punishment in the 1980s. As the liberal attitudes of the 1960s gave way to the conservative politics of the 1980s, the public became increasingly disenchanted with the unfulfilled promises of the medical model. Concerns were voiced that rehabilitation was not working, and the Martinson report[48] appeared to confirm the worst suspicions. As the crime rate continued steadily upward, society became increasingly frustrated with the system's ineffectiveness as well as impatient with the offender's ability to change.

In retrospect, the extent to which public policies or correctional practices were to blame may have been overstated, in light of the fact that the post-World War II baby boom had reached its primary crime-risk age (late teens to young adulthood). It is possible that demographic patterns alone might have produced rising crime, regardless of sentencing procedures or correctional approaches. But the timing was ripe for reassessing America's response to crime. Pressures to "get tough" and assure that offenders received their "just deserts" mounted. In a number of states, indeterminate sentences and the hope they held out for early release were replaced by determinate (flat, fixed) sentences, often accompanied by the abolishment of discretionary parole.

But the shift from rehabilitation to retribution did not necessarily produce the intended effects. Without the advance planning needed to accommodate longer and more punitive sentences, the justice model was no more equipped to achieve its goals than its predecessor. Just as the funds were never forthcoming to implement the medical model effectively, the facilities needed to incarcerate greater numbers of inmates for longer periods of time under the justice model were not appropriated. Correctional institutions were unprepared for the massive influx of offenders into already strained facilities. Nor were the courts willing to tolerate vastly overcrowded institutions.

When facilities began drastically exceeding their capacity, the courts intervened, requiring that corrections keep the number of inmates being confined within mandated population caps. At the same time, correctional officials were becoming concerned about their ability to control inmates in the absence of the incentive that parole provided for good behavior. The answer to both crowding and control came in the form of gain time, whereby a specified number of days is automatically deducted from an offender's sentence for every month served without disciplinary infractions. This modification was essential to reduce prison populations to somewhat more manageable levels. However, gain time defeats the original purpose of the justice model to deter crime, incapacitate offenders, and assure that one's "debt to society" is paid by serving a full term without the possibility of early release.

Increasingly dissatisfied with gain time—yet still unwilling to raise taxes in support of massive prison construction—by the mid-1990s public policy-makers had taken yet another turn. Fueled by mounting fear of crime, intolerance of criminals, and exasperation with the system's response to both, a renewed focus on punishment took hold.[49]

Perhaps because crowding often diminished the length of time behind bars, there was a growing determination to intensify the distastefulness of imprisonment. Responses to the mounting punitive outcry gained steamroller momentum as, one after another, states jumped on the no-frills bandwagon and embraced humiliating practices; for example:

- Mississippi legislators voted in 1994 to return to striped uniforms with the word "convict" emblazoned on the back.[50]

- Alabama, Arizona, and Florida reinstated various forms of chain gangs in 1995,[51] followed by jails and prisons in a number of other locales.

- By 1997, once-basic staples of prison life ranging from weight lifting to TV programming were banned in many facilities throughout the country.[52]

Some of these changes have been more symbolic than substantive. There is likewise some disagreement over whether legislators are *responding* to public opinion or *reshaping* it with "get-tough" rhetoric designed to project a no-nonsense image at election time.[53] Moreover, to the extent that correctional officials need to "curry favor with legislative bodies, they may endorse deprivations that have no functional role in prison administration."[54]

Regardless of the reasons or motivations behind it, reaction from the field of corrections to such legislative micromanagement has been uniformly negative. Correctional administrators have been overwhelmingly unsupportive of no-frills mandates for at least two reasons: (1) Many of the prohibited activities fill what would otherwise be idle time. (2) They also serve important management functions—the "carrots" that can be offered to promote good behavior or withdrawn to control misbehavior.[55] While perhaps politically popular, such measures have been criticized by correctional officials as a "nasty" return to long-abandoned practices[56] that are based on "misconceptions" and "false impressions."[57] As at least one critic observed, "the corrections system is turning back the hands of time when the rest of the world is moving forward."[58]

However, the fact that correctional executives themselves have largely been opposed to what they have condemned as "harsh and mean-spirited" measures has not often made much of an impact.[59] By and large, leaders in the field have been relatively uninfluential in shaping the public policy agendas that guide correctional management. To the contrary, much of the public still harbors a misconception of prisons as so-called "country clubs." Nothing could be further from the truth. "Prisons are not country clubs: the guests are involuntary, the conditions generally spartan, and the routine deadly dull."[60]

It is too soon to judge how the correctional conglomerate will be affected by everything from the nationwide economic recession to the 2008 presidential election reflecting a somewhat more liberal policy-making agenda. But if, indeed, the past is prologue to the future, it is possible that the philosophy of corrections will again be reassessed in the face of both disenchantment with the justice model and inability to pay for it.

As an enterprise that deals with the disenfranchised of society, corrections has continually struggled to gain attention and support. Nevertheless, everything in life is relative. When viewed in comparison to the conditions faced by past reformers, corrections no doubt has made great strides. But the challenge for the future has shifted in recent years—from continuing progressive reforms to curtailing regressive reactions.

SUMMARY

While the victim's role in the criminal justice system has become more active today, it is far removed from the primitive practice in which the victim was responsible for seeking harsh retribution. With the rise of religion, crime was viewed as a sin that violated divine law and God's will, resulting in punishments that were brutal, inflicting extreme pain, suffering, and often death. The more "fortunate" were confined to convict ships or banished.

As the concepts of trials and courts developed, gaols were used to confine suspects until the king's court could convene or punishment could be carried out. Despite the fact that their occupants were still technically innocent, these early jails maintained virtually intolerable living conditions. Men and women, young and old, healthy and sick were forced to live together and pay fees for even the most minor necessities—a system later copied in American jails.

Adhering to strict Puritan religious beliefs, the first American colonists likewise employed extremely severe punishments for criminal offenses. Mutilation, branding, stocks, and pillories were all commonly used. Just prior to the American Revolution, the first U.S. prison—Newgate—was established in an abandoned copper mine, where conditions were as abysmal as those of the English gaols.

With the Age of Enlightenment and pioneering work of John Howard, public attention was called to the plight of law violators. Emphasis was placed on punishment in proportion to the offense. Fundamental rights were formally recognized in the U.S. Constitution, and the first U.S. penitentiary was established by the Quakers at the Walnut Street Jail. But the penitence-oriented philosophy of the Pennsylvania system was challenged by the greater economic benefit of congregate work in the Auburn system. Adopting the stern discipline, imposed silence, and hard work practiced at Auburn, corrections in the United States entered a period marked by abuses and exploitations that were not to be challenged until the beginning of the reform era in 1870.

Reformers promoted innovations ranging from indeterminate sentencing to parole and inmate education. Despite their forward thinking, throughout much of the early twentieth century, corrections focused predominately on the generation of profits through inmate leasing, contract labor, prison farms, and factories. With the rise of unions and the Great Depression, however, society could no longer afford competition from free inmate labor. The industrial era thus ended with legislative action restricting the sale of inmate products. Although interest in inmate industries is reviving, the focus today is more on providing meaningful work and career training than on strictly economic gains.

Following the introduction of psychoanalytic and social work techniques, corrections moved into the rehabilitative era. This emphasis on offender treatment reached its peak during the 1960s, with national studies, federal funding, and judicial recognition of inmates' rights. But liberal politics eventually gave way to the conservative agenda of the 1980s. Society became increasingly disillusioned with rising crime, recidivism, and the ineffectiveness of rehabilitation. Thus the medical model was replaced by the justice model, with its determinate sentencing structures.

But correctional facilities were no more equipped to implement the justice model than its predecessor. As institutions filled well beyond capacity, court-ordered population caps forced early release through gain time, thereby defeating the purpose of assuring that offenders received their "just deserts." These often contradictory historical fluctuations make it difficult to forecast just where corrections will be tomorrow, as society again reevaluates its priorities. In the meantime, the challenge is to adapt to more punitive sanctions without abandoning more positive solutions.

FOR FURTHER DISCUSSION

1. Determine how the concept of "benefit of clergy" relates to inequities that are still apparent today in the criminal justice system.

2. Compare society's vengeance-related primitive punishments to the contemporary justice model of public policy-making, and explain why it would not be in society's best interests to regress to medieval punishment practices.

3. Relate debtors' prisons and banishment or exile to the manner in which the U.S. addresses the issues of homelessness and mental illness today.

4. In terms of the historical era during which it was developed, discuss why the U.S. Constitution included the Bill of Rights.

5. Compare the Pennsylvania system to the Auburn system, especially in terms of how well each was suited to the social, political, and economic climate of the era in which they developed, and why one became more prevalent in the U.S.

6. Look further into the history of Elmira and Zebulon Brockway, and determine whether he can most accurately be characterized as a benevolent reformer or a repulsive dictator.

7. After watching the classic movie *I Was a Fugitive from a Chain Gang*, explain why the power of prison staff and administrators must be curtailed, and provide several recommendations for ways to do so.

8. From the taxpayer's perspective, argue for expanding prison industries. Then play the role of a union leader, discussing why prison industries are unfair competition with the free marketplace and need to be curtailed.

9. Explain what social, economic, and political forces propelled American public policy from the medical model to the justice model. Given economic conditions today, analyze the likelihood of yet another policy paradigm shift.

PART 2

Correctional Services, Practices, and Institutions

While recognizing that offenders are responsible for their own actions, we must also recognize our responsibility for providing the best possible correctional services.[1]
Correctional Service of Canada

ONE OF THE DIFFICULTIES IN THE field of corrections is that the general public is not aware of what goes on behind prison walls, inside jails, or within the caseloads of probation and parole. Police officers—working directly with the public and easily identifiable by uniforms and marked cars—apprehend and arrest offenders, but what happens after that is obscured in the dark recesses of correctional institutions and caseloads.

Moreover, society's clamor for punishment appears to give little support to community-based sentencing alternatives that do not involve institutional confinement. Outside of the correctional system, few may recognize the merits of such options as diversion, probation, or electronically monitored home confinement. Nor do most people appreciate just how restrictive community supervision actually can be, or just how much confinement actually can cost. Nor is the public clear about what correctional institutions should be accomplishing. Although everyone is concerned when prisons and jails fail to "rehabilitate" offenders, society has recognized the futility of achieving long-term behavioral changes. Consequently, it has left correctional institutions with a basic incapacitation mandate. Such a social compromise creates a more realistic mission for corrections but a less optimistic outlook for its clients.

Throughout the next chapters, these issues are explored as we look at both community-based and institutional corrections. Beginning with community-based alternatives in Chapter 4, we see how the least visible component of corrections works. The advantages and disadvantages of diverting offenders from the justice system are discussed, along with how electronically monitored home confinement can serve as an intermediate option for those who would otherwise be incarcerated. Even in the midst of the justice model's emphasis on punishment, institutional crowding has, if nothing else, necessitated continual use, and even expansion, of such alternatives.

As the oldest and most frequently used sentencing alternative, probation is the next focus of attention. We will look at who is eligible for probation, what restrictions probationers are subjected to, what services they are provided, and how they are supervised. Of course, not everyone functions effectively under community supervision, so we must also consider under what circumstances this privilege can be revoked. The unsuccessful termination of probation brings us to Chapter 5 and the next level on the sentencing scale—short-term confinement in jail.

Just as the public is not often aware of what actually occurs within community corrections, there is equal uncertainty about the function of jails. Yet there are far more jails than prisons in the United States and, as a unit of local government, jails are closer to the communities they serve. Because there are so many of them, they vary widely—from small, rural facilities to the megajails of major metropolitan areas, and from antiquated, unsanitary facilities built in the past century to the modern direct-supervision jails constructed in the past few years.

The jail population reflects similar disparities. Jail inmates range from those who are convicted to those still awaiting trial, from those serving short sentences for minor offenses to those awaiting transfer to prison for major violations, and from alcoholics and drug addicts to juveniles, vagrants, and the mentally ill. In the midst of such diversity, we will see how jails cope administratively with everything from classification to crowding.

This portrait of the jail is naturally followed by a description of those institutions reserved for offenders with longer-term sentences—state and federal prisons. Since they are less numerous than jails, there is more standardization among prisons. But, as we see in Chapter 6, they, too, can vary widely—ranging from minimum-security farms, ranches, or work-release centers to the maxi-max institutions that we traditionally tend to associate with the term "prison." Additionally, we take a look inside the prison compound to see how it is organized, how it operates, and how it controls inmates.

After exploring these institutional features, we encounter the challenges created by the continually escalating prison population. A review of overcrowding leads us to examine just who is in prison and why they are there, which leads to discussing in Chapter 7 the dynamics of the prison population. Looking at the totality of the population, we begin to see that prisons, like jails, may not always be housing those who most need to be kept in secure confinement. From that perspective, we view offenders with special needs—from childbearing females to those who are substance abusers, developmentally disabled, mentally ill, physically challenged, or geriatric offenders. Again, this raises the question of what society expects its correctional institutions to accomplish, and what will have been achieved upon their release.

In summary, whether the topic is community-based or institutional corrections, the bottom line is that a society concerned with crime and recidivism basically has two choices. We can attempt to prepare inmates for a law-abiding lifestyle during confinement, or we can avoid the debilitating effects of institutional life by retaining offenders under control in the community. Both approaches are explored in the following chapters, beginning with community-based treatment alternatives, moving to short-term confinement in jail, and concluding with incarceration in prison. Both options have advocates as well as opponents, benefits as well as drawbacks. But, without an understanding of community-based as well as institutional corrections, it is impossible to make informed public policy choices.

CHAPTER 4

Community-based Alternatives

From the very beginning, the direction of the correctional process must be back toward the community. It is in the community that crime will be committed or a useful life lived.[1]

Ramsey Clark

CHAPTER OVERVIEW

Over the past two decades, community-based alternatives have come to imply excessive leniency—"coddling criminals," "wrist slapping," "being soft on crime"—which is quite the opposite of the public's demands for "just deserts." In fact, programs that used to be called "alternatives to incarceration" are now labeled "intermediate sanctions" or "punishments," presumably because society does not interpret "alternatives to incarceration" as sufficiently punitive.[2] It has even been proposed that probation be recast as a "surveillance and supervision" program to satisfy the public's thirst for punishment.[3]

But renewed emphasis on the harsher sentencing practices of the justice model has provided a false sense of security. On the one hand, it was anticipated that potential offenders would think twice before engaging in crime if they knew the severity with which they would be punished. Moreover, even if would-be offenders were not deterred by the threat of punishment (and most were not), there was satisfaction in knowing that incapacitation would prevent further involvement in crime during the period of confinement. Quite true; also quite shortsighted. Upon release, offenders are returning to the very place they came from—free society. How secure are we in the belief that, having been exposed to the debilitating effects of prison life and now stigmatized as ex-offenders, they will make the dramatic changes necessary to become law-abiding citizens? If the answer is "Not very," then community-based approaches assume greater significance in achieving the goals of the justice system. This does not mean that community corrections is a panacea for solving the crime problem. But, even if a community-based approach does not do anything to improve offenders, at least it is not doing anything to worsen them. It is highly unlikely that the same could be said of incarceration.

Certainly, there are some offenders whose crimes are so violent and whose behavior is so uncontrollable that prison or jail is the only feasible option. Nevertheless, there are many others who are harmed more than helped by incarceration. Even in the midst of the "get-tough-on-crime" era, community-based alternatives to secure confinement were never abandoned. In part, this was a result of the inability of new prison construction to keep pace with demand. Overcrowding has called attention to the need to reserve costly prison beds for truly violent, hard-core, chronic offenders. But, beyond the practical limitations of space in secure confinement, there remains a fundamental ray of hope in the ability to sanction behavior properly without severing bonds with the community.

Everyone benefits if selected, low-risk offenders can pay their debt to society through community-based alternatives such as diversion, home confinement, community-based treatment, victim restitution, community service, or probation. The offender avoids the social isolation and stigmatizing impact of imprisonment. Society avoids the economic impact of unproductive confinement in high-cost facilities. However, without awareness of its benefits, community corrections can easily be dismissed as a disagreeable economic compromise rather than a directed effort to control behavior cost-effectively.

To what extent community-based alternatives will be maintained if demands for stiffer sentences do not abate remains uncertain. In that regard, such programs cannot afford to be viewed as "freedom without responsibility" or "sanctions without accountability." Rather, they must be seen as involving real penalties that are as stringent as incarceration would have been.[4] While community-based corrections has suffered from image problems, evidence began emerging by the early 1990s that society may not be as unsupportive as we might think, with four out of five people in one national survey favoring community-based programs over prison for nondangerous offenders.[5] Especially in light of the economic recession that has recently curtailed government spending, community-based approaches will continue to represent a significant function in the correctional system, even if for economic rather than egalitarian reasons.

PRETRIAL INTERVENTION

pretrial intervention (diversion): diverting a case out of the justice system at a point prior to adjudication.

Most of the programs discussed in this chapter involve options for keeping offenders out of correctional institutions after adjudication,[6] but **pretrial intervention** is completely different. It diverts the entire case out of the criminal justice system *before* trial. When first-time, nondangerous offenders are viewed as good risks, they may be eligible for voluntary supervision in the community without being convicted, especially if no constructive purpose would be served by conviction and sentencing.

As the term *pretrial* implies, the system has intervened to remove the case from the criminal justice process before adjudication. In essence, the alleged offender is being offered a second chance to avoid prosecution in exchange for voluntary participation in some treatment, counseling, training, or educational program in the community. This type of diversion has been practiced extensively for many years in juvenile court, and various forms of diversion have also been used in the adult system since the 1960s. By 1973, the National Advisory Commission on Criminal Justice Standards and Goals had recognized diversion as an appropriate alternative when "there is a substantial likelihood that conviction could be obtained and the benefits to society from channeling an offender into an available noncriminal diversion program outweigh any harm done to society by abandoning criminal prosecution."[7] Today the growing drug court movement is creating treatment-oriented diversion opportunities for many offenders.[8]

We tend to think of corrections as the last phase of the criminal justice system. Thus, it may appear contradictory to include diversion within the correctional caseload. But in Chapter 1 we saw that corrections (specifically, the local jail) is also responsible for pretrial detention—confining those awaiting trial who are not released pending adjudication. Similarly, alleged offenders who have been diverted out of the system before trial could be considered correctional clients. Although they have been accused of criminal behavior, it has been determined that their needs can best be met without official processing, through programs offered in the community.

The Diversion Process

Pretrial intervention is commonly referred to as *diversion*, since the suspect is diverted from official processing, thereby minimizing penetration into the justice system. It occurs without any finding of guilt or innocence—in other words, without subjecting the defendant to trial. Clients of diversion therefore cannot technically be considered "offenders," since they have not actually been convicted.

Pretrial intervention represents the system's first opportunity to make a positive change in the defendant's lifestyle, at a point before more serious criminal behavior patterns become firmly established. Through community-based alternatives, the intent is to help resolve whatever problems attracted the attention of criminal justice authorities.

Diversion can occur at any phase of processing prior to adjudication—whenever officials decide not to invoke the criminal justice process. Much of the willingness to employ diversion is based on the availability of accessible options. In the absence of options, the process simply becomes diversion *from* the system, rather than *to* a more appropriate alternative.

Particularly if the victim is more concerned with being compensated for losses than seeking a criminal conviction, the prosecutor may arrange an agreement whereby the alleged offender repays the victim in exchange for dropping the

alternative dispute resolution: a neutral third party attempts to reach a compromise between the victim and offender in order to resolve the case outside of the criminal justice system.

charges. In recent years, such approaches have become standardized practice, known as **alternative dispute resolution** or victim–offender reconciliation. Resolutions can range from victim compensation to community service or simply offering an apology, in order to "personalize and humanize the criminal justice system."[9] Such programs are similar to the arbitration of labor–management conflicts. Negotiation between the victim and alleged offender is mediated by an impartial third party, in an effort to reach a satisfactory resolution for everyone.

With the flood of drug-related cases overwhelming the criminal justice system in recent years, a popular diversionary program in many jurisdictions has emerged in the form of drug courts.[10] Such special-docket courts are based on the assumption that drug users benefit more from being treated for their addiction than from being tried and incarcerated. The drug courts diagnose problems related to substance abuse, make treatment referrals, and closely monitor the client's progress. Similar options have also now emerged in the form of mental health courts and even "veterans courts," designed to apply collaborative efforts to the needs of military veterans whose crimes are committed in the aftermath of their service.[11] Whatever form they take, many communities are opting for diversionary approaches to common problems from alcohol abuse to family crisis—all of which are better addressed by interventions outside of the justice system.[12] Of course, a defendant's failure to comply successfully with program requirements can result in reactivating the case by proceeding with adjudication.

Advantages and Disadvantages of Diversion

To both the defendant and the system, pretrial diversion offers benefits. Untried offenders who truly are committed to making positive changes in their lives may appreciate this "second chance," as well as the opportunity it presents to get help for their problems. However, that does not mean that all diversionary options are necessarily treatment oriented. Victim compensation, for example, while a form of repaying one's debt to society, does not necessarily address the underlying causes of whatever crime was involved. As described below, diversion is not without drawbacks as well as advantages:

- *Stigma.* Even pretrial interventions that do not address the root causes of behavior at least do no further harm to the defendant. By providing an option to official processing, the stigma of being labeled "criminal" is avoided. Having a criminal record is a serious obstacle to employment, social relationships, and even family stability. To defendants facing the prospect of conviction and possible jail or prison time, participating in a diversionary program avoids being labeled throughout life as "convicts" or "ex-offenders," along with all the limitations and restrictions that entails.

- *Leniency.* On the other hand, the fact that diversion reduces the consequences of criminal behavior raises the criticism that it is too lenient, doing little to hold offenders accountable for their actions or to deter future crime. But some diversionary programs are actually harsher than the penalty that would probably follow conviction. For example, withholding adjudication through drug court participation might require lengthy treatment, frequent urinalysis, specified meetings, and so on, whereas conviction might entail only a few weeks in jail.

As this example illustrates, we often overlook the fact that community corrections has "significant sanction value" that is "compatible with the demand for retribution."[13] To be taken more seriously as a form of punishment, however, community-based alternatives must demonstrate that they are "tough with the enforcement of court orders—most of all, in quick, decisive and uncompromising reaction to noncompliance."[14]

- *Normality.* Although the effectiveness of diversion remains debatable, the effects of prison are all too well known. The restrictive, abnormal environment of correctional institutions could not differ more from life in free society, and the strain it puts on families can be overwhelming. Operating in the open environment of the free world—where the offender can maintain employment, family stability, and community ties—diversion offers an alternative to the counterproductiveness of incarceration in a normal setting at considerably less cost to the taxpayer.

- *Costs.* Compared to the expense of going to trial, the skyrocketing costs of constructing and staffing correctional facilities, the sophisticated technology needed to maintain prison security, the welfare payments to families who lose their breadwinner, and so on, diversion is a fiscal bargain. Cost-effectiveness is particularly attractive when budgets are being reduced and operating funds are limited. While economic considerations alone should not determine how

EXHIBIT 4.1
Community-based options such as diversion, probation, and electronic monitoring provide lower-cost alternatives to the high price of prisons.

extensively pretrial intervention is used, if more beneficial results can be achieved in the community without endangering public safety, lower costs represent an added incentive to experiment with such options.

- *Efficiency.* Beyond lower costs, diversion presents an opportunity to enhance the efficiency of the criminal justice system. Given the fact that the courts are already overburdened with serious violent crimes, the system would probably crush under its own weight if all previously diverted, less serious offenses were suddenly added to its workload.

- *Flexibility.* Many of the crimes committed by offenders reflect personal circumstances ranging from homelessness and alcoholism to mental illness and emotional distress. These are not problems that generally can be addressed effectively through the criminal justice system. Without the opportunity for diversion and the expanded community resources which it embraces, such cases would probably be dealt with through rather limited, generally punitive, and often inappropriate responses.

- *Discretion.* On the other hand, too much unregulated discretion can produce forced treatment on those who have committed no crime or for whom there is not enough evidence to convict. Avoiding a conviction is not the objective of diversion. Rather, it is a tool to facilitate the treatment of whatever underlying personal problems may have promoted the offender's illegal behavior. Pressuring defendants into pretrial diversion programs not only raises ethical questions, but also creates a situation whereby defendants may involuntarily abdicate many of their due process rights—most significantly, the right to trial and protection against self-incrimination. Although it is important to note that diversion is not conviction, this is a legal technicality that may blur in practice.

- *Net-widening.* Finally, the extent to which diversionary options are available is itself a source of concern. If, for example, the defendant would have been subjected to less interference or less supervision in the absence of diversionary options, are these programs truly serving the purpose for which they were intended? In this regard, it has been noted that "innovations designed to reduce the overall intrusiveness of the system, no matter how well-intentioned, often backfire and instead add to its capacity for social control."[15]

  When police, prosecutors, and judges are aware that offenders can obtain help for their problems rather than simply serve time, there is some danger that the system will extend its reach into borderline behavior that would otherwise have been overlooked. For example, when they are aware that the court's options are limited, police officers might ignore a situation involving possession of a small amount of drugs by a young person—concerned that it would be unproductive for this person to be incarcerated for such an offense. But, when drug treatment is well known as an available diversionary program, the police may be more likely to make an arrest in order to obtain help for the offender. This illustrates the concept of **net-widening**—when a new program broadens official intervention rather than improving the shortcomings of the existing system.

If diversion results in bringing more clients into the system and/or dealing with them more harshly, it becomes a form of net-widening. On the other hand, it could be argued that the system's initial reluctance to interfere with obviously law-violating behavior before the availability of diversionary options was equally inappropriate and could not be justified simply because effective response alternatives were lacking. In any case, pretrial interventions continue to be useful alternatives that are often benevolent to the offender as well as beneficial to the victim and the community.

net-widening: the potential for unintentionally expanding the scope or intensity of criminal justice intervention into people's lives.

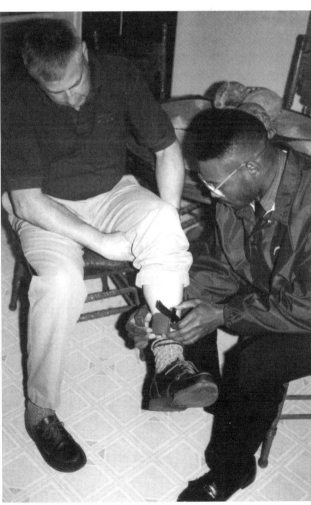

EXHIBIT 4.2
An ankle transmitter enables offenders who qualify for electronic monitoring to work in the community and live at home.

Source: Courtesy of Kenneth R. McCreedy.

LEARNING GOALS

Do you know:

5. at what stages in criminal justice processing electronic monitoring can be used and with what types of clients?

6. what the advantages and disadvantages of electronic monitoring are, and how net-widening can reduce its advantages?

electronic monitoring: verification through electronic transmitters and receivers that the offender is adhering to restrictions of home confinement.

HOME CONFINEMENT AND ELECTRONIC MONITORING

Home confinement through **electronic monitoring** is an innovation that has considerable potential for reducing prison populations, but at the same time for "widening the net." With technological advances in recent years, it has become possible to combine diversion with confinement in one's residence, verified by electronic monitors. In fact, as illustrated in Exhibit 4.3, home confinement under electronic monitoring can be employed at virtually any point in the criminal justice process following arrest—from pretrial to post-sentencing, and even post-incarceration.

During the period of confinement, participants are placed on a form of curfew, restricted from leaving their place of residence. Exceptions are made during work hours if the client is employed, or for such legitimate reasons as performing community service, grocery shopping, or attending authorized activities (for example, treatment programs, church services, or medical appointments). Otherwise, the client is expected to remain at home, as verified by computerized devices or, more recently, cellular or satellite systems such as GPS tracking.

EXHIBIT 4.3
Key decision points in the criminal justice system where electronic monitoring is used.

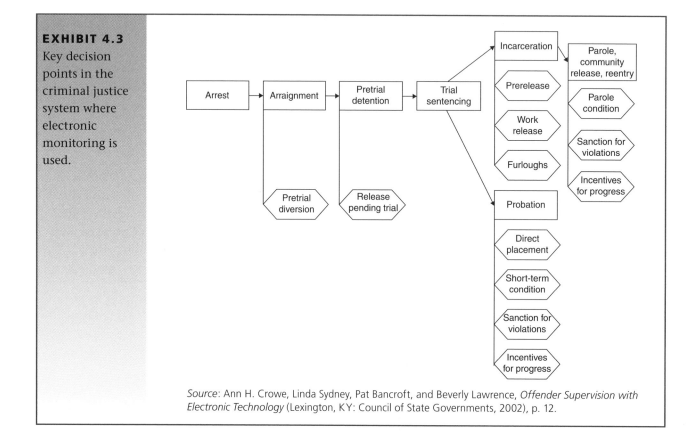

Source: Ann H. Crowe, Linda Sydney, Pat Bancroft, and Beverly Lawrence, *Offender Supervision with Electronic Technology* (Lexington, KY: Council of State Governments, 2002), p. 12.

Electronically Monitored Clients

Because of its diverse uses and flexibility, it is not surprising to find that electronically monitored home confinement is being employed with more and more offenders. Yet less than 3 percent of clients in the correctional conglomerate are under such surveillance.[16] When electronic monitoring initially gained popularity, most of its clients were either convicted or accused of major traffic offenses (usually DUI—driving under the influence), property crimes, or drug offenses (possession or distribution).[17] Since eligibility criteria vary among states, the thousands of offenders being monitored today represent a wide range of criminal behavior. While its benefits and drawbacks have been debated, electronic monitoring has become a key ingredient in response to prison crowding and overloaded probation and parole caseloads.

Advantages and Disadvantages

Much of the popularity of this approach has resulted from the combination of increasingly punitive public attitudes toward crime and decreasingly available space in correctional institutions. With society in no mood to "coddle criminals," alternatives to prison crowding must be tough, without compromising public safety. When enforced by electronic monitoring, home confinement meets the public's demand for retribution and protection without abandoning the system's desire for more productive and less expensive offender processing.

Unlike institutional confinement, home confinement also provides greater potential for treatment. (In reality, however, that potential is rarely fulfilled, since treatment is not often a component of such programs.) Particularly during economic downturns, electronically monitored home confinement is especially attractive. As shown in Exhibit 4.4, the average daily cost for such clients is well below the price

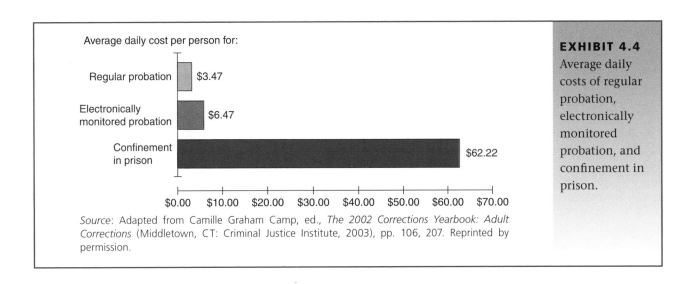

Average daily cost per person for:

Regular probation — $3.47

Electronically monitored probation — $6.47

Confinement in prison — $62.22

$0.00 $10.00 $20.00 $30.00 $40.00 $50.00 $60.00 $70.00

EXHIBIT 4.4 Average daily costs of regular probation, electronically monitored probation, and confinement in prison.

Source: Adapted from Camille Graham Camp, ed., *The 2002 Corrections Yearbook: Adult Corrections* (Middletown, CT: Criminal Justice Institute, 2003), pp. 106, 207. Reprinted by permission.

of maintaining them in prison, and many programs charge the participants fees to offset expenses.

Beyond monetary considerations, social benefits represent additional advantages. The offender can remain employed, continue any treatment initiated in the community, avert family breakup, and avoid the negative effects of incarceration. Moreover, home confinement is well suited to dealing with special needs offenders who might be particularly vulnerable in prison or jail settings (for example, those who are mentally retarded, pregnant, youthful, or terminally ill). It is also a speedier and more flexible response to handling vast numbers of clients than would ever be possible through new facility construction.

Despite its appealing features, home confinement through electronic monitoring is not without drawbacks.[18] To the extent that it becomes a cheap alternative to prison, a number of questions are raised, among them the net-widening potential mentioned earlier. For example, if nonviolent, low-risk offenders become primary targets for house arrest, the net of social control is extended to embrace those who are actually least likely to have been sentenced to prison, which is in fact what some research has demonstrated.[19] If such intermediate sanctions are not reserved for the truly prison bound, cost-effectiveness is dramatically reduced. Moreover, the "widened net" in this case can extend beyond the individual offender to his or her family as well, particularly when electronically generated calls come in at any time of the day or night.

In that regard, the intrusiveness of electronic monitoring into private residences has also been criticized. One's home in essence becomes a prison, generating Orwellian "Big Brother" concerns. In response, some maintain that home confinement certainly provides greater privacy than prison or jail and that, in any event, participation is voluntary. But others ask "What's next?" In fact, for over two decades some community corrections programs have been using telemonitoring, where "visual contacts with offenders are produced via telephone from the offender's home," with a breath-alcohol monitor attached to the video to ensure abstinence of alcohol use.[20] Moreover, such technology has implications for drastically changing the people-oriented practice of community corrections into a computer-driven emphasis on surveillance.

Not everyone who disagrees with electronic monitoring is opposed to the severity of its intrusiveness. Quite the contrary, there are those who do not believe that it is sufficiently harsh. At the same time, offenders who are not eligible because of the fees involved and the necessity to have a telephone at home have raised the issue of potential discrimination. Nor is electronic monitoring a fail-safe means of preventing criminal activity on the part of those being monitored.

These are but a few among the many issues that must be addressed in the future, keeping in mind that "it is all too tempting to employ the equipment simply because the means are available to do so."[21] In the meantime, just as home confinement was originally created as an alternative to incarceration, prison remains as an alternative to home confinement.

PROBATION SERVICES

As a community-based approach, **probation** has the advantage of dealing with problems in the environment where they originated. It also avoids the breakdown of social ties that occurs as a result of being incarcerated. When the objective is to help offenders to function better in society, it is more effective to work *with* social relationships than to sever them. In short, it is easier and more efficient to maintain the offender's integration as a part of society than to attempt reintegration upon release. It is also less expensive, since it costs considerably more to maintain a prison inmate than it does to supervise someone in the community.

The courts have recognized these advantages in their sentencing practices, making probation the most widely used correctional disposition in the United States. Of all adults under correctional control, more than half (58 percent) are on probation, representing over 4 million clients.[22]

In contrast to diversion, which is intervention before trial, probation is an actual sentence for a *convicted* offender. As we have seen, probation can also be combined with home confinement and electronic monitoring. In addition, it is often combined with a suspended sentence, whereby the judge sentences a defendant to prison or jail time and then suspends the sentence pending satisfactory completion of probation. In this way, offenders are presumed to be more motivated to comply with the conditions of probation by knowing what awaits should they fail to do so. Thus probation is *a conditional sentence served under supervision in the community.*

Among the conditions that may be imposed on probationers are such restrictions as keeping reasonable hours, remaining employed, and supporting one's family, along with rules that apply to a particular case, such as abstaining from alcohol and drugs or participating in mandated treatment. Community service work or other forms of restitution can likewise be required. Generally, there is a wider variation among probation rules than among parole regulations, since the conditions of probation are generally set by individual judges rather than by a single state agency as in the case of parole.

Although probation is commonly considered a part of the correctional conglomerate because it is a post-conviction sanction, it is technically a judicial function, in which convicted offenders are formally placed under supervision of the court. In practice, however, probation officers are usually employed by the state department of corrections, although in a number of jurisdictions they remain attached to the court system.[23]

History of Probation

Probation as we now know it in the United States originated in 1841 when a Boston cobbler, John Augustus, began visiting the courts. As a temperance crusader, he was

probation: a conditional sentence served under supervision in the community.

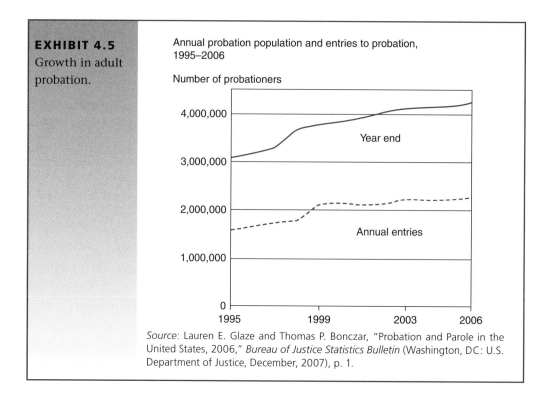

EXHIBIT 4.5
Growth in adult probation.

Annual probation population and entries to probation, 1995–2006

Number of probationers

Source: Lauren E. Glaze and Thomas P. Bonczar, "Probation and Parole in the United States, 2006," *Bureau of Justice Statistics Bulletin* (Washington, DC: U.S. Department of Justice, December, 2007), p. 1.

interested in reforming alcoholics. Convinced that he could help, Augustus would provide their bail or pay their fines, asking the judge to place them under his supervision. He would assist them with remaining sober, finding work, and staying out of trouble. As more and more petty criminals were released to his supervision, his house was literally filled with people he had bailed, almost none of whom violated his trust.[24]

As the next "Close-up on Corrections" describes, Augustus was responsible for reporting back to the court on their progress. The judge usually took his account into consideration when deciding a disposition, and reformed offenders were spared incarceration in a correctional facility. Because of his pioneering efforts, John Augustus is considered the "father of probation." As a result of his efforts, the first probation statute was passed in Massachusetts in 1878, and by 1954 all states had some form of probation. Moreover, despite recent trends in public attitudes favoring incarceration, probation caseloads have continued to grow dramatically, as shown in Exhibit 4.5.

CLOSE-UP ON CORRECTIONS
The Work of John Augustus

In the month of August, 1841, I was in court one morning, when . . . an officer entered, followed by a ragged and wretched looking man, who took his seat upon the bench allotted to prisoners.

I imagined from the man's appearance that his offense was that of yielding to his appetite for intoxicating drinks, and in a few moments, I found that my suspicions were correct, for the clerk read the complaint, in which the man was charged with being a common drunkard. . . . I conversed with him for a few moments, and found that he was not yet past all hope for reformation. . . . He told me that if he could be saved from the House of Correction, he never again would taste intoxicating liquors, [and] there was such an earnestness in that tone, and a look of firm resolve, that I determined to aid him. I bailed him, by permission of the court. He was ordered to appear for sentence in three weeks from that time. He signed the pledge and became a sober man; at the expiration of this period of probation, I accompanied him into the court room. . . . The judge expressed himself much pleased with the account we gave of the man, and instead of the usual penalty—imprisonment in the House of Corrections—he fined him one cent and costs amounting in all to $3.76, which was immediately paid. The man continued industrious and sober, and without doubt has been by his treatment, saved from a drunkard's grave.

Source: John Augustus, *A Report of the Labors of John Augustus, for the Last Ten Years, in Aid of the Unfortunate* (Boston: Wright and Hasty, 1852), reprinted as *John Augustus, First Probation Officer* (New York: Probation Association, 1939), pp. 4–5.

Contemporary Practices

Because probation is a function of various levels of government, its staff size, organizational structure, and availability of services vary widely throughout the country. Most jurisdictions administer probation through the state department of corrections. But, in others, probation is the responsibility of independent boards, separate departments, the courts, county government, or various combinations thereof.[25]

Many states have centralized probation at the state level in order to make service more uniform and assure that it is available in those counties that otherwise could not afford a probation staff. In these states, the pattern is often to have parole and probation combined administratively. But large counties and metropolitan areas generally maintain their own probation staffs, as does the federal government.

As a result of these differences, there is little uniformity with regard to the quality of probation services throughout the country. In contrast to these administrative factors, staff educational requirements are somewhat more standardized among jurisdictions. Following the lead of federal probation in 1930, most jurisdictions now require a bachelor's degree for entry-level probation or parole officers.[26] Moreover, if there is one qualification that probation officers have in common virtually everywhere, it is the ingenuity to maximize use of community resources. In addition to their counseling and casework functions, officers must be aware of employers who can offer jobs, as well as providers of many other services needed by their clients, from temporary shelter to drug treatment. It is through such personnel and community networking that probation manages to supervise over 4 million clients, while often unsupported and understaffed.

Conditions of Probation

Among the reasons why the public has not been overly enthusiastic about probation is the common misconception that it involves unrestricted freedom. Probation is often equated with "wrist-slapping, stern lecturing, or a judicial shrug."[27] In reality, however, probationers lose a considerable measure of privacy and liberty. Moreover, they are required to meet a number of conditions, such as:

- remaining within the geographic jurisdiction of the court;

- reporting to a probation officer on a prescribed schedule;

- refraining from association with certain types of people (e.g., known criminals) or places (e.g., bars);

- not possessing a firearm or committing a new offense;

- cooperating with the probation staff.

The judge can also mandate such further requirements as maintaining a curfew, fulfilling financial obligations, and remaining employed or seeking employment. These *general* conditions of probation are directed toward controlling the offender's behavior.

specific conditions of probation: restrictions or mandates that apply to the unique circumstances or needs of a probationer.

In addition, **specific conditions of probation** tailored to the client's particular situation or needs may be added that are more individualized or treatment oriented. For example, family support and/or victim compensation can be required, along with participation in various training, educational, drug treatment, alcohol detoxification, or counseling programs. Offenders are also increasingly being required to pay fees that offset at least some of the cost of their supervision.[28] Probationers can additionally be subjected to periodic random drug and alcohol tests to assure that they have not lapsed back into previous patterns of behavior. As detailed in the next "Close-up on Corrections," however, when extreme conditions are mandated, they may be overturned on appeal.

CLOSE-UP ON CORRECTIONS
Shaming through Probation

In Pittsfield, Illinois, a rural farm community, Judge Thomas Brownfield ordered a person convicted of aggravated battery to post a sign on his property that said "Warning: A Violent Felon Lives Here. Travel at Your Own Risk." The judge reasoned that a lengthy prison stay was too harsh for this defendant and gave him probation instead and a requirement to post this sign. . . . [The] condition was later reversed by the Illinois Supreme Court.

Source: Kathleen M. Simon and Ruth Ann Strickland, "An Alternative to Incarceration: Contemporary Use of Shaming Penalties in the United States," in Roslyn Muraskin, ed., *Key Correctional Issues* (Upper Saddle River, NJ: Prentice Hall, 2005), p. 170.

Probation Eligibility

The fact that probation does not appear to work equally well with all clients raises the issue of who should be eligible for it, as well as for whom it would be most beneficial. Because probation is less severe than incarceration, it might be assumed erroneously that it is reserved for those convicted of misdemeanors rather than felonies. Such is not the case.

In fact, not only is probation an available option for sentencing felony offenders, but there are actually as many felons as misdemeanants on probation. Of the total number of adults on probation, 49 percent are felons and 48 percent are misdemeanants. (The status of the remainder involves some other type of offense.)[29] This is likely because pretrial intervention or intermediate sanctions such as fines and community service are used more often in misdemeanor cases. Additionally, as states have attempted to reduce jail and prison crowding, probationers have increasingly been coming from the ranks of offenders who pose greater public safety threats.[30]

In deciding whether to impose probation or incarceration, judges obviously take a number of factors into consideration in addition to the offense. Anticipating future behavior is never an exact science. Even sophisticated "prediction tables" cannot always anticipate the risk an offender poses to society. With the exception of cases in which sentencing guidelines strictly preclude a judge from issuing probation for certain crimes, determination of whether an offender receives probation or incarceration is largely a value judgment based on the use of discretion.

Presentence Investigations

To assist in their decision making, judges have traditionally relied on a *presentence investigation (PSI) report*. While plea bargaining, mandatory minimum terms, and sentencing guidelines have reduced the impact of PSIs on sentencing decisions, such reports still can play an important role, particularly with regard to assuring that prior crimes are taken into consideration.[31]

The **presentence investigation** is a report generally prepared by a probation officer, although some jurisdictions contract this task to the private sector. In recent years, with determinate sentencing and overworked probation staffs, PSIs are often limited to a mechanistic check of prior offenses. But the initial intent was to conduct an in-depth probe not only of criminal history but also of the defendant's family, educational, medical, and social background, with a view toward working out an effective treatment program. Regardless of whether its contents are more broadly or narrowly focused, the PSI report is presented to the judge in order to guide disposition of the case.

presentence investigation: a report of pertinent facts, prepared to assist the judge with making a sentencing decision.

LEARNING GOALS

Do you know:

12. how the job functions of probation officers can create role conflict?
13. the difference between brokerage and casework models of probation services?
14. with what types of clients and under what circumstances probation is most successful?

PROBATION FUNCTIONS

As outlined in Exhibit 4.6, the probation officer's job can involve elements of investigation, counseling, service coordination, and rule enforcement. In addition to developing the presentence investigation, probation officers are responsible for the supervision of clients on their caseload. Unfortunately, as a result of the extensive amount of time required to research and prepare thorough PSIs, the time available for client supervision is often less than is necessary to do this complex portion of the job effectively.

Probation supervision includes not only casework and counseling, employment assistance, and personal planning, but also enforcement of the rules and regulations that constitute the conditions of probation. Thus the role of probation officers involves both *support* and *surveillance*—a combination of social worker and law enforcer.

However, it is difficult for one person to fulfill such demands equally effectively. For example, an officer who becomes overly empathetic toward the offender's problems and devotes considerable effort to resolving them might well be tempted to "look the other way" in the face of minor rule violations. On the other hand, strict rule-enforcing officers may be less inclined to offer much assistance, perhaps even waiting for a chance to "catch" the offender "messing up." Balancing these two contradictory expectations is a challenging task that can lead to **role conflict** for probation officers.

role conflict: the contradictory expectations of an occupational role—e.g., needing to assist as well as monitor a probationer.

For this reason, a team concept is used in some jurisdictions, with services as well as surveillance provided by teams of officers, each specializing in a particular aspect of the probation function. Additionally, some agencies separate responsibility for client supervision from presentence investigation. This enables some officers to prepare PSI reports exclusively, whereas others deal only with the supervision of probationers.

EXHIBIT 4.6 Job tasks involved in probation work.

Investigation

- Presentence investigation reports
- Case documentation
- Violation reports

Counseling

- Initial interview
- Individual supervision
- Family counseling
- Personal counseling
- Financial planning

Service coordination

- Job training
- Educational opportunities
- Employment assistance
- Transportation
- Shelter and subsistence
- Treatment programs

Enforcement

- Probation violation
- Probation-revocation recommendation
- Individual enforcement

Regardless of how the task is organized administratively, the probation staff must find the proper balance between control and treatment. This balance may shift over time—initially emphasizing greater control and then gradually reducing the level of supervision. Ultimately, the most important objective is to help clients change their behavior, thereby promoting both self-control and community protection.

Brokerage and Casework Models

Among the major aspects of the probation officer's work is employment counseling. Locating a job for probationers can be a significant challenge, especially for those who do not have good work habits or prior employment records. Thus it is essential for probation staff to be knowledgeable about and take maximum advantage of all resources available in the community. Various treatment programs, family counseling services, work incentives, educational assistance, mental health facilities, and social work agencies are all of potential help.

This reflects what has been called the *brokerage or resource management* approach—where the "supervising officer is not concerned primarily with understanding or changing the behavior of the offender, but rather, with assessing the concrete needs of the individual" and arranging for the receipt of "services which directly address those needs."[32]

In contrast, a *clinical, casework approach* focuses more on diagnosis and treatment, toward the goal of changing the offender's law-violating behavior. Based on the original philosophy and humanitarian efforts of John Augustus, the casework method shaped the delivery of probation services for many years. Informal counseling skills are still used by the probation officer in day-to-day work. But, in terms of more formal or long-term counseling, most officers are too burdened by heavy caseloads and paperwork to do much more than immediate crisis intervention. Moreover, some would maintain that the authoritative setting of probation is inappropriate to the practice of casework techniques, which again raises the issue discussed earlier of separating probationary functions through teamwork. (For a summary of the differences between the casework and the brokerage/resource management models of probation, see Exhibit 4.7.)

Assessing Effectiveness

The effectiveness of probation can be evaluated from two perspectives—the quality of services provided by staff and the success rates of their clientele. Measuring the diverse services rendered by a probation department is a challenging task. The quality of PSIs, casework, treatment, and community coordination are difficult to assess. In the absence of objective criteria, observing the success or failure of clients over a period of time has been one method used to evaluate probation.

In that regard, those with several prior felony convictions tend to be less successful on probation than other offenders. Of felons assigned to probation in one national

EXHIBIT 4.7		**Brokerage**	**Casework**
Comparison of brokerage (resource management) and casework models of probation.	Goal	Community integration	Individual rehabilitation
	Focus	Practical services	Treatment assistance
	Approach	Addressing specific, immediate survival needs of the client	Diagnosing/treating problems causing the client's behavioral difficulties
	Method	Linking needs of clients with available resources in the community (for example, training, education, employment, health care)	Clinical, therapeutic sevices (for example, counseling, group work, psychological or social work techniques)
	Officer's role	Coordinating community resources	Establishing a one-on-one relationship with the client
	Skills needed	Administrative, organizational, managerial	Counseling, treatment casework
	Relationship to clients	Advocate	Counselor

study, for example, 43 percent were rearrested for another felony violation within three years of sentencing.[33] Similarly, research indicates that the rate of recidivism varies with a number of client-related factors, as described in the next "Close-up on Corrections."

CLOSE-UP ON CORRECTIONS
Does Probation Work?

In reality there are two stories about probationer recidivism rates. Recidivism rates are low for adults on probation for *misdemeanors*—data suggest that three-quarters successfully complete their supervision. However, recidivism rates are high for *felony* probationers, particularly in jurisdictions . . . where supervision is minimal.

Recidivism rates vary greatly from place to place, depending on the seriousness of the underlying population characteristics, length of follow-up, and surveillance provided. A summary of 17 follow-up studies of adult felony probationers found that felony rearrest rates ranged from 12 to 65 percent.

Source: Joan Petersilia, "Probation in the United States: Practices and Challenges," *National Institute of Justice Journal* (September, 1997), p. 4.

While the effectiveness of probation has undoubtedly been curtailed by inadequate resources, obtaining sufficient funding ultimately depends on whether probation can prove its value, in a "Catch 22" situation that depends on measuring its results.[34] Nevertheless, long-term research has found that, compared to those incarcerated, the risk of reoffending is reduced for those in community-based alternative programs, and the addition of a treatment component produces a further reduction in recidivism.[35]

Rule Enforcement and Revocation

In addition to their counseling and supportive functions, probation officers are authority figures responsible for ensuring that the offender complies with the conditions established when the judge awarded probation. Probation is a privilege, not a right. Violation of the conditions required to maintain that privilege can result in its revocation. It is the probation officer's function to determine that whatever restrictions and mandates the court required are, in fact, being upheld.

There are two ways that a probationer can be released from supervision: discharge or **revocation**. Discharge generally means that the client has successfully completed the probationary period. However, some jurisdictions have developed the practice of discharging persons "not amenable to probation" rather than sending them to prison, which is somewhat similar to a "dishonorable" or "undesirable" discharge from the military services. In contrast, revocation means that the privilege of probation has been withdrawn and that another disposition must be made of the case, such as incarceration.

Generally, there are two reasons for recommending probation revocation: commission of a new crime or a **technical violation** of the rules. In some jurisdictions, revocation is relatively automatic with the commission of a serious offense, although there may be exceptions. Technical violations involve breaking one or more of the conditions of probation. Whatever the general and specific conditions are for a particular offender, violation can result in a recommendation of revocation. Of course, every form of misconduct does not result in removal from the community—in fact, one study found that, although 49 percent of probationers violate their conditions, only 20 percent are incarcerated as a result.[36]

revocation: withdrawing probation as the result of committing a new offense or failing to comply with conditions.

technical violation: breaking any of the rules established as conditions of probation.

Legal Issues

Nor is probation automatically terminated upon an officer's recommendation. Both probationers and parolees facing revocation have a number of due process rights—among them a formal hearing. At this revocation hearing, the judge and the offender hear the probation officer's recommendation for revocation (based on detailed information in the violation report), and the judge makes a decision.

In 1967, the U.S. Supreme Court determined in the *Mempa v. Rhay* case[37] that the probationer is entitled to representation by an attorney before being resentenced after a probation revocation. With this ruling, the court began to emphasize the revocation process as a "critical phase" in the justice system, which falls within the due process protections of the Fourteenth Amendment. The criticality of the hearing, of course, refers to the fact that it can involve the loss of liberty, since having probation revoked may result in a jail or prison sentence.

Due process protections were extended further in the 1973 *Gagnon v. Scarpelli* case,[38] which initiated a two-stage hearing process. In addition to the actual revocation hearing, this case established a preliminary hearing in order to determine whether there is probable cause to revoke probation (similar to the function of a preliminary hearing, when the defendant is originally accused of a crime). At both the preliminary hearing and the subsequent revocation hearing, the probationer also has certain due process rights, including:

- prior notice of the hearing;

- written notice of the alleged violation;

- the right to:

  - attend the hearing

  - present evidence and witnesses

  - be judged before a neutral and detached official.

But, despite these protections, just as there are disparities in sentencing, they also occur in probation revocation. Petty, unrealistic, or irrelevant conditions invite violations, which do not necessarily reflect poor adjustment. It is in such instances that appellate courts have intervened, particularly when the conditions established do not specifically address the needs of the client or circumstances of the crime.

On the other hand, some rather unusual conditions have been upheld when they related directly to the client's offense. Examples include such a seemingly strange requirement as mandating weight loss (as described in the next "Close-up on Corrections"). In essence, the courts tend to overrule conditions that are irrelevant to the case and uphold those that have a direct bearing on the original conviction.

CLOSE-UP ON CORRECTIONS
The Case of the Portly Probationer

> The 505-pound man's initial brush with the law came following the closure of his weight-loss business—ironically called "Inches Be Gone." Although slapped with probation after an ensuing forgery conviction, he cited his weight as the reason he was unable to pay restitution . . . The judge subsequently ordered him to shed pounds as a condition of probation. When he twice violated the condition . . . the offender was sentenced to 93 days in jail, despite his attorney's contention that the court's order to lose weight was cruel and unusual.
>
> *Source:* "Portly Prisoner Poses Peculiar Problem," *Corrections Alert*, Vol. 2, No. 20 (January 29, 1996), p. 1.

General conditions of probation also have been subject to challenge, especially when they are vague or ambiguous. How, for instance, does one objectively determine whether the client is "cooperating" with the probation officer? What about the client who lives on a state border and "travels out of state" to seek employment in the nearest city, which happens to be across the state line? When such questions are raised, they can provide the basis for legal challenges regarding fairness and practicality, as well as denial of due process, especially if reasons for revocation appear to be based on petty harassment.

PROBATION TODAY

LEARNING GOALS

Do you know:
18. how classification helps probation officers manage large caseloads?
19. the difference between traditional and intensive supervision probation?

Although they supervise the majority of all convicted offenders, probation agencies do not receive a majority of correctional expenditures. As a result of escalating numbers of clients without proportionally increasing resources, one of the primary difficulties in the field of probation is large **caseloads**. In fact, 92 percent of probation directors responding to a national study indicated that they needed more officers to handle increased caseloads.[39] The American Probation and Parole Association (APPA) recognizes that differences among clients in terms of risk factors, service needs, supervisory conditions, and the like mean that the workload demands of one probation officer may be quite different from those of another.[40] Nevertheless, the 50 cases per officer that APPA recommends for supervising moderate- to high-risk clients[41] is considerably less than the 127 average caseload reported nationally.[42]

caseload: the workload of a probation (or parole) officer, measured by the number and types of cases being supervised or investigated.

In California alone, probation caseloads had grown so much by the late 1990s—to more than 500 per officer—that over half of the probationers in Los Angeles were being tracked solely by computer, with no face-to-face contact.[43] In fact, the situation had grown to the point that some probation officers were reporting caseloads of 3,000 offenders, and more than half of the state's probationers were "likely to serve their entire term without ever meeting or even speaking with a probation officer."[44]

Caseload Classification

One of the ways that strained probation staffs are attempting to cope with ever-increasing caseloads in the absence of accompanying fiscal increases is through classifying cases according to the level of supervision needed. Clients vary in terms of the number and types of contacts that they need, based on such factors as the nature of their offense, their prior record, the variety and intensity of their problems, and the potential risk they pose. **Caseload classification** recognizes these distinctions, providing differing levels of service and supervision according to the nature of the client. For example, some states vary the intensity of probation from

caseload classification: separating cases according to the intensity of supervision needed by the client.

maximum to medium, minimum, and even mail-in supervision. Others screen cases upon intake to divert low-risk clients into non-reporting status.

While there is no direct evidence that lower caseloads reduce recidivism, the amount of time in supervision does appear to have a positive effect, along with how that time was spent (i.e., on surveillance that would increase technical violations, or counseling that would improve adjustment).[45] Workload reduction alone is not sufficient to achieve maximum effectiveness unless there is a commitment to specific treatment programs. But it is apparent that officers laboring under excessively high caseloads simply cannot provide the necessary time and attention to their clients.

EXHIBIT 4.8
Whether clients are on regular or intensive supervision probation, officers must meet with clients, provide supportive assistance, and monitor their compliance with conditions of probation.

Source: Courtesy of Kenneth R. McCreedy.

Intensive Supervision Probation

Many of the first efforts designed to classify and manage probation caseloads actually contained early versions of what has now become known as **intensive supervision probation** (ISP). Florida, for instance, passed legislation in 1983 to slow down prison admissions through "community control"—a punishment-oriented program of intensive supervision combining home confinement with strong surveillance[46] which remains in place today.

As public policy toward crime became increasingly punitive without an accompanying expansion of prison space, the need emerged for an intermediate sanction—something stronger than traditional probation but not as harsh as incarceration. For selected offenders, the solution came in the form of more intensively supervised probation.

To meet these objectives, ISP programs differ from more traditional probation in a number of respects. As its name implies, ISP requires a more intense level of supervision, which is achieved through such measures as:

- manageable caseloads;

- frequent face-to-face contacts;

- home confinement and electronic monitoring;

- regular visits to the client's home and workplace;

- verification of treatment program participation;

- drug and alcohol screening;

- clear revocation guidelines that are administered consistently and firmly.

In addition, those on ISP may also be required to make restitution payments, perform some type of community service, and pay supervision fees. But, as ISP programs have expanded in response to pressures created by prison and jail crowding, they have changed from a focus on treatment and service delivery to an emphasis on control and surveillance.

In that regard, early studies of ISP programs were generally quite positive, indicating lower recidivism rates for serious crimes, high rates of successful completion, and greater cost-effectiveness.[47] However, at least one major national study more recently found that effectiveness was related to whether the program set out to reduce costs and prison crowding or to provide a stricter form of traditional probation.[48]

ISP programs have also been noted for often limiting participation to low-risk, property offenders—thus potentially inflating their success rate. In fact, research indicates that "offender selection is one of the most problematic areas of ISP."[49] When ISP becomes a form of net-widening, many of its objectives are defeated. Moreover, when recidivism does occur, it is not necessarily a reflection of the fact

intensive supervision probation: a form of probation with closer monitoring, through more frequent contacts, more stringent conditions, and smaller caseloads.

that the public is not being protected. Given the stringent conditions of ISP, there is more opportunity for technical violations to occur. In that respect, it has been argued that removing offenders from the streets because of technical violations precludes further criminal behavior, thereby enhancing public safety.[50]

On the other hand, ISP's heavy emphasis on surveillance functions might be producing an underestimate of its potential. If the proper clients were selected and focus on treatment was expanded, it is possible that ISP could be more effective. This issue was addressed in a study examining ISP programs for serious offenders with prior records at three locations in California. The results revealed that, at all sites, offenders who participated in treatment programs had lower recidivism rates than those who did not.[51] Others agree that, although ISP should be continued, its emphasis should shift toward a more integrated approach, since the punitive conditions of ISP provide short-range crime control, whereas "rehabilitation has been associated with long-term behavioral change."[52] As we will see in upcoming chapters on jails, prisons, and their effect on the inmate population, that is sound advice.

SUMMARY

Community-based alternatives to incarceration were developed in an effort to deal more effectively with the offender's problems where they originated, to avoid breaking social ties, and to prevent exposure to the negative effects of secure confinement. As prison crowding and fiscal shortages provided additional incentives to retain offenders under community supervision, much of what had previously been called "community-based alternatives" became known as intermediate sanctions, reflecting more punitive attitudes and concerns that such programs assure the safety and protection of society.

Pretrial intervention represents the least intrusive community-based intervention, since it diverts the case out of the criminal justice system prior to adjudication. In addition to providing a "second chance," diversion avoids the stigma of a criminal record. It also takes advantage of community resources and enhances the flexibility and cost-effectiveness of the justice system. However, it has been criticized as, on the one hand, being too lenient and, on the other hand, having the potential for net-widening.

One form of community-based supervision that has become popular in both pre- and post-adjudication phases of the justice system is home confinement, which is often combined with electronic monitoring to assure compliance with curfew restrictions. Use of this alternative has been increasing dramatically as an alternative to prison crowding, since it enables community-based treatment without compromising public safety, at a cost considerably less than that of incarceration. But it also has raised questions with regard to net-widening, and the intrusiveness of electronic monitoring has been especially vulnerable to the criticism that government is now invading our private residences. At the same time, there are those who do not believe that home confinement is a sufficiently serious penalty.

While home confinement and electronic monitoring have been very recent developments, probation originated over 150 years ago with the work of John Augustus. Since probationers are *convicted* offenders, they represent felons or misdemeanants, in contrast to the unconvicted status of those diverted through pretrial intervention.

In determining whether to sentence someone to probation or incarceration, judges often rely on a presentence investigation report, which contains information on the offense and the offender's background, along with a recommended disposition. In addition to preparing such reports, probation officers are responsible for supervising clients, which involves both support and surveillance functions. Officers vary in terms of their supervisory styles, with some focusing on casework counseling, while others act more as "brokers," linking the needs of clients with resources in the community. Recently, however, overall emphasis has shifted to supervision and surveillance as officers struggle to monitor compliance in the face of ever-increasing caseloads.

Probationers can be released from supervision either through discharge (successful completion) or by revoking probation and making another disposition of the case. Those facing revocation have certain due process rights, including a two-stage hearing. Revocations involving technical violations have tended to be upheld by the courts if the conditions established were related directly to the offender's circumstances.

As probation officers struggle with high caseloads, efforts have been undertaken to classify cases according to the level of supervision needed. Likewise, intensive supervision probation (ISP) has emerged as a more punishment-oriented alternative to traditional probation. Often combined with home confinement and electronic monitoring, ISP provides more frequent face-to-face contacts, close monitoring, and consistently enforced rules.

These alternatives are among the varieties of programs that serve as intermediate sanctions. They are becoming increasingly attractive as society continues to explore mechanisms for dealing with prison overflow, keeping costs in line with what taxpayers will support, and providing help to those who can remain in the community without endangering public safety. For those who cannot, there will always be prisons and jails—as explored in the next chapters on institutional corrections.

FOR FURTHER DISCUSSION

1. Locate information about the operation of a drug court in your state and use it to illustrate this initiative's diversionary aspects, advantages, and disadvantages.

2. Develop a hypothetical scenario to illustrate the concept of net-widening, and then explain how cost-effectiveness is affected when net-widening occurs.

3. Using different assessment criteria, show how the same probationers could be viewed as both failures and successes.

4. Discuss whether the effectiveness of probation should be based on the recidivism of its clients and, if not, provide suggestions for alternative approaches.

5. Argue for and against a "zero tolerance" policy for probationary rule enforcement.

6. Provide a case study to illustrate why revocation may not always be the best alternative when a condition of probation is violated.

7. Depending on what population clients are being drawn from (i.e., traditional probation or those prison-bound), discuss how creating an intensive supervision probation alternative might or might not be cost-effective.

8. Explain why high recidivism and revocation rates are almost inevitable with intensive supervision probation.

Jails: Pretrial Detention and Short-term Confinement

A better public understanding of the jail as a community agency which can begin the process of punishment and treatment to be culminated in the community stands as one of the big challenges of local corrections in the future.[1]

Kenneth E. Kerle

CHAPTER OVERVIEW

Before society had police, courts, or prisons, there were local jails. Because jails are the oldest component of the criminal justice system, however, they have also been the most neglected. Tracing their origins back to the abysmal conditions and corrupt fee system of the English gaols, American jails have endured a legacy of insufficient funding, inappropriate facilities, idle inmates, inadequate staffing, and a public largely indifferent to it all.

Modern, reform-minded jail administrators have faced the extraordinary challenge of overcoming these historical obstacles and bringing today's jails into the twenty-first century. It has not been an easy task, for, despite the length of time they have been with us and how many people they incarcerate, jails are not highly visible.

Just as corrections is the least known function of the criminal justice system, jails represent the "silent majority" of the correctional system—"silent" because of their low profile and lack of attention, and "majority" because they actually process more clients than any other correctional institutions. While the average stay in jail is much shorter than in prison, jails admit 18 times more inmates than prisons.[2] In the year 2009, for example, jails admitted almost 13 million people, even though their total population was only 767,620.[3] Moreover, all jail inmates do not necessarily go on to prison, but practically all prison inmates have experienced time in jail.

Beyond their lack of visibility, jails must struggle with a role that has never been well defined. If society is uncertain about whether corrections should be a symbol of deterrence, a place of incapacitation, or a method of rehabilitation, the role of the jail is even more unclear. With a mixture of sentenced/unsentenced, convicted/ unconvicted, and felon/misdemeanant populations, jails must balance multiple missions. Their functions range from the first stop for the police after making an arrest to the last resort for a community when no other resources exist to deal with the problem. As a result, anyone from homeless hitchhikers to serial killers can be found in jail.

But, where challenges seem endless, the potential for change is equally limitless. With obstacles also come opportunities. Creative administrators have begun to seize these opportunities to make a positive impact on the status of the nation's jails. Particularly in major metropolitan areas, the dirty, dark, decrepit jails lingering from the past century have begun to be replaced by clean, well-lighted, modern facilities that no more resemble the traditional image of jails than today's computers resemble yesterday's typewriters. Under the "new-generation" approach, jails are structured to produce a normal environment. They are secured by doors rather than bars. They are staffed by officers trained in direct-supervision techniques. But, most of all, they confirm that there is, indeed, hope on the horizon for turning jails from virtual dungeons into viable detention centers.

Admittedly, there is still a long way to go toward securing the public attention, funding, and support that jails require to fulfill their potential. The day may come when society realizes that more effectively dealing with those in jail may well reduce the demand for so many prisons. But, until that time, there is reassurance in knowing that, no matter what the future holds for jails, it will inevitably be an improvement on the past.

LEARNING GOALS

Do you know:
1. what a jail is and why the number of jails in the U.S. has been decreasing?
2. what size of facility makes up the majority of the nation's jails (in contrast to where most inmates are confined)?
3. what regional jail consolidation is and what impact it has had?

NUMBER AND TYPES OF JAILS

No one knows exactly how many jails operate in the United States. As surprising as this may seem, it relates to our uncertainty about the function of jails. Because we do not agree on what jails should be *doing*, it is difficult to determine what types of facilities are performing whatever that role is. Facilities that are called "jails" range from massive detention centers to small "lockups," "holdovers," or "drunk tanks" in police stations. In this chapter, the term *jail* is limited to locally administered confinement facilities that hold persons awaiting trial (for more than 48 hours) or those serving short sentences. In addition to their pretrial functions, jails have traditionally been defined by their limitation to sentences of one year or less, although jails in a number of jurisdictions are now authorized to hold sentenced inmates for longer periods of time.

According to this definition, there were some 3,365 jails in the United States during 1999,[4] but that number had dropped to only 3,168 by 2007.[5] This does not mean that fewer people are going to jail. Nor does it mean that there is less need for jails. Rather, it reflects two trends: (1) the number of small jails that are being closed or consolidated into large detention centers, and (2) the number of extremely old jails that are being phased out of service. In fact, during recent years, facilities with fewer than 50 inmates accounted for virtually all of the decline in the total number of jail jurisdictions.[6]

Jail Size

This trend reflects the fact that the large number of relatively small jails has been a major obstacle in the path of modernization. As Exhibit 5.1 illustrates, facilities housing fewer than 100 inmates actually make up the majority (59 percent) of the nation's jails. This might create the assumption that most of the people in jail are confined in small facilities. But they are not. Despite their dramatically fewer numbers, as Exhibit 5.1 also shows, large jails account for far more inmates.[7] Just 6 percent of the nation's jails—the largest facilities—house over half (51 percent) of the total population.[8] In other words, a small number of large jails hold the majority of inmates.

In very small, rural jails, even segregating only the most obvious groups (male/female, young/old, felons/misdemeanants) can create crowded conditions, despite the fact that the total population may well be within the facility's overall capacity. Moreover, it is virtually impossible to provide the training, range of treatment

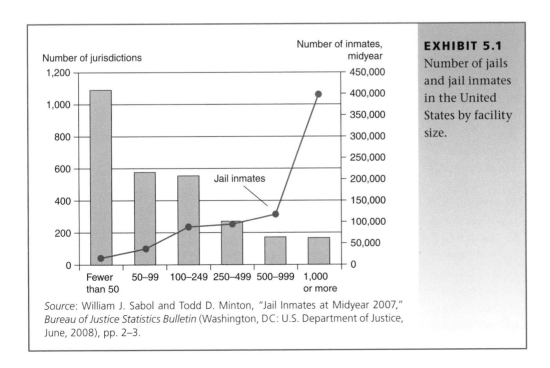

EXHIBIT 5.1
Number of jails and jail inmates in the United States by facility size.

Source: William J. Sabol and Todd D. Minton, "Jail Inmates at Midyear 2007," *Bureau of Justice Statistics Bulletin* (Washington, DC: U.S. Department of Justice, June, 2008), pp. 2–3.

services, and varieties of personnel that are available in larger, urban jails.[9] The most pressing issues facing small jails include staff shortages, lack of round-the-clock coverage, maintenance difficulties, and inability to provide adequate physical separation of special inmates (e.g., juveniles, elderly, mentally ill, etc.). The lack of ability to properly classify and separate inmates also can accelerate additional operational problems such as attacks, assaults, and the introduction of weapons and other unauthorized items.

Consolidating Small Jails

For many of these reasons, there has been considerable movement in recent years toward the consolidation of small jails into larger regional detention centers. Just as the centralization of purchasing reduces the cost of items to each department involved, regional **jail consolidation** enhances cost-effectiveness, along with providing expanded and improved services.

jail consolidation (or regionalization): the merging of several small jails into one regional facility.

Some states are even taking the lead by encouraging local jails to regionalize. In Virginia, for example, the state has reimbursed up to half of the new construction or renovation costs when three or more jurisdictions consolidate. As a result, 12 regional jails in Virginia represent a total of 24 counties and 11 cities that otherwise would have to maintain their own small jails. The savings in construction and operating costs alone have been cited as "economically staggering."[10] Likewise, the West Virginia Jail Authority (a state agency) sets inspection and training standards for that state's ten regional jails.[11]

Such collaborative efforts also enable a jail to offer programs that jurisdictions functioning independently could not afford to staff or operate. In addition, through

EXHIBIT 5.2
With many small jails being phased out or consolidated, those confining 1,000 or more inmates (such as this megafacility in Tampa, FL) represent the type of jails that are increasing throughout the United States.

Source: Courtesy of the Hillsborough County (Florida) Sheriff's Department.

regionalization, it is possible to assure that minimally acceptable standards are met. Wide variations in staffing patterns, training programs, operational procedures, and inmate services can be reduced significantly.

Thus it is not surprising to find that the type of facilities that have been declining the most in recent years are jails housing fewer than 50 inmates. At the other extreme, **megajails** confining 1,000 or more inmates are rapidly increasing. In short, while we still have far more very small jails, they are dropping in number. By the same token, while we still have few very large jails, they are increasing in number.

megajails: very large local detention facilities, generally housing 1000 inmates or more.

NATURE AND FUNCTIONS OF JAILS

LEARNING GOALS

Do you know:

4. what types of inmates jails have authority to confine?
5. what percentage of the jail population is pretrial (versus convicted)?
6. for what types of offenses most people are in jail?

Researchers have noted that today's jails "hold a myriad of inmates for widely diverse reasons."[12] But that was not always the case. As described in Chapter 3, early English gaols originated as places to confine those who were awaiting either trial or imposition of the death penalty. (In contrast to modern times, defendants then could expect to wait much longer for the former than the latter.) Those on death row are now housed in state prisons. But local jails have retained their pretrial function to this day. In terms of conviction status, the bulk of the jail population breaks down into two general categories: (1) *accused* defendants awaiting trial; and (2) *convicted* offenders serving short-term sentences.

Pretrial Detention and Convicted Offenders

Since incarceration is considered a form of punishment, it would be logical to expect that jails would house more convicted offenders serving sentences than accused suspects waiting for trial. That is not the case. To the contrary, those in pretrial or unconvicted status now represent well over half (62 percent) of the jail population, clearly surpassing the number serving sentences in jail.[13]

Obviously, jails have little control over the sentences of those convicted. But efforts have been made to reduce pretrial populations through such alternatives as release on recognizance, pretrial intervention, and electronic monitoring. However, as pretrial release rates declined throughout the late 1990s, the unconvicted population has been steadily climbing. In fact, it is the increasing number of pretrial detainees that accounts for the majority of the jail population growth in recent years.[14] As a result of such trends, the majority of the jail population is technically innocent in the eyes of the law.

Other Jail Inmates

Beyond confining pretrial detainees and those serving short sentences, as illustrated in Exhibit 5.3, jails also are responsible for:

- booking those arrested;
- holding convicted offenders awaiting sentencing;
- holding sentenced offenders awaiting transfer to other correctional facilities;
- readmitting probation, parole, and bail/bond violators or absconders;
- holding illegal immigrants pending further processing.

Of these functions, holding inmates waiting to be transferred to prison is among the most controversial. In recent years, it has become a source of conflict between some local and state jurisdictions. As prisons fill above capacity, an overflow of sentenced inmates can quickly back up in already crowded jails. For example, in 2007, local jails were holding over 80,000 state and federal prisoners.[15] When states refuse to accept such inmates in a timely manner, it can create conflict between the local jail and state prison officials. As noted in a lawsuit filed by several sheriffs against a state department of corrections, "holding felons for long periods in local jails is not only illegal, but dangerous, expensive, and unfair."[16]

The jail also serves other purposes for which it was not intended. For example, jails can hold juveniles (pending their trial in adult court or transfer to other

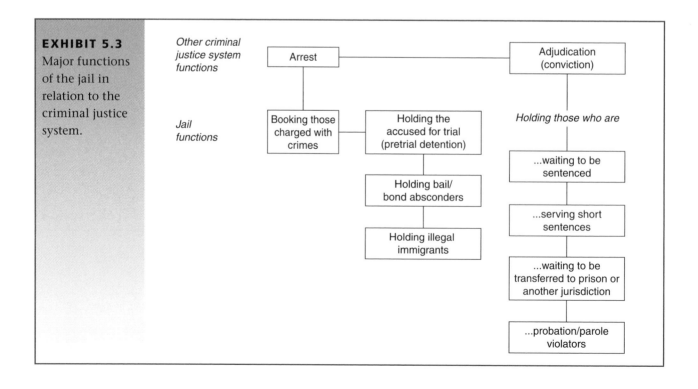

EXHIBIT 5.3
Major functions of the jail in relation to the criminal justice system.

correctional facilities), probation and parole violators (pending their revocation hearings), the mentally ill (pending their transfer to mental health facilities when such resources are available), and indigent transients—who, unfortunately, are usually not pending transfer anywhere but back on the streets, since the jail is often the only facility available 24 hours a day to shelter them.

Offenses of Jail Inmates

From this wide assortment, it is apparent that the jail serves many purposes and confines a diverse population. Although the public may be under the impression that local jails are incarcerating primarily hardened, violent offenders, that assumption is challenged by the data in Exhibit 5.4.

While the types of offenses for which people are confined in jail vary with local policies, a national picture of the jail population presents some interesting findings. In terms of their most serious offense, only one-fourth of the population is confined for such violent offenses as murder, kidnapping, rape, robbery, or assault.[17] Of these, most are in *pretrial* status, because those suspected of such violent crimes are less likely to qualify for bail or release on recognizance and, once convicted, they are more likely to receive an extensive prison sentence.

Thus, as Exhibit 5.4 illustrates, three out of four inmates are *not* in jail for the types of violent personal crimes most feared by society but, rather, for property crimes, drug-related offenses, or public order offenses (such as traffic violations, obstruction of justice, weapons charges, or—most commonly—driving while intoxicated). This is not meant to imply that jail crowding should be reduced by legalizing drugs or that drunk driving is not a significant threat to public safety. But it does point out that the public's perception of the "typical" jail inmate may not conform with who is actually in jail.

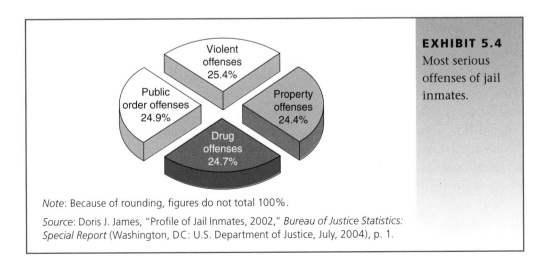

EXHIBIT 5.4
Most serious offenses of jail inmates.

Note: Because of rounding, figures do not total 100%.

Source: Doris J. James, "Profile of Jail Inmates, 2002," *Bureau of Justice Statistics: Special Report* (Washington, DC: U.S. Department of Justice, July, 2004), p. 1.

Alcohol and Drug Abusers

As is apparent from this inmate profile, much of the jail's population is experiencing some type of difficulty with either alcohol or drugs (along with related medical and mental health issues). Moreover, many jail residents are homeless or transient drifters. Since public intoxication remains an offense in most jurisdictions, a sizeable number of these people find themselves incarcerated for drunkenness, vagrancy, or disorderly conduct. A chronic drinker who has been arrested dozens of times can cumulatively spend a decade in jail on short-term sentences. Despite some efforts to replace "drunk tanks" with detoxification centers and to decriminalize public inebriation, the "common drunk" remains a headache for local jails.[18]

Moreover, crackdowns on DWI offenders, as well as "zero tolerance" drug enforcement policies, have contributed substantially to the jail population. In one recent national survey, more than two-thirds of jail inmates (68 percent) met the criteria for substance abuse or dependence.[19] But that does not mean that jails are well equipped to help alcohol and drug abusers. It has been reported, for example, that only 4 percent of jailed DWI offenders receive treatment, compared with 46 percent of those on probation. Even when such self-help efforts as AA are included, the numbers increase to only 17 percent of those in jail, in contrast to 62 percent of those on probation.[20] While nearly two-thirds of jails make self-help programs available, far fewer (43 percent) offer specific substance abuse treatment in the form of detoxification, professional counseling, or residential treatment.[21]

Despite research indicating that drug treatment is more effective than punitive sentences,[22] substance abusers remain warehoused in jails that are ill suited to handle their problems. Moreover, as long as public policy continues to focus more on building jails than developing treatment programs, the cycle of drug- and alcohol-related crime can be expected to continue.

Jail Turnover

Regardless of the offense, in many jurisdictions the jail is not authorized to hold inmates serving longer than one year. Thus, as a general rule, those with a sentence of a year or less will serve it in jail, while those with longer terms will serve their time in prison. As with most general statements, however, there are exceptions. Some jurisdictions enable inmates to serve a number of years in jail.

Nevertheless, in contrast to the length of stay in prison, the average length of stay for jail inmates is measured in days, rather than months or years. That obviously produces a consistently high level of turnover. In fact, on an annual basis, there are about as many *admissions to* as *releases from* jails. Stated another way, on average it takes the U.S. prison population two years to turn over once, whereas the jail population turns over 20 to 25 times each year.[23] Simply releasing the right person in the midst of such a constant influx and outgo of inmates can be challenging. Moreover, this continual turnover has far-reaching implications for jail management, programming, and inmate supervision.

DIRECT-SUPERVISION (NEW-GENERATION) JAILS

If you bought a computer several years ago, you probably have already found that it is obsolete. Newer, faster, more sophisticated models are constantly replacing each previous "generation" of computers. As society progresses and new advancements are made, one might expect that similar changes would be reflected in our jails. But even facilities constructed as recently as 25 to 30 years ago "are not radically different, in most respects, from the nation's first penitentiary—the Walnut Street Jail of 1790."[24] They may be cleaner. They may be better lighted. They may include more high-tech security. But their basic features have remained essentially the same.

Philosophy

In response to the need for a "new generation" of correctional facilities, several jails were constructed during the mid-1970s that no more resemble traditional jails than manual typewriters resemble today's computers. The rationale behind this movement is based on several fundamental principles:

• Over half of those in jail have *not yet been convicted*. It is therefore questionable whether pretrial inmates should be punished by subjecting them to worse conditions than what they would experience if convicted and sentenced to prison.

• The *physical design* of a correctional facility shapes inmate as well as staff behavior. When people are degraded to the point of putting them in cages otherwise reserved for animals, it should not be surprising if their reactions more closely resemble animal than human behavior. When staff are overstressed by the noise, tension, and depressing environment of the jail, it should not be surprising if they become frustrated and look for better opportunities elsewhere.

• The *control of behavior* within a correctional facility should be a function of staff rather than inmates. When jail personnel cannot adequately observe what all inmates are doing at all times, gaps are created. Inmates will be quick to fill the vacuum, with the strong preying on the weak.

- The fundamental purpose of jails is to *maintain custody* of those who have been deprived of their liberty. In other words, the role of the jail is not to inflict greater punishment than the loss of freedom. Exposure to substandard living conditions, sexual attacks, demeaning treatment, and inmate dominance are not what the courts have authorized as part of an inmate's "sentence."

In response to these problems, the courts have often intervened to mandate jail improvements. As successful cases challenged the constitutionality of confinement conditions, many localities were forced to upgrade their jail facilities. Rather than waiting to react to court decisions, however, the new-generation philosophy assumes a *proactive* approach—creating facilities that not only meet basic standards of human decency, but come as close to replicating a "normal" environment as can be achieved in confinement.

Architecture and Inmate Supervision

The two major features that set new-generation facilities apart from traditional jails—and to which much of their success in behavioral control can be attributed—are *architectural design* and *management style*. These features work hand in hand to shape behavior and are reflected in the three generations through which jails have progressed:[25]

first-generation jails: facilities with multiple-housing cells lined in rows along corridors which join together like spokes of a wheel.

1. **First-generation jails** are those we would most typically think of if asked to describe a jail. Inmates are confined in multiple-housing cells that are lined in rows along a corridor. The end of each row comes together toward a central

EXHIBIT 5.5
Direct supervision jails are based on the concept that inmates will act more normally when they are confined in a more normal environment. As shown here, this means the absence of bars, natural lighting, and a more open environment.

Source: Courtesy of Mark Goldman and Associates.

control area, similar to the spokes on a wheel (see Exhibit 5.6). Officers patrol the corridors (or "catwalks") on an intermittent, infrequent basis. They cannot observe everyone in all cells at any one time, and their interaction with inmates is primarily through bars as they pass by. As a result, activities often occur in the cells without staff knowledge or control. Because of the linear layout of the cells and the lack of constant supervision, the inmate management style of first-generation jails is known as *linear remote (or intermittent) surveillance.*

2. In the **second-generation jails**, inmate housing surrounds a secure control booth (see Exhibit 5.7). Officers can see directly into the housing units. Thus, rather than physically patrolling corridors, staff can observe inmates directly from their glass-enclosed booth. Although this design increases visual

second-generation jails: a secure, glass-enclosed control booth surrounded by inmate housing, where officers interact with inmates through an intercom.

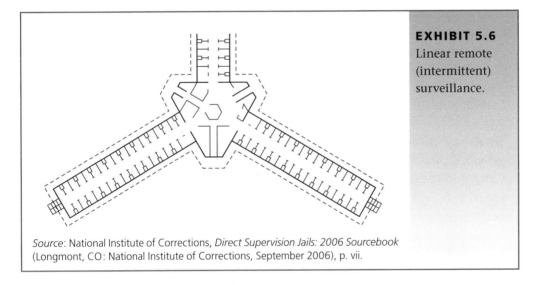

EXHIBIT 5.6
Linear remote (intermittent) surveillance.

Source: National Institute of Corrections, *Direct Supervision Jails: 2006 Sourcebook* (Longmont, CO: National Institute of Corrections, September 2006), p. vii.

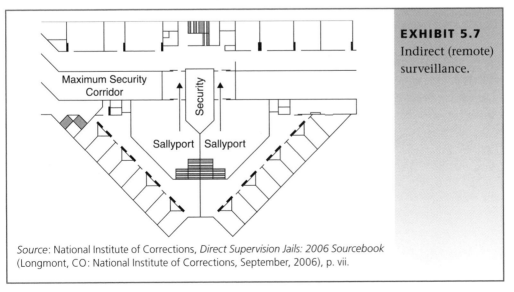

EXHIBIT 5.7
Indirect (remote) surveillance.

Source: National Institute of Corrections, *Direct Supervision Jails: 2006 Sourcebook* (Longmont, CO: National Institute of Corrections, September, 2006), p. vii.

surveillance, isolation in the booth reduces verbal interaction. Communication with inmates is accomplished through an intercom. Because of the lack of personal contact, the inmate management style of second-generation jails is known as *indirect (or remote) surveillance*.

third- (or new-) generation jails: housing units located around an open area where an officer is stationed; known as direct-supervision since no barriers interfere with interaction between inmates and officers.

3. The **third- (or new-) generation jails** combine the principles of continual surveillance with personal interaction. Individual housing units are located around an open, dormitory-style area, where an officer is stationed permanently (see Exhibit 5.8).[26] No barrier separates personnel from residents. Inmates freely move throughout the unit, under the continual supervision of the officer in charge. It is for this reason that new-generation jails are known as *direct-supervision* facilities. As one advocate of direct-supervision jailing notes:

> It's a throwback to the old days, when cops used to walk a certain beat every day, [and] the people of the neighborhood would develop a relationship with him. . . . Gradually, the neighborhood would accept him and feel comfortable enough to share their daily life and concerns with him. This kept the officer informed and intimately aware of neighborhood dynamics. . . . Having an officer in the pod [unit], among the inmates at all times, resembles in many respects walking a neighborhood beat.[27]

To reduce unnecessary movement and related staffing costs, all services are provided directly in the unit—meals, telephones, showers, laundry, counseling, visits, and the like.[28] Although the relative freedom may give the impression that security is lacking, new-generation jails concentrate security on the outside perimeter. Internal security devices are designed to be as unobtrusive as possible.

Physical Features

Visitors to a direct-supervision facility are almost immediately struck by how unlike their typical image of a "jail" it looks. The atmosphere tends to be calmer and less

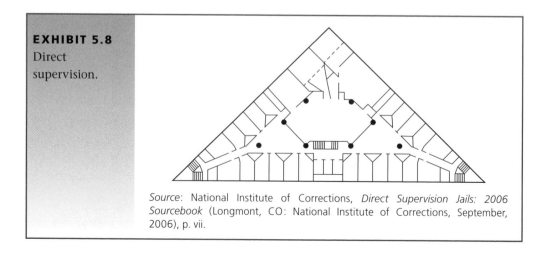

EXHIBIT 5.8
Direct supervision.

Source: National Institute of Corrections, *Direct Supervision Jails: 2006 Sourcebook* (Longmont, CO: National Institute of Corrections, September, 2006), p. vii.

tense than in traditional jails. The floors are carpeted. Windows provide natural light. There are no communal cells with bars. Instead, there are individual rooms with doors.

The initial reaction to direct-supervision facilities is how totally contrary they are to our concept of what jails have been (and, to some, what many believe they should still be today). But, in addition to the fact that a sizeable portion of jail inmates are accused citizens rather than convicted criminals, there are specific operational reasons for each of the amenities provided. For example:

- *Carpeting (or vinyl tile), acoustical tile, and open spaces* reduce noise and the tension it creates by absorbing sounds.

- *Solid walls and doors* (instead of gates and bars) eliminate the constant irritation of metal clanging against metal.

- *Natural lighting and soft colors* create a soothing behavioral effect and reduce the impression of an institutional environment.[29]

Through such measures, new-generation jails attempt to provide more natural surroundings, based on the belief that the environment in which we live is self-reinforcing. In other words, the conditions to which people are exposed have a significant effect on their behavior—with normal conditions producing more normal behavior.

Nevertheless, it has been their physical features that have provoked the greatest criticisms of direct-supervision jails. As public attitudes toward offenders have hardened over recent years, critics maintain that such facilities are too "plush"— that they are "coddling" criminals. In response, some jurisdictions have modified the physical structure by removing carpeting, replacing porcelain fixtures with stainless steel, increasing the ratio of inmates to officers, and even replacing unique wall colors with industrial beige and white paint. But, in direct-supervision facilities, "positive expectations are generated in part by an environment that is non-institutional in appearance," and when such jails have compromised physical design principles they have also experienced less successful results.[30]

Costs and Effectiveness

The appearance of direct-supervision jails may give the impression that they are more expensive to construct and operate than traditional jails. But evidence indicates that exactly the opposite is the case. Such facilities are both easier to manage and more economical.[31] Cost savings are achieved in a number of ways, including:[32]

- the use of *standard, commercial-grade* fixtures rather than high-security, vandal-proof materials;

LEARNING GOALS

Do you know:
11. why direct-supervision jails do not result in higher operating costs?
12. why direct-supervision/new-generation jails cannot function effectively with "old-generation" management?

- the efficiency resulting from the *need for fewer staff,* since personnel are in constant contact with the inmates and are not required to transport them as often because most services are offered directly in the housing unit;

- the *reduced use of sick leave* by personnel;

- the *lower maintenance costs* resulting from the absence of vandalism and graffiti.

Although cost savings are certainly a high priority for any responsible jail administrator, they usually come only at the expense of reducing the quality of service. But again, direct-supervision jails represent an exception to this rule of thumb. As noted previously, these facilities provide a more natural environment, with the anticipation that inmate behavior, in turn, will be modified. Evidence of this **self-reinforcing effect** is extensive:

self-reinforcing effect: the concept that one's environment influences behavior, with more normal conditions promoting more normal responses.

- *Violent incidents* and aggressive behavior overall are reduced.[33]

- Inmates report *feeling safe,* not needing weapons, and an absence of sexual assaults.[34]

- The numbers of *suicides, attempted suicides, and escapes* are considerably lower.[35]

- Significantly *fewer formal rule violations* occur,[36] *disciplinary reports* are substantially lower,[37] and overall disciplinary problems are significantly reduced.[38]

- *Vandalism and destruction of property* are almost completely eliminated. For example, in one facility, the number of TV sets needing repair dropped from "two per week to two in two years."[39]

- Staff express satisfaction with being *free to work* "without constant supervision," as well as having *greater control* over the inmate population.[40]

- Administrators report *improved staff morale* and *lower stress* as benefits.[41]

Perhaps such encouraging outcome measures are fundamentally a reflection of the improved interaction between inmates and officers in new-generation facilities. As one inmate remarked, "Most officers in the pod treat me with dignity and respect, as opposed to being treated like a non-person in other parts of the jail."[42]

Nevertheless, these positive results do not mean that direct-supervision jails are intentionally designed for the purpose of treatment or rehabilitation. Rather, they are simply designed to improve security and prevent inmates from deteriorating further as a result of their jail exposure. But they can promote positive outcomes by providing a setting in which any treatment programs that are offered have a better chance to work. As one researcher noted, the most radical aspect of these facilities is that they challenged—and ultimately changed—long-held assumptions about inmate behavior and responsiveness to treatment.[43] Through the creation of a more normal environment, it is expected that those confined will behave more normally, and research thus far has tended to confirm this expectation.

Training and Management

The residents, of course, are quite receptive to direct-supervision jails. Beyond their basic comforts, they are much safer facilities in which to be confined. No longer do inmates constantly have to fear for their safety or make weapons for their own defense. Officers, however, sometimes experience difficulties with the transition to a new-generation jail. Those who have become accustomed to being physically separated from the inmates quite naturally feel safer being on the "other side of the bars." As a result, they may initially resist being placed directly into a housing unit which "seemingly places officers at the mercy of inmates."[44]

Employees are not permitted to carry weapons inside of any correctional facility, because of the potential that weapons would encourage attacks on staff and potentially fall into the wrong hands. When officers are separated from inmates by secure metal bars, this is not viewed as a major disadvantage. But it is an entirely different situation when removing the bars requires staff to interact face to face with inmates continuously, relying only on verbal skills to control their behavior. In fact, as shown in the next "Close-up on Corrections," competent staff is one of the fundamental principles of direct supervision.

CLOSE-UP ON CORRECTIONS
The Nine Principles of Direct Supervision

1. Effective control.
2. Effective supervision.
3. Competent staff.
4. Safety of staff and inmates.
5. Manageable and cost-effective operations.
6. Effective communications.
7. Classification and orientation.
8. Justice and fairness.
9. Ownership of operation.

Source: Originally adopted by the American Jail Association Board of Directors, November 14, 1992, and reaffirmed on May 3, 2008.

Training is therefore critical to the effective implementation of direct-supervision jails. Such training focuses on the underlying principles of new-generation jailing, the significance of staff to its success, and the interpersonal skills needed to deal with inmates in such an environment. With direct supervision, officers are taught to respond in a proactive way to minor issues before they become major problems, rather than dealing in a reactive way with the consequences.

By being in constant contact with inmates, officers "get to know them well. They learn to recognize and respond to trouble before it escalates into violence . . . [and] negotiation and communication become more important than brute strength."[45] In fact, after staff have experienced the reduced tension and improved inmate behavior of such jails, they may well be reluctant to work in any other type of facility.

Just as officers must be prepared for their new role in direct-supervision jails, supervisors must also become familiar with a new management style. In traditional jails, lower-level staff tend to have routine assignments, management is centralized, and upper-level administrators make all important decisions. In contrast, new-generation jailing will only be effective when management adopts a more **decentralized** approach.

decentralization: an administrative style that gives lower-level staff more autonomy and decision-making input.

As the personnel in charge of the units, officers require greater autonomy to carry out their job. Thus they must be granted more authority to participate in jail management, make their own decisions, and provide leadership within their unit. In other words, "you can't run a new generation jail with old generation management."[46] Physical design is only half of the formula for the success of direct-supervision jails—as in any correctional facility, it is staffing and training that are really the key ingredients. In fact, it is when these critical features are compromised that direct-supervision jails have failed to fulfill their expectations, despite the most advanced architectural design.[47]

LEARNING GOALS

Do you know:

13. at what level of government most jails function, and where the exceptions are?
14. how the elected sheriff model of jail management differs from the appointed administrator model?

JAIL ADMINISTRATION AND OPERATIONS

While the number of direct-supervision facilities increases each year, the vast majority of jails still reflect varieties of first- and second-generation architecture. The major reason that there is so little consistency in terms of everything from size to facility design is that jails are primarily financed, operated, and controlled by local governments. (Although there are federal jails for inmates serving short sentences or awaiting trial on federal charges, they represent very few of the nation's jails.[48]) Because most jails are local facilities housing a relatively short-term, transient population, they are not often high among local funding priorities.

Counties and municipalities are relatively free to set their own policies and procedures with regard to jail operations. Again, however, there are exceptions. In most states, jails are a function of local government. But in six states—Alaska, Connecticut, Delaware, Hawaii, Rhode Island, and Vermont—jails are a responsibility of the *state level* of government.[49] In addition, even when the jail is locally controlled, states may intervene in jail operations. Some, for example, require that jails adhere to state-mandated standards; others provide fiscal incentives to improve jail conditions. There are, however, still other states that neither provide funding nor require standards of their local jails.

Two Models of Jail Administration

Despite these exceptions, as a result of their English origins, most of the nation's jails are administered by a sheriff at the county level of government. Like their predecessors, sheriffs are generally responsible for both enforcing the law and administering the jail. Again, however, there are the inevitable exceptions. In some counties, the sheriff's functions do not include law enforcement but, rather, are limited to jail administration, court security, and serving legal documents.

As an elected official, the sheriff is ultimately accountable to the citizens. This can be advantageous to the jail if the public is concerned about maintaining safe, sanitary, and humane conditions of confinement. But voters often place a higher priority on reducing crime than improving jails, and the sheriff who does not respond to public pressures is not likely to be reelected. Professional sheriffs take their responsibilities for jail administration as seriously as their law enforcement duties. In some places, however, the jail has been neglected in favor of higher-visibility enforcement activities that are more likely to generate votes.

In an effort to balance law enforcement and correctional responsibilities more equitably, some counties have either created separate budgets for law enforcement and correctional functions or actually abolished the office of sheriff, establishing in its place a local department of corrections that is independent from the county's police department. Under this arrangement, both the police chief and the corrections director are appointed by the county administrator rather than elected by the public. In this type of management system, the jail has a separate administrator advocating its needs and may not be as subject to political pressures.

Staff: Setting the Tone for Inmates

Regardless of how the jail is administered, it is the operational personnel who are in day-to-day, continuous interaction with the jail's population. Inmates are completely dependent upon them—for everything from the time they eat, to what they can keep in their cells, to whether they can get an aspirin for a headache. Staff control virtually every aspect of an inmate's life during confinement, in accordance with the rules and regulations of the facility.

Effective administrators today recognize that "a jail's most important resource is staff."[50] In that regard, personnel have progressed from being viewed as "turnkeys" or "guards" to **correctional officers**—inmate managers and leaders,[51] who are recognized for their critical role in facility operations. (For more insights into this issue, see the next "Close-up on Corrections.") Because of their tremendous diversity, jails vary considerably with regard to how extensively they have improved

correctional officers: the title preferred for uniformed, operational staff working in custodial facilities (in contrast to the outdated term "guard").

employee compensation, training, screening, and management practices over the years.[52] But physical facilities notwithstanding, any jail will be only as good as the people staffing it.

CLOSE-UP ON CORRECTIONS
Guards or Correctional Officers?

> Are we guards or correctional officers? . . . A "guard" is one who watches over, protects and prevents escape, etc., but more than that, a "guard" is a technician trained to do a rather specific task, maintain security/custody. On the other hand, an "officer," by definition, is one who . . . serves other people in a wholistic way, concerned about the total person . . . and the surrounding environment. They learn how to care for the physical health of a person, how to promote mental/emotional well-being, and how to lift the spirit by promoting self-esteem. They learn how to provide a safe and secure environment. Above all, they are respecters of persons, individuals and their rights.
>
> *Source*: Larry W. Bergman, "Corrections as a Wholistic Profession?,"
> *The Keepers' Voice*, Vol. 15, No. 1 (Winter, 1994), p. 43.

LEARNING GOALS

Do you know:

15. what intake procedures are conducted upon arrival in jail?
16. in contrast to prison, why jails are particularly vulnerable to suicides?
17. how public policy changes resulted in more of the mentally ill being confined in jails?

intake: procedures involved in officially admitting an inmate to jail.

booking: the process of creating an administrative record of an arrest.

Intake Procedures

To the extent that first impressions are lasting, it is during initial **intake** that the jail has the greatest potential for making a positive or negative impression. The attitudes of staff, the way inmates are handled, and the level of professionalism displayed during the receiving process do much to establish the frame of mind for the inmate's adjustment to jail. An offender who is roughhandled physically, demeaned verbally, or simply treated discourteously during intake is likely to form lasting impressions of distrust and disrespect that will influence subsequent interactions with the jail's personnel. On the other hand, when new arrivals are treated with dignity, courtesy, and respect, the effect can often be reinforcing in terms of how they, in turn, interact with staff.

Inmates are usually received by way of an outside enclosure called a sallyport, through which the police or sheriff's car transporting the offender passes. (To accommodate those coming directly from court, many jails have an enclosed walkway connected to the courtrooms, which reduces security risks involved during outside transportation.) Once the vehicle is inside and the gate secured, the suspect is taken to the receiving area of the jail.

At this point, the arrest form is checked during the intake and **booking** process, since legal problems can arise when a person is deprived of liberty without adequate documentation. Assuming that immediate medical attention is not needed, most jails then conduct a pat-down or **frisk search** (often followed later by a full strip search). All valuables confiscated are carefully recorded, placed in an envelope, and signed for on a property receipt. Since cash and expensive jewelry are not permitted in most jails, these items are placed in a property storage room, to be collected upon release.

Basic information is then taken—such as name, address, physical description, occupation, specific charges, name and phone number of anyone to be notified in case of emergency, attorney's name and address, and name and address of those who may be expected to visit. In addition, some jails record a particularly personal item of information that only the individual being admitted would be likely to know, such as mother's maiden name. The purpose of this is to ensure that, upon release, the correct person is being discharged, since several inmates may share exactly the same name and even bear a physical resemblance, especially in very large jails.

Photographing and fingerprinting follow next, with a complete set of prints sent to the FBI to check on outstanding warrants and file with the National Crime Information Center. This enables jail personnel to determine whether the person poses any identifiable security or safety risks.

frisk search: physical "pat down" of a clothed subject to determine whether weapons or other contraband items are being concealed.

EXHIBIT 5.9
Fingerprinting is an essential part of the booking process, since it establishes positive identification and enables accurate checking for prior offenses.

Source: Courtesy of the Broward County (Fort Lauderdale, FL) Sheriff's Office.

Operational Considerations

Once an inmate is admitted, there are numerous legal and security-oriented issues to be addressed—such as providing opportunities to make arrangements for bail and to contact an attorney, monitoring visits, inspecting incoming packages, controlling the use of medicines, conducting searches, etc. More detailed discussions of these operational practices are contained in Chapter 7, since most of them also pertain to prisons. But it is noteworthy that, in many respects, jails incur greater security risks than prisons. Not only is there a constant flow of inmates into and out of the jail, but the extensive pretrial population must be transported to all of their preliminary court appearances, as well as to and from the courtroom during each day of their trials. Such continuous movement presents an obvious security challenge, requiring professional staff who remain alert to the potential for escape.

Treatment and Industrial Programs

In the past, inmates lingered unproductively in jails, making security matters even more difficult as residents sought outlets for their boredom. In part, this is a reflection of the jail's early history as a holding facility which did not include reform or rehabilitation among its goals. Moreover, both treatment and constructive employment are particularly difficult in jails because of the high turnover of the population as a result of their short-term confinement. But, "without appropriate programs that focus on changing the criminal behavior of inmates, the jail becomes a 'revolving door,' releasing individuals into the community simply to readmit them in a few months, weeks, days, or even hours, when they are arrested for another crime."[53] Progressive administrators today are therefore attempting to provide activities that promote job skills, occupy time, and in some cases even reduce the cost of jail management.

Most jails now at least have available reading materials, recreational opportunities, and organized religious programs. Many have also added various forms of educational classes, correspondence courses, group counseling sessions, and even self-paced, computer-assisted instruction.[54] Even television is now programmed with topics ranging from drug and alcohol dependency to educational improvement, employment readiness, parenting skills, and anger management, in an effort to turn idle TV watching into useful skills training.[55]

In addition, productive labor has expanded under such initiatives as federally sponsored industrial programs, through which inmates have been able to accrue privileges, learn job skills, and earn wages that go toward repayment of custodial costs and compensation to crime victims.[56] Beyond reducing idleness, these programs are designed to improve work habits, develop new skills, and generate revenues or reduce costs. Since they engage inmates in activities ranging from landscaping to assembling electronics components, such labor is now expanding well beyond the routine facility maintenance functions to which jail inmates had largely been limited in the past.

Medical Services

In recent years, court cases resulting from deaths related to lack of proper medical attention, along with increasing pressure for adequate standards, have focused more attention on health care in jails.[57] Although they are voluntary, the standards established by the Joint Commission on Correctional Health Care have also influenced improvements in institutional medical services. For example, the importance of an initial medical exam is perhaps best illustrated by the fact that some suspects who have been arrested for apparent drunkenness were later found to have had a fractured skull, diabetes, or other illnesses or injuries which caused physical behavior that could easily be misinterpreted as intoxication.

Moreover, infectious diseases (such as hepatitis, tuberculosis, and AIDS) are common among those most frequently brought into jail, and treatment is often unavailable to them in the community. Recognizing this, a special task force has been established by the Centers for Disease Control and Prevention to focus on the public health risks related to tuberculosis among people behind bars. In fact, jails are deep reservoirs of numerous health-related issues and communicable diseases. As a result, effective diagnosis and treatment intervention are essential—not just for the good of individual jail patients, but also for the ultimate benefit of the entire community by interrupting the spread of infection and optimizing the health of the general public.[58]

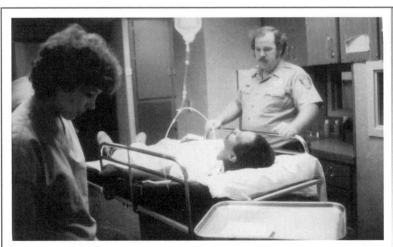

EXHIBIT 5.10
Today's jails are responsible for providing both routine health care and emergency medical services to an inmate population with many serious communicable diseases and health care needs.

Source: Courtesy of the Miami-Dade (Florida) County Department of Corrections and Rehabilitation.

CONTEMPORARY JAIL ISSUES AND CHALLENGES

When determining the primary challenges facing contemporary jails, the importance of health care—along with the next issue to be discussed, suicide—cannot be overestimated. Both rose to the surface in 2007, when sheriffs and jail administrators representing all sizes of facilities from throughout all areas of the country assembled to identify their primary concerns. The result was that inmate health and mental health issues took first place on their list of priorities.[59] That is largely because the mentally ill constitute such a large portion of the jail population. Moreover, there are a number of features about jail confinement that promote the potential for suicide.

Suicide Vulnerability

Because jails are especially vulnerable to suicides, an essential aspect of intake processing is identifying those displaying signs and symptoms that indicate they are intent on taking their own life. This is a particularly significant problem for all jails, but especially smaller facilities.[60] Although the rate has been steadily declining in recent years (see Exhibit 5.11), suicide still accounts for nearly one-third of inmate deaths in local jails. In contrast, it is the cause of less than 6 percent of the deaths in state prisons.[61] Nor do statistics on jail suicides reflect the many additional but unsuccessful attempts that were prevented by alert staff.

The question is why those in jail are so vulnerable to the potential for suicide. The answers are numerous. Many jail inmates are suffering from various forms of mental illness, which can be aggravated by exposure to jail, as the tragic case in the

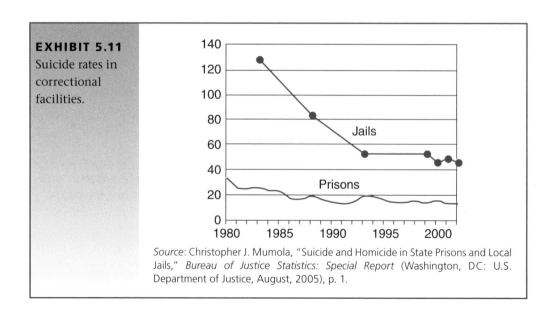

EXHIBIT 5.11 Suicide rates in correctional facilities.

Source: Christopher J. Mumola, "Suicide and Homicide in State Prisons and Local Jails," *Bureau of Justice Statistics: Special Report* (Washington, DC: U.S. Department of Justice, August, 2005), p. 1.

next "Close-up on Corrections" reveals. But, even among otherwise mentally healthy inmates, the jail includes more of the types of people most prone to suicide than are found among the general public in free society—such as young, unemployed, unmarried males.

CLOSE-UP ON CORRECTIONS
Tragedy behind Bars

In a northwestern state a young man encountered a snowstorm as he drove from his office to a distant town. For reasons perhaps caused by his psychiatric problems, together with the stress of driving in a snowstorm, the man developed a sense of helplessness and confusion. He parked outside of a hospital and made a phone call to his father asking for help because he was confused and did not know what to do. His father told him that he would send his brother to be with him and that he should wait at the hospital for him. So he sat and waited. The desk receptionist observed the young man sitting in the snow without a coat during the blizzard and decided to call the police.

The police officer who responded to the call accused him of being on drugs and therefore took him away to the small local jail. At the prisoner's request, the officer called the boy's father who informed him of the boy's psychiatric history. Unconcerned with this information, the officer told the boy's father that he was going to hold the young man on suspicion of drug possession. The young man was placed in a cell without being booked or charged with any crime. At that time, a traffic accident was reported and because he was the only one on duty, the officer left the man alone in the cell for the rest of the evening. The prisoner was frightened and begged the officer not to lock him up. The officer did not return that evening. When shifts changed, the replacement officers discovered the prisoner was dead; he had hanged himself by his shoelaces.

Source: David Lester and Bruce L. Danto, *Suicide behind Bars*
(Philadelphia: Charles Press, 1993), pp. 7–8.

Moreover, admission to jail can be a traumatic experience for someone who has never been incarcerated before. By the time offenders go through the full legal process and are sentenced to prison, they have more or less accepted and adjusted to the reality that they are facing a period of confinement. But the uncertainty of how long they will be kept in jail—combined with an immediate sense of loss and hopelessness, frustration, and depression about their situation—can promote suicidal thoughts, as reflected in data indicating that a quarter of all jail suicides occur within the first 24 hours of incarceration.[62] As the next "Close-up on Corrections" reveals, there are many features of the jail environment itself that make inmates more susceptible to suicide than their prison counterparts. Added to this is the fact that a sizeable percentage of arrestees commit their offense while intoxicated or under the influence of drugs.[63] When the effects of the alcohol or drugs wear off, depression can set in, along with realization of the seriousness of their situation. In fact, nearly half of jail suicide victims in one study were identified during intake as having a history of substance abuse,[64] and another reported that all of the victims studied had used excessive amounts of alcohol and drugs prior to their admission to jail.[65] This is consistent with research indicating that addictive and mental health disorders are in some way involved in more than 9 out of 10 suicides.[66]

CLOSE-UP ON CORRECTIONS
How the Jail Itself Influences Suicidal Behavior

- *Authoritarian environment.* Those not familiar with regimentation can encounter traumatic difficulty in the jail setting.
- *No apparent control over the future.* Following incarceration, many jail inmates experience feelings of helplessness and hopelessness. They feel powerless and overwhelmed.
- *Isolation from family and friends.* Support may seem far away, especially with restricted visiting and telephone privileges.
- *Dehumanizing aspects of incarceration.* Confinement in even the best of jail facilities is dehumanizing. Lack of privacy, inability to make your own choices, strange noises and odors, and the stress of overcrowding can all have a devastating effect.
- *Heightened fears.* Based on stereotypes of jails seen on television and in movies, fears heighten inmate anxieties.
- *Reaction to "special housing" assignment.* Inmates housed in isolation and/or special housing are often locked down for 23 or more hours per day with few privileges. Under these conditions, they may react with frustration, panic, despair, or rage.
- *Shame of incarceration.* Feelings of shame are often inversely proportionate to the gravity of the offense committed. Frequently, such feelings develop in those persons who have never been arrested before or who have a limited arrest history. It is not uncommon for jail suicides to be committed by intoxicated persons held under "protective custody" until sober, or by individuals arrested for traffic violations, disturbing the peace, or other minor offenses.

   Source: Summarized from "Suicide Risk despite Denial (or When Actions Speak Louder than Words)," *Jail Suicide/Mental Health Update*, Vol. 16, No. 1 (Summer, 2007), p. 4.

Suicide Prevention

To prevent jail suicides, it is essential for intake staff as well as custodial officers to be familiar with warning signs and suicidal profiles. The role of intake is especially critical, yet the booking area in jails is often chaotic and noisy, with staff pressured to quickly process large numbers of arrestees. As a result, jail intake lacks the "two key ingredients for identifying suicidal behavior—time and privacy."[67]

Even after inmates have completed intake and been assigned to housing, staff need to remain alert to subtle signals as well as sudden behavioral changes. Suicide prevention is an ongoing process, and in this regard the close observation available in direct-supervision units presents obvious advantages over the remote, intermittent surveillance of traditional facilities.[68]

When the possibility of suicide is suspected, it is essential to take immediate action. Unfortunately, the ability of many jails to deal with mentally disturbed suicidal inmates may be limited to isolating them from the general population. But this approach can be counterproductive, since isolation "tends to create fear and suspicion . . . further undermining their mental state" and increasing the potential for suicide.[69]

Precautions taken to respond appropriately to suicide risks will depend on the situation. Based on the seriousness of the symptoms, responses can range from simply talking with the inmate, to removing any items that could be used for self-destruction, to arranging for more frequent (or even constant) monitoring, to reassignment in special management units or "suicide-proof" cells.[70] The most serious cases, of course, should also be referred for psychiatric evaluation. But, no matter how trivial they may seem, no suicidal threats can be taken lightly in the vulnerable atmosphere of the jail.

The Mentally Ill in Jails

Beyond identifying those prone to suicide, intake screening has long been noted as "one of the most significant mental health services that a jail can offer."[71] That is because, for a number of reasons, the mentally ill are overrepresented in the jail population. Nearly two out of three (64 percent) of those in jail have some type of mental health problem,[72] and the situation has only been getting more serious in recent years. For example, men in urban jails are now "three times more likely to be afflicted by such illnesses as schizophrenia, severe depression, and mania than the population at large."[73]

As a result, the National Coalition for the Mentally Ill in Criminal Justice reports that there are actually more mentally ill people in jails than in mental health hospitals.[74] The situation has come to the point that "the three largest de facto psychiatric facilities in the United States are now the Los Angeles County Jail, Rikers Island Jail in New York City, and Cook County Jail in Chicago."[75] In fact, one judge estimates that "Psychiatric inmates languish in jail eight times longer than other inmates. They wait for court-ordered evaluations. They wait for medication to make them competent to stand trial. They wait for beds in treatment facilities."[76]

Jails today are additionally faced with growing numbers of "dually diagnosed" offenders—those suffering from a combination of mental health and substance abuse problems. Estimates indicate that three out of four inmates with a mental health diagnosis also have a co-occurring substance abuse disorder.[77] With sheriffs and jail administrators ranking inmate medical and mental health services as the greatest challenge they face,[78] the situation has become so serious that some are even beginning to call for jails to be certified as mental health institutions.[79]

Even if the resources are not available to properly treat them (as is often the case), it is important that such inmates be identified to better assure their safety during confinement. But accurate identification does not account for why the mentally ill represent such a sizeable portion of the jail population. To answer that question, it is necessary to look deeper into public policy fluctuations over the past several decades.

Deinstitutionalization of Mental Health Services

For many years, psychiatric patients were warehoused in large, substandard mental health institutions. In response to their poor treatment, there was a major move throughout the country during the 1960s to close these "insane asylums" and replace them with community-based mental health facilities. This process of **deinstitutionalization** did, in fact, result in closing many of the worst mental hospitals. But the local outpatient treatment services envisioned to replace them were not as readily forthcoming:

deinstitutionalization: replacing large, centralized institutions with smaller, community-based facilities that function on an outpatient basis.

> In 1955, there were over half a million severely mentally ill patients in public psychiatric hospitals. In 1994, there were 71,619. Based on population growth, estimates are that, without a change in approach, there would have been over 885,000 patients in state hospitals in 1994.[80]

Where have they gone? As communities closed their mental health institutions without providing other alternatives, many former patients were found wandering the streets, vulnerable to arrest. Of the hundreds of thousands of people who are homeless in America, it is estimated that at least a third are mentally ill.[81] In addition, closer restrictions designed to ensure that only the truly ill are confined to mental hospitals have made involuntary commitment procedures more difficult.[82] Combined with lack of sufficient local treatment resources, these circumstances have resulted in what has become known as "criminalization" of the mentally ill.

Criminalization of the Mentally Ill

With changes in public laws, many behaviors of the chronically mentally ill have become criminalized—including homelessness, vagrancy, and disorderly conduct.[83] While most of those with mental disturbances are no longer being warehoused in substandard mental health institutions, many are still being warehoused in jails—"the only place left to 'put' them and the only institution that cannot say 'no.'"[84] As one mental health advocate summarized the situation, "We have not 'deinstitutionalized' the mentally ill. We have 'transinstitutionalized' them, shifting the mentally ill from hospitals to jails and prisons."[85]

This criminalization raises serious public policy questions in terms of how appropriate jails are for responding to mental illnesses.[86] Additionally, such revolving door policies are costly. Tax dollars are paying for police officers to repeatedly arrest, transport, and process mentally ill defendants, jail costs associated with treatment and crisis intervention, salaries of judges, court staff, prosecutors, and defense attorneys, and many more hidden costs.[87] As one study found, stabilizing the homeless and mentally ill saved $16,000 annually per person in terms of social, mental health, and jail expenses.[88] Moreover, there can be serious repercussions when the mentally ill are released back into the community without follow-up.

Despite the fact that they are poorly financed and equipped to deal with it, not all correctional facilities are simply ignoring this unwanted responsibility. Some are making substantial efforts to provide behavioral health care.[89] In Milwaukee, for example, an outpatient community support program combines therapeutic services and money management with day reporting and close monitoring.[90] In several states, jail officials collaborate with mental health professionals to divert potential inmates from confinement to community-based treatment.[91] In a number of jurisdictions from California to Alabama, mental health treatment courts have been established on the basis of successful drug court models.[92] But, in many other places, mentally disturbed clients land in jail, which prompted the American Jail Association to adopt the resolution highlighted in the next "Close-up on Corrections."

CLOSE-UP ON CORRECTIONS
The Mentally Ill in Jail

WHEREAS, the growing number of inmates with mental illness and the lack of appropriate resources in jails to screen, treat, and properly house these individuals, strain daily jail operations and weaken staff morale. Additionally, the problem compromises the safety of staff and inmates alike, exacerbates crowding, and increases the costs of operating our nation's jails.

WHEREAS, the American Jail Association feels strongly that the jail setting is not the proper therapeutic milieu for effective, long-term treatment of mental illness. . . .

THEREFORE, BE IT RESOLVED that the American Jail Association urges its members to improve the response to people with mental illness who come into contact with the criminal justice system by developing and promoting programs, policies, and legislation that accomplish the following goals:

- Improve collaboration among stakeholders in the criminal justice and mental health systems;
- Integrate mental health and substance abuse services to more effectively address the needs of individuals who have co-occurring mental health and substance abuse disorders;
- Focus efforts toward providing the mental health system with resources and training regarding the criminal justice system;
- Recognize that the solution to this complex problem depends on an effective and accessible community mental health system;

- Support efforts to establish mental health courts that would effectively divert nonviolent offenders from the criminal justice system into appropriate treatment and/or supporting services.

Note: The resolution also calls for Congress, federal agencies, and local government officials to increase funding programs, collect information, facilitate partnerships, and improve research on this topic.

Source: "Newly Adopted Resolutions," *American Jails* (July/August, 2003), p. 7.

LEARNING GOALS

Do you know:

18. how inmates are managed through classification?
19. what the difference is between the "design" and "rated" capacity of jails?
20. what can be done to reduce jail crowding?

classification: the separation of inmates into groups according to characteristics that they share in common.

Inmate Classification

Just as certain inmates may need special attention because they are suicidal or mentally disturbed, there are other groups who also need to be housed separately to promote the safety of all inmates and the security of the institution. This is what is meant by **classification**—the "systematic grouping of inmates into categories based on shared characteristics and/or behavioral patterns."[93] Proper classification helps to promote inmate safety, as well as smooth operation of the facility.

However, correctional facilities did not always group inmates separately. As we saw in the early origins of the jail, men and women, young and old, and even sick and healthy inmates were all housed together. In the history of correctional institutions, inmates were first separated by sex and then by age. It has only been much more recently that classification has progressed to more sophisticated dimensions. In modern jails, classification serves to segregate:

- *pretrial* defendants from *convicted inmates*;
- *sentenced* from *unsentenced inmates*;
- *males* from *females*;
- *adults* from *juveniles*;
- *violent* from *nonviolent inmates*;
- *general population* from *special needs inmates* (e.g., drug/alcohol abusers, emotionally disturbed, sexual predators, elderly, physically disabled).

The information used to classify inmates comes from a number of sources, including observations and interviews, along with review of available court reports, the inmate's personal history, and medical or psychological screening records. Staff look at such things as the offense committed (or charged), and the offender's legal status, background, medical/mental health issues, gang affiliations, etc. This establishes a basis for making decisions in terms of everything from housing assignment to degree of supervision needed and eligibility for various work, educational, or treatment programs. (The objective classification techniques that are increasingly employed in both prisons and jails today are discussed in greater detail in Chapter 8.)

Service Fees

Regardless of what specific programs or services an inmate might receive, most jail operations are no longer provided exclusively at taxpayer expense. With nearly every state authorizing the assessment of inmate fees, 90 percent of U.S. jails are charging inmates for everything from health care to work release.[94] Such fees not only generate annual revenues in the millions of dollars, but also reduce demand for services. For example, when inmates are required to make a co-payment, it has been determined that demand for medical services has dropped by as much as 60 percent.[95] Nevertheless, there are concerns that such fees can also discourage inmates from seeking necessary treatment and that they are not as cost-effective as might appear, since the administrative burden of collecting fees "is not matched by the revenues generated."[96]

Facility Crowding

Regardless of who is paying for them, even the best-intentioned and most sophisticated programs cannot achieve their objectives in institutions that are seriously crowded. When space is limited, just having enough room for screening, booking, and classification becomes a luxury. Moreover, when space is severely restricted, inmates must be "fit in" wherever a spare bed can be found (or added). Under such conditions, the integrity of the classification system is quickly compromised.

A correctional facility is generally considered to be crowded when it exceeds either design capacity (the number of inmates that it was originally constructed to confine) or **rated capacity** (the number of inmates that an acknowledged expert, such as a state prison inspector, estimates the jail can safely hold, which is generally a less conservative figure).

As inmates became more active in challenging crowded conditions, the courts became increasingly active in correcting the situation. Many of the nation's jails are still subject to court-mandated **population caps**, and others are under court order or **consent decree** for a number of conditions related to crowding—such as fire hazards or lack of sufficient medical services, staffing patterns, visiting practices, library services, or inmate classification.

The fact that the judicial branch of government has determined that the situation is so serious as to warrant court action is itself illustrative of the severity of the problem. New construction, expansion of existing facilities, community supervision, day reporting, and early release are among the many options that have been used to reduce crowding. However, many of these innovations are short-term, stop-gap

rated capacity: the number of inmates that a facility can safely hold, according to expert opinion.

population cap: a court-ordered maximum number of inmates that can be housed in a facility.

consent decree: response to a lawsuit whereby correctional officials agree to voluntarily remedy shortcomings, rather than contest the allegations.

measures, and new facilities often fill to capacity quickly. The issue cannot be addressed effectively without systemwide attention to everything from public policies and sentencing practices to consideration of the community-based alternatives described in Chapter 4. In fact, jails have begun placing so many of their clients under various forms of community supervision that nearly 10 percent of the population is now actually supervised outside of the jail in some type of community service, work or treatment programs, electronically-monitored home confinement, or similar options.[97]

But jail administrators cannot be the only personnel who take responsibility for the crowding crisis. To the contrary, the jail itself can implement very few changes to alleviate crowding, since it does not enact penal codes, prescribe sentences, or determine release dates. In fact, jails actually have little or no control over the two primary determinants of the jail population—the number of bookings and the average length of stay.[98] Moreover, there is little the jail can do when judges become less willing to grant bail, more offenders violate probation or parole conditions, and state prisons slow down transfer of sentenced inmates as a result of their own crowded conditions.

There are, however, many other decision-makers in the local justice system who exercise discretion in small ways that can add up to sizeable reductions in the jail population without releasing serious offenders. Several examples are highlighted in the next "Close-up on Corrections."

CLOSE-UP ON CORRECTIONS
Systemwide Strategies to Alleviate Jail Crowding

Law Enforcement

Decisions surrounding local arrest practices—whether to arrest, transport to jail, book, or detain for bail—are critical determinants of jail population size. In that regard, police can increase use of citations for minor offenders and divert those with special problems to community treatment programs.

Jail Administrators

While they have little direct control over admissions and length of confinement, jail administrators nevertheless can help to reduce crowding by:

- assuring ready access to pretrial release screening and bail review;
- keeping judges continually informed of the status of the jail population;
- establishing timeframes for case disposition through an automated tracking system;
- supporting such options as electronic monitoring or day reporting;
- collaborating with lawmakers on legislation that would offer alternatives to jail sentences, allow deferred sentencing, and increase jail funding.

Prosecutors

Early case screening by prosecutors can reduce unnecessary confinement by eliminating or downgrading weak cases as soon as possible. Greater use of risk assessment, diversion, and delegated release authority would also contribute to reducing the jail population.

Pretrial Services

Providing background information on defendants, release-on-recognizance recommendations, and case flow information can help to reduce crowding.

Judiciary

Judges make more decisions affecting jail populations than anyone else. As such, they can:

- make greater use of alternatives to jail, including pretrial release and diversion programs;
- make magistrates available 24 hours per day, seven days per week for release decisions;
- expedite court proceedings whenever possible;
- provide intake staff who can screen out people inappropriate for jail (including the mentally ill) and place them in alternative programs.

Probation and Parole

Probation and parole agencies can improve case-processing efficiency by streamlining presentence investigation procedures, expediting revocation decisions, and using incarceration only as a last resort.

State Departments of Corrections

Partnerships with prison administrators can better assure that sentenced inmates are transferred to state custody in a timely manner.

Overall Criminal Justice System

An "expediter team" could scan the jail roster each day to identify inappropriate detentions as well as those eligible for nonfinancial release. Most importantly, establishing a criminal justice coordinating committee composed of key stakeholders could facilitate systemwide discussion, oversight, and collaboration.

Sources: Compiled from Bureau of Justice Statistics, *A Second Look at Alleviating Jail Crowding: A Systems Perspective* (Washington, DC: Bureau of Justice Statistics, October, 2000), pp. 31–63; Gary F. Cornelius, *The American Jail: Cornerstone of Modern Corrections* (Upper Saddle River, NJ: Pearson Education, 2008), pp. 36–38; National Institute of Corrections, *Jail Population Reduction Strategies* (Longmont, CO: National Institute of Corrections, April, 1995), pp. 16–22; and Neil Vance, "Real Reductions in Jail Populations Require Comprehensive Actions," *American Jails* (November/December, 2005), pp. 71–72.

While these illustrations are indicative of the significant steps being taken, managing crowding requires a comprehensive understanding of the dynamics that create changes in jail occupancy levels.[99] Jail crowding is a complex challenge that cannot be adequately addressed by one or two isolated changes. Rather, it requires comprehensive strategies based on information gathered from sources ranging from surveys of criminal justice officials to analysis of arrest databases, court files, and aggregate trends.[100]

The long-term plight of crowded jails will be resolved only when jails are reserved for those who actually need to be confined behind bars—who are not there simply because the system is slow in processing them or because there is no other resource in the community to deal with their problems. Moreover, as long as society continues to respond to the symptoms rather than the causes of behavior for which people are confined, the public will continue to be disenchanted with the performance of its jails. As long as jails remain the primary vehicle for responding to such social problems as mental illness, alcoholism, and drug abuse, their role will continue to be unclear, their performance will continue to be unsatisfactory, and their space will continue to be filled beyond capacity. Direct-supervision/new-generation jails can change living conditions for those confined, but only a new generation of public policies can challenge long-held practices concerning who should *be* confined.

SUMMARY

As the oldest component of the justice system, jails have historical legacies which remain evident today in antiquated facilities that have long outlived their usefulness. While more small jails are being consolidated into regional detention centers, there are still far more jails housing 50 inmates or fewer than megajails confining 1,000 or more. However, the largest facilities still hold the greatest percentage of the overall inmate population.

Of those in jail, less than half are convicted offenders, while the remainder are accused defendants awaiting trial. Jails also book arrestees, hold those awaiting sentencing or transfer, and readmit probation, parole, or bail/bond violators. Many inmates confined in jail have not been involved in violent crimes but, rather, are being held for drug-related, public order, or property offenses. In fact, alcohol and drug abusers represent a sizeable portion of the jail's clients, despite the lack of adequate resources to address their problems while incarcerated. Since jails generally do not have authority to confine offenders with sentences of more than one year, there is a high turnover among the inmate population.

In order to improve management and operational practices, a number of jurisdictions have embraced a new generation of jailing, which attempts to create as "normal" an environment as can be achieved in confinement. Architecture, physical amenities, and management style all work together to shape behavior in such jails. In contrast to the intermittent or remote style of surveillance in traditional facilities, these jails rely on direct supervision. Officers interact directly with inmates, unobstructed by bars or glass enclosures. While such facilities have been criticized as too "plush," their basic intent is not to promote comfort but to provide a safe and secure environment where staff rather than inmates are in control. Consequently, they tend to experience lower rates of violent incidents, suicides, escapes, and vandalism.

Because jails are administered primarily at the local level of government, they represent considerable diversity with regard to everything from size to facility design and management style. However, one thing that all jails have in common is reliance on proper staffing, which is why the proper selection, compensation, training, and development of personnel are so essential to achieving the jail's mission.

Inmates are admitted to jail through the process of intake, which includes booking, recording information, searching, photographing, and fingerprinting. For those who have been admitted, many jails now provide recreational, educational, and counseling services, and some have initiated jail industries to enable inmates to engage in productive work.

The availability of medical services is a necessity in jails, not only to provide treatment to the inmate, but also to curtail the spread of infectious diseases. Because suicide is the primary cause of death in jail, personnel must be alert to its signs and symptoms, taking immediate precautions whenever the potential for suicide is suspected. Like those vulnerable to suicide, the mentally ill are overrepresented among the jail population, largely as a result of the deinstitutionalization of mental health facilities. Because of the lack of resources to deal with them in the community, the mentally ill are often confined in jails, which are poorly suited to address their needs.

To better ensure safety and security of all inmates, the jail population is classified according to their conviction/sentencing status, sex, age, offense, security risk, etc. But it is difficult to provide proper classification in crowded facilities, where limited space does not always enable the proper separation of inmates. Jails are considered crowded when the number of persons they are holding exceeds either the facility's design or its rated capacity. A number of severely crowded jails are operating under court order or consent decree to reduce their population. While new construction, community supervision, and early release all have been employed to address the crowding problem, without a coordinated, systemwide approach, these are likely to be temporary stop-gap measures. Nor is the situation much better in prisons, as we will see in the following chapters.

FOR FURTHER DISCUSSION

1. Put yourself in the position of the administrator of a jail with fewer than 50 beds. Discuss what the benefits as well as challenges would be if your jail was to consolidate with those of several other equally small surrounding jurisdictions.

2. Determine what the breakdown is of pretrial versus convicted inmates in your local jail and discuss measures that could be implemented to reduce the pretrial population.

3. Identify what resources are available in your community for chronic alcoholics, drug abusers, and the homeless. To the extent that such resources are lacking or insufficient, discuss the impact on your local jail.

4. Put yourself in the position of a jail administrator who wants to build a direct-supervision facility, but the county commission has heard about the amenities associated with these facilities and is opposed on the basis that they are "too plush." Develop arguments that you can use to persuade the commissioners to support you.

5. Discuss how everything from staff selection and training to supervisory practices and performance evaluations will need to change in order to effectively implement direct-supervision jailing.

6. Explain why correctional staff consider it derogatory to be referred to as "guards" rather than "correctional officers."

7. Describe measures that jails could take to reduce their vulnerability to suicide, including why direct-supervision jails are considerably less vulnerable in this regard.

8. Explain what is meant by the "criminalization of the mentally ill," along with what initiatives a community could implement to reduce this dilemma.

9. Discuss what can be done by the courts, probation/parole, and the prosecutor's office to reduce jail crowding in your community.

Prisons and Other Correctional Facilities

We ask an awful lot of our prisons. We ask them to correct the incorrigible, rehabilitate the wretched, deter the determined, restrain the dangerous, and punish the wicked. We ask them to take over where other institutions of society have failed. . . . We ask them to pursue so many different and often incompatible goals that they seem virtually doomed to fail.[1]

Charles H. Logan

CHAPTER OVERVIEW

Just as jails are the last resort for a community that has no other alternatives to deal with its social problems, prisons represent the last resort for a criminal justice system that has exhausted all other alternatives. Although a first-time offender may be sent to prison for a serious offense, the majority of prison inmates have had previous experience with the criminal justice system. Some had been afforded a "second chance" through probation; others had served prior time. But, whatever their previous experience, it was obviously unsuccessful in changing long-term behavior—leaving the prison to attempt to accomplish what other sanctions failed to achieve. In most cases, however, it is equally unable to do so. About the only thing that prisons are able to achieve with consistent success is suppressing further involvement in street crime during the period of incarceration. Whether the offender becomes better or worse as a result of the experience is no longer the primary issue.

Prisons provide the direct, external control demanded when such indirect social controls as norms, values, and even laws proved ineffective. As the most visible image of corrections, it is prisons that first come to mind when the public considers responses to crime. Like anything that is unfamiliar to us, isolation behind thick walls and barbed-wire fencing, with high-powered rifles protruding from guard towers, creates an aura of mystique. As a result, we are at the same time both fearful of and fascinated by our prisons.

NUMBER AND TYPES OF INSTITUTIONS

Prisons range from large, high-security complexes to community-based work-release units and small, rural road camps. Like jails, some date to the turn of the twentieth century, whereas others are much more modern. But, because they do not trace their history as far back as jails, prisons overall have been more recently constructed. They are also far less numerous than jails, thereby enabling greater uniformity.

Federal, State, and Military Facilities

Since jails are a function of the local level of government, every county and municipality potentially has the authority to operate a jail. Prisons, however, are a responsibility of the *state* and *federal* levels of government, which represent only 51 jurisdictions. Whether an inmate will be confined in a state or federal institution depends not on the seriousness of their crime, but rather on whether they violated a state or federal statute.

While all states have at least several facilities, the 1,406 government-operated state and federal prisons in the U.S.[2] reflect only about half of the number of jails. Adding the 415 facilities that are privately operated brings the total to 1,821 prisons nationwide, still far less than jails.[3] Although contracting with the private sector to operate prisons for state and federal government is a relatively recent development, private facilities accounted for nearly all of the growth in the number of prisons during the past few years.[4] (For a detailed discussion of the history, development, and controversies involved in the privatization movement, see Chapter 15.)

In addition, the U.S. Army, Navy, Air Force, and Marine Corps maintain correctional facilities for some 1,794 imprisoned military personnel.[5] Some of these inmates have been turned over to the military for trial, sentencing, and imprisonment after committing crimes in civilian jurisdictions. Others have been convicted of violations of the Uniform Code of Military Conduct (e.g., desertion, disrespect for a superior officer, or being absent without official leave). In this regard, military corrections differs somewhat from its civilian counterparts, since the primary objective is often restoration of the offender to active duty.

Costs of Imprisonment

Asking how much it costs to build a prison is somewhat like asking how much it costs to buy a car—it all depends on what you want. How expensive any particular correctional institution is to build and operate will depend on a number of factors—where it is located, the number of inmates it confines, the number of personnel needed to adequately staff it, how secure it is designed to be, the extensiveness of programs offered, and so on. In general, the larger and more secure a prison is, the more expensive it will be. Construction costs range from more than $92,000 *per bed* for maximum-security state prisons, to more than $39,000 *per bed* for minimum-security facilities.[6] But that is just for initial construction. Annual operating costs average well over $22,000 per inmate.[7] As a result, prisons represent the bulk of all correctional expenditures. (See Exhibit 6.1.) Because the majority of prisons operate at the state level of government, it is not surprising to find that the primary brunt of this fiscal burden falls to state governments, which bear nearly two-thirds of total correctional costs.[8] Moreover, the burden is ever-increasing. State correctional spending has been climbing in recent years at a rate that outpaces almost all other expenditures, including both education and health care.[9]

Undoubtedly, imprisonment is an expensive option. For what it costs to keep an inmate in maximum custody for a year, a student could attend one of the best universities in the country, dozens of offenders could be supervised on probation or parole in the community, or hot meals could be provided to thousands of needy people. It is for such reasons that this country's extensive use of incarceration frequently comes under fire.

But some argue that the costs of prison must be balanced against the costs of crime. At least one study estimates that, given losses to victims, court costs, and police expenditures (multiplied by the average crime rate per offender), it is

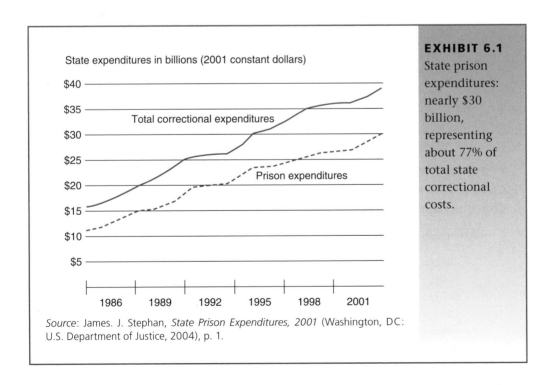

State expenditures in billions (2001 constant dollars)

Total correctional expenditures

Prison expenditures

1986 1989 1992 1995 1998 2001

EXHIBIT 6.1
State prison expenditures: nearly $30 billion, representing about 77% of total state correctional costs.

Source: James. J. Stephan, *State Prison Expenditures, 2001* (Washington, DC: U.S. Department of Justice, 2004), p. 1.

actually less expensive to keep someone in prison.[10] Nevertheless, others point toward many additional factors beyond incarceration that account for lower crime rates, and point out the many "hidden costs" associated with imprisonment—ranging from welfare payments to child endangerment when a parent is absent.[11] Regardless of whether or not sizeable fiscal savings can actually be achieved by incarceration, the fiscal as well as social costs of imprisonment must be weighed against the alternatives.

Offender Fees

Despite economic arguments pro and con, the fact remains that current public policies emphasize the use of imprisonment. As correctional costs have skyrocketed in recent years, some jurisdictions have turned to the private sector in an attempt to operate prisons more cost-effectively (a topic discussed further in Chapter 15). In addition, "the notion that offenders should contribute to their own supervision costs has gained widespread political support" in recent years.[12] To some, charging offenders for their confinement brings back memories of the inequities involved in the fee system that was common during the early history of corrections. Thus, it is not surprising to find that there is significant debate surrounding these practices, which have been subjected to court challenges and criticized as being "impractical, unprofessional, or inherently unfair."[13]

In desperate efforts to offset escalating costs, however, more and more facilities are charging inmates fees for everything from room and board to medical treatment.[14] Especially in tight economic times, when universal health care is not available to those in free society and most insurance plans require co-payments, legitimate arguments can be mounted for assessing health care fees. But, as the next "Close-up on Corrections" reveals, there are equally valid arguments on both sides of this issue. In fact, the position of the National Commission on Correctional Health Care is that access to health care in correctional facilities is so fundamental that it should be available regardless of ability to pay.

CLOSE-UP ON CORRECTIONS
Charging Inmate Fees for Health Care—You Decide

Some of the arguments for charging inmates a fee for health services are:

- The cost of medical care is an increasingly heavy burden on the financial resources of the facility. . . .
- Sick call is abused by some inmates . . . making it more difficult to provide adequate care for inmates who really need the attention.
- Inmates who can spend money on a candy bar or a bottle of shampoo should be able to pay for medical care with the same funds—it is a matter of priorities.
- It will do away with frivolous requests for medical attention.

- It cuts down on security's problems in transporting inmates to and from sick call. . . .
- It instills a sense of fiscal responsibility and forces the inmate to make mature choices. . . .

On the other hand, some of the arguments against charging inmates a fee for health care services are:

- A fee-for-service program ignores the significance of full and unimpeded access to sick call and the importance of preventive care.
- Inmates are almost always "indigent" . . . [and] "extras" become extremely important to one who is locked up twenty-four hours each day. The inmate may well choose to forego treatment of a medical problem in order to be able to buy the shampoo or toothpaste.
- The program sets up two tiers of inmates—those who have funds to get medical care and commissary privileges, and those who have to choose between the two.
- Avoiding medical care for "minor" situations can lead to serious consequences for the inmate or inmate population [and can] . . . lead to the infection of others.
- Because of crowded conditions, there is a risk of spreading infections. . . .
- Charging health service fees as a management tool does not recoup costs; rather, when looking at the increased administrative work involved or the long-term effect of the program, charging health service fees can cost more to implement than what is recovered.

Source: National Commission on Correctional Health Care, *Position Statement: Charging Inmates a Fee for Health Care Services* (October, 2005), available at http://www.ncchc.org/resources/statements/healthfees.html.

Whether it is medical care, educational programming, vocational training, or some other type of treatment, however, the fact remains that maintaining prison security is far more expensive than providing inmate services. Moreover, when government revenues are diminishing at the same time that demands continue mounting, there is considerable support for requiring users to pay for the services they receive— even if the "users" are inmates and the "services" are food, clothing, and shelter in a prison cell.

SECURITY CLASSIFICATIONS

Regardless of whether they are paying "rent" for being there, prison inmates face minimum terms that are longer than one year. The maximum, of course, can extend to life behind bars, and states that provide for capital punishment also hold inmates awaiting execution on death row.

Because they confine inmates ranging from nonviolent property offenders to serial killers, prisons operate at varying

LEARNING GOALS

Do you know:
3. the difference between various security levels in correctional institutions?
4. at what level of security most inmates are classified?

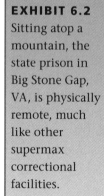

custodial classification: the level of externally imposed control to which an inmate is assigned.

levels of **custodial classification**. For security purposes, they are classified as maximum, close, medium, and minimum—depending on the level of control they exert.

The custodial classification of a particular institution is based on such factors as how heavily the outside perimeter is controlled, the presence or absence of "guard" towers, the extent of external patrols, the number of detection devices, the control of housing areas, and the level of staffing. An entire facility may be classified at one level (e.g., maximum), or various levels of security may be established for different units within an institution. Thus within the same compound might be found sections designated as maximum, close, medium, or even minimum security.

Maximum/Close Security

Maximum-security facilities are often located in remote rural areas and surrounded by a walled (or heavily fenced) outside perimeter, armed guard towers, searchlights, alarms, electronic detection devices, and similar control measures. External security

EXHIBIT 6.2
Sitting atop a mountain, the state prison in Big Stone Gap, VA, is physically remote, much like other supermax correctional facilities.

Source: Courtesy of the American Correctional Association.

is physically obvious, and internal security is tight as well. Movement within the institution is closely restricted. Visits are limited and carefully controlled. Inmate counts are conducted frequently (as often as every two hours). Because surveillance is so continuous, privacy is essentially eliminated.

Larger, more populated states usually have one or more maximum-security prisons. In states with fewer institutions, part of a medium-security compound might be designated for maximum internal security. In still other locations, an additional category of *close security* has been added, which is not quite as restrictive as maximum but more closely supervised than medium.

At the most extreme level, a number of states have now added *supermax* prisons, where impersonal controls keep staff at a distance, virtually all privileges have been stripped away, and "segregation is the end in itself."[15] Inmates in these facilities are confined to their cells up to 23 hours a day under extremely tight security. Denounced as the "Marionization" of U.S. prisons—after the notorious federal penitentiary in Illinois where the practice originated[16]—such facilities have been criticized for imposing "extreme social isolation," "limited environmental stimulation," and "extraordinary control over every movement."[17] Even prison wardens themselves are not completely supportive of these institutions. While research indicates that they believe such facilities increase order and control in the prison system, at the same time, the majority do not feel that they rehabilitate violent inmates, reduce recidivism, or deter crime.[18] In fact, some studies raise the possibility that, rather than deterring inmates from future criminality, harsher prison conditions may actually stimulate further involvement in crime.[19] To better understand why, take a brief glimpse into supermax confinement in the next "Close-up on Corrections."

CLOSE-UP ON CORRECTIONS
Conditions in Highly Restrictive and Supermax Prisons

Stripped naked in a small prison cell with nothing except a toilet; forced to sleep on a concrete floor or slab; denied any human contact; fed nothing but "nutri-loaf"; and given just a modicum of toilet paper—four squares—only a few times. Although this might sound like a stay in a Soviet gulag in the 1930s, it is . . . Wisconsin in 2002 . . . where the state contends these conditions are "uncomfortable, but not unconstitutional."

Source: Fred Cohen, "Penal Isolation: Beyond the Seriously Mentally Ill,"
Criminal Justice and Behavior, Vol. 35, No. 8 (August, 2008), p. 1020.

Inmates have described life in a supermax as akin to living in a tomb. At best, their days are marked by idleness, tedium, and tension. But for many, the absence of normal social interaction, of reasonable mental stimulus, of exposure to the natural world, of almost everything that makes life human and bearable, is emotionally, physically, and psychologically destructive. . . . As one federal judge noted, prolonged supermax confinement "may press the outer bounds of what most humans can psychologically tolerate." . . .

> The extraordinary security controls, isolation, and lack of in-cell as well as out-of-cell programs and activities . . . are pointlessly harsh and degrading, particularly if imposed for long periods of time. In some states, the conditions are so extreme—e.g., lack of windows, denial of reading material, a maximum of three hours a week out-of-cell time, lack of outdoor recreation—that they can only be explained as reflecting an unwillingness to acknowledge the inmates' basic humanity.
>
> *Source*: Human Rights Watch, "Supermax Prisons: An Overview,"
> available at http://www.hrw.org/reports/2000/supermax/.

Medium Security

A medium-custody institution usually has layers of wire fencing, along with a strong perimeter that can include guard towers or booths. From the exterior, some medium-security physical plants may not be noticeably different from maximum prisons. But they contain fewer restrictions inside the fences—fewer counts, more privileges, greater freedom of movement, and more interaction with other inmates. However, all of these "liberties" are relative to the virtual isolation of those in maximum confinement. There will still be such controls as alarms, closed-circuit television, and locked gates, with the flow of traffic restricted to certain specified areas.

These types of institutions house a wide variety of offenders—virtually anyone who is not dangerous enough to require maximum or close security, but not a sufficiently low risk to be entrusted to a minimum level of security. Because their inmates enjoy less restricted movement, medium-security prisons also tend to offer more training, treatment, and work programs.

Minimum Security

In contrast, a minimum-custody facility has extremely little external control or regimentation. It frequently contains only a single fence or no exterior obstruction at all. There are no towers or outside patrols. Inside, there are no cells, bars, or other obvious security measures. Housing is generally arranged in dormitory fashion. The physical structure itself may look like a farm, ranch, or college campus.

In fact, some minimum-security facilities are not even referred to as "prisons" but, rather, as halfway houses, camps, work-release centers, or prerelease centers. Especially in urban areas, where minimum-security facilities are located directly in the community, they are often known by the generic term "community residential centers," which can "be used as a pretrial detention option, as a condition of probation, as part of a sentence of confinement, as a transitional setting for offenders about to be released into the community from jail or prison, and as an intermediate sanction for violations of community supervision requirements."[20]

In this type of setting, security relies more on proper classification than on physical restrictions. In other words, only those sufficiently trustworthy are assigned to minimum custody, so there is little need for elaborate hardware or electronic security systems. Administrators concerned with reducing the public's fears about being neighbors to a community-based facility are sensitive to the need for both careful screening and proper supervision. In that regard, residential programming has been described as "strict, intensive, and accountability-oriented."[21] Verifying the close supervision, one offender who was fulfilling the last months of his sentence at a community residential center stated on national television that serving time there was harder than in prison.[22] In minimum security, the stern imposition of external control is replaced by the firm expectation of self-control.

Inmates in such institutions may hold jobs or attend classes in the community by day, returning to the facility after work or school. Often the programs offered are a combination of work release and drug or alcohol treatment. Although those returning from outside assignments are likely to be searched, much of the facility's security depends on the "honor system," which most tend to respect in order to avoid losing their greater freedoms and privileges.

Those confined in minimum security tend to be nonviolent offenders serving short sentences, those who have earned a lower custody classification through good behavior in higher-security facilities, or inmates preparing for release. In terms of the latter, phasing inmates into the community through minimum security near the end of their sentence enables them to resume life in free society while still under some supervision and lessens the trauma of readjustment.

Security Distribution

Maximum-security prisons undoubtedly have the greatest public notoriety. Institutions such as San Quentin, Alcatraz (now closed), and Attica have been the subject of numerous books, songs, television programs, and movies. But despite this publicity, as shown in Exhibit 6.3, only slightly over one out of three inmates serve their time in maximum or close custody.[23]

Women's Facilities

Virtually every state has maximum-, medium-, and minimum-security institutions for men. But, because of their fewer numbers, there is less custodial classification among women's prisons. Those convicted of a wide variety of offenses representing a considerable range of seriousness therefore may be confined together. In fact, a number of states do not have enough female offenders to justify more than one women's prison. Thus, it is not unusual to find a women's prison housing minimum-, medium-, and maximum-security inmates. This

LEARNING GOALS

Do you know:
5. what factors distinguish female from male correctional facilities?
6. what the advantages and disadvantages of coed prisons are?
7. how an inmate's custody classification is determined and why it might change?

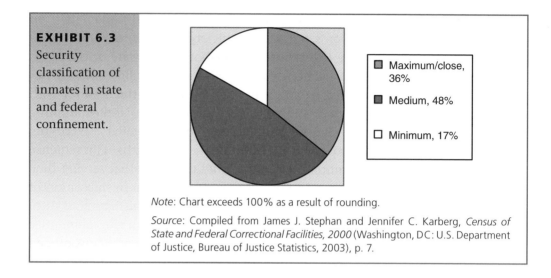

EXHIBIT 6.3
Security classification of inmates in state and federal confinement.

Maximum/close, 36%

Medium, 48%

Minimum, 17%

Note: Chart exceeds 100% as a result of rounding.

Source: Compiled from James J. Stephan and Jennifer C. Karberg, *Census of State and Federal Correctional Facilities, 2000* (Washington, DC: U.S. Department of Justice, Bureau of Justice Statistics, 2003), p. 7.

also means that women's facilities are likely to be more geographically remote than male facilities, requiring families to travel considerable distances for visiting. As described in more detail in Chapter 9, facilities for female offenders also lack the number and variety of treatment, educational, and training programs found in male institutions.

Co-correctional (Coed) Prisons

co-correctional (coed) institutions: facilities where men and women are housed within one compound, with access to the same programs (although not shared living quarters).

Although it would be extremely costly to establish services in women's prisons that are equivalent to those received by men, one way to better assure parity between male and female offenders would be to incarcerate them together in **co-correctional (coed) institutions**. The first experiments with coed prisons for adults date back to the mid-1970s, when the Massachusetts Correctional Institution at Framingham and the Federal Correctional Institution at Fort Worth, Texas, became co-correctional.

In an effort to achieve greater cost-effectiveness (as well as provide a more natural environment for both male and female inmates), some 93 state and federal prisons operate on a coed basis, housing over 77,000 inmates of both sexes.[24] Men and women in such facilities are prohibited from sharing living quarters or engaging in sexual contact. In some institutions, they may interact socially during meals or recreational periods, or while attending various institutional programs. However, rules governing unacceptable conduct are quite specific and carefully supervised. Although the public may have visions of these facilities as havens of sexual freedom where rampant promiscuity results in many illegitimate births, nothing could be further from reality. Moreover, it may be preferable to deal with the few instances of improper heterosexual contact in coed institutions than the widespread homosexuality characteristic of single-sex prisons—especially since research indicates that, from a psychological perspective, coed prisons help both male and female inmates better fulfill some of their interpersonal needs.[25]

For both male and female inmates, serving time in coed facilities has benefits as well as drawbacks. Men are not pressured to portray the hardened, macho image required to avoid appearing weak in a male institution. They tend to behave better in the presence of women and engage in fewer fights, since proving one's toughness does not become the "badge of honor" that it is in male institutions. For women, such facilities provide a greater range of recreational, educational, training, and work programs than would traditionally be available in female prisons. However, researchers have found that women do not tend to take advantage of these expanded opportunities and, because there are more men than women, programming is still largely targeted toward men.[26]

In fact, research evidence concludes that co-correctional facilities overall are not as beneficial for female offenders: "Serving time with men evidently reinforces traditional sex stereotypes, since women tend to concentrate on relationships and not self-improvement, and recreate dysfunctional relationships similar to those that got them into trouble on the outside."[27] If, as these studies suggest, traditional co-correctional facilities are not actually beneficial to women (and perhaps even somewhat detrimental), a more effective approach may be implementation of such gender-responsive guidelines as those developed by the National Institute of Corrections.[28]

Classification Procedures

Whether male or female, all inmates undergo some form of custodial classification. Essentially, the classification process is designed to determine the level of externally imposed control needed by those whose behavior indicates that they have not developed sufficiently strong internal controls. As we saw earlier, classification separates inmates into groups according to characteristics they share in common. Those sentenced to serve their time in prison represent a wide range of seriousness in terms of both their current offense and their prior criminal history. Prison inmates are therefore primarily classified according to the degree of security they require.

During initial intake, an evaluation assessment is conducted, often at a central reception or diagnostic center, where new inmates are transferred upon arrival. The reception process itself ranges considerably in terms of sophistication. Some systems may simply review the official documents accompanying the inmate's transfer (court papers, arrest forms, the presentence investigation report, etc.). Others may conduct an in-depth interview with the offender, along with a psychological evaluation, medical examination, intelligence and aptitude testing, and vocational interest measures.

With this information, staff determine custodial classification, housing assignment, and what (if any) types of educational, treatment, or work programs the inmate will be offered. Throughout this process, efforts are made to predict both security risk and treatment potential. Greatest emphasis, however, is on determining the level of risk or dangerousness of the offender, both to protect other inmates and to promote the order and safety of the total institution. For example, in deciding a person's custody classification, the U.S. Bureau of Prisons ranks offenders on such factors as severity of current offense, expected length of incarceration, type of prior commitments, history of escape attempts, and history of violence, along with additional internal management considerations, such as racial balance and degree of crowding in various facilities.

Reclassification

Initial classification does not preclude a change in status at a later time. The process is not foolproof, and it may turn out that someone was either overclassified or inappropriately classified at too low a level of security. Additionally, as inmates prove themselves worthy of greater trust over the years, their security level could be reduced. It is in the institution's interest to classify offenders at the lowest classification that is safely feasible. The less security, the less expensive the inmate's supervision and, simultaneously, the closer the correctional process is to reintegrating the offender into society. Thus, during the period of their incarceration, prisoners may be reclassified and assigned to new housing, jobs, or programs any number of times.

But, as we have seen in terms of how classification operates in jails, the process does not always work effectively, particularly when a system is faced with such severe crowding that inmates must be placed where there is room rather than where they can function most effectively. In that regard, there is evidence that a majority of new inmates are classified as minimum-custody upon intake, although limited space in such facilities may not necessarily enable them to be confined there.[29]

incarceration rate: the number of people in prison for every 100,000 residents in the population.

NUMBER OF INMATES

Without sufficient bedspace, the integrity of the entire process is compromised, with inmates being placed wherever there is room, rather than where they are properly classified. This has become a dilemma in many facilities, as the **incarceration rate** of inmates in state and federal prisons steadily increased over the past several decades, reaching a record high of 1,540,804[30] in 2008. While the pace of prison growth has slowed somewhat in recent years (see Exhibit 6.4), many facilities are still seriously overcrowded, even if they are not necessarily under court order or consent decree. For example, nearly 40 percent of state prisons are operating at more than

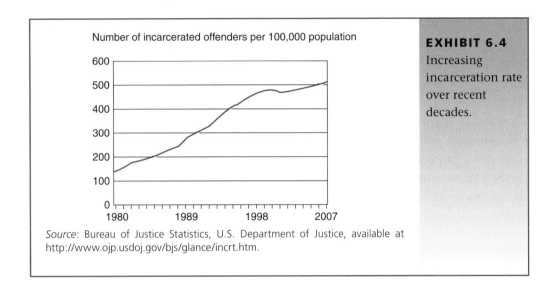

Number of incarcerated offenders per 100,000 population

EXHIBIT 6.4
Increasing incarceration rate over recent decades.

Source: Bureau of Justice Statistics, U.S. Department of Justice, available at http://www.ojp.usdoj.gov/bjs/glance/incrt.htm.

100 percent of their highest capacity, and an equal number of states are between 90 percent and 99 percent of capacity.[31]

Prison Crowding

Numbers and charts do not, of course, begin to portray the widespread misery of living conditions to which inmates are subjected in overflowing prisons. To the contrary, it has been observed that overcrowded facilities "[h]ave adversely affected conditions of confinement, jeopardized prisoner safety, compromised prison management, and greatly limited prisoner access to meaningful programming."[32]

As described in the next "Close-up on Corrections," it is apparent that crowding affects every aspect of institutional life. The consequence of housing too many people in too little space means that inmates are double-bunked in small cells designed for one or sleeping on mattresses in unheated prison gyms, day rooms, hallways, or basements. Others may sleep in makeshift trailers, tents, or even converted ferries. Space that had once been devoted to work, study, and recreational programs is being turned into dormitories.[33]

CLOSE-UP ON CORRECTIONS
Impact of Crowding

The greater the crowding, the greater the negative impacts. A smaller percentage of inmates has any kind of job or educational placement. Less recreational space means more people competing for a ball or a game opportunity. The waiting list to see doctors and counselors lengthens. More prisoners are crammed into cells where they spend more hours per day. Less space and less privacy generate more friction and conflict. . . . Moreover, the prevailing ethos is not sympathetic to prisoners. To the contrary, there is political pressure to cut back on or cut out "amenities" like weight lifting and college programs and to establish "no frills" prisons. . . . And such cuts, of course, contribute to the spiral of decline.

Source: James B. Jacobs, "Prison Reform amid the Ruins of Prisoners' Rights," in Michael Tonry, ed., *The Future of Imprisonment* (New York: Oxford University Press, 2004), p. 182.

Under such conditions, it is not surprising to find that inmates have fewer opportunities for everything from visits to training or treatment programs. But, even more importantly, there are serious health and safety risks associated with packing more inmates into less space: Studies have linked crowding with higher rates of violence, aggression, stress-induced mental disorders, and even suicides.[34] Additionally, crowded institutions promote such communicable medical problems as colds, infectious diseases, tuberculosis, and sexually transmitted diseases.[35]

Nor are prison staff able to exert as much control over the population of excessively crowded facilities:

> As the numbers of prisoners increase, the space normally used for recreation or education is diverted to dormitory use. Incidents of violence between prisoners increase, and control of the institution gradually slips to the most aggressive groups. . . . The exhaustion of services and the limitation on recreational activities further lead to tension, boredom, and conflict. . . . Eventually, there is a degradation of morale among the staff, greater staff turnover, and a vicious cycle of diminished control.[36]

Moreover, the greater potential for violence in crowded facilities is not limited to incidents between inmates. More than one out of three assaults are against staff members,[37] and the rate (14.6 per 1,000 inmates) has been increasing over recent years.[38] Under crowded conditions, it becomes increasingly difficult to maintain

EXHIBIT 6.5
Along with increased violence and mental health issues, overcrowded prisons promote contagious infections ranging from colds to tuberculosis.

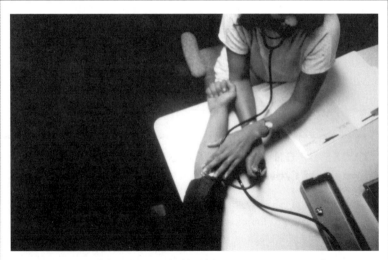

Source: Courtesy of the Miami-Dade (Florida) County Department of Corrections and Rehabilitation.

orderly behavior and, as staff become more fearful for their safety, it may not take much for the use of force to escalate. As the national Commission on Safety and Abuse in America's Prisons observed:

> Corrections officers feel they work under the constant threat of spontaneous violent outbursts; they literally feel under siege. That feeling can lead officers, especially new and inexperienced ones, to overreact and use force when talking would be more effective, or to use more force than necessary to resolve a situation. And these altercations can start or perpetuate a cycle of strikes and retaliation.[39]

While greater emphasis on staff training and interpersonal communication skills can help to diminish the potential for overreaction, the overall cycle of prison violence cannot be effectively curtailed without addressing the underlying causal factors related to overcrowding.

Responses to Crowding

Reactions to the crowding crisis have included both the expansion of existing facilities and the construction of new institutions. In recognition of the futility and expense of this approach, a range of additional options has been advocated—from a front-end reduction in the number of people *going into* prisons to a back-end increase in the number *coming out*.

The intent of **front-end solutions** is to keep more people from being incarcerated, through use of the community-based alternatives (diversion, electronic monitoring, probation, etc.). On the other hand, **back-end approaches** are designed to release more of those already confined, through such options as time off for good behavior, parole, weekend confinement, and other forms of early or temporary release.

Some would argue that neither front- nor back-end solutions have been pursued very vigorously. In any event, these approaches have yet to significantly reduce the continually escalating size of the inmate population, raising questions about the fundamental purpose of prisons.

front-end/back-end approaches: addressing the prison crowding crisis by either reducing the numbers going into prison (front-end) or increasing the numbers coming out (back-end).

THE PURPOSE OF PRISONS

Exactly what does society expect its prisons to accomplish? There is no consensus on the answer to that question. As a result, we cannot evaluate the effectiveness of our prisons, because we are not entirely sure what they should be doing—in other words, "If you don't know where you're going, how will you know when you get there?"

As described in earlier chapters, correctional institutions were first developed to provide a more humane alternative

LEARNING GOALS

Do you know:
10. what goals society has had for prisons over the years and how they have changed today?
11. to what extent the public supports punishment versus rehabilitation for inmates?

to corporal or capital punishment. In line with their Quaker-initiated origins, the first prisons were viewed as a place where inmates could read the Bible, reflect upon past wrongdoings, and repent for their sins. As one historian put it, "the founders of the American prison were idealists who believed that prisons and other total institutions could be used to change human beings for the better."[40] Ultimately, idealism turned into realism.

With the advent of the industrial era, achieving penitence gave way to attaining profits. Then, as the promise of the medical model renewed hope for rehabilitation, the purpose of prisons shifted again. The degrading pictures of chain gangs, forced labor, and physical punishment diminished in favor of the uplifting potential of counseling, therapy, and treatment. There are probably few who would advocate a return to the barbaric practices of the past. But society's frustrations with the apparent inability to accomplish long-term behavioral changes in prison, coupled with the fears generated by increasing crime rates, again called for a new prison agenda. In essence:

> Each generation has criticized the prisons and penal philosophies of its predecessor and has offered new rationales and management theories. . . . Time and again in American history, men and women have looked to penal institutions for solutions to individual and social problems. Time and again, they have been disappointed.[41]

Social Compromise

By the early 1980s, the justice model's concern for retribution, deterrence, and certainty of punishment had found a receptive public audience. From the unfulfilled promises of the medical model came an unconditional plan for change. If it was too much to hope that prisons could improve people, at least they could incapacitate them. If rehabilitation was an impossible expectation, at least retribution would ensure that "justice was served." If criminals were not mindful of penalties, at least they would be reminded through punishment. And, if this did not deter them, at least they would pay their debt.

When society came to the conclusion that the situation was out of control, it settled for these compromises. Essentially, we elected to "pull drowning people out of the river without going upstream to find out why they are drowning in the first place."[42] The problem is that they are "drowning" for many complicated reasons that we cannot comprehend, cannot respond to effectively, or simply do not wish to address. Thus we continue to pull offenders out of the social mainstream and put them into secure institutions. There they find a fertile environment to nourish isolation, frustration, and antisocial behavior—as we see in the upcoming "Close-up on Corrections."

EXHIBIT 6.6
While long-term social isolation behind bars has been our primary response to crime, there is no consensus among Americans on what prisons should be accomplishing.

CLOSE-UP ON CORRECTIONS
Prison Life and Human Worth

There is a slang phrase which probably originated far from prison but which applies better to prison life than do any other two words in the English language—"put down." It eloquently describes the emotional effect of being squelched, and . . . it tells sadly, bitterly just what prison is. To the person who never has served time, it is hard to realize just how much of a daily humiliating "put-down" prison life can be, even in a well-run institution.

It is not necessary to look for a venal warden, or even a merely inept one. It is not necessary to look for sadistic guards, political chicanery from the governor's office, inadequate food, or stingy budgets from an uncaring legislature. . . . When we look for such factors, we are missing the real guts of the problem, which is that in the best of prisons with the nicest of custodians and the most generous of kitchens, the necessary minutiae of management tend to deny and even insult the basic needs of individuals. . . . Sooner or later, the prisoner must lose his spirit, or he must rebel.

Source: Paul W. Keve, *Prison Life and Human Worth* (Minneapolis: University of Minnesota Press, 1974), pp. 15, 41–42.

Public Opinion

However, there is some doubt that the public in general is truly as punitive as advocates of the justice model would like to believe. For example, when people throughout the country were asked whether they thought the crime rate could be lowered by spending money on social and economic problems or on prisons, police, and judges, it might be reasonable to assume that they would be overwhelmingly in favor of the latter. Not so. Overall, only 27 percent supported criminal justice spending, in comparison to the 68 percent favoring social and economic options.[43]

Likewise, once offenders are incarcerated, public support for rehabilitation (72 percent) far outdistances that for punishment,[44] and policy-makers themselves appear to be most supportive of rehabilitative goals, as well as serving the needs of those with mental health and substance abuse problems.[45] But that does not mean that the public believes prisons are doing a good job—82 percent rated the ability of prisons to rehabilitate inmates only "fair" or "poor."[46] In that regard, some maintain that the dominance of blacks in today's prisons has resulted in these institutions virtually being "written off as useless by the larger white society . . . serving no useful purpose for those confined."[47] Moreover, support for treatment-oriented imprisonment does not necessarily equate with a willingness to pay for it.

LEARNING GOALS

Do you know:
12. how politics influence the administration of prisons?
13. the differences between operations, program services, and support services units within a correctional institution?

director (or commissioner) of corrections: the chief executive officer who administers a statewide prison system, appointed by the governor.

PRISON ORGANIZATION

The fact that society's true sentiments may not always be accurately represented in public policy does not necessarily mean that public opinions are not reflected in the way prisons are operated. Quite the contrary, the attitude of the public influences political leadership, which, in turn, is responsible for appointing correctional leadership. For example, every state's **director (or commissioner) of corrections** is appointed by the governor. Thus the type of administration that prevails at any institution is ultimately a reflection of public preferences, as expressed through the political process. Prison directors themselves also develop a reputation for having a certain operational "style" and are attracted to locations where elected politicians and public sentiments are consistent with their approach.

Political Influence

This system of political influence can be a positive benefit when it works to the advantage of its stakeholders. However, it can also be a negative factor when "politics" unduly interfere with correctional practices. For example, following a highly visible escape or institutional disturbance, the correctional administrator or warden may be fired, serving as a political scapegoat for public disenchantment with the system. Moreover, when a new governor is elected, it is almost certain that new cabinet appointments will be made, including the director of corrections.

This is a legacy dating back to the time when states were small, the correctional "system" consisted of one prison, and the warden was the sole correctional administrator, appointed by and responsible to the governor, under a system of political patronage. Thus, much of the early history of prisons reflected mediocre performance by those who were appointed more for their political connections than their prison-related capabilities. "There were some [who] . . . administered with intelligent dedication, but part of the reason for their outstanding leadership was the wasteland of mediocrity around them."[48]

Today, some correctional agencies are still politically motivated, which can result in appointing a director with little knowledge of or experience in corrections. But, even when more qualified candidates are appointed, it is essential for them to know the political system and be able to work adeptly within it. When a career correctional expert is placed in a turbulent political environment and does not understand the political maneuvering required to survive, the outcome can be disastrous.

It is for such reasons that those in charge of state correctional systems experience an average longevity of just over three years,[49] often regardless of their talent. In fact, a recent survey found that nearly one out of every three corrections directors had occupied their current leadership position for a year or less.[50] This brief tenure is "hardly long enough for the inexperienced appointee to learn the job and assess the adequacy and competence of staff available, let alone weigh the need for change."[51]

As a result, it is not uncommon to find directors who have experienced a virtual career of "musical chairs," having been in charge of corrections in any number of states. Even where there is more stability in the upper ranks, it may be attained at the cost of continually adjusting to the changing political climate. Needless to say, such instability is neither personally desirable nor organizationally productive.

Institutional Structure

Relatively frequent leadership turnover is one of the few organizational features that many correctional facilities have in common. In contrast, the specific manner in which prisons are organized and operated varies according to their size, purpose, and degree of security. In that regard, correctional institutions range from large, sprawling prison complexes to road camps or halfway houses that hold as few as 10 or 20 people. The manner in which they are organized likewise varies.

In medium-to-large facilities, the organizational administrative structure is likely to be divided into at least three general components:

- **Operations** (also called custody or security);

- **Program services** (also called treatment or inmate programs);

- **Support services** (also called administrative or staff services).

operations: the component of a facility that encompasses custodial staff and activities related to providing security and inmate supervision.

program services: the component of a facility encompassing those responsible for providing inmate programs and treatment.

support services: the component of a facility encompassing all of the maintenance, management, planning, and staff services that support treatment and custody.

In larger institutions that provide their own in-house medical staff (rather than contracting with an outside provider), there is also likely to be a separate unit for health services. While large facilities will undoubtedly have multiple layers of management and greater specialization of job functions, a streamlined overview of a hypothetical table of organization for a medium-sized prison is presented in Exhibit 6.7.

Operations.   The operational division of a prison includes all of the employees and activities directly related to providing both internal and external security, as well as inmate supervision. Authority is assigned on the basis of rank—starting with officers (or "line" staff) and moving up the supervisory hierarchy to sergeants, lieutenants, and captains. Ultimately, all sworn personnel report to a deputy or assistant warden for operations. However, it is expected that they will do so through the "chain of command," beginning with their immediate supervisor and working upward if the issue cannot be resolved.

The number of operational staff will vary with the size of the facility, as will the officer/inmate ratio. Throughout the country, there is an average of one correctional officer for every 4.8 inmates in state confinement.[52]

Program Services.   Within the program services division are units providing inmate programs and treatment: for example, vocational training, education,

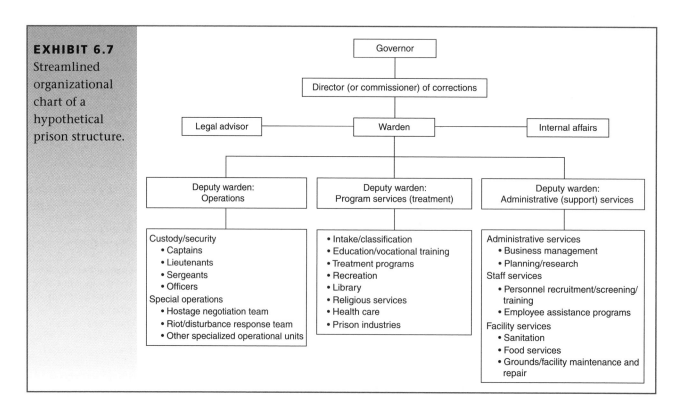

EXHIBIT 6.7 Streamlined organizational chart of a hypothetical prison structure.

prison industries, the library, recreation, casework, counseling, and the like. Other responsibilities related to inmate welfare are also likely to fall within this division, such as the maintenance of records, the chaplain's office, and the classification unit. In contrast to the operational division, personnel in program services tend to be nonsworn civilians (although sworn staff on specialized assignments may be included).

Because of differences in backgrounds, job classifications, and the nature of their work, there is considerable potential for mistrust between operational and program personnel. The goals of custody and treatment differ substantially, and each needs to understand the other in order to avoid conflict and maintain collaborative relationships in the interest of the overall institution.

Administrative (Support) Services.   A prison's administrative (or support) services encompass the many activities that assist treatment and custody functions. In some facilities, this unit may be further divided into two separate sections: one addressing *facility maintenance* and one focusing on *staff support*. Within facility maintenance are such services as physical plant maintenance (electricity, water, heat, sanitation, etc.), clothing issue and laundry, food preparation, fire protection, locksmithing, and other functions related to the physical complex. Business management, accounting, purchasing, planning, research, and new construction may be considered support services, or these functions can be provided through a separate administrative unit. Support services related to staff include the recruitment, screening, and training of personnel (described in Chapter 13), as well as various employee assistance programs.

Organizational Culture.   All of these operational, administrative, and supportive functions of a prison simply reflect how the facility is officially organized in the table of organization. Some facilities may have a detailed and complex organizational chart, while others may simply reflect the fundamentals outlined above. Regardless of a prison's size or complexity, however, all facilities have an informal organizational culture that is often even more powerful and influential than the formal structure. At times in contrast to official policy, the informal culture establishes its own values, norms, and practices—i.e., what is considered "acceptable" or "unacceptable" within that organization. Since a prison's culture is largely a feature of its employees and their interactions—especially those in leadership positions—a detailed discussion of organizational culture can be found in Chapter 13, which emphasizes the proactive approach that administrators need to take in order to promote and maintain a positive institutional culture.[53]

Career Opportunities.   Regardless of how a prison is organized administratively, the overall compound of any large institution functions as a community within itself. Because of their self-contained nature, correctional institutions therefore offer a wide variety of career opportunities. Thus, in order to operate effectively, they need everyone from teachers, health care professionals, psychologists, social workers, and correctional officers to the less visible people working behind the scenes, such as clerical staff, dieticians, electricians, and maintenance personnel. As a result, wide varieties of career opportunities are available, even for those who do not desire security-related work. In fact, corrections has been among the top growth industries for a number of years.[54] Even during recent economic downturns, correctional positions have been among the least affected.

Inmate Control

Regardless of the institutional design or number of employees, inmates will always attempt to exert control unofficially. It is, of course, the inmates who outnumber officers and civilian staff. But the extent to which inmates rather than staff are in charge of a prison depends in part on the capacity in which inmates are used within the institution.

In the past, it was common for many of the clerical and technical jobs in prisons to be assigned to inmates, particularly when budgets were too limited to hire enough staff. In fact, well into the twentieth century, some states went so far as to rely on "inmate guards" to maintain order among the prison population. For an inside account of how brutal these unofficial "staff" could be in dealing with fellow inmates, see the following "Close-up on Corrections."

CLOSE-UP ON CORRECTIONS
Inmate Control over Inmates

Inside the prison, a general alarm sounded. . . . While the guards milled about, testing the heft of their three-foot black batons . . . another group [was] forming in the gym. About 150 inmate trusties, known in Texas prisons as building tenders, plus 150 of their aides and chums were also preparing to restore order. They were the inmates who really ran the asylum: the meanest characters the administration could co-opt into doing the state's bidding. While rocks smashed against the gym's barred windows . . . the boss tender ordered his troops to tie white bandannas on their heads so they wouldn't be confused with the rioters. . . . "They're carrying trash-can lids, pipes, clubs, weight-lifting bars," he recalls, "The adrenaline's really flowing, flowing so much it's spooky. . . ."

The rioters [were] fleeing toward one corner of the yard. And pursuing them were the building tenders. One of the tenders, who calls himself Tommy B., remembers what happened next: "We had clubs, bats, chains, knives, everything, and we formed what we called a 'whupping' line." The only way to the safety of the gym was down that gantlet, and the rioters, now edging toward panic, began running through. . . . Inmate Ronnie . . . was inside the main building as the "whupped" staggered in. "Some of the guys you couldn't recognize, and a lot were unconscious. I wasn't sure if they was alive or dead." The inmates who could walk staggered back to the cell blocks; the others were carried inside to wait for ambulances.

Source: "Inside America's Toughest Prison," *Newsweek*
(October 6, 1986), pp. 46–48.

Even in prisons where inmates were prohibited from using physical force against other inmates, they might be used for such sensitive assignments as making deliveries, picking up supplies or equipment, bookkeeping, or accounting. Needless to say, these practices were open to considerable abuse. Freedom to travel outside the compound made the introduction of contraband quite tempting. Moreover, even **trusties** in clerical jobs could use their positions to personal advantage—as a basis for gaining authority over other inmates by extending favors to them.

As the corruption resulting from such practices captured administrative attention, strong arguments were made to provide sufficient fiscal support to enable prisons to function without extensive dependence on inmate skills. As a result, inmates now tend to work in much less sensitive areas and have generally been absolved of any custodial supervision over other prisoners. But, even today, many institutions rely extensively on residents for carpentry, plumbing, general maintenance, and other nonsecurity-related tasks.

Eliminating inappropriate job assignments has not, however, eliminated inmate influence. Particularly in those institutions that assign new correctional officers to work without sufficient training, security personnel may well find themselves relying on "friendly" inmates to teach them their job. The American Correctional Association now has standards that call for the provision of a minimum of 40 hours of training prior to job assignment (followed by an additional 120 hours).[55] But in addition to the fact that this is clearly a minimum requirement, as we will see in later chapters, compliance with ACA standards is voluntary. Until training standards are mandated everywhere, there will be places where officers are overly dependent on inmates to learn their job.

trusties: inmates assigned to various work details within a facility as a result of their trustworthy status.

Informal Social Control

In every facility, there is informal control among the inmates that enables the institution to run smoothly. Some have a personal stake in a trouble-free prison—whether they are in positions of responsibility or simply want to "do their own time" as quietly as possible. Because of this personal investment, they will take steps to preserve the system and will help to keep other inmates in control. Naturally, administrators must be alert to ensure that the "peacekeepers" themselves do not physically take authority into their own hands (as we saw earlier in the case of the building tenders).

LEARNING GOALS

Do you know:
14. how informal social control works among the inmate population?
15. how participatory management has been used in prison settings?
16. how inmate self-governance relates to Maslow's hierarchy of needs?

informal social control: the self-imposed controls that inmates exert over each other, apart from official sanctions.

But, even if it is not formally endorsed by the administration, this type of **informal social control** is imposed by the inmate body upon itself and can help to run the prison without disturbance. In return for healthy self-government, the administration may extend certain privileges to the inmate population, ranging from work release to conjugal visits. Participants in such programs will carefully guard these benefits and informally pressure others to conform when their behavior threatens the system. Everyone knows, for example, that, if those on work release take advantage of this liberty by attempting to escape, the privilege will be revoked for everyone. Similarly, engaging in disruptive behavior results in additional supervision, restriction, and scrutiny that inmates do not want forced upon them.

Participatory Management

There have been efforts to formalize such inmate self-control through various degrees of official recognition—from simple "suggestion boxes" to full-fledged "inmate councils" with decision-making power. The idea behind increased involvement of inmates in institutional procedures is based on the principles of **participatory management**.

participatory management: a decentralized approach whereby decision-making involves those affected by the outcome, to promote their commitment.

According to participatory management, people are more likely to be committed to decisions or policies which they were involved in making. If, for example, the warden determines that high-fat foods will be eliminated, the change will probably meet with considerable resistance. If, on the other hand, inmates themselves become sufficiently concerned about the unhealthy effects of such foods that they propose a ban on them, the change will encounter greater support. The idea is that people inherently resist being *told* what to do (often regardless of whether or not they actually favor doing it). But, when the idea is *theirs*, they have "ownership" of it and are therefore more likely to support it.

Because of the need for security-related restrictions, prisons are obviously not the ideal environment for inmate participation in facility management. Quite the contrary, correctional institutions are usually well noted for exercising "total control" over everything from the movement of inmates to the timing of meals.

But prison administrators have also recognized that such impotence can produce disastrous consequences when resulting frustrations explode into violence. Moreover, officers dealing with inmates on a day-to-day basis experience their frustrations firsthand as they attempt to resolve seemingly endless complaints before situations escalate into serious disruptions. In addition, the courts have become more active with regard to intervening on behalf of inmates when prison conditions fall below constitutionally acceptable levels of safety, sanitation, or security. From this perspective, the advantage underlying some form of inmate participation is that it enables the administration to respond *proactively* to concerns before they get out of hand.

Inmate Self-governance

Recognizing the benefits of involving inmates in prison management is not a new concept. But failure to install sufficient protections and controls resulted in abolishing many early efforts, as a few powerful inmate leaders began using the process to further their own self-interests.

In any **inmate self-governance** experiment, adequate administrative controls are essential. Caution must be exercised in determining to what extent the governing body will be able to exercise authority, assuring that established limits are not exceeded. Self-governance is a form of participatory management—a method of involving inmates in decisions and negotiating problems and grievances with them. As such, it is a form of *sharing* power and decision-making with inmates, not *abdicating* authority to them.

Inmate governing councils have existed in varying forms in a number of institutions. One of the most widely used has been that in which elected inmates discuss policies and complaints with management staff. In this form of inmate involvement, elected representatives do not have the power or authority to change policies or implement new procedures. Rather, they simply bring to administrative attention issues that are of concern to the resident population. For example, they might forward inmate grievances, make suggestions, identify problem areas, help work out unnecessary conflicts, and interpret administrative decisions to the general population.

The results can be favorable to all involved when proactive adjustments are made in response to the inmates' concerns. When this is done, not only can potential disruptions be curtailed, but inmates also begin to see that the administration cares about their welfare, potentially resulting in improved relationships with staff.

inmate self-governance: involving inmates in prison management by sharing some degree of power and decision-making authority with them.

Self-governance Critique

Of course, not all forms of inmate self-governance are equally effective. The question then becomes why it is that so many experiments with inmate involvement in institutional management have not succeeded. One might assume that those institutions where inmates have a greater "say" in rules and regulations affecting them would tend to be less disruptive. To the contrary, there is "little evidence . . . to support the belief that prisons where inmates enjoy more self-government are better than prisons where they enjoy less."[56] The reasons for this apparent contradiction are as varied as the types of inmate self-governance that have been implemented. But they may well relate to such issues as timing, authority, relationships, and inmate maturity:

• *Timing.* It is not uncommon for inmate governance to be implemented as a result of the threat of a riot or a strike. In such a situation, the population has apparently reached such a high level of frustration with existing administrative procedures or institutional conditions that they believe these are the only tactics that will get the attention of those in charge. In other words, they are reacting (or at least threatening reaction) to the lack of an administrative climate that proactively seeks to address grievances before they build up to the point of violence. If inmates are to be involved in facility management, the time to do so is *before* complaints escalate to such a dangerous point. Otherwise, the perception is created that the administration is abandoning its responsibilities by "giving in" to demands, thereby opening the door for exploiting such signs of "weakness."

- *Authority.* Particularly if the expansion of inmate participation is seen as a concession by management, inmates may tend to get somewhat carried away with their newfound source of power and authority. Those who have been docilely subservient for many years may well find it difficult to cope with any amount of power without abusing it. Obviously, it must be emphasized in both written policy and unwritten practice that inmate involvement is *advisory* only. It must be clear that inmates are not *running* the facility but, rather, simply making suggestions for how it could be administered better. Reducing inmate roles to an advisory capacity still involves some risks, however, since those representing the population have the power to bring forth or withhold issues for administrative consideration.

- *Relationships.* Even the most clear-cut guidelines restricting the authority of the inmate governing body will produce ineffective results if the system is nothing more than a public relations "gimmick." If the primary concern is improving the image of administration instead of making fundamental changes in response to legitimate concerns, the effort will be self-defeating. When communication consists of one-way, inmate-to-staff "gripe sessions," trust and confidence in the process quickly disappear. Not only are two-way dialogue and feedback needed, but staff must also take inmate concerns seriously and make good-faith efforts to act on those that can reasonably be changed without jeopardizing institutional safety or security.

- *Inmate maturity.* Needless to say, those inmates selected to represent the prison population in any form of participatory government will play a crucial role in whether or not the process works. Especially when inmate representatives are given too much authority, the process can break down as a result of their lack of experience with power, resulting in their inability to use it responsibly. Many of those in prison are simply not accustomed to making their own decisions or taking personal responsibility for their actions.

In this regard, Maslow's hierarchy of needs is a useful tool for assessing the motivation of inmates to participate in and benefit from self-governance. As illustrated in Exhibit 6.8, Maslow maintains that our behavior is determined by our personal motives or needs, which can be arranged in a hierarchy:

- *Physiological* (or physical) needs—food, clothing, shelter—dominate initially. These are our most powerful motivators until they are at least somewhat satisfied.

- Once our needs for physical well-being are gratified, *safety* dominates—the need to be secure and free of risk, danger, or concern for our physical needs.

- When both physiological and safety needs are relatively well met, we are motivated by the need for *social* affiliation—to belong to various groups and to be accepted by them.

- But, once we belong to a group, we often want to be more than a member— perhaps a leader, trusted advisor, or at least someone held in respect, reflecting our need for *esteem*.

- Finally, it is no longer sufficient to be recognized by others, which leads to our desire for *self-actualization*—that is, to become everything within our capability, to be "all that we can be."

Very few people reach the top of Maslow's hierarchy (self-actualization), and prison is certainly not the ideal environment for achieving one's full potential. Nor are the majority of inmates likely to be functioning on the level of self-esteem, since many tend to characterize themselves as "losers," "dropouts," or "failures." In essence, neither the interpersonal development of most inmates nor the prison setting itself tends to encourage the pursuit of upper-level needs. It is therefore likely that the bulk of the inmate population is functioning at the physiological, safety, or at most social levels of Maslow's hierarchy.

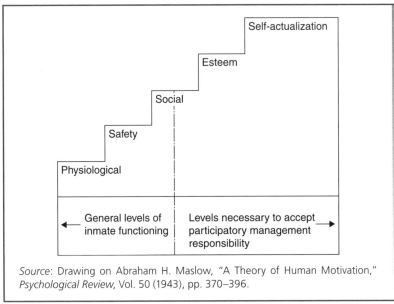

EXHIBIT 6.8
Maslow's hierarchy of needs as it relates to inmate involvement in participatory management.

Source: Drawing on Abraham H. Maslow, "A Theory of Human Motivation," *Psychological Review*, Vol. 50 (1943), pp. 370–396.

However, participatory management will be effective only insofar as the participants are sufficiently emotionally mature—that is, motivated at the upper levels of Maslow's hierarchy.[57] Only when the participants are mature enough to accept the responsibilities of being involved in making their own decisions will true participatory management work effectively. Otherwise, it is similar to parents involving their children in making daily decisions about what to eat, when to go to bed, or anything else concerning their welfare. They are simply not mature enough to make such decisions in a responsible manner.

This, of course, does not negate the need to be responsive to inmate complaints. But it is perhaps for this reason more than any other that the ideals of actual participation in management have met with so much failure when implemented in the reality of the prison environment. Nor, as the next chapter reveals, is the nature of the environment itself conducive to the rationality of behavior that we associate with life in free society. Prisoners may or may not be substantially "different" from the rest of society. But they are imprisoned, and that, if nothing else, distinguishes them from everyone else.

SUMMARY

As a responsibility of the state and federal levels of government, prisons are less numerous than local jails. But, while prisons are typically more standardized than jails, they still reflect considerable diversity—from high-security custodial institutions to minimum-security community residential centers. In addition, the military operates correctional facilities confining enlisted personnel and officers.

Compared to other alternatives, prisons are the most expensive component of the correctional system. Most of their costs are paid by the state level of government, although some jurisdictions have begun to collect fees from inmates to offset expenses. Generally, prisons confine those serving sentences in excess of one year. The type of institution in which an inmate will serve time is determined by the person's security classification. Those requiring the greatest amount of control are assigned to maximum security, which imposes a high level of both external and internal restrictions. At the other extreme, the most trustworthy offenders are assigned to minimum security, which provides far greater freedoms and privileges.

Because they serve a much smaller population, women's prisons tend to include a wider range of custodial security and are more geographically remote than male facilities. Additionally, their smaller size often prohibits offering the diversity of programs provided within men's prisons. In an effort to address this problem economically, some facilities are now coed, with male and female inmates confined within the same compound. They do not share living quarters but may be allowed to interact socially and share the same programs, which involves both advantages and disadvantages.

Whether male or female, the offender's custody level is determined through the classification process, which identifies the person's level of risk or dangerousness. During classification, inmates are processed into the system, and assigned to housing. However, they may be reclassified at any time during their confinement.

In recent years, the number of inmates sentenced to state and federal correctional institutions has been increasing at a steady pace, causing many facilities to become overcrowded. The effects of crowding not only reduce the availability and quality of inmate programs and services, but also pose serious health and safety risks. Responses to the crowding issue have ranged from expansion and new construction to "front-end" alternatives designed to keep people out of prison, and "back-end" approaches to release more of those already confined.

Organizationally, state departments of corrections are headed by a director (or commissioner) appointed by the governor. As a result, there is potential for political influence, and directors are often replaced with the election of a new governor. The state director appoints the warden (or superintendent) of each facility, who is responsible for assuring that the organizational units within the prison (operations, program services, and support services) are working together toward mutually compatible goals.

Although the management of prisons is formally in the hands of the warden, the inmate population also has considerable informal control. To prevent inmates from exercising too much unofficial authority, efforts have been made to restrict them to less sensitive work assignments and to remove them from direct supervision over other inmates. However, prisoners still exert significant informal social control, which in some institutions has been formalized through participatory management. Where participatory management has expanded into inmate self-governance, some difficulties have occurred— particularly when officials abdicate authority to the inmates rather than share power with them. Many offenders simply may not be sufficiently mature to accept the responsibilities of self-governance in a responsible manner. Moreover, the security-conscious nature of the prison environment is not always conducive to the types of rational behavior associated with life in free society, as we will see more clearly in upcoming chapters.

FOR FURTHER DISCUSSION

1. Compare the costs of building a prison in your community to opening a homeless shelter or a substance abuse treatment center.

2. Debate the pros and cons of charging inmates fees for health care. Devise a compromise that would address as many points by both sides as possible.

3. Go online to view the statement of Human Rights Watch (September 22, 2009) concerning the impact of supermaximum-security prison facilities and debate whether they should be abolished.

4. Discuss what front-end and back-end approaches could be employed to reduce prison crowding without unduly endangering public safety.

5. Determine whether there are any options for removing the political influence from correctional administration.

6. Conduct an online search of the Department of Corrections website in your state and identify how many different varieties of jobs are found in both institutional and community corrections throughout your state.

7. Use Maslow's hierarchy of needs to explain why many experiments with inmate self-government have been unsuccessful and develop an alternative to address inmate concerns without violating Maslow's concepts.

8. After watching *The Shawshank Redemption* movie, discuss why it is equally dangerous to give inmates assignments that are too sensitive and to control a prison too rigidly or punitively.

CHAPTER 7

Dynamics of the Prison Population

Punishment has become normalized, affecting large social groups rather than just the behaviorally distinctive deviants in the shadows of social life.[1]
Bruce Western, Mary Pattillo, and David Weiman

CHAPTER OVERVIEW

We tend to speak of the "correctional population" as if it were a singular entity. Indeed, with so many people now serving time in correctional facilities, there is a tendency to view them in terms of gross numbers and abstract generalities. As more than one and a half million people flood the nation's prisons, this human tsunami blurs their individual characteristics. Engulfed by such overwhelming numbers, it is often difficult to keep in mind that each and every one of these hundreds and hundreds of thousands of people is a unique person—with a particular demographic makeup, individual background, criminal record, litany of strengths and weaknesses, and a potential to change that differs from that of every other inmate in the system. Just as excessively large college classes cannot effectively address the personal needs and learning styles of each individual student, neither can even the most committed prison administrators effectively respond to the widespread diversity represented by those confined to overcrowded and underfunded facilities.

From the perspective of the inmate, the ordeals of adjusting to imprisonment and the obstacles to readjusting upon release are challenging for anyone. But they can be particularly difficult for inmates with special needs—from childbearing females to those who are elderly, physically or mentally disabled, alcoholic, drug addicted, or AIDS infected. The negative effects of incarceration can be profound even for healthy males (who represent the majority of inmates in prison), but the destructive impact can be even more significant for other groups.

Women, for example, do not react to the conditions of confinement in the same manner as men. Their concerns, social relationships, and adaptation to imprisonment are somewhat different. Although still in the vast minority among the institutional population, their numbers are increasing. Consequently, there is a need for both greater consideration of their unique requirements and greater parity of services in comparison to those extended to men.

Other groups that were also incarcerated in smaller numbers in the past include AIDS-infected and elderly inmates. But with longer mandatory sentences, as well as the spread of AIDS in society at large and the growing number of senior citizens, more and more of these offenders are appearing in correctional facilities, and bringing with them special medical needs.

Still others, such as alcoholics and the mentally ill, have always been represented in sizeable numbers among those under correctional supervision. The necessity to provide better care and treatment for them is no less acute today. Now, however, they are joined by growing numbers of drug-addicted offenders. Although corrections has made strides in providing treatment for such clients, demand still exceeds capacity.

To some extent, the lack of correctional services for inmates with special needs reflects similar shortcomings in the community at large. Once removed from society through incarceration, however, inmates with special needs become an even lower priority on the public agenda—essentially a minority within a minority. Some are subject to victimization by other inmates in a subculture where the weak are quickly overcome by the strong. Some simply languish in a system hard pressed to meet basic necessities of conventional inmates, much less divert scarce resources to those with special needs. It is an unfortunate irony that, in many cases, attention is largely directed toward them reactively in proportion to the growth of their numbers, rather than proactively in an effort to prevent their numbers from growing.

LEARNING GOALS

Do you know:
1. what nation has the highest incarceration rate?
2. the characteristics of a typical prison inmate?
3. for what types of offenses prisoners are serving time?

TODAY'S PRISON POPULATION

Just as there are concerns that people such as vagrants, alcoholics, and the mentally ill are being detained in jails inappropriately, the question has been raised as to whether prisons are being reserved for those who truly deserve to be behind bars. For example, the perception that only high-risk, dangerous offenders are going to prison is challenged by one study which found that only 18 percent of new admissions could be ranked "serious" on the basis of the offense for which they were committed.[2] Yet it is also true that some inmates enter prison with a long criminal history (even though the offense for which they are admitted may be nonviolent). Moreover, nearly a third of all prison admissions in recent years have been for violations of parole or some other type of supervised release.[3] Such issues have come under considerable debate as it has become apparent that the United States is now in its fourth decade of continually increasing prison populations and, as a result, maintains the world's leading incarceration rate. (See Exhibit 7.1.)

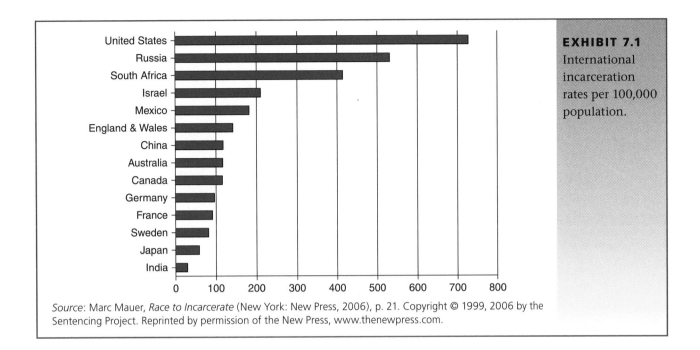

EXHIBIT 7.1
International incarceration rates per 100,000 population.

Source: Marc Mauer, *Race to Incarcerate* (New York: New Press, 2006), p. 21. Copyright © 1999, 2006 by the Sentencing Project. Reprinted by permission of the New Press, www.thenewpress.com.

Inmate Characteristics

With so many people incarcerated, it is reasonable to ask just who exactly is in all these prison cells—or, if trends continue in the same direction, the more pertinent question may become who is *not*. The typical profile of a state prison inmate in the U.S. is a black male (47 percent) who is:

- under the age of 35 (57 percent);

- unmarried (83 percent);

- uneducated (less than high school, 43 percent);

- employed (55 percent), but making less than $12,000 (54 percent).[4]

It is notable, however, that the rate at which women have been incarcerated in recent years is increasing faster than the rate for men. Beyond these demographic statistics, more in-depth insights into the complexity of today's prison population reveal greater numbers of dangerous offenders with antisocial tendencies, substance abusers, those with serious mental illness, sexual predators, illegal immigrants, and people with radical religious and/or political beliefs—all of which bring their own issues and challenges into correctional institutions.[5]

Inmate Offenses

Given this profile, it may not be surprising to find that most of those in prison are generally familiar with the criminal justice system. In fact, the vast majority

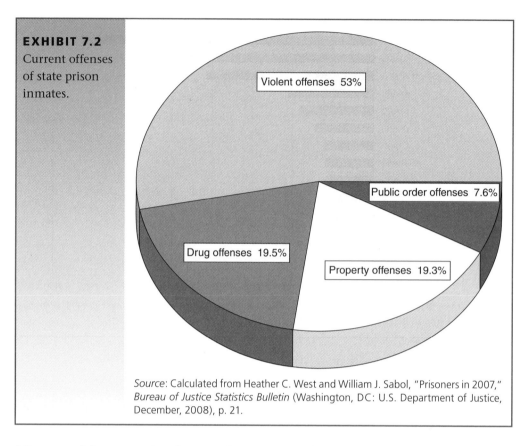

EXHIBIT 7.2
Current offenses of state prison inmates.

Violent offenses 53%

Public order offenses 7.6%

Drug offenses 19.5%

Property offenses 19.3%

Source: Calculated from Heather C. West and William J. Sabol, "Prisoners in 2007," *Bureau of Justice Statistics Bulletin* (Washington, DC: U.S. Department of Justice, December, 2008), p. 21.

(75 percent) have previously served time on probation or behind bars.[6] The half who have been incarcerated previously are referred to as "churners"—i.e., those engaged in "reentry cycling."[7]

In terms of the type of violation for which they are presently incarcerated, slightly more than half of those in state prison (53 percent) are serving time for violent offenses—predominantly murder (13 percent) and robbery (14 percent). As shown in Exhibit 7.2, most of the remainder are incarcerated for either property crimes (19 percent) or drug offenses (19 percent).[8] The question then becomes what return society expects for the costly investment it is making in large-scale institutional confinement of so many offenders. While that is not an easy question to answer, taking a closer look at just who these inmates are begins to shed some light on why they are there.

FEMALE OFFENDERS

In comparison to males, females have always been (and continue to be) less frequently convicted of crimes and incarcerated in correctional facilities. Some maintain that this

LEARNING GOALS

Do you know:

4. for what types of crimes women are more likely to be arrested?

5. what proportion of inmates in prison and jail are female?

6. what offense is largely accounting for increases in female arrest and incarceration rates?

7. how concerns about children affect women in prison?

reflects a tendency of the justice system to treat women with more leniency. For example, when a woman is the sole support for her children, the decisions of criminal justice officials may be influenced by realizing the hardship that imprisonment would create for the family. On the other hand, some believe that females—especially those engaged in the types of serious crimes usually committed by men—are dealt with more severely by a system that views such acts as particularly unacceptable for women.

Beyond potentially chauvinistic attitudes, the fact remains that women do not generally pose as clear a danger to society. In comparison to men, they are far more likely to be arrested for property offenses than for violent crimes.[9] However, women are beginning to appear more often in police reports and, subsequently, prison populations.

Women in Prison

Given their more limited involvement in crime, it is not surprising to find that women constitute only 7 percent of all prisoners nationwide[10] (although they also represent 11.6 percent of the jail population).[11] This, of course, means that there are far fewer female prisons. A total of only 98 federal and state prisons exclusively house women, which represents just 8 percent of all prisons.[12] In addition, the nonviolent property crimes that are more characteristic of female offenders are

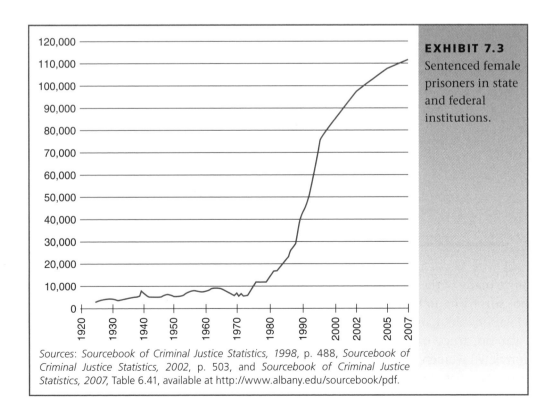

EXHIBIT 7.3
Sentenced female prisoners in state and federal institutions.

Sources: Sourcebook of Criminal Justice Statistics, 1998, p. 488, Sourcebook of Criminal Justice Statistics, 2002, p. 503, and Sourcebook of Criminal Justice Statistics, 2007, Table 6.41, available at http://www.albany.edu/sourcebook/pdf.

more likely to make them candidates for probation, community service, restitution, or other non-incarceration alternatives.

Although the rate of imprisonment for males is considerably higher, the number of women serving time has increased significantly in recent years (see Exhibit 7.3), and the female inmate population continues to grow at a faster pace. In fact, there is some empirical evidence that the criminal justice system takes more punitive action against women offenders.[13] To get a better idea of what may be accounting for this discrepancy, we need to take a closer look at what types of female offenders are being incarcerated.

In many respects, the characteristics of female inmates resemble those of their male counterparts. Like male prisoners, women tend to represent minorities who are relatively young and unmarried (either single, separated, divorced, or widowed). Compared to men, however, they are less likely to have been employed prior to their arrest, and much more likely to have been on some form of government assistance.[14] They are also more likely to have suffered physical and sexual abuse while growing up.[15] (For a profile of the typical female offender, see the next "Close-up on Corrections.")

CLOSE-UP ON CORRECTIONS
National Profile of Women Offenders

- Disproportionately women of color.
- In their early-to-mid-thirties.
- Most likely to have been convicted of a drug-related offense.
- From fragmented families that include other family members who also have been involved with the criminal justice system.
- Survivors of physical and/or sexual abuse as children and adults.
- Individuals with multiple physical and mental health problems.
- Unmarried mothers of minor children.
- Individuals with a high school or general equivalency diploma (GED) but limited vocational training and sporadic work histories.

Source: Barbara Bloom, Barbara Owen, and Stephanie Covington, *Gender-responsive Strategies: Research, Practice, and Guiding Principles for Women Offenders* (Washington, DC: U.S. Department of Justice, National Institute of Corrections, 2003), p. 8.

Since many of these characteristics are also reflective of drug-related offenders, it is not surprising to find that nearly three times more women are in prison for drug violations than any other offense.[16] In that regard, it has been suggested that the "war on drugs has translated into a war on women."[17] Moreover, when drug-convicted women are released, they may be subjected to a lifetime ban on welfare benefits, a penalty that affects tens of thousands of children.[18]

Concerns for Children

In fact, if there is one major factor that separates women from men in prison, it is worrying about their children. That is not to imply that men are unconcerned, but, despite social progress toward achieving sexual equality, child-rearing largely remains a female responsibility. The majority of women in correctional facilities (64 percent) lived with their minor children prior to being incarcerated, while only 44 percent of male inmates did so. Together, this accounts for almost 1.5 million children under 18 years of age.[19] Since we have already seen that most female prison inmates are unmarried or separated, it is apparent that many of these mothers are single parents. Additionally, half of them were unemployed in the month before their arrest, and 18 percent had been homeless at some point in the past year.[20]

While male inmates have traditionally counted on the mother of their children to look after them, women cannot necessarily depend on the father to do so. For example, 9 out of 10 male inmate fathers report that their children live with the mother, but only 28 percent of inmate mothers have their children living with the father.[21] As a result, the male offender's family may remain relatively intact, whereas a woman's family can be seriously disrupted when she is removed from the home.[22] Added to the "pains of imprisonment" for females, therefore, is the further frustration, conflict, and guilt of being separated from and unable to care for their children. As one mother put it, "I can do time alone okay. But it's not knowing what's happening to my son that hurts most."[23]

Maintaining Maternal Bonds

Not only do many female offenders harbor concerns for children on the outside, but some give birth in prison as well. Since there is no national policy determining what happens to those born to women behind bars, the vast majority are separated from their mothers immediately at birth and placed in the custody of relatives or foster care. Only a dozen states permit infants born in prison to remain with their mother for any amount of time—usually just until the mother is released from the hospital.[24] However, nine states have developed special nurseries to enable children to bond with their mothers for up to 18 months.[25]

While they may not permit live-in arrangements, most states do attempt to nurture mother–child relationships during visiting.[26] Many have a room or an area set aside to simulate a "home setting," and most provide special activities for visiting children. For example, in addition to arts, crafts, and games, some facilities sponsor storytelling sessions, summer camp, reading programs, birthday celebrations, and holiday events. Several even permit overnight visits on camping trips in conjunction with programs such as Girl Scouts behind Bars. In other places, inmates and their children are allowed to cook meals in the kitchen, take naps together, and enjoy outside playgrounds or picnic areas.[27]

Yet, because there are fewer women's prisons, female offenders are likely to be incarcerated at a greater distance from their children than males. In fact, the average female inmate is more than 160 miles farther from her family than a male inmate.[28] To maintain parental bonds in facilities too remote for regular visitation, some states now have "video visitations" that enable inmate mothers to visit with their children technologically through videoconferencing.[29] But, despite these brief reprieves, women often find the loneliness of prison filled with anxious thoughts about the collateral consequences for their "prison orphans."[30]

This anxiety about how their children are getting along without them is not without cause. Studies show that children of incarcerated parents have lower than

EXHIBIT 7.4
For women especially, prison can be a lonely, soul-searching experience generating a sense of helpless abandonment.

Source: Courtesy of the American Correctional Association.

average self-esteem, express anger and defiance, are more likely to end up behind bars themselves, and have a much greater than average chance of getting pregnant and experiencing learning or emotional problems.[31] Likewise, parental incarceration has been identified as a risk factor for childhood problems ranging from truancy to depression, anxiety, and violence. Moreover, the adverse effects extend into adulthood, with the children of prison inmates more likely to be arrested, use drugs, be unemployed, and lack educational credentials.[32]

Even more importantly, research tends to show that, when the incarcerated parent is a man, "the effects are moderate, compared to when the incarcerated parent is a woman."[33] In recognition of such risks, some states extend outreach efforts, social services, and group support to the children of offenders. Likewise, the American Correctional Association's policy on crime prevention calls for considering the children of offenders as integral partners in treatment programs.[34]

Some may think that the children of alcoholics, drug abusers, or other more serious offenders might be better off growing up without their influence, but this is not what studies tend to show. It is more likely that imprisonment of parents is harmful to children, even when they come from dysfunctional families. Once the parent is removed from the household, the quality of alternative care arrangements for the children may be worse, which only enhances the trauma of separation.[35] Moreover, parental imprisonment may be just one of many cumulative risks that prison orphans experience—ranging from poverty to family violence, substance abuse, peer stigma, and fluctuating residences and/or caregivers.[36] While the impact of any one of these risk factors might not be significant, their cumulative effect can be devastating.

Adding further baggage are feelings of abandonment. During imprisonment, more than half of female prison inmates never have personal contact with their children,[37] and such separation can provoke considerable stress on both sides of the bars. Additionally, in a society where women who violate the law are not only social outcasts but almost automatically assumed to be inadequate parents as well, the inmate mother's self-respect is inevitably bound to suffer.

In the prison population, however, female offenders are hardly the only ones labeled as "social outcasts." To the extent that prisons are being used to deal with social problems ranging from drug and alcohol abuse to mental illness that are not being addressed effectively in the community, they will contain the most marginalized and impoverished groups in society.[38]

INFECTIOUS DISEASES IN CORRECTIONS

In recent decades, a disease that knows no gender, racial, or class boundaries has created a devastating impact behind bars.

LEARNING GOALS

Do you know:

8. why the rate of AIDS and hepatitis is higher within correctional institutions than among the general public?

9. what responses correctional administrators have implemented to reduce the spread of HIV/AIDS?

10. what position the courts have taken with regard to the mandatory testing of inmates for HIV/AIDS and the separate housing of those who test positive?

No particular social or demographic groups are inherently at risk of contracting AIDS. Rather, it is the high-risk *behaviors* in which they engage that place them in danger. Nor is anyone immune. Many of those being infected today, such as women and children, are the inadvertent victims of those who have been involved in such high-risk behaviors as sharing drug needles or engaging in unsafe sexual practices.

Yet, while AIDS has received the most notoriety, it is likely that even more inmates are infected with various types of viral hepatitis—the results of which can range from minor discomfort (hepatitis A) to acute liver failure (hepatitis C). Of those behind bars, it has been estimated that 22 percent to 39 percent are infected with the hepatitis A virus, with 16 percent to 41 percent showing signs of hepatitis C infection[39] (compared to less than 2 percent of the general population).[40]

HIV: the human immunodeficiency virus, transmitted through bodily fluids, which over time can develop into AIDS.

As with hepatitis, without mandatory testing it is impossible to know exactly how many inmates are infected with **HIV**, since the virus can linger undetected for years before developing into AIDS. But we do know that the rate of confirmed AIDS cases in state and federal prisons is more than double that of the general population.[41] The difference between the rates of AIDS cases in prison and in the general population has, however, been steadily shrinking since 1999 (when the correctional rate was five times higher).[42]

Some of this differential is a reflection of the fact that correctional institutions confine a population with a higher concentration of individuals who have histories of high-risk behavior, particularly IV drug use. In that regard, the National Commission on AIDS points out that, "By choosing mass imprisonment as the federal and state governments' response to the use of drugs, we have created a de facto policy of incarcerating more and more individuals with HIV infection."[43]

Since there is not yet a vaccine to prevent either AIDS or hepatitis C,[44] the vital concern with regard to these infectious diseases is to reduce their proliferation. A number of approaches have been implemented in response to this concern, primarily:

- *educating* both inmates and staff with regard to how the disease is spread;

- *issuing condoms* to protect inmates engaged in homosexual activities from contracting the disease;

- *testing* (either voluntary or mandatory) to identify those who are infected;

- *separately housing* those in various stages of the disease.

Education and Training

Virtually all prisons and jails report offering some type of AIDS training or educational materials.[45] Such initiatives are essential to provide facts concerning how the disease is transmitted—thereby promoting change in high-risk behaviors. In addition, they can help to eliminate the myths surrounding casual transmission that can lead to overreaction and unwarranted discrimination.

Ideally, programs should be offered for both inmates and staff in a *proactive* manner—well before widespread concern promotes panic. Among inmates, for example, at least one study has found that there is considerable confusion about the manner in which AIDS can be transmitted. Moreover, lower levels of knowledge are also associated with higher perceptions of the risk of contracting AIDS while incarcerated.[46] In other words, the less inmates know about objective facts concerning AIDS transmission, the more fearful they are of acquiring the virus in prison.

Condom Distribution

While support for AIDS education is widespread, there is one particular policy of some facilities that is another matter entirely—the distribution of condoms. On the one hand, this practice has been widely criticized as giving official sanction to unauthorized sexual activities. But, on the other hand, there are advocates who maintain that, since it is virtually impossible to prevent inmates from engaging in homosexual behavior, it is better to provide them with protection than to risk spreading the disease throughout the institution. As one doctor practicing in corrections has argued: "Facilities that have decided to issue condoms to inmates have not decided to permit sex. Instead, the programs are established as an acknowledgment that sex occurs. In the absence of such programs, I challenge prison administrators to stop sex altogether."[47]

HIV Testing

Like the condom issue, testing inmates for HIV has both supporters and critics. Advances in HIV treatment that delay the onset of AIDS underscore the need for early detection and intervention. In light of this medical incentive, more people in the general population are undergoing diagnostic tests. But, of course, they are doing so of their own free will. Within corrections, few would argue against providing tests and follow-up medical services on a *voluntary* basis for those requesting such help—as evidenced by data showing that 47 states and the Federal Bureau of Prisons make testing available upon request.[48] But it is the *mandatory* testing of everyone that is in dispute.

This involuntary means of identifying HIV-positive inmates has increasingly come under fire from both sides of the issue. On the one hand, some inmates have demanded mandatory mass testing for everyone's protection. In opposition, others have challenged such practices as an invasion of their right to privacy. Thus far, the courts have neither uniformly upheld nor denied either side.

In one case, for example, an appellate court refused to order correctional officials to administer AIDS tests to all inmates and staff on the basis that "the risk alleged by the inmates was based on unsubstantiated fears and ignorance."[49] From the opposite perspective, a prisoner in another jurisdiction challenged the constitutionality of the state's policy of testing all inmates for the AIDS virus.[50] In this case, the court ruled that the inmate's invasion of privacy was "far outweighed" by the prison's interest in treating those infected and taking steps to prevent further transmission of the disease.[51] In yet another case, the outcome was more ambiguous, with the court finding that the prison administrators had no evidence on which to base an AIDS testing procedure.[52]

Overall, however, the courts have been relatively consistent in upholding the constitutionality of state laws permitting mandatory testing. But, at the same time, they have supported the right of correctional administrators to refuse to implement mandatory testing. Thus, current judicial reasoning appears to be that testing is not constitutionally *required* under the Eighth Amendment (which forbids cruel and unusual punishment); but neither is it *prohibited* under the Fourth Amendment (which protects privacy). As a compromise between the extremes of mandatory and voluntary screening, some states target AIDS testing toward high-risk groups (such as IV drug users, homosexual men, and prostitutes).

Some jurisdictions have discontinued mass screening for reasons ranging from funding shortages to the realization that its drawbacks outweighed any benefits. In that regard, the American Correctional Health Services Association has gone on record as opposing mandatory testing, based on the concern that it is "costly and serves no useful public health function."[53] With less mass testing, there are undoubtedly inmates in prison who have undetected AIDS. But that does not mean that they necessarily contracted the disease in prison. To the contrary, although correctional facilities may be perceived as fertile breeding grounds for the spread of HIV, a number of studies suggest that this is not the case. Research to date indicates that relatively few inmates become HIV-positive as a result of activities that took place in a correctional facility.[54]

Separate Housing

Regardless of whether inmates are screened upon arrival or submit to testing voluntarily, once AIDS is detected, the issue becomes what actions are appropriate to take. As the National Commission on AIDS has observed, "there is certainly no point in screening without a clear notion of what is to be done with information uncovered in the screening process."[55] From a humanitarian point of view, it is obviously essential to provide medical care, although this can be quite costly. But it is the question of where to locate inmates who have tested positive that has become most controversial.

As with mandatory/voluntary testing, correctional administrators are again caught between two contradictory arguments in this regard. On the one hand, inmates free of AIDS have raised Eighth Amendment challenges, maintaining that it is "cruel and unusual punishment" to be unprotected from others with this communicable disease. But at least one court has held that prisoners must specifically show how the conditions of confinement they are challenging put them at risk of contracting AIDS.[56] In a similar case, inmates demanded mandatory screening and housing segregation of those who test positive. The judge rejected their arguments, ruling that the state had taken reasonable precautions to minimize the risk that inmates would contract the virus.[57]

At the same time, HIV-positive inmates have questioned whether it is a violation of *their* rights to be housed separately from the general population. In this respect, one court has declared that inmates shall not be segregated solely because they are HIV-positive, although they may be isolated on a case-by-case basis according to security or medical needs.[58] But, in another case, the court supported the argument of correctional administrators that "the segregation of infected prisoners was mandated to protect both the AIDS victims and other prisoners from tensions and harm that could result from fears of other inmates."[59] While most judicial rulings have upheld the constitutionality of separate housing, as with testing "the courts have concluded that the Constitution neither requires nor prohibits segregation."[60]

Legal Implications

As these cases reflect, such disputes have raised a number of legal issues. An immediate legal implication of a separate housing policy is that it readily identifies those with HIV, thereby compromising the confidentiality of AIDS testing. Laws and court rulings vary in terms of how strictly they protect the confidentiality and anonymity of those tested for HIV. States with such protections generally limit notification to the inmate and attending physician. Only a few jurisdictions have official policies of notifying correctional officers.

Staff, however, are not always satisfied with these confidentiality provisions. As one officer has argued, "the nation now has right-to-know laws dealing with dangerous and toxic substances in the workplace . . . [A]n inmate with AIDS is a dangerous person, and his or her blood is definitely a toxic substance."[61] In response, it has been pointed out that "disclosures may, in fact, lull correctional officers into a false sense of security, leading them to believe that all infected prisoners have been identified."[62]

In addition to revealing the confidentiality of their health status, separately housing those who are HIV-positive can have further repercussions. The National Commission on AIDS notes that not only is there "no legitimate public health basis for segregating prisoners with HIV," but also those who are so isolated:

- often lose access to religious services, work programs, visitation rights, libraries, educational and recreational programs, and drug/alcohol treatment;

- serve in virtually solitary confinement within small prisons, and in larger institutions are often grouped together indiscriminately, regardless of their security classification.[63]

It is therefore not surprising that such practices have represented a sizeable proportion of the lawsuits related to AIDS. Undoubtedly, these cases have generated some of the impetus toward the current trend away from segregation—toward the "mainstreaming" of HIV-positive inmates with the rest of the general population. But, beyond the threat of legal action, this change in housing policy has resulted from a combination of additional factors, including increased costs, less fear, more compassionate attitudes, and the rising numbers of inmates with HIV infection or AIDS—which is making segregation both impractical and infeasible.

A compromise between the extremes of complete integration and total segregation has been recommended that would take into account both high-risk behavior and HIV/AIDS infection. This approach would classify the person according to a multivaried continuum reflecting institutional behavior as well as the health status of those who are HIV-positive. Housing and supervision would then be designed to both reduce opportunities for high-risk activities and provide for the medical needs of those who are becoming progressively ill.[64]

In summary, there are no clear-cut guidelines on how corrections should respond to the threat of AIDS. As a result, some administrators have experimented with preventive measures, ranging from providing condoms to promoting education. Identification approaches likewise have varied from requiring mandatory mass testing, to selectively screening high-risk groups, to simply making tests available on a voluntary basis. In reaction to the results, some systems have implemented housing segregation policies. Others have explored compromises, such as increasing segregation on the basis of how far the disease has progressed. Many have either continued or returned to mainstreaming those who are HIV-positive with the rest of the population. The only thing that is sure about AIDS is that, until there is a cure, the issues surrounding it will undoubtedly continue to create further conflict, confusion, and court cases.

LEARNING GOALS

Do you know:
11. what percentage of prison inmates are in need of drug treatment?
12. what sanction is most often imposed by the justice system for those convicted of drug offenses?
13. to what extent those in prison or jail are participating in drug treatment programs?

SPECIAL NEEDS OFFENDERS

Beyond childbearing women and those who are afflicted with HIV/AIDS, there are any number of inmates with special needs in the correctional setting. Some (such as those who are alcohol- or drug-addicted or mentally disordered) represent a sizeable portion of the correctional population. Others merit attention either because they have often been overlooked as a result of their limited numbers (e.g., the physically impaired) or because their growing numbers are causing concern (e.g., the elderly). While these groups certainly do not exhaust all categories of special offenders, they do illustrate the scope of unique challenges that correctional administrators face.

Drug Abusers

It is well known that IV drug use with unsanitary needles is a major transmitter of AIDS and hepatitis, but drug abusers and **addicts** are not found solely among those with HIV. Over half of those in prison admit to having used drugs in the month before their offense, and one in three property offenders committed their offense in order to get money for drugs.[65]

Perhaps because poverty and discrimination can be so degrading to self-esteem, drug abuse has traditionally been associated with low-income and minority groups. While the use of drugs knows no social or racial boundaries, minorities are disproportionately affected. Growth in the minority population of juvenile detention facilities, for example, has been linked to the "extremely large increase in the number of these youth referred to juvenile court for drug offenses," along with "a substantial change in how juvenile courts respond to [such] cases."[66] Like the adult justice system, the juvenile system is becoming more inclined to incarcerate those involved in drug offenses. And, if offenders do not find effective treatment for their problem in juvenile facilities, it can be anticipated that they will appear later in the adult correctional system.

Institutional Profile. In fact, there is already evidence that such trends are occurring among the nation's jails. Because jails are more likely than state prisons to house young, first-time, or minor drug offenders, it is not surprising to find significant percentages of drug users among the jail population. Nearly three-fourths (70 percent) of jail inmates meet criteria for substance abuse or dependence[67] (including alcohol as well as drugs).

It is apparent that the adult criminal justice system, like its juvenile counterpart, is becoming tougher on drug crimes. The majority of adults convicted of drug offenses are being sentenced to confinement (67 percent)—either in jail (30 percent) or prison (37 percent).[68] Moreover, the average sentence for drug offenders going to prison (51 months) is greater than for anything except violent crimes.[69] Thus, drug violators have contributed significantly to the growth of both jail and prison populations over recent years (see Exhibit 7.5), despite the fact that treatment is far less expensive than imprisonment. Nor do these figures include substance abusers who happened to be convicted of other crimes. As one doctor put it, "addiction is a stigmatized disease that the criminal justice system often fails to view as a medical condition."[70]

Treatment Programs. Throughout the country, almost two-thirds of America's prisoners meet medical criteria for a substance use disorder.[71] As a result, it is not surprising to find the U.S. Office of National Drug Control Policy reporting that up to 85 percent of state prisoners need drug treatment, but only 13 percent will receive it while incarcerated.[72] Likewise, one national survey discovered 84,000 offenders on

addict: someone with an alcohol or drug dependence, a physical tolerance requiring increasingly larger doses, and an overpowering desire to continue taking the addictive substance.

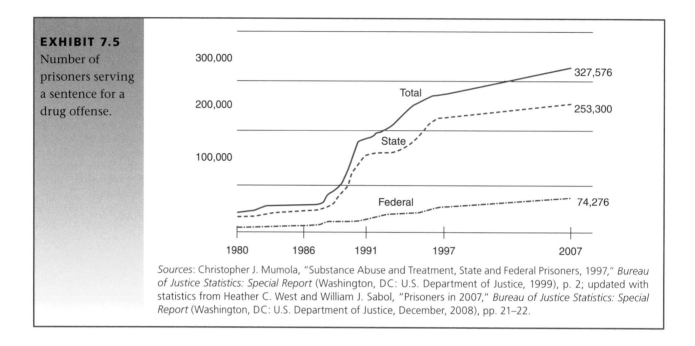

EXHIBIT 7.5
Number of prisoners serving a sentence for a drug offense.

Sources: Christopher J. Mumola, "Substance Abuse and Treatment, State and Federal Prisoners, 1997," *Bureau of Justice Statistics: Special Report* (Washington, DC: U.S. Department of Justice, 1999), p. 2; updated with statistics from Heather C. West and William J. Sabol, "Prisoners in 2007," *Bureau of Justice Statistics: Special Report* (Washington, DC: U.S. Department of Justice, December, 2008), pp. 21–22.

program waiting lists for drug treatment,[73] and that was before the national fiscal crisis beginning in 2008 had its devastating impact on correctional programming.

Among the programs that have been offered in correctional institutions, the focus has ranged widely—from group counseling, intensive therapy, and self-help groups to the use of acupuncture and comprehensive therapeutic community approaches. (For an overview of what strategies are most likely to work, see the next "Close-up on Corrections.") But a major weakness of many drug rehabilitation efforts in corrections is that they operate without the benefit of postrelease treatment and continuing support. Research has found that drug treatment alone, without an accompanying range of rehabilitation services, "can rarely effect stable, long-term behavioral change."[74] For example, it does little good to send an abuser home drug free and presumably "cured" without any prospect of employment. Incarceration can compel abstinence from drugs and address withdrawal symptoms. However, it is unlikely that long-term effectiveness will be achieved if the underlying social and psychological causes of physically addictive behavior are not confronted— or if interventions end with the offender's institutional sentence.

CLOSE-UP ON CORRECTIONS
What Works in Correctional Drug Treatment?

The National Institute on Drug Abuse has identified the following principles of effective approaches to drug abuse treatment in corrections:

1. Recognize that drug addiction is a brain disease that affects behavior.

2. Recovery from drug addiction requires effective treatment, followed by management of the problem over time.

3. Treatment must last long enough to produce stable behavioral changes.

4. Assessment is the first step in treatment.

5. Tailoring services to fit the needs of the individual is an important part of effective treatment.

6. Drug use during treatment should be carefully monitored.

7. Treatment should target factors that are associated with criminal behavior.

8. Criminal justice supervision should incorporate treatment planning, and treatment providers should be aware of correctional supervision requirements.

9. Continuity of care is essential for drug abusers re-entering the community.

10. A balance of rewards and sanctions encourages prosocial behavior and treatment participation.

11. Offenders with co-occurring drug abuse and mental health problems often require an integrated treatment approach.

12. Medications are an important part of treatment for many drug abusing offenders.

Source: Bennett W. Fletcher and Redonna K. Chandler, *Principles of Drug Abuse Treatment for Criminal Justice Populations* (Washington, DC: National Institute on Drug Abuse, U.S. Department of Health and Human Services, September, 2007), pp. 1–5. See also Peter D. Friedmann, Faye S. Taxman, and Craig E. Henderson, "Evidence-based Treatment Practices for Drug-involved Adults in the Criminal Justice System," *Journal of Substance Abuse Treatment*, Vol. 32 (2007), pp. 267–277.

Alcohol Abusers

A long-standing problem that has plagued society well before the current war on *illegal* drugs concerns the abuse of a *legal* drug—alcohol. Because it is so widely, inexpensively, and legally available (at least for adults), alcohol in some ways may actually be a greater threat. Certainly, it generates more police activity. When figures for DUI arrests, drunkenness, and liquor law violations are compiled (over 2.7 million), they far exceed those of any other offense category.[75] This does not mean that many people do not consume alcohol in a socially responsible manner. It is when overuse begins to damage health, deteriorate family relationships, affect employment, and generate crime that it becomes a problem.

Like the use of illicit drugs, the use of alcohol often begins at young ages, even though it is legally restricted for those under 21 in all states. But illegality does not prevent consumption. Alcohol is, in fact, the "drug of choice" among young people. While only 2 percent to 4 percent of high school seniors report using hard drugs on a monthly basis, almost half (47 percent) admit to monthly use of

> **LEARNING GOALS**
>
> Do you know:
> 14. why alcohol is in many ways a greater threat than the use of illegal drugs?
> 15. how the use of alcohol compares to the use of illegal drugs among inmates?

alcohol.[76] As with illegal drugs, abuse of alcohol does not necessarily result in addiction. But among those who are particularly susceptible genetically or psychologically, problem drinking can lead to addiction or **alcoholism**.

alcoholism: the disease associated with abuse of legal drugs (e.g., beer, wine, or liquor), which may be inherited genetically, as well as promoted by social and psychological factors.

Institutional Profile. Within state correctional facilities, a slightly higher percentage of inmates reported being under the influence of alcohol (37 percent) than drugs (33 percent) when they committed their crime.[77] As shown in Exhibit 7.6, this is similar to the percentages of jail inmates and probationers who were also drinking at the time of their conviction offense. Moreover, the combination of alcohol with other drugs (polydrug use) is also appearing more frequently among correctional populations.

Of course, being "under the influence" during the commission of a crime does not inherently mean that the person is an alcoholic. It may only indicate that the offender becomes more susceptible to criminal behavior or cannot control impulses when drinking. On the other hand, there are alcoholics who are completely convinced of their ability to "handle" increasingly large amounts of liquor, managing to function without detection in society and not seeking help until alcoholism has begun to destroy their life. As a result, alcoholism is to a great extent a hidden disease, with no accurate measures of its prevalence.

Treatment Programs. As with drug addiction or any other social problem, prevention is a far better remedy than intervention after the fact and, as with these other maladies, behavior is often symptomatic of deeper underlying problems. Treatment of alcoholism must therefore be based on the realization that drinking may be a manifestation of other difficulties (although now there is

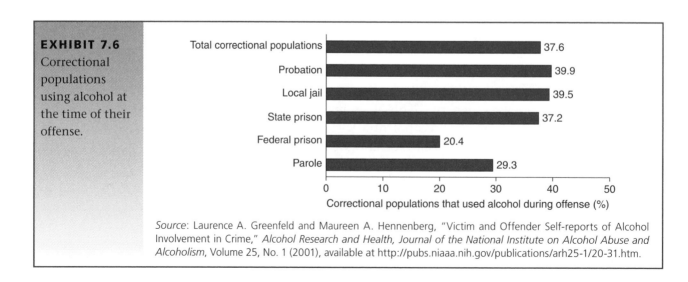

EXHIBIT 7.6
Correctional populations using alcohol at the time of their offense.

Correctional populations that used alcohol during offense (%)

Population	%
Total correctional populations	37.6
Probation	39.9
Local jail	39.5
State prison	37.2
Federal prison	20.4
Parole	29.3

Source: Laurence A. Greenfeld and Maureen A. Hennenberg, "Victim and Offender Self-reports of Alcohol Involvement in Crime," *Alcohol Research and Health, Journal of the National Institute on Alcohol Abuse and Alcoholism*, Volume 25, No. 1 (2001), available at http://pubs.niaaa.nih.gov/publications/arh25-1/20-31.htm.

additional evidence pointing toward a genetic link through which alcoholism is inherited).

In any event, conventional therapy emphasizes strengthening the patient psychologically so that alcohol is no longer a convenient "crutch" for solving problems or relieving emotional tensions. As with drug intervention, treatment approaches range from psychotherapy to special diets designed to counteract vitamin deficiencies, along with self-help groups. In both cases, treatment is more likely to be effective if it is not conducted in isolation but, rather, includes a more comprehensive family-focused approach. In the final analysis, however, the effectiveness of any intervention is ultimately dependent on an accurate diagnosis, which is not always feasible, especially in light of the fact that substance abuse often occurs in conjunction with mental health disorders (as illustrated in Exhibit 7.7).

Mentally Disordered Offenders

Throughout history, society has reacted to those who have mental disorders with a mixture of fear, mistrust, and repulsion. In the Middle Ages, it was thought that they were possessed by evil spirits and, if fortunate enough to escape burning at the stake, they faced banishment from society. In later years, ashamed families would hide mentally disordered relatives in basements or attics. When society began to assume more public responsibility for their care, they were again secluded—

LEARNING GOALS

Do you know:

16. how society has responded over the years to those with mental disorders?
17. how the developmentally disabled differ from the mentally ill?

in large remote institutions closed off from public scrutiny. Eventually, concerns were voiced about both the conditions in which they were being confined and the types of disorders for which they were being held. Mental institutions often became dumping grounds where the elderly, handicapped, and undesirable

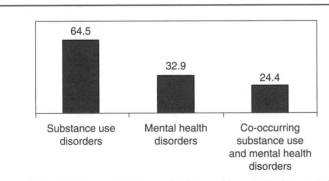

EXHIBIT 7.7
Percentage of inmates with substance abuse and mental health disorders.

Source: National Center on Addiction and Substance Abuse, *Behind Bars II: Substance Abuse and America's Prison Population* (New York: National Center on Addiction and Substance Abuse, Columbia University, February, 2010), p. 23, available at http://www.casacolumbia.org/articlefiles/575-report2010behindbars2.pdf.

were virtually imprisoned.[78] Even among those with legitimate mental problems, it was determined that many suffered from conditions that could be treated as effectively on an outpatient basis.

Much of this criticism came to a climax during the civil rights movement of the 1960s—when widespread support was generated for protecting the interests of the disenfranchised, including the mentally ill. As a result, the deinstitutionalization of large mental hospitals began with various forms of community mental health legislation in the 1970s. However, somewhere along the way to replacing institutional confinement with community-based treatment, society ran out of money or interest or both. Earlier we saw the impact of this transition in terms of how jails have in a sense become a "second-rate mental institution."

As with alcoholics and drug addicts, when society cannot or will not effectively care for certain groups, they often become correctional clients. In that respect, public attitudes toward the mentally ill have not changed dramatically over the years—still reflecting a combination of suspicion, fear, and aversion. Moreover, the term "mentally disordered" encompasses a wide range of behaviors, from the mildly disoriented or neurotic to those who are severely psychotic and completely out of touch with reality. While this term is used broadly to refer to conditions that differ from what is considered "normal," it is important to make clear distinctions between the developmentally disabled and the mentally ill.

Developmental Disability.   Previously known by such terms as "mentally defective" or "feebleminded," and more recently as "mentally retarded," **developmentally disabled** is a clinical classification resulting from an

developmentally disabled: those with mental capacity that was retarded at an early stage of development (identified by an IQ of less than 70).

EXHIBIT 7.8 With the closure of many large-scale mental health institutions, those with mental disorders can often be found wandering the streets—homeless, hungry, and vulnerable to arrest.

abnormally low IQ (70 or below) and a deficiency in two or more adaptive life skills.[79] There is not necessarily any relationship between such a disability and criminal behavior. But the limited intelligence of the developmentally disabled severely restricts their employment opportunities. It also tends to make them susceptible to being led into crime by others, and when they do break the law, they often do not have the mental capacity to do so without being detected.

Because of their nominal intelligence, when such persons engage in crime, they may not be held accountable for their actions in a court of law, just as a small child would not be held criminally responsible due to lack of ability to distinguish right from wrong. As a result, it is not surprising to find that their proportion of the institutional population in corrections is quite small.[80] Given their limited numbers, programs for them are very scarce—found in less than half of the states.[81] Although there is no "cure" for mental retardation, with special assistance, some can be helped to improve the level of their development toward achieving greater social independence.

A far greater danger for them than lack of treatment, however, is their potential for being victimized in prison. Not only are they subject to verbal ridicule and physical abuse by other inmates, but to conceal their deficiencies, they often avoid participating in institutional programs. In addition, they are generally slower to adjust to prison routines and find it more difficult to comprehend rules and regulations. Often, they simply do not understand what is expected of them. Staff who are not sensitive to the developmentally disabled can therefore mistakenly assume that an inmate is being defiant when actually the person cannot cognitively comprehend the officer's instructions, as illustrated in the following "Close-up on Corrections." Since these offenders are skillful at hiding their disability in an effort to appear "normal," they tend to accumulate more disciplinary infractions and thus are more likely to be denied parole.[82]

CLOSE-UP ON CORRECTIONS
Dealing with the Developmentally Disabled

On one particular hot summer weekend, fifteen minutes before he was to be relieved, Officer Terry . . . asked inmate Ness to assist him [in cleaning up the mess hall]. . . . About twenty minutes later, C.O. Terry returned to the mess hall to check on the work. When he saw what inmate Ness was doing, he first couldn't believe it and then he got angry. Inmate Ness had continued to sweep the garbage back and forth all over the floor, but was not putting it in a pile. In fact, the area that needed cleaning was now larger. Barely able to control his anger, C.O. Terry yelled, "NESS, WHAT THE HELL IS WRONG WITH YOU? WHAT ARE YOU—STUPID? WHAT DO YOU THINK YOU'RE DOING?" Inmate Ness became visibly nervous and stammered, "I, I, I ain't stupid." C.O. Terry disregarded the inmate's remark and stated, "YOU'RE TRYING TO BUST MY CHOPS BECAUSE YOU KNOW I WANT TO GET OUT OF THIS PLACE. LISTEN, NESS, I'M NOT GONNA TELL YA AGAIN, GET THIS MESS PICKED UP NOW!" . . .

Inmate Ness then grabbed a garbage can and began walking around the mess hall picking up a handful here and there, never really making any progress on the scattered mess. After five minutes, Officer Terry returned and once again . . . screams, "O.K., YOU MORON, THAT'S IT, GET OVER HERE." Before the inmate moves, he yells back, "I, I AIN'T NO MORON." C.O. Terry yells, "YOU ARE TOO, NOW GET OVER HERE." Inmate responds, "I AIN'T NO MORON." C.O. Terry yells, "I'M GIVING YOU A DIRECT ORDER TO GET YOUR BUTT OVER HERE RIGHT NOW." Inmate Ness shakes his head violently side to side, indicating that he's not moving. C.O. Terry calls for officer assistance.

Source: Thomas Tiberia, "Helping Correction Officers Recognize and Interact with Handicapped Offenders," *American Jails*, Vol. 6, No. 2 (May/June, 1992), pp. 31–32.

To prevent such difficulties, some departments have established procedures for identifying developmentally disabled offenders and placing them in special units where they can receive the structured direction, appropriate care, equitable discipline, and life skills training that will help them become more independent upon release.[83] But, unfortunately, they are more likely to be either unrecognized or mainstreamed with the general population and supervised by personnel who are not aware of their special condition.

LEARNING GOALS

Do you know:

18. how the prevalence of mental illness in the general population compares to that in prisons and jails?

19. why it is difficult for corrections to provide proper treatment for mentally ill inmates?

Mental Illness.   Unlike the relative simplicity of identifying developmental disabilities, the complexities of mental illnesses defy easy classification. In terms of seriousness, mental illness can range from harmless senility to violence-prone psychosis. In this discussion, the term *insanity* is used to differentiate mentally ill offenders from those with varieties of less severe disorders. Although it obviously has a medical interpretation, in the criminal justice system insanity is a legal term—a status that is decided by the court, taking into consideration the opinions of medical experts.

In the past, defendants ruled incompetent to stand trial or declared legally insane during trial could be confined in a mental health institution for an indeterminate period of time. In fact, it has been said that "there were places in the 1950's where the mean length of stay was 20 years, and the mean type of discharge was a funeral."[84] But a 1977 Supreme Court ruling (*Jackson v. Indiana*) held that those found incompetent for trial cannot be held indefinitely and established that any such commitment must be justified by treatment progress. However, even if released under criminal law, the patient may be recommitted under civil law.

mentally insane offenders: those designated by the courts as meeting the legal criteria of insanity, which can absolve the offender of criminal responsibility.

If at some point a **mentally insane** patient is determined by medical staff to be "cured," there may well be nothing to prevent his or her release, since technically the person was not "convicted" in a court of law. In an effort to prevent untimely releases from mental health institutions of those who could otherwise be held in a correctional institution, Michigan passed the first "guilty but mentally ill" legislation in 1972. Several other states have followed suit. Although these statutes vary, the basic intent is to establish factual guilt or innocence in a court of law (regardless of the insanity outcome), which would therefore enable a correctional sentence to be imposed, thus preventing the offender who is declared mentally insane from escaping criminal responsibility.

In addition to mental health institutions, the criminally insane may be confined in a special forensic hospital (i.e., a psychiatric hospital that is also a secure correctional institution). In smaller states and localities, a separate psychiatric ward may be set up within an existing prison. Contrary to past practices, the legally insane are no longer confined indiscriminately with the general population.

But that certainly does not mean that there are no mentally ill inmates among the general population. An inmate may suffer from any number of mental disturbances without being declared legally insane. There are no valid statistics documenting exactly how many mentally ill offenders are behind bars. Estimates of mental health problems range from 45 percent of federal inmates to 56 percent of state prisoners and nearly two out of three in the jail population.[85] If these statistics seem high, that is because they are. In contrast to the general public, for example, state prison inmates are three times more likely to have symptoms of mental health disorders.[86]

Today the United States has far more mentally ill men and women behind bars than in all state hospitals combined.[87] But that was not always the case. As shown in Exhibit 7.9, hospitalization of the mentally ill used to far surpass imprisonment rates. By the 1970s, however, this pattern had started to reverse itself as the rate of mental hospital inpatients declined dramatically while the incarceration rate climbed just as dramatically. As a result, corrections now holds the vast majority of the institutionalized population in this country. Regardless of the numbers, however, whether or not they get help is another matter.

Treatment Potential. Treatment is both essential from a compassionate point of view and a practical management necessity, since certain psychiatric disorders generate violent outbursts. In fact, state prison inmates with mental health problems are twice as likely to be injured by fighting and nearly twice as likely to be charged with a rule violation involving verbal or physical assault.[88] But sophisticated psychiatric and psychological treatment is costly and, when available, may be limited to only the most severe cases. As illustrated in the tragic and ironic story in the next "Close-up on Corrections," help is not always forthcoming.

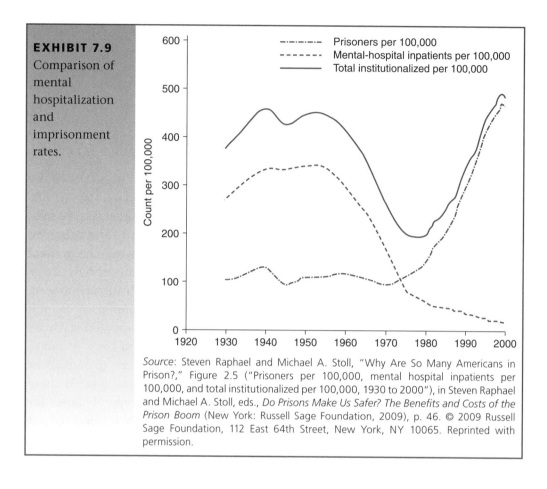

EXHIBIT 7.9
Comparison of mental hospitalization and imprisonment rates.

Source: Steven Raphael and Michael A. Stoll, "Why Are So Many Americans in Prison?," Figure 2.5 ("Prisoners per 100,000, mental hospital inpatients per 100,000, and total institutionalized per 100,000, 1930 to 2000"), in Steven Raphael and Michael A. Stoll, eds., *Do Prisons Make Us Safer? The Benefits and Costs of the Prison Boom* (New York: Russell Sage Foundation, 2009), p. 46. © 2009 Russell Sage Foundation, 112 East 64th Street, New York, NY 10065. Reprinted with permission.

CLOSE-UP ON CORRECTIONS
Brothers on Opposite Sides of the Bars

Interviewed behind thick plate glass in the Departmental Disciplinary Unit, where he has been for more than two years for a series of offenses, including assaulting a correction officer, Tom Walker says his violent behavior and series of suicide attempts are symptoms of his mental illness and cries for help amid an atmosphere of hopelessness. "They look at us as a hassle," Walker said. "They just want to punish us for our actions. They don't want to deal with the reasons we do these things."

Nearly 200 miles away in coastal Maine, Bob Walker [his brother] leads a tour of the red-brick jail that he supervises, and points to a pockmarked cell wall. It marks the spot where he used a sledgehammer to destroy a series of small hooks that could be used by at-the-brink inmates to anchor a cord and hang themselves. He said locking up mentally unstable inmates for 23 hours a day in solitary confinement contradicts sound correctional policy—and common sense.

When Tom Walker is released from prison, his brother hopes he will move to Maine, where he will help him rebuild his life. But he worries whether his brother will leave alive. "I'm praying these people are listening. . . . It sickens me to think that a whole department would ignore somebody saying, 'Look, I want to kill myself today.' And they'd be like, 'Yeah, OK, whatever.' "

Source: Thomas Farragher, "Brothers Took Divergent Paths to Opposite Sides of the Cell Door," *The Boston Globe* (December 11, 2007), available at http://www.boston.com/news/local/articles/2007/12/11/brothers_took_ divergent_paths_to_opposite_sides_of_the_cell_door/?page=2.

Estimates indicate that less than half of the inmates with severe mental illnesses—and less than one-quarter of those with more moderate mental illnesses—receive treatment for their condition while incarcerated.[89] Responses to mental illness in financially pressed agencies are likely to be limited to simply containing behavior. Appropriate treatment, however, extends beyond merely segregating, supervising, and medicating inmates. Moreover, as with addiction, effective intervention cannot end upon release—a fact recognized in a class action lawsuit filed on behalf of mentally ill inmates in New York City, where discharged offenders were being dropped off near subway stations between 2:00 a.m. and 6:00 a.m. with $1.50 and two subway tokens.[90] That litigation charged officials with routinely releasing patients who received mental health treatment behind bars without making any provision for continuing their care and medication in the community, thus causing many of them to deteriorate and commit new offenses.[91]

It might seem that an obvious solution would be to transfer such cases to state mental health hospitals better equipped for their care. But, since the deinstitutionalization movement, that is far more easily said than done. Before an inmate is accepted, state mental health laws now often require that, in addition to the person being legitimately mentally ill, "clear objective evidence must also exist that the inmate is a real and immediate danger to himself or herself or to others; or that the inmate is unable to attend to his or her basic needs. . . . This standard, when rigidly applied . . . effectively precludes the transfer of many inmates . . . to mental institutions."[92]

Moreover, without sufficient psychiatric staff, it is difficult to determine just who is mentally ill. It is often the correctional officer who is the first to notice such indicative changes as "poor grooming and hygiene, decreased appetite, or crying spells," along with "talk of suicide."[93] Clever inmates, however, have been known to feign symptoms in order to get attention or to be transferred to a different housing assignment, making it difficult to distinguish manipulators from the truly mentally disturbed. Additional challenges include those with co-occurring disorders—i.e., whose mental health issues are compounded by substance abuse, and who may also be experiencing serious medical problems.

Even when treatment staff are available, custodial security and therapeutic services do not always work hand in hand in the correctional conglomerate. Rarer still is the "integrated service delivery" advocated by treatment professionals.[94] Yet, if nothing else, incarceration does provide an opportunity to "identify, diagnose, and begin to treat the mentally ill."[95]

Physically Challenged Offenders

The needs of physically challenged offenders obviously differ substantially from the requirements of those who are psychologically damaged, but in both cases, correctional systems are likely to be ill equipped to meet them. The physically impaired (or disabled) include those who do not enjoy the benefits of being able to see, hear, speak, or walk, or who in some other way face a major restriction as a result of some disability. In the past, they were referred to as "handicapped," terminology that has changed with greater realization that there is often nothing "handicapping" them more than social attitudes toward their condition.

The burden of accommodation has likewise shifted over more recent years. Previously, disabled offenders had to adjust to correctional facilities as best they could. Now, as a result of the Americans with Disabilities Act (ADA), it is correctional agencies that must adjust.

disabled: those who are physically or mentally encumbered by an impairment which substantially limits some portion(s) of their major life activities.

ADA defines the **disabled** as "anyone with a physical or mental impairment substantially limiting one or more major life activities, [who] has a record of such impairment, or is regarded as having such an impairment."[96] Especially because of the prevalence of mental disabilities among inmates, this raises significant issues for corrections. Under the law, such inmates cannot be excluded from "programs and services available to the rest of the population."[97] Other provisions relate to the requirement that reasonable accommodations must be made for the disabled unless it would pose an "undue hardship" on the organization. This means that new buildings must be constructed in such a manner that they are accessible to those with disabilities, and existing buildings must be made accessible.

An additional feature of the law prohibits a public entity from denying program benefits because facilities are inaccessible. Since this requires specific programming to be accessible, it is obviously a more comprehensive challenge. Rulings by the 8th U.S. Circuit Court of Appeals, however, have cast doubt on whether Congress exceeded its authority in legislating certain program and service requirements of ADA,[98] giving correctional administrators a legal basis for refusing requests for accommodations that they cannot afford. Regardless of how far correctional facilities are required to go in terms of accessibility, accommodating needs of the disabled and providing them with equal opportunities can have far-reaching fiscal and operational implications, as vividly illustrated in the next "Close-up on Corrections."

CLOSE-UP ON CORRECTIONS
Meeting the Needs of Disabled Offenders

Custody and Security

Officers should be taught how to properly strip search a wheelchair-bound paraplegic, disassemble wheelchairs and prostheses, and otherwise conduct a proper shakedown. . . . Questions will arise concerning requirements for leg cuffs on paraplegics, waist chains across colostomy bags and even handcuffs for those on crutches. Custody should consult medical personnel when making these decisions.

Personal Safety

First, disabled inmates need to be protected from other inmates. . . . Second, [they] need to be protected in case of fire or natural disaster. Building evacuation planning and emergency response must include special consideration for the disabled. Wheelchairs and crutches can block exits, leading to panic and injury. Plans must include the steps to be taken to safely evacuate this population without slowing the evacuation of other inmates.

Programs

A major challenge . . . is providing the disabled with meaningful work, study and recreational opportunities. All too often, no attempt has been made to put these inmates to work, and they have been forced to sit back and watch other inmates earn incentive wages and days off their sentences without an opportunity to do likewise.

Medical Service

Another issue is helping with activities of daily living. These include dressing, bathing, feeding, and transporting. . . . Ideally, medical staff such as nurses' aides provide all such required assistance. However, in the real world of limited budgets and insufficient staff, inmates frequently are used for these activities. . . . Any inmate involvement in daily living assistance must be closely monitored by professional staff to ensure inmates are properly trained and that they do not exploit those they are assigned to assist.

Housing

Simply putting up handrails in the showers is no longer adequate. . . . The square footage requirement for handicapped inmates is greater. Lockers must be low enough to be reached from a wheelchair, and writing tables must be high enough for a wheelchair to pull under. . . . While their numbers are few and their needs are great, the system must be prepared to accommodate them.

Source: Herbert A. Rosefield, "Enabling the Disabled: Issues to Consider in Meeting Handicapped Offenders' Needs," *Corrections Today*, Vol. 54, No. 7 (October, 1992), pp. 111–114. Reprinted with permission of the American Correctional Association, Alexandria, VA.

LEARNING GOALS

Do you know:
22. why there has been such growth in the proportion of elderly inmates in prison?
23. what alternatives to incarceration have been proposed for geriatric prisoners?

The Elderly in Prison

Just as the population in general is aging, so is that of our correctional institutions. As a result of medical advances and healthier lifestyles, average life expectancy continues to climb. Senior citizens are already a rapidly growing segment of the population, as those in the post-World War II "baby boom" begin to enter retirement. Young people still are far more disproportionately likely to be criminal offenders, although crime among the elderly is no longer as totally unheard of as it was in the past. But, especially in light of trends toward longer mandatory sentences, prison populations are getting older.

In fact, the number of inmates past the age of 55 is increasing at twice the rate of the total prison population,[99] generating needs for everything from physical therapy and cardiac medication to special diets and wider cell doors for wheelchairs and walkers. While 55 may not seem "elderly" among those in free society, most prisoners have had inadequate (or nonexistent) health care throughout their lives,[100] often combined with years of substance abuse, smoking, and other lifestyle

EXHIBIT 7.10
While the prospect of dying in prison may be the ultimate form of loneliness, having outlived relatives and friends, geriatric inmates often have nowhere to go even when humanitarian release is available.

Source: Courtesy of the American Correctional Association.

patterns that promote the aging process.[101] Overlooking the special needs of **geriatric inmates** has been criticized as nothing less than "institutional thoughtlessness."[102]

As the elderly become a larger percentage of prison inmates, correctional administrators will be faced with unique challenges to address their needs. If aging inmates are simply mainstreamed with the overall population, they will be vulnerable to being preyed upon by younger, healthier inmates. They are also less likely to be able to participate physically in recreational and vocational programs. Nor can they in many cases eat the same foods as other inmates, since aging is often accompanied by more restrictive diets. Meeting the housing, recreational, rehabilitative, and nutritional needs of geriatric inmates thus presents issues that corrections will be confronting head on in the years ahead.

But perhaps most significantly, as more and more older offenders are confined behind bars, long-term health care will become an increasingly greater concern, just as it is already within the general population in free society. Most geriatric inmates have some chronic condition that requires frequent medical attention,[103] and meeting such needs is costly. It has been estimated that the average expense of medical care and maintenance for inmates over 55 is about three times the norm,[104] and one study points toward "enormous hidden costs and consequences" for taxpayers as prisons are "transformed into expensive old-age homes."[105] In fact, one institution spent $200,000 to care for just one geriatric inmate who had open-heart surgery, an angioplasty, and treatment for a stroke (which did not include the cost of physical therapy that he received to regain his speech and the use of his right leg, or the daily cost of managing his heart disease, diabetes, and hypertension).[106]

While some states have opened geriatric prisons,[107] others advocate secure nursing homes, electronic monitoring, or compassionate release for the elderly,[108] especially those who are terminally ill—for financial if not humanitarian reasons. As one study of geriatric inmates put it, many offenders view the prospect of dying in prison as "the ultimate personal failure."[109] Realistically, however, long-term inmates are not always in a position to accept such well-meaning gestures to live their remaining days in the dignity of free society. Many older prisoners have outlived their relatives and used up their savings. Faced with the fear of loneliness and the inability to survive on the outside, one 92-year-old offender actually took his own life after release, because he simply "didn't have any other place to go."[110]

geriatric inmates: those requiring special consideration for housing accommodations, medical care, and/or dietary needs as a result of the changes accompanying aging.

SUMMARY

Since the United States maintains the world's highest international incarceration rate, one might well ask what types of offenders are occupying all of those prison cells. Typically, the profile of a state prison inmate is a relatively young, unmarried black male who has not graduated from high school and was employed at a low-paying job before confinement. While society has not clearly expressed what it expects its prisons to accomplish with these offenders, shifting from the medical model to the justice model has reduced the emphasis on rehabilitation.

Because of women's "minority" status among institutional populations, the needs of women have not often been a high priority. Female offenders in particular have historically been arrested, convicted, and incarcerated less frequently. However, the rate of growth among female prison inmates is escalating faster than that of their male counterparts. Much of that increase is attributable to drug-related offenses. But, regardless of the reasons, women are becoming a larger proportion of clientele in the correctional conglomerate, and although they are still in the minority, they bring separation anxiety and special childbearing considerations into correctional facilities.

Like women, those with HIV infection are appearing more frequently in correctional populations. With the spread of AIDS throughout society, it is not surprising to find that this disease has been on the increase among inmates, particularly since those convicted of drug offenses are likely to be sentenced to confinement. Correctional responses to reducing the transmission of HIV have included educational programs, issuing condoms, HIV testing, and separate housing. Legal challenges have focused primarily on mandatory testing and the segregation of HIV-positive inmates. Thus far, however, the courts have ruled that mandatory testing and/or segregation is neither required under the Eighth Amendment nor prohibited under the Fourth Amendment.

Alcohol and drug abusers represent another component of correctional clientele that is growing at alarming rates. While treatment programs are available in many facilities, they are not reaching everyone in need. Additionally, they are not usually followed up by postrelease assistance and community-based monitoring.

Along with those experiencing problems with alcohol or drugs, mentally disordered offenders represent a sizeable component of correctional populations, especially since the deinstitutionalization of mental health services. Developmentally disabled offenders differ from the mentally ill in that their mental capacity has been subdued at an early stage of development, which renders them easily susceptible to apprehension. Within correctional institutions, the developmentally disabled represent special considerations, since they are slower to adjust to prison and learn what is expected of them—behaviors which can be misinterpreted as defiance.

In contrast, the criminally insane are so designated by the courts, using legal criteria related to one's capacity to distinguish right from wrong. Those legally determined to be insane may be confined in mental health facilities, forensic hospitals, or the separate psychiatric ward of a prison. Nevertheless, there are many others incarcerated who are not legally designated "insane," but nevertheless suffer from various forms of mental illnesses. While it has become more difficult to transfer such inmates to a mental health hospital, correctional facilities are nevertheless ill equipped to meet the challenges they present.

In the past, corrections as well as the general public has been slow to respond to the physically impaired. With implementation of the Americans with Disabilities Act, however, public agencies are now legally prohibited from discriminating against the disabled. While the physically impaired are still a small portion of correctional clientele, however, the elderly population is rapidly expanding.

Along with the overall aging of society in general, longer prison sentences are resulting in greater numbers of geriatric inmates. As this trend continues, corrections will be faced with meeting their unique requirements in terms of everything from housing assignments to dietary restrictions and recreational provisions. Moreover, the long-term health care of aging inmates will become increasingly costly. In fact, meeting the special needs of all groups of offenders discussed in this chapter presents a significant challenge for correctional administrators who are already hard pressed to meet even the basic requirements of more "traditional" offenders.

FOR FURTHER DISCUSSION

1. Go online to find the incarceration rates of three different countries and compare them to that of the U.S. Aside from higher crime rates, explain why the U.S. rate is so much higher than that of most western industrialized countries.

2. Discuss whether mothers of infants should or should not be permitted to keep their children with them behind bars and, if so, for how long. Include the interests of the newborn child, the mother, prison management, and society in your response.

3. Given the profile of female offenders, determine what proactive, community-based approaches could be implemented to reduce the growing numbers of women behind bars.

4. From both a moral and a cost-effectiveness standpoint, argue for and against distributing condoms in correctional facilities.

5. Debate both sides of the issue of whether inmates who are HIV-positive should be segregated from the general population.

6. Play the role of a prison policy development committee that is charged with deciding what approach to take with regard to testing inmates for AIDS, and, if the committee determines that some form of testing should be implemented, identify what policies should govern use of the results.

7. Go online to look at your state's correctional budget, especially what is being spent on inmate programming. Then assume that reduced revenues now require you to reduce the budget by 10 percent. Identify where you will make the cuts, provide a rationale for what you selected, and discuss the long-term implications of your choices.

8. Determine what treatment initiatives could be pursued with a family-focused approach to alcoholism that could not be addressed by an isolated focus on the individual offender.

9. Go online to locate mental health facilities that are available to your community, and identify what procedures are necessary to commit someone to their care.

10. From the website of the Americans with Disabilities Act (www.ada.gov), determine what accommodations a new prison would have to comply with if it were being built today.

11. Calculate what it would cost to incarcerate someone with a serious medical illness (e.g., cancer, heart disease, or diabetes) for a year, and from both a humanitarian as well as a legal perspective, explain why it is necessary for corrections to absorb this cost.

PART 3

Correctional Institutions: Custody, Treatment, Confinement, and Release

The possibility should at least be examined that the reason for the high levels of violence in American prisons may have as much to do with the way in which prisons have been managed and staffed on the cheap, and the fairness and dignity with which prisoners are treated, as it has with the qualities that criminals bring with them into prison.[1]

Roy King

T₀ ₐ SOCIETY FEARFUL OF CRIME, it is undoubtedly reassuring to know that convicted offenders are confined behind bars. In the short term at least, the public can take some comfort in knowing that an offender cannot continue to victimize society while serving time in a correctional facility. But a short-term sense of safety does little to address long-term solutions. Very few offenders die in prison, which is another way of saying that almost all inmates are eventually released to society—replacing our sense of comfort today with a renewed concern for our safety tomorrow.

In the upcoming chapters, we explore this issue by looking at just what does happen when an offender is incarcerated. The logical starting point is an inside view of prisons and their custodial procedures. If nothing else, correctional institutions are expected to retain inmates in custody. In Chapter 8, we will see how this is accomplished—from the formal controls achieved through physical restrictions, rules, and regulations to the informal controls encouraged through supervisory relationships between staff and inmates.

However, the overall objective of protecting society is better served in the long run by treatment. Thus, in Chapter 9, we turn our attention to the various clinical, educational, and training approaches that have been provided within correctional institutions. Some of these efforts focus on improved behavioral adjustment. Others emphasize developing self-respect and social responsibility. Still others target the need for marketable job skills. Regardless of their specific approach, all have in common the goal of better preparing the offender for a law-abiding lifestyle upon release.

But, as we will see in Chapter 10, the ability to accomplish this far-reaching goal is constrained by the very environment within which such programs are offered. Correctional institutions are notorious for the negative impact they have on those confined. Even the most humane, progressive institutions are, in the final analysis, just that—institutions. They are not rehabilitation centers. They are not job training facilities. They are not personal treatment programs. They are, first and foremost, institutions—where residents are closed off from normal relationships, unable to make even the most minor personal decisions, and pressured by others to fit into the inmate society and conform to its "informal code" of conduct. For many, prison reinforces rather than reduces antisocial tendencies. As a result, it is perhaps not surprising that so many offenders return to a life of crime but, rather, more surprising why some do not.

It is to the issue of life after confinement that Chapter 11 is devoted—considering such issues as how well institutional regimentation prepares one for success upon release, how likely former inmates are to recidivate, and how the shift from the medical model to the justice model has influenced the nature of parole in terms of release criteria, time served, and postrelease supervisory practices.

Exploring this transition from confinement, it becomes apparent that a society reassured by incapacitation is unlikely to welcome the reintegration of those same offenders back into the community. But that is exactly where nearly all are eventually returning. And it is when they are released that the public must confront the issue of how prudent it is to dismiss long-term solutions for a short-term sense of security.

CHAPTER 8

Custodial Procedures

The clanging of the metal doors to the main entrance . . . is unlike any sound you have ever heard. It is loud, heavy, and harsh. An exclamation point hammering home the fact that you are now inside a prison.[1]

Grace L. Wojda et al.

CHAPTER OVERVIEW

Providing safety, maintaining security, and preventing escapes are the major functions of custodial institutions. This requires such practices as counting, controlling movement, conducting searches, staffing tower observation points, regulating contact with the outside, and managing inmate behavior. Some inherent restrictions are built into the physical plant itself. Others result from custodial procedures implemented by staff. All emphasize maintaining compliance with rules and regulations. When such compliance is not achieved, the results can be disastrous—ranging from escapes or violent assaults to riots or other disturbances. But custodial features represent only one aspect of maintaining institutional control. Often overlooked are the more informal, noncoercive controls emerging from the relationship established between correctional officers and the inmate population.

For many years, the fact that those dealing directly with the inmates have significant potential for achieving a positive impact on their behavior was largely overlooked. But it has now become clear that operational staff are perhaps even more influential than treatment staff because of their continuous interaction with those incarcerated. Like the teachers a child encounters at school, treatment personnel play a major role. But teachers cannot completely replace the impact of the family, with whom the child interacts more intimately on a daily basis. In a correctional institution, it is the operational staff who are to some extent the inmate's surrogate "family"—whose firm-but-fair supervisory style can go far toward creating a more receptive environment for treatment.

This recognition of a broader role for line staff began the transition from punitive, rule-enforcement "guards" to the modern concept of "correctional officers" whose responsibilities extend beyond custody toward establishing an interactive relationship based on mutual respect. That does not mean overlooking security measures but, rather, developing the type of respectful relationship that is more likely to produce enough voluntary compliance to reduce the need to rely exclusively on coercive techniques. With even the most efficient custodial procedures, it is difficult to control those who do not voluntarily consent to be controlled. Thus, in the long term, developing effective working relationships not only promotes treatment but serves security objectives as well. It is this combination of conventional control and informal influence that best enables an institution to achieve its custodial mandate.

FUNCTIONS OF CUSTODY

LEARNING GOALS

Do you know:
1. the primary function and purposes of custody?
2. how custodial security is related to treatment effectiveness?

The primary function of custody is to provide external control for those who do not have sufficient internal controls to function effectively in free society. Ideally, custody should provide only that amount of external control which is directly necessary. It is for this reason that correctional institutions function at various levels of security—from minimum to maximum. Even for those who are initially assigned to a high-security classification, the level of control can be reduced gradually for those who increasingly demonstrate the ability to function on their own as they better internalize self-control.

While correctional facilities represent the ultimate form of control, less restrictive social controls are also maintained by many other institutions in society, such as family, schools, churches, and civic organizations. It is through these institutions that we learn morals, values, and socially acceptable behavior. It is when the socializing influences of these other institutions fail that correctional control takes over—which is not, however, to say that it is any more effective.

In correctional facilities, custodial procedures are designed to control individual behavior for the overall well-being of the institution. More specifically, the immediate operational objectives of custody are to:

- prevent escape;

- maintain order and safety;

- promote efficient functioning of the facility.

In the long term, the types of behavioral restraints involved in maintaining custody are also designed to shape the offender's behavior upon reentry into society. Undoubtedly, other programs offered during confinement—counseling, vocational training, work release, and the like—contribute significantly to this long-term goal. But it is custody that enables such programs to function.

Custody–Treatment Relationships

In terms of the discussion of Maslow's hierarchy of needs (see Chapter 6), it is apparent that at least some minimal level of physiological well-being, safety, and security must be established before higher-level motivations can be fulfilled. In more practical terms, it is difficult, if not impossible, to develop meaningful programs when work schedules are "frequently interrupted by violence" or classrooms become "battlegrounds."[2] If an inmate is constantly concerned about self-protection and institutional disruption, the appropriate environment for working, learning, or changing behavior is simply lacking. As one officer put it:

> Security doesn't mean keep them from going over the wall. It means you try to make the guy feel secure, that he's not going to get killed or hurt. . . . So he doesn't have to worry about something happening. . . . If they want to go out, they'll find a way. It's not that kind of security.[3]

In fact, there is a strong relationship between being able to maintain security and being willing to provide inmate programs. As most staff fully recognize, effective treatment initiatives cannot exist in a dangerous or disorderly facility. At the same time, the availability of a variety of institutional programs actually helps staff better manage the institution. In short, custody and treatment go hand in hand.

Of course, even under the best of conditions, correctional institutions are far from the ideal environment for the implementation of meaningful treatment programs. But, in those facilities where basic control is absent, treatment faces a formidable obstacle. On the other hand, the most secure institution might keep the inmates closely confined to their cells, but that would make it next to impossible to provide effective inmate programming. Nor does such restriction prepare inmates for the interaction with others that is inevitably encountered upon release. Consequently, the institution is faced with finding the appropriate balance between program operations and security needs.

Security Techniques

Different correctional facilities seek to achieve this balance in different ways. To some extent, emphasis will depend on the security classification of the institution. Certainly, more freedoms and opportunities for program participation are available in minimum-security facilities. However, that does not mean that services must be sacrificed to achieve custodial security. To the contrary, *custody* is a necessary condition for *treatment*.[4]

Custody is achieved in part through the architectural features and security hardware of the physical plant itself. But even the most architecturally sound institution designed for the highest level of security also requires such control procedures as separation, restricted movement, counts, searches, and the regulation of everything from visiting and correspondence to tools and property.

Throughout the remainder of this chapter, we will see how physical features, combined with control techniques, function together to maintain custodial security.

ARCHITECTURAL DESIGN

The physical design of a correctional facility largely reflects its philosophy. As an example, look at the forbidding prison "fortresses" surrounded by thick, impenetrable concrete walls that were built in the twentieth century. The cold, uninviting atmosphere of such a sternly institutional structure immediately communicates a morbid impression of the prison as a symbol of punishment.

Although prison architecture has progressed beyond such harsh origins, the need to incorporate security remains a primary consideration. The challenge now has become integrating the "dual mission" of treatment and

EXHIBIT 8.1
Towering fortress-like walls presented a forbidding perimeter for high-security prisons constructed during the early twentieth century.

security into facility design.[5] In addition, the American Correctional Association has established certain minimum standards that institutions seeking the endorsement of ACA accreditation are required to meet. Although the internal and external security measures built into prisons today may be somewhat more subtle, upon entering a prison there is little doubt about where you are. For an inside account of the impact of prison security on a newly arriving visitor, see the next "Close-up on Corrections."

CLOSE-UP ON CORRECTIONS
Welcome to Lebanon

More than the miles of razor-sharp concertina wire that surround the institution, more than the guard towers that loom over the compound, it is the clanging of the three-inch thick steel doors that defines what life is like inside the prison.

In some respects, your first view of Lebanon is disappointing. There's no shoving and pushing going on. Nobody is manacled. The inmates don't march in lock step; the officers don't even carry guns. In fact, it all seems pretty tame.

But a senior correctional officer quickly puts things into focus. "This is not a boys' camp," he says, "You never forget what they're here for." Adds another officer, "You can't totally relax in here. If you do, you're a fool." . . .

Tuesday is laundry day. . . . In the space of 35 minutes, all 2,000 inmates walk the length of the prison, deposit their old sheets and pillowcases in large hampers, pickup clean linen, and head back to their cells. It is the single biggest mass movement among the inmates that takes place at Lebanon, and it presents . . . security problems.

During the exchange, inmates are required—as always—to walk along the right-hand wall. . . . The sheets are . . . folded and placed over the left shoulder, allowing the officer to watch the inmates' hands and ensure that no weapons or contraband are being transported.

The most obvious security problem, however, is the simple fact that 2,000 inmates are in one place at one time. That's a lot of men to watch.

Source: Grace L. Wojda, Raymond G. Wojda, Norman Erik Smith, and Richard K. Jones, *Behind Bars* (Alexandria, VA: American Correctional Association, 1991), pp. 3–1, 11.

External Security

Simply by looking at the external physical plant, it is often possible to determine the security classification of a correctional institution. The higher the security classification, the more specific "reminders" there will be of the institution's custodial function.

As noted earlier, maximum-security institutions have traditionally had a **perimeter** composed of high walls. Building miles and miles of walls around a prison compound has, however, become extremely expensive. More recently, walls have tended to be replaced by the type of fencing common in medium-custody facilities, topped with rows of razor wire for added security.

perimeter: outside boundary of a correctional facility, formed by walls, fences, and/or layers of razor wire.

At various points throughout the perimeter, guard towers are located, sometimes surrounded by bulletproof glass and equipped with search-lights. From these towers, armed officers with binoculars constantly survey the area for signs of disturbances, escapes, or anything else that is out of the ordinary. In fact, it has been said that, "if there is any doubt as to the nature of the institution . . . the inmate may merely glance at the walls. The tower guard symbolizes the stern hand of the community that has placed him in exile."[6]

In addition, ground posts may be situated between towers on the outside perimeter. These are staffed during times when there is low visibility from the towers, such as during fogs or storms. In some very high-security facilities, ground sensors—designed to sound an alarm or alert personnel when activated—may also be installed in areas inside the perimeter fences that are off-limits.

Regardless of their specific features, however, all prisons are designed to separate convicted offenders from law-abiding citizens. Essentially, they are places where social isolation is "a matter of policy" as well as a somewhat misguided "approach to rehabilitation."[7]

Internal Security

To further enforce the isolation of prisoners, the entrance to correctional facilities (called the sallyport) is secured by a series of locked gates, with passage in and out controlled by the officer on duty. Search procedures for those entering the compound will vary according to the security classification of the prison. However, even prisons with the same security level may vary the intensity of searches according to the particular administrative policy of the institution. Procedures range from a superficial "frisk" to the use of a metal detector or the inspectroscope equipment used to screen carry-on baggage for airline security. The limitation of using such equipment in corrections is that, while it can detect metal weapons, it does not identify drugs or nonmetallic contraband items. Now, however, there is a handheld device called the WANDD (weapons and nonpermitted devices detector) that can detect contraband ranging from plastic knives to cell phones.[8]

Inside the prison, the physical plant is constructed to limit and monitor movement throughout the compound. In addition to the ground posts and guard towers, this can be accomplished through closed-circuit TV monitors, centralized locking devices, control booths, alarms, magnetic data strips, and computer-controlled door access. In fact, closed-circuit TV now has the capability to use artificial intelligence, which detects unusual movements and automatically reports trends to a control center.[9] Moreover, it will not be long before existing methods of electronic security are surpassed by biometric recognition—use of various parts of the body (e.g., retina, voice, fingerprints, etc.) to confirm personal identification.[10] For an inside look at some of the sophisticated technology that is increasingly being used to maintain security, see the next "Close-up on Corrections."

CLOSE-UP ON CORRECTIONS
Technological Advances Anticipated Tomorrow

While some may sound like fictional gadgets from a *Star Wars* movie, all of the following initiatives are either ongoing research projects or upcoming priorities of the National Law Enforcement and Corrections Technology Center:

- *cell phone detection*—technology to detect, locate, and neutralize the illicit use of cell phones and other electronic equipment in correctional facilities, without interfering with staff radio frequencies;
- *tracking and monitoring systems*—monitoring the location of staff and inmates with radio frequency technology;
- *improved contraband detection*—incorporating multiple technologies into a single transportable device to detect a broad range of contraband;
- *staff identification, location, and duress alert*—technology to continuously locate staff so they can be helped in case of emergency;
- *wireless inmate surveillance and monitoring*—detection systems that automatically alert officials when specific actions occur (e.g., escape attempts, violence, and other criminal activities) and notify staff of unauthorized absence from approved areas or unauthorized presence in forbidden areas;
- *complex data integration*—automated technologies to integrate and analyze complex data sets (e.g., inmate telephone calls, visitation records, gang records, inmate financial transactions) in order to identify criminal activity and security threats;
- *biohazard protective apparel for correctional officers*—workday apparel to protect staff against commonly encountered body fluid hazards (e.g., blood, feces, and urine);
- *prevention of airborne disease transmission*—sterilization units that disinfect areas of a facility by using ultraviolet light to break down bacteria in food, air, and water.

Source: Compiled from Thomas V. Williams, Francis R. Ford, and Chuck Dunn, "UVGI Airborne and Surface Pathogen Control in a Large County Jail," *American Jails* (January/February, 2009), pp. 63–67, as well as information on websites of the U.S. Department of Justice, National Institute of Justice (http://www.ojp.usdoj.gov/nij/topics/corrections/technologies/institutional-priorities.htm) and NIJ's National Law Enforcement and Corrections Technology Center (http://www.justnet.org/Pages/InstitutionalCorrectionsTechnologyPriorities.aspx).

Not all facilities have such high-tech equipment, but virtually every maximum or medium institution will have a system of double door security monitored from control booths, whereby no two consecutive doors or gates can be opened at the same time. Movement therefore occurs sequentially, from one security post to the next, with the rear gate always closing behind you before the upcoming gate is opened. In this way, if a disturbance occurs during movement, it can be separated from the rest of the population, or one entire area of the compound can be closed off to keep an uprising from spreading further.

Vulnerability Analysis

All of these security features—from external hardware to internal rules and regulations—function together to promote the custodial security of the institution. They help to assure that those who are not authorized to do so neither come in nor get out. At an even more sophisticated level, vulnerability analysis has now enabled techniques employed in homeland security to be adapted to the correctional environment. Using both performance and policy compliance measures, this unique technique defines threats and identifies potential vulnerabilities, actually putting a quantifiable number on the level of risks in the physical protection system:

> The key to an effective vulnerability analysis program is to evaluate staff compliance with policy and the performance of security systems (both physical and human). . . . Sound correctional policies and procedures are the foundation for institutional security, but an ongoing assessment of staff and system performance is necessary to ensure the safety of staff, inmates, and the public.[11]

CONTROL PROCEDURES

Even the best and most modern physical plant represents only part of what is needed for secure custodial control. The structure and hardware work hand in hand with the people and procedures used to ensure institutional security. Electronic gadgetry cannot replace the need for operational procedures that provide further controls within the physical structure.

As correctional administrators have cautioned, it is not the hardware that catches escapees or breaks up fights. In the end, security is primarily dependent on personnel.

Facilities differ considerably with regard to how restrictive they are and how rigorously rules are enforced. Obviously, those with high-security classifications will have the most severe restrictions and will be less tolerant of infractions. But again, even within prisons of similar custodial classification, there will be variations in terms of how extensively inmates are segregated, how strictly movement is controlled, how frequently counts and searches are conducted, how much effort is devoted to property and tool control, or how often visits are permitted. Moreover, the specific rules and regulations governing inmate behavior will vary in terms of content, enforcement, and resulting penalties. But, regardless of the implementation differences, there are certain general techniques that are relatively universal.

segregation:
physical isolation of an inmate from the general population to minimize interaction with others.

Principles of Segregation

Just as the prison itself is physically separated from the outside world, **segregation** within the institution isolates inmates from each other. It is based on the premise that *minimizing interaction* between inmates also minimizes their opportunity for disruptive behavior—including everything from planning escapes and dealing in contraband to engaging in fights and assaults.

In the most secure prisons, each inmate is confined in a separate cell. Unlike the individual living units of new-generation jails, however, the cells do not open into a dayroom to which inmates have free access. Rather, movement in and out of the cell is strictly regulated—often confined to brief periods of recreation or visiting—and always under the close supervision of a correctional officer. While such an approach serves the security interests of the institution, there are trade-offs in terms of the psychological effects of isolation, as well as the limits it imposes on the development of social skills or participation in institutional programs.

With the pressures of crowding in recent years, more and more inmates are being doubled up in cells originally intended for single occupancy. As a result, many facilities have two or more inmates in a cell, while others use the dormitory concept. Group living has definite social and psychological advantages over single-cell isolation. But here, too, there are trade-offs, since it is far more difficult to control group behavior, particularly when observation is limited to an officer occasionally passing by the cellblock on routine "patrol."

Types of Segregation

Of course, not everyone is equally capable of living amicably in a dormitory, and the weak are easy prey for the strong in such an environment. Thus segregation also can be used to respond to problems created by group living. For instance, an inmate who fears for his safety in a dormitory can request isolation for personal protection. Some inmates are administratively assigned to **protective custody**, as in high-profile cases or those involving former judges, police, or correctional officers whose safety in the general population would be in jeopardy. Once someone is assigned or moved to protective custody, it is, however, very difficult for him to assimilate into (or return to) the general population, since that person now has a reputation for being unable to stand up for himself.

Administrative segregation refers to any number of reasons for which an inmate may be separated other than disciplinary infractions. Examples might include those experiencing deteriorating mental health, undergoing "mood swings," or requiring gradual reentry following hospitalization. In essence, any circumstances that call for greater attention and supervision than would be available in the general population could result in administrative segregation. In such cases, the inmate has not necessarily done anything that would be a violation of institutional rules.

In contrast, **disciplinary segregation** *is* used for punitive purposes in response to rule infractions. Disciplinary segregation may include various levels of supervision (ranging from "close" to "maximum"), but it is most often associated with solitary confinement. Under solitary conditions, inmates spend all but a few recreational

protective custody: segregation either requested by an inmate in fear of danger, or assigned by staff concerned about an inmate's safety in general population.

administrative segregation: separate confinement for inmates who need closer attention or supervision than is feasible in general population.

disciplinary (or punitive) segregation: the isolation of disruptive inmates whose rule infractions endanger safety and security.

hours in their cells, and additional privileges may also be restricted. Inmates are confined to such conditions for a specified length of time following a disciplinary hearing (unlike administrative segregation, which is more subject to staff discretion). The function of disciplinary segregation is to isolate and control those whose behavior presents a problem for others or for the overall security of the facility.

Without violating constitutional protections, there are a relatively limited number of benefits and privileges that can be withdrawn through disciplinary action. When these have been exhausted, there may be no other alternative but to separate the offender physically, protecting others from assaults, homosexual attacks, or strong-arm tactics. Thus segregation can be used to confine those who are threatening to others, dangerous to themselves, or in need of protective custody from other inmates.

EXHIBIT 8.2
While disciplinary segregation isolates and controls a facility's behavioral problems, it can be an emotionally overwhelming experience for the inmate.

Controlled Movement

Another way that inmates are physically restricted is through closely **controlled movement** within the institution. This is an important feature of custody, since every time inmates are moved—particularly in groups—there is a potential security risk (as noted in the laundry situation described in the first "Close-up" of this chapter, "Welcome to Lebanon"). In addition, it is essential to know where all inmates are at all times, which becomes increasingly difficult with frequent movements.

The amount of movement allowed within a facility will largely depend on the institution's security classification. In minimum-security facilities, there are few restraints—inmates are permitted to go relatively freely from their living quarters to work assignments, recreation areas, and dining halls. But maximum-security prisons reduce the potential for escapes by (among other things) closely supervising and very strictly limiting movement. The basic concept is that the *less* inmates need to be moved, the easier it is for an institution to maintain security. But the security advantages of restricted movement must be weighed against the disadvantages of excessive boredom accompanying prolonged confinement.

controlled movement: restricting freedom of movement in order to better ensure institutional security.

Individual Movement. In the past, a system of passes was typically used to control movement. For example, a prisoner needing to go from a work assignment to a counselor would get a pass from a correctional officer, which would include the time of departure and designated location. The pass would then be signed by the correctional officer at the identified destination. Upon the inmate's return, the officer would note the time and file the pass.

This manual method of recording movement has many shortcomings. It is "time-consuming, subject to error," and potentially dangerous, since each time officers log one person's transfer they are "temporarily unable to keep a close watch on other inmates."[12] More recently, a modern high-tech approach that automatically records all transfers has become available as an alternative to the pass system. Each inmate wears a bracelet which contains a bar code that is scanned at various locations throughout the facility whenever the inmate is moved. Like the bar code reader used at supermarket checkout counters, an electronic scanning device produces a printout that records precisely when and where the inmate was moved throughout the day. In fact, the same system can be used to obtain books from the library or to charge items purchased at the commissary (facility store) to an inmate's account.[13]

External Transportation. To limit the need for transportation outside of the prison, most large institutions provide as many services as possible within the compound. For example, through the use of "telemedicine," medical professionals have been able to confer with inmate patients without ever setting foot in the facility or transporting the inmate. (See the next "Close-up on Corrections".) Judges can likewise conduct various types of legal proceedings through two-way video monitoring. In fact, some correctional facilities even treat mentally ill inmates through "telepsychiatry."[14] However, there will always be a need for some external movement in order to transport inmates to other correctional facilities, hospitals, trials, funerals, and so on.

CLOSE-UP ON CORRECTIONS
Telemedicine in Action

In 1995, a Colorado Department of Corrections inmate was transported from a state correctional facility to a Denver hospital for a follow-up appointment related to an earlier knee injury. During the trip to the hospital, he managed to release himself from his restraints. When the vehicle arrived and the deputies opened the door, the inmate bolted, knee injury notwithstanding. He sprinted through the hospital parking lot and escaped into a residential neighborhood, and has not been seen since. His timing in this escape was fortuitous, since in early 1997 his correctional facility implemented a telemedicine program which would have eliminated the need to transport him off-site.

Telemedicine involves linking primary care and specialty doctors with inmates via video or other electronic media for selected medical consultations, which eliminates the need to transport some inmates to an outside medical facility. Telemedicine can be used to increase access to health care (particularly in remote areas), improve access to specialists, and provide faster diagnosis and treatment.

The overall impact of this technology falls into three categories—cost savings, reduced escape attempts, and improved medical care, with access to more specialized services. Telemedicine also entails a number of intangible benefits—e.g., one facility in Virginia which now provides cardiology-related care through telemedicine has noticed a reduced number of chest pain complaints because inmates know they will no longer be taken off-site for diagnosis.

Sources: Compiled from Kevin Raines, Joni Toenjes, and Allan Liebgott, "Telemedicine . . . It's Not Just for Rural Jails," *American Jails* (May/June, 1998), pp. 9–21; Mark F. Fitzgibbons and Tracy Gunter-Justice, "Telemedicine and Mental Health in Jails: A New Tool for an Old Problem," *Corrections Today* (October, 2000), pp. 104–107; and Barbara Drazga, "Telemedicine and Corrections," *Correctional News* (July/August, 2000), p. 43. See also "Telemedicine Can Reduce Correctional Health Care Costs: An Evaluation of a Prison Telemedicine Network," available online at http://www.ncjrs.org/telemedicine/toc.html.

Although staff do not carry weapons while supervising inmates within the facility, those transporting inmates to the outside are almost always armed. The inmates themselves are restrained by handcuffs, which are sometimes attached to waist chains. Leg irons may also be used to control a prisoner's stride and eliminate a foot race.

Not only are outside trips well planned, but in particularly dangerous situations, a "chase" vehicle may follow the transporting vehicle to provide backup assistance in case an escape is attempted. Given the risks, costs, and labor involved, it is not surprising to find correctional agencies increasingly contracting with private companies for transportation services. But not all inmates being transferred from one facility to another justify such expensive, high-security arrangements. In fact, as part of a cost-cutting initiative, some low-risk inmates traveling to minimum-security facilities in the federal prison system may ride without escort on public buses.[15]

Conducting Counts

The purpose of restricting internal and external inmate movement is naturally to keep track of precisely where everyone is at all times. The location of inmates is also confirmed periodically through headcounts. In the past, **counts** were only able to be conducted physically by correctional officers. But here, too, technology now exists in terms of a sensor device worn like a wristwatch that not only has an automated headcount feature but can also be used by the inmate to signal for help in a dangerous situation.[16]

counts: periodic verification of the number of inmates in custody, conducted most frequently in maximum security prisons.

Counts are one of the most important functions of custody. Because the count is so significant, other activities stop when it is conducted. In facilities without sophisticated technology, inmates may be required to stand in order to be properly identified. But, regardless of the specific procedures employed, officers need to be careful to identify each inmate personally. Assuming, for instance, that a bulky form under blankets on a bed is actually the cell's occupant gives an escaping inmate valuable time until the next count is conducted. On the other hand, inefficient counting which erroneously indicates that an inmate is missing can cause serious disruption of normal institutional operations while a needless recount or search is mounted. Any count that does not match the number on the official roster (whether over or under) results in everyone being "locked down" in the living units while a rapid recheck is made and another full count is conducted. If the discrepancy still exists, emergency search procedures are activated.

Escapes

Having exactly the right number of inmates in custody at any given time is critical to every correctional institution. Any fewer than there should be results in activating an escape alarm, notifying law enforcement agencies, and closing down normal operations while an extensive search is mounted. For a firsthand account of the adrenalin-pumping response to a missing inmate, see the next "Close-up on Corrections."

CLOSE-UP ON CORRECTIONS
Inmate's Escaped!

It's been another long, slow day at work, which is routine around here. The inmates are mostly out on one of many labor details; picking up litter along the roadsides, paving new streets, or doing maintenance jobs in and around the institution. Pretty soon, they'll trickle in, go down to the mess hall to eat and then prepare for the evening's activities. I am getting antsy, looking forward to a long weekend. . . .

[T]he daywatch supervisor bursts into the control center where I am assigned. "Owens!" he cries, "I think David . . . is missing! Let's do a quick count and make sure!" Although I'm alarmed, I'm hardly surprised. Several weeks of excruciating boredom drift by, and now suddenly, it is time to act, to remember procedure, to try to keep a cool head while all hell breaks loose around me. I run down the hall to alert the others, then head back to the Control Room. Mr. D. comes running back in, agitated, "O.K. . . . I think we have an escape, let's do it!" He then starts barking orders, and everyone scrambles to lock down the institution and commence the search. . . .

I grab a loaded .357 and jump into the van to search outside the perimeter. The neighborhood consists mostly of ramshackle houses and ancient trailers, many of which are abandoned. As I begin looking around, several of the residents nearby peer out from their homes, their eyes filled with fear and wonderment. My nerves are acting out; I keep hearing sounds inside this one trailer, so I draw my weapon and creep back. I know who this guy is, but I don't know what he'll do if cornered. . . .

It is getting late now, and he has yet to be found. The dragnet has widened over several counties. I have an official from the central office who is riding with me, so I am careful to follow procedure closely. I call in my position to the command post, and am told to return. I am disappointed that I'm unable to return with him as my prisoner, but that feeling is routine. "Next time," I say to myself. I think of the looks on the people's faces as they saw me invade their neighborhood, and I hope for them there won't be a next time. But I know there will, when I least expect it.

Source: Doug Owens, "In Search of Dignity," *Keeper's Voice*, Vol. 13, No. 1 (January, 1992), pp. 23–24.

The overdramatized television and movie accounts of prison breakouts would lead us to believe that escapes are accompanied by elaborate plotting, high suspense, and violent outcomes. But, in real life, escape attempts take many forms. In one case, a telephone call from a "probation officer" requested the release of a prisoner, but a return call to the officer indicated that no such request had been made. The prisoner himself was discovered telephoning from the institution's pay phone.

Many escape attempts are simply "walk-aways," often in conjunction with visiting, outside work assignments, or a low level of institutional security. While there are few escapes from inside the walls of high-security facilities, those are the ones that make the headlines. But, as shown in Exhibit 8.3, almost all escapes are from minimum-security facilities or in conjunction with furloughs, work release, or home confinement.

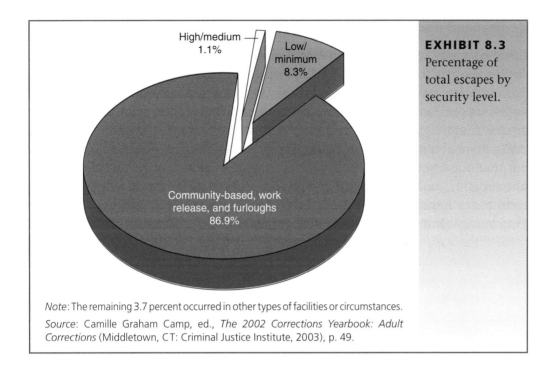

High/medium
1.1%

Low/
minimum
8.3%

Community-based, work
release, and furloughs
86.9%

EXHIBIT 8.3
Percentage of
total escapes by
security level.

Note: The remaining 3.7 percent occurred in other types of facilities or circumstances.

Source: Camille Graham Camp, ed., *The 2002 Corrections Yearbook: Adult Corrections* (Middletown, CT: Criminal Justice Institute, 2003), p. 49.

Most are eventually apprehended.[17] Although escapees do not usually avoid capture for very long, there are always the isolated exceptions. For example, one man who escaped in 1957 from an Alabama prison (where he was serving a 14-year term for stealing pigs) was discovered living in Detroit some 45 years later—although Alabama officials were no longer interested in reincarcerating him.[18] Today, chances of eluding the authorities are not as great. With the "electronic bulletin boards" available in recent years through such nationally broadcast television programs as *America's Most Wanted*, the high visibility given to dangerous escapees assists in their recapture.

CONTRABAND AND SEARCHES

The type of search resulting from an escape extends throughout the institution as well as to the outside community. But other more restricted searches are conducted within the facility on a daily basis. These can include both cell searches and personal (body) searches.

Searches of cells or dormitories (generally referred to as "shakedowns") are conducted routinely, with frequency depending on the facility's security level. The purpose of conducting cell searches is to detect contraband. It therefore stands to reason that the searches should not be so routinely scheduled that inmates are well aware of when they will occur.

LEARNING GOALS

Do you know:
10. what types of searches are conducted in a correctional institution?
11. the definition of contraband?
12. under what conditions cells can be searched?
13. the differences between frisk, strip, and body-cavity searches?

Contraband Control

Contraband consists of any item (or quantity of item) that is not authorized within the institution or an authorized item that is altered from its original state. For example, a certain amount of food may be permitted in one's cell, but hoarding large amounts would be prohibited. A normally authorized item that has been altered could be something as simple as a pen or a plastic eating utensil that is melted down and sharpened into a "shank" (weapon). Some unauthorized items are traditionally forbidden in all correctional institutions, such as liquor, drugs, knives, guns, or other items that could be used as weapons. But, with modern technology have come new additions to contraband lists, such as the rapidly growing problem of smuggling of cell phones.[19]

Facilities vary widely, however, in terms of what is and is not considered contraband. Some go so far as to prohibit such seemingly innocent things as family photos. Some permit inmates to keep a specified amount of money (although it would be a violation to be in possession of a quantity greater than the authorized amount). Others do not permit any money at all in order to discourage theft and gambling. When inmates wish to make purchases from the commissary, the transaction is made by computerized account system through which no actual cash changes hands. Moreover, it is becoming increasingly common practice to require inmates to purchase virtually all authorized personal property from an approved commissary sales list.

The purpose of removing contraband from the facility is to reduce the potential for escapes, fights, threats, and assaults that it creates, thereby promoting the safety and security of both inmates and staff. Moreover, dealing in contraband allows some inmates to have power over others by controlling illicit resources that are in demand. But contraband can never be eliminated completely. There are simply too many sources through which it can pass into the institution—from an embrace during visiting, to interaction with the vendor on a food delivery truck, to contact with a staff member in need of extra money.

Cell Searches

The right to be free from illicit searches is protected under the Fourth Amendment. In free society, it would therefore not usually be legal for a police officer to search your home without a court-issued warrant based on probable cause. But it is entirely different in a correctional facility. While inmates do not lose their constitutional protections, they do not enjoy as much privacy, because of the overriding need to maintain institutional security. Within a correctional facility, general searches can be authorized at any time without specific cause. Thus, searches may be conducted:

- *routinely*, at certain predetermined (but unannounced) times;

- *randomly*, at undetermined, unannounced times; or

- deliberately, based on *reasonable suspicion*, such as information received from a reliable informant.

Correctional officers do not need a warrant or probable cause to justify a search. But they cannot recklessly destroy property in the process of the search. Nor can searches be used to single out any particular person for harassment by, for example, continuously focusing on one cell to the exclusion of all others for no particular reason.

Inmates can be ingenious at finding unsuspected hiding places, particularly in the many cracks and crevices of older institutions. Conducting a thorough cell search can therefore become quite physically disruptive. Tearing apart what is for all practical purposes an inmate's "home" will create ill will if the contents are left carelessly scattered around. Moreover, it is particularly irritating to inmates if their personal possessions are disturbed only to confiscate some insignificant item on the contraband list.

Personal Searches

Since contraband must be transported to one's cell, personal body searches are also routine features of prison life, particularly when an inmate enters or leaves the facility. The intrusiveness of personal searches ranges from a simple frisk (or "pat-down"), to an unclothed strip search, to a body-cavity search. A frisk search is an external inspection of a fully clothed person. It is the least intrusive, since the officer only feels exterior surfaces to determine if any items are being concealed within one's clothing, hair, shoes, and so on.

Much more intrusive is the strip search, in which the naked body and its cavities are visually inspected from all angles. Because strip searches can be very personally degrading, they need to be conducted in a manner that retains as much dignity as possible.

As inmates became increasingly creative in their efforts to conceal contraband, the need for internal body-cavity searches emerged. In fact, body-cavity searches have yielded items ranging from drugs to ammunition, weapons, and tools. Because this is the most intrusive type of search, it demands justification based on reasonable suspicion. Special permission from a higher authority (such as the prison warden) is generally required, and such searches can be performed only by appropriate medical staff. However, a recent technological innovation may one day put an end to exploratory body-cavity searches. Called the body orifice scanning system, it enables the inmate to simply sit in a chair specially designed to detect metal contraband that is concealed internally.[20]

Inmate Supervision

It may seem somewhat illogical to discuss careful contraband control when, at the same time, items such as knives and industrial scissors are available to trusties working in the prison kitchen or sewing shop. Even if these implements are carefully monitored to assure that they do not leave the area, they could be used in a stabbing attempt while in the hands of inmate workers. Careful classification screening is therefore essential when determining such work assignments.

In addition to cautious selection, those on various work details must be closely supervised, particularly when assignments involve work outside the prison compound. Otherwise, those on external work details can be used as a "trafficking service" in contraband items or an underground "messenger service" between other inmates and the outside. Even within the prison, certain work details can provide opportunities for graft, corruption, and contraband trading if officers do not maintain close oversight of inmate activities.

Nor is the correctional officer's responsibility limited to those engaged in work assignments. Throughout the day, the inside of the institution is supervised by operational personnel assigned to each school, factory, or shop, as well as such other areas of the prison as the infirmary, counseling offices, and recreation yard. During these assignments, officers are responsible for constantly observing all activities to detect signs of danger. It is largely through training and experience that operational staff develop the insights and intuition that alert them to the warning signs of imminent danger. But, in the final analysis, it is not so much the explicit control of staff as the implicit cooperation of inmates that enables the system to operate effectively.

CONTACTS WITH THE OUTSIDE

LEARNING GOALS

Do you know:

14. why inmate contact with the outside must be restricted but not eliminated?
15. how correctional institutions restrict an inmate's mail, phone, and personal contacts?

Beyond controls that restrict freedom within the compound, everyone confined to a correctional institution is subject to some degree of isolation from the rest of society. Yet it is largely through visits, phone calls, and letters that inmates maintain ties with the outside.

On the one hand, it is important to retain such communication because of its constructive influence on inmate behavior and morale. External contacts help to reduce the negative impact of socializing only with other criminals day after day. They promote a more civilizing atmosphere, help to maintain social bonds, and assist with eventual readjustment to society.

On the other hand, however, such interactions present security risks. They can facilitate both escapes and the introduction of contraband. The key is to find the proper balance between restricting outside contacts and jeopardizing institutional security. As a result, limits have been placed on phone calls, written correspondence, and visiting.

Telephone and Mail

Although all correctional institutions permit inmates to use the telephone, the number of calls authorized is generally limited according to one's security classification. Minimum-security facilities might have a centrally located telephone for all to use with few restrictions. In contrast, medium and maximum custody are more likely to involve individual arrangements for telephone access, such as using modular outlets to enable a phone to be moved into cells during designated times.

Since prisoners do not have the immediate convenience of picking up the phone, texting, or emailing, written correspondence is important to them. Anyone who has ever been away from home in an unfamiliar environment for an extended period of time can appreciate how much letters from family help to ease loneliness, tension, and anxiety.

In the past, all incoming mail and packages were very closely scrutinized—to the point of censorship. Arbitrary censorship has now been replaced by practices that can be justified on the basis of institutional security, such as inspection for contraband. As prison populations expanded, it became increasingly difficult and labor-intensive to read and censor all correspondence, so prisons came to rely on spot-checks for contraband. While letters from attorneys, judges, or other government officials cannot be either censored or read, inmates may be required to open such correspondence in the presence of a correctional officer if transmission of contraband is suspected.

Visiting Policies

Approved visiting lists will generally be limited, although immediate family members are almost always included, and one's attorney can visit at any time. Other relatives and friends may need further justification, particularly in maximum-security institutions.

In addition to who can visit, prisons regulate how often they can come. Again, the number of visits allowed may depend on custody classification. Moreover, a severely crowded facility may need to further restrict the frequency of visits simply because of operational inability to manage the necessary movements. For such reasons, research indicates that visitation policies have become more restrictive in recent years.[21]

Beyond the obstacles presented by institutional regulations, it may be difficult for an inmate's family to visit when the prison is located in a rural area far from home and is not accessible to public transportation. It is a dedicated family member who will go to the expense, take the time, and suffer the humiliation often involved in visiting someone in prison—which is hardly conducive to maintaining family unity.

Part of the reluctance to visit those in prison relates to the abnormal atmosphere surrounding the conditions under which outside contact takes place. Privacy is virtually nonexistent. Visits are supervised and carefully monitored by uniformed correctional officers to reduce the introduction of contraband. Inmates are searched before and after each visit, and visitors themselves may be subject to frisk searches as well.

In very high-security situations, visitors and residents are placed in two different rooms. They are separated by a window of plate glass, with a telephone device used for communication. Visits in a lower-security environment may be conducted around long tables, with inmates sitting on one side and visitors on the other, sometimes monitored by video surveillance cameras. The least restrictive are **contact visits**, which permit physical contact between inmates and visitors (within specified rules). Of course, with greater visiting freedom also comes greater potential for the introduction of contraband. As a result of such considerations, more and more facilities have installed video visitation systems,[22] which both minimize institutional security concerns and overcome the many difficulties and inconveniences encountered by visitors.

contact visits: the authorization of physical contact (within specified limits) during visits.

LEARNING GOALS

Do you know:

16. the difference between furloughs, contact visits, and conjugal visits?

17. the advantages and disadvantages of conjugal visiting?

Conjugal Visits

Even the most liberal and informal visiting procedures cannot replace the intimacy of sexual relationships. Confinement in prison can severely strain a marriage and actually represents grounds for divorce in a number of states. Some believe that sexual deprivations are to be expected as an inherent part of the punishment function of incarceration. Others express concern about the promotion of homosexual activities when

EXHIBIT 8.4
Inmates who do not qualify for contact visits might use these visiting booths to interact with those on the outside.

Source: Courtesy of Datapoint, Inc.

the legitimate expression of basic sexual drives is denied. In response to such concerns, several states have authorized inmates to participate in **conjugal visits**. But, while unsupervised visits from members of the opposite sex have been common in a number of South American and Scandinavian countries, that has not been common practice in the United States.

Although it was not openly admitted, conjugal visiting has actually been available in American prisons from time to time on an informal basis. South Carolina initiated such visits in the late nineteenth century, and Mississippi started the practice informally at the state penitentiary in Parchman early in the twentieth century. Over the years, several other states did likewise, but more recently, only five states have retained conjugal visiting.[23]

Research indicates that conjugal visiting has a significant positive effect on family stability, as well as a significant negative effect on involvement in prison violence.[24] Other advantages of conjugal visits include fewer pressures to engage in homosexuality, improved morale, and a strengthening of family bonds. The potential loss of conjugal visiting privileges is also a strong restraint upon behavior. But they are not without drawbacks. For one thing, if visits are limited to married inmates, everyone will not qualify, and the provocation of seeing others participate may promote homosexuality among those who are ineligible. Additionally, some wives may not participate for a variety of reasons, particularly if the process is viewed as degrading. Participants also are faced with issues surrounding pregnancies and sexually transmitted disease.

For the correctional institution, both administrative and operational issues are involved. Administratively, there are concerns surrounding the verification of marriages and the question of whether or not to accept common-law relationships. Operationally, potential problems include the difficulty of controlling contraband and enforcing appropriate behavior, along with resentment on the part of those who do not have access to conjugal visits.[25] Thus the question becomes whether the benefits outweigh the risks. For more insights into the answer, see the point–counterpoint debate in the next "Close-up on Corrections."

conjugal visits: authorization of visits enabling sexual relations, to maintain family bonds and reduce prison homosexuality.

CLOSE-UP ON CORRECTIONS
Conjugal Visits—A Matter of Logic

Besides preparing inmates for re-entry, private family visits can also maintain and strengthen family bonds. At the same time, such visits are a behavior management program that rewards positive behavior among inmates. . . .

For many now drug-free inmates, this may be the first time they are accepting their parental responsibilities. Thus, although parents and children living for a few days in a motel-type setting on the prison grounds or furloughed to a nearby motel may be a very artificial setting, such visits could begin to address some of the problems that every family must solve to function properly.

[A review of] all previous studies on visitation concluded that an inmate who receives visits is six times less likely to recidivate. . . . Besides the family, private family visits can be beneficial to prison administration and staff by providing inmates incentive to follow prison rules. Such a program is by far one of the best ways to reward positive inmate behavior.

Source: Charles Sullivan, "Private Family Visits Are a Matter of Logic," *Corrections Today* (June, 2003), p. 18.

Costs Outweigh Benefits

Instead of promoting healthy family bonding, the unsupervised nature of conjugal visits may actually lead to an increased risk to the physical safety of family members in some cases. . . . Supervised visitation that enables interaction in a more secure environment may better serve families involved in such dysfunctional relationships. . . .

[Moreover], conjugal visitation increases the risk of spreading sexually transmitted diseases by an already identified high-risk population. . . . States that have initiated such visitation programs are forced to address the tough moral and ethical dilemma of permitting conjugal visitation for offenders known to be infected. . . .

Conjugal visitation also presents an ethical dilemma by increasing the chance of pregnancy when the incarcerated partner often lacks the ability to provide financial and emotional support to the partner and resulting child. Children born as the result of conjugal visitation are denied important emotional bonding with the incarcerated parent. . . . Additionally, there is a disinclination of the public to accept programs that provide extra privileges to convicted felons at a cost to the taxpayer.

Source: Reginald A. Wilkinson, "The Cost of Conjugal Visitation Outweighs the Benefits," *Corrections Today* (June, 2003), p. 19.

Furloughs

furloughs: brief temporary release, with the inmate expected to return to confinement when required.

Many correctional administrators who are opposed to conjugal visits favor the use of **furloughs** instead. Essentially, furloughs involve a brief period of *temporary release*—often over a weekend—with the understanding that the prisoner will return to the institution at a specified time. Because a large portion of those incarcerated are single or divorced, more inmates will qualify for furloughs. Moreover, the emphasis with furloughs is on broader social reintegration rather than the exclusive sexual focus of conjugal visits. Another benefit is that, rather than seeing their parent in a prison setting, children can interact with mom or dad at home during furloughs.

Offering inmates temporary freedom does, however, entail obvious dangers. Although efforts are made to select those awarded furloughs carefully, there is always the possibility that the desire to live on the outside again will be too great to resist. Absconding is generally not as great a problem as might be expected, since there is considerable pressure from other inmates to abide by the rules so that the privilege is not revoked for everyone. In fact, only about 1 percent of furloughs result in either escape or commission of a new crime.[26]

But there is always the potential of awarding a furlough to someone who does not have sufficient self-control to avoid becoming involved in crime. This concern was propelled into a major national issue that affected the 1988 presidential election—when an inmate who was granted a weekend pass in Massachusetts (Willie Horton) engaged in a series of violent crimes that ultimately reflected upon the campaign of former Governor Michael Dukakis.[27]

As a result of the public outcry following the Horton case, a number of legislatures implemented much more restrictive measures governing furlough eligibility. The tightening of furloughs following this public backlash created a situation of "zero tolerance"—similar to reducing the driving speed limit to 10 mph to prevent traffic crashes. While their use had begun to increase in a number of states by the 1990s,[28] even the designation of "furlough" has changed to "transitional control," presumably in an effort to portray an unpopular practice in a more positive light.

Like conjugal visits, furloughs are not without risks. The challenge is therefore to strike a reasonable compromise between an overly lenient policy that can incur public safety risks and one that overly restricts the benefits of family preservation to a handful of the most model prisoners.

INSTITUTIONAL RULES AND DISCIPLINE

LEARNING GOALS

Do you know:

18. what disciplinary procedures are employed when an inmate violates the rules?
19. what rights inmates have when facing severe disciplinary action?
20. what sanctions can be imposed for rule violations?

All of the procedures discussed thus far—from segregating prisoners within the institution to restricting their contacts with the outside—are designed to control inmate behavior. Not all prisons are so rigidly controlled. All do, however, have provisions for shaping individual behavior for the benefit of the overall population. As we saw with movement, counts, and outside contacts, these provisions will be more relaxed in minimum-security facilities. But inmates in higher-custody classifications presumably lack the self-control necessary to constrain their own behavior. The purpose of institutional rules and regulations is therefore to regulate conduct and maintain order through externally imposed restrictions.

Rules and Regulations

One of the first things that a newly arriving inmate receives upon initial reception is the rulebook outlining the "dos and don'ts" that are expected during the period of confinement. Rules are designed to promote adjustment to the institutional routine and thereby maintain order. The nature of inmate rules will vary depending on the size and security classification of the facility. But virtually all institutions will have at least some number of general rules governing such things as:

- *inmate–officer relationships* (e.g., addressing employees respectfully, immediately obeying orders issued by officers);

- *relationships with other inmates* (e.g., no fighting, assaults, homosexual behavior, or conspiring with other inmates);

- *prohibited activities* (e.g., no profanity, gambling, trafficking, bartering, trading, attempting escape, running, etc.);

- *prohibited items* (e.g., no unauthorized items that are designated as contraband);

- *personal hygiene/grooming* (e.g., requirements regarding personal attire and cleanliness);

- *outside contacts* (e.g., mail, phone, and visiting restrictions);

- *overall institutional regulations* (e.g., prohibited areas of the compound, personal property limitations, disciplinary and grievance procedures, the schedule of daily routines governing eating, sleeping, and so forth).

In addition to these general rules, some institutions extend regulations to very precise details. But the longer and more complex the list of rules, the more difficult they are to enforce. Additionally, the more rules are viewed as petty harassments, the more likely they are to be violated. On the one hand, too much rigidity can promote resistance. On the other hand, too little regulation can produce confusion and lack of control.

Rule Enforcement

Whatever the institution's specific rules are, it is up to the operational staff to assure that they are being observed and, if not, to deal with infractions. How firmly regulations are enforced will vary considerably, depending on the institution, the situation, and the particular officer involved. Ultimately, it is through both formal disciplinary measures (i.e., rule enforcement) and informal communication that a process for managing inmate behavior develops.

disciplinary action reports: paperwork submitted by a correctional officer to officially document a rule violation.

Correctional officers have the day-to-day authority to enforce rules. That does not mean that they have the power to inflict formal punishment for disciplinary infractions. Operational staff have some limited authority to handle minor misconduct. Major violations, however, are "written up" on official **disciplinary action reports** and submitted through the organizational chain of command.

Typically, major violations in prisons include gambling, sexual activities, fighting, and assaults. Anything involving physical harm or a major security violation is most likely to be officially referred for formal disciplinary action. But, as the employee guidelines of one prison state, "Minor matters of discipline, where no danger to life, security or property exists, shall be handled quietly and routinely."[29]

Disciplinary Procedures

When a major infraction is reported, upper-level command staff must determine if further action is warranted. If so, the inmate is afforded a hearing before either a

EXHIBIT 8.5
Major violations are logged into daily records, documented on disciplinary reports, and forwarded through the agency's chain of command.

Source: Courtesy of the American Correctional Association.

hearing examiner or a disciplinary committee. While some institutional committees are drawn from the ranks of custodial, treatment, and/or classification staff, others invoke the services of an outside hearing examiner. This has developed in response to concerns that using staff in disciplinary proceedings is inherently biased against the inmate, tending to favor institutional concerns. The outside hearing examiner is viewed as capable of conducting a more impartial tribunal. Additionally, committees can also take up excessive staff time, so using a hearing examiner may be more cost-effective. It also enables the examiner to concentrate on the cases at hand, rather than viewing the hearing as an inconvenience added to one's regularly scheduled job.

In the past, inmates had no universally recognized due process rights during disciplinary hearings. In fact, correctional administrators were free to impose penalties without a hearing. Needless to say, this widespread discretion was open to potential abuse, particularly in prisons with little public oversight or administrative restraints. In an effort to assure more objective and impartial proceedings, the Supreme Court ruled that inmates are entitled to certain due process protections when facing severe disciplinary action (e.g., that which would further restrict their freedom or extend their confinement). Thus, with the *Wolff v. McDonnell* case (1974),[30] inmates facing such penalties became entitled to:

- advance written notice of the charges;

- the right to a fair and impartial hearing;

- the right to present evidence and call witnesses on their behalf (when permission to do so "will not be unduly hazardous to institutional safety or correctional goals");

- use of counsel or counsel substitute for illiterate accused persons or those who otherwise cannot understand the proceedings;

- a written statement of the decision reached and the reasons for it.

However, more recently in the case of *Sandin v. Conner*, the Supreme Court modified its position, no longer requiring the procedural protections outlined in *Wolff v. McDonnell* in disciplinary cases where sanctions are limited to segregation (and therefore do not affect the inmate's "liberty interest" in being free from restraint).[31]

Inmates are not legally entitled to appeal the outcome of disciplinary hearings. Nevertheless, many institutions provide for an appeal to the prison warden, and some allow appeals beyond the institution to the state director of corrections. Nor does internal disciplinary action preclude subsequent criminal prosecution. If warranted by the offense, that would not constitute "double jeopardy."[32]

Disciplinary Penalties

Aside from solitary confinement or disciplinary segregation, the most severe penalty an inmate can receive is loss of credits reducing the length of their sentence (e.g., good time or gain time). No inmate wants to jeopardize a release date. Time credits therefore represent both a major incentive to maintain good behavior and the ultimate penalty for misconduct.

Moreover, many of the harsh punishments used in the past (such as bread-and-water diets and corporal punishment) have been ruled unconstitutional. Restricting visits, commissary privileges, recreation, and the like must also be done within legal limits. As a result, the loss of time credit is the one primary behavioral control mechanism that correctional personnel still have to induce compliance with institutional rules and regulations.

LEARNING GOALS

Do you know:
21. how officers exercise formal and informal controls to regulate inmate behavior?
22. what problems occur when officers either over- or underenforce institutional rules?

INMATE MANAGEMENT

Older, long-timer inmates who simply want to "do their time" as quietly as possible recognize that the rules exist largely for their own protection and therefore tend to support rule enforcement. Those who are younger, recent arrivals, and more militant, however, are more likely to view institutional regulations as a form of repression and a personal challenge. When cooperation and voluntary compliance are not forthcoming, it is the correctional officer's job to maintain control by initiating the disciplinary process.

Although officers must be observant to detect violations, the responsibility of managing inmates is certainly not restricted to simple visual surveillance. If that were the case, closed-circuit television could largely replace the need for human supervision. This point was vividly made in one minimum-security institution when a perimeter fence was installed: "Staff were taken from interacting with inmates and committed to operating and monitoring a fence. Perhaps it was not surprising that the fence did not reduce the number of escapes."[33]

It is the officer's ability to communicate verbally that is of greatest importance—a skill that is not confined to issuing orders but, rather, one which, when used properly, establishes an effective working relationship with the inmate population.

Rules and Relationships

Just as the rules themselves must be properly balanced between too much rigidity and too little regulation, officers also find that they must steer a middle course between severity and laxity in enforcing them. Institutional regulations represent the "tools of discipline." It takes experience, sensitivity, and training to learn how to use them properly, just as it takes practice and instruction to use any other kind of tool.

The extent to which regulations are enforced varies from institution to institution. But, even within the same facility, enforcement styles can vary from one shift to another and from one officer to another. It is the administrator's job to assure that there is general enforcement consistency, which cannot be achieved simply by telling operational staff that they are expected to "fully enforce all rules at all times." Like police officers enforcing society's laws on the street, correctional officers find that it is neither possible nor practical to do so. Faced with a wide variety of regulations, many of which are ambiguous, they have a great deal of discretion in deciding what rules will be enforced, against whom, and under what circumstances.

Formal and Informal Controls

It is not only by enforcing the rulebook that inmates are managed. As in free society, institutional behavior is controlled through both rules and relationships. Parents, for example, establish certain boundaries governing their children's actions. At one extreme, an excessively stern parent might immediately resort to punishment whenever a child crosses the established boundaries. At the other extreme, an overly lenient parent might avoid any type of punishment, trying instead to reason, bribe, or coax the child into compliance. In between these extremes are those who attempt to find a reasonable compromise—developing a nurturing relationship that communicates concerned support, guiding the child toward self-restraint but resorting to some form of discipline when these informal controls do not work.

Correctional officers likewise employ a great deal of discretion in the management of inmate behavior. Faced with choices between relying on rules and developing relationships, the actions they take can be directed toward:

- *formal controls:* initiating the disciplinary action process by officially "writing up" the offender through a disciplinary action report; or

- *informal controls:* using informal verbal communication to either prevent or deal with a situation, in an effort to foster voluntary compliance without the need to resort to official action.

Within a correctional institution, neither excessive reliance on formal disciplinary action (overenforcement) nor too much informality (underenforcement) tends to be an effective approach. Rather, the key is to find the proper balance between these two extremes.

Overenforcement

Some officers enforce rules strictly "by the book," writing up every inmate for even the most minor infractions. Such practices are obviously resented. That can create a dangerous process of retribution, as illustrated in the following scenario:

> At approximately 5:15 p.m., the officer on duty in C cellhouse was standing just inside the office door when an iron weight of about five pounds was dropped from an upper range. It landed on the metal screen covering the office. It is believed this was a measure of retaliation against the officer, who was performing his job in a manner seen as "overzealous" by inmates.[34]

Nor do inmates have to resort to physical attacks to avenge an officer's heavy-handed rule enforcement. Simply being uncooperative can cast a negative light on the officer's supervisory abilities. Such tactics vividly point out the difference between rule enforcement within correctional institutions and law enforcement in free society. Outside a court of law, police officers may never again encounter those against whom they take action. But it is entirely different in the enclosed environment of corrections, where officers must continue to interact on a daily basis with those against whom they enforce the rules. As a result, one's safety and even job security may be jeopardized by a "hard-line" approach.

In addition, correctional officers are closely scrutinized by their colleagues. Hard-liners do not earn much respect from their operational peers or supervisors. They are generally viewed by other staff members as being too weak to manage inmate behavior without using the rulebook as a crutch. Moreover, because of the resentment and retaliation that their actions may create among the inmates, those who rely excessively on the formal disciplinary process can place their co-workers in danger as well.

Underenforcement

On the other hand, there are those who rarely take any formal action at all. Such officers may simply be intimidated by fear, they may be overly sympathetic to the

CUSTODIAL PROCEDURES **231**

plight of those incarcerated, or they may be trying to avoid ill will. For whatever reasons, they attempt to remain in the good graces of the population simply by "looking the other way" when rules are violated.

Even those who may not be concerned about how they are viewed by the inmates can fall into a laid-back supervisory style if they believe that their disciplinary actions will not be supported by upper-level management. When officers are continually confronted with situations where they feel that their efforts were not backed up by the chain of command, it can become very frustrating. In some cases, lack of further action may be justified on the basis of mitigating circumstances that the officer was unaware of, but officers who believe that the administration "doesn't care anyway" are likely to be considerably less enthusiastic about taking action in the future.

Some prisoners use the greater freedoms they are afforded under such a laissez-faire approach to manipulate staff and see how much they can "get away with." Others find themselves victimized as strong inmate leaders emerge from the vacuum created when rules are not enforced. Officers likewise come to resent the additional burden placed on them when some are not carrying out their full responsibilities. Needless to say, neither inmates nor staff members respect those who actively avoid rule enforcement on a continuous basis.

Corrupt Alliance

To a certain extent, almost all officers will overlook some things. In light of the complex situations that they face, some flexibility in rule enforcement is always necessary. By its very nature, correctional work demands compliance from inmates in order to maintain control without generating resentment or hostility.

In other words, a willingness to tolerate violations of "minor" rules and regulations enables the officer to obtain compliance with the "major" areas of the custodial regime.[35] The resulting system of informal compromises has been cited as usurping official authority by developing a **corrupt alliance** between the inmates and custodial staff. In this respect, "corrupt" is not used in the sinister sense of exploitation for illicit gain but, rather, in the more benign sense of seeking a workable accommodation.

In normal settings it is in the subordinate's best interests to comply with the orders issued by those in charge. Whether the order is issued by a parent or an office manager, there is a certain "sense of duty" that motivates compliance. But correctional institutions are not normal settings, and inmates are primarily confined to their custody because they have not demonstrated such internal moral controls in the past. In prison, "the custodians find themselves confronting men who must be forced, bribed, or cajoled into compliance."[36]

LEARNING GOALS

Do you know:

23. why the relationship between officers and inmates has been called a "corrupt alliance"?
24. how officers can use interpersonal communication skills to manage inmate behavior proactively?

corrupt alliance: the working relationship that occurs when minor violations are overlooked in an implicit "bargain" with inmates to comply with major regulations.

Needless to say, submission through physical force is no longer permissible. Nor, as we have seen earlier, are there many incentives left with which to "bribe" inmates into compliance: "Mail and visiting, recreational privileges, the supply of personal possessions—all are given to the inmate at the time of his arrival. . . . The prisoner, then, finds himself unable to win any significant gains by means of compliance, for there are no gains left to be won."[37]

Beyond this lack of incentives, the close working relationships established between officers and inmates throughout the course of weeks, months, and (in some cases) years can serve to inhibit stern reactions to misbehavior. Moreover, we have seen that those writing too many disciplinary reports are often frowned upon by their supervisors. As a result, a situation can be created in which the officer,

> under pressure to achieve a smoothly running tour of duty not with the stick but with the carrot . . . finds that one of the most meaningful rewards he can offer is to ignore certain offenses or make sure that he never places himself in a position where he will discover them . . . [i]n effect . . . buy[ing] compliance or obedience in certain areas at the cost of tolerating disobedience elsewhere.[38]

Balanced Enforcement

The disobedience tolerated represents relatively minor rule infractions, the excessive enforcement of which could be viewed as unnecessary harassment. In addition, officers who find themselves chronically overworked in overcrowded prisons with an overwhelming number of rules must develop some system of prioritizing simply to survive. Whether the result is considered a "corrupt alliance" achieved by implicit bargaining or a "calculated arrangement" accomplished by impartially balancing priorities is largely a matter of perspective.

Ultimately, the enforcement of discipline must be reasonable, steering a middle course between severity and laxity, and neither ignoring nor overenforcing the rules. Since regulations are not absolutes, it is essential to employ a common-sense approach to discipline in which they are subject to interpretation.

Consistency

There are some who would maintain that a consistent inmate management style means treating everyone exactly alike. But such an approach is no more effective with inmates than it would be if parents responded to all of their children in precisely the same manner, or if employers used the same tactics in supervising all of their employees.

As with everyone else, the needs and behavioral motives of inmates differ widely. Some will respond promptly to a mild verbal warning. Others will openly defy even a direct order. The key is to remain fair and objective without showing favoritism. In other words, the most effective officer is one "who is flexible, who adapts to various situations, who can change from authority figure to counselor, depending on the type of interaction required, who has the good judgment to realize which rules and regulations need to be rigidly enforced and which ones can be bent."[39] Moreover, when inmates are treated firmly, fairly, and consistently, they may well reciprocate when the tables are turned and an officer needs help—as actually happened in the true story featured in the upcoming "Close-up on Corrections."

In addition to variations among inmates, the particular circumstances involved may also call for considerably different responses. An emergency situation obviously requires immediate take-charge action, whereas a minor infraction could be handled on a more informal basis. Developing a **consistent management style** means responding to a similar circumstance or type of behavior in a similar manner whenever it occurs, as opposed to treating all inmates and situations alike.

consistent management style: responding in a uniform manner to similar situations (instead of using the same approach at all times).

CLOSE-UP ON CORRECTIONS
When the Tables Are Turned

Officer Richard Sawyer was working in the minimum security unit . . . when he began to feel sick. He leaned against a wall, turned to an inmate and said, "I'm not feeling well. . . ." Seconds later, Sawyer began to slide down the wall to the floor. The inmate helped lower him to the floor and called for assistance from other inmates. Before passing out, Sawyer asked the inmate to phone for help.

Several inmates helped place Sawyer in a more comfortable position and began checking his vital signs. Although they had access to his keys, they knew it would take too long to find the right one to open the unit and run for help. They also were unsure how to use the unit's security phone system. Finally, one inmate took the officer's radio and called for assistance. . . . Help arrived a short time later and Sawyer was taken to a nearby emergency room, where he regained consciousness. . . .

One reason for the assistance he received may have been Sawyer's good relationship with the inmates: "I had an excellent relationship with them—not in terms of friendship, but in terms of being able to talk. . . . I always had good communication back and forth with most inmates in the facility, and that might have helped a lot."

Source: "Inmate Comes to Officer's Aid," *On the Line*, Vol. 16, No. 4 (September, 1993), p. 2.

Informal Controls

Effective correctional officers realize that the ultimate objective of discipline is developing control from within—rather than imposing external rules and regimentation. Thus the question becomes how order can be promoted without either ignoring or excessively writing up inmate violations. The answer involves how officers use both informal disciplinary action and verbal communication skills.

Simply because an infraction is not officially recorded on a disciplinary action form does not necessarily mean that it was ignored. In addition to a verbal warning, officers may be able to reduce television privileges, remove an inmate from a work detail, or initiate similar informal responses to misconduct. Although the range of privileges that can be restricted is somewhat limited and temporary in nature, there are means short of official action that can be used to achieve compliance.

But it is obviously far more effective to prevent violations *proactively* than to deal *reactively* with misbehavior after it occurs. In other words, it is best to encourage voluntary compliance in order to reduce the need to resort to official action. This is quite a challenge when dealing with those whose lack of internal restraints often has much to do with why they are incarcerated. It calls for developing appropriate interpersonal working relationships that are neither too close nor too distant.

Social Distance

Naturally, there must be some social distance between officers and inmates. There is a fine line between properly displaying some degree of empathy and improperly becoming overly sympathetic. Those who become emotionally involved with prisoners are inevitably vulnerable to deception and manipulation, since inmates are quick to identify staff weaknesses and prey upon them. It is for such reasons that officers are well advised to avoid such things as using nicknames to address inmates, making "deals," discussing their personal life, giving legal advice, or becoming overly familiar with inmates.

At the other extreme, there are those who are coldly detached—performing their duties in a routine, bureaucratic manner, and making it clear that they are unapproachable, regardless of the inmate's personal needs. Like the physician who must maintain a caring but clinical relationship with patients, correctional officers must balance personal concern with professional caution. Those who are successful in doing so develop a style of **detached commitment**, whereby their professional commitment to the well-being of the inmate is tempered with a degree of personal detachment that promotes objective judgments and rational decision making.

detached commitment: maintaining an appropriate balance between concern and caution by ensuring that interpersonal relationships do not interfere with professional judgments.

Interpersonal Communications

Since so much of an officer's time is spent interacting with inmates, the development of effective interpersonal communication skills is an essential ingredient of the job. The manner in which officers build and maintain relationships with inmates will have much to do with their success or failure in managing behavior. It will also largely determine whether they can proactively control inmates or whether they must rely on reactive measures.

In corrections, staff are sometimes so inundated with ongoing requests and complaints that their listening skills diminish over time. As with listening to the narrator on a guided tour, it is difficult to maintain the same enthusiasm with the last group in the evening as the first group in the morning. Day after day, correctional officers hear the same troubles, gripes, and pleas—often from the same inmates, and many times concerning things that the staff can do nothing about. But simply being there to listen is often just the "safety valve" that is needed to prevent an inmate's frustration from exploding into violence.

Thus the ability to listen may be an officer's most effective asset. As noted earlier, verbal communication is not limited to a one-way issuing of orders and commands. Rather, it involves engaging in a two-way dialogue that establishes an effective working relationship. **Active, nonevaluative listening** can be a far more powerful management tool than reactively responding. Quite simply, a good inmate manager is a good inmate listener.

active, nonevaluative listening: energetically involved in listening without passing judgment on what is being said.

Unit Management

In fact, proactive management of inmate behavior is one of the hallmarks of an initiative that has transformed administrative and operational practices in a number of prisons throughout the country—i.e., the concept of **unit management**. Similar in many respects to the principles of direct-supervision jailing, unit management (originally called "functional unit management") was likewise initiated by the federal government during the mid-1970s. Although designed originally to decentralize classification and treatment services, unit management is not a treatment program. Nor is it a custodial strategy. Rather, it is a system whereby custody and treatment work hand in hand within a setting that promotes their close cooperation in achieving two primary goals:

unit management: decentralizing a large prison into semi-autonomous living units where staff are empowered to establish objectives and make decisions concerning inmates assigned to the unit.

- to establish a safe, humane environment for both staff and inmates that minimizes the detrimental effects of confinement;

- to deliver a variety of counseling, social, educational, and vocational training programs designed to aid offenders in making a successful return to the community.[40]

The units themselves consist of a small, self-contained living area and staff offices. They can be either general units that house a variety of general population inmates, or specialized units serving a particular group, such as alcohol or drug abusers. Thus unit management offers a flexible approach to the management of varying types of offenders. Whether they present special risks or special needs, inmates can be placed accordingly and their situation can be addressed appropriately.

Within the unit, staff can review and be authorized to approve visitors, correspondence lists, job assignments, and requests for program changes. During team meetings, program decisions are arrived at jointly, with employees listening to the inmate and explaining their decisions. On a day-to-day basis, staff interact closely with inmates, taking a proactive approach that enhances communication, enables closer observation, and promotes order and control. While that approach may be more costly, the extra expenses are made up in savings as a result of less overtime, fewer repairs to damage from vandalism, fewer disturbances, and even less litigation.[41] More of the operational details of unit management are described in the next "Close-up on Corrections."

Because the centralized power typical of correctional agencies is redistributed under this concept, the unit manager serves as a "subwarden," and each unit is in a sense a "mini-institution," operating semi-autonomously within the confines of a larger institution. All decisions and problems concerning the inmates are handled in the unit. The idea is to decentralize authority by dividing the prison into smaller, more manageable components.

One of the major advantages of unit management is that it "works as well in high security institutions as it does in low or medium security facilities."[42] Moreover, studies have found that, in such facilities, there are fewer inmate-on-inmate assaults, fewer escapes while on furlough, and considerably less custody–treatment rivalry among staff.[43] But success is perhaps best illustrated by the fact that unit management is operational in at least 33 states,[44] and thus far no correctional system that has adopted this approach has later abandoned it.[45]

CLOSE-UP ON CORRECTIONS
Unit Management—Objectives and Operations

The concept of unit management is designed to:

- divide large groups of inmates into smaller, well-defined clusters;
- increase the frequency of contact and the quality of relationships between staff and inmates;
- provide better observation of inmate activities, detecting problems before they become critical;
- improve inmate accountability and control;
- provide different programs, strategies, and interventions for each inmate;
- place special emphasis on institutional adjustment, work skill acquisition, interpersonal communications, positive self-esteem, self-motivation, problem-solving techniques, realistic goal-setting, education, and training.

But, like any correctional intervention or management strategy, unit management will only be effective to the extent that it adheres to the basic requirements for its success, which include:

- *Leadership.* Since unit management involves decentralizing power and decision-making more broadly throughout the organization, top-level administrators must be supportive and committed to the concept.
- *Unit plan and mission.* Each unit requires a written plan specifically defining its purpose, which provides documentation of the goals against which progress is measured.
- *Population size.* Each unit's population size is based on its mission—i.e., a general unit can accommodate 150–250 inmates, and a special unit can accommodate 75–125 inmates.

- *Staffing.* In each living unit (i.e., dormitory or cellblock), staffing consists of a unit manager, one or two case managers, one or two counselors, and a secretary, along with full- or part-time mental health staff and 24-hour correctional officer coverage.
- *Assignment stability.* Inmates and unit staff are permanently assigned to the unit (barring changes in the inmate's status). Correctional officers are stationed for a minimum of nine months.
- *Training.* Unit personnel receive formal, ongoing training regarding their roles and responsibilities.
- *Interdepartmental cooperation.* Because unit management cannot work in a vacuum, interdisciplinary cooperation is essential.
- *Monitoring and evaluation.* A systematic approach to the evaluation of unit management is necessary to determine if its goals are being achieved, with outcomes analyzed and refinements made in order to maximize efficiency and effectiveness.

> *Sources*: Compiled from W. Hardy Rauch and James D. Henderson, *Guidelines for the Development of a Security Program* (Washington, DC: National Institute of Corrections, 1987), pp. 14–15; and Robert B. Levinson, *Unit Management in Prisons and Jails* (Lanham, MD: American Correctional Association, 1999), p. 9.

SUMMARY

Because many of those in prison have not displayed sufficient self-control to function effectively in society, an elaborate system of external controls is imposed to maintain security. In that regard, the operational objectives of custody are to prevent escape, maintain order and safety, and promote efficient functioning of the institution. Moreover, custody is a necessary condition for effectively implementing treatment programs.

Custodial security is achieved through the architectural design and technological hardware of the physical plant, as well as the control procedures maintained by prison staff. Externally, high-security facilities feature perimeter walls, fences, and razor wire, along with guard towers, ground posts, locks, alarms, and other electronic devices. Internally, control procedures include inmate segregation, controlled movement, periodic counts, cell searches, personal searches, and control of everything from equipment to communication. Since these provisions are less rigid in minimum-security facilities, they are the most vulnerable to escapes. Most inmates who abscond, however, are eventually apprehended.

To detect contraband items, cell searches are conducted routinely, randomly, or for reasonable suspicion. Personal searches are also conducted, which range in intrusiveness from a simple frisk, to a full strip search, to a body-cavity examination. To further reduce the risk of escape or the introduction of contraband, correctional institutions control inmate contact with the outside. Use of the telephone is restricted, cell phones are banned, mail is checked, and the number of visits is limited. Some states permit conjugal visits to reduce homosexual activities, improve morale, and strengthen family bonds. But not all inmates qualify for conjugal visits, which can create resentment. Some institutions therefore favor social integration through the use of furloughs, although this approach also presents risks of absconding or committing new crimes.

In an effort to achieve orderly group life, a number of rules and regulations govern inmate conduct within correctional institutions. Officers are responsible for enforcing the rules, and they possess considerable discretion in this regard. Although minor infractions may not be fully enforced, major violations are written up through official disciplinary action reports. If it is determined that further action is necessary, the inmate is afforded a hearing before a disciplinary committee, which has the authority to impose sanctions when a penalty is warranted.

Attempting to obtain compliance without taking official action can create an accommodation between officers and prisoners, whereby officers accept some degree of minor misconduct as a trade-off for the observance of major rules. This is the result of an effort to avoid either over- or underenforcing the rules. Overly strict enforcement is viewed by the inmates as unnecessary harassment, whereas nonenforcement diminishes respect for both the officer and the rules. In any event, the ultimate purpose of discipline is developing internal self-control.

Yet formal regulations represent only one aspect of maintaining institutional control. Often overlooked are the more informal, noncoercive controls emerging from the relationship established between correctional officers and the inmate population. Encouraging voluntary compliance involves the need to develop an appropriate interpersonal working relationship with the inmates. But officers must be careful to maintain a certain social distance, balancing personal concern with professional caution.

Much of an inmate's frustration, anxiety, and tension can be reduced simply by having someone who is willing to listen without passing judgment. In that regard, establishing a two-way dialogue rather than a one-way dictation of commands not only lessens potential hostility but creates a more proactive management atmosphere. Unit management likewise demonstrates potential for both controlling and changing inmates while they are within correctional custody. In fact, it is this potential for changing behavior that is explored more extensively in the upcoming chapter.

FOR FURTHER DISCUSSION

1. Explain what is meant by the observation that custody and treatment go "hand in hand" in an effective correctional facility.

2. Go online to find photographs of several prison facilities (old as well as new), and from the pictures alone discuss what messages their architectural styles convey.

3. Play the role of a member of the technology committee of your state department of corrections and, based on an Internet search, recommend to the director what new equipment that is now available (or being developed) should be purchased.

4. Provide an example to explain how prison officials might abuse the use of administrative segregation to circumvent legal restrictions on the use of disciplinary segregation.

5. Following the walk-away escape of four long-term offenders after visiting hours, the director of corrections was dismissed and you have been asked to fill the position—provided that you can assure the governor that there will be no escapes during your administration. Discuss your response to this demand in terms of what you would need to do to meet it, what it would cost (not necessarily fiscally), and what the long-term implications would be. Then decide whether you should accept the position.

6. Go online to read the story of Eugene Richardson, a man who escaped from a Florida work-release center in 1979 and was recaptured some 30 years later. Based on the facts of his case, his life over the past 30 years, and theoretical perspectives related to both rehabilitation and retribution, determine what you think the state of Florida should do with him.

7. Debate the pros and cons of conjugal visiting versus furloughs. Based on these facts, determine which you would prefer if you were a prison administrator.

8. Describe how both underenforcement and overenforcement of prison rules by one officer can jeopardize the safety of others, as well as why it is in an officer's best interests to be firm, fair, and consistent in that regard.

9. In terms of staff enforcement of prison rules and regulations, explain why Sykes's use of the term "corrupt alliance" does not imply "corruption" as we would normally use the word.

10. Discuss how the principles of unit management in a prison relate to direct-supervision jailing.

CHAPTER 9

Treatment and Related Programs

We must accept the reality that to confine offenders behind walls without trying to change them is an expensive folly with short-term benefits—winning battles while losing the war.[1]

Former United States Supreme Court Chief Justice Warren Burger

CHAPTER OVERVIEW

Treatment in correctional institutions involves all of the programs and services that bring socializing influences to bear on the inmate. Viewed comprehensively, it refers to all of the processes that promote the normal socialization of people in free society—such as schools, religion, and recreation—as well as the psychological, psychiatric, and social work services that are traditionally associated with the term *treatment*. To the extent that they contribute to the inmate's socialization, a wide variety of factors can be broadly viewed as treatment—from the work habits learned in prison industries, to the educational credentials earned in GED classes, to the discipline instilled by compliance with institutional regulations.

Despite society's shift from the rehabilitative emphasis of the medical model to the more punitive focus of the justice model, corrections has not abandoned the broad scope of treatment. In part, this may be a reflection of practical considerations. A prison in which training, education, work, or religious activities are lacking is one in which boredom and idleness prevail, compounding the already difficult task of maintaining custody and control. Institutional programs not only enable better inmate management than custodial staff alone can provide, but also help neutralize feelings of anger and frustration.

In addition, despite the presumably voluntary nature of treatment under the justice model, it is inevitably the corrections component of the criminal justice system which is criticized when ex-offenders become recidivists. Even if the public views the mission of corrections as restricted to incapacitation, it does not seem to be willing to absolve prisons of at least some blame when they fail to make positive changes among those confined. The legal responsibility of prisons may be limited to carrying out the sentence imposed by the court. But the public's protective demand is ultimately to return the offender to society as a law-abiding citizen. In that regard, "education, mental health, substance abuse, and other rehabilitative programs . . . are not a bleeding heart coddling of inmates, but rather, are directly related to public safety and are cost beneficial."[2]

Moreover, correctional administrators themselves continue to express a belief in rehabilitation. Basic literacy, GED, and vocational training programs are among the "amenities" that have been least favored for reduction or elimination by prison wardens.[3] Another national survey found that, while "maintaining custody and institutional order are dominant concerns," there was also clear "support for rehabilitation as a secondary but fundamental goal," with wardens expressing a desire to expand inmate treatment opportunities.[4] As we will see in this chapter, however, treatment in the traditional clinical or casework sense is sadly lacking in most correctional facilities. After all, we now speak of "state prisons" rather than "correctional institutions."[5]

While treatment is not confined to a single program or service, neither is it merely a process for helping the inmate adapt to imprisonment with a minimum of irritation and anxiety. Rather, it is related to what every officer, counselor, work supervisor, chaplain, or other institutional employee does that has a positive impact on long-term social adjustment. Even in those facilities lacking sophisticated clinical or therapeutic programs, much can be done on a routine day-to-day basis to promote treatment efforts by introducing socializing influences into lives that have often been characterized by dysfunction and disorganization. In other words, to achieve effective postrelease results, the correctional process must be directed toward "changing behavior, rather than just containing behavior."[6]

INMATE CLASSIFICATION

Through the classification process, inmate risks and needs are identified. Classification decisions therefore become the basis for assigning inmates to varying programs and institutional security levels. We may not think of classification as a part of life in free society, but there are also many ways in which it functions outside of prisons. For example, every time that you go to the "express" or "cash-only" checkout line in a grocery store, classification is being used to expedite your transactions.

LEARNING GOALS

Do you know:
1. for what purposes inmates are classified?
2. how the emphasis of classification has changed over time?
3. on what basis classification decisions are made and how they affect the offender?

Within corrections, classification refers to the grouping of inmates according to characteristics that they share in common and their level of security risk. It is therefore a helpful tool in managing large numbers of cases more efficiently than they could be handled on an individual basis. Through identification of general patterns and the grouping of services to match them, the unique requirements of large numbers of people can be better met. Thus classification groups offenders for the purpose of maximizing resources, minimizing risk, and/or promoting change. Related treatment goals can range from learning auto mechanics through vocational training, to becoming functionally literate through computer-assisted instruction, to improving social adjustment through group therapy.

Determining treatment needs, however, is no longer the predominate objective of classification. With greater emphasis on the justice model in recent years, along with the impact of both overcrowding and funding cutbacks, correctional administrators have focused more on running safe, secure, industrious, and lawful institutions than on treating those confined there.[7]

Reception and Diagnosis

Historically, inmates were classified first on the basis of gender and then by age; later, they were separated according to the severity of their offense. Over time, the classification process has become much more sophisticated, to the point where it is so complex that it is often computerized now.

diagnostic reception center: a central intake location where new inmates are interviewed, tested, examined, and evaluated for classification purposes.

Today, the initial step in classifying prison inmates is the diagnostic process that occurs in a **diagnostic reception center** during reception and intake. Incoming inmates are interviewed, tested, examined, and evaluated. Additionally, the content of their presentence investigation report, as well as other background information, is reviewed. Before the adoption of classification on a statewide basis, judges could sentence offenders to a particular prison within the state. Thus classification was essentially a function of the court. Today, state-controlled classification places everyone sentenced by the courts under the central authority of the state department of corrections.

EXHIBIT 9.1
The classification of prisoners by sex, age, health, and crime is a relatively new development. Earlier, facilities comingled men and women, along with children, as well as violent criminals and nonviolent debtors.

Source: Courtesy of the Federal Bureau of Prisons.

Classification Decisions

On the basis of diagnostic information, decisions are made concerning an inmate's housing, level of security, program assignments, and special needs (such as anger management training, alcohol/drug treatment, psychiatric referral, and so forth). This is how classification is designed to operate, but the process is far from being either foolproof or completely objective. The sheer volume of cases can create routinized decisions that are based more on efficient processing than effective prognosis. It is in part for such reasons that more clearly defined, objective criteria are now being used in many correctional classification systems.

Regardless of how they are made, classification decisions have a long-term impact on the offender. Everything from job placement, to educational programming, to parole eligibility is tied to classification outcomes. In essence, classifying people "channels destinies and determines fate,"[8] at times becoming a self-fulfilling prophecy.

Relationship to the Medical Model

The reception–diagnostic process was compatible with the medical model's focus on the unique pathologies of individual offenders. Since this perspective was based on a belief that criminal acts were essentially a "cry for help," early and accurate diagnosis was necessary, along with appropriate therapeutic intervention as determined by the treatment plan established during classification.

Whether or not the inmate desired treatment was not the point. The offender's own motivation to seek help—or lack thereof—was largely ignored. Rather, the treatment plan was based on the classification committee's view of inmate *needs*, as opposed to what the person *wanted* or had the motivation to *do*. Realizing that "going along with the system" would provide the only avenue to freedom naturally created a strong incentive for doing what was prescribed, even if that might mean simply going through the motions to demonstrate eligibility for release. Although there is some evidence that court-ordered treatment can be even more effective than voluntary treatment,[9] with the shift from the medical model to the justice model, mandated treatment was deemphasized in favor of voluntary participation.

> **LEARNING GOALS**
>
> Do you know:
> 4. how classification relates to both the medical model and the justice model?
> 5. what occurs when inmates are "overclassified"?
> 6. what the benefits and drawbacks are of using objective models for classification decision-making?

Risk- versus Needs-based Classification

Throughout the history of classification progress, professional treatment personnel were needed to make the initial diagnosis and develop related custody and treatment plans. This was not only costly, but also vulnerable to subjective opinions. As early as 1967, the President's Task Force on Corrections expressed a desire for a more objective and easily administered classification tool, "capable of administration in general day-to-day correctional intake procedures, that would group offenders according to their management and treatment needs."[10]

To streamline procedures and improve objectivity, there has been a move in recent years toward more empirically valid classification measures. However, in the process of making this transition, the differences between classification instruments designed to identify treatment needs and those designed to determine behavioral risk seem to have become blurred. As a result, there is concern that risk assessment instruments are being misused to predict treatment potential.[11]

Methods that are used to classify for treatment purposes are directed toward understanding causes of criminal behavior and identifying specific targets for change. In contrast, objective risk-based systems use standardized decision-making criteria that are focused more on classification for institutional management or inmate adjustment to confinement. As researchers have cautioned, risk and needs should not be combined into one measure,[12] and before they can be used effectively, it is essential that we fully understand exactly what various classification instruments are intended to do.[13]

Relationship to the Justice Model

It is not surprising that objective classification models have gained support under the justice model, when sentencing guidelines and selective incapacitation prediction formulas have also become popular. All of these numerical formulas, models, and prediction devices may owe much of their prominence to concerns for achieving consistency and rational decision-making, along with our fascination with the capabilities of computers and mathematical problem-solving. If decisions are numerically derived, there is a tendency to view them as more valid and trustworthy, despite the fact that the variables being analyzed are still a product of human choice. In that regard, it has been noted that "the objectivity of a classification system is a matter of degree, for the creation of these systems involves subjective judgments, and all of the systems currently in existence incorporate at least some subjective staff judgment."[14]

objective prediction models: using a limited number of standardized, quantifiable decision-making criteria to reduce the subjectivity of classification.

Certainly, the variables taken into consideration in **objective prediction models** are considerably more moderate in scope than the widespread tests and measures upon which previous classification decisions were based. As outlined in the next "Close-up on Corrections," criteria are limited to relatively few clearly defined and legally based variables that are designed to predict one's institutional adjustment and future behavior. For example, the instrument developed by the National Institute of Corrections includes:

• past institutional violence;

• severity of current offense;

• severity of prior convictions;

- escape history;

- prior felonies;

- stability (age, education, employment);

- time to release.[15]

Notable by their absence are indicators related to clinical assessments of offender needs. Objective prediction models are therefore directed more toward determining the necessary level of institutional security than individual treatment prescriptions. Thus their acceptance in the field represents another reflection of the movement from the rehabilitative focus of the medical model to the custodial orientation of the justice model.

CLOSE-UP ON CORRECTIONS
Objective Classification Instruments

Correctional classification systems have moved away from so-called "subjective" models to "objective" systems. Subjective models tend to rely on informal criteria that often lead to inconsistency in decision-making. However, objective systems depend on a narrow set of well-defined legal factors (e.g., severity of current offense, prior convictions, etc.) and personal characteristics (e.g., age, marital status, etc.). These items are weighted and assigned differential values within a well-defined instrument that is then used to assess an inmate's level of risk or program needs.

Standardized instruments that are used in objective classification meet the following criteria:

- *validity:* capable of assigning a custody level that reflects the inmate's true risk for disruptive and violent behavior within the facility;
- *reliability:* consistently achieving similar classification decisions for comparable inmates;
- *equity:* decision-making items that are nondiscriminatory and reflect commonly accepted societal values;
- *utility:* a system that is efficient, simple to use, and easy to understand.

    Source: Paraphrased from James Austin, *Objective Jail Classification Systems: A Guide for Jail Administrators* (Washington, DC: National Institute of Corrections, 1998), pp. 3, 10. See also James Austin and Patricia Hardyman, *Objective Prison Classification: A Guide for Correctional Agencies* (Washington, DC: National Institute of Corrections, 2004).

Institutional Implications

As described in the objective classification guidelines developed by the National Institute of Justice, improved classification of inmates has been an essential component of the response to prison crowding:

> With proper classification . . . only those inmates requiring high levels of security are placed in costly, tight custody facilities, while those evidencing less threat can be assigned to lower security institutions. Appropriate classification also can assist in determining which inmates can be considered for early release or for retention in the community with appropriate supervision. Most importantly, effective classification helps assure the safety of the public, agency staff, and prisoner population.[16]

By removing personal opinions and subjective judgments, objective models are designed to be more equitable to all inmates, as well as more valid and reliable predictors. As correctional facilities have become increasingly crowded, however, it is not always feasible to place inmates in the institutions and programs that are best suited for them. It has, for instance, been noted that "[a] state with 75% maximum security spaces will tend to classify 75% of its intake population as maximum security."[17] Moreover, some systems tend to violate one of the cardinal rules of classification by "overclassifying"—that is, "unnecessarily placing many inmates in higher levels of security than required, given the risks they pose."[18] It has been found that this is especially problematic for women. In fact, concerns have been expressed that the same instrument does not necessarily work equally well for both male and female inmates, resulting in an excessive number of "overrides," whereby staff substitute their own judgment when classifying women.[19] Likewise, overclassification becomes an issue in systems where those convicted of certain offenses (such as murder) are automatically assigned to maximum security, even though "offense is a relatively weak predictor" of disciplinary infractions or escape risk.[20]

Assessment of Objective Classification

While the process may not always work as intended, the aim of a properly implemented risk-based classification system is to match the security and treatment needs of the inmate with the resources available within the correctional system. To the extent that objective classification can reduce needless overclassification without increasing misconduct or escapes, it can represent a significant accomplishment—especially in light of the potential relationship between misclassification and rule infractions, adjustment difficulties, and limited treatment progress. In that regard, objective classification has been credited with helping to reduce violence, escape attempts, inmate manipulation of housing assignments, and staffing costs.[21]

But there is also some resistance to objective classification techniques, since they change the role of classification personnel from diagnosticians and therapists to something closer to that of accountants or bookkeepers. Such an impersonal approach can dehumanize classification, to the point where it simply becomes a bureaucratic process devoid of personal discretion.

Nor do classification experts themselves agree on the "best" way to classify inmates. Some caution against relying on one instrument in a "one-size-fits-all" approach, arguing for discretionary input within the framework of an objective instrument.[22] Others continue to question whether removing the human element from classification decision making is truly more *equitable* or whether *efficiency* is merely disguised as equity. In other words, do the rigors of empirical analysis produce more equitable results than the richness of clinical assessments?

Regardless of the answer, once classified the inmate is faced with adjusting to the decisions made during the intake process. Offenders may find themselves assigned to a minimum-, maximum-, or medium-security institution; to a facility with a wide range of programs and services or to a place where an hour a day of solitary recreation is the single diversion; to a prison with a variety of employment opportunities or a location where work is confined to routine maintenance duties. Given these variations, the remainder of this chapter focuses on the change-oriented activities, services, and programs typically provided in correctional facilities.

FAITH-BASED PROGRAMMING

Ever since the powerful religious impact of the Quakers on the first penitentiary at the Walnut Street Jail, religion has played a significant role in prison life. Over 200 years later, virtually every state in the U.S. offers faith-based instructional programs and worship services,[23] attracting greater participation than any other types of programs. Perhaps that is because religion performs essential functions in prison life—ranging from dealing with guilt to finding a new way of life and coping with loss, especially the loss of freedom.[24]

Historically, chaplains represented the first example of what could be considered treatment staff in correctional institutions. During the early development of prison systems, they were the unofficial therapists, dedicated to "saving souls," before there were teachers, social workers, or counselors.[25] Even in facilities with limited or nonexistent treatment programs, inmates virtually always have access to a chaplain. As seen in the next "Close-up on Corrections," it is the chaplain who is there to break bad news, soothe sorrows, and make life somewhat more tolerable for those incarcerated—who holds out promise for a future better than the past.

CLOSE-UP ON CORRECTIONS
The Chaplain's Message

The chaplain walked along the fence, staring through his wire-frame glasses. He seemed like a messenger of death. I wanted to turn away and pretend I'd never seen this man of the cloth before. But like so many of my fellow prisoners, I had: this very priest had brought me the news of the sudden deaths of my mother, brother, and sister.

He pressed his hands against the fence, his eyes searching intently for someone in the yard. I had nothing—no basketball to bounce, no handball to hit, no weights to lift—to distract me from my inner pleading, "Not me again!"

First relief, then sadness swept over me when I saw the chaplain trying to get Freddie's attention on the basketball court. "Hey, Freddie," he said. "Buddy, I have a bit of bad news for you. I need to speak to you just for a minute, OK?" But Freddie only played harder. I watched fear pinch his eyes as he tried to concentrate. The other players upped the pace of the game as if to shield him from the chaplain's voice. This was their way of supporting their friend for as long as he needed to deny that the chaplain's news was for him.

Source: Jarvis Jay Masters, *Finding Freedom: Writings from Death Row*
(Junction City, CA: Padma Publishing, 1997), p. 80.

Inmate Acceptance

Unquestionably, chaplains play an indispensable role in correctional institutions. But, while chaplains have always been involved in prisons, their acceptance has never been complete or unreserved. Some inmates consider religion as representing the authority of an "establishment" of which they are not a part. On the other hand, inmates who are experiencing guilt and remorse can seek out religious programs for support and forgiveness. With little but time on their hands, even some of the most seemingly hard-core inmates do—in the original Quaker tradition—indulge themselves in reading the Bible and attending faith-based programs. There are those who undoubtedly find a measure of personal solace in religion. Others find it a useful aid to help them adjust to their situation, or simply a "crutch" to lean on in hard times. Still others may actually use religious conversion as a manipulative tool to convince officials of their reform and eligibility for release. But regardless of their motives, it is not uncommon for prisoners to "find God" during their incarceration.

Staff Acceptance

By the same token, chaplains have not been universally well accepted by prison staff. Some operational personnel may look upon the chaplain as a threat to security, since the job calls for being on somewhat "friendly" terms with the inmates. A chaplain who is naive with regard to the manipulative capabilities of inmates can become an "easy touch." For example, in one small rural prison, the chaplain was told by the inmates that they did not have pens to write to their loved ones. The prisoner communicating this sad news indicated that his wife would gladly donate pens if the chaplain would pick them up. Inside each of the pens was a small quantity of marijuana. As illustrated by this "con game," chaplains must become skillful at separating legitimate from illegitimate inmate anxieties. They must minister to the religious needs of the population while being alert to the security concerns of the institution. Doing so requires maintaining a delicate balance between being useful and being used.

Current Challenges

Finding dedicated people to fill a position that is often underpaid, unappreciated, and overworked can be a challenge. In addition, as prison populations reflect greater cultural and ethnic diversity, faith-based personnel representing the traditional Catholic, Jewish, and Protestant denominations may not be as relevant to the broader-based religious orientations of the inmates. Although it is no longer assumed that a chaplain's training must reflect the specific religious denomination of the inmate being counseled, it is equally inappropriate to overlook the need for greater diversity among religious staff. In that regard, some correctional institutions maintain a religious advisory board, composed of faith-based representatives from throughout the community, which serves as a potential source of volunteers.[26] Others have implemented such creative approaches to meeting religious needs as broadcasting faith-based programs through the facility's television sets.[27]

Treatment Impact

As the most consistent representative of treatment over the years, chaplains have contributed significantly to corrections. Just having someone to talk to, share grief with, or listen to problems can exert a powerful influence. Imprisonment can be a lonely, soul-searching experience. It is often faith-based personnel who make existence there more bearable. Moreover, finding structure in religion provides many offenders with the internal stability needed to make a successful adjustment not only to prison, but also to society upon release.[28] In that regard, research indicates that "religion seems to give hope, meaning, optimism, and security" to people, is "positively related to personal and emotional well-being," "has beneficial health effects,"[29] and, most significantly, also appears to have a positive influence on recidivism.[30]

EXHIBIT 9.2
For those behind bars, religious study can be a source of hope, optimism, and potential change.

Source: Courtesy of the Roanoke County (Virginia) Sheriff's Office.

Faith-based programming now extends well beyond worship services and religious education, embracing a wide variety of initiatives—everything from ethics and personal growth to practical skills and support groups. In fact, faith-based cognitive programs blend biblical perspectives with cognitive therapeutic techniques. In this "healing environment" faith-based counselors encourage self-awareness and teach new ways of thinking through cognitive restructuring:

> For example, Thinking Error No. 2 is Victimstance, which is defined as the tendency to see oneself as a victim of circumstances such as social conditions, family history, past negative experiences, etc. It involves blaming others for one's actions instead of accepting responsibility for bad choices. For insight into this behavior, students are directed to look at the story of Adam and Eve's disobedience . . . [and] are led to see that failure to admit crime and accept responsibility is a barrier to rehabilitation.[31]

Thus the oldest and most modern approaches to treatment have established a unique working partnership. But, as religious principles have merged more and more intimately with secular programming, criticisms have emerged with regard to everything from invalid evaluations of their effectiveness to pressuring inmates to join faith-based prison communities. As one inmate put it, "the Christians do lots of stuff the state used to do, like vocational programs, but now they're only for believers."[32] Additionally, questions have been raised about the constitutionality of using public funds for faith-based initiatives. For some insights into how this issue might be addressed, see the next "Close-up on Corrections."

CLOSE-UP ON CORRECTIONS
Principles Governing Faith-based Initiatives in Government-funded Settings

- The primary criterion for whether any provider is eligible to participate in the delivery of government-funded social service must be its effectiveness in meeting the needs of beneficiaries.
- If any individual objects to the religious character of the faith-based organization that is providing services, the individual should have the option of participation in alternative programs without negative consequences. . . .
- The same standards of financial accountability should be applied to religious as to nonreligious providers of services regarding the use of government funds.
- Nondiscrimination with respect to religion must be maintained in all relations between government and organizations providing services. . . . [W]ell-established Constitutional principles should govern the relationship (see *Bowen v. Kendrick*, 487 U.S. 589, 1988).
- Existing legal and civil rights protections for all beneficiaries and providers of government-financed social services must be preserved; but faith-based groups must be allowed to maintain employment standards that support their quality and character.

Source: Pat Nolan, "Prison Fellowship and Faith-based Initiatives," *On the Line*, Vol. 25, No. 5 (November, 2002), p. 2.

EDUCATION, VOCATIONAL TRAINING, AND OTHER SERVICES

Following religion, the introduction of education was the second major change in the history of correctional institutions. Nor has the need for inmate education diminished over the years. An estimated 40 percent of state prison inmates and nearly half (47 percent) of jail inmates do not have a high school diploma or GED—rates that are more than double those of the general population in free society (18 percent).[33] Additionally, many prisoners are functioning below basic literacy levels,[34] meaning that they are unable to perform such everyday activities as filling out a job application, reading a newspaper, or balancing a checkbook. Lack of education may or may not have promoted their involvement in crime. Nevertheless, it is clear that their postrelease employment opportunities will be severely limited in a culture where high school education is a minimum requirement for most jobs. In today's society, functional literacy is essential for basic survival.

Nor are the difficulties resulting from inadequate education restricted to employment limitations. Those who have insufficient schooling have probably also missed the socialization and cultural conditioning that are equally important. Education is not just learning knowledge or skills, but also the development of work habits, feelings of accomplishment, and the self-discipline it takes to succeed.

Institutional Programs

Promoting literacy and marketable job skills saves money in the long term by better equipping inmates with the resources they need to survive in free society. Making inmates productive is the first step to keeping them out of prison, and making them literate is the first step toward making them productive.[35] In that regard, an examination of 97 published articles revealed "solid support for a positive relationship between correctional education and lower recidivism."[36] The National Institute for Literacy reported that correctional education programs reduced the probability of reincarceration by 29 percent, with a similar 33 percent reduction for those who participated in vocational training.[37]

The primary purpose of academic education and vocational training programs in correctional facilities is to provide offenders with the tools of literacy, a trade, or specific job skills. But important secondary advantages include enhancing the inmate's work habits, pride, dignity, and self-esteem. Merely being able to read a story to a child during visiting can be an uplifting experience for a formerly illiterate inmate.[38] For those who have experienced a lifetime of being "losers," these indirect benefits often prove to be even more significant than more immediate objectives. For a personal account of how this happened in one case, see the inmate's story in the following "Close-up on Corrections."

CLOSE-UP ON CORRECTIONS
Plea from a Prisoner

The youngster appeared in front of my tiny "house" on an afternoon when I was short on patience and long on aggravation. All of his possessions were inside a pillowcase slung over his shoulder. "I'm your new cellie," he informed me. "Jackson's my name and crack's my game."

"Perfect . . ." I mumbled to myself, looking at a kid half my age. . . . Just what I needed, a 20-year-old street punk sharing my 5′ × 9′ cubicle. . . .

Fortunately, we worked different jobs, and different shifts, allowing occasional cell privacy. . . . Jackson stayed on his bunk, pacified by television.

There was no animosity on my part, just no interest in lame conversation.

One thing I did notice. He would perk up when the guard came around our cell at mail call. But there was never anything for Jackson. A couple of times he had commented sarcastically about all the letters I wrote, and the stack of magazines and books cluttering my shelf space.

A day came when Jackson did get a letter. Lying on my lower bunk, I could hear him above, rattling the pages while I flipped through a new magazine. He swung his bare feet off the upper bunk and hopped to the floor. . . .

With unusual meekness he asked, "Say man, you got a minute?"

"What for?"

"Would you read my momma's letter to me?"

I was just able to hold back the question, You can't read? But surprise surely registered on my face. It always comes as an astonishing revelation to encounter an adult American who is functionally illiterate.

"Sure," I told him. The letter was two simple pages from a mother worried about her boy confined in a harsh world of bricks and bars. He was silent after I read the final few words: "We love you son. Be careful and come home soon, Momma."

"Would you help me write back to her?" he asked. Gone was the cocky criminal, replaced by a sad, vulnerable youngster barely out of his teens. I hesitated, then made a decision.

"Yeah, I'll write the letter, but it's going to cost you."

"How much?" he asked suspiciously. Everything costs something in the penitentiary.

"An hour of your time, every night at lock up. You're gonna learn to read and write."

He looked hard at me. "What's the catch?"

"You've got nothing but time," I reminded him. "Might as well get something out of being here."

"You won't tell nobody?" he asked sheepishly.

"Isn't anybody's business."

"Deal!" he said, sticking out his hand to seal the bargain. . . .

Jackson obviously hadn't absorbed much in the six years he attended school. The basic alphabet was a cloudy concept. His written vocabulary was barely double digit.

But within a few weeks, two things were readily apparent: I had a lot to learn about patience, and Jackson was a very bright young man.

He attacked our project with determination. Instead of watching "Gilligan's Island" reruns, he practiced the alphabet, printing out page after page of characters, then progressing to short words. He copied countless sentences from magazines and tried to decipher the words syllable by syllable. I watched with amusement and a little pride, as he discovered the magic of language. . . .

That was several years ago. Jackson has long since gone back to "the world" on parole. During two years "inside," he became an insatiable reader who kept a tattered paperback dictionary always within reach. Unlike most men who come to prison, he left a little better for the experience.

Source: Guy Marble, "Plea from a Prisoner," *Educational Leadership*, Vol. 50, No. 4 (December 1992/January, 1993), pp. 61–62. Reprinted with permission of the Association for Supervision and Curriculum Development. Copyright 1992 by ASCD. All rights reserved.

Educational Challenges

When educational programs are conducted within prison walls, unique challenges are presented. For one thing, maintaining order in the classroom is essential. It is

EXHIBIT 9.3
Just being able to read a story to a child during visiting can be a meaningful experience for someone behind bars.

Source: Courtesy of Volunteers of America.

not conducive to learning if inmates view classes as a break from normal discipline. Some institutions reserve separate cellblocks for those involved in various educational activities. Housing all inmates participating in a particular program together enables them to study together and mutually reinforce learning. In addition, it promotes security by minimizing the need for movement to and from classes. But, wherever they are housed, it is essential to avoid labeling students in such classes as "stupid" or "illiterate." As was clearly demonstrated in the last "Close-up," being **functionally illiterate** is a personal embarrassment that many inmates will attempt to conceal.

functionally illiterate: unable to function effectively in society as a result of being unable to read or write.

Computer-assisted Instruction and Distance Learning

Schools in correctional institutions are also unlike those in free society in another respect—they are not able to run on a regular, September-to-June calendar. Inmates arrive continuously throughout the year. Moreover, unlike the public schools, smaller facilities may not have the luxury of dividing classes by grade levels. Addressing the educational needs of inmates who function at varying grade levels was especially difficult before the introduction of **computer-assisted instruction** (CAI). With the programmed instruction available through CAI, however, many of the deficiencies in the academic offerings of correctional institutions can be eliminated.

computer-assisted instruction: offering programmed instruction on computers, individualized to the level of learners, who progress at their own pace.

As a self-paced instructional tool, CAI enables each student to progress at his or her own rate. It also enables the institution to address widely varying educational levels without the need for separate classrooms for each grade. CAI presents material in short and easy steps, keeps the learner actively involved and provides immediate feedback of results. Moreover, it is considerably more prestigious to work on a computer than to be in a regular classroom setting. Another major benefit is reduced staffing, which is a significant factor, given the shortage of prison teachers. With CAI, fewer instructors can serve more students.

Every correctional institution obviously cannot afford the investment in equipment and software that would be necessary to enable all inmates with educational deficiencies to participate in computer-assisted instruction. But distance learning presents another high-tech solution that is more cost-effective than on-site instructors. In those facilities where inmates have access to TV, instructional programming is also available via satellite broadcasts and DVDs featuring education programs that assist offenders with developing the skills needed to obtain employment and make a successful transition into the community.[39]

Post-secondary Education

In addition to basic remedial education, college coursework is also available now through distance learning, as well as arrangements with local institutions of higher education. But offering post-secondary education to inmates has generated protests among taxpayers who resent providing inmates with the advantage of college study while they have to pay the costs of educating their children. On the other hand, this argument overlooks the expense of continuing to support recidivating offenders who might be motivated by a college education to make a change in their lifestyle.

One summary of studies on this topic concludes that a significant body of research "demonstrates a positive correlation between higher education and post-release success."[40] Another meta-analysis indicates that, in more than 90 percent of the studies conducted over a 10-year period, recidivism was reduced for those who had participated in post-secondary education (averaging 46 percent lower than for those who had not taken college classes).[41] Nevertheless, public backlash can be a strong deterrent to offering educational programs that go beyond what is available in secondary schools.

This was perhaps best illustrated by the 1994 congressional action barring inmates from receiving Pell grants for post-secondary education. As a result, by 1995 a national survey of prison wardens found 68 percent reporting that college education programs had been reduced or eliminated in their facilities during the previous year.[42] By 2000, more than two out of three state and federal prisons were not offering such coursework.[43] Just five years later, however, post-secondary education seemed to be on the rise again—with 43 states and the federal government reporting the availability of at least some post-secondary programs.[44] Whether the trend will shift again with the cutbacks accompanying more recent budget deficits remains to be seen. But perhaps the major difference today is that funding comes from a variety of sources (including the inmates themselves), so post-secondary programs may not be as dependent on federal or state revenues as in the past. Moreover, much more can be done to make ex-offenders aware of educational opportunities upon release.[45]

Vocational Training

Work has been a central feature of prisons throughout the history of corrections—from the handicrafts assembled in the Walnut Street Jail, to the large prison industries of the nineteenth century, to the contract labor systems used throughout the South. While such labor may have instilled discipline, the demeaning work and dehumanizing manner in which it was supervised often did more to degrade self-esteem than to develop skills. Moreover, the primary purpose was not to promote an inmate's potential but, rather, to produce an institutional profit. As a result, "during the first half of the twentieth century, the unregulated use of prison labor led to exploitation of prisoners and unfair competition with free-world labor."[46]

Since its origin in the Elmira Reformatory (1876), **vocational training** has expanded to include everything from auto mechanics to welding, printing, construction trades, woodworking, agriculture, data processing, bookkeeping, and

vocational training: learning a marketable skill or trade through classroom instruction and/or on-the-job training.

cosmetology. Currently, over half of prisons and many jails have some type of industrial or vocational training.[47] But many correctional facilities are unable to accommodate everyone desiring to participate. In fact, such programs still enroll only about 10 percent of the prison population,[48] and the waiting list to get a job in prison industries can be "a couple of years long."[49] Even though more than two out of three prison inmates have work assignments, most involve janitorial duties or food preparation (26 percent), with only 4 percent involved in any type of industrial production.[50] While such jobs generally pay far less than $1 an hour, they are nevertheless highly coveted. As one former inmate noted: "In the outside world, you must work or starve. In prison, you work to keep from dying of boredom."[51]

In contrast to the days of pressing license plates, there is greater concern today that many offenders will end up back in the correctional system unless they are integrated into "meaningful occupations with a future."[52] In fact, it has been calculated that prisoners who participate in vocational training have about a 13 percent lower recidivism rate and that, down the line, such programs save some $12,000 per participant in criminal justice expenditures.[53] Moreover, as demonstrated in the upcoming "Close-up on Corrections," prison labor can also provide service to the community, as well as personal satisfaction to the inmate.

CLOSE-UP ON CORRECTIONS
Helping Themselves by Helping Others

> More than half of California's. . . . wild land firefighters are prison inmates earning $1 an hour as they work off sentences for nonviolent crimes. . . . The offenders are usually out of sight, laying more than a mile of hose, cutting fire lines and grubbing stubborn pockets of flame with shovels, rakes, pickaxes, and hoes. . . . Burglars and thieves risked their lives to rescue prized possessions from doomed houses. "The ceilings and light fixtures were coming down around us. You're wondering if you'll have to go out a window" to escape, said Greg Welch, serving seven years for selling drugs. . . .
>
> When they are not fighting fires . . . they're cleaning up parks, rebuilding trails, or making or renovating children's toys. Every day these inmates work, they get two days off their sentence. . . . "We save million-dollar homes for a dollar an hour," [said] Ricky Frank, sentenced to ten years for theft. "You get to help people. It's better than being locked up."
>
> *Source*: "Inmates Helped Quell California Wildfires," *Corrections Compendium*, Vol. 28, No. 12 (December, 2003), p. 20.

Private Sector Involvement

A promising response to the lack of readily available vocational training is the expanding private sector involvement in prison industries. In addition to removing certain restrictions on the sale of prison-made products, federal legislation in 1979 authorized the establishment of Prison Industry Enhancement (PIE) projects (discussed in Chapter 3). These initiatives now operate in 35 states and are generating millions of dollars in government revenues, inmate family support, and victim-compensation payments.[54]

Such partnerships between public prisons and private enterprises are not, however, problem-free. Major issues surround the challenges of recruiting employers into prisons, as well as determining salaries and benefits for inmate employees. Attracting industries into prisons would undoubtedly be promoted by lower salaries. But others argue that only union or prevailing wages will protect the free market from the unfair competition of prison-made products. Furthermore, such accepted practices of the private sector as collective bargaining can conflict with prison policies. In other words, the goals of private enterprise are not necessarily compatible with those of safe and efficient prison management.

Gender Discrimination

While correctional programming is insufficient in male facilities, it is even more limited in women's prisons, where research has cited inadequacies ranging from education to vocational training, prison industries, and law libraries.[55] As a result, programs in women's institutions may be limited to such stereotypical activities as sewing, typing, and the like—or, at best, other nontraditional programs that do not need sizeable enrollments to be cost-effective. In contrast, the more diverse, large-scale industrial and vocational training offered in male facilities provides better preparation for obtaining jobs and achieving upward mobility upon release. For example, research indicates that:

- women are generally offered a narrow range of stereotypical job training programs for conventionally "female" occupations, such as cosmetology and low-level clerical work;

- male prisons typically provide a greater variety of educational and vocational programs and training for more skilled (and better compensated) occupations;

- women in prison receive fewer institutional work assignments and lower rates of pay than male inmates, and men have greater access to work-release programs.[56]

- in comparison to the more than 35,000 professional/technical staff employed in male facilities, there are fewer than 3,000 in female facilities;

- in contrast to nearly 11,000 educational personnel in male facilities, fewer than 900 provide educational services for women.[57]

Under the equal protection clause of the U.S. Constitution, female offenders have filed suits in an attempt to obtain programs similar to those provided for male inmates. But, while one court ruling rejected that claim,[58] another found that state prisons receiving federal funds "are required by Title IX to make reasonable efforts to offer the same educational opportunities to women as men."[59]

Recreation

Unlike vocational training or other forms of treatment, virtually all inmates are entitled by court rulings to some form of recreation. Even in maximum security, inmates are afforded recreation, although it may be restricted to an hour of solitary workout under the close supervision of correctional staff. In lower-security facilities, recreational pursuits can range from individual or group athletics to arts and crafts, music, drama, table games, hobbies, television, and movies. However, some of these activities have generated considerable controversy and public criticism in recent years.[60] While the future of recreational TV may be in jeopardy, some institutions have turned television into a productive tool through programming that features instruction on everything from basic education to life skills and conflict resolution.[61]

Additionally, meaningful recreation may be one of the most beneficial activities in correctional facilities. Beyond occupying leisure time, recreation can help inmates cope with confinement and relieve the stress and anxiety of incarceration. Additional benefits range from developing interpersonal skills to enhancing self-esteem, problem-solving, and decision-making, as well as fostering cooperation and teamwork.[62] Moreover, people do not tend to get into trouble while busily occupied working off excess energy. Trouble inevitably starts during the boredom caused by too much leisure time.

EXHIBIT 9.4
Recreation can be a beneficial outlet for coping with the boredom and anxiety of confinement.

Source: Courtesy of the Broward County (Fort Lauderdale, FL) Sheriff's Office.

COUNSELING, CASEWORK, AND CLINICAL SERVICES

Everyone would not necessarily agree that religious services, educational programs, libraries, vocational training, or recreation meet a strict definition of "treatment." But there is little doubt that counseling, casework, and clinical services represent traditional long-term approaches to offender rehabilitation. Given their rehabilitative emphasis, one might assume that such treatment services were generally available in prisons under the medical model. That, however, was not the case.

Rhetoric versus Reality

Even at the height of the medical model, in-depth psychological counseling, social casework, and psychiatric therapy have never been prominent features of correctional institutions. A survey of state and federal prisons conducted in the mid-1950s, for example, found that the vast majority of staff held jobs related to the security needed to keep prisoners *in*, with less than 8 percent classified as people who were "there to get them ready to go out and stay out" (and even many of these were clerical positions).[63] At that time, there were only 23 full-time psychiatrists in U.S. correctional institutions—a number that would provide an average of 82 seconds of psychiatric help each month per inmate (assuming equal distribution throughout the country). The psychological staff numbered 67—able to provide about four minutes monthly for individual attention. The 257 caseworkers averaged less than 16 minutes per inmate each month.

By the mid-1960s, the percentage of treatment personnel had increased. But it was still estimated that more than 20,000 additional specialists were needed to address the "drastic scarcity" of treatment staff.[64] During a time that represented the peak years of the medical model, these figures do not say much for practical as opposed to ideological commitment to rehabilitation. In fact, most correctional administrators responding to a national survey in 1975 maintained that treatment programs had never really been tried, because they had not been adequately funded.[65] Others have observed that:

> It is not uncommon for an institution that houses a thousand or more inmates to define itself as being committed to rehabilitation when there is no full-time staff member who holds an advanced degree in any of the helping professions, or, when there are full-time and more or less adequately qualified staff members, to find that the ratio of inmates to qualified treatment staff is a hundred or more to one.[66]

As a prominent critic put it:

> One might conclude [that] we went through a great renaissance in corrections in the 1960's—characterized by massive infusions of funds into rehabilitative programs, psychoanalysis, psychotherapy, intensive treatment programs, etc. This, of course, is a great myth. The language of rehabilitation was popular—the reality was virtually nil.[67]

Additionally, during this period of time, treatment represented an "invasion" of what had previously been a custody-dominated system. Those in the custodial ranks tended to view treatment personnel with varying degrees of skepticism, mistrust, or at best grudging tolerance. Mere acceptance was still a long way off, let alone the establishment of a mutual custody–treatment partnership.[68] For these and many other reasons, it would appear that the medical model focused more on rhetoric than rehabilitation.

Treatment Availability Today

Undoubtedly, staffing over recent years has increased well beyond 23 psychiatrists, 67 psychologists, and 257 caseworkers—but then so has the number of people behind bars. On average, state and federal correctional facilities today have one psychologist on staff for every 750 inmates—which means that, hypothetically, each clinician would be responsible for the treatment of approximately 200 severely mentally ill offenders.[69] At the same time that the inmate population has been escalating, the availability of mental health services in the community has been declining. In 2002, it was observed that, over the previous decade, "forty state mental hospitals have closed, while more than 400 new prisons have been opened."[70] More recently, a direct inverse relationship for the past three decades has been documented between escalating numbers of prisoners and declining populations of mental hospitals.[71] In other words, the number of people in mental health facilities has dropped at essentially the same rate as that at which the number of people in prisons has grown. This shifts more and more of the mental health burden to the correctional conglomerate. Yet, as Exhibit 9.5 illustrates, custodial/security staff still far outnumber educational or professional/technical personnel employed in America's prisons. Even where treatment staff are available, many of them work in classification, where they are *processing* prisoners rather than *counseling* them.

Nor has treatment been recognized as a constitutional right. The Supreme Court has held that correctional administrators cannot maintain an attitude of "deliberate indifference" to the serious mental, physical, or emotional illness of offenders. But treatment may be limited to those with an identified medical necessity, as well as to procedures that can be provided within reasonable time and costs.[72] In fact, the courts rejected a sex offender's argument that the failure of prison officials to provide a therapeutic program tailored to his needs constituted cruel and unusual punishment.[73] In short, legal opinion to date has not supported a constitutional right to treatment for adult prisoners.

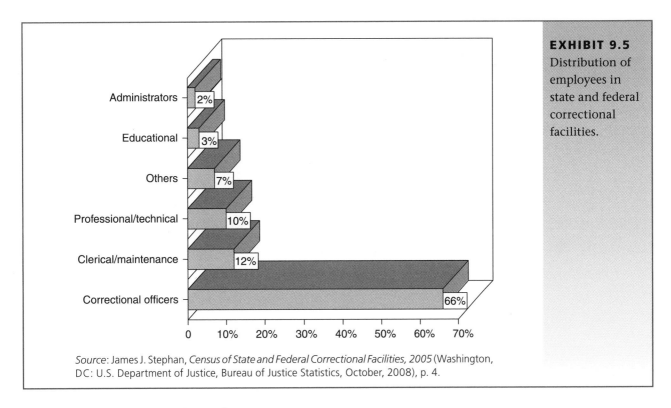

EXHIBIT 9.5
Distribution of employees in state and federal correctional facilities.

Source: James J. Stephan, *Census of State and Federal Correctional Facilities, 2005* (Washington, DC: U.S. Department of Justice, Bureau of Justice Statistics, October, 2008), p. 4.

Changing Treatment Orientation

Additionally, the overall objective of treatment has changed in recent years. With emphasis shifting toward the public safety orientation of the justice model, it has been observed that the major rationale for prison programming is no longer treatment, but security. Thus a program's impact on future criminality has become secondary to "more immediate concerns of keeping inmates busy and out of trouble." As a result, prison programs today are more likely to be viewed "as a means of riot prevention than crime prevention."[74]

On the other hand, it must also be acknowledged that many inmates do not actively seek treatment with a great deal of enthusiasm. They may well procrastinate even in the face of very clear expectations about the types of programs they must participate in to earn various privileges (such as parole, work-release opportunities, a lower security classification, etc.). Then, when it becomes apparent that entering a specified program is the only avenue to achieve these objectives, it may be difficult to be accommodated. Under such circumstances, packed "therapy sessions" are more likely to provide attendance certification than an avenue for meaningful change. In essence, treatment means change, and change is contrary to established lifestyles.

Generic Counseling

Counseling represents the one type of treatment that has been most commonly available in correctional facilities, and remains so today. (See Exhibit 9.6.) In fact,

counseling: establishing a supportive relationship with a client to achieve mutual understanding and address the client's problems.

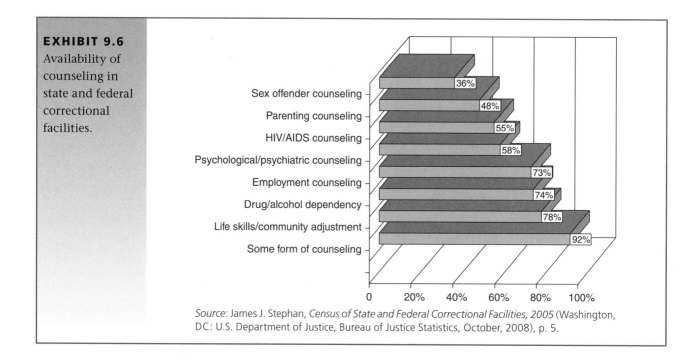

EXHIBIT 9.6
Availability of counseling in state and federal correctional facilities.

Source: James J. Stephan, *Census of State and Federal Correctional Facilities, 2005* (Washington, DC: U.S. Department of Justice, Bureau of Justice Statistics, October, 2008), p. 5.

generally speaking, counseling could be considered an approach used in almost every correctional setting. As a result, the word *counseling* can be very misleading when used in corrections.

In the outside world, counselors are considered to be those with appropriate academic credentials and a license to practice, who address a client's problems through such professionally recognized practices as individual or group therapy. In corrections, however, this title can take on a much broader meaning and might not actually refer to someone with formal educational preparation in counseling. (For a look at how counselor credentials can affect long-term outcomes, see the following "Close-up on Corrections.")

Of course, there are uncertified personnel who can and do perform generic counseling functions. Correctional officers, for example, probably conduct more "cellblock counseling" than any other staff members, since they are readily accessible to the inmates for more extended periods of time than the official treatment personnel. But the title "correctional counselor" within a facility might be attributed to anyone from professionally licensed clinical practitioners to unlicensed civilian personnel who handle inmate requests for commissary items, passes, medical attention, and so on.

CLOSE-UP ON CORRECTIONS
Selecting the Right Staff

The National Science Foundation report on rehabilitation describes the example of an experiment designed to test the effectiveness of group counseling. Offenders were randomly assigned to groups that received counseling or that did not. Parole performance at 12, 24, and 36 months was examined, and it appeared that offenders who had received counseling did not do any better than those who had not received counseling. However, upon closer scrutiny, it was found that the individuals providing counseling were not trained counselors. In addition, for many counselors there appeared to be little personal commitment to or involvement in the counseling. . . . In reality, the program did not provide the kind and quality of counseling that was ostensibly the object of the research.

Source: Alexis M. Durham III, *Crisis and Reform: Current Issues in American Punishment* (Boston: Little, Brown, 1994), pp. 149–150.

Clinical Counseling

Unlike those who engage in informal "counseling" without professional training, some correctional staff are certified counselors with academic credentials in psychology. In contrast to the long-term therapy provided by psychiatrists searching for deep-rooted causes of behavior, the "present orientation" of psychologists deals with how behavior is being expressed. The goal is to help the offender better resolve problems and manage conflicts in the here and now, rather than to completely resolve them.[75]

Basic to psychological therapy are the methods used to preserve one's ego or sense of worth—that is, defense mechanisms, such as *rationalization*. All of us have rationalized our behavior at some time, seeking to justify what we do. Whether this defense mechanism is socially harmful or not depends on what is being rationalized—the shoplifter's theft of merchandise because "that store is ripping off customers anyway," or the student's inability to remember historical dates because "they don't really matter."

Offenders are often noted for the defense called *projection*—transferring the blame for one's own shortcomings to others. Such projections are essentially excuses to avoid accepting responsibility. A common pattern among correctional clients, for example, is the projection of blame on society or "the system." Using this line of thinking, offenders can convince themselves that they are not in trouble because of their own fault but, rather, because of cops who were "out to get" them, judges who were "corrupt," a victim who "asked for it," or a lawyer who was "incompetent." The reality or unreality of these attitudes is not the issue—the fact remains that they exist.

Counseling Challenges

In treating criminal behavior, clinical psychologists attempt to divert the offender from socially unacceptable activities. This is done by channeling aggression, frustrations, and other stress and tensions in more socially acceptable directions. However, problem-solving through counseling in the correctional setting is often directed more toward facilitating the inmate's adjustment to the institution than toward long-term adjustment to life in free society.[76] This does not necessarily mean that counselors take an overly narrow view of their role, but the limited availability of treatment personnel in correctional institutions can impose a system of prioritizing. And, obviously, the difficulties of incarceration are immediate concerns.

Beyond large caseloads, counselors face a number of additional challenges unique to the institutional setting. Correctional counselors must be able to cope with everything from lack of administrative support and a heavy volume of paperwork to the difficulty of maintaining confidentiality, the potential for being "conned" by manipulative clients, and the necessity to work with those who have been "coerced" into treatment. Given these considerations, the effective correctional counselor is one who is both patient and persistent, skilled and streetwise, optimistic and realistic. With appropriate interpersonal relations skills and concerted effort, almost anyone can establish rapport. However, successful termination—bringing the client to the point of being able to function independently—requires exceptional skills.

LEARNING GOALS

Do you know:

16. why group rather than individual methods tend to prevail in correctional treatment?

17. the advantages of peer counseling and self-help groups?

group therapy: working with small groups, guiding interaction, exploring problems, and developing social skills by building supportive relationships.

Group Methods

Because individual counseling is conducted in one-on-one sessions between the client and therapist, it does not enable as many inmates to receive services as group methods, where a number of clients can be involved simultaneously. The key difference between group and individual counseling is the presence of other clients during the intervention process. In addition to being more economical and meeting the needs of a greater number of inmates, group techniques provide an opportunity for obtaining feedback and reinforcement from one's peers.

In its pure sense, **group therapy** is a treatment process in which a trained therapist (often a psychiatrist or clinical psychologist) works with small groups, guiding interaction, exploration of problems, and development of social skills through the establishment of supportive relationships within the group. Group therapy, group counseling, guided group interaction, sensitivity training, and psychodrama are among the group-oriented techniques that were introduced into correctional institutions in the decades between the late 1940s and the mid-1960s. While some of these techniques (such as psychodrama and sensitivity training) may be used less frequently today, group methods in general have become a widely used alternative in correctional settings, within both institutions and community-based services such as probation, parole, and halfway houses.

self-help groups: those uniting together to seek help for a shared problem such as alcohol abuse (e.g., AA) through positive peer reinforcement and supportive relationships.

Self-help Groups

Beyond merely participating in groups initiated by the correctional administration, inmates have for many years been involved in **self-help groups** of their own creation. In fact, as one counselor put it, "in the end, all counseling is self-help," since counselors can only facilitate and stimulate change.[77] The basic premise of these affiliations is that people with similar needs can be a source of mutual support. Both within and outside correctional institutions, prisoners and ex-offenders have become involved in such groups as Alcoholics Anonymous (AA), Narcotics Anonymous (NA), and Gamblers Anonymous. In addition to treatment-oriented groups, they have also participated in such social organizations as the Jaycees and various religious associations.

There are a number of advantages to the peer involvement of such self-help groups. For one thing, many of the members recognize that they have a problem with which they need help. Whether the motivation to change is the result of external intervention or internal self-awareness, these groups involve positive peer pressure through association with other people undergoing similar problems. The person comes to realize that he or she is not alone in experiencing such difficulties, and that others can help in developing the inner strength necessary to overcome the problem. Such groups also provide a vehicle through which the offender can learn responsibility, decision-making, problem-solving, and other life skills. In fact, in one state where budget cuts have eliminated most drug treatment programs, the only types of treatment available to prisoners in need of such services now will be AA and NA.[78] An additional benefit of these groups is the fact that they operate both inside prisons and within the outside community and can therefore serve as a "bridge" back into the mainstream of life for newly released ex-offenders.

Behavior Modification

Because prisons are closely controlled environments, they represent a setting that is adaptable to **behavior modification**. This treatment technique is based on the assumptions that criminal behavior is learned, and that it can be altered through a system of rewards and punishments in an institutional setting. However, it has also been criticized for reducing human dignity through manipulative, stimulus-followed-by-response types of interaction.

Most often used in juvenile facilities, behavior modification has often taken the form of a "token economy." In this system, tokens that can be used to purchase institutional privileges are awarded for good behavior and taken away for misconduct. One of the difficulties, of course, has been identifying effective reinforcers of approved behavior, since what may be motivating to one person may have little relevance to another. The process is also vulnerable to manipulation by inmates who quickly "learn the system" and superficially comply without altering their fundamental behavior. Additionally, there is concern that even valid changes which do occur may be

LEARNING GOALS

Do you know:

18. how techniques employed in the name of modifying behavior have been used as well as misused?

19. why social casework is more frequently used in community-based corrections than in institutional settings?

20. what therapeutic communities are?

behavior modification: changing behavior through the conditioning power of such reinforcements as rewards and punishments.

temporary features of the rigidly controlled environment of prisons, rather than long-term behavioral improvements that carry over to the freedom of life on the outside.

Most disturbing, however, is the fact that some of the correctional procedures dubiously referred to as "behavior modification" have at times gone well beyond what was originally meant by the term—turning into "fiendish forms of punishment."[79] Examples in the past have included the use of electroshock, aversive therapy, mind-altering drugs, and psychosurgery. In response to the abuse of these techniques, litigation was generated that has helped to eliminate many of these forms of "behavior modification" from prison systems.[80]

Drug Therapy and Other Behavioral Controls

Tranquilizing drugs, however, remain utilized because of their sedative effect in controlling violent, angry, or unruly offenders. Officials admit that nearly 10 percent of the state prison population receives psychotropic medications, and in five states that figure is nearly double (20 percent)[81]—despite criticisms that such tranquilizing drugs represent a subtle means of repression by disguising control as therapy.[82] In fact, it was only in 1990 that the Supreme Court determined that "a prison could not forcibly medicate a mentally ill person as punishment nor . . . forcibly medicate a mentally healthy inmate to achieve security objectives."[83]

The administration of drugs as a substitute for treatment has been one of the unfortunate by-products of an inadequate number of therapeutic personnel. But, even when used more for the control of personality disorders than for managerial convenience, medications are not always administered appropriately. Moreover, with the advent of managed care and contracted medical services, there is added concern that fiscal factors may be preventing offenders who truly need such medications from receiving them.

Reality Therapy

reality therapy: treatment directed toward facing the reality of the situation and becoming responsible for one's own actions.

If there is one area of correctional treatment that has been almost as controversial as behavior modification, it is **reality therapy**. Originally, reality therapy was developed by a psychiatrist who became disenchanted with traditional therapeutic techniques and created a system diametrically opposed to orthodox psychoanalytic approaches.[84] It takes the position that excuses for deviant behavior should be faced realistically, and that the most appropriate therapeutic approach is getting involved with the client, rejecting irresponsible behavior, and encouraging acceptance of responsibility for one's own actions.

Some of the key words in reality therapy are "responsibility," "involvement," "here and now," and "facing the consequences." Focus is on discussing the client's current situation as one of his or her "own choosing," while still making the person feel loved and worthwhile. The idea is that aggressively dealing with reality in a therapeutic frame of reference can communicate love (sometimes called "tough love") and generate self-respect through firm but caring steps.

More recently, several new forms of reality-based behavior therapy have emerged that appear to hold considerable potential—including anger management and cognitive-restructuring programs. Such efforts emphasize changing inappropriate behavioral responses and antisocial thought patterns that have played a significant part in igniting the offender's conflicts with society.

On the one hand, this technique may be helpful in encouraging young offenders to take responsibility for their problems and regain control over their lives. But, on the other hand, its weakness may lie in oversimplification of human behavior and the potential for worsening some types of mental illness by expectations that are too demanding.

Cognitive Restructuring

One of the most recent therapeutic trends has been in the area of cognitive restructuring—attempting to change, first, the way people think and, ultimately, the way they act. The basis of this theory is that criminals do not think like law-abiding prosocial people. Rather, their erroneous thinking process "rationalizes and justifies" their behavior by making excuses, blaming others, and playing the role of victim.[85]

Therapists have identified a number of these common errors or distortions in cognitive processing that can have serious implications for subsequent behavior.[86] Programs that use this approach are based on the premise that changing thinking patterns changes self-image, and ultimately, behavior. Through cognitive restructuring, offenders learn how to identify and alter their thought patterns. They learn that "by controlling their thinking and changing their perceptions of events around them, they gain the ability to make appropriate choices."[87] Prosocial reasoning, self-control, and problem-solving strategies are emphasized in an open, empathetic atmosphere.[88]

One such program, for example, works with violent juvenile offenders to help them develop insights into and strategies for dealing with such characteristic problems as anger, lying, and projecting blame. They learn how to take responsibility for their actions and to defer immediate gratification. Self-reflections are used to explore the inmate's thought processes, and participants eventually begin to see how "certain events trigger cycles or patterns of thinking." The object is then to "design and practice interventions to derail the cycle and avoid the thought patterns that led to violent behavior."[89] As one participant summarized the process, "I guess I don't have to do the same old stuff if I don't think the same old way."[90]

Psychiatric and Psychoanalytic Treatment

Psychiatric treatment or involvement in corrections is generally limited to initial diagnosis, treatment prediction, and subsequent consultation with the

psychiatric treatment: long-term therapeutic techniques directed toward uncovering deep-rooted causes of behavior, often through psychoanalysis.

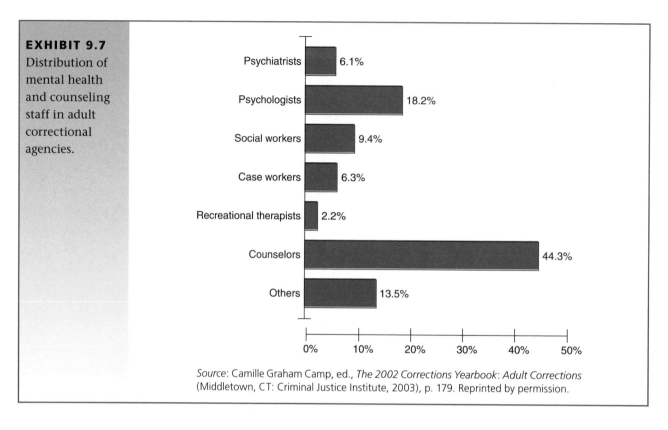

EXHIBIT 9.7
Distribution of mental health and counseling staff in adult correctional agencies.

Psychiatrists 6.1%
Psychologists 18.2%
Social workers 9.4%
Case workers 6.3%
Recreational therapists 2.2%
Counselors 44.3%
Others 13.5%

Source: Camille Graham Camp, ed., *The 2002 Corrections Yearbook*: *Adult Corrections* (Middletown, CT: Criminal Justice Institute, 2003), p. 179. Reprinted by permission.

psychologists, social workers, and other counselors who make up the bulk of institutional treatment staff. As shown in Exhibit 9.7, the extremely small number of psychiatrists working in the correctional field suggests that long-term psychoanalytic techniques designed to uncover deep-rooted causes of behavior have not frequently been employed in prison settings. Within the criminal justice system, most psychiatrists function outside of corrections in the pretrial and courtroom phases of the process—to determine whether defendants are of sufficient mental competence to be held legally responsible for their actions.

When an extremely disturbed inmate is in need of mental health services, referral is usually made to a psychiatric hospital for treatment. In fact, some correctional departments, in conjunction with the state mental health agency, maintain a separate forensic facility exclusively for the criminally insane. (For a more detailed account of how the mentally ill are handled in corrections, see Chapter 7.)

Social Casework

Historically, the partnership between social work and corrections began early in the twentieth century, when private charities and reform groups were becoming increasingly involved with offenders. As the field progressed toward development of the concept of self-determination, social work became the art of "helping people help themselves."

Because of this emphasis on empowerment of the individual client, however, social work has not been as amenable to the authoritative setting of institutional corrections. As a result, **social casework** is used more frequently in community-based corrections (particularly probation and parole), minimum security institutions, juvenile facilities, and diagnostic processing, as opposed to the direct delivery of services in high-security prisons.

Social work techniques typically include social casework and group work, along with practices ranging from community organization and individual problem-solving to Freudian diagnostic and therapeutic approaches. But generally the emphasis is more on dealing with an inmate's immediate situation than on in-depth psychotherapy. Caseworkers help clients maintain constructive relationships, solve problems, and function independently.[91]

social casework: providing services through social work practices, often designed to achieve self-determination and individual empowerment.

Nontraditional and Interdisciplinary Techniques

The psychoanalysis practiced by psychiatrists, the casework methods used by social workers, the group and individual therapy performed by psychologists, and the informal counseling conducted by many others all represent traditional approaches to working with people. Those who have become disenchanted with these orthodox procedures have advocated such nontraditional concepts as transactional analysis, primal therapy, systematic desensitization, nondirective therapy, and—more recently—even acupuncture, pet therapy, and transcendental meditation,[92] along with many others. Generally, these new techniques have been directed toward a certain group representing a proportionally small segment of the total correctional caseload. For an exception, see the nontraditional strategy described in the upcoming "Close-up on Corrections," where productivity, decision-making, and accountability are emphasized throughout confinement in preparation for the realities of life on the outside.

CLOSE-UP ON CORRECTIONS
Preparing on the Inside for Life on the Outside—Missouri's Parallel Universe

Recognizing the disconnection between life inside and outside of prison, the Missouri Department of Corrections has overhauled its approach to prison management. The new strategy, "parallel universe," is based on the notion that life inside should resemble life outside, and that inmates can acquire values, habits, and skills that will help them become productive, law-abiding citizens.

In conventional prison management, institutional control eliminates any opportunity for prisoners to make decisions and be held accountable. Avoiding punishment becomes the primary occupation, and two important skills that offenders need are overlooked—making decisions, and accepting their consequences. But in Missouri, the structure of prison life has been re-engineered to include four interactive components:

1. *Productivity:* Every inmate is engaged in activities that parallel those of free society. During "work hours," they go to school, jobs, and treatment programs. During "nonwork hours," they participate in community service, recreation, and activities such as victim–offender mediation, victim impact classes, and projects designed to repair the harm suffered by victims.

2. *Prevention:* Everyone must adopt relapse prevention strategies and abstain from unauthorized activities, including drug/alcohol use and sexual misconduct. Because they are aware of their risk of reoffending, they are better able to make responsible decisions.

3. *Decision-making:* Most offenders can earn opportunities to make choices, and are held accountable for them.

4. *Motivation:* Offenders are recognized for good conduct and can improve their status by obeying rules and regulations.

From an institutional management standpoint, this approach also has obvious advantages, since most inmates do not commit crimes while productively engaged in work or school activities. But the real evidence of its effectiveness occurs when they are released.

Upon admission, felons in the Missouri prison system could be considered failures on a number of counts. The vast majority were high school dropouts. Many were unable to obtain or hold a job. Most had abused drugs and/or alcohol. But since Missouri prisons adopted components of the parallel universe, many failures have been transformed into successes. Now more than 98% of the inmate population is engaged in some combination of full-time education, work, and/or treatment. Lawsuits initiated by prisoners have dropped substantially. But perhaps most impressive . . . recidivism was reduced by one-third (from 33% to 20%).

Postscript: In 2008, Arizona's parallel universe program (where it is known as "Getting Ready") received an innovations in American government award from the John F. Kennedy School of Government at Harvard University.

Source: Compiled from Dora Schiro, "Correcting Corrections: Missouri's Parallel Universe," *Sentencing and Corrections: Issues for the 21st Century* (Washington, DC: U.S. Department of Justice, May, 2000). See also Dora Schiro, "Getting Ready: How Arizona Has Created a 'Parallel Universe' for Inmates," *American Jails*, Vol. XXIII, No. 6 (January–February, 2010), pp. 15–19.

None of the traditional or nontraditional approaches works with everyone, but each seems to work with someone. Some offenders are reformed through psychiatric help, others because they learned a job skill, others because they found religion, and still others simply because someone took an interest in them. It is apparent that no single type of treatment is demonstrably superior to any other one. No single program or process represents the ideal solution for every client. Each has its unique strengths and weaknesses. Each works better with some offenders or at some point in their lives than others.

Although treatment personnel might like to draw from a broad array of techniques, the extensive training needed to become a professional in any one area creates a narrowly focused perspective. As a result, most identify with one or two approaches, neglecting the larger body of knowledge outside of their professional discipline. Similarly, budgetary constraints combined with political ideologies often result in correctional institutions adopting a narrowly limited range of techniques to offer everyone within their custody. Given this "one-size-fits-all" approach, it is not surprising that researchers have often reported disappointing results. However, a review of some 700 studies indicates that, when offenders participate in programs that are appropriate to their specific needs, reductions in recidivism range from 25 to 30 percent.[93]

Therapeutic Communities

Some institutional settings have embraced a much wider variety of treatment alternatives that are not based on a single method. An example of such a multifaceted approach is the prison that functions as an overall **therapeutic community**. As the next "Close-up on Corrections" describes, these "communities" are based on the concept that multiple interdisciplinary techniques focusing on prosocial values, combined with a treatment-oriented custodial staff and a supportive peer culture, can produce an institutional environment directed toward behavioral change.[94] In this manner, everyone works together toward providing a cohesive, supportive network, with each component reinforcing the others.

In fact, some therapeutic communities extend into postrelease aftercare, which has been reported to have positive results with drug-involved offenders.[95] While there has been some exception taken to "premature" belief in the substantial impact of therapeutic communities,[96] studies have reported lower recidivism when their graduates are compared to those of prison-based treatment groups.[97]

therapeutic community: a comprehensive treatment environment, where multifaceted techniques are combined with treatment-oriented custodial staff.

CLOSE-UP ON CORRECTIONS
Inside a Therapeutic Community

Upon entering a therapeutic community (TC), one does not see the trappings of an institution, clinic, hospital, or even a treatment program per se. Instead, elements of a home, school, and business are apparent and a variety of housekeeping, educational, and vocational activities are in progress. The environment more largely resembles an energetic village than an institution or service setting.

Individuals change when they are totally involved in the community. Indeed, the word "involvement" is not used casually by residents or staff. Both participation and involvement are related to program stages. Individuals in the induction, primary treatment, and reentry stages are at different points in the program plan.

In comparison to prisons, therapeutic communities are non-bureaucratic. There is a minimum of clearly defined rules, and decision-making is decentralized to facilitate the goal of individualized treatment. In their relations with clients, staff members are expected to minimize status distinctions, to encourage open and spontaneous communication, and to develop close, personal relations in an effort to gain client cooperation. Misconduct is interpreted as symptomatic of an underlying problem, and any punishment is consistent with therapeutic recommendations. Punishment is thus minimized and highly individualized.

The client is expected to develop a life as similar as possible to life in the free community through involvement in the work, educational, religious, and recreational programs provided. Relations within residential units are expected to resemble family relations. Group therapy sessions are conducted within the residential unit, and each cottage is largely a self-governing unit, with administrative and maintenance problems resolved by means of group decisions.

What distinguishes TCs is the "community" or group as the primary facilitator of growth and change. Other features they have in common include the use of ex-offenders and ex-addicts as staff, use of confrontation and support groups, a set of rules and sanctions to govern behavior, and promotion of prosocial attitudes. Participation generally lasts for an extended period, during which clients are shielded from competing demands of street, work, friends, and family. It may be this intensive, multifaceted focus that explains why TCs are more likely to be successful in the long run.

Source: Adapted from George DeLeon, *The Therapeutic Community: Theory, Model, and Method* (New York: Springer Publishing, 2000), pp. 119, 347, and Douglas S. Lipton, "Prison-Based Therapeutic Communities: Their Success with Drug-Abusing Offenders," *National Institute of Justice Journal* (February, 1996), p. 13.

The Future of Prison Programming

Every approach does not work equally effectively with every offender. The question then becomes just what *does* seem to work best? The next "Close-up on Corrections" provides some answers—identifying the fundamental principles of effective intervention. Especially with so much focus today on the negative aspects of corrections and the failures among its clients, it is important to keep in mind that properly structured programs based on appropriate treatment techniques *do* hold promise and have potential to alter lives.

CLOSE-UP ON CORRECTIONS
Principles of Effective Correctional Intervention

1. *Organizational culture*—well-defined goals, ethical principles, staff cohesion, and a history of effectively responding to issues.
2. *Program implementation/maintenance*—consistent with organizational values, based on empirically defined needs, thorough literature review, and pilot trials.
3. *Management/staff characteristics*—professionally trained (with previous experience); selected on the basis of rehabilitative beliefs, relationship styles, and therapeutic skills.
4. *Client risk/need*—assessed by instruments of proven predictive validity which include a

wide range of dynamic risk factors or criminogenic needs (e.g., antisocial attitudes), as well as offender responsivity to different styles and modes of service.

5. *Program characteristics*—targeting a wide variety of criminogenic needs for change (i.e., factors that predict recidivism), using empirically valid behavioral therapies, with the ratio of rewards to punishments at least 4:1, and provision for relapse prevention.

6. *Core correctional practice*—including anti-criminal modeling, effective reinforcement, problem-solving techniques, structured learning, skill-building, effective use of authority, cognitive self-change, relationship practices, and motivational interviewing.

7. *Inter-agency communication*—aggressive referrals and advocating for offenders so that they receive high-quality services in the community.

8. *Evaluation*—routinely conducting program audits, consumer satisfaction surveys, process evaluations of changes in criminogenic need, and follow-ups of recidivism rates.

Source: Compiled from Edward J. Latessa, Francis T. Cullen, and Paul Gendreau, "Beyond Correctional Quackery: Professionalism and the Possibility of Effective Treatment," *Federal Probation* (September, 2002), p. 45.

But, with the change from the therapeutic focus of the medical model to the incapacitation emphasis of the justice model, enthusiasm for prison-based rehabilitative efforts has diminished. What the future holds remains to be seen, but it is apparent that the orientation of prison programming has shifted from treatment to security.

It is equally clear that, if insufficient resources were available to implement the mandates of the medical model, it is not very realistic to expect more during times of greater fiscal restraint. Prison-based programming has simply not kept pace with the dramatic growth in institutional populations.[98]

Additionally, the fiscal crisis that emerged in 2008 has undoubtedly had an impact, as budget deficits forced many facilities to downsize or discontinue nonessential initiatives. With at least 22 states scaling down correctional funding in their fiscal year 2010 budgets, one of the most prevalent cost-saving strategies has been to eliminate or reduce programming.[99] Yet research indicates that "effective treatment results in savings to society that outweigh the costs of treatment by a factor of at least 4 to 1."[100] In fact, when managed effectively, alcohol and drug treatment have been cited as saving $7 for every $1 spent.[101]

Nor are limited resources and lessened enthusiasm the only challenges correctional treatment faces. Prison-based rehabilitative programs are inherently difficult to manage and administer, regardless of the specific modality, qualifications of staff, or sincerity of participants. Correctional institutions "are simply ill-suited for intensive treatment programs."[102] Moreover, transferring treatment progress to the real world from the artificial environment of a correctional institution represents a significant challenge. For example, providing drug treatment in prison is "commendable but incomplete" without ongoing relapse prevention upon release, just as offering job training programs is less likely to be effective without a link to the outside world of work.[103] In many respects, the better option may well be to expand the availability of treatment programs outside of the correctional conglomerate. As one researcher has pointed out, "instead of advocating treatment in prison, we should be trying treatment *instead of prison*."[104]

SUMMARY

Some would maintain that correctional treatment is limited to therapeutic intervention by licensed professionals following a clinical diagnosis. In contrast, this chapter has reflected a broader perspective encompassing many of the programs and services provided within correctional facilities that promote socializing influences among the inmate population.

Whatever one's perspective of treatment, within corrections the process begins with initial classification. Through proper classification, the institution is better able to manage large groups of offenders, meet individual needs, prioritize services, and distribute scarce resources. Recently, objective models have been used to streamline classification. But concerns have been expressed that such a highly structured process dehumanizes classification, substituting administrative efficiency for an in-depth assessment. Additionally, prison crowding can prohibit placing inmates in those facilities and programs best suited to their needs. Nevertheless, classification outcomes have a long-term impact on the offender.

Regardless of how an inmate is classified, religious services represent one form of "treatment" to which everyone is entitled. Beginning with the Quakers, religion has always played a key role in corrections. Although chaplains are not always fully accepted by either inmates or staff, they can be very influential. Beyond providing worship services and faith-based studies, one of the most significant roles of the chaplain is simply being a willing listener.

Following religion, education and vocational training were the next major rehabilitative programs to be introduced into correctional institutions. Because so many inmates have not completed high school or are functionally illiterate, they are especially in need of remedial education. Computer-assisted instruction has been helpful in this respect, since it enables classes to be provided on an ongoing basis, tailors learning to the individual's capability, and progresses at the student's own pace.

Work has been a central feature of prisons throughout the history of corrections. But it has only been in relatively modern times that employment and vocational training have been directed toward developing marketable job skills rather than making financial profits. Although wide varieties of vocational programs are available throughout corrections today, they are still insufficient to meet the demand. Efforts have therefore been under way to encourage the private sector to become involved in establishing prison and jail industries.

While such vocational opportunities are limited, virtually all inmates have access to recreation, which encompasses everything from team sports to arts and crafts, music, drama, table games, hobbies, television, and videos. Recreation programs not only relieve boredom and idleness, but can also help to reduce the stress and anxiety of incarceration.

The more traditional forms of treatment provided in corrections include counseling, casework, and clinical services. Even during the height of the medical model, however, such programs were not readily available, and many treatment personnel find themselves more immersed in routine processing than direct service delivery. Of all forms of treatment, counseling represents the most commonly available (although the term *counseling* is sometimes interpreted broadly in correctional settings). In contrast to one-on-one counseling sessions, group therapy can serve more clients in a less threatening atmosphere. Inmates themselves have also formed such self-help groups as Alcoholics Anonymous and Narcotics Anonymous.

Another form of treatment, behavior modification, was originally designed to change behavior through the conditioning power of rewards and punishments. However, efforts to modify behavior have at times extended to such aversive techniques as electroshock and mind-altering drugs. Although many of these practices have been terminated as a result of legal intervention, tranquilizing drugs are still used in some settings to control violent, angry, or disruptive inmates.

Numerous additional techniques have been attempted at one time or another—ranging from reality therapy to cognitive restructuring. However, long-term psychoanalysis has not been frequently employed in corrections. Similarly, social work has not been a part of the treatment program of many correctional institutions, in part because its focus on self-determination and individual empowerment can conflict with an authoritative setting. Social casework has, however, been used much more extensively in juvenile facilities and community-based corrections.

Historically, correctional institutions have offered a limited range of treatment techniques, despite the fact that no one alternative will work equally well with all inmates. In an effort to provide a multifaceted approach that incorporates a number of disciplines, therapeutic communities direct the total environment toward behavioral change. A broader array of treatment alternatives certainly presents greater potential for meeting the needs of any particular person. But, with society's move from the medical model to the more punitive justice model, issues surrounding how best to diagnose, treat, and change behavior are not predominate concerns of the correctional conglomerate today.

FOR FURTHER DISCUSSION

1. Discuss the benefits and drawbacks of both objective and subjective classification models, especially from the perspectives of both efficiency and effectiveness. Aside from the operational attributes of various models, explain the role of public policy in shaping classification decision-making.

2. It has been stated that the overall aim of an appropriate classification system is to "match the security and treatment needs of the inmate with the resources available within the correctional system." Develop several hypothetical cases to describe what can happen when necessary resources are unavailable in this regard, especially in terms of the potential negative consequences.

3. Recently, there has been some controversy about whether classification systems are gender-neutral, or whether a separate system is needed to more effectively classify women. Look at the classification materials available on the website of the National Institute of Corrections and argue for or against gender-specific classification.

4. Go online to locate several evaluations of faith-based programming in correctional facilities, and critique their objectivity, methodology, and findings.

5. Especially with respect to the constitutional separation of church and state, debate whether the merger of religious principles with correctional programming through faith-based initiatives is appropriate in government-funded correctional facilities.

6. Locate research findings on the impact of post-secondary education in correctional facilities. Then go online to review the reasons behind congressional action barring inmates from receiving Pell grants in 1994. From the information you obtain, debate both sides of the issue of post-secondary correctional education.

7. Visit the website of your state's department of corrections to see what prison industries are operating in your state and what commodities they are producing.

8. Either visit or go online to find a local correctional facility in your area and look at their table of organization to determine how many treatment staff they employ. Then find out how many inmates they service and calculate how much treatment time per week, on average, each inmate is hypothetically able to receive.

9. Discuss what behavior modification means from a psychological perspective, as opposed to the manner in which it is often employed (with tranquilizing drugs) in correctional facilities.

10. Especially in terms of their holistic approach, explain why such alternatives as therapeutic communities or Missouri's parallel universe may be more likely to be effective than specific individual techniques.

11. Review the primary principles of effective therapeutic intervention developed by Gendreau and others and determine why they are so integrally related to treatment effectiveness.

CHAPTER 10

The Effects of Institutional Life

It's difficult to conceive of a better plan to render people incapable of living in society than isolating them in the abnormal world of high-security prisons.[1]
Michael G. Santos

CHAPTER OVERVIEW

The effects of being incarcerated are difficult for those in free society to fully appreciate. They range from the simple irritation of being required to eat the same monotonous food at precisely the same time day after day to the serious impact of being restricted from normal social relationships. They include the dehumanizing influence of everything from being subjected to strip searches to losing material possessions, personal privacy, and individual autonomy. They transform adult men and women into "little boys and girls who are assumed to need maximum supervision and guidance for even the simplest of activities."[2] They are the product of an environment in which inmates are secluded from the outside, subservient to the staff, subdued by the rules, subjected to the control of other inmates, socialized into the prison subculture, and silenced by the lack of public concern.

Under such conditions, hopelessness, frustration, and alienation find fertile breeding grounds. Some express their feelings in passive resignation, others in physical rebellion. Assaults, homicides, and suicides occur in virtually every correctional institution. Although considerably less frequent, riots represent the ultimate expression of built-up hostilities. The public is inevitably shocked when violence flares into a widespread riot. But it is perhaps more surprising that such major disturbances are relatively unusual events.

Those in free society might argue that, by stripping the offender of human dignity, imprisonment will make the type of lasting, negative impression that will serve as a strong deterrent to recidivism. Quite the contrary, instead of leaving with a determination to avoid another prison term, many become accustomed to prison life and resigned to the inevitability of returning to it. Some become so acclimated to the prison routine and so apprehensive of their ability to "make it" on the outside that, ironically, they are reluctant to leave.

Given the fact that even the best of the treatment techniques described in the previous chapter take place within such a dehumanizing environment, it is little wonder that they have been less than totally successful. Undoubtedly, there are those who have overcome the effects of prison to become law-abiding citizens. But they may well have done so despite—rather than because of—their experiences in confinement. In many respects, imprisonment represents more an obstacle to overcome than an opportunity to reform. It may simply be illogical to expect corrections to change behavior, given the incongruity of trying to teach offenders to adjust to society by removing them from it.

THE PROCESS OF PRISONIZATION

Through the process of **prisonization**, inmates become socialized into prison life. It involves adapting to the culture, values, norms, and behavioral expectations of the prison environment and begins virtually immediately upon entry. In fact, incarceration promotes prisonization among both new and experienced inmates. The entering inmate is stripped, showered, deloused, given a uniform, assigned a number, and issued the rulebook. Personal property is searched, inspected, and inventoried. Items that are not allowable are stored or shipped elsewhere. Hair is cut to standardized regulations. Stripped of these sources of individual identity, the depersonalization of imprisonment begins. As one inmate describes it, "one of the cruelest aspects of a penitentiary is the way it leaves one isolated and lonely despite the overcrowded surroundings."[3]

Reactions to the prisonization process range from physical or mental rebellion to abnormal hunger and capacity to sleep.[4] But free will and self-direction can be repressed only so far, even in the most regimented institution. In opposition to the authoritative controls of the administration, inmates create their own status hierarchy, code of conduct, and subcultural value system—governing everything from verbal communications to sexual activities. It is not long before new inmates learn how personal autonomy finds expression within confinement. They quickly determine who wields power, controls privileges, and imposes punishments. It is not long before those imprisoned realize that they are subject not only to the formal rules and regulations established by the official administration, but also to the informal code imposed by their fellow prisoners. And, among the inmate population, violation of the inmate code is a far more serious infraction than violation of the official regulations.

Importation versus Deprivation

But just how does prison socialization take place? Is it simply a result of confining together large groups of offenders who share similar values, attitudes, and behaviors?

> **LEARNING GOALS**
>
> Do you know:
> 1. what "prisonization" is?
> 2. how the importation model and the deprivation model differ in terms of their explanation of inmate socialization?
> 3. what behaviors characterize an "institutionalized" personality?

prisonization: becoming socialized into institutional life by adapting to the culture, values, norms, and behavioral expectations of the prison environment.

EXHIBIT 10.1
Despite overcrowding, the prisonization process leaves inmates feeling isolated, lonely, helpless, and depersonalized.

importation model: maintains that the prisonization process is a feature of characteristics that inmates bring (import) into prison.

If so, according to the **importation model**, the attributes of prisonization are *imported* (i.e., brought into the institution) by the particular types of people who commit crime. Thus, we would not expect to find the same behaviors if prisons confined those of a different socioeconomic class or value background.

Certainly, one's moral values are bound to be affected by close, continuous association with others who do not adhere to socially acceptable norms. But is there also something about the nature of correctional institutions that creates an unnatural response among those who would otherwise not react the same way in a different environment? If so, according to the **deprivation model**, the behavior of those confined may reflect a normal response to being abnormally *deprived* of everything from physical amenities to social status and personal self-esteem.[5] According to the deprivation perspective, the pains and stresses associated with incarceration confront inmates with adjustment problems that call for a collective solution—which they pursue through the inmate subculture.[6]

deprivation model: maintains that the prisonization process is a result of adapting to the deprivations of an abnormal institutional environment.

Regardless of which theory is subscribed to, it is apparent that prisons produce a unique culture that reflects either "response to the deprivations of prison existence or . . . re-creation of [one's] external environment within the walls."[7] Actually, it may be a little of each, with the two models complementing rather than contradicting each other.

The Stanford Prison Experiment

A landmark experiment conducted with two dozen male college students acting in roles as inmates and officers may shed some light on this issue.[8] Those selected were mature, emotionally stable, intelligent students from middle-class backgrounds. None had any criminal record. In fact, they appeared to represent the "cream of the crop" of their generation. By the flip of a coin, half were assigned to play the role of "prisoners." The other half were designated as "guards," instructed to make up their own rules for maintaining law, order, and respect in the mock prison setting established by the researchers. How do you think you would react if placed in the role of an inmate or correctional officer? According to this experiment, your response might be quite different from what you would expect. See the next "Close-up on Corrections" for the chilling details of what actually happened.

The outcome of that experiment tends to support the deprivation model in a number of respects. The student inmates displayed many of the same prisonization characteristics as their real-life counterparts, despite the fact that their backgrounds were not at all representative of the typical prisoner. Additionally, the officer "guards" quickly assumed roles that reflected a repressive environment. As a result, the researchers concluded that we underestimate the power and pervasiveness of situational controls over behavior.[9]

At the same time, it should be noted that this brief experiment involved not "hardened criminals" but defenseless students, who were placed in an environment that was very different from that to which they were accustomed. In contrast, inmates entering correctional institutions today are more likely to have progressed through a number of intermediate sanctions or shorter terms in jail prior to experiencing prison. It would therefore be expected that their "criminal identity" would be better developed.

Nor did those playing the role of "guards" have the benefit of the academy training and more rigorous selection that would be characteristic of a real setting. In that respect, the experiment's most significant message may actually be the danger inherent when unskilled, untrained, and unsupervised personnel control the destiny of the powerless. As a result of such factors, the effects on the students were rather drastic and spontaneous, whereas becoming "prisonized" in reality is a more long-term process—with inmates gradually becoming accustomed to the "wide range of restrictions, deprivations, and indignities that institutionalized life imposes."[10] Yet the frightening message of the Stanford experiment was reinforced again in the 2004 scandal at Abu Ghraib prison during the Iraq war.

CLOSE-UP ON CORRECTIONS
The Pathology of Imprisonment

The "prisoners" were unexpectedly picked up at their homes by a city policeman in a squad car, searched, handcuffed, fingerprinted, booked . . . and taken blindfolded to our "jail." There they were stripped, deloused, put into a uniform, given a number, and put into a cell with two other prisoners, where they expected to live for the next two weeks. The pay was $15 a day, and their motivation was to make money. . . .

At the end of only six days, we had to close down our mock prison because what we saw was frightening. It was no longer apparent to most of the subjects (or to us) where reality ended and their roles began. The majority had indeed become prisoners or guards, no longer able to clearly differentiate between role-playing and self. There were dramatic changes in virtually every aspect of their behavior, thinking, and feeling. In less than a week, the experience of imprisonment undid (temporarily) a lifetime of learning; human values were suspended, self-concepts were challenged, and the ugliest, most base, pathological side of human nature surfaced. We were horrified because we saw some boys (guards) treat others as if they were despicable animals, taking pleasure in cruelty, while other boys (prisoners) became servile, dehumanized robots who thought only of escape, of their own individual survival, and of their mounting hatred for the guards.

We had to release three prisoners in the first four days because they had such acute situational traumatic reactions as hysterical crying, confusion in thinking, and severe depression. Others begged to be "paroled," and all but three were willing to forfeit all the money they had earned if they could be paroled. By then (the fifth day), they had been so programmed to think of themselves as prisoners that when their request for parole was denied, they returned docilely to their cells. . . . By the last days, the earlier solidarity among the prisoners (systematically broken by the guards) dissolved into "each man for himself." Finally, when one of their fellows was put in solitary confinement (a small closet) for refusing to eat, the prisoners were given a choice . . . give up their blankets and the incorrigible prisoner would be let out, or keep their blankets and he would be kept in all night. They voted to keep their blankets and to abandon their brother.

About a third of the "guards" became tyrannical in their arbitrary use of power, in enjoying their control over other people. They were corrupted by the power of their roles and became quite inventive in their techniques of breaking the spirit of the prisoners and making them feel they were worthless. Some of the guards merely did their jobs as tough but fair correctional officers. . . . However, no good guard ever interfered with a command by any of the bad guards; they never intervened on the side of the prisoners, they never told the others to ease off because it was only an experiment, and they never even came to me as prison superintendent or experimenter in charge to complain. . . .

The consultant for our prison . . . [was] an ex-convict with 16 years of imprisonment. . . . [He] would get so depressed and furious each time he visited our prison, because of its psychological similarities to his experiences, that he would have to leave. A Catholic priest who was a former prison chaplain . . . talked to our prisoners after four days and said they were just like the other first-timers he had seen.

Source: Philip G. Zimbardo, "Pathology of Imprisonment," *Society*, Vol. 9, No. 2 (1972).

The Impact of Incarceration

As the mock prison experiment illustrated, the pervasive effects of incarceration can occur in even a very brief period of time. Consider, then, how detrimental the effects of long-term imprisonment can be, especially for those in maximum custody, where everyone is subjected to rigid regulations, inmates are taught to line up and move in unison, aggression is met with aggression, orders dictate every movement, lights never go out, life is highly structured around a well-regulated routine, and there are few individual decisions to be made—other than whether to go along or resist.

In such a setting, close emotional relationships are nonexistent. Little things—from the food menu to TV programming—take on an exaggerated importance. The minimal standard of living drains the very meaning from life. Goals and aspirations become readjusted downward or given up completely. As the next "Close-up" describes in vivid detail, long-timers learn to live from day to day. Combined with the lack of opportunity to make decisions, the strict rules produce people who are "emotionally crippled."[11] In the words of one inmate: "Surviving imprisonment requires patience and humility. . . . Despite the dangers of assault, the struggle is more mental than physical; the real threat is to your sanity."[12]

CLOSE-UP ON CORRECTIONS
Reflections on Survival

> I was now a member of the prison system. I knew nothing about what was going on, only that I had maximum time to do, if I ever got out. . . . I adjusted as best I could. As I changed over the years, the system affected me more than I ever thought it would. I quickly adjusted my beliefs and changed my habits and my personality to fit my new hell. I developed an emotionless face and learned to trust no one. . . . I became preoccupied with surviving and avoiding violence. I focused on food, water, cigarettes, and survival: the basics of life.
>
> No staff member taught me these lessons. I learned them to survive. Now they're a part of me.
>
> *Source:* K.C. Carceral, *Behind a Convict's Eyes: Doing Time in a Modern Prison*
> (Belmont, CA: Wadsworth/Thomson Learning, 2004), p. 22.

The Institutionalized Personality

The result is a dehumanizing environment that forms an **institutionalized personality**. The inmate becomes similar to a robot, moving according to a routinized pattern, losing all initiative, living on a day-to-day basis, blocking off the past, and avoiding the future. To the extent that the institutionalized inmate looks forward to anything, it is only to such simple diversions from the dullness of routine as a weekly movie. As one inmate describes this depersonalization, "The longer a person remains in prison, the less likely it is that he will be able to share sincere feelings with anyone."[13]

institutionalized personality: promoted by the dehumanizing prison environment, a personality characterized by automatic responses, routinized patterns, loss of initiative, submissiveness, and lack of emotional investment.

It may be difficult for those on the outside to appreciate how issues as seemingly minor as getting a smaller portion of food or disagreeing over what TV program to watch can explode into violent attacks. But, as explained in the next "Close-up," such apparent overreactions to trivial details are not nearly as irrational when viewed from within the confines of a totally controlled environment.

CLOSE-UP ON CORRECTIONS
Fighting over Food

I have seen inmates fight over things that people take for granted on the street. For example, "fried chicken nights" in institutional cafeterias present an opportunity for violence. Fried chicken is one of the few meals that can actually provide both taste and nutrition. . . . The result is a larger percentage of inmates who go to the cafeteria. Crowded lines of men pushing and shoving can often turn into a melee of violence. At the same time, inmates will often place their trays on a table momentarily to fill their drink cups. I have seen inmates bludgeoned or stabbed because they took a piece of chicken from another convict in the sixty to ninety seconds it may take to get a drink.

Source: Stephen Stanko, "Surviving in Prison," in Stephen Stanko, Wayne Gillespie, and Gordon A. Crews, eds., *Living in Prison: A History of the Correctional System with an Insider's View* (Westport, CT: Greenwood Press, 2004), p. 173.

The transformation to an institutionalized personality represents the inmate's accommodation to long-term control through processes that have been variously described as "desocialization,"[14] "prisonization,"[15] imposed socialization,"[16] "total institutionalization,"[17] or adapting to the "pains of imprisonment."[18] It is largely generated by the abnormal features of the prison environment, particularly those tangible as well as intangible things that the prisoner is deprived of—including everything from personal property to goods and services, civil rights, heterosexual relationships, personal status, autonomy, and security. Contrary to what those in free society may believe, it is not the extent to which inmates are deprived of material possessions that imposes the greatest punishment. Rather, it is the deprivation of being locked away from family and friends, being "totally out of control of one's life," that "dwarfs the significance of television, stereos, and designer jeans."[19] As one inmate described it:

> The everyday pain caused by the loss of the simple things tears away at the human soul. The drive to work, pumping gas, traffic, deciding what to wear . . . cooking, mowing the lawn—the list is endless. What people in society may see as tasks and chores, a prisoner might very well see as dreams and wishes.[20]

Personal Adaptations

Just as people on the outside find ways of adjusting to hardships, those on the inside do as well. Many institutionalized offenders simply attempt to get along in such a regimented society by "playing the nods" with supervisors and "doing their own time" with peers. They conform to the norms and values considered socially acceptable by other inmates—for example, disdain for the system and those in authority, use of vulgar language, name-calling, distrust of fellow prisoners as well as staff, and acceptance of the status quo.

The resulting stereotypical pattern of behavior allows inmates to "get into the routine" with a minimum of irritation and anxiety. In some respects it is similar to breaking the spirit of a wild horse in order to shape its response to the commands of the rider. As with the horse and rider—who develop a working accommodation with each other—the subsequent relationship is characterized by routines of dominance, surrender, and behavior on cue. For inmates, this conformity creates a facade of courtesy toward authority figures and promotes flat, noncommittal responses to others which are lacking any emotional investment. While developing an impenetrable "prison mask" is a practical survival strategy for coping with confinement, such adaptations also carry long-term psychological baggage. Constantly needing to hide feelings from others can make inmates forget that they have any feelings at all, thus destroying the potential for intimate relationships and creating a permanent distance between themselves and other people.[21] In the end, the most common overall effect of imprisonment is "a slow, water-drip disfigurement of the human spirit. The greatest tragedy is that those who adjust to it best are damaged most."[22]

ADJUSTING TO CONFINEMENT

To some extent, everyone is affected by this wearing-down process of imprisonment. It is, after all, a normal reaction to abnormal conditions.[23] Those who are younger, more emotionally vulnerable, and confined for longer periods of time will be particularly susceptible. But, even among the physically strong and emotionally healthy, few escape the long-lasting influence of incarceration. Of course, not everyone reacts exactly the same way to the dehumanizing effects of imprisonment. Nor do all correctional institutions exert the same impact. In local jails, for example, the shorter terms of confinement—combined with the high turnover of the population—do not enable the intense, long-term interactions that promote prisonization.

> **LEARNING GOALS**
>
> Do you know:
> 4. what types of inmates are most susceptible to the negative effects of imprisonment?
> 5. what factors contribute to an inmate's adjustment to confinement?
> 6. what attitudes, values, and defense mechanisms influence one's behavior in prison?

The treatment or custodial orientation of a facility also can be influential. Generally, research has suggested that the counterproductive influences of the inmate subculture are diminished in settings focused more on treatment than custodial control. For example, the prisonization process seems to be reduced among inmates who are "actively involved in prison-based therapeutic communities."[24] On the other hand, when people are locked into cages and treated like animals, it should not be surprising that their behavior is less than civilized. In other words, behavior often conforms to expectations.

Individual Adjustments

adaptive behaviors: responses through which inmates adjust to the institutional setting, often through psychological defense mechanisms.

Because of the unique nature of this interaction, it is not surprising to find a wide range of **adaptive behaviors**. Some simply try to maximize their personal benefits and minimize discomforts. Some try to remain aloof, not risking involvement and maintaining a social distance from the rest of the population. Some project a tough "convict" veneer designed to keep predators at bay.[25] Others rebel, become aggressive, or exploit fellow inmates—exercising whatever control they can exert over those who are even more powerless. Still others rebel passively, sullenly biding their time until release.

First-timers may be particularly vulnerable to intimidation by other inmates, as well as more cautious and apprehensive in their dealings with staff. Likewise, youthful offenders tend to react to institutional conditioning even more intensely than their older counterparts—potentially developing antisocial grudges, feelings of inequality, and a diminished self-concept that can shape their outlook for years to come.

Tolerance for Anxiety

An inmate's tolerance for anxiety is another factor to be taken into consideration in predicting institutional behavior. Many are worried about their spouse, family, or loved ones. A disturbing letter from home (or lack of correspondence) can create a state of severe anxiety. Yet those incarcerated can do nothing about anything on the outside—they are utterly powerless.

During the first few months of incarceration, inmates routinely experience high levels of anxiety. These tend to level off as the offender adjusts to institutional routines and then rise again nearing release as the inmate confronts the uncertainties of what will be faced in free society. In fact, psychologists have determined that those who are profoundly institutionalized may become "extremely uncomfortable" when their previous autonomy is returned—finding that they no longer know how to do things on their own or how to refrain from doing things that are harmful or self-destructive.[26] As a result, some may even attempt to escape (or do something else to jeopardize their legal release) shortly before they are scheduled for parole.

Attitudes and Values

There is little doubt that the coercive nature of imprisonment does much to shape inmate responses to it. Nevertheless, there are also certain attitudes and values prevalent among the population that influence behavior. To some degree, these represent traits that may have brought offenders into contact with the law on the outside, although they can also be further nurtured by the institutional environment. For example, many inmates have experienced a lifetime of difficulty with appropriately responding to authority—particularly if they were products of dysfunctional families or abusive homes, where violence was an acceptable means of exerting power. To such offenders, the constant supervision, adherence to the demands of those in power, and subservient role of inmates in prison further reinforce their distrust and disrespect for authority. Their reference to correctional officers as "screws" reflects what they perceive the staff as doing to them. Officers are authority figures who are out to "get" them.

Defense Mechanisms

Nor is it only the correctional staff who "have it in" for them. The very fact that they are in prison is often blamed on someone else—or simply "the system" or society in general. In a social structure where inmates see themselves as "born to lose," it is easy to assume the self-concept of scapegoats. Unwilling or unable to accept personal accountability, offenders find it convenient to neutralize blame by rationalizing their actions (e.g., "I needed the money"; "People who never get caught steal a lot more than I did"). Through various forms of rationalizing their guilt and/or projecting blame on others, they can psychologically:

• avoid responsibility ("It wasn't my fault"; "I just went along with the gang");

• deny injury ("They can afford it"; "Nobody got hurt");

• blame the victims ("They had it coming"; "They should have done what I said");

• minimize guilt ("Yes, I sold drugs, but not to kids").[27]

In part, such attitudes are further reinforced by the inmate's concept of the social system as composed of those who got caught and those who got away. Those incarcerated were just unfortunate enough to get caught. In a world filled with perceptions of exploitation and injustice, those society has labeled as "offenders" often view themselves as "victims." Whether it was a teenager "asking" for sex, a poverty-ridden family, or an abusive childhood, their self-image as the unwitting victims—the "innocent pawns" of society—enables them to avoid accountability.[28] This line of thinking may seem quite convoluted to law-abiding citizens in free society. But, in the words of one inmate, "the more hostile the environment, the more they saw themselves as victims, and the less responsible they felt for their own actions."[29]

Those who share certain values, attitudes, beliefs, ethnicity, or other similar traits often group together into subcultures within free society. The same occurs within prison walls. And, just as different patterns of behavior, standards of conduct,

LEARNING GOALS

Do you know:

7. how the inmate subculture operates within prisons?

8. what functions are served by the inmate code?

9. what action Congress has taken to reduce prison rape?

and even language characterize subcultures on the outside, the same is true in prison.

Inmates organize into a separate **inmate subculture**, which emerges in reaction to the deprivations, frustration, and isolation of institutional living. It serves as an expression of autonomy in a setting that attempts to suppress individuality. It provides a self-defensive solidarity in an environment where a "we versus they" social boundary prevails. It helps to integrate newcomers into the inmate society. But, mostly, it unites the "kept" against their "keepers."

inmate subculture: the organization of prisoners into a cohesive subgroup characterized by unique values, attitudes, language, and standards of conduct.

Prison Language (Argot)

This society is manifested in a unique language, as reflected in the terms used to identify various inmate roles (for example, "straight," "tough," "wolf"). It should, however, be noted that inmate slang is neither universal nor static but, rather, is continually evolving at each institution. Any examples therefore represent prison **argot** in one area of the country at one particular point in time. As with the secret codes of childhood games, learning the inmate argot not only enables prisoners to communicate with each other in a language unfamiliar to outsiders, but also establishes an identity which only they can share. Moreover, within the terms used in the language of the inmate subculture are elements of:

argot: the unique vocabulary used in communication between inmates.

- mockery of the system (e.g., "the man," "goon squad");
- superficial resignation to authority (e.g., "play for the gate," "play the nods");
- the inmate social hierarchy (e.g., "right guys" versus "straights");
- adherence to the inmate code ("Don't snitch," "get-backs").

But, to the extent that language is simply a means of communicating and reinforcing values, it is the inmate code of conduct that most significantly identifies the prison subculture. In opposition to the institutional rules and regulations, it sets informal standards for controlling behavior in a manner designed to counteract official authority.

The Inmate Code

The informal social control maintained by inmates through adherence to the **inmate code** serves the vested interests of powerful and long-term prisoners. Those who have been around the institution long enough to know the routines and the authority structure can achieve power by gaining the trust of administrative officials and the acquiescence of other inmates. It is through the inmate code that such compliance is maintained.

inmate code: informal regulations governing inmate conduct that are in opposition to the formal rules of the institution.

As shown in the following "Close-up on Corrections," the code defines what actions are acceptable or unacceptable among fellow inmates. By establishing these prescriptions for "dos and don'ts," the inmate code clearly distinguishes between the values of the official administration and those of the unofficial social system. The resulting "we and they" distinctions expressly prohibit any support for the administration. Relationships with officials are permitted only for exploitative purposes, and the greatest status is reserved for those who most vigorously oppose their "oppressors."[30] (While the convict code is more potent among male inmates, there is a female version that retains many similarities but has some distinct aspects as well.)[31]

CLOSE-UP ON CORRECTIONS
The Inmate Code—in Their Words

Do:

- Mind your own business
- Watch what you say
- Be loyal to convicts as a group
- Play it cool
- Be honorable
- Do your own time
- Be tough
- Be a man
- Pay your debts

Don't:

- Snitch on another convict
- Pressure another convict
- Lose your head
- Attract attention
- Exploit other convicts
- Break your word.

Source: Jeffrey Ian Ross and Stephen C. Richards, *Behind Bars: Surviving Prison* (Indianapolis, IN: Alpha Books, 2002), p. 72.

Don't trust the guards or the things they stand for—don't be a sucker. Guards are hacks or screws. The officials are wrong and the prisoners are right.

Source: Gresham M. Sykes and Sheldon L. Messinger, "The Inmate Social System," in Richard A. Cloward et al., eds., *Theoretical Studies in the Social Organization of the Prison* (New York: Social Science Research Council, 1960), p. 8.

In the words of one inmate:

the *prisoner mentality* . . . concerns itself with which prisoners are *solid*. . . . Solid men never provide information to law enforcement and are prepared to respond to all problems with lethal force. . . . Just don't rat, and handle all problems *like a man*. Those are the understood values of the prison community. And anyone who questions them or does not abide by them is suspect.

Source: Michael G. Santos, *About Prison* (Belmont, CA: Wadsworth, 2004), p. 74.

In free society, breaking the laws of the community results in punishment, as well as an inferior social status for the offender. In much the same manner, violation of the inmate code produces alienation from fellow prisoners, reduced status on the social hierarchy of the institution, and punitive sanctions. In fact, it can result in severe physical retaliation, as we will see later in the vicious treatment of "snitches" when inmates broke into the protective custody unit during the Santa Fe, New Mexico, riot.

Violence in Prison

Newly arriving inmates (referred to in a predatory manner as "fish") are rapidly initiated into the code of conduct through exaggerated accounts of what lies ahead, intimidation by other inmates, situations where they are required to "prove themselves," and both real and fabricated threats concerning what happens to those who are noncompliant. Moreover, visual observations quickly reinforce the power of inmate control:

> The first day I got to Soledad, I was walking from the fish tank to the mess hall and this guy comes running down the hall past me, yelling, with a knife sticking out of his back. Man, I was petrified. I thought, what the f— kind of place is this?[32]

Along with being oriented to the inmate code, the new offender is "sized up"— evaluated according to such features as age, race, offense, fighting ability, and social connections. The prisoner who does not establish his "turf," demonstrate his masculinity, or prove capable of defending himself during this initial assessment process is likely to be relegated to a low position on the inmate hierarchy—subject to manipulation, intimidation, and domination throughout his sentence.

With others always poised to take advantage of a weakness, it is not surprising that prisoners become hypervigilant, distrustful, and suspicious.[33] In fact, research indicates that the vast majority of inmates experience feelings of vulnerability and victimization, "creating a mental state in which they are constantly on guard against danger that one cannot hope to locate, to anticipate, or to guard against."[34] As a result, it is not surprising that, when Americans think about someone they know being incarcerated, the vast majority (84 percent) say they would be concerned about the person's physical safety.[35] In the words of one inmate, "This place welcomes a man who is full of rage and violence. Here he is not abnormal or perceived as different. Here rage is nothing new, and for men scarred by child abuse and violent lives, the prison is an extension of inner life."[36]

Prison Rape Reduction

One of the most brutal and prevalent forms of violence behind bars—inmate rape—ultimately reached national attention. In 2003, Congress passed the Prison Rape Elimination Act (PREA), which established programs in the U.S. Department of Justice to:

- Collect prison rape statistics throughout the country, with special focus on those prison systems where the incidence of rape greatly exceeds the national average (for a look at some of the research that has been conducted under PREA, see the next "Close-up on Corrections");

- Disseminate information and procedures for combating prison rape—including prevention, investigation, and punishment;

- Provide grant funding to state and local programs that enhance the prevention and punishment of prison rape.[37]

CLOSE-UP ON CORRECTIONS
Prison Rape-related Research

Under the Prison Rape Elimination Act, the National Institute of Justice has coordinated studies to:

- Identify policies and practices to prevent sexual violence in prisons and jails;
- Study medical and psychological effects of sexual violence on inmates;
- Develop screening instruments to identify potential victims or perpetrators;
- Examine techniques for the investigation and prosecution of sexual assaults on inmates;
- Investigate the potential connection between sexual violence and other violent behavior;
- Evaluate programs and technologies designed to prevent prison rape;
- Examine staff-on-inmate sexual misconduct, specifically aimed at research on cross-gendered supervision and strip and pat-down searches of inmates.

Source: Andrew L. Goldberg and Doris Wells, "NIJ's Response to the Prison Rape Elimination Act," *Corrections Today* (June, 2009), p. 91.

Additionally, this legislation created a PREA Commission to examine all related physical, medical, mental, and social issues, as well as to propose national standards for investigating and eliminating prison rape. If established by the U.S. attorney general, these standards become applicable to the Federal Bureau of Prisons, and states which adopt them by statute may receive increased federal funding (or, alternately, may lose funding for failure to do so). Moreover, prison accreditation processes would be required to examine rape prevention practices as a critical component of their facility reviews. In an effort to put pressure on the U.S. attorney general to implement the PREA regulations, 35 inmates at one Virginia prison, "fed up with rape and sodomy," have filed federal lawsuits seeking an end to prison violence.[38]

ADAPTATIONS OF WOMEN

While women's facilities are not as violent, female inmates face many of the same debilitating effects of imprisonment as men.

LEARNING GOALS

Do you know:
10. in contrast to men, how women adapt to the conditions of confinement?
11. what conditions of confinement are like for female inmates?

EXHIBIT 10.2 Women behind bars adapt to prison deprivations somewhat differently than men.

There are differences, however, in the manner in which they adapt to the institutional environment. These distinctions result from both dissimilarities between male and female correctional institutions and inherent differences between the sexes.

Generally, women find institutional adjustment more difficult than men do, for a number of reasons. They tend to value privacy more and, consequently, experience greater difficulties adjusting to communal living, the intrusion of rules, and the degrading nature of body searches.[39] At the same time, they experience the anxiety of being separated from their children and do not have much support from spouses and significant others on the outside. For many, in fact, confinement is often accompanied by divorce or desertion.[40]

Others fear being abandoned and worry about the inability to cope with the loneliness they might experience upon release. Thus female inmates are more likely to substitute emotional intimacy with other inmates for the loss of family and social ties. These bonds are often expressed in **quasi-family** patterns, with certain inmates taking on the roles of mother, father, and children within the institution.

quasi-families: the prevailing subculture pattern of female prisons, in which inmates assume family member roles (e.g., children, parents, etc.).

Inmate Relationships

The value of family life—and the woman's role within it—are so firmly established in American culture that female inmates try to avoid the alienating and dispiriting effects of imprisonment by creating family structures. Unlike men, who tend to form gangs, women establish power and emotional relationships through the model that they were familiar with on the outside—the family. In other words, they imitate the "real world" that they came from or, in some cases, try to capture the intimacy of close family relationships that they missed on the outside:

This is an affectionate world of families . . . [where] some women play the parts of men . . . cutting their hair short, wearing slacks, walking and talking in a masculine way. . . . Other women play the traditional role of mother or wife. . . . [T]hey wander into relationships . . . much like friendships we have on the outside—where, for instance, you guide and counsel a friend as though he or she were your own child. The difference in prison is that you most often call that friend your "child" or your "mother" openly. It is a family that allows a sense of belonging and eases the loneliness of feeling isolated. . . . It creates a common bond that eases the pressures of doing "hard time."[41]

Although some of these adaptations to confinement may result in deep emotional attachments, they may or may not be sexual in nature, and can endure as friendships rather than romance.[42] Thus, homosexuality in female institutions is characterized more by mutual affection and caring relationships than the violent submission to force of homosexual behavior in male prisons. In contrast to male prison subcultures, the resulting subculture among female inmates is more an attempt to establish a substitute social reality in which they can play roles related to life on the outside. While participating in such "pseudo-families" enables women to escape into a fantasy world where they can avoid the realities of prison life, it also distracts them from "addressing the real problems in their actual lives."[43]

Prison Conduct

Overall, women's facilities reflect a greater degree of cohesiveness than male prisons, at least in part because the female subculture serves as a source of emotional support.[44] Women are less likely than men to experience sexual attacks during incarceration, and also appear to be less victimized in general by other inmates.[45] However, this does not mean that women's institutions are peaceful, tranquil environments that are managed with ease. Quite the contrary, a number of correctional staff tend to prefer being assigned to male institutions—despite the fact that they may fear for their safety more when working in male prisons. "The reasons usually given for this preference are that the male inmates are perceived as more cooperative and respectful than female inmates, who are usually seen as more manipulating and emotional."[46]

There is also debate about why female inmates seem to accrue more disciplinary infractions than their male counterparts. There is some evidence that rules in women's prisons may be more strict and cover more petty details than those in male institutions, and that staff may be less tolerant of violations.[47] In that regard, minor misbehavior can assume more significance in a female institution. Petty violations might not generate as much concern in a male facility, where more serious infractions (such as physical assaults) demand more frequent attention. As a result of their emotional bonds, women also differ in their reaction to staff disciplinary actions: "Male inmates generally do not care if another inmate is disciplined or 'locked up'—it's 'every man for himself.' Female inmates, however, tend to support the inmate involved in the misconduct or fight [even if they themselves were uninvolved]."[48]

Women likewise relate to staff in a somewhat different manner than men. In contrast to their male counterparts, women tend to "ask more questions, question authority . . . and challenge decisions. Staff who are inexperienced with these differences become irritated" and therefore are more likely to write up female inmates for disciplinary infractions.[49] On the basis of such realities, 70 percent of prison administrators in one study recommended using a different management style for women—one that involves greater capacity to respond to expressions of emotion, along with a willingness to communicate openly in a less authoritarian manner.[50]

Conditions of Confinement

Although conditions of imprisonment for women have come a long way from the abusive practices of the past, they still have a long way to go in many respects. In fact, the issue of staff sexual misconduct has received increasing attention in recent years. Sexual misconduct can take many forms, including inappropriate language, verbal degradation, intrusive searches, sexual assault, unwarranted visual supervision, denying privileges, and the use (or threat) of force.[51] Particularly among women who enter prison with an abusive past, such mistreatment can trigger a retraumatization that can further result in depression, anxiety, and other disabilities that diminish the offender's ability to participate in rehabilitative programs during confinement, as well as reintegrate effectively upon release.[52]

Because they serve a more limited population, female institutions are also substantially smaller in size. The average daily population of male prisons (700) is almost double that of female institutions.[53] That does not necessarily mean that female facilities are less crowded. But they are generally less likely to suffer from the impersonal conditions of male facilities. The physical environment of women's prisons is less oppressive, and there is more emphasis on rehabilitation. At the same time, however, female institutions are less likely to be able to economically justify a wide variety of treatment, training, recreational, vocational, or educational programs.

Gender-responsive Treatment

In recent years, some improvements have undoubtedly been made to upgrade services provided in female prisons, particularly in such areas as health care, drug treatment, and accommodating children. (See, for example, the upcoming "Close-up on Corrections.") Although needs still tend to outdistance available resources,[54] the American Correctional Association has developed policy guidelines calling for equity in terms of correctional services for male and female offenders. In any event, whatever strategies are pursued in an effort to better meet the needs of female offenders, the results are destined to have a wide collateral impact—on entire families and intergenerational cycles of crime.[55]

CLOSE-UP ON CORRECTIONS
The New Women's Prisons

Coffee Creek, Oregon, is a special facility for mother–child bonding. Situated outside the secure perimeter in a secluded wood, it functions as a day school with a bona fide Head Start program, where inmates work with at-risk youths. Female offenders learn valuable parenting skills while children reap the rewards of motherly attention.

Another fresh transitional-housing application is found at the new Denver Women's Correctional Facility, which includes "reintegration" apartments. These residential-style units, each with its own outdoor patio, are arranged around a central common room and children's play area. As they near release, inmate mothers are placed in these apartments with their children for stays ranging from a day to a week, allowing counselors to monitor their progress.

At the Kentucky Correctional Institute for Women, spatial provisions include places for women to retreat (designed as a result of awareness of the ways in which women deal with conflict, primarily by withdrawal). Medical and psychiatric services take precedence because a large number of women have experienced sexual or physical abuse and arrive at the prison with sexually transmitted diseases, as well as psychological problems and issues of mistrust. The treatment they receive in prison may be the only serious attempt to intervene in generational cycles of criminality.

Source: Compiled from "Inmates/Women/Mothers: The New Women's Prisons," *Correctional News* (March/April, 2002), pp. 14–15.

PRISON GANGS (SECURITY THREAT GROUPS)

Since male facilities tend to be more hostile settings, it is not surprising to find that they are more likely to have **inmate gangs** and display gang-related violence. In fact, the "sizing up" of new "fish" is in some respects similar to the initiation rights performed before accepting new members into a gang—where torturous rituals seek to assure the prospective member's "machismo."

With the emergence of gangs, the prison subculture is no longer as simple as "us" (inmates) against "them" (staff). Inmate solidarity has not disappeared. But, beyond overall resistance to institutional authority, specific allegiance to inmate associations has developed, largely along racial, ethnic, or religious lines—as evidenced by such gangs as the White Mafia, Aryan Brotherhood, Afro-American Society, Black Guerrilla Family, Black Muslims, Mexican Mafia, La Nuestra Familia, and Latin Kings. Just as with gangs in free society, such divisiveness further intensifies power struggles within correctional institutions, generating an ongoing cycle of violent vengeance.

LEARNING GOALS

Do you know:
12. why inmates join gangs?
13. what current term is used for prison gangs?
14. what activities are engaged in by inmate gangs?
15. what prison administrators are doing in response to security threat groups?

inmate gangs: powerful security threat groups that polarize the population, engage in corrupt activities, and promote collective violence.

Like their counterparts on the outside, prison gangs are often united by shared values. Given the fact that gangs in free society tend to attract those seeking acceptance, recognition, and a sense of belonging, it is apparent that fertile recruiting grounds exist among those in confinement. The racial or ethnic pride promoted by a gang can serve as a substitute for lack of personal identity. Status in a gang can upgrade low self-esteem. Viewing those in power as "oppressors" can provide a cause for uniting militant inmates. The protection and excitement offered by a gang can serve a functional purpose and fill voids in an unsafe and boring existence. As one inmate put it, "in the penitentiary, strength comes through alliances—the more people with whom one is connected, the less vulnerable he will be to predation."[56] In essence, gangs meet unfulfilled needs. (This may well be a primary reason that gangs rarely form in female institutions, since the quasi-family structure described earlier fulfills the unmet needs of female inmates.) But, whatever the reasons for their existence, male gangs also seriously jeopardize the order and safety of correctional institutions.

EXHIBIT 10.3 Although prison gang members may vividly advertise their affiliation, much of their motivation for joining gangs relates to unfulfilled personal needs for acceptance, recognition, and self-esteem.

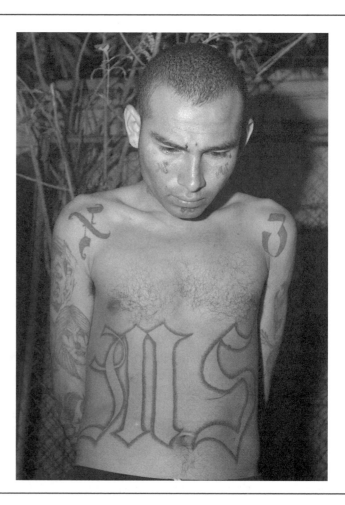

Gang Activities and Influences

While gangs share values such as loyalty, unity, and identity, they likewise reward the antisocial activities of their members.[57] It is for this reason that they are now also known as "security threat groups." As such, they have become a significant problem in correctional institutions throughout the United States. It has been estimated that, fueled by tens of thousands of members, they are responsible for at least half of prison disruptions,[58] and, even in jails, research has uncovered a much higher prevalence of gang membership than previously suspected.[59] In some places, the threat has become so serious that inmates have actually sued correctional agencies over inadequate protection and psychological injury from gangs.[60]

Large states such as California, Illinois, New York, and Texas are especially susceptible because of the size of their prison populations and the influence of gangs on the outside. Among the street gangs that are infiltrating correctional institutions today are the Bloods, Crips, Vice Lords, Hells Angels, Skinheads, and Latin Kings.[61] In fact, there is more and more overlap between groups defined as "prison gangs" and those identified as "street gangs," which is also complicating parole supervision of gang members.[62] While many gangs may originally have been formed for self-protection, finding strength in unity has bolstered their power. Without targeted intervention, they can disrupt all aspects of prison life as they compete for control through strategies ranging from intimidation and extortion to assault, rape, and murder.[63]

Institutional Responses

In Texas alone, the two most violent years in the history of the correctional system resulted in 52 inmate homicides and over 7,000 inmate and staff assaults—with 92 percent of the homicides and 80 percent of the assaults attributed to gang-related activities.[64] In response, Texas has implemented strategies ranging from hiring more staff to providing additional training, aggressively prosecuting in-house violence, and placing confirmed prison gang members in administrative segregation. Other states are providing cognitive-restructuring training to redirect gang members toward more prosocial lifestyles. Even experiments with behavioral contracting (e.g., promising "no further gang activity" in exchange for institutional privileges) have been tried,[65] along with the strategies outlined in the upcoming "Close-up on Corrections." Although these tactics have undoubtedly helped to ease the impact of prison gangs, officials still continue to view them as a serious ongoing threat.

CLOSE-UP ON CORRECTIONS
Correctional Responses to Security Threat Groups

- Using inmate informants;
- Noting gang affiliation in an inmate's file, which enables transfer to a high security facility;

- Segregating prison gang members and isolating their leaders;
- Interrupting the internal and external communications of gang members;
- Vigorously prosecuting criminal acts committed by prison gang members;
- Locking down entire institutions;
- Transferring key members out of state (also known as "bus therapy").

Source: Mark S. Fleisher and Scott H. Decker, "An Overview of the Challenge of Prison Gangs," in Richard Tewksbury, ed., *Behind Bars: Readings on Prison Culture* (Upper Saddle River, NJ: Pearson Prentice Hall, 2006), p. 416.

Well-organized gangs can exert considerable control over such illicit prison enterprises as gambling, sex, and drug transactions. They can intimidate other inmates through coercion, threats, and physical violence. But, aside from their strong-arm tactics and corrupt activities, one of the greatest threats of gangs to institutional security is their ability to unite the inmate population into polarized groups prepared for collective violence.

PRISON UPRISINGS

LEARNING GOALS

Do you know:
16. how to define a prison riot?
17. when and where the first prison riot occurred?

Correctional institutions may be physically isolated from the outside world. However, they are not immune to the influence of the social, political, racial, and ethnic tensions that also have an impact on society in general.

The explosion of urban street riots in Los Angeles following the acquittal of police officers involved in the beating of Rodney King revealed the mounting hostility that had been lurking beneath a surface of superficial tranquility. If frustrations can erupt into such outrage in free society, the "chemistry for violence" is that much greater in prison. The words of a former director of corrections, although written decades ago, echo a warning no less relevant today:

> All around us, the ghetto streets have periodically burst with violent indignation at the demeaning inequities suffered by the have-nots. If we listen closely to what the ghetto rioters are saying, we find that they are not just angered by their lack of jobs and income, but angered more by those societal conditions and attitudes which frustrate their efforts to improve their lot and enhance their dignity. When such people come into our prisons, they find there a microcosm of the ghetto's frustrations, denied opportunities, and purposeless living. To bring this explosive potential to a critical point needs only the right leadership and the right incident for a spark.[66]

Expressions of personal frustration can take many forms. Some seethe inwardly—resisting authority in subtle ways and mouthing silent words of defiance. Others are much less constrained—belligerently challenging "direct orders" and asserting their individuality at all costs. Still others act out aggressively by physical attack—destroying property, or assaulting staff or other inmates. In fact, prison violence has to some extent come to be viewed as almost a routine expectation, for reasons ranging from overcrowding and understaffing to changes in good-time and parole policies.[67] As one official phrased it:

> If you put poor, underprivileged young men together in a large institution without anything meaningful to do all day, there will be violence. If that institution is overcrowded, there will be more violence. If that institution is badly managed . . . [including] poor mental health care, there will be more violence.[68]

But these forms of violence are largely *individual*, self-defeating expressions of frustration or discontent. As long as inmates are predominantly loners who usually cooperate with institutional procedures, controls can be concentrated on the relatively few mavericks. It is when prisoners unite into close-knit groups under leaders promoting intentional, collective violence that the stability of the "fragile truce" between the keepers and the kept is clearly endangered.[69]

Riots and Disturbances

Among the public, corrections is narrowly judged by its ability to maintain custody and control. Losing either is a correctional administrator's worst nightmare. Unless the prisoner is particularly notorious, there is generally little public attention paid to an individual escapee, and quickly regaining custody of the absconder can restore public confidence. Riots, however, are a far more notable threat. Unlike the solitary escapee, riots represent the correctional authority's loss of control over "a significant number of prisoners, in a significant area of the prison, for a significant amount of time."[70]

The intensive media scrutiny occurring when such a widespread disturbance breaks out can devastate the image of corrections. That would be a relatively minor price to pay, however, if instantaneous notoriety generated long-lasting public support for change. If so, it would be possible that positive by-products could result from destructive events. But the impact is likely to be a fleeting concern expressed by demands for tighter security, rather than a fundamental commitment directed toward substantial improvements.

Perhaps because of this inability to learn from the past, riots and disturbances are as old as prisons themselves. In fact, the first recorded U.S. prison riot predates the American Revolution. It occurred in 1774 at the Newgate Prison built over an abandoned mine shaft at Simsbury, Connecticut.[71] Since then, correctional institutions throughout the country have been plagued by hundreds of riots and numerous smaller disturbances.

However, serious uprisings have diminished considerably in recent years. Modern prisons have become much more "riot-resistant" than they were in the years when

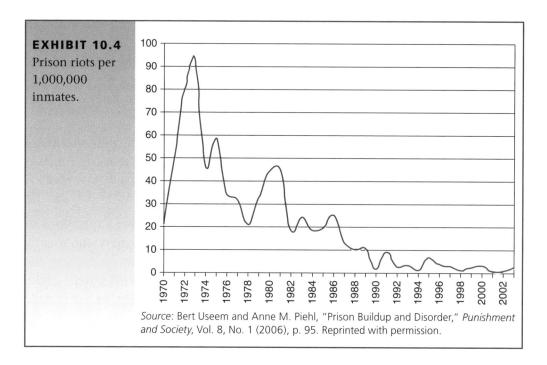

EXHIBIT 10.4
Prison riots per 1,000,000 inmates.

Source: Bert Useem and Anne M. Piehl, "Prison Buildup and Disorder," *Punishment and Society*, Vol. 8, No. 1 (2006), p. 95. Reprinted with permission.

Attica and Santa Fe exploded. In addition to better hardware, SWAT units, and riot control training, today's prisons have more sophisticated planning strategies for quickly terminating such disturbances. As a result, rioting is "less likely, and if it occurs, more controllable."[72]

Causal Factors

Inmates have never won a prison riot, either in the short-term sense of maintaining their freedom or in the long-term sense of drawing lasting attention to their plight. Knowing the ultimate outcome, why do they engage in such futile actions? There is no single answer or simple explanation. Although some riots may be well-planned protests, most appear to be more spontaneous events. One study found that riots are more likely in older, larger, and maximum-security institutions, as well as those where there is less recreation, fewer meaningful work opportunities, and less contact between the warden and inmates.[73] But it has also been noted that:

> it isn't necessary to have a callous or inept warden to have a riot. It isn't necessary to have sadistic guards, bad food, or any of the other classic grievances that supposedly provoke a riot. Those will be only surface complaints. The real problem is that even in a prison with good food and humane custodians, life is still a put-down, day after day. Boredom, pettiness, and repetitive meaningless activities are inherent in prison existence, and it should be no surprise that at some point the inmate population has had all it can stand.[74]

In other words, prison riots are to a considerable extent natural consequences of unnatural circumstances. Just as an active volcano is bound to erupt, prisons are virtually destined to burst into violence periodically. In much the same way that geological factors alert us to the potential for volcanic eruption, there are also signals that can warn perceptive staff of an oncoming disturbance. For example, in the two days preceding the 1987 riot at the U.S. Penitentiary in Atlanta, there was evidence that a riot might be impending. Inmates had remained dressed overnight, and the outgoing mail volume was several times heavier than normal, much of it containing photographs.[75] Later it was learned that inmates were mailing the photos home to prevent loss or destruction in the riot. See the next "Close-up on Corrections" for other changes in institutional atmosphere that can serve as early warning indicators of inmate unrest.

Predisposing Conditions

Although there is no single overall explanation that accounts for all prison riots, various features of prisons can either *reduce* or *reinforce* the potential for violent explosion. In other words, there are certain **predisposing conditions** that can serve to make an institution vulnerable to organized violence. For example, the American Correctional Association has identified a number of underlying contributors to institutional disturbances:[76]

predisposing conditions: factors in a correctional institution that promote the potential for a riot.

- *environmental stressors:* regimentation, personal deprivations, freedom limitations, boredom, idleness, brutality, racial conflicts, and gangs;

- *substandard facilities:* overcrowded living quarters, depersonalized surroundings, poor or monotonous food, and inadequate plumbing, heating, lighting, or ventilation;

- *inappropriate staffing:* insufficient numbers of staff to provide basic services, as well as inadequate management, security, and supervision;

- *public apathy:* indifference, punitive attitudes, singular focus on incapacitation, and lack of concern for treatment—prompting feelings of alienation as inmates see themselves increasingly ostracized from society;

- *inadequate funding:* the basis of many of the staffing, physical plant, and program deficiencies that set the stage for potential problems.

Each of these impediments provides fuel to smouldering issues and can turn them into full-scale disruptions. But it is their unification in a manner that destroys the fundamental social order of the institution that research points to as the primary causal factor.[77]

CLOSE-UP ON CORRECTIONS
Early Warning Signals: Conditions Conducive to Unrest

- Dining hall indicators:
  - alteration of noise levels;
  - removal of food staples;
  - refusals/requests not to attend meals.
- Housing unit indicators:
  - increase in contraband;
  - alteration of noise levels;
  - increase in misbehavior reports/incidents;
  - increase in cell change requests;
  - increase in assaults on staff.
- Recreation yard indicators:
  - large gatherings of ethnic, racial, or other groups;
  - polarization of known inmate rivals;
  - increase in verbal defiance of staff members;
  - decrease in yard attendance.
- Other indicators:
  - increase in buying of staples from commissary;
  - alteration of visiting activity;
  - increase in smuggling of contraband by visitors;
  - increase in manufacture/possession of weapons;
  - increase in sick call attendance;
  - increase in protective custody admissions.

Source: Condensed from Department of Correctional Services, *Early Warning System: Introduction and Implementation Manual for Employees* (Albany, NY: Department of Correctional Services, n.d.), pp. 5–9.

Pleas for Dignity

While many conditions serve to predispose correctional institutions to riots, perhaps the most pervasive underlying factor is the simple lack of personal dignity. As was expressed in the riots at both Attica and Santa Fe, "prisoners came to believe the only way to prove their humanity was by dying. . . . They saw nothing short of death that would regain their individuality and give them an identity."[78] Stated in their own words, "If we cannot live like people, we will at least try to die like men" (Attica); "If I'm going to die, I'm going to die like a man" (Santa Fe).

Undoubtedly, such alienation exists in many prisons, along with the additional institutional conditions and social forces described above. The question thus may be not why there are so many prison riots but, rather, why there are so few. As one correctional official put it, "dignity and respect should not be currency in human relationships to be doled out as a reward or withheld as punishment."[79]

Precipitating Event

Inmates may well endure any number of predisposing conditions for quite extensive periods of time without erupting into organized violence. At some point, however, a completely unanticipated event may precipitate mass action in violent response. Creating a strong perimeter with extreme pressure inside is the basic technique for building a bomb. It is also the recipe for creating a riot. Then all that is needed is to ignite the fuse.

Any number of **precipitating events** can serve as the spark that ignites a riot. An altercation between an inmate and an officer, a momentary breach of security, a fight between two inmates, or any variety of other random incidents can trigger a riot. Even publicized accounts of events outside the prison can serve as precipitating events, as in the case of federal immigration actions that set off the Atlanta and Oakdale riots of 1987. In fact, it is probably due to the alert attention of correctional officials that widespread violence throughout the country did not spread into correctional institutions following the verdict in the 1992 trial related to the Rodney King case.

When a number of predisposing conditions come into contact with both a precipitating event and a breakdown in security, the stage is set for a riot. Such was the case in Attica—where, in 1971, the longest and most lethal riot in correctional history resulted in the deaths of 32 inmates and 10 staff members. Attica thrust corrections into the national spotlight for nearly five days, during which Americans were forced to become aware of things about its correctional system which had, until then, remained secluded from public scrutiny. In terms of the specific grievances of rebelling inmates, conditions undoubtedly have improved. In Attica, as elsewhere throughout the country, officers are now better trained, physical facilities have been upgraded, and more inmate programs are available. But progress is relative to previous conditions. As one Attica commentator noted, "no matter how badly we fare, the legacy we pass on cannot be worse than the one we inherited."[80]

precipitating event: the incident that ignites the violent outburst resulting in a riot.

Stages of a Riot

While the nature of prison riots has largely been attributed to the behavior of rebellious inmates, some recent research takes a different perspective, arguing that what happens during the disturbance itself will influence its scope and outcome. Particularly, the way that prison administrators "prepare for and handle this type of crisis can make the difference between a small-scale disturbance and a full-fledged riot."[81] Although riot activities are not easily categorized into uniform patterns, they do generally tend to proceed in five stages:

1. *Initial explosion:* the spontaneous (or, in some cases, planned) uprising during which inmates gain control of part of the institution.

2. *Organization:* the emergence of inmate leadership, as staff mobilize to prepare to respond.

3. *Confrontation:* the stage when inmates are confronted, either through negotiation or by force. This phase can range from long-drawn-out discussions to quickly issuing a warning, followed by an ultimatum and a show of force. Tactics employed may depend on whether hostages have been taken.

4. *Termination:* the point at which custodial control is regained, through firepower, nonlethal force, or negotiated agreement.

5. *Explanation:* the subsequent investigation, designed to identify what caused the disturbance and assure the public that necessary remedies are being undertaken.

Riot Control: Planning and Negotiating

To prevent widespread property damage, injuries, and loss of life, the best point at which to intervene in a riot is before the inmates can become organized under strong leadership. Unfortunately, that is also the time when correctional staff may be equally disorganized. As a result, institutions have devoted more attention in recent years to developing riot control plans designed to locate and isolate the disturbance, evacuate unsafe areas, and quickly resolve the situation.

Rioting inmates know who has the advantage of weapons and firepower. In such a situation, "negotiation" takes on a different connotation from labor mediation, where the power of both sides is more equally balanced. In prison disturbances, negotiation is more a form of "keeping them talking" until group cohesion begins to break down, and then offering an honorable and face-saving way out for the inmate leadership.

Lengthy negotiations with rioters have always been politically unpopular, particularly in light of the disastrous results at Attica following four days of extended discussions. In addition, if disorders are not dealt with immediately and decisively, the initiative is lost. It is for such reasons that most riots in the past have been resolved by use of force, show of force, or force combined with other factors.[82] However, more recent research revealed that half were settled through some form of negotiation.[83] In one such example (Oakdale, Louisiana), surrendering inmates cleaned up the yard, planted flowers, and formed a gauntlet through which the hostages were released—receiving flowers and open signs of affection as they passed through.[84]

Riot Prevention

Once a major disturbance has occurred, there is generally considerable reluctance to "give in" to any demands that were not part of an official negotiation agreement.

Especially if lives were lost, the public is not likely to support responses which appear to send a message that endorses violence as a means of achieving change. In fact, during the explanation phase, a "scapegoat" is often identified (such as the warden or director of corrections) whose physical dismissal may also serve as a symbolic dismissal of the entire incident.

Obviously, the days following a riot are not the ideal time to address conditions underlying the disturbance. What is needed are not *reactive responses* after the damage has been done but, rather, *proactive procedures* designed to prevent riots from occurring in the first place. Admittedly, there may be little that correctional administrators can do to alleviate either public apathy or persistent stressors inherent in the prison environment. Nor can much be done without taxpayer willingness to support the funding to improve everything from physical facilities to staff salaries. But there are less costly steps that can be taken to reduce the tension, anxiety, and frustration that make an institution particularly vulnerable to rioting. As illustrated in the next "Close-up on Corrections," many of them relate to improvements in prison leadership and administrative policy.

CLOSE-UP ON CORRECTIONS
Actions that Reduce Riot Risks

- Maintain clarity of purpose among state authorities, prison administration, and corrections staff. Do not undertake changes in policy without clear support and the financial and political resources to carry out the policy.
- Train and protect staff, to maintain high morale and loyalty.
- Do not impose arbitrary or poorly explained disamenities or penalties on inmates.
- Treatment of inmates by staff and administration should strive to maintain legitimacy in terms of legal standards. Prisoners should not have a reason to develop an ideology that unites inmates in the belief that prison conditions or staff actions are illegitimate and would be rectified if people "knew what was happening inside."
- Respond quickly, firmly, and consistently to inmate actions that infringe rules or challenge prison authorities.

Source: Summarized from Bert Useem and Jack A. Goldstone, "Forging Social Order and Its Breakdown: Riot and Reform in U.S. Prisons," *American Sociological Review*, Vol. 67 (August, 2002), pp. 520–521.

One example is simply providing access to a formal grievance procedure to respond to inmate complaints before minor irritations become major issues. Of course, if inmates do not have confidence that the grievance procedure will result in action, it may only serve as a further source of frustration. Although there will undoubtedly be complaints that are not within the authority or fiscal ability of the administration to resolve, efforts can be made to explain the reasons for inaction.

Language of the Unheard

In this regard, *effective communication* with the inmate population represents another aspect that can be addressed without additional resources. In fact, from one perspective, a riot can be viewed as a method of communicating—"a dramatic one that is seldom used unless other forms of communications have been tried and failed."[85] Perhaps Martin Luther King stated it best when he described riots as "the language of the unheard."[86]

In an atmosphere of open, two-way interaction, inmates do not have the need to resort to violence to get administrative attention. Active listening is not only an effective overall management strategy, but also a good riot prevention tool.[87] While even the best communication process is not likely to create an atmosphere of true mutual trust within a prison, listening and responding to inmate problems demonstrates administrative concern, allows for the airing of legitimate complaints, and enables staff to detect signs of impending unrest. In other words, "the most effective approaches to prevention are founded on good management, visibility and accessibility of top administrative staff, and constant alertness to symptoms of possible problems."[88]

This does not, however, mean that communication should focus on nurturing sources of intelligence information through informants (or "snitches," as they are disreputably referred to by prisoners). Extensive use of inmate "tipsters" creates an environment of paranoid suspicion, encourages corrupt practices, and is demeaning to employees and inmates alike. Moreover, the "snitch system" can put the lives of informants in grave danger. The worst example of the sadistic cruelty with which inmates have reacted to informants was demonstrated in the 1980 Santa Fe, New Mexico, disturbance—when rioters broke into the section of the institution holding those in protective custody. The viciously brutal treatment of informants by the rioters is described in the following "Close-up on Corrections."

Beyond accounting for 33 inmate deaths, rioters in Santa Fe violently expressed their vengeance through widespread property damage, creating the most costly disturbance in U.S. prison history. Totaling some $36 million, the "cost of the event reached almost exactly one million dollars an hour; the riot lasted thirty-six hours."[89]

CLOSE-UP ON CORRECTIONS
"Get-backs" for "Snitches" in Santa Fe

The first killings took place in Cell Block 3, soon after the block was under inmate control. In one case, inmates armed with steel pipes gathered in front of the victim's cell. One of the assailants said, "We've got to kill this son-of-a-bitch, man. . . . We've got to kill him. . . . He snitched on [inmate's name]." They beat and then knifed him to death. . . .

Another unpopular resident of Cell Block 3, seeing what was coming, jammed the door of his cell so successfully that it couldn't be opened for two days after the prison was recaptured.

But it did him no good. He was shot in the face through the window of his cell with one of the grenade launchers taken from the control center.

These murders created a model for retribution against "snitches" and enemies. Thereafter, it was as if inmates vied with each other to produce imaginative modes of murder and mutilation. . . . Begging for his life, [one] victim was kicked and then bludgeoned to death with a pipe. . . . Another victim had his eyes gouged out, a screwdriver driven through his head. . . .

Inmates killed no hostages. . . . [T]he guards may actually have been less hated by the inmates than the "snitches" were. . . . The demonstrative means used to kill "snitches" suggest a virtually ritualistic "purging" of traitorous elements. . . . Guards, on the other hand, however disliked, do what they are expected to do in imprisoning inmates, and do not bear the stigma of treason.

Source: Bert Useem and Peter Kimball, *States of Siege: U.S. Prison Riots, 1971–1986* (New York: Oxford University Press, 1989), pp. 105–107.

Postscript: Although no correctional officers were killed, it should be noted that they did suffer "stabbings, beatings, and brutal degradation during their captivity."

Source: Adolph B. Saenz and T. Zane Reeves, "Riot Aftermath: New Mexico's Experience Teaches Valuable Lessons," *Corrections Today*, Vol. 51, No. 4 (July, 1989), p. 66.

The Aftermath

Undoubtedly, $36 million could have been used much more effectively for remedies directed toward preventing the disturbance than for repairs to the resulting damages. However, it is inevitably easier to generate public concern and fiscal support *after* an institution explodes into all-out violence—when the ambiguity of unheeded warnings is replaced by the clarity of undeniable consequences. As a prison manager noted: "Every time there's a riot, half of us cries and half is happy because we know it means more attention and probably more money for everything—salaries, programs, you name it"[90]—a benefit of which the prisoners themselves may well be equally aware. In the words of one inmate, "What incentive is there to keep prisons safe and humane? Violence and hatred in prison mean more money, more guards, more overtime, and more prisons."[91]

In the face of the immediate fiscal cost of institutional disruptions, it is easy to become distracted from the greater long-term social costs incurred by the more subtle day-to-day threat of brutality and degradation. Some would contend that exposure to such conditions is "just deserts"—that it is fitting for those who were victimizers in the free community to become victims themselves in the prison community. Aside from basic human dignity, what that argument conveniently overlooks is the fact that their membership in the prison community is temporary. Thus "permitting them to serve their punishment in an atmosphere at least as free from terror and violence as the outside world is a test of our collective self-respect, and ultimately, a matter of our collective self-interest."[92] For insights on ways to do so, see the next "Close-up on Corrections."

CLOSE-UP ON CORRECTIONS
Preventing Violence behind Bars

Recommendations of the national Commission on Safety and Abuse in America's Prisons for preventing violence include:

- *Reduce crowding:* Set and meet reasonable limits on the number of prisoners that facilities can safely house.
- *Promote productivity and rehabilitation:* Invest in programs that are proven to reduce violence and change behavior over the long term.
- *Use objective classification and direct supervision:* Incorporate violence prevention in every facility's fundamental classification and supervision procedures.
- *Use force, non-lethal weaponry, and restraints only as a last resort:* Dramatically reduce the use of this equipment by using non-forceful responses whenever possible, restricting the use of weaponry to qualified staff, and eliminating the use of restraints except when necessary to prevent serious injury.
- *Support community and family bonds:* Re-examine where prisons are located and where prisoners are assigned, encourage visitation.

Source: John J. Gibbons and Nicholas de B. Katzenbach, *Confronting Confinement: A Report of the Commission on Safety and Abuse in America's Prisons* (Washington, DC: Vera Institute of Justice, 2006), p. 37.

SUMMARY

Inmates are socialized into the institutional setting through the process of prisonization, by which they adapt to the culture, values, norms, and behavioral expectations of the environment. Some maintain that this process is a feature of similar values, attitudes, and behaviors that offenders bring into the prison setting (importation), while others attribute it to natural adjustments made to an unnatural environment (deprivation).

Whatever the cause, the result is often adaptation through development of an "institutionalized personality"—characterized by such noncommittal features as routinized behavior, automatic responses, loss of initiative, submission to power, and avoiding any emotional investment. To those exhibiting such a personality pattern, seemingly minor diversions or incidents can take on exaggerated importance.

But everyone does not accommodate to imprisonment in exactly the same manner. Individual characteristics, environmental conditions, and interaction between the two all shape one's adjustment. Defense mechanisms ranging from outright rebellion to rejection of authority, projecting blame on others, and rationalizing behavior also assist the inmate in psychologically coping with confinement.

In response to the dehumanizing nature of institutional conditions, the inmate subculture serves to protect personal identity and autonomy. Through this subculture, inmates reinforce values, attitudes, and standards of conduct that are in direct contrast to those of the administration. The subculture is distinguished by a unique language (argot), as well as an inmate code of conduct that establishes informal regulations in opposition to the formal rules of the institution. Women, however, adapt to confinement somewhat differently than men, and the conditions they are exposed to in female prisons also differ in a number of respects.

Beyond their organization into a separate subculture, inmates also unite through gangs (which is predominately a feature of male institutions). Prison gangs polarize the population along racial, ethnic, and religious lines. In addition to their involvement in corrupt activities, gangs present a serious concern for order and safety as a result of their well-organized collective violence.

When correctional officials lose control of a number of prisoners in a sizeable area of the compound for a significant amount of time, an institutional riot has occurred. Many underlying conditions can promote the potential for a riot—from the regimentation, deprivations, and lack of personal dignity of the environment itself to crowding, substandard physical facilities, inadequate staffing, public apathy, and perceptions of inequities. Such predisposing conditions may be tolerated for long periods of time. Then a completely unanticipated event can suddenly provide the "spark" that precipitates a riot.

Once the institution explodes into a violent uprising, riots generally progress in stages—moving from organization under inmate leaders, to confrontation with authorities, to termination (through firepower, nonlethal force, or negotiated agreement) and subsequent explanation. In addition to improved riot control planning, correctional officials can take proactive steps to address predisposing conditions. Examples include implementing formal grievance procedures and encouraging two-way communications between inmates and staff.

Beyond the loss of life and injuries resulting from riots, extensive property damage can require massive fiscal investments to restore the institution to a fully operating condition. Undoubtedly, such funding could have been spent more productively to remedy conditions provoking the disturbance, rather than to repair the subsequent damage.

FOR FURTHER DISCUSSION

1. Put yourself in the position of a progressive prison warden who wants to reduce some of the negative effects of incarceration. Without jeopardizing safety or security, what could you do to minimize the "prisonization" of inmates?

2. Critique the methodology of the Stanford Prison Experiment, especially in terms of the extent to which it represented prison reality. If you were able to replicate the experiment today, knowing what you do about the first time it was conducted, what would you do differently that would keep the project realistic while reducing the negative psychological implications?

3. What are some of the things that prison administrators could do to reduce the development of an institutionalized personality?

4. Arrange a visit to a prison or jail and observe how staff treat the inmates— i.e., the language they use to address them, the manner in which they interact (or avoid interaction), the extent to which they exert authority, etc. Determine whether your observations overall are positive or negative and, if negative, what is needed to move staff–inmate interaction toward a more positive approach.

5. Discuss how it is possible for inmates to view themselves as "victims," when in fact they are incarcerated for victimizing others.

6. Go online and see if you can find more examples of the inmate code, argot, or testimonials from inmates themselves about what life is like behind bars. Discuss what functional role the code and argot serve for the inmates, as well as what impact it has on prison management.

7. Look up the blog for the Prison Rape Elimination Act sponsored by the National Institute of Corrections (http://community.nicic.org/blogs/prea/default.aspx) and read the latest updates, or go to the Office of Justice Programs website (http://www.ojp.usdoj.gov/programs/prisonrapeelimination.htm) and determine what the current status is in terms of PREA implementation. Discuss whether prison rape can ever be completely eliminated.

8. Explain why "gender responsiveness" should be a consideration in establishing prison policies, classification procedures, and other administrative aspects of operating a women's prison.

9. If you were the warden of a women's prison, discuss what types of approaches you would use that would differ from the practices employed in a male prison.

10. Debate both sides of the issue regarding whether pregnant women should be allowed to keep their newborn babies in prison (and, if so, for how long). Expand the debate to include women who did not come to prison pregnant but have children less than a year of age. Include discussion of what should happen to children during the time before their mother is released.

11. Using whatever information you have (or can locate online) about intervention and prevention of gang development in free society, discuss what strategies might be effectively transferred to corrections in order to reduce the growth of gangs behind bars.

12. Combine what you know about the prisonization process, deprivation model, and development of an institutionalized personality to explain Martin Luther King's statement that riots are "the language of the unheard." Given these factors, explore what prison administrators can do proactively to reduce the potential for violent uprisings.

CHAPTER 11

Transition from Confinement to Community

It is not surprising that most inmates who leave prison become reinvolved in crime. After all, they had serious needs prior to imprisonment; most of them went untreated in prison; and now they face a staggering number of personal and financial problems at release.[1]

Joan Petersilia

CHAPTER OVERVIEW

Given the effects of prison life described in Chapter 10, it is apparent that incarceration is far from the optimal means of preparing offenders for a law-abiding lifestyle in the community. No matter how punitive the public may be, the fact is that, at some point, nearly all inmates are eventually eligible for release. The inevitable may be temporarily postponed, but in most cases it cannot be totally prevented.

As we saw in previous chapters, those in confinement are isolated from the rest of society, both physically and psychologically. They are constrained by strict rules. They are constantly supervised. Their movements are closely regulated. They "survive" the experience by adaptation. Some become subservient automatons. Others become rebellious activists. Most subscribe to an inmate behavioral code that is counter to the norms and values of official authority.

At the other extreme, those of us in free society are physically integrated with that society. Our actions are unhampered by direct scrutiny. We are free to come and go as we wish. We are able to live our lives much as we please, guided only by self-discipline and the implicit deterrence of social controls. In exchange for these freedoms, however, society imposes certain requirements. Thus, former inmates rejoining free society must be able to replace external with internal constraints. They must substitute compliance with social laws for adherence to inmate codes. In other words, they have to adapt to community integration from controlled isolation.

An inmate cannot be subjected to the rigidities of a tightly controlled institutional environment one day and walk confidently into the freedom of society the next without mishap. Yet that is exactly what is expected in the absence of parole: "One day these predatory inmates are locked in their cells for 23 hours at a time and fed all their meals through a slot in the door, and the next day they're out of prison, riding a bus home."[2]

Making the transition between these two extremes is obviously not an overnight process that can occur effectively without assistance. Much like the decompression process for deep-sea divers, who cannot rise too quickly to the surface, the parole process is designed to deescalate external controls gradually in order to ease reintegration into the community. And, given the magnitude of the upcoming prison exodus, focusing on reintegration may be "our best hope for keeping crime rates down, as nearly 600,000 inmates a year—1,600 a day—leave prison and return home."[3]

CHANGING NATURE OF PAROLE

Parole involves both regulatory and rehabilitative functions. Much like probation officers with their dual responsibilities (discussed in Chapter 4), parole officers face the need to balance their supportive and surveillance duties. Beyond the dual nature of its mission, however, parole has also encountered vocal opposition as public sentiments have shifted.

Under the medical model, it was assumed that there was an optimum time for releasing an offender from incarceration. With indeterminate sentencing, establishing when an inmate should be released was largely the subjective decision of the paroling authority.

In the absence of clear, objective guidelines, eligibility for parole became the source of complaints about apparent inequities. In some cases, parole policies have even been cited as causing prison riots. Attica was a prime example—where the official investigation concluded that "the operation of the parole system was a primary source of tension and bitterness within the walls."[4] In Attica and elsewhere, those who were satisfied with decisions of the parole board were out in the community, while those turned down for parole remained in prison venting their frustrations. Nor was the credibility of the decision-making process enhanced by high rates of recidivism or the public outrage that followed when a parolee engaged in a particularly notorious crime.

Movement to the justice model's determinate sentencing was designed to eliminate the uncertainty of prison terms based on the release-through-parole feature of indeterminate sentencing. As a result, 16 states have abolished parole,[5] and mandatory release is now increasing, while discretionary parole releases are decreasing.

This does not mean that parole no longer exists. However, paroling authorities are now more likely to be responsible for *supervising offenders* in the community

parole: supervised release from prison before sentence expiration, under conditions that permit reincarceration if violated.

following mandated discharge than for *making decisions* about when to release them. Despite more restrictive functions and a less supportive public, parole remains a key component of the correctional conglomerate. For as long as the environment of correctional institutions differs so extremely from free society, assistance is needed to prevent released offenders from becoming repeat offenders.

Historical Background

The word *parole* originated with the French term *parole d'honneur*, which means "word of honor."[6] But, because inmates are not generally considered to be highly honorable, parole has always been controversial.

As noted earlier, Captain Alexander Maconochie experimented with a **mark system** that enabled inmates to earn freedom through credits awarded for hard work and proper behavior. For this and similar progressive but provocative efforts, Maconochie was removed as superintendent of the Norfolk Island (Australia) penal colony. Returned to Britain, he was subsequently dismissed from prison service for employing methods that were too lenient. Maconochie's visions lived on, however, in the Irish ticket-of-leave concept pioneered in 1854 by Sir Walter Crofton. Under this system, inmates earned release by gradually progressing through a series of stages involving reduced discipline, which could eventually earn them a **ticket of leave**—or what we now know as parole.

Parole Developments in the U.S.

Massachusetts was the first state to officially establish parole service when an agent was appointed in 1846 to assist released prisoners. By legislative action some 20 years later, Michigan became the first state to introduce indeterminate sentencing. This was necessary in order to enable correctional officials to provide early release on parole, under the philosophy that "the prisoner's destiny should be placed . . . in his own hands."[7]

During the 1870 meeting of the National Prison Association, Zebulon Brockway argued that preemptory (fixed) sentences should be replaced with indeterminate sentences. With such a change, prisoners could be released early, after demonstrating evidence that they had been reformed, rather than merely awaiting the lapse of time. He further suggested providing some type of supervision for three years after release from prison. Brockway later became superintendent of the Elmira Reformatory, where parole was an integral feature from its opening in 1876.

By the 1950s, all states had implemented indeterminate sentencing, and all jurisdictions throughout the country had adopted some form of parole. But a quarter-century later, the tide began to turn. Public disillusionment with the medical model's indeterminate sentencing was fueled by reports citing the futility of rehabilitation, along with alarming recidivism rates. As a result, in 1976 Maine became the first state to fully embrace determinate sentencing and abolish parole.

mark system:
Alexander Maconochie's idea of enabling inmates to earn early release for hard work and good behavior.

ticket of leave:
forerunner of parole, the Irish system of gradually reduced custody stages, whereby prisoners could earn a ticket to leave prison before sentence expiration.

Since then, a number of states and the federal government have adopted some form of structured sentencing, and those with determinate sentencing practices have largely eliminated release on parole.[8] Recently, however, discretionary parole release began to make a comeback in some states, as shown in Exhibit 11.1.

Parole Defined

While some form of parole remains the primary method through which inmates are released from prison, the nature of parole has changed considerably from its early origins. Generally, parole is considered to be *supervised conditional release* from a correctional institution prior to sentence expiration, under requirements that

Sanctioning/ correctional emphasis	1920 – 1970	1970 – 1980	1980 – 2000	2000 – 2003
Rehabilitation	X			
Desert		X		
Incapacitation/ deterrence			X	
Evidence-based interventions				X
Parole discretion	Extensive	Reduced or eliminated	Some increase but with high structure	Increasing in some states

EXHIBIT 11.1 Overview of sentencing trends and parole discretion.

Source: Peggy B. Burke, ed., *A Handbook for New Parole Board Members* (Washington, DC: National Institute of Corrections, April, 2003), p. 9.

permit reincarceration if violated. In other words, parole is simply a continuation of one's sentence in the community. The inmate is released under supervision and expected to abide by certain provisions, violation of which could result in revocation of parole. The conditions imposed are quite similar to those required of probationers—such as remaining drug and alcohol free, reporting periodically to a parole officer, avoiding criminal associations, obeying the law, and the like.

LEARNING GOALS

Do you know:

4. how the functions of parole have changed in recent years?

5. what conflicting objectives are expected of parole?

PAROLE AUTHORITY

Unlike probation, which is primarily a judicial function of the courts, parole is an *executive function* of correctional authorities. In fact, under indeterminate sentencing practices—when parole boards had virtually unlimited discretion to determine release dates—correctional officials in many respects had a greater impact than judges in terms of establishing the length of sentences. In states that still maintain discretionary release, parole functions include:

- *selection:* reviewing cases to identify which inmates should be released from prison before the expiration of their sentence;

- *preparation:* classroom sessions, counseling, and other assistance designed to prepare new parolees for the decisions and self-discipline needed to resume life in free society;

- *supervision:* assistance and oversight provided in the ex-offender's home environment to ease transition from the institution, as well as monitor behavior in the community;

- *termination:* either through routine dismissal of the case upon successful completion of parole or revocation for violation of parole conditions.

Today, correctional authority is more limited to parole supervision and termination, with release determination often a function of legislative guidelines. But there is some debate over whether this actually represents a departure from past practices, rather than new terms for old practices.

Objectives of Parole

Ultimately, the major focus of parole has been on reducing recidivism. In the past, parole attempted to achieve this objective by a combination of selecting the most appropriate candidates for release and providing them with support and supervision as they made their transition into the community. With responsibility for selection diminishing, the focus of parole today is directed more toward postrelease procedures. But parole is still expected to help the offender successfully reintegrate into the community, while at the same time safeguarding the public by continuing to control the parolee under community supervision.

As with probation, parole officers struggle to find a balance between providing supportive assistance and monitoring activities so that public safety is not compromised. In fact, it is ironic that the effectiveness of parole is largely judged on the basis of whether its clients return to prison—since it is incumbent upon parole authorities to do exactly that when a client is not functioning effectively in society. Moreover, as we will see, parole can neither be fully credited with its successes nor blamed for its failures.

Eligibility for Parole

Under indeterminate sentencing, once an inmate has served whatever minimum sentence was established, he or she is generally eligible to be considered for release. Unless the sentence specifically includes a stipulation that it is issued with no possibility of parole, even those with "life" sentences are eligible for early release in a number of states. That does not, however, mean that inmates can initiate an application for parole. While they may voluntarily turn down an opportunity to be paroled, they have no direct control over when it will be offered.

Nor does eligibility mean that parole will be granted automatically. Discretionary parole is legally considered a *privilege* rather than a *right*. No constitutional right to be released on parole has been recognized by the courts.

Those turned down for consideration may be routinely scheduled for a rehearing after a designated period of time. While some offenders are paroled at the first opportunity, particularly notorious criminals may proceed through numerous rehearings unsuccessfully. For example, parole hearings are still conducted periodically for Charles Manson, under California's provision for rehearing the cases of those serving life terms every three years.

One might think that inmates repeatedly denied parole are likely to be the most serious, potentially dangerous offenders. While that may be true, it does not mean that everyone who is denied fits that description, especially as states have become increasingly conservative when making release decisions. In one state, for example, the percentage of inmates who were released after a parole hearing declined from 70 percent in 1990 to 38 percent a decade later.[9] As a result, some discouraged inmates may actually opt to waive their parole hearings, finish their sentences, and be released unconditionally. However, in states that do not provide for life without parole, only death in prison can completely assure that an inmate will not be released.

While parole eligibility may well have been restricted with public safety in mind, as one report on the impact of this policy concluded:

The result is that the inmates who pose the greatest threat to public safety are denied parole, while minor offenders, least in need of supervision, are under the watchful eye of a parole officer. . . . The very thing the public wants—community safety—is jeopardized when inmates are released without the supervision and support of parole.[10]

It is indeed ironic that long-termers who ultimately exit prison upon the expiration of their sentence—often from maximum security and without community supervision—are often those who need the scrutiny of parole the most. See the next "Close-up on Corrections" for the tragic account of one such case. While some may denounce the availability of parole as "too lenient," it is the desire to prevent such unfortunate events that motivates many to support postrelease supervision.

CLOSE-UP ON CORRECTIONS
The Truth about Polly Klaas

Richard Allen Davis was a dangerous, violent felon. He was sentenced to life in prison in 1976 for kidnaping and other violent crimes. His criminal record was littered with instance after instance of predatory behavior. The paroling authority in the State of California knew this. His disregard for human life and safety, even while in prison, was a profound reminder of the need to keep this individual isolated from the community as long as possible. While in prison, the parole board reviewed his case six times, and six times the parole board rejected any possibility of release.

But the forces of change were at work in California. Politicians pledged to be "tough on crime." The obvious answer—"Abolish parole." And they got their wish. The requirement of earning the approval of the parole board before even a dangerous offender could be released was abolished. New standard sentences mandated automatic release after service of a set portion of the sentence. Offenders already incarcerated came under the provisions of the new law.

Release dates were churned out by the prison system's computers for thousands of prisoners then in custody. When the computers had done their job, there was no turning back. Richard Allen Davis had already served the amount of prison time that the new law and its mandatory release provisions demanded. . . . On the night of June 27, 1993, Richard Allen Davis walked out of prison, a free man. Less than four months later, in the safe darkness of a girlhood slumber party, Richard Allen Davis . . . kidnaped and brutally murdered a little girl. Her name was Polly Klaas.

No one can say with certainty all that would have happened to Richard Allen Davis if parole had not been abolished in California. But there is overwhelming evidence that if the parole board had still been in control of release, Richard Allen Davis would have been in prison the night that Polly Klaas was murdered.

Source: American Probation and Parole Association, *Abolishing Parole: Why the Emperor Has No Clothes* (Lexington, KY: American Probation and Parole Association, 1995), p. 2.

Parole Boards

Parole selection in most states is administered by a **parole board (or commission)** appointed by the governor (which may be subject to confirmation by the legislature). Given the relatively small size of most paroling authorities, tremendous discretionary power is concentrated in very few hands. (In fact, throughout the entire country, there are only slightly more than 200 full-time parole board members.)[11]

Much of the concern surrounding parole has centered on how that power has been used. In the past, it was not uncommon for appointments to become a reward for political service to the successful gubernatorial candidate. As a result, the integrity of the parole process has, at times, been compromised when parole commissioners have been suspected or accused of corruption—awarding parole on the basis of political, personal, and/or financial motivations.

To reduce the potential for political involvement, recommendations of the President's Crime Commission in 1967 called for appointments based solely on merit, with qualifications including "broad academic backgrounds, especially in the behavioral sciences."[12] Yet, decades later, parole boards in most states are still being cited for making appointments according to political patronage, without relevant background or educational requirements.[13] One study found that, in 29 states, "there were no professional qualifications, defined by statute, for parole board membership."[14] Even among the remaining 21 jurisdictions, statutes establishing qualifications may be written in "very general terms," thus giving the governor rather "wide latitude and generous discretion."[15]

The result has been a system of "patronage appointments" that have seldom produced parole boards with "deep expertise in the behavioral sciences" or with the credentials that would give us confidence in their professionalism.[16] As one analysis concluded, this lack of professional competency has been a "skeleton in the closet" of paroling authorities.[17] Moreover, unlike sentencing judges, parole board members are not required to make their decisions on the basis of specific rules, explain their decisions on the record, or subject their findings to appellate review.

parole board (or commission): a state administrative body appointed by the governor which has authority to grant and/or revoke parole.

SELECTION PROCEDURES

When an inmate is eligible for discretionary release, the prison or institutional treatment staff generally prepare a pre-parole progress report for the board's review.[18] This report usually includes such information as:

- a summary of the inmate's *case history* (including prior record, presentence investigation report, classification results, and the like);

- the *institutional programs* in which the offender has participated;

LEARNING GOALS

Do you know:

8. what due process protections are involved in parole decision-making?
9. on what basis parole boards make selection decisions?

- evidence of *adjustment* during confinement (particularly any disciplinary action taken);

- a *proposed plan* for postrelease transition (such as employment and residence);

- other documents relevant to *behavioral predictions* (such as a psychological profile);

- a *recommendation* by the institutional staff for or against parole, along with supporting reasons.

Due Process Considerations

Due process procedures surrounding parole hearings have undergone changes over the years. Surprisingly, however, these modifications have not been a result of court intervention. Quite the contrary, courts have been reluctant to interfere in what they have traditionally viewed as the administrative decision-making function of parole boards.

The courts have not recognized that inmates have a constitutional right to parole. Nor have they established due process requirements in the parole selection process. For example, in one particular case (*Menechino v. Oswald*),[19] an inmate challenged his parole denial on the basis that he should have been entitled to counsel, the right to cross-examine and produce witnesses, notice concerning the information being reviewed, and specific grounds for the denial. The court ruled that these due process rights did not apply to parole hearings, under the rationale that:

1. denying parole did not alter the status of the inmate (i.e., the inmate did not possess something that was being lost); and

2. the parole board's interests in rehabilitation and readjustment were not contrary to those of the inmate (i.e., the board was not in an adversarial position with regard to the inmate).

Nevertheless, although not legally required, most parole hearings today do allow the inmate to be represented by an attorney and to introduce witnesses. The proceedings are generally recorded in written transcripts, with the inmate advised in writing of the final decision (although, again, this is not constitutionally required).[20] Recommendations of the American Correctional Association further call for consistently applied written criteria on which to base decisions, along with informing those denied of both their future hearing date and recommendations for improving their prospects at that time.[21]

Selection Criteria

The popular perception of parole boards may be that they make every effort to select inmates who have good potential for early release. But that is not exactly how the system operates. This does not mean that parole boards do not take their mission seriously or that they are overly lenient. But, given the candidates they are faced with assessing, their function is often limited to screening out the worst risks, rather than selecting the best.

Despite boards having access to literally volumes of records, reports, data, interview transcripts, and other information concerning the offender, determining parole eligibility has ultimately been a product of the individual judgments of parole board members. Factors deemed important by any single member might include anything from cleanliness to church attendance.

Some members refuse to parole anyone who steadfastly maintains innocence despite having been convicted. Others base decisions on rehabilitative considerations—reviewing the inmate's outlook, self-improvement, change in work habits, and similar indicators of capacity to adapt to society. Some place heavy emphasis on victim impact statements and anticipated public reaction if the offender is paroled. Still others will reluctantly support releasing a high-risk offender nearing sentence expiration, using the rationale that it is preferable to be released under supervision than unconditionally. In the absence of solid, tangible evidence, parole boards have acted largely on faith in the inmate's intentions and capacity to "make good."

In short, all of these varied decision-making criteria reflect the individual preferences, values, beliefs, and biases of parole board members. Given this extensive discretion, combined with concerns about the political independence and professional qualifications of those entrusted with it, it is not surprising that the parole selection process has been subject to complaints and controversy.

Decision-making Criticisms

Needless to say, inmates denied parole have often been dissatisfied with what they consider arbitrary and inequitable features of the process. Particularly when inmates are not personally involved in parole decision-making, it is difficult to appreciate how an anonymous group of people can fairly determine an unknown inmate's destiny. Even those who have an opportunity to present their case through a personal interview are sent out of the room while discussions of the case take place (being recalled only to hear the ultimate decision and a summary of the reasons for it). This protects the confidentiality of individual members' actions. But it does not enable the candidate to hear objective discussions of the case, evaluations of strengths and weaknesses, or guidance in terms of how to modify behavior in order to improve subsequent chances for successful consideration. Without such insights, it is unlikely that those denied parole understand the basis for the decision or attach any sense of justice to it.

Parole boards are also subject to manipulation by clever inmates. For example, some prisoners initially fake illiteracy, reasoning that, when they later appear to be doing extremely well educationally, they will have tricked the parole board into "believing they had worked hard to make a positive change in their lives."[22] Nor are criticisms of parole limited to the inmate population. Friction between prison wardens and parole boards can be generated because of differences in viewpoints. Like the candidates themselves, prison officials may wonder why some were paroled whereas others were not. On the other hand, parole boards may view some of those supported by institutional staff as being the "warden's pets" or advocated for release in order to manage the facility better. In essence, no matter what the board's decision, it is unsatisfactory to *someone*.

Impact of the Justice Model

Beyond inmate discontent and staff disagreement, however, it has been ordinary citizens who often express the most vocal dissatisfaction with parole. For it is not the long-term successes but the legendary failures that capture public attention. As a result of a few notorious cases, public opinion has had a substantial impact on stimulating change toward the determinate sentencing of the justice model.

In retrospect, it is perhaps surprising (but not illogical) to discover that it was actually inmates who originally advocated determinate sentences—to avoid being coerced into rehabilitation and to better assure that those convicted of similar offenses received similar prison terms. As one inmate phrased the frustration of his fellow prisoners, "Don't give us steak and eggs. . . . [F]ree us from the tyranny of the indeterminate sentence!"[23] But the complaints of inmates about involuntary treatment or sentencing inequities might well have fallen on deaf ears had the public been satisfied with the existing system.

To many observers, however, by the late 1970s and early 1980s the system simply did not appear to be working:

- The unspecified length of indeterminate sentences created strong suspicion that potential law violators were not being deterred by the certainty of punishment.

- High rates of recidivism provided evidence that criminals were apparently not being rehabilitated.

- The likelihood of early release on parole generated concern that offenders were not paying their "just deserts" to society.

Parole itself was termed a tragic failure and a cruel hypocrisy. It was viewed as deceiving both the inmate looking for help and the public looking for protection,[24] providing neither security to the law-abiding nor fair treatment to law violators.[25] The premise that parole safeguards society by keeping criminals in prison until they are ready for release was dismissed as nonsense.[26] Although the criminal justice system can never be free of failures, parole was charged with providing more than its share of them. As a result, an increasingly conservative society—lacking trust in rehabilitation and fearful of rising crime rates—called for fixed, determinate sentences with a more objective method of establishing release dates (preferably upon completion of full sentences). Yet, as the next "Close-up on Corrections" reveals, abolishing parole does not necessarily improve public safety.

CLOSE-UP ON CORRECTIONS
Which of These Alternatives Makes You Feel Safer?

Scenario 1: Parole as Part of Responsible Sentencing

A prisoner, convicted of assault upon his wife, received a sentence of 7 years that included eligibility for parole after service of 3 years in prison. . . . The board deemed a minimum of 5 years in prison as appropriate. Concerned that the wife might still be endangered if the prisoner were to be released, the board ordered polygraph testing of the offender and interviewed fellow inmates about threats made in their presence. . . . In addition, the board invited the wife to a confidential interview so that they could hear directly from her about her concerns. Convinced that the wife was still at considerable risk, the board continued the prisoner in custody, and indicated that they would not consider release until he had completed an anger management program, identified a residence in a completely different part of the state from his wife, and agreed that he would accept a "no contact" condition if parole were to be granted at a later date. Because the wife indicated that his episodes of violence usually occurred while the offender was drinking alcohol, the board also required alcohol screening and treatment as a condition of parole. In all, the offender served 6 years in prison, was released under strict conditions designed to protect the wife, and completed his sentence in the community without incident.

Scenario 2: The Impact of Abolishing Parole

This same prisoner has been convicted of assault in the same state. However, the state has now abolished parole in order to be "tougher" on crime. As the result of a plea, the offender has . . . pled guilty to simple assault, an offense that allows the judge to impose a sentence of 4 years. With good time credits, he will serve 24 months in prison before he is released. He has boasted many times to his cellmates that he will make his wife "pay" when he gets home, but no one ever learns of these threats. Indeed, he has even made threatening phone calls and sent letters to his wife, but she does not know where to turn. She never appeared in court for fear of angering her husband, and does not know the name of the judge in the case, who, in any event, has rotated off the criminal bench. . . . Unaware that her husband was to be released, she was home the day he arrived from prison. Her husband is drinking heavily again, and has instigated several arguments that have resulted in further injury to her and her children. [Based on an actual case.]

Source: American Probation and Parole Association, *Abolishing Parole: Why the Emperor Has No Clothes* (Lexington, KY: American Probation and Parole Association, 1995), p. 15.

Conditional versus Unconditional Release

With the transition from the medical model to the justice model, the method by which inmates are released from confinement has changed, although not necessarily in the manner anticipated. Ever since the first indeterminate sentencing legislation was enacted more than 125 years ago, inmates have been released from correctional institutions either:

- *conditionally:* with continued freedom dependent upon adhering to the requirements established by the paroling authority; or

- *unconditionally:* with no conditions attached, because the offender had served the full sentence, been pardoned, had the sentence commuted, or received some other form of legal modification.

Beyond the simple expiration of the sentence, unconditional release can occur as a result of clemency extended by the executive branch of government (i.e., the governor of a state or the president of the United States, although parole boards in some states have this power as well). **Executive clemency** ordinarily takes the form of a:

executive clemency: granting an offender mercy by the governor of a state or the president of the U.S. through a pardon or sentence commutation.

- *Commutation.* The sentence is reduced, such as when "time served" is substituted for a longer original sentence. However, a commutation does not necessarily lead to release—as, for example, when life imprisonment is substituted for a death sentence.

- *Pardon.* The offender's conviction is forgiven. While pardons do not erase the criminal record, they do restore the rights of citizenship. Originally designed to undo miscarriages of justice (e.g., when a person was wrongfully convicted), pardons are often unconditional. But conditional pardons can be issued which are dependent upon subsequent performance of the person being pardoned. Most significantly, pardons reinstate the civil rights of convicted offenders—such as the ability to hold an elected or appointed political office, as illustrated in the next "Close-up on Corrections," which describes the case of an ex-offender being considered by the governor of Massachusetts for a judicial appointment.

CLOSE-UP ON CORRECTIONS
Judging the Value of Redemption

Swirling through the halls of Boston's juvenile court, lawyer Rick Dyer glad-hands everyone. . . . He stops to huddle with a group that includes a probation officer and a social worker. They are discussing Dyer's client, a troubled 16-year-old. . . . Dyer has won a promise that the boy will receive trauma therapy. . . . "He's always fighting for the kids," says the probation officer.

It's no wonder. Nearly 50 years ago, Dyer was such a kid. At ten, he began sniffing glue, then moved up to alcohol and heroin. His rap sheet details more than ten years of felony convictions. . . . Yet today Dyer is a respected member of the bar. . . . He has been sober for three decades.

Now a growing number of influential Bostonians are urging the governor of Massachusetts to make Dyer a judge. They argue that appointing him to the bench would send a powerful message of hope, forgiveness, and redemption. If appointed, Dyer would likely be the first judge in U.S. history to bring with him not only a record of drug abuse, but also a personal understanding of what it's like to be homeless, on welfare, and behind bars. "There is a lot to be said for having people in the system who have lived the life and come out on the other side of it," says former Massachusetts Governor Michael Dukakis, who in 1983 granted Dyer a full pardon, clearing the way for him to become a member of the bar.

Source: Linda Himelstein, "Judging the Value of Redemption," *Parade* (June 27, 2010), p. 14.

Corrections can maintain supervisory authority only over those offenders who are *conditionally released*. **Conditional release** is similar to the situation of probationers who face the imposition of a suspended sentence for failure to abide by the conditions of probation. Likewise, parolees face the possibility of returning to prison to complete their original term if parole is revoked for failure to comply with the conditions attached. Those receiving unconditional release, however, are no longer under any legal authority of the correctional system.

conditional release: releasing an inmate under certain conditions, violation of which can reactivate the unserved portion of the sentence.

Parole Trends Today

The movement toward determinate sentencing presumably was designed to achieve certainty in punishment—with fixed, flat terms replacing flexible ranges. One might therefore assume that more full sentences would be served, more unconditional releases would occur, and parole populations would decline. Nothing could be further from reality.

Despite the intent of the justice model, inmates continue to be released from prison before serving their full potential terms. The average time served by those released from state prisons is still only about half of their original sentence.[27] Nor are unconditional releases replacing conditional supervision. Most of those coming out of prison are still being released under some form of conditional supervision in the community. (See Exhibit 11.2.) Nor is the number of people on

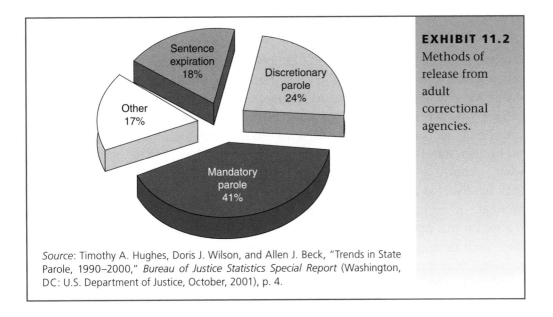

EXHIBIT 11.2
Methods of release from adult correctional agencies.

Source: Timothy A. Hughes, Doris J. Wilson, and Allen J. Beck, "Trends in State Parole, 1990–2000," *Bureau of Justice Statistics Special Report* (Washington, DC: U.S. Department of Justice, October, 2001), p. 4.

parole diminishing. Quite the contrary. The parole population has reached a record high of over 800,000.[28] What can account for these discrepancies?

As was described in earlier chapters, the major element that public policy changes failed to take into account when shifting to determinate sentencing was prison space. Under the justice model, more offenders have been more likely to be sentenced to at least some time in a correctional institution. Yet sufficient funding has not been available to accommodate them through new construction or expansion of existing facilities.

The primary method for dealing with this escalating inmate population has become the awarding of "gain time" or "good time." These terms are widely used interchangeably. But, technically, **gain time** refers to time that is *automatically* deducted by law, based on the length of the sentence, the length of time served, and/ or the seriousness of the offense. For example, some states credit an increasing number of days per month the longer a person remains incarcerated. Under such a system, an inmate could earn five days each month during the first year of imprisonment, six days per month during the next year, and so on. On the other hand, **good time (also called "incentive" or "meritorious" time)** is *earned* for proper institutional conduct. In some jurisdictions, it can also be awarded for participation in certain treatment, training, educational, or work programs.

gain time: time deducted from an original sentence, according to a formula established by legislative action.

good time (also called "incentive" or "meritorious" time): sentence reductions authorized by state statute that can be earned for proper conduct and/ or program participation.

LEARNING GOALS

Do you know:

13. how mandatory and discretionary parole differ?
14. how objective prediction instruments have changed parole decision-making?

Mandatory versus Discretionary Release

If the primary intent of the justice model was to increase the severity of sentencing, its goal will not be realized until institutional crowding is eliminated. For example, one study found that inmates released in nonparole states actually served seven months *less*, on average, than those with similar characteristics who were released in states using discretionary parole.[29] If, however, the major intent was to achieve certainty in sentencing, the justice model's mission is closer to accomplishment. That is not meant to imply that the full sentence imposed by the court is the one that will be served. But, after crediting inmates with time deductions, it is a straightforward mathematical calculation to determine one's earliest possible release date. Assuming that the prisoner does nothing while confined to jeopardize time credits, release is virtually automatic at that point.

Thus, in states with determinate sentencing, inmates now become eligible for what is known as **mandatory supervised release** (or mandatory parole) when they have served their original sentence minus any gain-time or good-time credits accrued. In most states, this means that, although the inmate must be legally released at that point, the state can require continued supervision in the community until such time as the full length of the sentence would have been served. In that respect, there is more than some truth to the observation that new language has simply been introduced for ongoing practices—with "supervised release" replacing

mandatory supervised release: the conditional release of offenders to community supervision when they have served at least their minimum sentence, minus time credits.

"parole," but very little actually changing with regard to the parole officer's supervisory role.[30] Another indicator that meaningful change may not have actually occurred is the earning of good time for program participation—a practice that bears close resemblance to basing parole decisions on treatment progress.

Mandatory supervised release is essentially a form of what has been described earlier as conditional release. The ex-offender is subject to conditions which, if violated, could result in reincarceration to serve out the remainder of the sentence (i.e., that portion which was relieved by time credits). It is therefore not the postrelease supervisory function of parole that has changed with the justice model. Nor is that unfortunate, since replacing conditional with unconditional releases could create far greater public safety hazards.

What has been fundamentally altered is how release decisions are made. As the term *mandatory supervised release* or *mandatory parole* implies, more inmates are now coming out of prison because the statutory authority to confine them has expired. In other words, they have served at least their minimum sentence, minus time credits. It is this mandated element that distinguishes it from the traditional form of discretionary parole. Once gain-time or good-time credits have been deducted from the original sentence, release becomes a compulsory result of mathematical calculations, as opposed to a discretionary decision of parole boards.

In the mid-1970s, nearly three out of four persons discharged from prison (about 72 percent) were released on the basis of parole board decisions.[31] But, more recently, discretionary parole has been accounting for only about one-third of prison releases (a percentage which has been dropping through much of the past decade).[32] As illustrated in Exhibit 11.3, at the same time that discretionary releases have been *decreasing*, mandatory releases have been *increasing*.

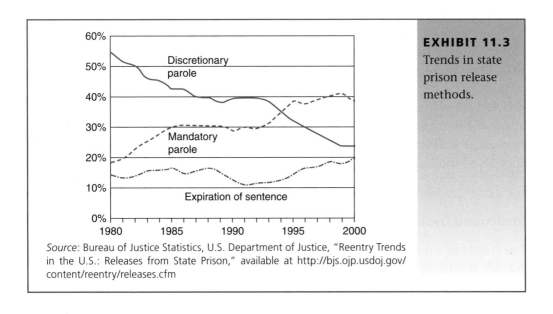

EXHIBIT 11.3
Trends in state prison release methods.

Source: Bureau of Justice Statistics, U.S. Department of Justice, "Reentry Trends in the U.S.: Releases from State Prison," available at http://bjs.ojp.usdoj.gov/content/reentry/releases.cfm

Parole Implications

Despite the significance of this change, few of those in free society fully understand it. The scenario in the next "Close-up on Corrections" provides a vivid example of how such misconceptions can fuel public anger.

It is easy to see how the public has become confused. Obviously, the trend over recent years has been toward less discretionary and more mandatory supervised releases. But that does not mean that parole board decision-making has been completely abolished. The majority of states still have various forms of indeterminate sentencing. And, even in states with determinate sentencing, parole boards must continue to address those inmates sentenced earlier under indeterminate statutes.

CLOSE-UP ON CORRECTIONS
Let's Get It Straight—Who's Doing the Releasing?

All too frequently, the media fail to understand and clearly distinguish between basic concepts. . . . As a result, the public does not get an accurate story. Few reporters understand the difference between . . . discretionary release and mandatory release, or the function of earned time or gained time and its effect in radically altering a sentence structure.

This example provides a valid illustration. A California man who had raped and severed the arms of his victim was widely reported to have been on parole release after serving only a portion of his sentence. The public voiced understandable outrage at the thought that parole board members would consider early release for such an individual. In fact, the inmate was not released as a matter of discretion, but because the law mandated it. Virtually no media reports pointed out that important aspect of the story.

Source: John J. Curran, Jr., "A Priority for Parole: Agencies Must Reach Out," in American Correctional Association, *Correctional Issues: Probation and Parole* (Alexandria, VA: American Correctional Association, 1990), pp. 34–35.

While the releasing authority of parole boards has been declining steadily, it has not been completely destroyed. It has, however, been subject to much greater *accountability*—"parole has been called on to be more responsive to the competing concerns of offenders, victims, and the public."[33] Consequently, parole discretion also has been subject to much greater control. Not only are paroling authorities more restricted in terms of which inmates can be selected for release, but today they also function under more structured release decision-making guidelines.

objective parole decision-making: the use of instruments that structure parole board discretion by replacing the subjective decisions with objective risk prediction formulas.

Structured Decision-making

The trend toward structuring the discretion of parole boards toward more **objective parole decision-making** reflects much of the same reasoning as the sentencing guidelines and objective classification procedures discussed in Chapter 2. In other words, it is designed to replace the *subjectivity* of personal decisions with the *objectivity* of formulas that predict risk on the basis of empirical research.

The search for valid instruments to identify what types of offenders represent the best risks for parole began well before our current infatuation with the capabilities of computers. As early as the 1920s, rudimentary forms of parole prediction tables began to appear.

During the 1960s and 1970s, as corrections assumed a more legalistic direction guided by constitutional issues, increasing emphasis was placed on due process considerations, definable standards, and defensible procedures. Parole was no exception. By the late 1970s, for example, a number of states had moved to parole contracting, whereby a target date is determined which becomes the parole release date if all provisions are met by the inmate. These contracts set specific goals in such areas as education, training, counseling, and institutional behavior.

By the 1980s, most states had adopted various forms of written guidelines governing the granting of parole.[34] Some of these documents are essentially lists of criteria that parole board members are implicitly supposed to take into account in making release decisions. Others are much more explicit statistical tables that assign specific weights to various factors, with the total score determining the candidate's prognosis for success or failure on parole. All are designed to base the granting of parole on more objective criteria. However, with the movement toward less discretionary parole and more mandatory supervised release, such instruments today are more likely used to determine postrelease risk factors so that the releasee is assigned to the proper level of supervision.

One of the most popular statistical risk prediction tables has been the salient factor score, originally pioneered by the U.S. Parole Commission in the 1970s. Under this system, scores of varying weights are assigned to six factors pertaining to the offender's background (shown in Exhibit 11.4). As that chart indicates, better risks are reflected by high scores (e.g., those who are older or who have no prior convictions). Low scores, on the other hand, reflect greater risk of subsequent violations.

While many states have relied upon salient factor score sheets in the past, the use of such generic decision-making guidelines has declined today. Even in the few states that do still use them, the risk assessment score tends to function only in an advisory capacity. At least in part, this is because they primarily measure "*static criminal history items*" (such as age, gender, and prior record)—none of which can be changed. At the same time, they overlook more *dynamic* factors related to the offender's criminogenic needs (such as interpersonal relationships, personality characteristics, and social achievement)—all of which are subject to change.[35] One of the newer instruments that does include both static and dynamic factors, the level of service inventory—revised (LSI-R),[36] is becoming an increasingly popular tool for making release decisions as well as determining postrelease treatment priorities, service provision, and level of supervision imposed.

Of course, mitigating or aggravating factors that have a bearing on the case are not reflected in the mechanical calculations of statistical scores. As with sentencing

EXHIBIT 11.4
Salient factor
score sheet.

Item A: *Prior convictions/adjudications (adult or juvenile)*   _____

None	=3
One	=2
Two or three	=1
Four or more	=0

Item B: *Prior commitment(s) of more than thirty days (adult or juvenile)*   _____

None	=2
One or two	=1
Three or more	=0

Item C: *Age at current offense/prior commitments*   _____

Age at commencement of the current offenses

26 years of age or more	=2*
20–25 years of age	=1*
19 years of age or less	=0

Exception: If five or more prior commitments
of more than thirty days (adult or juvenile),
place an 'x' here _____ and score this item   =0

Item D: *Recent commitment-free period (three years)*   _____

No prior commitment of more than thirty days
(adult or juvenile) or released to the community
from last such commitment at least three years
prior to the commencement of the current offense   =1
Otherwise   =0

Item E: *Probation/parole/confinement/escape/status violator this time*   _____

Neither on probation, parole, confinement, or
escape status at the time of the current offense,
nor committed as a probation, parole, confinement,
or escape status violator this time   =1
Otherwise   =0

Item F: *Heroin/opiate dependence*   _____

No history of heroin/opiate dependence   =1
Otherwise   =0

Total Score   _____

Note: For purposes of the salient factor score, an instance of criminal behavior resulting in a judicial determination of guilt or an admission of guilt before a judicial body shall be treated as a conviction, even if a conviction is not formally entered.

guidelines, structured parole guidelines do not eliminate discretion in the decision-making process. Much as with sentencing guidelines, the intent is to enable some flexibility within a standardized framework. That is because even the most sophisticated statistical techniques cannot fully substitute for human judgment. While objective instruments can provide valuable tools to guide human decision-making, they cannot replace it. Nor can any process, no matter how sophisticated, perfectly predict the future.

POSTRELEASE SUPERVISION

In addition to more closely structuring decision-making, objective guidelines have also been used to determine the level of supervision needed by those reentering the community. Again, this is not unlike another practice discussed earlier—the classification of probation caseloads. We have already seen how classifying probationers according to the level of risk they pose enables staff to allocate scarce resources more appropriately and manage heavy workloads more efficiently. In much the same manner, objective prediction instruments can serve similar functions for parole officers.

LEARNING GOALS

Do you know:
15. how the supervisory functions of parole and probation officers differ?
16. what transitional services assist offenders preparing to return to society?
17. how today's reentry population differs from previous releasees?

In fact, the supervisory responsibilities of parole staff are in many respects quite similar to those of probation officers. Their clients, however, are not necessarily similar. Parolees are generally more difficult to supervise than probationers. Whereas probationers have been considered sufficiently hopeful to avoid being sent to prison, parolees have been incarcerated as poor risks for probation. In addition, they have adapted to institutional life. Many have learned to acquiesce to authority on a superficial basis while maintaining a behavior pattern that is basically unchanged. Others have learned to manipulate their way through prison life. All were ineligible for probation (or failures from it) and often negatively conditioned by their prison experience.

While that does not make them unsalvageable, having been removed for some time from the community not only increases the difficulty of their supervision but also subjects them to additional personal stresses not encountered by probationers. Despite their indifferent external demeanor, freedom can have an overwhelmingly emotional impact on those institutionalized. Successful planning for parole must therefore begin well before an inmate exits the prison gate, although that is not often the case. In fact, underfunding has made parole in many jurisdictions "more of a legal status than a systematic process of reintegrating returning prisoners."[37] Moreover, the greater numbers of inmates being released in recent years has placed an increasing strain on the system, "challenging parole authorities to provide more services with fewer resources."[38]

Prerelease Planning

From their perspective, ex-offenders have already been rejected for years by the mainstream of society. When they encounter continued rejection upon reentering a hostile environment, feelings of inadequacy and failure are reinforced. It may not take long for even the most hopeful parolee to find the optimism of "starting over" overcome by the realism of being stigmatized. The ultimate effect is often a self-fulfilling prophecy, as those society expects to fail do exactly that. In the words of one ex-offender:

They walk through the gate in the big brick wall, which confined them for months or years or lifetimes, only to hit the wall of solid self-righteousness that so many people erect . . . perhaps in an attempt to feel that they are somehow morally superior to all of us ordinary folk out here breathing common air.[39]

At the same time, just as the community must be prepared to accept ex-offenders, they, in turn, must be prepared to be realistic about what they will confront and what adjustments they must make upon release. Those who have adapted well to years of institutional life face the formidable challenge of reorienting to an entirely different lifestyle in free society. Few can successfully make that adjustment alone. As one inmate put it, "after decades of living in the abnormal subculture behind fences, it's no wonder that so few succeed upon release. Prisons condition prisoners to fail."[40]

For an inside view of the fear and apprehensions of someone being released, read the next "Close-up on Corrections," which puts you in the place of a long-term inmate leaving prison (and also illustrates the unrevealing "social veneer" described previously). As that scenario points out, in the final analysis, it is in everyone's best interests to extend the help needed to prevent releasees from becoming readmissions.

Because the reception extended to ex-offenders is often more antagonistic than accepting, however, it is important for the parolee to locate supportive peer associations. Relying on such groups can do much to make the transition from confinement less frightening. While it may be difficult to imagine a "hardened ex-con" fearing anything—much less the expectation of imminent freedom, as

CLOSE-UP ON CORRECTIONS
Hesitant to Go Home

Next Wednesday you will be walking out those front gates as a free man. This last time around cost you ten years. It was your third hitch. You have spent thirty of the last forty years of your life behind bars. Sixty-two years of life's ups and downs have softened your disposition. You have no excuses left; you feel that the time you got was coming to you. In fact, the last hitch was one you purposely set up.

You had been released on a cold gray morning in February. There was no one on the outside waiting for you; your friends were all in prison. You had been divorced for over fifteen years and your former wife had remarried. Your parents were dead, and your two sisters had given up on you long ago. Besides, there were too many decisions to make in the free world. You were not used to all of that freedom; it was frightening. No one cared about you like they did inside the joint.

You got a job as a busboy in a restaurant, but the hustle and bustle was too much, and besides, no one wanted to make friends with an old ex-con. Finally you had all you could take, so you stole all the money from the cash register one night during a lull in the business. You did not spend any of it, but instead went home, had a beer, and waited. In less than two hours, the police arrived at your apartment. Once the restaurant manager realized you and the money were missing, it was not long before you were arrested. You refused an attorney and told the judge that you would keep committing crimes until he sent you back. He reluctantly sentenced you to ten years. You passed up parole each time it came around.

So here you are again. You have been measured for your new suit of street clothes and your one hundred fifty dollar check for transitional expenses has been processed. The labor department representative has arranged for you to have a stock-clerk job in a small grocery store in a nearby town. Your social worker has also arranged for you to stay in a small apartment near where you will work. You remember your last prerelease counseling session with her and how she offered all the words of encouragement a young, energetic, and well-meaning counselor could muster. You just smiled and nodded your approval. What good would it have done to burst her idealistic bubble? She could never understand how frightening the outside world had come to be for you. All of her friends lived in the free world; none of yours did.

You would like to make it on the outside if you could, but the odds are against you. And besides, it's just too lonely out there. You know you ought to feel happy about leaving prison, but the truth is, you are miserable about it. You would like to be able to make it on the outside, but deep down inside, you feel you are doomed before you start.

Source: Michael Braswell, Tyler Fletcher, and Larry Miller, *Human Relations and Corrections*, Third Edition (Prospect Heights, IL: Waveland Press, 1990), pp. 83–84. © 1990, 1985 by Waveland Press. Reprinted by permission of Waveland Press, Inc.

we saw in the last scenario, even with official assistance, parole can be a very lonely experience. In large part, that is because those behind bars have largely lost contact with the outside world. As one inmate described the postrelease survival potential of a 45-year-old inmate who had done 25 years:

You still have the mindset of a 20-year-old. You see that time is running again, and it's running fast, not standing still like it did in prison, where time never moved. The shock, the stress, the strain of the fast pace can get you down and you can end up returning to what you know best . . . what you're most comfortable with.[41]

In the upcoming "Close-up on Corrections," an inmate's plea to advice columnist Ann Landers is further evidence that the prospect of getting out can create more panic than the possibility of staying in. Particularly in terms of the critical role of self-help groups, note her response.

CLOSE-UP ON CORRECTIONS
Prerelease Panic

Dear Ann:

I am coming to the end of a five-year prison sentence in a state correctional facility. I need to know how to deal with society after my release. I'm not sure about how I should conduct myself around people I haven't seen in five years. What will be expected of me? . . .

When I apply for a job and am asked if I have a criminal record, what should I say? I'm afraid if I mention this I won't be hired. On the other hand, if I lie and they find out the truth, I will probably be fired.

It seems that there should be some kind of counseling in prison to prepare people like me for the outside. Some inmates I know who have been in prison for a long time are actually afraid to leave because they don't think they'll fit in out there. Almost 90 percent of these prisoners end up coming back, mainly because they were not prepared to face the outside world.

If you can be of any help to people like me, it will be greatly appreciated by the thousands of inmates who are struggling with the same problem.

F.C., Cranston, R.I.

You are not alone. I've dealt with this problem in my column before. There is a self-help group for ex-offenders that can answer your questions and give you more guidance on living on the outside. It can also refer you to local groups around the country that offer job training and placement, as well as counseling. For more information, send a self-addressed, stamped envelope to The Fortune Society, 39 W. 19th St., New York, N.Y. 10011. Its members do an excellent job.

Source: Ann Landers, "Support Group Can Help Ex-prisoners," published in newspapers throughout the country on February 7, 1992. Permission granted by Ann Landers and Creators Syndicate.

Preparing the Offender

As that inmate's letter indicates, not all institutions offer prerelease guidance before discharge.[42] But some correctional facilities do make an effort to prepare offenders for what to expect and how to cope upon release. In fact, much of the success of reintegration depends on how well the inmate is prepared prior to release. This can be accomplished through a variety of prerelease counseling and planning programs, as well as through work release or by phasing out through prerelease centers.[43]

In some cases, prisoners are phased out through gradual reduction of their security classification. In this manner, the last months of the sentence are served in a minimum-security facility or prerelease center—where there are fewer rules governing behavior, less staff monitoring, and greater trust placed in the inmate. The goal is to enable those about to be released to take more personal responsibility for decision-making, as well as encourage them to replace external staff control with internal self-control.

Inmates in such community reentry centers may spend daytime hours at work assignments or educational programs in the community. Thus they are able to become better accustomed to the freedoms of outside life. They can "practice" living in society while remaining under supervision during their unoccupied time. Beyond these general functions, additional assistance is provided in terms of plans to obtain housing, employment, transportation, and other essentials for surviving on the outside.

Not all correctional agencies have a prerelease center or sufficient bedspace in it to meet demands. But arrangements can be made for work release without transferring inmates from their assigned institution. Particularly where preparation for parole is viewed as a long-term process, opportunities for work release may be provided well in advance of anticipated departure. They enable inmates to be employed on salary in the community during the day, while returning to the facility at night.

Work release is an alternative to total confinement that has a number of advantages—among them, enabling offenders to help support their families and reducing the financial burden on taxpayers. Perhaps most important, it enhances the inmate's job skills, confidence, sense of responsibility, and ties with the community.

Not everyone, however, is equally enthusiastic about it, nor is work release without risks. Despite its advantages, not all correctional systems have adopted work-release programs. Even where it is available, the number participating is extremely small, representing only 2 percent of the total prison population.[44] Undoubtedly, there have been isolated problems with inmates absconding or returning under the influence of alcohol or drugs. But, for the most part, it would appear that the benefits of reintegrating the offender into society through work release outweigh the drawbacks. Except for the extremely few prisoners sentenced to death or confined to life without parole, virtually everyone is subject to potential release at some time. With those who are eligible, it would seem logical that the time to take the risks associated with work release is while they are still subject to continued custody.

Today's Reentry Population

Offenders being released today are often returning to the community "with contagious diseases, chronic medical and mental health problems, and histories of substance abuse."[45] Beyond their own personal problems, they are also ill prepared to assume such family roles as financial provider, caregiver, or partner in a relationship.[46] Not only are today's releasees ill prepared for their return to free society, but they also differ from their predecessors in a number of ways.

On average, current parolees have served a longer prison sentence under harsher conditions with less availability of treatment, training, and educational programs. They are more likely to be gang members, mentally ill, and alcohol or drug abusers. They are more disconnected from family and friends, as well as less educated and employable.[47] In the year before their scheduled release, only about 1 in 10 had participated in formal prerelease initiatives designed to help them transition to the community.[48] Obviously, none of this points toward a good prognosis for reintegration.

To the extent that shorter sentences—combined with education, training, treatment, and prerelease initiatives—increase the potential for success on parole, these are foreboding facts. At all levels of the correctional conglomerate, budget cuts have curtailed programs that provide offenders with the skills necessary to prepare for reintegration into society.[49] As shown in Exhibit 11.5, the percentage of

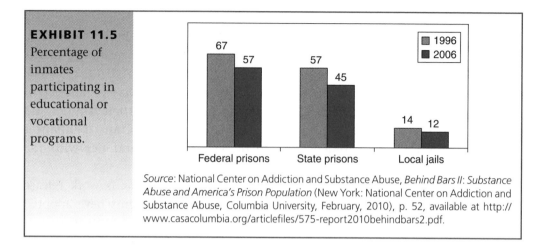

EXHIBIT 11.5
Percentage of inmates participating in educational or vocational programs.

Source: National Center on Addiction and Substance Abuse, *Behind Bars II*: *Substance Abuse and America's Prison Population* (New York: National Center on Addiction and Substance Abuse, Columbia University, February, 2010), p. 52, available at http://www.casacolumbia.org/articlefiles/575-report2010behindbars2.pdf.

the inmate population participating in vocational or educational programs is dropping in virtually all correctional facilities—local, state, and federal. Yet some 650,000 people are released every year from our prisons,[50] and even this number pales in comparison to the 7 million being released annually from American jails.[51]

Thus, at the same time that corrections is required to manage the reentry process for increasing numbers of offenders, the very programs upon which successful reentry is built have been scaled back or eliminated as a result of shifting priorities driven by budget cuts.[52] As described in the next "Close-up," needs are far outpacing the ability to respond. In essence, although more people are being released after experiencing severe conditions that potentially "threaten greater psychological distress and long-term dysfunction," they are returning to communities that are "already disadvantaged by a badly frayed 'safety net,'" unable to provide needed supportive resources.[53]

CLOSE-UP ON CORRECTIONS
Reentry Realities versus Resources

People are released from prison and jail with complex needs . . .

* Three out of four have a substance abuse problem, but formal treatment prior to release is received by only 10 percent coming from state prisons and 3 percent from local jails.
* Two out of three lack a high school diploma, and 40 percent have neither a diploma nor a GED. Only about 1 out of 3 gets vocational training at any point during incarceration.
* Over half (55 percent) have children under the age of 18.
* About 20 percent are released from prison without community supervision.

. . . and they return to communities that are particularly ill-equipped to help them succeed . . .

* In Connecticut, almost half of the prison and jail population is from just a handful of neighborhoods in five cities, which have the most concentrated levels of poverty and nonwhite populations in the state.

- In Chicago, only 24 percent of organizations that provide services to reentering individuals were located in any of the six communities to which the highest numbers of people are returning.
- In California, a study found significant gaps between the needs of parolees released in the state and available services, with only:
    - 200 shelter beds for more than 10,000 homeless parolees,
    - 4 mental health clinics for 18,000 psychiatric cases,
    - 750 treatment beds for 85,000 released substance abusers.

Source: *Report of the Re-Entry Policy Council: Charting the Safe and Successful Return of Prisoners to the Community* (New York: Council of State Governments, 2003), synopsis available at http://www.reentrypolicy.org/publications/1691;file.

Conditions of Parole

While communities may be poorly prepared to support reentry, since parole is a form of conditional release, its clients are subject to mandated restrictions. For the most part, the conditions of parole are quite similar to the probation stipulations described earlier. As with probation, *general conditions* refer to the standard requirements governing behavior that are imposed uniformly. Designed to reduce the chances of renewed involvement in crime, they may require steady work, restrict travel, limit personal associations, prohibit the use of alcohol, require periodical reporting to a parole officer, and the like. Although they are not identical throughout the country, these general conditions will be imposed on all parolees within their jurisdiction.

LEARNING GOALS

Do you know:

18. what general conditions are usually established for parolees?
19. what functions parole officers perform?

In addition to such universal requirements, *specific conditions* can be added for a particular client to address any unique treatment needs or behavioral restrictions. For example, a habitual DUI (driving under the influence) offender may also be required to attend Alcoholics Anonymous sessions regularly, to abstain completely from the use of alcohol, to refrain from driving a car, and even to submit to random breath, blood, or urinalysis testing.

As we saw earlier, general trends in the overall parole process have also been moving toward greater objectivity. As a result, parole authorities have begun to reduce the number of conditions, focusing more on those related to crime control than on those related to social activities. Regardless of what the requirements are, however, the client must agree in writing to abide by them.

Functions of Parole Officers

It is the parole board in the state's central office that authorizes general conditions by which clients must abide. But it is the parole officer in the field who is responsible for assuring that they are upheld. Previously, field services were an administrative unit of the parole board. Since the 1970s, however, community supervision has become increasingly independent and is now usually housed separately (primarily within the state department of corrections).[54]

On the part of the officer, field services call for—among many other attributes—skills in working with the client and his or her family, developing relationships with law enforcement agencies, and becoming thoroughly familiar with available resources in the area. As with probation supervision, the parole officer's role involves similar conflicts between providing support and imposing sanctions. But encouraging *change* is actually what both are designed to accomplish.[55]

To achieve change, parole officers are simultaneously expected to:

• furnish assistance to help the ex-offender readjust;

• monitor signs indicating how well or poorly that adjustment is occurring; and

• take appropriate action to control behavior when necessary.

In some jurisdictions, they are getting assistance in that regard from a powerful but unlikely source—the courts. The upcoming "Close-up on Corrections" describes a unique strategy designed to bring the prestige and resources of the judiciary to bear on the challenges of making a successful transition from prison—reentry courts, which is the parole equivalent of drug courts. While this initiative is just beginning to make an impact, at least one early assessment indicates that the extensive supervision provided to the client (e.g., monthly court appearances, individualized attention, and three to four face-to-face contacts per week) improves chances for success, even among drug and sex offenders, who are not traditionally considered good parole risks.[56]

CLOSE-UP ON CORRECTIONS
Transition through Reentry Court

The reentry court concept involves drawing upon the authority of the court to promote positive behavior by offenders returning from prison, much as drug courts manage the behavior of drug offenders. Two of the key components in drug courts are that they represent the exercise of judicial authority toward a beneficial end, and that offenders respond positively to the fact that a judge is taking an interest in their success. Frequent appearances before the court, combined with the offer of assistance and predictable consequences for failure, assist offenders in taking the steps necessary to get their lives back on track.

The reentry court involves applying these principles at another stage in the justice process—as inmates leave prison. But the core elements are similar:

• *Assessment and planning.* Following assessment of inmates' needs, corrections officials—working in conjunction with the reentry court—establish linkages to social services, family counseling, health care, housing, job training, and work opportunities to support successful reintegration.

- *Active oversight.* The reentry court sees clients frequently—probably once a month—beginning right after release and continuing until the end of their parole (or other form of supervised release).
- *Management of supportive services.* A case management function brokers a broad array of supportive resources, including substance abuse treatment, job training, faith institutions, housing assistance, and community services.
- *Accountability to the community.* Mechanisms for drawing upon diverse community perspectives are incorporated, such as a citizen advisory board.
- *Graduated and parsimonious sanctions.* A predetermined range of sanctions for violations of release conditions is swiftly, predictably, and universally applied (although they would not automatically require return to prison).
- *Rewards for success.* Milestones in the reentry process trigger recognition and rewards through positive judicial reinforcement (e.g., graduation ceremonies, early release from supervision).

Based on the concept that the judiciary provides a powerful public forum for encouraging positive behavior, the expectation is that focusing on reentry issues in the courts will help reduce the recidivism rate of returning prisoners and will encourage a broad-based coalition to support their successful reintegration.

Source: Compiled from Office of Justice Programs, "Reentry Courts: Managing the Transition from Prison to Community," *A Call for Concept Papers* (U.S. Department of Justice: Office of Justice Programs, September, 1999), pp. 1–9.

Collateral Consequences of Conviction

Until their civil rights are restored, those convicted of a felony in many states lose their right to vote, hold public office, join the military, serve on a jury, or obtain a passport. In fact, as public policy-makers adopted more punitive sentencing under the justice model, they likewise embraced more collateral sanctions. By the mid-1990s, for example, it was found that, over the previous decade, there had been increases in the number of states:

- permanently denying convicted felons the right to vote;
- allowing termination of parental rights;
- establishing a felony conviction as grounds for divorce;
- restricting the right to hold public office;
- requiring lifetime registration for certain sex offenders;
- establishing occupational barriers for those with various criminal convictions.[57]

LEARNING GOALS

Do you know:
20. what collateral consequences of conviction affect parolees returning to the community?
21. how occupational licensing restrictions limit employment for ex-offenders?

But these are only the state-specified losses. Among the many other collateral consequences of conviction and incarceration[58] is the less-publicized loss of family ties over years spent behind bars, often in remote locations far from the offender's home community. As a result, many parolees have neither the supportive family nor the financial resources to help them get resettled. Thus, many ex-offenders are homeless upon release. As one observer described it, temporarily they are "staying on someone's couch, but it won't last long."[59] For those classified as sex offenders, however, even a friend's couch may be off-limits, since state residency restrictions often prohibit them from living in proximity to everything from schools and day care centers to parks and bus stops. In one city, the situation became so desperate that homeless sex offenders set up a sizeable "tent city" in virtually the only location legally available for them to live—under a causeway bridge.[60]

Since employment is often contingent on a stable residence, homelessness makes it even more difficult to find a job. Research indicates that the quality and quantity of employment are among the most consistent predictors of success on parole.[61] Yet many jobs are restricted because of the ex-offender's ineligibility. Those who have not participated in institutional education programs will especially find doors closed to them, since even entry-level jobs today tend to require at least a high school diploma. In one state alone, it has been estimated that about half of the prisoners released on parole are illiterate, and about 85 percent are substance abusers[62]—hardly good qualifications for seeking postrelease employment.

Even those with the required educational credentials, however, will find that they are faced with another collateral consequence of conviction in the form of **occupational licensing** restrictions. Often based on "good moral character," such restrictions effectively exclude ex-offenders. In fact, it is estimated that 40 percent of the jobs in at least one state are off-limits to ex-offenders.[63]

Given how dramatically the number of occupations that exclude convicted felons has been increasing, it is not surprising to find that more than three out of four ex-offenders in another state remain jobless one year after release.[64] In some states, positions requiring licenses are difficult (or impossible) to obtain by those with a criminal record and can include a long list of occupations—everything from dentistry, firefighting, and police work to funeral director, security guard, barber, nurse, pharmacist, veterinarian, teacher, plumber, or sanitation worker. While states have the power to lift these bans by providing "certificates of rehabilitation," only six states have provisions for removing occupational barriers to ex-offender employment.[65] Further compounding these barriers are fluctuations in the employment market itself:

> The kinds of jobs for which former prisoners are most likely to get hired—blue-collar and manufacturing jobs—are decreasing as a share of the workforce. The jobs for which former prisoners are least likely to get hired, (involving contact with children, the elderly, and direct customer contact), are increasing as a share of the workforce.[66]

occupational licensing: requiring a license to do certain types of work, which may specify being of "good moral character."

EXHIBIT 11.6
The work that inmates perform while confined in correctional institutions does not often prepare them for employment in free society.

Moreover, Congress has provided federal and state courts with the ability to deny tax-supported federal benefits to those convicted of drug possession or trafficking. Among the benefits that can be denied are grants, contracts, loans, and licenses. Thus students can lose college loans, pilots can lose their FAA license, business-owners can lose federal contracts, and researchers can lose academic grants.[67]

Additionally, denial of welfare benefits and public housing—combined with restrictions on employment prospects—can present a virtual "brick wall" for returning ex-offenders.[68] Beyond these pragmatic barriers is yet another collateral consequence of a felony conviction that has generated widespread controversy in recent years—the disenfranchisement of millions of potential voters on the basis of their criminal record. (See the next "Close-up" for the American Correctional Association's arguments against this practice.)

CLOSE-UP ON CORRECTIONS
National Public Correctional Policy on Restoration of Voting Rights for Felony Offenders

Introduction

People convicted of crimes are expected to become responsible citizens after being discharged from correctional supervision. However, many individuals are excluded from exercising their civic rights because they are banned from voting in many jurisdictions. The laws that prohibit offenders from voting, even after they have been discharged from correctional supervision, frustrate offenders in their attempt to fully re-enter society successfully . . . and disproportionately exclude a large number of people from participating fully in society.

Policy Statement

The American Correctional Association affirms that voting is a fundamental right in a democracy, and it considers a ban on voting after a felon is discharged from correctional supervision to be contradictory to the goals of a democracy, the rehabilitation of felons, and their successful re-entry to the community. Therefore, ACA advocates:

- Restoring voting rights for felony offenders once they have been discharged from incarceration or parole;
- Developing protocols for federal, state, and local correctional agencies that inform inmates near their release about the means by which their voting rights will be restored and provide education and assistance to felony offenders in completing the restoration process to regain their civil rights; and
- Developing state election agency procedures that permit eligible felony offenders to vote in elections after completing and filing all necessary paperwork.

Source: Unanimously ratified by the American Correctional Association Delegate Assembly, January 12, 2005.

While some 5.3 million Americans (1 of every 41 adults) are currently or permanently disenfranchised,[69] several states are beginning to restore voting rights, as well as remove arbitrary restrictions on job opportunities for ex-offenders. Some jurisdictions have also begun prohibiting the denial of employment or licensing because of a conviction unless it involves unreasonable risk or there is a direct relationship between the offense and the specific type of job or license.

Combined with legislatively imposed restrictions is the basic hesitancy of many employers to "take a chance" by hiring ex-offenders. For example, a survey of employers in several major U.S. cities found that nearly two out of three said they would "definitely" or "probably" not knowingly hire someone with a criminal record.[70] Another study determined that 40 percent of employers would "never" hire anyone with a felony drug conviction.[71] Finding jobs for parolees is also especially difficult in times of high unemployment, when even those without the stigma of being "ex-cons" have a hard time finding meaningful work. Despite federal tax credits and bonding programs that insure employers who hire ex-offenders,[72] sometimes it is almost impossible to place parolees in jobs with a livable salary, much less opportunities for career advancement. As one review of research on this topic concludes, "discrimination against ex-offenders translates into fewer job opportunities and lower earnings."[73] Such "invisible punishments" have become so pervasive that the American Bar Association has recommended that state legislatures codify these sanctions and notify defendants of their consequences before offering a guilty plea.[74]

In essence, offenders leave prison with multiple disadvantages—ranging from social stigma to fractured families. But, when society piles on further postrelease penalties and discriminatory practices, the resulting hurdles and barriers can become insurmountable. The ironic effect of such collateral consequences may well be that large numbers of "former inmates with few social supports, family attachments, or economic opportunities may ultimately increase crime rates more than they were lowered by the expansion of the penal system in the first place."[75]

Reentry Initiatives

By 2009, it had become apparent that the magnitude of reentry challenges, coupled with the widespread numbers of communities that were being affected, called for federal intervention. In response, Congress appropriated well over $100 million under the Second Chance Act to support initiatives ranging from mentoring and reentry demonstration projects to transitional services, reentry courts, technological training, and prison education programs. (For more details, see the next "Close-up on Corrections.")

CLOSE-UP ON CORRECTIONS

Key Provisions of the Second Chance Act

- *Demonstration grants:* funding state and local governments to promote reintegration, including employment services, substance abuse treatment, housing, family programming, mentoring, and methods to improve release and revocation decisions using risk assessment tools.
- *Mentoring grants:* funding to nonprofit organizations for mentoring or transitional services.
- *Offender reentry substance abuse treatment:* funding for drug treatment in prisons, jails, and juvenile facilities.
- *Family drug treatment programs:* funding for family-based treatment programs for incarcerated parents with minor children.
- *Federal reentry initiative:* providing information on health, employment, personal finances, release requirements, and community resources to inmates released by the Federal Bureau of Prisons.
- *Reentry research:* requesting the U.S. Department of Justice's National Institute of Justice and Bureau of Justice Statistics to conduct reentry-related research.
- *National adult and juvenile offender reentry resource center:* establishing a national resource center to collect and disseminate information and provide training on and support for reentry efforts.

Source: The Second Chance Act of 2007, H.R.1593 (1060), available at http://www.fedcure.org/information/HR1593.shtml (accessed July 5, 2010).

While this federal funding is providing much-needed fiscal resources, some localities are also turning to a unique restorative justice approach to structured

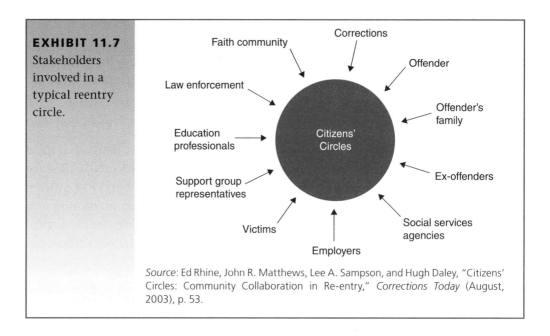

EXHIBIT 11.7 Stakeholders involved in a typical reentry circle.

Source: Ed Rhine, John R. Matthews, Lee A. Sampson, and Hugh Daley, "Citizens' Circles: Community Collaboration in Re-entry," *Corrections Today* (August, 2003), p. 53.

reentry that involves not only the correctional system, but collaborative partnerships with the community as well. For example, through citizens' circles involving a broad-based array of local representatives (see Exhibit 11.7), the root causes contributing to the parolee's involvement in crime are addressed, offender accountability is established, and linkages are developed with those in the community who have a direct stake in the outcome, using the principles of restorative justice:

> The process itself is based on negotiation and consensus-building between the offender and circle members. The circles embrace local citizens, support systems, community agencies, the corrections department, and the offender in decision-making and case management related to rehabilitation and re-entry. Circle members meet on a regular basis . . . [and] offer a powerful forum for citizens to communicate their expectations for successful re-entry. They also help offenders recognize the harm their behavior has caused . . . and develop a viable plan of action to promote responsible citizenship. . . . Most importantly, the circle helps offenders understand that acceptance back into the community requires the fulfillment of certain obligations and commitments.[76]

In this way, the community can exert its capacity to provide informal social control, build supportive relationships with ex-offenders, and promote prosocial lifestyles. At the same time, ex-offenders can obtain opportunities to alter their self-image, earn redemption, repair the harm they have caused, and rebuild community trust through civic engagement.[77] Especially with larger numbers of ex-offenders returning to a relatively small number of neighborhoods, strengthening community support systems has become a key ingredient in their successful reintegration.[78]

Field Supervision

Once survival needs have been addressed, attention turns to monitoring the parolee's reintegration progress. Much of this component of the job relates to enforcing established conditions. In recent years, the parole officer's monitoring functions have been supplemented by such techniques as drug-testing, house arrest, and electronic monitoring. It is, however, noteworthy that "such techniques seldom contribute to rehabilitation; they just help identify the failures more quickly."[79]

Ideally, both the officer and the client would view parole conditions as tools to shape behavior rather than as limits being imposed. Of course, that is not often the case. When it is obvious that the parolee is becoming unresponsive and in danger of getting into further trouble, the officer may well recommend revocation. If a new offense is committed, such action will be virtually certain.

As with probation, parole officers might be reluctant to take formal action upon a first violation, especially when it involves a technical or minor matter. But, unlike probation officers, parole officers are dealing with more serious and/or repeat offenders and therefore do not tend to exercise as much discretion. Public criticism has not gone unnoticed when a client's criminal actions capture media headlines. Unfortunately, that is when parole is most likely to make the news. In that regard, parole has taken its share of criticism from many quarters: "Crime-control advocates have denounced parole supervision as largely nominal and ineffective; due-process advocates have criticized parole revocation as arbitrary and counterproductive; social welfare advocates have decried the lack of meaningful and useful rehabilitation services."[80]

While parole has not responded with equal vigor to all of these concerns, authorities have become increasingly responsive to the need to protect community safety. Thus more parole agencies have turned to intensive supervision programs, tightening standards, and adopting a **sanction orientation** that stresses quick and uncompromising response to noncompliance.[81] This does not mean that parole officers have now become police officers, or that they take pleasure in recommending revocation, or that they have abandoned rehabilitative goals. But, if a client "cannot or will not change within the environment of the community, then the sanction orientation requires that community corrections must, for the sake of community protection, immediately . . . act to change the environment in which the criminal functions."[82] As a result of this emphasis, it has been concluded that "parole as it is currently practiced focuses almost entirely on detecting and punishing failure."[83]

sanction orientation: community supervision that emphasizes public protection through swift and sure enforcement of rule violations.

Parole Revocation

Since parole is a form of conditional release, it can be revoked for failure to maintain the conditions upon which it was awarded. But, while the supervising officer can make such a

LEARNING GOALS

Do you know:
22. what due process protections are required for parole revocation?
23. why measures of recidivism are not always valid indicators of the effectiveness of parole?

EXHIBIT 11.8
Monitoring the offender's reentry into the community is an essential function of parole officers.

recommendation, only the parole board is authorized to revoke parole. In other words, those with the authority to grant parole are also those with the power to repeal it.

In contrast to parole selection, however, inmates *are* entitled to certain due process protections in parole revocation proceedings. The rationale for this distinction is, as the Supreme Court has phrased it, that there is a "difference between losing what one has and not getting what one wants."[84] That is, those denied the opportunity to be *released* on parole are not subject to a change in status. They remain in the institution to which they are already confined. On the other hand, those denied the opportunity to *remain* on parole may suffer a substantial change in status.

Due Process Protections.   For many years, parolees had no legal means of challenging the discretion of parole board revocation actions. The concept then was that parole was extended by the "grace" of the executive branch of government and that it could be withdrawn at any time. The granting of parole is still legally considered a privilege. Nevertheless, the Supreme Court determined in the 1972 *Morrisey v. Brewer* case[85] that revocation of parole represents a "grievous loss" which falls within the due process provisions of the Fourteenth Amendment. This does not extend to parolees the full due process protections of defendants facing adjudication in a criminal court. Parole revocation is *not* considered either a stage of criminal prosecution or an adversarial proceeding. But the Supreme Court's ruling did establish that parole revocation must include two stages:

1. a *preliminary hearing*, at which point it is determined if there is *probable cause* to believe that a violation of parole conditions was committed; and if so

2. a full *revocation hearing*, at which the parolee must be afforded:
   • written notice of the alleged violation,
   • disclosure of the evidence related to the violation,
   • an opportunity to be heard in person and to present witnesses and documentary evidence,
   • an opportunity to confront and cross-examine adverse witnesses (unless good cause can be demonstrated for prohibiting confrontation),
   • judgment before a neutral and detached hearing body (such as a parole board), and
   • a written statement regarding the evidence relied upon and the reasons for revoking parole.

Note that one of the fundamental due process protections—the right to counsel—is not included among these requirements. This issue was addressed the very next year (1973) in the *Gagnon v. Scarpelli* case.[86] But that ruling did not extend due process protections to the provision of counsel for indigent clients facing possible probation or parole revocation. Rather, it was held that the decision to appoint counsel could be made by the state on a case-by-case basis, using its discretion as to whether the parolee's version of an issue being disputed can only be fairly presented by an attorney.

Nor have any court decisions thus far mandated the provision of a revocation appeal process. It may therefore be surprising to find that, although not constitutionally required, about half of the states (48 percent) do offer an opportunity to appeal.[87] Overall, both legally and administratively, trends point toward affording greater due process rights when liberty will be restricted.

Revocation Results. The next question is what consequences might occur if parole is revoked. Many would immediately answer that the offender would be returned to prison to complete the remainder of the original sentence. That is certainly a possible outcome, particularly if another crime has been committed. In fact, the readmission of parolees accounts for a substantial share of prison crowding, representing over one-third of new admissions.[88] In recognition of this, Connecticut has substantially reduced the number of technical violations that can send a parole violator back to prison, such as not having a job or missing a meeting with a parole officer.[89] Likewise, by 2010, the budget crisis and overcrowded prisons in California had resulted in implementing reduced restrictions for nonviolent parolees, in the hope that fewer would be sent back to prison.[90] But reincarceration is not the only possibility when parole is violated. To the contrary, in many states the parole board may also elect to restore parole status—with either no change or a modification of conditions.

Recidivism

recidivism:
indication that a former offender has returned to crime, as demonstrated by rearrest, reconviction, reincarceration, parole revocation, or other measures.

Ultimately, it is effectiveness measures upon which parole—and, for that matter, much of the entire correctional system—is judged. Such measures and judgments are often based on **recidivism** rates.

To *recidivate* means to "revert" or "repeat." The question is, what is being reverted to or repeated? One of the major challenges to answering that question is the fluctuating definition of recidivism rates. For example, recidivism could be defined as:

- *Rearrest.* Are criminals considered "recidivists" when they are rearrested? If so, does the type of crime make any difference? Would a juvenile car thief be considered a recidivist if taken back into custody for running away from home?

- *Reconviction.* What about those rearrested who are not reconvicted? Can they be classified as recidivists if they are innocent in the eyes of the court?

- *Reincarceration.* Even if reconvicted, does it matter whether or not they are reincarcerated? What if their punishment is just a fine?

- *Parole violation.* Are parole violators recidivists? What if they only committed a minor technical violation?

- *Parole revocation.* Are those whose parole is revoked recidivists? What if they are not reincarcerated?

Recidivism rates will usually be highest when measured by rearrest and lowest when measured by return to prison for a new crime. For example, one national study found that within three years of their release:

- 67.5 percent of the prisoners were rearrested for a new offense (almost exclusively a felony or a serious misdemeanor);

- 46.9 percent were reconvicted for a new crime;

- 25.4 percent were resentenced to prison for a new crime;

- 51.8 percent were back in prison, serving time for a new prison sentence or for a technical violation of their release, such as failing a drug test, missing an appointment with their parole officer, or being arrested for a new crime.[91]

In addition to questions concerning what criteria to consider as recidivism, there is the further issue of how long a period of time should be taken into consideration. In other words, how long should offenders be monitored to establish valid recidivism rates? One year? Two years? Ten years? The rest of their lives? Using different failure measures and follow-up periods will obviously produce different outcomes. These are among the complications that make it not only difficult to measure recidivism, but also virtually impossible to compare studies which use varying definitions of it.

If successful discharge is any indicator, parole may not be as ineffective as sensationalized media accounts might lead us to believe. The likelihood of successfully completing parole, however, depends on a number of variables. For example, success rates are higher for discretionary parolees (54 percent) than for those who received mandatory parole (33 percent). Parole outcomes also vary by a number of other factors. In that regard, success rates are higher among those who are:

- first prison releases (63 percent success rate) rather than re-releases (21 percent);

- age 55 or older (54 percent), rather than under age 25 (36 percent);

- female (48 percent), rather than male (39 percent).[92]

Research likewise indicates that the profile of the typical violator is that of a "single male who does not seek or obtain a job following release, has a known history of abusing alcohol and/or drugs, has not taken academic or vocational courses while incarcerated, is a minority, and more often, is a repeat offender."[93]

In summary, the effectiveness of parole depends on many factors—from what variables are being measured to what types of offenders are being assessed over what period of time. It is for such reasons that standardization of recidivism criteria is necessary if accurate evaluations of parole are to be obtained. But, even with nationally standardized guidelines for determining recidivism, there are no uniform standards for making revocation decisions. As a result, it has been noted that high or low revocation rates are more a product of "the system's sensitivity to violations" than of any significant difference in the behavior of offenders—thus we cannot necessarily equate low revocations with successful rehabilitation.[94]

Nor can parole be held completely accountable for either its successes or its failures. Among many other variables that will have an impact on the postrelease conduct of parolees is the willingness or unwillingness of state legislatures to provide funding for meaningful programs during confinement. In that regard, it has been noted that effective programs—ranging from therapeutic communities for drug addicts to basic education and vocational training for the general population—have been shown to reduce recidivism rates among participants by 8–15 percent.[95] As a result, reinvesting in such programs is a key feature of the recommendations for reforming parole and reentry practices featured in the next "Close-up on Corrections."

CLOSE-UP ON CORRECTIONS
Recommendations for Reforming Parole and Reentry Practices

- *Reinvest in prison work, education, and substance abuse programs.* There is ample evidence that treatment can reduce recidivism if the programs are well designed, well implemented, and targeted appropriately.
- *Reinstate discretionary parole where it has been abolished.* Inmates released by a parole board have higher success rates, and discretionary parole also serves to refocus prison staff and correctional budgets on planning for release, not just opening the door at release.
- *Front-load post-prison services during the first six months after release.* It makes no sense to spend $23,000 a year on an inmate (even three times that if he or she is in maximum security) and then, on the day of the inmate's release, spend from zero dollars (for unconditional releases) to about $2,500 a year for the average parolee.
- *Implement a "goal parole" or earned discharge system.* Factors such as work, education, and treatment incentives would be built into the system, and parolees could earn time off their parole term by succeeding in prosocial activities. Research shows that informal social controls—those interpersonal bonds that link ex-inmates to churches, jobs, law-abiding neighbors, families, and communities—are strong predictors of reduced recidivism. And, even if most parole boards no longer retain the discretion to set the date of release, all of them set the conditions of release.
- *Establish procedures by which some ex-offenders can put their criminal offending entirely in the past.* In terms of this issue, the U.S. has the worst of both worlds—higher rates of application of the criminal process, combined with no way to move legally beyond its stigmatizing effects.

Source: Summarized from Joan Petersilia, "Hard Time: Ex-offenders Returning Home after Prison," *Corrections Today* (April, 2005), pp. 70–71.

Perhaps most influential, however, is the acceptance or rejection of the client by the community. In that regard, it has been noted that "there is always an instinct to shun the disgraced, especially when they appear to be blameworthy. . . . But we must help them all, for their sake and our own."[96] Beyond the offender's desire and capacity to change, the success of parole is ultimately dependent on everything from correctional practices to community responsiveness.

SUMMARY

Originating with Maconochie's "mark system" and Crofton's "ticket of leave," parole was initiated in this country at the Elmira Reformatory in 1876. By the 1950s, every state had implemented the indeterminate sentencing necessary to enable offenders to be released on parole. But, some 25 years later, trends began to change. Several states moved back to determinate sentencing, abolishing or limiting the functions of parole. Nevertheless, whether based on mandatory or discretionary discharge, parole retains its role of supervising those released prior to sentence expiration, under conditions that permit reincarceration if violated. In that respect, parole is still grappling with contradictory expectations—i.e., safeguarding the community while serving the client, and extending support without overlooking surveillance.

Unlike probation, parole is a responsibility of the executive branch of government. In most states it is administered by a board or commission appointed by the governor. Given the board's extensive power, recommendations have been made to enhance the qualifications of board members, with appointments made solely on the basis of merit.

It has been the decision-making component of parole that has experienced both the greatest criticism and the greatest change over recent years. Extensive information is taken into account in deciding whether or not to grant parole. But personal preferences, values, and backgrounds of individual board members can influence the process. The final selection decision may come down to a basic trust or mistrust with regard to both the inmate's intention and capacity to change. As a result, parole decisions have been vulnerable to criticism. Concerns have been raised that discretionary parole does not provide sufficient deterrence or punishment, has been used to coerce inmates into treatment, and creates disparities in the sentences of offenders convicted of similar crimes.

All of these issues have generated pressure to return to determinate sentencing, with release specified by sentence length rather than subject to parole board discretion. But, in light of the severe prison crowding that followed changes in sentencing practices, good-time and gain-time provisions have been established. Once these time credits are deducted from the sentence, release is essentially mandatory. But, because the full original sentence was not served, release is still conditional on the offender's good behavior under community supervision. Current trends clearly point toward a significant increase in such mandatory supervised releases. At the same time, discretionary releases are decreasing. Even where parole boards still have discretion over release decisions, objective parole prediction devices (e.g., the salient factor score) are often used to reduce the subjectivity of decision-making.

Despite these changes in the selection process, parole retains its postrelease supervisory functions. Much of the parole officer's initial work with a client involves arranging to meet basic survival needs, such as locating housing and employment. The hesitancy of employers to hire ex-offenders, combined with occupational licensing restrictions and educational and experience limitations, often makes it difficult to obtain suitable employment for parolees. In addition to addressing these needs, officers are also responsible for monitoring the reintegration process.

When the parolee is not adjusting successfully to the freedom of the community, it is also the officer's duty to recommend revocation if warranted by evidence that conditions are being violated. The sanction orientation which such actions reflect maintains that the welfare of all involved requires swift and sure enforcement of rules. In contrast to the parole selection process, those facing possible revocation are entitled to certain due process rights.

Although parole is judged largely on the basis of recidivism rates, such figures can be misleading. Differing failure measures over differing follow-up periods have produced vastly differing results. The effectiveness of parole is not only difficult to quantify but ultimately influenced by everything from programs offered during confinement to community attitudes toward ex-offenders.

FOR FURTHER DISCUSSION

1. Is the fact that Maconochie was dismissed from service related to the relatively brief tenure of correctional administrators today (especially those with farsighted thinking)? If so, what do we need to do to assure that innovative reformers do not become outcasts from the correctional system?

2. List the implications that would result if parole were (or if it is) abolished in your state. Then divide your list into positive and negative repercussions. If the negatives appear to outweigh the positives, determine what we could do to reverse the equation.

3. Identify what could be done to make parole more effective, not just in terms of reducing recidivism rates, but also with regard to better preparing offenders for release and supporting them afterward.

4. Envision yourself working as a parole officer in an agency that places so much emphasis on keeping recidivism rates low that officers themselves are pressured to do so, and your performance is rated on that basis. Discuss what you are likely to do in order to please your superiors, as well as whether this approach is in the best interest of the offender and/or the community. Use the results of your discussion to argue for or against judging the success of parole on the basis of recidivism rates.

5. Explain why parole can neither be fully credited with its successes nor fully blamed for its failures.

6. Go to the paroling authority website in your state and determine how parole board members obtain their positions and (if possible) what credentials are required. Assess the results in terms of what you know about the authority and responsibilities of parole board members.

7. Explain why potential parolees have no due process protections when applying for parole, but do enjoy such protections if they are facing revocation, as well as why the American Correctional Association recommends written criteria on which to base decision-making (although that is not required constitutionally).

8. Determine how the impact of subjective opinions, values, and attitudes of parole board members could be reduced (if not eliminated) in the parole selection process.

9. As contradictory as it may seem, explain why inmates joined much of the general public in arguing against discretionary parole and indeterminate sentencing. Especially in terms of the public's interest, discuss whether abolishing parole is really the best course of action.

10. Go online to see if you can determine how many pardons the governor in your state issued last year. Then look up some of the cases involved and discuss whether you think the governor made the right decision. Are there other cases in the news in your state that might be good candidates for future pardons? If so, argue the merits for and against such gubernatorial clemency.

11. Identify what the good-time and gain-time provisions are in your state, and then discuss the benefits and drawbacks of this option for reducing time served.

12. Explain why discretionary releases from prison have been decreasing at the same time that mandatory releases have been increasing (indicating what type of mandatory release is the most frequently occurring).

13. In addition to parole, use several examples from throughout the correctional conglomerate to illustrate how discretionary decision-making has been replaced by structured decision-making in recent years. Discuss the advantages as well as disadvantages of this trend.

14. Discuss the pros and cons of including dynamic as well as static items on such parole decision-making instruments as the salient factor score sheet.

15. Describe how those entering society from prison today tend to differ from their predecessors, particularly in terms of how well equipped they are to face the challenges they will inevitably confront.

16. Using drug courts as an example, discuss what role reentry courts can play in easing the transition of ex-offenders into the community.

17. Do online research to determine what collateral consequences of conviction apply to released offenders in your state. Then discuss what implications they have for successful reintegration.

18. Determine what voting rights ex-offenders have in your state. If their rights are curtailed, find out what former offenders must do to restore their voting rights. Argue for and against maintaining (or initiating) such restrictions.

19. Discuss how the principles of restorative justice can be applied to the reentry process.

20. Go online to document how many prison entries are a result of probation or parole violations (either nationwide or in your state). Then identify what could be done to reduce this proportion of the prison population.

21. Envision yourself as a researcher conducting a study of prison discharges. Establish the methodology that you would use to measure recidivism, in terms of both time and criteria. Then critique your selections.

PART 4

Juvenile Corrections, Staff Concerns, Legal Issues, and the Future

In the final analysis, passing on the leadership reins should be the end result . . .
of a process that is designed . . . to inspire future leaders to maintain the passion
when the torch is passed to them.[1]

Jeanne B. Stinchcomb, Susan W. McCampbell, and Leslie Leip

PREVIOUS CHAPTERS DESCRIBING CORRECTIONAL SERVICES, FACILITIES, and programs have focused on practices and procedures related to adult offenders. A few things are still missing, however, in a comprehensive overview of where corrections is today—as well as where it should be heading in the future. To complete that picture, the remaining chapters turn toward topics that are destined to exert a significant impact on the correctional horizon—from the growing population of juvenile offenders to the underlying impact of everything from the correctional workforce itself to the court decisions affecting their work. Combined with the insights provided in earlier chapters, it is apparent that the issues and initiatives discussed here will be influential in shaping both current trends and future projections.

Ultimately, it is America's youth who will forge that future. Yet the involvement of juvenile offenders in the justice system persists at alarming rates. Since many current prisoners and probationers had their first contact with the law as juveniles, it stands to reason that much of the hope for reducing adult correctional populations rests with the juvenile justice system. But, as with adults, we will see in Chapter 12 that even the best intentions are not always fulfilled in reality. Nor will we find that youthful offenders have escaped the impact of the justice model. Not only are more juveniles being transferred into the adult criminal justice system, but the juvenile system itself is beginning to look more like its adult counterpart. Regardless of the underlying reasons, the substantial impact of juveniles on the future justifies their significance as a topic of special consideration.

Whether adult or juvenile, unique or traditional, institutional or community-based, convicted offenders ultimately come under the supervision of the correctional workforce. As Chapter 13 emphasizes, it is staff who are the key ingredient in the correctional conglomerate. "Even the best policies, the latest technology, and the newest innovations depend on people for effective implementation and successful outcomes."[2] From the executive director to the entry-level officer in the cellblock or the probation or parole officer in the community, it is only through the dedication of qualified employees that corrections can function effectively. It is these faceless names on organizational charts who actually operate the system 24 hours a day, seven days a week, often with little compensation and even less recognition. It is therefore fitting to consider how they are recruited, selected, trained, and supervised. For it is these hundreds of thousands of men and women who are the vital factor— not just in terms of how corrections performs today but, more importantly, what potential it has for tomorrow.

Aside from staffing, there may be nothing more likely to shape tomorrow's correctional practices than liability and litigation—the subjects of Chapter 14. To the extent that the past is prologue to the future, a logical starting point for discussion of what lies ahead is legal issues, since past and present correctional operations have often been substantially altered by judicial intervention. The courts have been somewhat more restrained in recent years, and legislative actions have been taken to discourage frivolous lawsuits. Nevertheless, it is reasonable to assume that the future will continue to be affected by legal actions as well as economic conditions and social change. A prime example is the continuing public debate and legal challenges surrounding the death penalty. Chapter 14 therefore considers major legal cases that have influenced the correctional system, as well as lingering controversies that await resolution.

Certainly, no consideration of the future would be complete without devoting attention to the fundamental mission of corrections and how it has changed over time. Again, by looking at past trends, public opinions, and legislative actions in Chapter 15, we can begin to glimpse what tomorrow may hold. Will more proactive crime prevention reduce the system's reliance on reactive responses? If not, will we continue to struggle with the dilemma of finding the right balance between punishment and treatment? Will corrections forever be plagued with excessive caseloads and crowded facilities? Will it remain a government function or increasingly become a component of the private sector? Will promising treatment techniques ignite new hope for its potential? And, most critically of all, will corrections be able to attract and retain the quality of personnel necessary to meet the challenges of change? If so, there is hope for a future that is brighter than the past. But, whatever the outcome, there is no one with a greater stake in assuring its success than each and every one of us.

CHAPTER 12

Juvenile Corrections

To say that juvenile courts have failed to achieve their goals is to say no more than what is true of criminal courts in the United States. But failure is most striking when hopes are highest.[1]
President's Commission on Law Enforcement and Administration of Justice

CHAPTER OVERVIEW

The future ambitions and far-reaching aspirations of any society depend on its children. The children of today will become tomorrow's leaders, workers, and parents. Unfortunately, some will become its criminals as well. In addressing any social problem, prevention holds far greater promise than intervention after the fact, and crime is certainly no exception. When prevention fails and young offenders confront social authority, they are sending a signal that something has gone wrong. Many will overcome their difficulties simply by maturing and growing up. Others will not. For them, encounters with authority will escalate if that "something" is not corrected. For a certain number of them, confrontations will become increasingly serious and frequent, until any hope for change is all but abandoned.

Before that point of no return is reached, children who come into contact with the justice system present more promise than their adult counterparts. By their very definition, "juveniles" are considered different from adult "criminals." If nothing else, they are younger—and therefore presumably less responsible for their actions, as well as more amenable to change. Involvement in the juvenile justice system can therefore offer the potential for addressing their problems and redirecting their behavior at an early stage. On the other hand, it can further alienate and embitter them, fostering the resentment and frustration that propel juvenile offenders toward adult criminality.

In fact, it was in recognition of the unique needs and potential for change among young people that the juvenile court was originally established. In an effort to create an environment where the "best interests" of the child would be served, the juvenile court was meant to be an advocate rather than an adversary of the offender. The intent was to promote the welfare of the child rather than to punish the offender for wrongdoing. But, somewhere along the path toward serving their best interests, it became apparent that children were receiving neither the benevolent protection promised by the juvenile court nor the due process protections afforded to adults.

At the same time, juveniles were engaging in far more serious offenses than the original founders of the juvenile court had ever envisioned. To their victims, it makes little difference whether it was a juvenile or an adult who had raped, assaulted, or robbed them. Thus demands for greater procedural protections in juvenile court, combined with increasing fear of juvenile crime, have resulted in a juvenile justice system today which more closely resembles its adult counterpart.

The question of whether juveniles should be punished or protected remains a continuing source of debate. Although it is unlikely that basic issue will be resolved, the manner in which it is addressed will have long-term implications—not only for young offenders themselves, but also for the collective future of our entire society.

LEARNING GOALS

Do you know:
1. how children were treated historically in comparison to adults?
2. why reform schools were established?
3. how industrialization, immigration, and urbanization influenced the child-saving movement?

HISTORICAL BACKGROUND

While we are now accustomed to thinking of children as different from adults, that was not always how young people were treated. Throughout medieval society, the idea of childhood simply did not exist. In fact, it has only been within relatively recent history that children have clearly been distinguished from grown-ups. Previously, young people were considered virtually "miniature adults"—they were dressed like adults, employed in the same backbreaking work, and subject to similar (or in some cases even more severe) punishments for misbehavior.

In one of the first efforts to separate juveniles from adults, Massachusetts opened a public reform school for delinquent boys in the mid-1840s. But at this time there were no juvenile courts, so youthful offenders were sent to such reformatories to avoid a conviction that would otherwise result in a sentence to be served in an adult prison. Although reform schools provided an alternative to incarceration with adults, conditions there were harsh. Children were subjected to strict discipline, long hours of work, and severe punishments. Many of these institutions were actually designed more for industrial production than for nurturing or rehabilitation, and their exploitation of child labor was shameful.[2] Likewise, sweatshops, mines, and factories had become notorious for their abuse of children. By the end of the nineteenth century, conditions cried desperately for improvement.

EXHIBIT 12.1 In the mid-nineteenth century, children above the age of seven were treated much like adults, often exploited in sweatshops and factories, where they worked long hours under harsh conditions for little pay.

The Child-saving Movement

As cities expanded, urbanization required accommodating a continuous influx of people, many of whom did not share the same customs or even speak the same language. Crime, poverty, overcrowding, and unemployment escalated dramatically. But, perhaps more important, these trends toward industrialization, immigration, and urbanization threatened what had become well-entrenched standards of the "American way of life," firmly rooted in middle-class, rural values.[3]

Under such conditions, it became increasingly apparent that the economic, social, and physical impact of life in crowded ghettos of urban immigrants was creating a negative influence on childhood development. Intervention into the lives of such economically and culturally deprived children was therefore justified as essential to "rescue" them from a destiny of doom, which became known as the **child-saving movement**—essentially, a reaffirmation of faith in traditional institutions, including parental authority and home-based education, which had become "contaminated" by urban living.[4]

In retrospect, some have criticized the motives of such social reformers as a hostile reaction against immigration and urbanization that was largely based on self-serving rather than child-saving interests. But, at the time, child-savers were cast as righteous campaigners responding to the immorality that was viewed as the cause of delinquency among immigrant children. Nor could their timing have been better.

Beyond the social disruptions occurring in America, child-saving emerged when the role of women was expanding. As women began to seek careers outside of the home, intervention into the welfare of children became an acceptable option for them. At the

child-saving movement: intervention into the lives of disadvantaged urban children, justified to "rescue" them from urban problems at the turn of the century.

same time, new criminological theories offered hope that behavior might be amenable to change. And who better to begin with than the youngest offenders?

Origin of the Juvenile Court

As a consequence of these widespread social influences supporting a different approach to wayward children, the first juvenile court was established in Chicago in 1899. Focusing on *dependency* and *neglect* as well as *delinquency*, reformers envisioned "rescuing" the child from a host of undesirable conditions. To accomplish this, the law provided for:

- separate hearing of children's cases in a court of chancery rather than criminal jurisdiction;

- detention of children apart from adult offenders;

- a juvenile probation system.[5]

Separate detention and probation already existed in some locations, and the concept of chancery (i.e., civil) jurisdiction had also been established previously.[6] But, while the individual elements of the Illinois legislation may not have been so revolutionary, the impact of their combined effect has been felt throughout the country—resulting in the development of a distinct *juvenile justice system* in virtually every state in the United States.

The Power of *Parens Patriae*.   To achieve its wide-ranging mission, the new juvenile courts emphasized an individualized approach to justice. A prominent objective of the court was to develop a diagnosis and personalized treatment plan designed to meet each child's specific needs, which took priority over deciding "guilt" or "innocence."

parens patriae: a Latin term referring to the king as ultimate parent over all subjects, which is the foundation for juvenile court authority over the welfare of youth.

To protect rather than prosecute, the court relies on the authority of ***parens patriae***—a Latin term that refers to the king as the ultimate parent (*parens*) over all subjects in the country (*patriae*). In the United States, the concept of *parens patriae* derived from the state's power to sever children from their pauper parents under the Poor Laws. With no welfare support available in the nineteenth century, the only alternative for indigents was refuge in the poorhouses. Since that was obviously not a healthy atmosphere in which to raise children, the state could remove children from indigent families and place them out as apprentices.

Under *parens patriae*, the juvenile court was invested with responsibility for and authority over the welfare of its clients. Moreover, the jurisdiction of the juvenile court extended well beyond offenses that would be considered criminal if committed by an adult—into such nebulous areas as truancy, begging, and incorrigibility. In many cases, the behaviors targeted were "most directly relevant to the children of lower class migrant and immigrant families."[7] As a result, the conduct of youth need not be considered particularly serious to justify juvenile court processing. In the name of *parens patriae*, the power of the state assumed priority over the rights of the parents, and the broad but vague authority of the juvenile court far exceeded that of its adult counterpart.

Procedural Informality.   According to this philosophy, the juvenile court did not require an adversarial model of justice, wherein the defense competes against the prosecution. To the contrary, juvenile court was designed to be the defendant's *advocate* rather than *adversary*. As with a reasonable and knowledgeable parent, the court's intent was to serve the "best interests" of the child.

Underlying this concept is the assumption of youthful dependency and vulnerability, which entitles children to certain privileges and protections not afforded to adults. But, at the same time, it restricts the child from legal safeguards provided in the adult criminal justice system. According to this view, the state—serving in the parental role—is in the best position to determine what treatment is needed to guide the child back on a proper path.

Much of the justification for this diversion from the adversarial model of justice is based on the desire to prevent stigmatizing the child and to provide flexibility in prescribing treatment. Removed from a punishment orientation, the court was committed to avoiding the labeling of children as "criminal." In exchange, less formal procedures would be employed to determine the facts of the case. The ultimate outcome was to benefit the child, uninhibited by procedural formalities. In fact, distinctions between the adult and juvenile justice systems extended to the very terminologies used to describe legal procedures, as reflected in Exhibit 12.2.

Prevention and Treatment.   Under this unique approach, it was not the specific offense bringing the child to the court's attention that was of primary concern but,

Criminal Justice System	Juvenile Justice System	
Crime	Delinquent act	**EXHIBIT 12.2** Contrasting terminologies of the criminal and juvenile justice systems.
Arrest	Take into custody	
Warrant	Summons	
Criminal complaint/indictment	Petition	
Plea bargain	Adjustment	
Trial	Hearing (or adjudication)	
Guilty verdict	Adjudicated delinquent	
Convicted	Found involved	
Sentencing	Disposition	
Incarceration	Commitment	
Jail	Detention center	
Prison	Training school	
Inmate	Resident	
Parole	Aftercare	

rather, the underlying circumstances. Since the individual's behavior was seen as the product of preexisting causes, the court's mission was to discover and address what was actually causing misconduct. But the potential to do so was greater the sooner intervention occurred.

Thus an important component of the juvenile court related to the ability to identify "predelinquent" children and impose upon them treatment designed to "correct their wayward tendencies."[8] It was for this reason that the court's mandate included a wide variety of deviant behaviors directed toward "children who occupy the debatable ground between criminality and innocence."[9] The rationale for such intervention was largely based on the desire to prevent more serious infractions in the future.

Overall, the court's objective was "not so much to punish as to reform, not to degrade but to uplift, not to crush but to develop."[10] Equally glowing pictures were painted of the juvenile court's advantages over its adult counterpart: "The old courts relied upon the learning of lawyers; the new courts depend more upon psychiatrists and social workers. . . . Justice in the old courts was based on legal science; in the new courts it is based on social engineering."[11]

due process movement: the trend toward extending greater due process protections to juveniles, begun with landmark Supreme Court decisions in the 1960s.

With its innovative emphasis on prevention and diagnosis, its noncriminal basis in the doctrine of *parens patriae*, and its ability to deviate from procedural formality, the juvenile court held out promising hope—for personalizing the justice process and making a substantial impact on the delinquency problem. Unfortunately, its promise did not measure up in practice.

LEARNING GOALS

Do you know:

8. why youthful offenders were characterized as suffering "the worst of both worlds" in terms of their treatment in the justice system?
9. how the due process movement has affected juvenile justice?
10. how delinquents differ from status offenders?
11. for what types of offenses youths are processed in juvenile court?

JUVENILE JUSTICE TRANSFORMATION

As was observed by the early 1970s, "today's juvenile court personnel have shed the naive expectations of early reformers."[12] After more than half a century of experimentation, the juvenile court had neither curtailed the growth of juvenile crime nor fulfilled its commitment to protect rather than punish its clients. To the contrary, it was becoming apparent that, in juvenile court, youths actually receive "the worst of both worlds," getting "neither the protections accorded to adults nor the solicitous care and regenerative treatment postulated for children."[13]

By the 1960s, a newly emerging juvenile justice paradigm was directed toward exactly the opposite—reducing intrusion of the court into children's lives.[14] Spearheaded by the **due process movement**, the power and intervention of the court were restricted, based on the notion that rights should not be sacrificed in the name of rehabilitation.

As a result of growing concerns over the arbitrary manner in which cases were being handled, a number of significant decisions regulating juvenile justice practices have been handed down by the Supreme Court. As outlined in Exhibit 12.3, these changes have generally brought the procedures in juvenile courts more in line with those used in the adult system. While they have not fully transformed the juvenile justice system into a miniature version of criminal courts, they have had considerable impact. Like the sentencing guidelines, objective classification procedures, and parole decision-making models addressed earlier, they have introduced greater structure into what was previously a highly discretionary process.

Juvenile Court Caseload

Much of the difficulty experienced by juvenile courts relates to the widespread array of behaviors that can bring a youth into the justice system. In addition to offenses that would be considered "criminal" if committed by an adult (what is officially termed **delinquency** today), youths can be held accountable for **status offenses**—behavior that is illegal only for those under the age of majority. While hundreds of thousands of those under the age of 18 are arrested each year for running away from home, loitering, or curfew violations, the major status offense that brings youths into the juvenile justice system is truancy. However, this is not meant to imply that juvenile offenders do not also engage in serious criminal activities.

delinquency: a juvenile court adjudication finding a minor involved in an offense that would be a crime if committed by an adult.

status offenses: activities that are illegal only for those under the statutory age of majority (e.g., truancy).

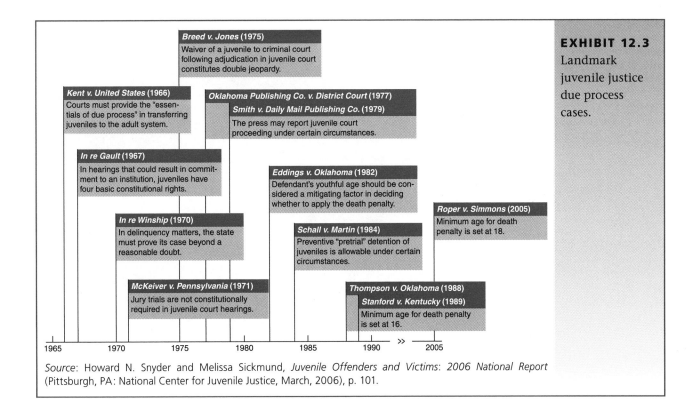

EXHIBIT 12.3 Landmark juvenile justice due process cases.

Breed v. Jones (1975)
Waiver of a juvenile to criminal court following adjudication in juvenile court constitutes double jeopardy.

Kent v. United States (1966)
Courts must provide the "essentials of due process" in transferring juveniles to the adult system.

Oklahoma Publishing Co. v. District Court (1977)
Smith v. Daily Mail Publishing Co. (1979)
The press may report juvenile court proceeding under certain circumstances.

In re Gault (1967)
In hearings that could result in commitment to an institution, juveniles have four basic constitutional rights.

Eddings v. Oklahoma (1982)
Defendant's youthful age should be considered a mitigating factor in deciding whether to apply the death penalty.

Roper v. Simmons (2005)
Minimum age for death penalty is set at 18.

In re Winship (1970)
In delinquency matters, the state must prove its case beyond a reasonable doubt.

Schall v. Martin (1984)
Preventive "pretrial" detention of juveniles is allowable under certain circumstances.

McKeiver v. Pennsylvania (1971)
Jury trials are not constitutionally required in juvenile court hearings.

Thompson v. Oklahoma (1988)
Stanford v. Kentucky (1989)
Minimum age for death penalty is set at 16.

1965   1970   1975   1980   1985   1990   2005

Source: Howard N. Snyder and Melissa Sickmund, *Juvenile Offenders and Victims: 2006 National Report* (Pittsburgh, PA: National Center for Juvenile Justice, March, 2006), p. 101.

Delinquents in Juvenile Court

In fact, it is the hard-core, chronic offenders who capture media headlines, creating a distorted perception of the "typical" youthful lawbreaker. But, although they are responsible for a disproportionate share of violations, habitually violent juveniles do not by any means represent the bulk of clients processed in juvenile courts. As Exhibit 12.4 indicates, most delinquency cases handled by juvenile court are for property crimes (primarily larceny), followed by public order offenses. Although violent juvenile crime is a growing concern, most cases appearing in juvenile courts are considerably less serious (especially if status offenses are also taken into account).

But one lesser-known statistic that should be cause for concern is the fact that more than two out of three of those processed in the juvenile justice system meet clinical criteria for at least one mental health disorder.[15] As shown in Exhibit 12.5, their conditions range from mood disorders to substance abuse, and girls are at higher risk than boys in all categories. Such alarming statistics indicate that many juveniles require mental health and/or substance abuse treatment that the justice system is often ill equipped to provide.

Pre-adjudication Detention

As in the adult system, seriousness of the offense will be taken into consideration when determining whether to release or detain a youth prior to court appearance. **Predisposition (or pre-adjudication) detention** can be either in protective

predisposition (or pre-adjudication) detention: the decision to maintain custody of a youth prior to adjudication (similar to pretrial detention in the adult system).

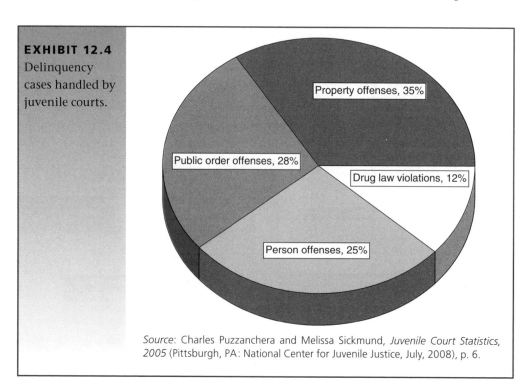

EXHIBIT 12.4
Delinquency cases handled by juvenile courts.

Property offenses, 35%

Drug law violations, 12%

Person offenses, 25%

Public order offenses, 28%

Source: Charles Puzzanchera and Melissa Sickmund, *Juvenile Court Statistics, 2005* (Pittsburgh, PA: National Center for Juvenile Justice, July, 2008), p. 6.

custody (such as a foster home or runaway shelter) or in a secure custodial facility (what would be termed "pretrial detention" for adults). In general, youths are likely to be detained if they present a threat or risk if returned to the community.

Detaining juveniles prior to their court disposition has been legally challenged. But, in the 1984 *Schall v. Martin* case, the Supreme Court upheld the preventive detention of juveniles for their own or society's protection.[16] This does not mean that juveniles can be held indefinitely, and the child is entitled to a subsequent detention hearing where a judge determines whether to authorize release or continue with confinement.

Nevertheless, many disturbed young people are confined in juvenile detention without any pending criminal charges, merely because mental health treatment is not available to them. In fact, a congressional report revealed that two-thirds of juvenile detention facilities hold youth waiting for community mental health treatment, some as young as seven years of age—and representing a price tag of nearly $100 million.[17] Moreover, because many of these children are either suicidal or violently aggressive, they present serious management and safety challenges for facilities that are often ill equipped to cope with their needs. As one administrator put it, "we have become the depository of last resort for all acting out, behaviorally challenged, developmentally disabled [youths] when others don't know how to handle them."[18]

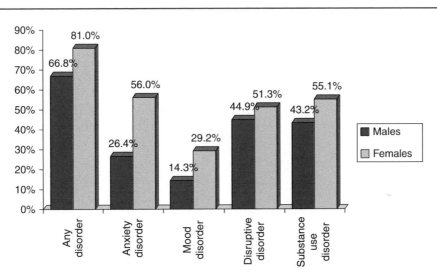

EXHIBIT 12.5 Mental health disorders among males and females in the juvenile justice system.

Source: Jennie L. Shufelt and Joseph J. Cocozza, "Youth with Mental Health Disorders in the Juvenile Justice System: Results from a Multi-state Prevalence Study," *National Center for Mental Health and Juvenile Justice: Research and Program Brief* (June, 2006), p. 2.

In that regard, it appears that the juvenile justice system is following the same trends toward criminalization of the mentally ill as its adult counterpart. The major difference is that the negative impact is considerably greater when the client is younger.

Juveniles in Adult Jails

A major issue facing the juvenile justice system in recent years has become *where* those held prior to disposition of their case are being confined. Because of the small numbers of offenders requiring custody in the past, many jurisdictions did not provide separate juvenile detention facilities. Rather, they housed youths in adult jails—where they could face deplorable conditions and even death, as described in the next "Close-up on Corrections."

EXHIBIT 12.6
Juveniles can be taken into custody for a wide variety of reasons unrelated to criminal conduct, and many of these disturbed youths are confined in detention when they should actually be in mental health facilities.

CLOSE-UP ON CORRECTIONS
Juveniles in Jail: Deadly Lessons Learned

- In Ohio, six adult prisoners murdered a 17-year-old boy while he was incarcerated in the juvenile cellblock of an adult jail.
- In Florida, a 17-year-old mildly retarded boy who had pleaded guilty to sexual battery was strangled to death by his 20-year-old cellmate.
- In Ohio, a 15-year-old girl ran away from home overnight, then returned to her parents, but was put in the adult county jail by the juvenile court judge to teach her a lesson. On the fourth night of her confinement, she was sexually assaulted by a deputy jailer.
- In Idaho, a 17-year-old boy was held in the adult jail for failing to pay $73 in traffic fines. Over a 14-hour period, he was tortured and finally murdered by other prisoners in the cell. Another teenager had been beaten unconscious by the same inmates several days earlier.
- In California, a 15-year-old girl was taken to the local jail for staying out past curfew. After several days, she had a detention hearing, but was not released. When she went back to her cell, she committed suicide.

Source: "Children in Adult Jails—Fact Sheet," Building Blocks for Youth Initiative (Washington, DC), available at http://www.buildingblocksforyouth.org/issues/adultjails/factsheet.html

Given the impact of such an environment, it may not be surprising to find that juveniles in adult jails have the highest suicide rate of all inmates—double that of almost all other age groups in jail,[19] and nearly 20 times that of teenagers in free society.[20] Yet there are still thousands of juveniles confined in adult jails.[21] Many are serious offenders being transferred to adult court—stereotyped as sophisticated criminals, whereas in reality they are often emotionally even younger than their chronological age.[22] Nor is there even legal justification for those who are status offenders, first-timers, or minor delinquents being confined in adult facilities. In every respect, jails are unsuited for anyone in the midst of their social, psychological, and emotional development. As the situation was described over 20 years ago, "jails lack adequate physical plant facilities, adequate numbers of appropriately trained staff members, as well as adequate health, recreational, and other programs to meet the minimum standards of juvenile confinement."[23] Nevertheless, a national report by the Campaign for Youth Justice indicates that this dismal description remains no less true today.[24]

National Legislation

Recognizing the negative influence that jail confinement can have on juveniles, the federal **Juvenile Justice and Delinquency Prevention Act** of 1974 restricted the confinement of juveniles in adult facilities to limited situations. When the Act was amended in 1980, its provisions went even further—requiring the removal of all juveniles from adult jails and lockups by the end of 1985. But, because so many states were not in compliance by the deadline, it was extended

Juvenile Justice and Delinquency Prevention Act: federal legislation that has provided fiscal incentives to encourage state and local juvenile justice reform.

three years until 1988, and several exceptions were added—primarily allowing for short-term detention in certain serious juvenile cases, provided that they are separated from adult inmates by "sight and sound." In other words, juveniles and adults must be kept completely separate in terms of all institutional activities (e.g., sleeping, eating, recreation, education, health care), and direct-contact staff must be separate from those who service the adult population. Additional modifications in 1996 further clarified the "sight and sound" provisions and permitted exceptions for up to six hours before and after court appearances.[25]

However, responsibility for the juvenile justice system is a state and local function. Although this federal legislation therefore does not carry the weight of law, it does provide funding in exchange for an agreement to comply with its provisions. Compliance is monitored by the U.S. Department of Justice, Office of Juvenile Justice and Delinquency Prevention (OJJDP). States in violation face the possibility of having their federal juvenile justice funds terminated. In addition, lawsuits have been filed challenging state violation of the federal requirements. In one such case (*Hendrickson v. Griggs*), the judge issued an injunction to stop the state from detaining any more delinquent children until a plan was submitted to remove them from adult jails, noting that "it makes little difference . . . that these values were embodied in a funding program rather than a nationwide prohibition. If the state did not share Congress' priorities or did not wish to implement them, it could merely have refused to seek the OJJDP funding."[26]

For many years, reaction was slow and sporadic, for reasons ranging from deliberate defiance to lack of resources. By 2008, however, OJJDP reported that all states were now in compliance with the separation of juvenile and adult offenders in secure institutions, and all but two were in compliance with the jail removal initiative.[27] A significant loophole in the legislation, however, still permits jail confinement for youths who are charged as adults.

LEARNING GOALS

Do you know:

15. what percentage of those in short-term detention are being held before adjudication ("pretrial")?
16. what is meant by the "balanced approach" to juvenile justice?

Juvenile Detention Facilities

Short-term detention facilities are the juvenile equivalent of adult jails. They house over 26,000 youths in some 769 detention centers throughout the United States (most of which are state or locally operated).[28] Like those in adult jails, most of those in detention are awaiting disposition of their case—only 27 percent have been committed following adjudication in juvenile court.[29] Nearly three out of four are confined while awaiting adjudication (in adult terms, "pretrial"). As might be expected, the vast majority of those being temporarily detained are charged with delinquencies—that is, offenses which would be considered crimes if committed by an adult. Although 5 percent of those in detention are status offenders or nonoffenders,[30] this population has been declining in light of the Juvenile Justice and Delinquency Prevention Act's prohibition against the secure confinement of children who are dependent, neglected, or status offenders (with which all but two states are now in compliance).[31] Additionally, some jurisdictions have begun independent initiatives to reduce their reliance on juvenile detention.[32]

While children are in detention, there is an opportunity to learn as much as possible about them. For this reason, progressive facilities employ various tests and diagnostic procedures. Moreover, with half or more of the residents reporting depression, family/ peer problems, and drug or alcohol abuse,[33] it is apparent that treatment intervention is essential. Burdened with a wide array of social and emotional problems, and often victimized by emotional, physical, or sexual abuse, many detention clients are isolated children, handicapped by feelings of inferiority. In fact, it is not at all unusual for them to enter the system as runaways, seeking to escape abuse at home.

Detention Problems and Alternatives

Secure detention has long been plagued by problems ranging from substandard care to insufficient resources. In fact, just a few years ago, a juvenile died in detention after suffering for three days in severe pain with the classic symptoms of appendicitis.[34] Like their adult jail counterparts, many detention facilities are overcrowded and underfunded.

For these reasons, public or private **shelter care** is often a preferable option to secure confinement for short-term detention. Shelters are a type of residential home environment for dependent children, those who are neglected, or status offenders. In addition, several states are also using shelter care successfully for cases of minor delinquency pending court disposition. For those with special needs, such options

shelter care: open (nonsecure) youth shelters, group homes, or similar community-based facilities.

EXHIBIT 12.7
Unlike many juvenile detention facilities, this one is unique in terms of its small size, case management approach, family counseling, and staff interaction with the residents.

Source: Courtesy of Northwest Regional Youth Center, Missouri Division of Youth Services.

as group homes, mental health facilities, or other programs for youth with emotional disturbances often can provide more effective help than detention.

Adjudication

adjudication: a juvenile court hearing to establish the facts of the case.

Under the juvenile court's original philosophy, the intent of **adjudication** was to give personalized attention to determining the facts involved in each case and the individual needs of each offender. That, however, was long before anyone remotely envisioned that the court's annual caseload would ever approach the two million mark. Such a heavy workload can severely limit judicial attention, resulting in cases being decided in a matter of minutes. Obviously, this type of "assembly-line justice" negates the system's ability to provide the kindly, parental guidance envisioned by early reformers.

Additionally, society today is concerned that juvenile justice not only serve the needs of the child, but also be in keeping with the public good. As one advocate of the recent trend toward a more balanced approach has observed,

> We didn't want to assume that "in the best interest of the child" always meant an adversarial relationship with the best interest of the community. When a crime occurs involving a juvenile, we should try to come up with a penalty that is best for the kid and best for the community.[35]

For a look at how some communities are accomplishing this, see Exhibit 12.8. It describes how everyone involved—from the juvenile justice system to victimized communities and offenders themselves—can collaborate to achieve a balanced and restorative approach to juvenile justice.[36] As it demonstrates, the balanced approach maintains a strong emphasis on accountability and responsibility for all involved. For the offender, that does not mean either emphasizing leniency or demanding repression. Nor does it mean focusing exclusively on a middle ground between the two. Rather, it implies providing a more diverse range of options for responding to a similarly wide-ranging array of youthful problems and behaviors.

disposition hearing: the stage at which the juvenile court judge determines what consequences will be imposed or treatment required.

LEARNING GOALS

Do you know:

17. what general categories of disposition alternatives are available to juvenile courts?
18. the difference between secure and open custodial facilities?

Dispositions

At the **disposition hearing** (or what would be called sentencing in adult court), judges have a number of options, ranging in severity from nominal to conditional or custodial:

- *Nominal.* Particularly for first-time delinquents or those involved in less serious offenses, the judge may simply elect to issue a warning or reprimand, with no further repercussions if the youth avoids future contact with the law.

- *Conditional.* As the term implies, these sanctions require that the offender comply with some type of requirement (e.g., paying a fine, providing community service, making restitution to the victim, or completing a training, educational, or treatment

Accountability—When a crime occurs, a debt incurs. Justice requires that every effort be made by offenders to restore losses suffered by victims.

Juvenile justice system role: Direct juvenile justice resources to ensure that offenders repay victims and complete other relevant restorative requirements as a top system priority. *Intended outcome*: Efficient, fair, and meaningful restorative justice practices; increased responsiveness to victims' needs.	**Offender role:** Actively work to restore victims' losses and participate in activities that increase empathy with the victim and victims generally. *Intended outcome*: Understanding consequences of offense behavior; increased empathy; feeling of fairness in justice process.	**Community role:** Assist in the process by providing paid work opportunities for offenders, helping to develop community service work projects, and supporting victim awareness education. *Intended outcome*: More participation in and support for the juvenile justice system; message that victims receive priority.

Competency development—Offenders should leave the juvenile justice system more capable of productive participation in conventional society than when they entered.

Juvenile justice system role: Assess youths' strengths and interests and identify community resources to build on those strengths in a way that demonstrates competency. Engage youth in these activities and provide necessary supports for successful completion. Build prevention capacity through partnerships with employers, educators, and other community agencies. *Intended outcome*: More opportunities for youth competency development; improved image of juvenile justice; increased competency.	**Offender role:** Become actively involved in activities that make a positive contribution to the community while building life skills, make continuous progress in improving educational skills while using existing skills to help others. *Intended outcome*: Increased sense of competency and self-esteem; exposure to and interaction with positive adult role models; improved public image of youth.	**Community role:** Become partner with juvenile justice system in developing opportunities for youth to make productive contributions to the community while learning positive civic and other values. *Intended outcome*: Increased community involvement in and ownership of delinquency problem; new attitudes toward youth; completion of positive work in communities. Improved quality of life in the community.

Community protection—The public has a right to a safe and secure community; juvenile justice should develop a progressive response system to ensure offender control in the community and develop new ways to ensure public safety and respond to community concerns.

Juvenile justice system role: Ensure that offenders are carefully supervised by staff and a range of community guardians and that offenders' time is structured in productive activities; develop a range of supervision restrictiveness options, alternative responses to violations, and incentives for progress. *Intended outcome*: Increased public support for community supervision.	**Offender role:** Become involved in competency building and restorative activities; avoid situations that may lead to further offenses. *Intended outcome*: No offenses while on supervision; reduced recidivism when the period of supervision is over.	**Community role:** Provide input to juvenile justice system regarding public safety concerns; share responsibility for offender control and reintegration. *Intended outcome*: Increased feelings of safety in the community; increased confidence in juvenile community supervision.

Source: Office of Juvenile Justice and Delinquency Prevention, *Balanced and Restorative Justice: Program Summary* (Washington, DC: Office of Juvenile Justice and Delinquency Prevention, n.d.), available at http://www.ncjrs.gov/pdffiles/bal.pdf.

EXHIBIT 12.8
A balanced approach to juvenile justice.

program). Among the most frequently used conditional dispositions is formal probation. Like its adult counterpart, juvenile probation sets conditions—such as attending school, maintaining a curfew, and reporting to a probation officer. Also as with the criminal justice system, the utility of juvenile probation is limited by high caseloads, forcing greater reliance on practical requirements than treatment needs.

- *Custodial.* If custodial commitment is warranted, the court has two choices: *secure* or *nonsecure* facilities. Nonsecure or "open" facilities include foster homes, group homes, camps, ranches, and marine institutes. These are options for those who need some guidance, structure, and supervision, but not as much restraint and limitation as are found in juvenile correctional institutions or training schools. In terms of the length of time that youths committed to confinement must serve, there are many different models operating in various states throughout the country—ranging from determinate to indeterminate dispositions, with and without minimums and maximums. Moreover, in some states correctional agencies are authorized to release youths from confinement, whereas in others release decisions are reserved for either the judiciary or the parole board.[37]

Success Stories

As the juvenile court has struggled over the years with implementing appropriate dispositions for children accused of everything from truancy to manslaughter, it is easy to become discouraged by its failures. There is no doubt that many adult prisoners first came to the attention of the police as juveniles, and the earlier a youth enters the juvenile justice system, the more likely he or she is to continue to compile an extensive record. In that regard, the skyrocketing adult prison population could to some extent be viewed as evidence of the juvenile justice system's ineffectiveness.

But looking only at the failures obscures the many success stories of troubled youth whose contact with the system points them in the right direction. In commemoration of the juvenile court's centennial anniversary, the Office of Juvenile Justice and Delinquency Prevention profiled case studies of a number of success stories—youths who had been adjudicated for offenses ranging from shoplifting to attempted murder, but who turned their lives around and are now in such occupations as college administrator, journalist, author, professional athlete, district attorney, television broadcaster, corporate tax lawyer, superior court judge, and even retired U.S. senator. The next "Close-up on Corrections" highlights the senator's story.

CLOSE-UP ON CORRECTIONS
Second Chances—Senator Alan Simpson

At the kick-off rally for his 1978 campaign for the U.S. Senate, Alan Simpson spied a familiar face. Simpson waded into the crowd to meet his old friend, J.B. Mosley, and asked him to join his family and campaign workers around the podium. Modestly, he declined the offer. "This is your day," Mosley told the would-be senator. But Simpson could not let the moment pass. After his introductory remarks, he told the crowd there was someone present who had a great influence in his life and had helped him to make it to this moment—his probation officer, J.B. Mosley. The crowd was surprised, but also quite moved. "I tell you, I think I got every vote in that building," Simpson says with a chuckle.

The ex-senator fondly remembers the caring relationship he shared with Mosley during a time when Simpson describes himself as being "on the edge." . . . When he was 17, he and four of his friends loaded into his family's old car and drove off to shoot at mailboxes on a dusty rural road. He was a good shot—hitting a number of targets and blasting holes in the mail.

Ultimately, he pled guilty to destroying federal property. Since it was their first known offense, the judge sentenced Simpson and his co-conspirators to two years' probation and ordered them to make restitution. For the next two years, J.B. Mosley visited Simpson and his friends at home, in the pool hall, at school, and on the basketball court. Simpson remembers Mosley being a wonderful guy who would sit down with him, asking how he was doing, and keeping tabs on his scholastic work. "He didn't preach . . . he listened." . . .

Many years later, when he went back to practice law, people would see him and say, "I didn't think you had the guts to come back to this town after all you did around here." As Simpson recalls, "I would just smile and say, 'Well, everybody gets a second chance.'"

Source: Adapted from "Second Chances: Giving Kids a Chance to Make a Better Choice," *Juvenile Justice Bulletin* (May, 2000), pp. 19–20.

JUVENILE CORRECTIONS

The juvenile justice system may still in some respects adhere more to the philosophy of the medical model than that of the justice model. But, as with their adult counterparts, greater numbers of juveniles were confined in correctional institutions throughout the 1990s, although the custodial population has actually been declining slightly in recent years.

Nevertheless, nearly 110,000 youth are being held in public and private juvenile facilities throughout the country.[38] This represents a growth in custody rates over the past decade, with minorities accounting for much of the increase. In fact, this issue had become such a concern by the mid-1990s that provisions were added to the Juvenile Justice and Delinquency Prevention Act requiring states to determine whether the proportion of minorities in confinement exceeded their proportion in the general population and, if so, to initiate efforts to reduce their overrepresentation.[39]

While the male minority population has been declining in recent years, it has been increasing for females and, overall, still reflects 61 percent of those in custody.[40] Most youths confined are male (85 percent), although females are more likely to be

LEARNING GOALS

Do you know:

19. what demographic groups are most affected by changing juvenile custody rates?
20. how the populations of public and private juvenile facilities differ?
21. what problems are created by overcrowding in juvenile facilities?

held in custody for status offenses (representing 40 percent of the status offenders, compared to only 14 percent of the delinquent population).[41] Many are now also intergenerational offenders. In fact, the single greatest predictor of a male child's likelihood of incarceration is whether his father was incarcerated.[42]

Public versus Private Facilities

In terms of where they are confined, youths can be held in either public facilities or those operated by the private sector. Unlike adult correctional institutions, those operated by the private sector actually represent the majority (60 percent) of juvenile confinement facilities. But, although there are considerably more of them, they actually hold less than half as many juveniles as public facilities.[43] A closer look at how they differ from their public counterparts shows why.

Not only are private facilities smaller and far less likely to be overcrowded,[44] but they also differ in terms of security classification. Whereas public facilities are more likely to be detention centers or secure long-term facilities, those privately operated tend to be shelters, group homes, ranches, or wilderness camps.[45] Likewise, their populations differ. As shown in Exhibit 12.9, delinquent offenders (predominately male) are more likely to be housed in public facilities, whereas the much smaller number of status offenders (disproportionately female) are more likely to be confined in private facilities. In that regard, research indicates that, in contrast to white youths, minorities are more often placed in public residential facilities with the most restrictive confinement.[46]

Overcrowding

Overall, nearly one-third of youthful offenders are confined in facilities that are at or above their standard bed capacity, and most of them reside in public facilities.[47] When juvenile institutions are overcrowded, classification suffers, resulting in the potential for status offenders or minor delinquents to be mingled with serious

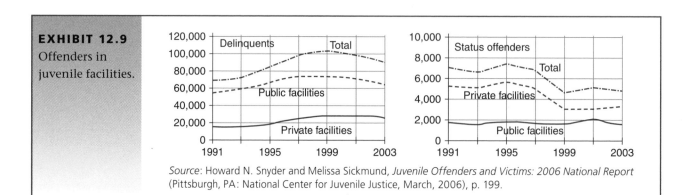

EXHIBIT 12.9
Offenders in juvenile facilities.

Source: Howard N. Snyder and Melissa Sickmund, *Juvenile Offenders and Victims: 2006 National Report* (Pittsburgh, PA: National Center for Juvenile Justice, March, 2006), p. 199.

offenders. This creates security deficiencies, to the extent that it diminishes the ability to separate predators from victims, making overtaxed facilities more dangerous and stressful for both clients and staff. Among employees, morale and commitment are bound to suffer as overburdened, underpaid staff are expected to meet the needs of youthful offenders ranging from drug abusers to depressed runaways. Among residents, more time is spent in lockdown, program quality suffers, and the primary focus becomes safety and security, thus compromising effective intervention and treatment.[48]

Since these concerns are overshadowed by the crowding in adult prisons that has dominated public policy agendas, it is difficult to generate concern about the plight of youthful offenders. Yet, in terms of the conditions in which they are confined, it is essential to be especially vigilant with juveniles, "because we are dealing with a population that is politically powerless, socially rejected, and easily exploited."[49]

Juvenile Institutions

Whether public or private, juvenile facilities vary widely— from state and local training schools to detention centers and various types of camps, ranches, and shelters. A national survey assessing the conditions of confinement in these diverse facilities reported mixed results. Apparently, juvenile institutions on average may be neither as bad as might be feared nor as good as might be hoped. For example, facilities were assessed as "generally adequate" in several important areas, including food, clothing, hygiene, recreation, and living accommodations. However, "widespread deficiencies" were found in terms of crowding, security, suicide prevention, and health screenings.[50] Even more recently, in conjunction with the Prison Rape Elimination Act, a nationwide study of adjudicated youth in large custodial facilities found that 12 percent had experienced one or more incidents of sexual victimization by another youth or staff member in the past year (or since admitted if confined less than a year).[51] As a result of such disturbing findings, it has been concluded that "improving conditions significantly will require broad-scale reforms affecting routine practices in most facilities."[52] That is a considerable challenge, especially given the varieties of clientele, funding arrangements, and administrative structures that characterize juvenile corrections in both public and privately operated facilities.

While private training schools are often supported by service fees, contributions, donations, and charitable foundations, they function under state license to assure compliance with minimum standards regarding health, sanitation, residential care, and institutional programming. But, because they are private, these schools generally have greater latitude than state schools. Therefore they can be somewhat selective in terms of the residents admitted so that their resources can be concentrated on specific types of problems.

LEARNING GOALS

Do you know:
22. what types of deficiencies characterize many juvenile facilities?
23. what programs and services are provided in juvenile facilities?
24. what impact institutions have on juvenile residents?

Although Supreme Court decisions prohibit racial discrimination in the selection process, private institutions do have the flexibility of setting minimum intelligence or educational requirements, prohibiting the admission of serious offenders, or restricting admission to only certain types of cases. As a result of such practices, private facilities are more likely to confine non-serious offenders, females, and non-Hispanic whites.[53] In contrast, public facilities do not have the option of specifying what types of cases will be admitted. State training schools must accept everyone committed to them and therefore must be equipped to handle a wider range of behavioral problems.

Accreditation of Juvenile Facilities

As in the adult system, one obvious means for improving the quality of juvenile facilities is through the American Correctional Association's accreditation process. Currently, only about 20 percent of public and private institutions for juveniles are accredited[54] (compared to more than 70 percent of adult facilities[55]). Perhaps in part this is because the courts have been less actively involved in litigation related to conditions of confinement for youthful offenders. Yet accreditation standards address many of the very issues that have plagued juvenile corrections, such as:

- *administration and management* (e.g., personnel training, staff development, records, and information systems);

- *physical plant operations* (e.g., building and safety codes, environmental conditions, programs, and services);

- *institutional operations* (e.g., security and control, safety and emergency procedures, rules, and discipline);

- *facility services* (e.g., food, sanitation, hygiene, and health care);

- *juvenile services* (e.g., classification, academic, vocational, and work programs, library, recreation, religious programming, mail, telephone, visiting, and release).[56]

However, as we will see later, unlike the accreditation of hospitals or schools, accreditation in corrections is a voluntary process for both the adult and the juvenile system. While becoming accredited entails numerous direct and indirect benefits (not the least of which is reduced potential for litigation), it is also a costly endeavor that generates no additional revenue. But, whether motivated by the desire for self-improvement or the demands of a lawsuit settlement, accreditation may hold the key to upgrading the conditions, services, and practices of juvenile institutions.

Custodial Operations and Treatment

The operation of juvenile institutions, whether public or private, accredited or unaccredited, encompasses a wide variety of functions—ranging from security to social services, education, recreation, treatment, food services, maintenance, and administration. In addition to state-mandated education for those of compulsory school attendance age, the counseling, group therapy, and other treatment programs discussed in Chapter 9 are even more important for juveniles. A number of juvenile institutions also operate vocational training programs. This is particularly beneficial for those who are already high school dropouts and need marketable employment skills.

In practice, a combination of education, work, and discipline has tended to characterize the typical approach of many state training schools, perhaps reflecting their reform school heritage. However, the courts have recognized that, unlike adults, juveniles committed involuntarily for rehabilitative purposes (which is presumably the primary rationale for the entire juvenile justice system) have a statutory and constitutional right to treatment.[57]

Precisely what is meant by "treatment" is, of course, another issue entirely. We have already seen that a wide variety of programs and activities have been loosely

EXHIBIT 12.10
Vocational programs for delinquent and at-risk youth help to develop pride and self-esteem, as well as marketable job skills.

Source: Courtesy of YouthBuild.

defined as treatment in adult prisons and jails. Moreover, despite the fact that rehabilitation was supposedly the major emphasis of the juvenile justice system, for the past two decades juvenile corrections professionals have been speaking sparingly about "correcting the behavior of young offenders and much more about education, skill training, social survival skills, community service and self-discipline. The word 'rehabilitation' is used less and less, and the word 'treatment' is almost extinct."[58]

Some might characterize such trends as reflecting a new approach that is more functional—equipping residents with the social accountability and personal skills that they lack. But, to others, they imply an enduring custodial orientation—emphasizing punishment, discipline, and control. Support for the latter view is found in evaluations of juvenile correctional facilities, which reveal "a continuing gap between the rhetoric of rehabilitation and its punitive reality."[59]

Effects of Confinement

Regardless of what types of treatment programs are available or how nonpunitive the facility's orientation is, confinement tends to produce significant negative effects for youth. Even among juvenile facilities, where efforts may be made to deemphasize the institutional atmosphere, training schools are, in fact, custodial environments. They are not rehabilitative centers. They are not educational facilities. They are, first and foremost, custodial institutions—where residents are subject to the authority of highly regulated living conditions.

In addition to the negative influence of custodial constraints, training schools have been cited as breeding grounds for abnormal behavior patterns ranging from homosexuality to theft. In this environment are concentrated varieties of delinquents who see life as socially unjust in the first place. Then these negative values are reinforced by their peers in a setting that too often lacks adequate responses to their problems and intensifies hostility. Separation from familiar settings, family members, and other social support systems promotes feelings of abandonment. Many have been rejected by their home, their school, and now their community as well. Such feelings of rejection can lower self-esteem, further underscoring their sense of failure.

Especially for first-time or status offenders, interaction with the institutional population itself can reinforce negative values. And, just as in adult prisons, the weak are prey for the strong. In fact, even those serving brief stays in short-term detention are vulnerable to abuse: "The weaker juvenile who is sentenced to detention may be subject to violent acts, victimized by extortion, and emotionally scarred. These youths need treatment and services, not a vindictive punishment."[60]

Virtually everyone is subject to the negative impact of institutional confinement discussed earlier with regard to adult prisoners—from lack of privacy to resentment of authority. However, the intensity of that impact can be considerably greater for children, in contrast to adults, as they are confined in the midst of their emotional and physical development. Even if the programs offered in such settings were implemented as originally intended, they would be hard pressed to overcome the combined detrimental effects of the repressive institutional atmosphere and the preexisting problems of the clients themselves. Thus it should not be surprising to find high rates of rearrest and new court referrals (ranging from 45 percent to 55 percent) among youths released from state incarceration.[61]

Shock Incarceration Programs

Because lack of self-discipline and disrespect for authority are common among youthful offenders, a number of states have tried to improve their juvenile justice track record by experimenting with an environment structured around a military-style boot camp. Also known as "shock incarceration," such programs are generally reserved for older adolescents and young adults, some of whom would otherwise be facing their first term in prison or jail. Like their military counterparts, **correctional boot camps** emphasize strenuous physical training and strict discipline.

Boot camps have enjoyed considerable emotional appeal. Their supporters range from veterans nostalgically recalling their own military training to policy-makers increasingly frustrated by the inability to control youthful offenders. But extensive emotional support is not necessarily based on effective experiential outcomes. In fact, "evidence has mounted indicating that boot camps are not the quick-fix, ready-made solution that early supporters had envisioned."[62]

Despite their widespread popularity, evaluation research has not given boot camps high marks. To the contrary, a multi-site evaluation of eight programs concluded that their impact on recidivism is "at best negligible."[63] A General Accounting Office review of research findings similarly reported that "graduates have only marginally lower recidivism rates," and "any differences tend to diminish over time."[64] Additionally, another multi-site assessment found that reoffending youth from boot camps actually committed new offenses more quickly than comparison groups.[65] Even when recidivism rates have been lower, the results appear to be a product of either the types of offenders selected or the intensive supervision they received afterward.[66]

While the reasons for such disappointing results are varied, concerns have been expressed that boot camps do not address long-term solutions to underlying problems.[67] As one therapist describes it, "You can scream at them and have them do as many push-ups as you want, but you are not getting at the pathology [of] their lack of values."[68]

Questions have also been raised about the relationship of boot camps to modern military training. Basic training for new recruits in the military has changed over time, and correctional boot camps may resemble an earlier model that the military has abandoned in its effort to improve an image that has sometimes been tarnished by arbitrary demands and degrading treatment.[69]

correctional boot camps: shock incarceration programs that promote respect for authority through military-style discipline and physical training.

Moreover, the discipline instilled in boot camps is only one component of what youthful offenders need to make long-term changes in their behavior upon release. In that regard, one boot camp director has noted:

> Within 90 to 120 days, the length of most boot camp programs, we cannot correct all of these young offenders' problems. Nor can we provide them with all the educational and vocational skills they have missed. . . . Boot camps were never intended to do all that. Consider military boot camps. They are not intended to make a young person into a fully functional soldier. Rather, they provide a foundation of discipline, responsibility and self-esteem [which] the military can build on during the advanced training that follows. Correctional boot camps are designed to do much the same thing.[70]

It is noteworthy that, where graduates do return to confinement at lower rates, the programs are longer, strongly focused on treatment, and followed by postrelease services.[71] Critics suggest that nostalgic legislators recalling their own military service forgot that boot camp was followed by further military service, as well as advanced training, and, when they were released, veterans returned to communities where they were welcomed and supported. In contrast, most correctional boot camp graduates return to impoverished communities without supportive aftercare. Thus any changes that might occur are unlikely to survive the "test of the streets" in the reality of a world "where drill instructors are replaced by drug dealers . . . where secure confinement is replaced by self-control . . . [and] where marching in straight lines is replaced by hanging on street corners."[72]

EXHIBIT 12.11
Building pride, discipline, and self-esteem is the primary focus of correctional boot camps.

Source: Courtesy of the Broward County (Fort Lauderdale, FL) Sheriff's Office.

Juvenile Aftercare

As the critics of boot camps note, it is not just what occurs within confinement that shapes behavior but, equally important, what follow-up services are provided upon release. In adult terms, this is what is referred to as "parole" or "mandatory supervised release." In the juvenile justice system, it is called **aftercare**. As the name implies, it is intended to provide continuing care, transitional services, and employment assistance for youths released from a correctional facility.

Unfortunately, aftercare is the function of an already overburdened juvenile justice system. With resources focused on the immediate needs of new cases and younger clients coming before the court, it is a luxury to divert attention to existing cases lingering in the system. Moreover, by the time they are released, some are close to or have already exceeded the age of majority. Thus, any further offenses they commit will be under the jurisdiction of the criminal justice system.

Aftercare is not provided in all jurisdictions, and when available, it is often plagued with administrative and operational difficulties. Additionally, like parole in the adult system, it can be so heavily focused on surveillance that staff lose sight of its supportive, reintegrative role. In an effort to improve the effectiveness of aftercare, a number of jurisdictions are shifting from an exclusive focus on the offender to a more comprehensive focus on the entire family context, as illustrated in Exhibit 12.12.[73] But even the most progressive, sensitive, holistic, and well-endowed aftercare program cannot erase the effects of confinement. In the end, the negative impact of incarceration is no less severe merely because the institution is called a "training school" or "detention center" rather than a prison or jail.

aftercare: follow-up services and supervision provided upon release from a juvenile correctional facility.

- Creating a therapeutic alliance with the family
- Reducing negativity and blaming in the family
- Creating new solutions for the family
- Motivating families to participate with their child in treatment
- Helping staff understand the youth's behavior in a family-systems context

EXHIBIT 12.12
Improving the reintegration of youthful offenders through a family-focused approach.

Parole counselors work with youths and their families to improve the way the family functions in support of youths' successful reintegration into their homes and community settings.

Source: Cheryl Stephani, "Systems Change and Shrinking Budgets: Improving a Juvenile Justice System despite Declining Resources," *Corrections Today* (February, 2004), p. 41. Reprinted with permission of the American Correctional Association, Alexandria, VA.

YOUTHFUL OFFENDERS IN THE CRIMINAL JUSTICE SYSTEM

As the public has become increasingly concerned about the growing involvement of teenagers in violent crime, judicial responses have likewise shifted toward a more punitive approach. Although proportionately few in number, these hard-core offenders account for a disproportionate share of juvenile crime. Many of them have already been processed through juvenile court for earlier offenses, often at quite young ages, and continue their criminal patterns as adults.

In recent years, public policy has demanded that experienced juvenile offenders, like adult criminals, be held responsible for their actions and pay their "just deserts." While the juvenile justice system has not dismantled the medical model to the same extent as in the adult system, there is little doubt that the justice model has had an impact here as well. Moreover, the extension of due process rights to juveniles has placed youths on a more equal footing with adults in the legal system, generating the implicit assumption that, "since children are to be accorded the same rights as adults, then children should be ready to assume adult responsibilities and accept adult-type punishments for their crimes."[74]

Juveniles in Adult Court

An obvious example of what has been termed the "adultification" of the juvenile justice system is the growing trend toward transferring juveniles accused of serious offenses to adult court.[75] In some cases, this is accomplished by discretionary **waiver**, through which the juvenile court relinquishes its jurisdiction. But a number of states now legislatively exclude certain violent offenses from being heard in juvenile court. In others, transfer to adult court is mandated when a young offender already has been adjudicated a specified number of times in juvenile court or has had a prior conviction in adult court. In cases where waiver is a discretionary decision, the factors generally taken into account include the juvenile's age, seriousness of the offense, previous court history, and considerations related to both rehabilitative prospects and public protection.

The percentage of cases being transferred to criminal courts is still a very small proportion (less than 1 percent) of the total delinquency cases petitioned to juvenile court. In fact, transfers leveled off during the mid-1990s and have actually declined in recent years—partly due to declining rates of violent juvenile crime and partly as a result of more serious cases being filed directly in criminal court under statutory exclusion legislation, thus bypassing the juvenile court completely.[76]

It may be surprising to those advocating a "tougher" stance against juvenile crime that transferring young offenders to the criminal justice system does not

waiver: the process whereby juvenile court can relinquish jurisdiction over a case, transferring it to adult court.

appear to notably increase the severity of sanctions that they are likely to receive, nor does it apparently reduce recidivism:[77]

> While transfer may increase the length of confinement for some of the most serious offenders, the majority of transferred juveniles receive sentences that are comparable to sanctions already available in the juvenile justice system. More importantly, there is no evidence that young offenders handled in criminal court are less likely to recidivate than those remaining in juvenile court.[78]

In fact, research indicates that transferred youth are more likely to reoffend and to reoffend earlier than those who were not transferred.[79] Moreover, as illustrated in the next "Close-up on Corrections," there is wide variation in terms of how such serious juvenile cases are being handled across the country. While the minimum age varies, there are three states (Indiana, South Dakota, and Vermont) that "allow the certification [to adult court] of a juvenile as young as ten years old."[80]

CLOSE-UP ON CORRECTIONS
Geographic Disparities

Oakland County, Michigan. In 1997, 11-year-old Nathaniel Abraham shot Ronnie Green, Jr. with a stolen rifle while he was allegedly shooting some trees. Abraham was convicted of murder in an adult court two years later. Although Abraham was eligible for a life sentence, the judge rejected it and sentenced him to a juvenile facility until he turned 21.

Shawnee County, Kansas. On September 24, 1997, 15-year-old Jason Johnston was charged with clubbing and stabbing his mother to death. Two years later, the judge ruled that Johnston be placed in the custody of the Juvenile Justice Authority until he turned 23, with a strong recommendation that he be placed in a mental health facility.

Palm Beach County, Florida. On May 26, 2000, 13-year-old Nathaniel Brazill shot his teacher, Barry Grunow, with a .25 caliber handgun in school. Palm Beach County prosecutors tried Brazill as an adult for first-degree murder. The jury found Brazill guilty of second-degree murder, and the judge sentenced him to 28 years in an adult facility.

Source: Elizabeth A. Klug, "Geographical Disparities among Trying and Sentencing Juveniles," *Corrections Today* (December, 2001): 100–107.

Juveniles in Adult Prisons

When offenders under the age of 18 are sentenced in adult court, where will their time be served? The answer depends on where you live. Some states are part of a growing trend toward "blended sentencing" options that combine the use of both systems. For those who are sentenced to prison, states likewise have varying correctional procedures. Housing options for underage inmates include straight adult incarceration, graduated incarceration, and segregated incarceration, as described in the upcoming "Close-up on Corrections."

CLOSE-UP ON CORRECTIONS
New Boys on the Block—Juveniles in Adult Prisons

State corrections responses available for persons under 18 who are sentenced to prison include the following:

- *Straight adult incarceration* enables underage inmates in correctional facilities to be confined with other offenders, with little differentiation in programming. Most states allow straight adult incarceration, although some require separate housing for those under 18.
- *Graduated incarceration* is employed in 12 states (Delaware, Georgia, Maryland, Missouri, North Dakota, Ohio, Oregon, Tennessee, Texas, Utah, Washington, and West Virginia). Inmates under 18 begin their sentences in a juvenile facility until they reach a certain age (usually 18). The offender can then be either released or transferred to an adult facility to serve the remainder of the sentence.
- *Segregated incarceration* assigns certain young offenders to specific facilities based on their age and programming needs. Eight states employ this approach (California, Colorado, Florida, Kentucky, New Mexico, New York, South Carolina, and Wisconsin). In some locations, these programs include specialized education, vocational training, and substance abuse treatment.

Source: Adapted from Kevin J. Strom, "Profile of State Prisoners under Age 18, 1985–97," *Bureau of Justice Statistics Special Report* (February, 2000), p. 10.

Those under the age of 18 who are currently in adult prisons are primarily minority (73 percent) males (92 percent) who are sentenced for a violent crime (69 percent).[81] However, over one-quarter (26 percent) are serving time for either property or drug-related offenses. Over recent years, their numbers have been steadily climbing—to the point where, on average, the increase in new admissions for underage inmates is greater than for offenders of all ages entering prison.[82]

But, because they still represent less than one-half of 1 percent of the state prison population, not much attention has been directed toward targeting programs for young inmates. In comparison to adult prisoners, they receive fewer visits, and their influx into state prisons "has resulted in few changes in policy or procedures, other than those mandated by law."[83]

Whether or not lack of programming is part of the explanation, they also tend to be involved in more disciplinary incidents than their adult counterparts. In addition, they are five times more likely to be sexually assaulted and twice as likely to be beaten in prison as in a juvenile facility.[84] Such findings have prompted the American Correctional Association to recommend that adult institutions confining youthful offenders should provide for:

- separate housing;

- high school education;

- life management skills;

- mandatory counseling and social skills training in such areas as anger management, drug and alcohol guidance, AIDS instruction, and parenting;

- an individualized schedule that extends from wake-up to lights-out.[85]

Likewise, a national study calls for developing specialized institutional programs for youthful offenders, ensuring that prison classification instruments are valid for juveniles, and enhancing the expertise of security staff in managing this younger, more energetic, and more impulsive prison population.[86] In the rush toward "adultification" of juvenile justice, what has perhaps been overlooked is the fact that changing the legal status of offenders does not change their biological or psychological condition. As one prison staff member said of underage prison inmates, "These are still kids!"[87]

ALTERNATIVE APPROACHES

The detrimental effects of contact with the juvenile justice system are not limited to those who are institutionalized. Simply being officially processed through the system labels the child as a "delinquent." Under the original philosophy of the juvenile court, of course, this was not supposed to happen. One of the fundamental reasons for establishing a separate juvenile justice system was precisely to avoid the stigma that inevitably accompanies involvement in the criminal justice system.

As we saw earlier, the due process movement called attention to the fact that young offenders were not receiving the solicitous care that had been the original philosophy of the juvenile court. To the contrary, it was becoming apparent that, for many, formal processing often produces more harm than good. Willingness to make referrals to this benevolent protector of the child's welfare might be greater if, indeed, such action would truly be nonstigmatizing, rehabilitative, and as paternalistic as originally envisioned. That not being the case, there are many who advocate strategies of **nonintervention**—keeping youth out of the system whenever possible, or at least minimizing the extent of penetration into the system. Reducing the court's intrusion into the lives of children has been promoted by efforts directed toward *diversion, decriminalization*, and *deinstitutionalization*.

nonintervention: whenever possible, avoiding intervention into the lives of youth, or at least minimizing how far the child penetrates into the system.

Diversion

One of the obvious ways to avoid the negative impact of being processed in the juvenile justice system is to divert troubled children out of it through referral to a nonjudicial agency better equipped to handle their problems. **Diversion** involves the disposition of a case without formal adjudication, on condition of fulfilling some type of obligation, such as obtaining counseling.

Today this concept is seen at **intake** in the centralized intervention services known as juvenile assessment centers, where cases are screened, processed, and referred to appropriate resources in the community. But there is evidence that diversion programs often "widen the net" of social control—"drawing clients from youth who previously would have had their cases dismissed or would not even have been referred."[88] The question then becomes whether such approaches are adding to the juvenile justice system rather than creating alternatives to it. It is also noteworthy that the word *diversion* itself has two meanings: diversion *from* something or diversion *to* something. Simply diverting children from court to some other juvenile justice-affiliated program or service does not remove them from the system. It only directs them into another part of it.

The concept underlying diversion is to employ the least restrictive means of dealing with the case that is in keeping with the welfare of the child and the protection of the community. But, in many communities, the range of services available is still quite limited—and weighted more heavily on the side of "most" rather than "least" restrictive alternatives.

Even where energetic attempts have been made to expand community-based treatment opportunities, invoking diversion raises the question of what legal rights the juvenile is entitled to when informal options are used. While informal adjustment of cases may remove the stigma of court adjudication, it can also subject youth to certain restrictions (e.g., informal probation) or treatment requirements in the absence of due process protections that would accompany formal hearings. On the other hand, there are those who maintain that providing alternative opportunities represents the original mission of serving the child's best interests. Again, as with the juvenile justice system in general, the issue comes down to whether troubled youth are gaining more than they are losing.

Decriminalization

One way to minimize the intrusion of the juvenile justice system would be to restrict the wide range of behaviors over which the court has jurisdiction. Earlier, it was mentioned that one of the original justifications for a separate juvenile court was based on identifying "predelinquent" children in order to address their difficulties before these preliminary tendencies escalate into more serious violations. That, however, was when considerable optimism still prevailed that official intervention would be more beneficial than harmful. To the contrary, it has now been suggested that court intervention may actually increase rather than reduce the future likelihood of engaging in serious criminal activity. As it became increasingly apparent that faith in good intentions was not justified in reality, many began to question whether "borderline" delinquent behavior, such as status offenses, should actually be dealt with in the juvenile justice system at all.

As a result, a number of states have created separate legal categories for status offenders (e.g., CHINS), designating that such children are in need of supervision rather than prosecution. But using different terms to classify them does not necessarily translate into substantial differences with regard to how they are treated. Moreover, simply attaching new labels to their behavior may be no less stigmatizing.

To address these problems, the National Council on Crime and Delinquency called for complete elimination of court jurisdiction over status offenders more than 30 years ago, based on the belief that community-based services are more beneficial than court-mandated supervision in addressing their needs.[89] This is what is known as **decriminalization**—removing noncriminal behaviors (i.e., status offenses) from juvenile court jurisdiction. Decriminalization is based on the belief that there is a need to confine the boundaries of official authority more closely, limiting the system's regulation of moral conduct and minor misbehavior.

decriminalization: reducing the scope of the juvenile court by removing noncriminal (status) offenses from its jurisdiction.

Further justification of decriminalization is cited by those who note that eliminating status offenses from juvenile court can reduce racial and economic disparity within the justice system. This does not necessarily mean that the system deliberately discriminates against the poor or minorities. But such groups have fewer options and resources available to them. They are less likely to be able to get decent jobs, afford private treatment, or take advantage of nonjudicial alternatives. As a result, their unaddressed problems are more likely to come to official attention.

Some maintain that, in the absence of other choices, something is better than nothing. This argument is based on the premise that, if no one else is willing or able to fulfill the needs of status offenders, the juvenile court is obliged to do so. But, to others, "doing nothing"—at least judicially—may not be such a bad idea, as one appellate court judge states in no uncertain terms:

> The situation is truly ironic. The argument for retaining beyond-control and truancy jurisdiction is that juvenile courts have to act in such cases because "if we don't act, no one else will." I submit that precisely the opposite is the case: *because* you act, no one else does. Schools and public agencies refer their problem cases to you because you have jurisdiction, because you exercise it, and because you hold out promises that you can provide solutions.[90]

Deinstitutionalization

Reformers have not been extremely successful in diverting status offenders from the system or decriminalizing their behaviors. But perhaps there is greater hope that they can at least be provided with more appropriate forms of treatment than custodial institutions. Just as decriminalization sought to remove less serious cases from the juvenile court, **deinstitutionalization** (or "decarceration") is directed toward removing low-risk, noncriminal offenders from secure confinement, providing services through community-based resources.

In Chapter 9, we saw how negatively the institutional environment affects adult prisoners. Earlier in this chapter, we saw that these results can be even more devastating for those who are still in their developmental years. In recognition of such disadvantages, the National Advisory Commission on Criminal Justice Standards and Goals recommended almost 40 years ago that states not only "refrain from building any more state institutions for juveniles" but also "phase-out present institutions over a five-year period."[91] Yet it was not until subsequent passage of the Juvenile Justice and Delinquency Prevention Act of 1974 that there was any real motivation for states to deinstitutionalize.

As with the removal of juveniles from adult jails, federal juvenile justice funding has been used as an incentive to promote the removal of status offenders from secure confinement. Compliance with the Act's mandates is monitored annually in all states participating in Juvenile Justice and Delinquency Prevention funding programs, and all except two are now in compliance.[92]

Alternatives to Institutions

However, it is one thing to remove status offenders from secure confinement, and quite another to identify appropriate community-based alternatives for them. Traditional options on the "continuum of care" have included home detention, afterschool reporting, restitution, shelter care, and various forms of community-based residential and nonresidential programs.[93] More recently, a number of nontraditional options have emerged—ranging from wilderness excursions to wagon train expeditions and maritime adventures. Through teamwork under difficult situations, such unique experiences are designed to build trust, confidence, and self-esteem.

Just as diversion attempts to provide the least restrictive means of processing a case, deinstitutionalization attempts to offer the least restrictive disposition. This concept recognizes that there is still considerable support for the potential deterrent effect of early intervention, but tries to assure that official intervention is as nonpunitive as possible. In fact, it was not actually the detrimental effects of incarceration that prompted Congress to pass the 1974 juvenile justice legislation but, rather, "the argument that deprivation of liberty for persons who have not violated the criminal code is unjust and unwarranted."[94]

However, it is difficult for preventive efforts and incarceration options to co-exist in a society that continues to place so much emphasis on institutional confinement.

In fact, "excessive reliance on incarceration" remains one of the pervasive problems in the juvenile justice system, "because inadequate resources have been allocated to the development of effective community-based services."[95] As yet another analysis echoed, "when placement in a secure facility is a jurisdiction's primary—or only—treatment option, it becomes an expensive catchall."[96]

This dilemma was recognized in Massachusetts when, in the early 1970s, the state closed virtually all of its large secure juvenile correctional institutions. Although it reserved secure placements in small treatment centers for a relatively few chronic, violent offenders, the vast majority of the state's juvenile population was deinstitutionalized. By 1975, only 10 percent of those not in aftercare were in secure settings. The remainder were primarily in nonresidential programs, group care, or foster care.[97] Clearly, this change placed young offenders in closer contact with the community. Perhaps more significantly, doing so did not appear to create any increased danger to the public. The state's network of community-based alternatives featured intensive supervision and surveillance and, despite concerns to the contrary, the reforms did not unleash a juvenile crime wave: "In 1985, Massachusetts ranked 46th among the 50 states with respect to their rate of serious juvenile crime," and among those who did reoffend there was a tendency to commit less serious crimes.[98]

Unintended Consequences

Although this experiment with deinstitutionalization has influenced other states, it never experienced widespread implementation. Moreover, all decarceration efforts are not equally successful and, overall, findings have been mixed.

Some observers are concerned that, however praiseworthy in theory, deinstitutionalization has produced unintended side effects. For example, as it has become more difficult to institutionalize status offenders in training schools, there is some evidence that parents have become more likely to coerce children into such alternatives as psychiatric hospitalization—in which case "youngsters are merely being shunted to different forms of institutional placement."[99]

Others assert that status offenders are "being cast to the urban streets, where they are exploited and victimized," as reflected in the findings of a task force which concluded that deinstitutionalization policies were directly contributing to the growing numbers of missing children.[100] From the opposite perspective, still others have found evidence of net-widening and "relabeling" (which refers to cases that previously might have been treated as status offenders being "relabeled" as minor delinquencies).[101]

As with the juvenile justice system in general, it appears that even the best intentions can produce consequences that are contrary to original ambitions. In that regard, "it must be said that at best we have been inefficient, and at worst we have been inhumane, and at all times we have been confused."[102]

SUMMARY

Social policies related to our treatment of children have emerged from a bleak history marked by harsh conditions. By the twentieth century, industrialization, immigration, and urbanization had combined to create problems of growing magnitude in American cities. The resulting poverty, overcrowding, unemployment, and crime obviously did not provide the best environment for raising children. Rather than addressing these underlying conditions, social reform was directed toward intervening in the lives of children in an effort to "rescue" them from the contaminating influences of urban life.

Thus the child-saving movement created the impetus for establishing the first separate juvenile court in 1899, based on the concept of *parens patriae*, which enabled the state to intervene in the place of parents on behalf of the welfare of the child. Serving the "best interests" of youths required that procedures be kept informal and flexible, since the court was designed to be an advocate rather than an adversary. The court's mission included early identification of predelinquent behavior, personalized diagnosis, and prescription of rehabilitative treatment. To further avoid the stigma of criminal processing, it relied on civil procedures and created a vocabulary of tranquilizing terms to distinguish the juvenile justice system from its adult counterpart.

But, some 60 years later, serious questions were raised about the court's fulfillment of its commitment to protect rather than punish. Given concerns that juveniles were sacrificing their rights in the name of rehabilitation (and that their "rehabilitation" often amounted to little more than incarceration), the due process movement sought to reduce the system's power and intrusiveness. During this period, a number of landmark Supreme Court decisions extended the due process rights to which juveniles are entitled. These rulings have not, however, fully transformed proceedings into the adversarial nature of the criminal justice system. There is still hope that, ideally, the juvenile court can guarantee legal rights through procedural safeguards without losing its personalized approach.

That potential is difficult to achieve, however, in a system which is empowered to take action in response to wide-ranging behaviors, from delinquent acts to status offenses. As a result, juvenile courts have been accused of being too punitive in their handling of minor cases, while at the same time being too lenient with serious delinquents. With increasing public concern focusing on chronic juvenile offenders engaged in violent crime, many high-risk cases are being transferred to adult court. Moreover, the juvenile court is now coming closer to resembling the justice model in terms of its dispositional practices. As a result, juvenile correctional facilities are witnessing a substantial growth in custody rates, particularly among minorities.

Juvenile institutions include both public and privately operated training schools. Public facilities must accept anyone committed to them, whereas private schools can be more selective, focusing on specific programs for particular types of offenders. If youths are confined for the express purpose of getting treatment, the courts have recognized their legal right to receive it. Unlike the focus of adult prisons, that of juvenile corrections is still assumed to be primarily rehabilitative rather than punitive. That does not, however, mean that the effects of confinement are not as detrimental for juveniles. Quite the contrary, the negative impact can be even greater for those who are confined in the midst of their emotional and physical development. Moreover, as increasing numbers of serious juvenile offenders are transferred to criminal courts, the adult correctional system is beginning to see considerably more youthful offenders confined in its facilities.

Because official intrusion into the lives of children appears to do more harm than good in many cases, there are those who advocate noninterventionist strategies. Supporters of this approach would keep youths out of the system whenever possible, or at least minimize the extent of their penetration into it. One way to do so is by diverting cases informally into nonjudicial community-based programs and services. Another is to decriminalize status offenses so that juvenile courts do not have jurisdiction over noncriminal conduct. Yet another alternative is to avoid institutionalizing status offenders. All of these approaches involve using the least restrictive means of dealing with minor indiscretions. But they depend upon community resources which are not always available and the use of which can create unanticipated negative consequences.

We have undoubtedly come a long way since the time when the concept of childhood simply did not exist. Yet in many respects, we still have a long way to go toward creating a juvenile justice system that is characterized as much by concern for kids as contempt for criminals. First, of course, we must distinguish between the two.

FOR FURTHER DISCUSSION

1. Discuss how the supposedly benevolent intentions of the "child-saving" movement could be alternately viewed as self-serving initiatives during a period of threat to the middle and upper classes.

2. Given its basis in the precedent of *parens patriae*, debate whether the juvenile court took on too much responsibility, and the extent to which its all-inclusive mission is related to the court's difficulties today.

3. Visit a local juvenile court, observe the proceedings, and determine whether the greater procedural informality of juvenile courts remains justifiable today, as well as whether juvenile justice might be better served through such alternatives as restorative justice.

4. While it is now over 40 years since the Supreme Court observed that offenders in juvenile court were receiving "the worst of both worlds," discuss how this issue has been addressed in the intervening years, in terms of both due process protections and rehabilitative opportunities.

5. Debate both sides of the issue concerning whether status offenders should continue to fall under the jurisdiction of the juvenile court and, if not, defend an alternative approach.

6. Go online to see if you can determine how your state is complying with provisions of the Juvenile Justice and Delinquency Prevention Act. Or look at statistics for your local jail to determine how many juveniles are being confined there, and for what reasons.

7. Schedule a trip to your nearest juvenile detention center and state training facility. Compare them in terms of everything from the physical structure and food services to how residents are treated, what programs are available, how professional the staff appear to be, etc.

8. You have just been appointed to a commission dedicated to reducing disproportionate minority representation in your state's juvenile correctional system. Without any significant additional funding, what would you recommend?

9. Discuss why so few juvenile correctional facilities are accredited (in comparison to adult prisons and jails), and determine what could be done to increase this number.

10. Debate whether the "adultification" of the juvenile justice system has primarily been a positive or a negative development, including recommendations for the future in this regard.

11. Discuss both sides of the confinement of youthful offenders in adult prisons, including what provisions need to be addressed if this practice is to be continued.

12. Go online and see if you can identify any of the cases involving youthful offenders sentenced to adult facilities in your state. If so, select two or three cases and find out what you can about the background of these offenders. Given what you learn, determine whether there is anything we can do proactively to prevent more of these young people from ending up serving long prison terms.

13. Find out whether your state operates a military-style boot camp for youthful offenders. If so, learn as much as you can about it and, based on evidence about the results of such programs in other states, decide whether it should be retained in your state as is, retained with specified modifications, or completely abolished.

14. Design a family-focused aftercare program for youthful status offenders that is targeted toward reducing recidivism and improving family functioning as well as quality of life.

15. Argue for and against establishing diversionary alternatives for drug-related crimes.

16. Identify what offenses might be appropriate targets for decriminalization, and debate the pros and cons of doing so.

17. Argue for and against deinstitutionalizing nonviolent property crimes.

CHAPTER 13

Staff—The Key Ingredient

The public rarely thinks about people in prison and thinks even less often about the men and women who manage and work in these same facilities . . . [who] shoulder tremendous responsibilities and face incredible challenges, usually without adequate resources and support.[1]

John J. Gibbons and Nicholas de B. Katzenbach

CHAPTER OVERVIEW

Throughout this book, numerous correctional processes, programs, and procedures have been discussed. They have focused on a wide variety of topics from a broad range of perspectives. But, however diverse the correctional conglomerate may be, it has one essential ingredient in common.

That crucial component is people. Those who make the decisions, establish the policies, and administer the correctional system are extremely influential. It is their leadership that shapes future visions and provides direction. Yet, in many respects, those who carry out the policies and deliver the operational services are in the long run even more influential. They are the employees who have the direct, day-to-day contact with correctional clients. Through them, prevailing theories, public opinions, and political actions are translated into practice. It is their level of professionalism and personal skill that can either help or harden an offender, promote or subvert operational programs, and strengthen or weaken correctional effectiveness: "Correctional administrators can (and do!) manage with crowded conditions, insufficient funding, political setbacks, and conflicting priorities. They cannot, however, manage without qualified, dedicated personnel."[2]

This does not mean that line-level staff are exclusively responsible for the system's successes or failures. Under the best of circumstances, it is difficult to implement policy intentions. But it can be virtually impossible when line personnel are faced with insufficient resources, uncooperative clients, and unsupportive supervisors. Staff members cannot achieve desired results without the fiscal resources necessary to do so. Being constantly short-handed, overworked, underpaid, and inadequately equipped eventually takes its toll on dedication and commitment.

Nor can operational personnel be held accountable for offenders who are unwilling to accept help or unmotivated to change their behavior. Dealing with reluctant clients is an acknowledged fact of life for correctional workers.

Confronting these inherent obstacles would be considerably less frustrating, however, within a supportive administrative environment. It is one thing to persevere in the face of an apathetic public and an unappreciative clientele. But line staff cannot be expected to perform competently in an organizational environment that is plagued with contradictory goals, unclear policies, inequitable rules, inconsistent administrative procedures, or autocratic management techniques.

While operational personnel are charged with direct delivery of services, it is the upper-level administrative and managerial staff who set the tone for how those services will be delivered. They determine how line staff will be selected, trained, motivated, evaluated, and supervised. Because tomorrow's supervisors and managers are recruited from within today's rank and file, these personnel practices will have long-term implications, shaping the future workforce for years to come.

CORRECTIONAL PERSONNEL

LEARNING GOALS

Do you know:
1. where most of the correctional workforce is employed?
2. what position is held by the vast majority of correctional employees?
3. in what respects the correctional workforce is changing?

Because it is in the "people business," corrections is a very labor-intensive enterprise. But, as the numbers of personnel expand to keep pace with growing client populations, it is also sometimes difficult to keep in mind that every number on every agency's table of organization represents an individual employee—a person with strengths and weaknesses, capabilities and limitations, and satisfactions and frustrations. The field of corrections invests tremendous resources in these people. In fact, about two-thirds of all operating costs are spent on employee salaries and benefits.[3] It therefore would not seem to make sense to dismiss all of that investment "with the flippant attitude that people are expendable."[4]

Numbers and Characteristics

Although we saw in earlier chapters that the bulk of correctional *clients* are under some form of community supervision, only about 12 percent of correctional *employees* work in probation or parole.[5] The overwhelming majority hold jobs in correctional institutions. Secure facilities are not only costly to construct, but also expensive to staff.

Some of these institutional employees are supervisors, managers, or administrators. Some are teachers, counselors, or other professional or technical staff. Some are clerical, maintenance, or other supportive employees. But, as shown in Exhibit 13.1, the vast majority are correctional officers who hold custodial/security positions in local, state, and federal correctional facilities.

With the growth of the correctional workforce, there have been a number of changes in the characteristics of these employees. Today, the stereotypical image of a correctional officer as a middle-aged, white male with less than a high school education could hardly be further from reality. That profile was typical of line staff in the past, but today they are younger, better educated, and more representative of women and minorities. Although males still reflect the majority of those on the correctional payroll, female representation has expanded to one-third of the staff working in both jails and prisons,[6] as well as over half (55 percent) of those working in probation and parole.[7] Nevertheless, women have been relatively recent additions to the workforce and thus remain underrepresented among correctional executives.[8]

In terms of race and ethnicity, comparable gains have been made, with minorities now representing nearly one-third of correctional personnel[9] (although again most are concentrated in lower ranks). While a college degree is not required by most departments, over one-third (37 percent) of the agencies responding to one national survey indicated that officers are entering correctional service with some college education.[10]

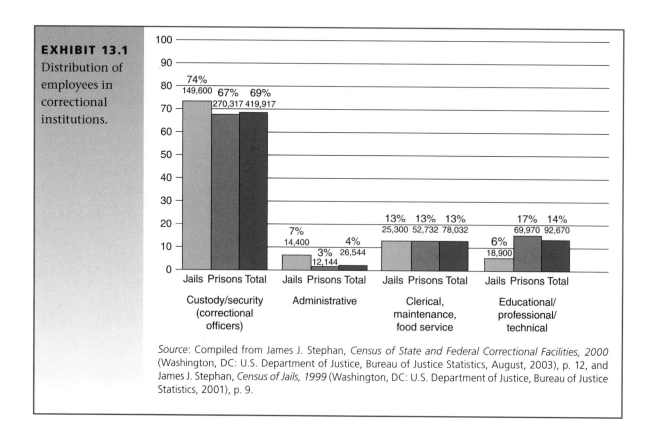

EXHIBIT 13.1
Distribution of employees in correctional institutions.

Source: Compiled from James J. Stephan, *Census of State and Federal Correctional Facilities, 2000* (Washington, DC: U.S. Department of Justice, Bureau of Justice Statistics, August, 2003), p. 12, and James J. Stephan, *Census of Jails, 1999* (Washington, DC: U.S. Department of Justice, Bureau of Justice Statistics, 2001), p. 9.

Gender Integration

Under equal employment laws, women and minorities cannot be denied correctional positions if they meet the qualification requirements. Particularly with respect to female employees, **gender integration** has created a major issue in which the male inmate's right to privacy in housing areas has confronted the female applicant's right to employment in male prisons.

Women were employed in corrections long before such concern surfaced, but earlier they were confined to duties within female facilities. Since there are far fewer women's institutions, employment opportunities for female staff were therefore quite limited. Moreover, because of the lack of job variety and promotional opportunities in these facilities, advancement potential for female employees was further restricted.

All of this changed in 1972 with the passage of amendments to the 1964 Civil Rights Act. Title VII of this Act prohibits employment discrimination on the basis of race, religion, sex, or national origin. The amendments added "were crucial to women's advancement in corrections work in two separate ways: First by covering public sector employment, and second by increasing the enforcement power of the EEOC [Equal Employment Opportunity Commission]."[11]

Bona Fide Occupational Qualification (BFOQ) Exception

The law does, however, provide for one exceptional circumstance under which some discriminatory practices might be allowed. That exception occurs when the employing agency can demonstrate that a particular race, religion, sex, or national origin is a *bona fide occupational qualification* (**BFOQ**) required to perform the job. This does not mean that employers can discriminate on the basis of general assumptions about women's suitability for correctional work. In fact, the law very narrowly defines BFOQ to apply only to certain unique situations, such as a movie role calling for a male actor, or a police officer being required to have a valid driver's license.

Nor have discrimination suits been limited to females working in male institutions. Comparable questions have been raised by male officers employed in female prisons, and the results have been similar. Overall, the courts "generally have concluded that employees' equal employment opportunity rights and institutional security take priority over inmates' limited privacy rights."[12] In fact, research reveals that, in most women's prisons in the United States, men are both employed as correctional officers and routinely assigned to supervise inmate living units.[13]

LEARNING GOALS

Do you know:

4. how Title VII of the Civil Rights Act has affected the correctional workforce?
5. what is meant by a BFOQ and under what circumstances it may be invoked?
6. how the courts have decided the issue of women's right to work versus male inmate privacy, and what, if any, restrictions are placed on their duty posts?
7. why staff sexual misconduct should be viewed as a security issue?

---

gender integration: more comprehensive inclusion of women throughout the correctional workforce.

BFOQ: a bona fide occupational qualification which might enable an exception to the equal employment provisions of Title VII of the Civil Rights Act.

Cross-supervision Challenges

Aside from the legal issues involved, prisons have never been the most adaptable environments for accommodating massive change. The integration of women into traditionally male-dominated institutions and job assignments has been especially controversial. In part, resistance has been based on fears that women would jeopardize safety and security, as expressed in the true story told in the next "Close-up on Corrections."

CLOSE-UP ON CORRECTIONS
The Gender Gap

[M]en frequently see corrections as a dangerous profession requiring machismo. They believe it is a place where women are especially unsafe. Because men are conditioned to protect women, they may feel that, in addition to working with the inmates, they have an added responsibility to protect the women officers.

These feelings can make men and women uncomfortable with each other. Women may feel patronized, as if they are merely being tolerated rather than appreciated and affirmed for their work. . . . A woman corrections officer recently told me she enjoyed counseling inmates who were close to release or community placement. She said that if she made a difference in the lives of even a few inmates, she felt her efforts were worthwhile.

However, some of her male counterparts thought she was getting too personally involved with the inmates. This baffled her, since she considered much of their contact with the inmates—bantering and favoring some inmates over others, for example—less professional than her counseling. To the male officers, her actions seemed too intimate and were thus inviting danger. . . .

The officer was comfortable with her approach. She was encouraging inmates' participation in an integrated community, a new experience for most of them. The inmates responded to her differently than they did to the men. To her, they expressed fears and confessed weaknesses they did not share with male employees.

Was she protecting the public by her actions or placing lives in jeopardy? The men viewed her activities as unnecessary and in a negative light. She saw her actions as positive. The differences here may be a result of differences in how each gender views the world.

Source: Adria Libolt, "Bridging the Gender Gap," *Corrections Today*, Vol. 53, No. 7 (December, 1991), pp. 136–138.

In fact, as recently as 2003, research revealed that a sizeable number of male officers feared that their female counterparts "maintained inadequate social distance" from male inmates, contributing to a "backdrop of male hostility and resentment."[14] More fundamentally, however, it appears that women represent a threat to the pride, homogeneity, and male ego associated with the close-knit world of correctional officers. To the extent that women can perform the job successfully, a serious challenge is posed to conventional beliefs that masculinity is a necessary requirement. As one male supervisor noted:

> It really hurts these guys to think that a woman can do their job. They've been walking around town like big shots—like they're doing a job only "real men" can do. Well, if the woman next door can do your job, then maybe you're not so tough after all. . . . [T]hese men have been going home to their wives for years saying "you don't know what it's like in there." Now some of their wives are joining up. The jig is up, so to speak.[15]

Ironically, one of the most unlikely sources of support for greater equality in the assignment of women came from correctional officer labor unions.[16] During the time that women were fighting for equality, union contracts in some states provided that seniority would be the sole criterion for making job assignments. Officers could bid for duty posts, and longevity was to be the only factor considered in selecting those to fill the most preferential assignments. However, when women began to join the corrections department, posts were classified as suitable or unsuitable for females in order to limit their direct contact with male inmates. The problem was that the noncontact posts designated as appropriate for women also happened to be among those most sought after by men, who were being denied their seniority rights under the contract as more and more women were joining the workforce. Unions therefore demanded an integrated seniority list.

Balancing Inmate and Employee Interests

The outcome reflects an attempt to minimize inmate privacy intrusions while balancing the rights of all employees with equal employment opportunities for women. The resulting compromises include such provisions as restricting opposite-sex strip searches and shower duty, teaming female and male officers in housing units, requiring opposite-sex officers to announce their presence, using partial shower and toilet screens, and the like.

Despite widespread initial resistance, female officers today are the beneficiaries of a legacy of decades of employment in a variety of correctional positions. Both federal and state correctional systems (including maximum-security prisons) have adopted "gender-neutral employment policies."[17] As a result, three out of four female correctional officers work in male facilities today.[18]

Inmate Reaction

Inmate reaction to the presence of women has been mixed but tends to be relatively positive. Some have neutral attitudes, under the theory that the rules are the same no matter who is enforcing them. While in the minority, others remain opposed—degraded by having a female "boss," concerned about lack of privacy, or frustrated by the presence of women in an environment where sex is prohibited. Overall,

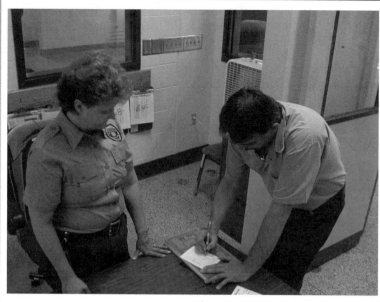

EXHIBIT 13.2
Women now routinely work side by side with male officers in correctional facilities.

Source: Photo by Joseph Fuller.

however, it appears that the majority favor female officers, feeling that they treat inmates with more respect, professionalism, and compassion,[19] and that they are equally capable of dealing with correctional job tasks.[20] Moreover, research indicates that male inmates are not as prone to attack female officers. A study of female officers working in male maximum-security prisons found that they are substantially less likely than male officers to be assaulted on the job.[21]

Staff Sexual Misconduct

That does not, however, mean that cross-gender inmate supervision has been without drawbacks. Correctional practices today commonly involve female officers supervising male inmates as well as male officers supervising female inmates. Within the close confines of a prison, it is not difficult for such working relationships to evolve into inappropriate intimacies, for staff to be manipulated sexually by inmates, or for inmates to be subjected to staff sexual demands. In fact, given the imbalance of power between employees and inmates, there is actually no such thing as "consensual" sexual activities behind bars.

This issue of staff sexual misconduct and undue familiarity with inmates has surfaced in recent years as attention has focused on a number of highly publicized class action lawsuits. In the past, when the courts were less likely to review such complaints or to decide in favor of the inmates, agencies had little incentive to aggressively investigate and seek remedies for staff sexual misconduct. Today, of course, that has changed, as evidenced by mounting numbers of cases in which plaintiffs have prevailed.

A survey by the National Institute of Corrections, for example, discovered that, within a five-year period, almost half of all state departments of corrections reported that they had faced lawsuits regarding staff sexual misconduct.[22] While some of these allegations eventually are determined to be unfounded, a United Nations study pointed out that sexual misconduct is relatively common in U.S. prisons, especially when compared to other industrialized countries. Moreover, reports by Human Rights Watch have detailed sexual harassment, abuse, and privacy violations in U.S. prisons, along with retaliation by staff against inmates for filing suits.[23]

In response, a U.S. General Accounting Office report called for directing more efforts toward improved reporting, monitoring, and investigatory procedures.[24] As a result, concerned correctional administrators today are doing everything from developing new policies to providing staff training, improving investigatory practices, and even working with their legislature to criminalize sexual contact with inmates. Additionally, the 2003 Prison Rape Elimination Act, among other things, requires the National Institute of Corrections to provide training, information, and technical assistance on staff sexual misconduct to correctional agencies throughout the country.

Nor is this merely a legal or personnel-related issue. In the final analysis, it has been suggested that staff sexual misconduct "should be defined as a security issue," inasmuch as such behavior "threatens the safety and security of everyone—staff and inmates alike."[25]

Implications of a Changing Workforce

Expanding the employment of women and minorities in corrections has produced a diverse workforce that is more reflective of the people and communities being served. But these changes have not always been easy to adjust to organizationally. In addition to a "new breed" of employee in terms of race, gender, and ethnicity, those beginning correctional work today are entering at younger ages and bringing with them the values of newer generations.

> **LEARNING GOALS**
>
> Do you know:
> 8. how the changing nature of the workforce is affecting correctional administration?
> 9. why employees leave correctional work, and whether such turnover is subject to change?

After the "traditionalists" who shaped early administrative practices came the "baby boomers," who in turn were followed by "generation X-ers" and, most recently, the "millennials." In contrast to the expectations of subsequent generations, however, the work-related expectations of traditionalists fit well within highly structured bureaucracies. Unlike the generations to follow, they were willing to take orders, knew their place in the chain of command, respected their superior officers, and were accustomed to "deferring the pursuit of personal autonomy to the power of institutional authority."[26] That is not true of their successors. In essence, "Traditionalists are classified as coming of age in a 'chain of command' environment, whereas for boomers it was 'change of command,' for x-ers, 'self-command,' and for millennials 'don't command—collaborate!'"[27]

This combination of an increasingly younger, better-educated workforce composed of a more diverse population reflecting the often conflicting values of new generations presents management challenges. Previously, correctional employees were considerably more homogeneous, sharing similar job-related values and attitudes. That was obviously a drawback in terms of generating change or meeting the needs of a diverse clientele. But it was advantageous in terms of managing, supervising, and accommodating like-minded employees. Along with the benefits of a more varied workforce, corrections is now faced with the challenge of adapting to the differences they represent.

Today's employees are considerably less likely than their predecessors to quietly endure an autocratic management style or to routinely implement unreasonable policies sent down through the chain of command. No longer are operational staff as willing to subserviently accept management practices that do not provide them with some degree of autonomy and recognize their worth as individuals. In fact, the National Jail Workforce Survey recently found that disapproval of how the agency is being managed ranked second in terms of what would most influence officers to leave.[28]

Staff Turnover

turnover: the rate at which employees leave an organization, either voluntarily or involuntarily.

Although the economic downturn in recent years has somewhat curtailed voluntary resignations, corrections has traditionally endured high rates of **turnover**. Depending on the state, separation rates have at times ranged up to 37 percent, with annual turnover rates for security staff averaging around 14 percent.[29] When they have better options, today's correctional employees are more likely than their predecessors to leave employment that is not satisfying to them.

Needless to say, no stable business could run efficiently with a continuous transition of employees coming and going. Moreover, when staff members leave within the first few years of their employment, turnover is especially costly, in light of the sizeable investment made in recruiting, selecting, and training them.

Undoubtedly, if the right people are not selected for the job, today's hiring mistakes become tomorrow's turnover statistics.[30] But considerable research has linked turnover, thoughts about quitting, and decisions to seek employment elsewhere with such administratively controlled factors as:

- insufficient opportunities for participation in decision-making;[31]

- inadequate supervisory support;[32]

- dissatisfaction with supervisors;[33]

- a "crisis of faith" in the management ability of ranking staff ;[34]

- poor communications between first-line supervisors and line-level employees;[35]

- lack of empowerment—i.e., ability to participate in and contribute to the organization.[36]

Most research on staff turnover points toward the negative impact of the work environment. Contrary to what might be expected, however, it does not appear to be either dangerous conditions or difficult inmates that lead most officers to quit. Rather, it is how employees are treated by management that best predicts turnover. For example, in one national study, more than three out of four jail staff said that having input into decisions, being treated fairly, and knowing that management listens to their opinions are all important to keeping them. But far fewer said that they enjoy such work conditions now.[37] In that regard, it has been noted that "people do not leave jobs; they leave bosses."[38]

Since everyone who wants to leave may not have the opportunity to do so, it is not surprising that organizational frustrations can become personally stressful. In fact, lack of recognition and problems with administrators have long been cited as major contributors to correctional officer stress.[39] Other stress-related research further confirms that autonomy on the job and participatory decision-making are associated with stronger organizational commitment and less job-related stress.[40] As one study concluded, the more empowered employees perceived themselves to be, the lower their level of occupational stress.[41] Thus, when bureaucratic management oppresses the self-direction, recognition, and organizational participation that employees are seeking on the job, it should not be surprising to find them dissatisfied, burned out, and resigning. While working with some inmates may simply be troublesome, working under some management practices may simply be intolerable.

episodic stress: the stress resulting from brief but traumatic incidents encountered on the job.

Officer Stress

Like a chronic cough, such management practices are among the sources of chronic, ongoing stress in the day-to-day work environment of corrections. Unlike **episodic stress**, **chronic stress** is not the result of a one-time crisis or emergency situation. It is not the adrenaline-pumping reaction to a riot, attack, or hostage-taking situation. Rather, it is the product of a slow, continual process of erosion that occurs over a period of years. Supervising inmates immediately comes to mind as a potential source of chronic stress within correctional institutions. But research reveals that it is actually employees who are more chronically stress provoking—from co-workers to supervisors, managers, and administrators. For example, one study reports that officers actually outranked inmates in terms of those creating major, continuing pressures and problems. Furthermore, in terms of how they are treated by supervisors, many indicate that they are either not recognized or are given attention only when something goes wrong.[42]

LEARNING GOALS

Do you know:
10. the difference between episodic and chronic stress?
11. how agencies traditionally have responded to officer stress and why such responses have been inadequate?
12. what can be done proactively to prevent correctional officer stress?
13. why correctional officers have joined labor unions and what impact this has had on agencies?

Time and time again, research has confirmed that the difficulty of work in correctional institutions is related more to problems involving staff relationships than to problems in dealing with inmates. Moreover, even when inmate interaction

chronic stress: the long-term, debilitating effect of ongoing pressures and problems in the daily work setting.

has been identified as a major stress inducement, the underlying source of the stress often is attributed to administrative problems such as unclear guidelines, inadequate communication, conflicting orders, lack of opportunity to participate in decision-making, inappropriate supervision, and the like.[43] In fact, lack of administrative support ranked among the highest sources of stress in all three states included in a national study of correctional officer stress.[44]

Organizational Responses to Stress

Correctional administrators have begun to recognize the debilitating impact of stress among their personnel. But that does not mean that they necessarily accept any personal responsibility for it. To the contrary, the primary organizational responses to stress are employee assistance programs and stress reduction training, both of which have significant limitations:

- *Employee assistance programs (EAPs).* Designed primarily to offer counseling and similar forms of individual treatment, EAPs assist employees in coping with problems—whether those problems are related to work, home life, substance abuse, or whatever. Such programs can be helpful in dealing with the post-traumatic stress resulting from critical incidents. But we have already seen that episodic incidents are not the most frequent stressors in corrections. Counseling is not likely to resolve chronic job-related stress, because it is treating the *symptoms* rather than dealing with the *causes*.

- *Training programs.* Stress reduction training typically includes information on nutrition, exercise, meditation, relaxation, and similar techniques for dealing with stress. As with EAPs, however, emphasis is on improving the employee's ability to cope with on-the-job stress by reducing its debilitating *effects* rather than taking steps to eliminate its underlying *causes*. In that regard, it is "not only foolish but also ineffective to treat correctional officer burnout as an individual pathology best addressed by measures such as relaxation techniques and employee assistance programs."[45]

When employees return from EAP counseling or stress training, where do they go? Right back into the same work environment that created their stress in the first place! True, they may be better equipped to cope with it (at least in the short term). But long-term chronic stress will not be resolved without a dedicated commitment to **proactive stress prevention**—that is, eliminating the work-related stressors, rather than treating the stressed-out workers.

The next "Close-up on Corrections" outlines simple techniques designed to address some of the administrative causes of stress. Notice that the emphasis is on keeping employees informed and involved. That is because a proactive organizational approach to stress prevention requires the inclusion of all ranks in the agency's problem-solving and decision-making network.

proactive stress prevention: addressing chronic organizational stressors before they produce negative effects on employees.

The ironic aspect of focusing on causes as opposed to effects is that it is not likely to be nearly as expensive. EAPs and stress reduction training programs are quite costly. In contrast, it is relatively inexpensive to uncover the supervisory, managerial, and administrative practices that are creating stress and take appropriate actions to change them. Rather than money, what it really costs to respond proactively to address employee stress is the willingness of administrators to confront organizational and managerial shortcomings. But, in many agencies, that is considered too high a price to pay.

CLOSE-UP ON CORRECTIONS
Administrative Strategies for Reducing Stress

The key ingredients in effective stress prevention planning are commitment, participation, and action, which means that managers concerned with reducing organizational stress must:

- make a *commitment to a proactive organizational approach*—to doing something about preventing stress by eliminating its causes;
- develop a *participatory change process*—strengthening commitment further through participation, and beginning to replace supervisory control by self-control;
- take the *necessary follow-up actions*—such as establishing clear expectations, communicating openly and honestly, making timely decisions, giving positive feedback, trusting staff, valuing their input, and treating them objectively.

Certainly, it is much easier to continue sending stressed-out employees to counseling sessions or training programs. It is less complicated to deal with the damaging *symptoms* of stress than to deal with its *causes*. But it is also much less effective.

Source: Adapted from Jeanne B. Stinchcomb, *Managing Stress: Performing under Pressure*, Vol. 2 (Lanham, MD: American Correctional Association, 1995), pp. 197–210.

Labor Unions

When an organization is unwilling or unable to respond to the concerns of its employees, it should not be surprising to find frustrated workers either leaving or turning to other avenues to resolve their complaints. One such alternative has undoubtedly been employee unions. Correctional officer unions have been strong for a number of years in some states.

Originally, unions were concerned predominantly with such extrinsic matters as salaries and working conditions. These items still remain serious issues on the bargaining table in a number of states. But union interests have begun to expand beyond money and fringe benefits. Unions are now becoming more actively involved in a wide range of issues affecting the health, safety, and well-being of their membership—ranging from equipment and training to disciplinary actions, promotional policies, and other administrative practices.

These intrinsic concerns are likely to become even more significant bargaining issues in the future for two reasons. First, unions are increasingly aware of the fact that, in a sluggish economy, demands for higher wages or additional benefits are often simply unrealistic. Second, as union membership becomes increasingly composed of the "new breed" of correctional workers described earlier, it can be expected that their concerns will begin to shift. In place of the extrinsic matters which had been emphasized by their predecessors, today's employees may be more likely to fight for qualitative issues surrounding work satisfaction, personal autonomy, job enrichment, and self-fulfillment.

From some perspectives, unionization has been viewed as reducing the capacity of administrators to manage the system, although less than half of the prison wardens in one survey reported that unions restrict their management style.[46] A national survey of jail administrators likewise found the vast majority indicating that unions had either no influence or a positive influence on everything from job assignments and training opportunities to salaries, disciplinary practices, and grievance resolution.[47]

Nevertheless, labor unions have won such concessions as overtime pay, compensation for being called back to duty, protection against extra-duty requirements, scheduling restrictions, and many other actions that have been perceived as infringements on management prerogatives. Yet, to some degree, it has been management's reluctance to share control and address grievances that has prompted employees to organize collectively. In the long run, however, both have mutual concerns at stake—the employees' best interests are served by working in a progressive organization, and management's best interests are served by organizing a progressive workforce. The more that each can fulfill their complementary roles, the less those roles will conflict.

ADMINISTRATIVE PRACTICES

It is especially ironic that labor and management are often adversaries, since most of today's administrators were yesterday's line staff. With a few exceptions that occasionally occur at the highest ranks, virtually all correctional managers and supervisors are selected from within the agency. (In fact, most systems have restrictions against lateral entry into all but the uppermost levels.) This pattern has long-term implications for how entry personnel are recruited, selected, and trained, since it is largely from the ranks of line-level officers that command staff are chosen.

Staff Recruitment

Historically, correctional agencies often tended to establish minimal requirements and accept anyone who could meet them. The rationale for such rudimentary practices typically related to the pressures induced by low public prestige, high turnover, and inadequate salaries.[48] But each of these justifications is amenable to change.

The Image Issue.   Some organizations are locked into the belief that it would be fruitless to set higher entrance standards because corrections suffers from an inferior image and is therefore relegated to taking virtually anyone who is willing to work there. Restricting standards to the lowest acceptable denominator, however, results in recruiting precisely that.[49] It is apparent that few of the best suited or most educated will be attracted to a job with requirements that are far below their level of qualification. Thus a self-fulfilling cycle is created—if only the least qualified are recruited, only the least qualified tend to apply. On the other hand, an agency that expects a high caliber of employee will be considerably more likely to attract better applicants.

Naturally, as standards are raised, more candidates will be rejected. That is why organizations concerned about attracting better applicants must be willing to search aggressively for them. Once an agency is recognized as a good place to work where people are proud to be employed and only the best are selected, it will be easier to appeal to suitable candidates. But, even under these ideal circumstances, it is essential to put considerable energy into the recruitment process, beyond just distributing posters and brochures. Making personal contacts, attending job fairs, establishing college internships, and the like are essential for successful recruitment.[50] With high visibility, a respected reputation, and intensive recruitment, the pool of prospective employees is likely to expand, thereby enabling greater selectivity.

Vacancy Pressures.   Much of the strategy for keeping entrance standards at minimal levels is designed to enable the organization to fill numerous vacancies promptly. That may be necessary because departments that are not at full capacity often will be required to employ officers on overtime, which quickly becomes very costly. Unfortunately, some agencies have come to accept high turnover as the price of doing business in corrections. In many cases, it is not.

Dealing with the turnover problem requires a twofold approach: first, finding out why employees are leaving, and then doing something about it. This does not necessarily mean trying to pry higher salaries from the taxpayers. Although better pay would undoubtedly help, people who enjoy their jobs will be more reluctant to leave, despite the attraction of more money elsewhere.[51] Throughout much of the remainder of this chapter, administrative techniques are addressed that could increase satisfaction without spending one additional dime. What is involved in reducing voluntary turnover is not greater cost but greater commitment. And the more that corrections can decrease voluntary resignations, the more it can increase entrance requirements.

Compensation Concerns.   In many states, it is readily apparent that few enter corrections for the monetary compensation it offers. While average starting salaries have been increasing, given the nature of the job and the qualifications necessary to do it properly, correctional personnel are not generally paid adequately.

This issue likewise has been used as a justification for reducing entrance standards. Yet research indicates that there are other techniques beyond lower standards or higher salaries that are both promising and less costly alternatives.[52] Moreover, there are any number of professions—from teaching to nursing or social work—that have traditionally not been well compensated. Nevertheless, in most states, these occupations have established and maintained relatively rigorous educational and training requirements. Even within corrections, the majority of probation and parole positions require a bachelor's degree, sometimes with additional experience as well.[53] In any event, if the job satisfaction concerns discussed throughout this chapter are addressed, salary may not be as significant a drawback to effective recruitment.

Entry-level Training

Regardless of how good the recruitment and selection process is at bringing the most qualified applicants into the agency, they cannot be expected to know what is required of them on the job without proper training. Gone are the days when a new employee was issued a uniform, a badge, and a set of keys, and sent to work

EXHIBIT 13.3
Although the correctional conglomerate offers a wide variety of challenging positions as well as job security, recruitment has often been hampered by a number of issues. To address this problem on a national level, a new website is under development, *discover-corrections.com*.

with no further instruction than "Good luck!" Officers are no longer relegated to learning the job through "helpful" inmates. Correctional work is not only more complex today, but also governed by a multitude of legal restrictions and organizational policies with which staff are expected to comply. When an untrained officer is involved in a situation that results in liability claims, the courts have been increasingly prone toward holding the employing agency liable for damages, using a "failure to train" rationale.

The American Correctional Association's entry-level officer standards call for a minimum of 160 hours of training within the first year of employment (with at least 40 of the 160 hours completed before job assignment), along with an additional 40 hours each year thereafter.[54] Given the complex demands and legal liability of correctional work today, these standards are just that—minimal. Moreover, unlike state certification statutes, ACA standards do not carry the weight of law. Although any correctional facility hoping to achieve ACA accreditation must meet these requirements, when only the basic mandate is met, the minimum required becomes the maximum provided.

The Professional Training Model

It is one thing to mandate a certain number of training hours for entry-level preparation, but quite another to assure that the training is provided in a timely manner. With pressures to fill existing vacancies quickly, the *historic approach* to training has been to immediately place new recruits directly on the job, postponing their enrollment in the academy until they could be spared to attend. Needless to say, once employees become a part of the workforce, they tend to become "indispensable," and sparing them at any time creates a hardship.

Most states now prohibit this approach, requiring preemployment training to be completed before job assignment. But all states do not cover jails in their training standards, and some may allow a designated grace period during which new recruits can legally work prior to enrollment in the training academy. Among the numerous disadvantages of postponing training, increased liability is the most significant.

Beyond legal vulnerability, lack of preemployment training puts officers in a very tenuous position. In essence, they are struggling to cope with a job where they are unsure of what rules to enforce, what behaviors are prohibited, and what actions to take. This can promote a dangerous reliance on the inmates for guidance. In addition, untrained officers do not tend to make receptive recruits when they finally do go to the academy, especially if they have already developed inappropriate work habits which must then be "unlearned."

For these and many other reasons, correctional organizations today are more likely to use the *traditional approach* to training. As shown in Exhibit 13.4, the traditional protocol that is now more widely accepted is to send recruits to training immediately upon employment. Thus, they are not assigned to work until successful completion of the academy. This is certainly a vast improvement over

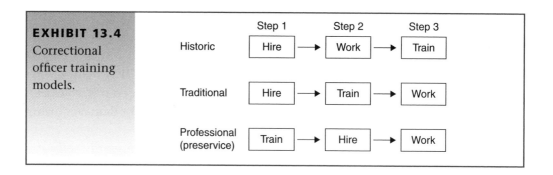

EXHIBIT 13.4 Correctional officer training models.

historic practices. But there are two fundamental drawbacks to the traditional approach: first, what it is costing the organization fiscally, and, second, what it is costing the field in terms of recognition as a profession.

Fiscally, the traditional approach is very costly. Since recruits are hired before training, everyone is on full salary throughout the academy, which can become extremely costly. In fact, custody and security expenses represent the largest component of correctional operating budgets,[55] most of which consist of personnel costs. Given the fact that corrections has routinely been underfunded, the potential for reducing such expenditures is appealing.

But perhaps even more important is what the traditional approach is costing in terms of corrections becoming recognized as a profession. The professionalization of corrections is a commendable goal that has been supported vigorously by virtually every state and national organization representing correctional personnel throughout the country. Realistically, however, it takes far more than vocal support to make it happen. Among other things, procedures for enacting and enforcing standards, licensing, and certification must be implemented.

One of the consistent hallmarks of any established profession is that the education, training, and certification mandated for entrance are required before employment. For example, a person interested in teaching would not apply to the school board and then expect to be sent to college. Someone interested in nursing would not apply to a hospital and then expect to be enrolled in nursing school. Those in occupations with state licensing requirements must meet established provisions before they can obtain their "license to practice."

It is therefore for both fiscal and professional reasons that some agencies are now turning to the **professional (or preservice) training model**. As with the traditional approach, recruits are fully screened to assure that they meet state and agency hiring standards before academy entrance. But that is where the similarity ends. As in existing professions, recruits are not hired under this model until they successfully complete the training necessary to be certified as correctional officers. The major advantage of this form of preservice training is therefore a combination of fiscal savings and the promotion of corrections as an acknowledged profession. As shown in Exhibit 13.4, the priority of training also increases correspondingly as the field moves from the historic to the traditional and, finally, to the professional/preservice approach.[56]

professional (or preservice) training model: requiring successful completion of entry-level training prior to employment, as in established professions.

Professional Certification

An additional step toward professionalization was taken early in the twenty-first century by the American Correctional Association with the development of its national certification program for correctional staff.[57] Designed to promote professionalism, encourage continued learning, and enhance the image of correctional personnel, this initiative offers employees the option of becoming certified, just as facilities can become accredited. After meeting specific prerequisites and passing a written exam, personnel working in either adult or juvenile corrections can be certified at one of four levels—officer, supervisor, manager, or executive—depending on their job classification (with additional specialty certifications available in certain areas). Just as in established professions, successful candidates subsequently must complete additional training or continuing education requirements in order to maintain their status and periodically renew their certification. While this process simply represents a "starting point for the arduous journey along the long road toward professional recognition," it is one step in that direction.[58]

LINE AND STAFF SUPERVISION

In most jobs, a new employee would have to work for some period of time at the operational level before becoming a supervisor. But, unlike entry-level employees in other occupations, beginning correctional, probation, and parole officers are immediately charged with supervisory functions—since they have legal authority over offenders. In that sense, officers are **line (or field) supervisors**—that is, they

line (or field) supervisors: entry-level employees who supervise offenders.

EXHIBIT 13.5 Becoming professionally certified in corrections requires requisite training and work-related credentials, along with successfully completing a certification examination.

supervise offenders at the line level of institutional operations or in the field (as in the case of probation or parole). They, in turn, are supervised by personnel at the next level of the organizational hierarchy, who are considered **staff (or first-level) supervisors**, since they represent the first level in the chain of command that has supervisory authority over other staff members. Within institutional corrections, staff supervisors are generally personnel at the rank of corporal or sergeant. Since they represent the organizational rank through which managerial policies are translated into operational practices, their capabilities will have a direct impact on how effectively policies are implemented.

To supervise inmates, officers must be able to motivate, discipline, direct, train, and evaluate behavior. To do so, they must be skilled in oral and written communication, judgment, sensitivity, leadership, and the like. But what is required of the first-level staff supervisor? The answer is essentially the same. Undoubtedly, staff supervisors have certain additional responsibilities, such as communicating with upper-level management, allocating personnel on a shift, and maintaining payroll records. In terms of their fundamental supervisory functions, however, there is a great deal of similarity.

In essence, both are supervising people—regardless of whether those people are offenders or officers. If a punitive or autocratic approach is learned at the entry level when supervising inmates, it is likely to be passed on to subordinates as one is promoted up the ranks. Thus, officers are likely to reflect the supervisory style of their own supervisor. Improving the supervision of offenders is therefore, in many respects, closely related to improving the supervision of officers. Staff members are entitled to be treated with no less equity and respect than would be expected of them in their supervision of offenders. And they are more likely to fulfill those expectations if they, in turn, receive appropriate treatment from their own supervisors.

Motivation

One of the most critical elements of good supervision is stimulating subordinates to perform at the best of their ability. This is what is known as motivation. People can be motivated either *externally* or *internally*. External motivators are rooted in the theory that behavior is shaped by how the supervisor responds to it. Responses include either rewards or punishments.

When personnel are treated in a manner that relies heavily on such negative external controls as punishment, they can become just as "institutionalized" as the inmates. On the other hand, when internal motivations are tapped, personnel are more likely to do a good job simply for the intrinsic benefits of doing so—such as feeling good about themselves, taking pride in their accomplishments, and enjoying a sense of personal satisfaction.

Traditionally, rewards in corrections have been rather narrowly interpreted as higher salaries, promotions, more benefits, or preferred assignments. What is often overlooked is the simple reward of a "pat on the back" for a job well done—in other words, some indication that the supervisor recognizes and cares about the employee's effort and quality of work.

As we saw earlier, Maslow's hierarchy demonstrates that people who have progressed beyond basic physiological and safety levels are not inclined to be motivated by money or similar extrinsic rewards. As the correctional workforce increasingly becomes composed of those with higher education and greater career options, the strength of these motivators is diminished. If supervisors are not able to create the type of environment where such employees feel needed, appreciated, and recognized, even the most lucrative benefits are unlikely to be powerful enough to motivate them to do their best. Essentially, when employees do not feel that management listens to them, involves them in decision-making, or values their opinions, "it is not surprising to find them becoming uncommitted and disengaged."[59]

Discipline

Added to the drawback of extrinsic motivators is the fact that, from the employee's perspective, it appears that punishments are applied more readily than rewards. It may well take years for even the most competent employee to obtain a salary increase, promotion, or additional benefits. On the other hand, when something inappropriate is done, the disciplinary system is activated much more rapidly. This is not meant to imply that some form of discipline is not at times warranted and necessary. Even when that is the case, however, the employee is considerably more likely to view disciplinary action as equitable when the supervisor's focus is not limited to punishing what was done wrong on a few occasions, but also includes praising what was done right on far more occasions.

Focusing on fear, threat, or intimidation becomes counterproductive—with employees as well as inmates. Rather than stimulating appropriate behavior, such negative conditions are more likely to generate low levels of morale, commitment, and effort. Again, that does not mean that supervisors should avoid correcting improper performance. But criticism should be constructive rather than destructive, emphasizing growth and development as opposed to suspicion and mistrust. Overall, the process of disciplining staff is not unlike that advocated in earlier chapters for inmates—that is, it should be carried out in a manner which is firm, fair, and consistent.

It is, however, somewhat more difficult to ensure that these criteria are met when disciplining staff. Because management staff is selected from the rank and file, a co-worker today can become one's supervisor tomorrow. Needless to say, it is never easy for a newly promoted supervisor to maintain neutrality and objectivity with former peers.

LEARNING GOALS

Do you know:

18. the difference between leaders and managers?

19. what crisis management is and why it is often characteristic of correctional agencies?

20. the relationship between proactively planning and reactively responding?

CORRECTIONAL MANAGEMENT AND LEADERSHIP

It is, of course, at the upper administrative ranks that overall direction is provided to guide everyone's efforts throughout the correctional system. Just as line officers tend to emulate the style of their supervisor, the agency's leadership and upper-level **management** set the tone for the entire organization. However, managers also have much more comprehensive responsibilities than supervisors, since they are responsible for organizing, administering, and coordinating a system designed to achieve the agency's goals. As such, they are responsible for systematically guiding each phase of the administrative process—from planning to budgeting, staffing, and program direction. But it should also be noted that, although certain officials carry the title of "managers," management is not the sole responsibility of any particular office. In essence, everyone throughout the organization contributes to the process of managing it.[60]

management: the process of organizing, administering, and coordinating a system designed to achieve organizational goals and objectives.

Strategic Planning and Leadership

planning: the art of predicting upcoming challenges and proactively addressing them.

A considerable part of the manager's job involves strategically **planning** how to achieve organizational goals and objectives, since it is planning that provides some degree of control over an agency's destiny. In fact, it is the visionary foresight involved in long-range planning and proactive decision-making that largely sets leaders apart from managers.

Regardless of how many policies are written or how much training is conducted, in the daily administration of a correctional organization, issues are bound to arise that generate conflict or confusion. Effective managers turn controversial issues into opportunities to make progressive change. True leaders proactively anticipate and deal with issues on the horizon before they actually surface and require reactive attention.[61]

Managers focus on keeping the existing system running smoothly, measuring their success by how well goals and objectives are met. But they may get so bogged down in the mundane and immediate matters that their view of the "big picture" is blocked. Leaders, on the other hand, focus more of their efforts on determining where the organization *should be headed* in the future. That is not meant to imply that they overlook the ongoing process for achieving goals and objectives. But, in contrast to managers with their technical emphasis on controlling what is happening "here and now," leaders are creative visionaries who are already contending with the challenges on the distant horizon. In other words, they direct more of their energies toward *leading* the path to the future than *managing* the process of keeping the organization on its present course.

As in many other fields, however, corrections has traditionally been "overmanaged" and "underled."[62] While the mechanics of strategic planning may be addressed at the upper levels of the organization, daily operations are often governed by the old adage "If it ain't broke, don't fix it," especially in times of fiscal cutbacks—when managers are forced to do more with less. But, aside from fiscal limitations, entrenched veteran managers who find change threatening may just want to "keep the lid on." This is understandable in view of external pressures from a turbulent political climate. Political instability contributes to an unwillingness to take risks and, in that type of climate, precedence becomes a good defense. As a result, tradition has a way of becoming ingrained in policy and procedure.

Crisis Management

Moreover, in the short run, it takes much less effort to wait until things fall apart before taking action. It is also more personally stimulating to respond to crisis situations immediately at hand than to plan ahead methodically so that crises can be prevented. For these and many other reasons, corrections has historically tended to take a reactive-oriented approach to **crisis management**. It is apparent that proactively planning is not nearly as enjoyable as reactively responding. But the less an organization does of the former, the more it will need the latter.

crisis management: responding reactively when an emergency occurs that could have been anticipated and avoided.

Management by crisis is not really "managing" anything. It is simply reacting to a situation that is blown out of proportion because of earlier reluctance to be proactive. In other words, the more proactive planning is put off, the more crisis reaction is needed. If nothing was fixed yesterday because it was not yet broken, today and tomorrow will find the manager continually trying to dig out of the resulting "reactive rut."

Decision-making

The manner in which plans are developed will have much to do with how well they can be implemented. Decisions guided by plans that are made by a select few at the top of the organizational hierarchy are likely to encounter resistance—and possibly even active sabotage—as they move down the chain of command toward the point of execution. A paramilitary, top-down approach may be appropriate for jobs that require few discretionary decisions, but work in corrections certainly does not fit that description. To the contrary, broader representation of all ranks in the planning and decision-making process is more likely to promote widespread "buy-in" and staff acceptance. That is because people are more likely to be committed to assuring the successful implementation of decisions they were involved in making.

Nor is the need to expand participation limited to those within the agency itself. Correctional administration differs from other types of public administration in terms of the many external stakeholders to which it must respond, from politicians and policy-makers to community leaders, each representing varying attitudes,

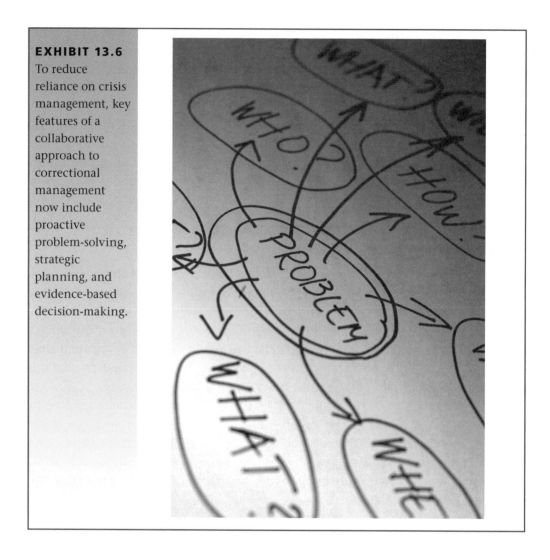

EXHIBIT 13.6
To reduce reliance on crisis management, key features of a collaborative approach to correctional management now include proactive problem-solving, strategic planning, and evidence-based decision-making.

opinions, and beliefs concerning crime and the treatment of criminals. As a result, a significant aspect of correctional leadership is interacting with the external environment to obtain public support for correctional policies and practices.[63]

Organizational Culture

In addition to creating external partnerships, one of the most important internal functions of correctional leaders is setting the tone for the agency's cultural environment. Even simply permitting employees to report for work in wrinkled, unkempt uniforms or letting trash accumulate on facility floors sends clear messages about what is or is not acceptable, whether staff are proud to be working there, and other positive or negative indicators of the organizational culture. Thus, it is largely through administrative actions, reactions, and inactions that powerful messages are communicated to staff which, in turn, shape the organization's culture.

Culture embraces the norms, values, and prevailing beliefs of an organization—i.e., what is considered acceptable or unacceptable, ethical or unethical, appropriate or inappropriate. It affects virtually every aspect of institutional life—from how staff members are treated by management, how they, in turn, treat each other, and ultimately how they treat inmates.[64] In fact, as the next "Close-up on Corrections" illustrates, culture is at the heart of many organizational issues. Since the cultural climate strongly influences behavior throughout the chain of command, it is essential that organizational culture is properly aligned with the agency's vision and mission.

CLOSE-UP ON CORRECTIONS
Understanding Organizational Culture

Without a clear understanding of internal culture, many problems in a correctional organization may inaccurately be blamed on uncompetitive compensation, poor communication, lack of teamwork, high caseloads, workforce diversity, or generational differences. These are often just the symptoms of deeper, more fundamental issues related to organizational culture.

For example, the investigation of the 2002 space shuttle *Columbia* disaster indicated that a melt-down of protective shields was only partially to blame. That was the technical reason. The underlying cause was more a reflection of management expectations than of malfunctioning equipment. Essentially, the tragedy occurred in an organizational culture where launch schedules took priority over safety considerations. Likewise, the congressional hearings related to the events of September 11, 2001, attributed much of the responsibility for the nation's lack of preparedness to intelligence-gathering agencies with isolated, uncooperative, and self-serving organizational cultures. In both cases, investigators called for changing the culture by changing the leadership. That is because competent leadership means being able to shape organizational culture.

Source: Jeanne B. Stinchcomb, Susan W. McCampbell, and Elizabeth P. Layman, *FutureForce: A Guide to Building the 21st Century Community Corrections Workforce* (Washington, DC: Bureau of Justice Assistance, U.S. Department of Justice, September, 2006), p. 19.

When correctional leadership is indifferent to what is going on at the line level, staff members get the message that their work is unimportant, and inmates will be quick to take advantage of the situation. For example, institutions with poor morale are more vulnerable to escape attempts than those with good morale. "And even all of the efforts of competent people at the institutional level can go for naught if the correctional department's central office is marked by incompetence."[65] Such an organizational culture can make even the most modern, well-designed prisons and jails unpleasant places to be—for both inmates and staff.

There is little doubt that the very nature of working in corrections means confronting insufficient resources, uncooperative clients, and an unsupportive public. These drawbacks eventually can take their toll on even the most dedicated personnel. Confronting such inherent obstacles would be considerably less frustrating, however, in a supportive administrative environment with a positive organizational culture.

It is one thing to persevere in the face of an apathetic public and an unappreciative clientele. But staff cannot be expected to maintain peak performance within an organizational culture that is plagued with contradiction, ambiguity, inequity, inconsistency, unethical behavior, or autocratic management.[66] On the other hand, administrators who display visionary leadership, take an active interest in daily operations, and assure that policies and procedures are enforced firmly, fairly, and consistently can create a positive climate, even in a less than desirable physical facility.

Although humane physical conditions are essential, staff are actually the key ingredient to managing any correctional facility effectively. And it is through leadership that the cultural foundation is established which will either uplift and encourage or crush and discourage every organizational employee. That, in turn, will have a decisive effect on long-term results throughout the entire correctional conglomerate.

SUMMARY

The majority of correctional employees throughout the United States work as officers in prisons and jails. Their stereotypical image has been changing as younger, better-educated people and more minorities and women have been entering the field in recent years. Such trends are both a benefit and a challenge to administrators, who must adjust to greater diversity in the workplace as well as meet the changing demands of new generations of workers.

Under Title VII of the Civil Rights Act, employers are prohibited from practicing discrimination. As a result, women have been employed increasingly in correctional agencies, creating conflict between equal employment rights and inmate privacy. Initially, this was resolved by restricting female job assignments to noncontact posts. But that practice has been opposed by males who were denied such preferential positions. The outcome has been a compromise involving broader integration of women throughout the workforce while minimizing intrusion on inmate privacy.

Today's "new breed" of employees with expanded career options may be more likely to join unions or leave unsatisfactory employment. But, until the recent economic downturn, corrections was often plagued by high turnover rates. When management can identify and rectify factors in the work environment that promote dissatisfaction, the organization is likely to experience less attrition, more productivity, and greater employee commitment.

Because there will always be some turnover, there will always be a need for active recruitment. Correctional recruitment has traditionally been hampered by constraints surrounding image, vacancy pressures, and compensation. Although these issues have often been used to justify reduced entrance standards, they are subject to change. Moreover, as corrections moves more toward the attributes of established professions, it will be more likely to embrace both certification standards and preservice training completed prior to employment.

Unlike most entry-level jobs, correctional officers become line supervisors immediately upon assignment. Like staff supervisors, they must therefore be able to motivate, discipline, and direct subordinates. While both rewards and punishments can be used to shape behavior, the latter unfortunately tend to be employed more frequently in corrections. Regardless of what approaches are used, however, it is through supervisors that management policies are translated into operational practices.

While supervisors implement policy, upper-level managers and leaders are responsible for developing it through the process of planning, decision-making, and allocating resources. The foresight of planning is essential to avoid the hindsight of reactively responding. Otherwise the organization falls into a pattern of management by crisis. To insure employee commitment, such plans and decisions are most effectively made with the active participation of those who will be responsible for their implementation.

Ultimately, it is the ability to maintain long-term visionary focus and planning foresight that distinguishes leaders from managers. But visions are merely dreams if not executed. In that regard, it is creating a positive, uplifting organizational culture to fulfill their vision that presents the greatest challenge for future correctional leaders.

FOR FURTHER DISCUSSION

1. Go online to the website of your state's department of corrections and determine what the requirements are for becoming a correctional officer. Given what you have learned about inmates and correctional facilities, debate whether these standards are sufficient.

2. Especially in a male prison, identify what obstacles female correctional officers are likely to face that are not encountered by their male counterparts and discuss how they might be overcome.

3. If you were a judge deciding whether the privacy rights of inmates should prevail over the equal employment opportunity rights of staff, discuss how you would respond.

4. Put yourself in the place of a warden who is faced with a staff member who has engaged in allegedly "consensual" sexual misconduct with an inmate. (The inmate supports the officer's story.) Determine how you would explain to the officer that this behavior is nevertheless inappropriate, as well as what you would do about it.

5. As a prison warden, identify what actions you could take to more effectively prevent staff sexual misconduct.

6. Select three people representing different generations in the workplace (e.g., baby boomer, generation X-er, and millennial). Conduct a debate among them about what qualifications an agency should look for when recruiting entry-level staff.

7. If you are working (even if not in corrections), determine what supervisory or managerial practices at your workplace make you think about quitting. Then determine what could be done to improve your chances of staying.

8. Discuss whether chronic or episodic stressors are more likely to create tension and anxiety for correctional staff.

9. Put yourself in the position of a correctional administrator, and identify what you could do to reduce (and ultimately prevent) job-related stress among your employees.

10. Although union and management often have differing opinions, explain why they fundamentally share mutual interests in the correctional workplace.

11. Debate the merits of increasing educational requirements for correctional employment with a hard-line warden who has a lot of vacancies to fill and limited funds for salaries.

12. Discuss the benefits and drawbacks of the professional approach to entry-level training with a correctional administrator who is considering switching from the traditional approach.

13. Go to the website of the American Correctional Association, determine what is required to achieve professional certification, and discuss whether these requirements are too limited, too elevated, or about right.

14. Use examples to explain the similarity between supervising inmates and supervising staff.

15. The warden you work for maintains that employees don't need to be "praised" for their performance, since "That's what their paycheck is for."

Based on what you have learned about motivation and extrinsic versus intrinsic rewards, challenge the warden's perspective.

16. Explain why "crisis management" is actually an oxymoron.

17. Discuss the importance of organizational culture in terms of recruiting and retaining qualified correctional staff, as well as administering an effective correctional facility.

CHAPTER 14

Legal Issues and Liability

The Constitution does not mandate comfortable prisons . . . but neither does it permit inhumane ones.[1]

Supreme Court Justice David Souter

CHAPTER OVERVIEW

Throughout this chapter, numerous examples are cited of how vigorously the courts have emerged from a long period of reluctance to address correctional operations. In fact, the years of most active intervention generated concern that the judiciary may have been overextending its interference. More recently, the general trend in correctional law has been directed toward achieving an equitable balance between inmate rights and institutional security. Nevertheless, the courts have made it clear that they will respond to valid inmate complaints when administrators are unable or unwilling to do so.

By no means are all of the controversies that result in litigation a reflection of inadequate or uncaring management. There are fundamental differences concerning issues ranging from the morality of the death penalty to methods of inmate discipline that will ultimately be settled in the courts. But it is also important to note that remedies do not need to be strictly dichotomous, "either-or" choices. In an effort to acknowledge the interests of both sides, the courts have attempted to protect the legal rights of inmates and staff while at the same time recognizing the legitimate needs of correctional institutions. However, that has been a relatively recent development. Earlier rulings tended to benefit one side over the other at differing points in the historical development of correctional law.

LEGAL ISSUES

Until the 1960s, corrections was largely insulated from legal scrutiny, and the courts were somewhat hesitant to intervene in correctional operations. During the lengthy period of the

LEARNING GOALS

Do you know:

1. the differences between the hands-off, involved-hands, and restrained-hands phases of correctional law?

2. on what basis the courts were initially reluctant to become involved in inmate litigation?

hands-off approach,[2] the inmate's legal status was virtually that of a "slave of the state"—who, upon conviction, no longer enjoyed the rights, privileges, and immunities of law-abiding citizens.[3] Beyond a limited view of inmate rights, the hands-off phase reflected judicial concerns about disrupting the balance of power between the executive and judicial branches of government, as well as a general acceptance of the presumed expertise of correctional administrators. In other words, during the hands-off phase correctional managers functioned relatively independently, because it was assumed that:

- while criminal suspects were entitled to constitutional rights at the trial phase, the courts would not respond to their post-conviction claims;

- since corrections was designed to benefit the offender, correctional staff would know what was best for the inmate;

- whatever was given to an offender was a "privilege"—not a "right"—and, as such, could be subject to conditions or taken away for any reason.[4]

hands-off approach: judicial reluctance to interfere with the correctional system, which lasted until the 1960s.

Involved Hands (or "Hands-on")

During the 1960s, however, widespread challenges to traditional authority emerged. Formerly disenfranchised groups began to demand equal rights, a voice in government, and protection under the law. It was therefore not surprising to find the courts also directing attention toward those most powerless and unprotected—correctional clients. This expanding recognition of individual rights prompted the **involved-hands (or hands-on) approach** to judicial activism, opening corrections to widespread constitutional review.

involved-hands (or hands-on) approach: a period of active judicial involvement in alleviating deficiencies of correctional institutions through legal action.

EXHIBIT 14.1 During the "involved-hands" phase of correctional litigation, the number of corrections-related lawsuits filed by inmates and their lawyers skyrocketed.

Under such scrutiny, many of the inmate rights discussed throughout the remainder of this section were enacted. Moreover, the emergence of a receptive audience was not overlooked by the inmates. As the inmate population has escalated, so has the number of suits they have filed in federal courts, at least until very recently, as we will see shortly.

Restrained Hands (or "Hands-off")

As the more conservative social climate of the 1980s replaced the liberalism of the 1960s, judicial intervention began to reflect a compromise between the extremes of the two earlier phases. That does not mean the flagrant violations that prompted the hands-on stage are being tolerated. But neither does it mean that management is as severely curtailed as was characteristic of the involved-hands phase. Rather, the **restrained-hands approach** characteristic of the past two decades has been more likely to attempt to seek a reasonable balance between the rights of inmates and the security interests of correctional administrators.

Using this "balancing test," the Supreme Court has ruled that certain restrictions on an inmate's constitutional rights are allowable if they are reasonably related to legitimate correctional interests, such as promoting institutional safety and security.[5] Nor are today's courts as quick to impose their own solutions. When a violation occurs now, they are somewhat more likely to give administrators an opportunity to correct the problem.

restrained-hands approach: judicial efforts to reasonably balance the rights of offenders and the security interests of corrections.

Current Legal Climate

Ever since the Supreme Court pronounced that "the Constitution does not mandate comfortable prisons,"[6] the stage has been set for turning an unsympathetic judicial ear toward inmate litigation. Fueled in part by media-driven denouncements of frivolous lawsuits, along with more conservative judicial appointments and a less tolerant public that has been vocally supportive of "no frills" prisons, the courts have retreated somewhat from their earlier activist position.[7]

As a result, it has become more difficult to mount successful constitutional suits challenging prison management.[8] This is largely because "more control over prisons has been given back to the states, and the courts are displaying more tolerance for minor violations of prisoners' constitutional rights,"[9] or at least they have narrowed their view of what conditions justify judicial intervention. Today the courts seem to require a much more pervasive pattern of wrongdoing to find conditions unconstitutional, and the inmates must shoulder a more substantial legal burden in order to prevail in court. Such trends demonstrate that the case law reported throughout the remainder of this chapter remains subject to ongoing refinement, in keeping with prevailing social, political, and public policy trends.

Impact of Successful Inmate Litigation

Whenever the courts redefine inmate rights, the outcome produces an accompanying redefinition of the power, authority, and liability of correctional staff. For example, when inmate rights are expanded, personnel are affected as well. Their power and authority are subsequently reduced, since they no longer have the autonomy to maintain practices that the courts have ruled as unconstitutional. At the same time, liability is increased, as organizations and their staff who are in violation of constitutional provisions become more vulnerable to civil litigation.

Lawsuits filed by offenders are a source of concern to both administrative and operational staff for other reasons as well. Inmates may petition the courts to seek redress for damages or to challenge practices on the basis that constitutional or civil rights have been violated. Thus, both the employing agency and its individual employees are subject to being named in lawsuits when their actions or inactions caused harm, injury, or death.

LEARNING GOALS

Do you know:

3. how court rulings on inmate rights redefine the power, authority, and liability of employees?
4. the difference between civil and criminal liability?
5. what types of damages can result from being held civilly liable?
6. what vicarious liability is and under what conditions it occurs?

ORGANIZATIONAL AND EMPLOYEE LIABILITY

Litigation can take the form of civil or criminal liability (or both), depending on whether a criminal law was violated. Criminal liability applies when, in the course of performing his or her job, an employee is found to have broken the law and is therefore held accountable in criminal court. For example, an officer who assaults and severely injures an inmate could be held criminally liable if the officer cannot establish that he or she was acting in self-defense.

Being prosecuted for a criminal act is not, however, the only form of liability that could result from this situation. Whether the officer is charged, convicted, and/or punished by the state, the injured inmate can still file a **civil liability** claim. As illustrated in Exhibit 14.2, there are several fundamental differences between criminal and civil law.

Criminal law violations are prosecuted by the state for the purpose of seeking punishment for disruption of social order. In contrast, civil action is initiated by the individual victim (or a group of victims, as in a class action lawsuit) in order to obtain compensation for damages, medical bills, pain, suffering, lost wages, and so on, or to change a particular organizational policy or procedure. Whereas a conviction of guilt in a criminal court may assist in establishing a subsequent civil case, acquittal in criminal court does not automatically absolve the defendant of possible civil liability.

civil liability: being held accountable in a civil court for actions or inactions that resulted in harm, injury, or death.

	Criminal	Civil
Action initiated by	the state	the victim
Invoked as a result of harm caused to	society overall	a particular person or class of persons
For the purpose of	punishment	compensation or organizational reform

EXHIBIT 14.2 Criminal and civil law comparisons.

Damage Awards

If an inmate (or a group of inmates pursuing a class action) is successful in a civil case against a correctional employee or agency, the court can award one of three types of damages:

- *nominal:* an insignificant amount of money (such as $1), which may be accompanied by a "cease and desist" injunction prohibiting similar behavior in the future;

- *compensatory:* a monetary award that is generally equated with the expenses incurred by the victim—to compensate for fiscal losses;

- *punitive:* a substantial monetary award that goes beyond mere compensation in an effort to punish the offender (or offending agency) "through the pocketbook," under the theory that suffering a major economic setback will prevent the behavior from reoccurring.

Since the ability of individual staff members to pay a large monetary settlement is limited, civil suits are often directed toward the employing governmental agency, which obviously has far greater fiscal resources. Since it is often an administrative rule or organizational policy that inmate lawsuits are challenging, most of their lawsuits are not filed directly against line officers. Additionally, an employing agency, supervisors, or administrators can be held liable for the actions of staff working under their command.

Vicarious Liability

vicarious liability: being held indirectly liable for the actions or inactions of another party that resulted in harm, injury, or death.

This involves another form of civil liability, which encompasses wrongdoing beyond one's own direct actions or inactions. Indirect or **vicarious liability** is created when:

- someone else (such as the employee's supervisor) knew or should have known what was occurring or about to occur;[10] but

- that person did nothing to correct the situation; and

- that lack of action was the proximate cause (as opposed to the direct cause) of subsequent harm, injury, or death.

Such vicarious liability can result from a variety of circumstances, such as:

- *Failure to train.* If, for example, in the previously cited case, the assaulting officer had recently been employed and had not yet been sent to the training academy, the officer could claim that he or she was not properly prepared for what to expect on the job and how to react appropriately. If the claim is successful, liability could transfer to the employing agency.

- *Negligent supervision.* In the same case, if the employee's supervisor witnessed the assault and did not intervene, the supervisor could incur liability as well. But a supervisor would not necessarily need to observe the incident visually to be held vicariously liable—if, for instance, the supervisor was well aware that this employee had engaged in assaultive behavior in the past and had taken no corrective action.

- *Negligent employment or retention.* As in the supervisory example, this is a form of the "known or should have known" feature of vicarious liability. Let us say that the employee had a long history of being fired by other correctional institutions for assaulting inmates. The courts could well maintain that the pattern of behavior was apparent had any effort been made to look into previous employment, thus holding the organization liable for negligent employment. If, on the other hand, the employee came into the agency with a clean record, but demonstrated a history of assaultive attacks following employment, the agency potentially could be held liable for negligent retention.

These are among the most difficult cases to defend. While correctional officials prevail in most prison litigation, at least one study indicates that inmates won slightly over half of cases in the category of administrative liability (e.g., failure to train, lack of supervision, deficient policies).[11] Yet, in the daily press of business, organizations and their employees do not always take these possible sources of liability into consideration. For example, look at the scenario presented in the next "Close-up on Corrections" and see if you can determine what, if any, consequences in terms of civil or criminal liability could result.

CLOSE-UP ON CORRECTIONS
Liable or Not?

Officer Johnson arrives on duty for the 11:00 P.M. to 7:00 A.M. shift. Immediately, he realizes that it is not going to be a good night. The sergeant is barking out a constant stream of orders. Phone lines are ringing incessantly. Officers are scurrying off to their posts. Metal is clanging against metal as sallyport gates continually open and close to admit and release coming and going staff. Things look even more chaotic than usual at shift change.

Johnson receives his orders—transporting an inmate from "D" wing to the downtown hospital. The inmate's condition is not exactly an emergency but has been ranked as a high-priority case. Officer Johnson realizes that, to do an outside transportation run, he will be required to carry a weapon, and his annual firearms qualification card expired last month. Momentarily, he debates over whether to just do the run without telling the sergeant, but he decides against it.

"Sarge, I hate to say this, but remember last month when they couldn't spare me to go to the range? Well, my firearms qualification is up."

The sergeant is in no mood to hear complaints or excuses.

"Yeah, well, this is sure a fine time to tell me that! You know what I have here tonight? Nowhere near enough to run this shift, that's what—three out sick, four on leave, and two more off for some training class."

"But, sarge, you know I have to check out a weapon for this run. Can't you give it to someone with a card?"

"Listen, I don't even know where the list is, and does it look like I've got time to hunt for it? Besides, the problem around here is we have too many stupid rules anyway. If that damn phone would just stop. . . ."

"But, sarge. . . ." The sergeant answers the phone, "Control Desk, hold on." Turning to the officer, he says, "Johnson, that's enough! Get going!" The sergeant goes back to the phone; the officer leaves for the transportation detail.

Officer Johnson pulls up to the hospital admission area. It is close to midnight and only a few people are milling around in the vicinity. They appear to be harmlessly going about their business. He breathes a sigh of relief and begins to remove the inmate from the vehicle. Without warning, two armed men emerge out of the shadows. They hit Johnson, force him to the ground, and take off with the inmate. One turns around briefly, pointing his weapon in the officer's direction. Johnson fires his revolver, and an innocent bystander is shot.

In this case, are there grounds for charging:

1. the officer with criminal liability?
2. the officer with civil liability?
3. anyone else with criminal or civil liability? If so, what type of liability would apply? Why?

(Answers appear at the end of the chapter.)

Liability Defense

The best protection against liability is a proactive rather than a reactive approach. It is being continually aware of what is going on within the organization, making it clear what is and is not acceptable through written policies and procedures, and taking all reasonable measures to assure that everyone fully recognizes the inmate's constitutional and civil rights. As in sports, the best defense is a good offense. "By addressing identified problems and concerns, the responsible administrator will sharply reduce vulnerability for civil litigation."[12] Managers, supervisors, and operational staff who avoid taking shortcuts, stay abreast of legal issues, and treat inmates with the same respect that they would desire if roles were reversed will achieve far more insulation from liability than any insurance policies could hope to provide.

THE CHANGING NATURE OF CORRECTIONAL LAW

Needless to say, everyone who works in corrections does not abide by such principles of professionalism. Nor is it always clear just how far inmate rights should be accommodated in terms of the operation of correctional facilities. Often it is only after the courts have decided key issues that correctional personnel actually have clear guidelines to follow. The remainder of this chapter reviews some of these significant areas in which the courts have shaped correctional policies and operational practices.

However, it is important to note that correctional law is continually changing. New cases are being decided on a regular basis and, thus, their resulting impact is always subject to change. In this dynamic environment, discussions of judicial influence on correctional policy can quickly become dated. Cases cited may have been superseded by more recent rulings, pointing correctional practices in alternate directions. The following material is therefore provided as illustrative demonstrations of how legal decision-making has affected correctional policy and practice at one point in time, and not necessarily as definitive statements of the current legal status of correctional practices.

Freedom of Religion

Under the First Amendment of the U.S. Constitution, the right to exercise religious beliefs is protected. Those in free society are readily able to attend whatever religious services they desire, to regulate their diet in accordance with religious practices, to wear or display religious materials, and so on. But enabling inmates to maintain such widespread freedoms would be difficult in a large institution encompassing many different religions and, in some respects, could jeopardize security as well. Thus, in keeping with the balancing test, inmates' freedom to fully exercise First Amendment rights may be reasonably restricted. In deciding to what extent such restrictions are constitutional, the courts have addressed a number of related questions:

- *To what extent can (or should) government subsidize religious activities?* Technically, the First Amendment prohibits state establishment of any religion, which could be interpreted as prohibiting the use of government funds for such religious activities as paying the salaries of chaplains. Yet, at the same time, government itself deprives some citizens of the full exercise of their religious rights—when, for example, they are stationed in remote areas on a military base or confined in a correctional facility. To address this state-created deprivation, the Supreme Court has held that provision of compensatory services in the form of prison chaplains is justifiable.[13]

Whether inmates must be provided with state-compensated clergy representative of their specific faith is, however, another issue. It has been ruled that corrections is not expected to maintain a "full complement" of religious personnel on the payroll but, rather, that a "representative selection" will suffice. This decision is based on the premise that chaplains "are hired to serve the spiritual needs of all prisoners and are not intended to be merely the emissaries of their particular churches."[14]

- *Exactly what qualifies as an actual religion?* To be safeguarded under the First Amendment, it is necessary to establish that the protections being sought do, in fact, apply to the practices of a recognized religion. The definition of *religion* is not limited to conventional faiths. For example, the courts have held that witchcraft meets the test of qualifying as a religion. On the other hand, the courts have refused to grant First Amendment protections to an inmate-created group called Church of the New Song (CONS), whose principles required them to be "served steak and wine from time to time."[15]

- *To what extent is the free exercise of religion protected?* Once it has been established that certain beliefs represent an acknowledged religion, the issue becomes to what degree correctional institutions can interfere with the unrestricted exercise of religious practices. This raises difficulties, since accommodating religious beliefs essentially means providing special treatment for certain groups.

  Some religious principles are relatively uncomplicated and easy to comply with in confinement. When Catholics were prohibited from eating meat on Fridays, for instance, it was not any major imposition to schedule fish to be served. On the other hand, pork is inexpensive and therefore frequently used in institutional meals. Both Jewish and Black Muslim religions have challenged this practice, although their claims "have met with mixed success because the dietary requests may pose both logistical and economic problems to prison administrators."[16]

  Generally, the courts have favored accommodating pork-free diet restrictions where those holding such religious principles represent a significant portion of the inmate population. However, it has also been held that eliminating pork completely from institutional menus is not required if inmates are provided with a sufficient variety of foods to enable them to "obtain a nutritionally adequate diet without violating their religious beliefs."[17] In deciding these cases, the administrative ease or difficulty of providing special diets will be a significant factor, as vividly portrayed in the next "Close-up on Corrections."

CLOSE-UP ON CORRECTIONS
Diet Too Complicated

A New York federal court refused to order the New York Department of Correctional Services to meet the dietary demands of Rastafarians (. . . a religion with roots in the culture of Jamaica). The demands were quite complex and included such things as no meat, sometimes (depending on the sect) no canned foods or dairy products, no foods treated with nonorganic pesticides or fertilizers, and food only cooked in natural materials, such as clay pots.

It made no difference to the court that the prison system provided Orthodox Jewish inmates with kosher or neutral diets and some special dietary accommodations for Muslims. The complexity of the Rastafarians' dietary requirements and the financial and administrative burdens that those requirements would create justified the differences [*Benjamin v. Coughlin*, 708 F. Supp. 570 (S.D.N.Y 1989)].

Source: William C. Collins, *Correctional Law for the Correctional Officer*
(Alexandria, VA: American Correctional Association, 2004), pp. 72–73.

- *Do inmates have a right to attend religious services?* Given the wide diversity of religions represented within large institutions, it is difficult to provide formal services for every conceivable group. When such services are offered, however, they cannot be confined to traditional faiths. On this issue, the Supreme Court has noted that an inmate is entitled to a "reasonable opportunity" to pursue his faith comparable to the opportunity afforded fellow prisoners who adhere to more conventional religious beliefs.

  Religions that represent sizeable numbers of inmates have traditionally been permitted to gather for services, provided that doing so does not represent a risk to institutional order and security. In fact, the practice of religion has been extended to enable Native Americans to participate in sweat lodge ceremonies.[18] Generally, courts have upheld the order-and-security constraint, ruling that freedom to exercise religious beliefs is not absolute, but is subject to restriction if prison officials can show that the restriction "is necessary to achieve a compelling government interest."[19]

  In other words, while everyone has the right to maintain his or her own personal religious beliefs, inmates do not have an unconditional right to exercise those beliefs during confinement. On the other hand, using the same reasoning, it has been held that a prison cannot arbitrarily prohibit the practice of an established religion unless it can prove that such practice creates "a clear and present danger to the orderly functioning of the institution."[20]

- *Are there exemptions from hair and beard regulations on religious grounds?* Those serving time in correctional institutions are often required to maintain short haircuts and a clean-shaven face. Officials have justified prohibitions against long hair and beards on the basis that they inhibit ready identification of inmates,

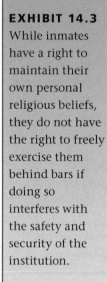

EXHIBIT 14.3
While inmates have a right to maintain their own personal religious beliefs, they do not have the right to freely exercise them behind bars if doing so interferes with the safety and security of the institution.

are unsanitary, and provide potential hiding places for contraband. Some groups, such as Native Americans, have challenged these regulations as a violation of their religious beliefs.

Court decisions have been somewhat diverse on this issue. When it is clearly established that religious beliefs are sincere, it is possible that the inmate's First Amendment argument will prevail. For instance, in one case involving a Cherokee Indian,

> [t]he court ruled . . . that even if the justifications themselves were legitimate, they were not warranted in this instance because less restrictive alternatives were available. The inmate could be required to pull his hair back from his face in a ponytail, for example, which would prevent his using it as a mask.[21]

But other rulings have upheld haircut and beard rules. A 1992 appellate court decision in the case of a Rastafarian hairstyle illustrates the greater discretion that is currently being delegated to correctional administrators. In that case, the court ruled that "it is not for us to impose our own ideas about prison management upon those who attempt the reasonable regulation of that nearly impossible task. . . . [T]he loss of absolute freedom of religious expression is but one sacrifice required by . . . incarceration."[22] On the other hand, as recently as 2004, the right of Muslim inmates to wear a one-inch beard was upheld.[23]

• *Is there a right to wear or use various types of special attire or articles (e.g., religious medallions, prayer rugs, shawls, or peace pipes)?* Concern for safety and security has also been used as a rationale for prohibiting the use or display of certain religious artifacts (especially those that could potentially be used as or shaped into weapons). In these areas, courts have tended to uphold reasonable regulations that are justified by the need for prison discipline and order. But, again, institutional policies cannot be used to discriminate against a particular religion. When something—such as the wearing of a medal—is permitted for one group, the same consideration must be extended to all denominations under the equal protection clause of the Fourteenth Amendment. Nor can the issue be avoided by arbitrarily prohibiting medals for everyone, unless sufficient reason to do so can be demonstrated.

In summary, while inmates are not entitled to freely exercise their religion behind bars, the courts have upheld some religious practices under certain circumstances. Nevertheless, various restrictions on the exercise of religious freedom within correctional facilities have been upheld when they are justified on the basis of:

• the need to maintain discipline or security;

• the proper exercise of authority and official discretion;

• the fact that the regulation is reasonable;

• the economic considerations involved.[24]

The extent to which correctional practices are defensible according to such criteria will continue to be defined by the courts. As a result, correctional institutions in various states have made faith-based accommodations ranging from diet and fasting to jewelry and clothing.[25]

Additionally, attempts have been made to influence these issues through legislative action in the form of the 1993 Religious Freedom Restoration Act (RFRA). However, even here the Supreme Court prevailed, nullifying RFRA's applicability to corrections four years later.[26] But Congress subsequently narrowed its focus and tried again, with passage of the 2000 Religious Land Use and Institutionalized Persons Act (RLUIPA). While much of this legislation relates to zoning and land use restrictions, it also prohibits correctional officials from "imposing a substantial burden" on the ability of inmates to worship as they please, unless a "compelling government interest" can be demonstrated. Thus far, RLUIPA has survived constitutional scrutiny, with the Supreme Court unanimously ruling in a 2005 case that its protections extended to such nontraditional religious practices as satanism and a racist Christian sect.[27]

Mail Privileges and Censorship

Another First Amendment right enjoyed by those in free society that is subject to modification during confinement is freedom of the press. The nature of incoming mail has been subject to regulation in order to detect contraband, uncover escape plans, avoid material that would ignite violence, and the like. Because of the labor-intensive and time-consuming process of implementing these constraints, further restrictions have often been placed on the volume of incoming mail that an inmate can receive. In addition, outgoing mail has been subject to such limitations as an approved correspondence list.

Today, correctional officials are required to more clearly justify such procedures, and, if an inmate's mail is rejected, case law has established certain due process procedures that must be followed:

- The inmate must be notified of the rejection.

- The letter's author must be allowed to protest the refusal.

- The complaint must be decided by an official other than the one who made the original decision to refuse delivery.[28]

Of course, such restrictions do not apply to correspondence with the courts, attorneys, or public officials. While these types of "privileged" mail cannot be read or censored, they can be opened and physically inspected for contraband in the presence of the inmate.

What is not so apparent, however, is how to handle sexually explicit publications. The First Amendment does not protect either pornographic material or that which "involves a clear and present danger of inciting . . . imminent lawless action."[29] Clearly, materials offering advice on such illegal acts as smuggling contraband, concocting homemade drugs or liquor, and the like can be prohibited. Sexually explicit publications can also be banned "on the grounds that the material is detrimental to rehabilitation and leads to deviate sexual behavior."[30]

Current Decision-making Standards

In deciding inmate cases involving constitutional challenges, courts have fluctuated over the years. Under the "restrained-hands" phase of judicial intervention, decisions have reflected a more balanced approach to the issue of First Amendment rights than inmates had enjoyed just a few decades ago. In fact, some might argue

EXHIBIT 14.4 An inmate's incoming mail may be opened to inspect for contraband—and drug-sniffing dogs can assist in determining what correspondence to open.

Source: Courtesy of the American Correctional Association.

that the "balance" is still off center—but this time judicial opinions are more likely to defer to the expertise of correctional administrators. At least in part, that is a result of the four-pronged standard that the courts now use when determining First Amendment claims:

1. Is the regulation being challenged related to a legitimate and neutral governmental objective?

2. Are there alternative means of exercising the right that are available to inmates?

3. What adverse impact will the asserted right have on correctional staff and other inmates?

4. Is the regulation an exaggerated response to the problem— that is, are less restrictive alternatives available?[31]

For the present time at least, this is the lens through which the courts are viewing both First Amendment claims and other constitutionally based challenges described in the remainder of this chapter.

Search and Seizure

The right to be free from "unreasonable" search and seizure is guaranteed by the Fourth Amendment. But the necessity to maintain institutional security through the detection of

LEARNING GOALS

Do you know:
12. when frisk, strip, cell, and body-cavity searches may be conducted without violating constitutional protections?
13. to what extent visitors can be subjected to searches?
14. under what circumstances employees can be required to undergo drug-testing?

contraband severely limits this right within correctional facilities. Frisk and cell searches can be conducted randomly at any time without cause, unless they are being used for an illegitimate purpose such as abuse or harassment. Inmate pat-downs and cell searches therefore do not tend to fall within Fourth Amendment protections. In contrast, there is a degree of protection against body-cavity searches. Because of their greater intrusiveness, such searches must be based on at least reasonable suspicion and performed only by authorized medical personnel.

Strip searches fall in between these two extremes. The Supreme Court has approved strip searches of inmates "following their exposure to the opportunity to obtain contraband" (e.g., after work release or a contact visit).[32] Moreover, at least one appellate court has ruled that "the correctional institution's interest in maintaining security and deterring and discovering contraband permitted it to conduct strip searches without reasonable suspicion or probable cause."[33]

Visitor Searches. Although visitors are shielded to a greater degree from restrictions and interferences than inmates, the degree of protection again will depend on the intrusiveness of the search. Visitors can be required to walk through a metal detector, to surrender any articles they are carrying to be searched (e.g., briefcases, umbrellas, purses), and to submit to a frisk search. But a strip search cannot be conducted without reasonable suspicion. Moreover, a visitor can refuse to be strip-searched even when reasonable suspicion exists. Although the visitor would then be denied admission to the facility, he or she could simply elect to leave. Nor is it permissible for an institution to require that visitors consent to a strip search as a condition for being admitted:

> A requirement that every visitor "agree" to a strip search as a condition of being allowed to visit jail inmates resulted in an award of $177,000 [in] damages against a Massachusetts sheriff. The court quickly rejected the argument that the visitor "consented" to the searches, saying that . . . the state cannot condition the granting of . . . a privilege (such as visiting) on someone giving up a constitutional right (in this case, the right to be free from unreasonable searches).[34]

Employee Searches and Drug-testing. Like the searching of visitors, that of employees is held to a higher standard than that of inmates. Employees can be frisk-searched on the basis of reasonable suspicion. But, for a body-cavity search, probable cause is needed, along with a search warrant.

Undoubtedly the most controversial area of employee searches in recent years has been the analysis of body fluids for the purpose of detecting drugs. There are no legal prohibitions against preemployment urinalysis for job applicants, and the majority of states now test officer applicants.[35]

Once candidates are hired, however, they enjoy greater due process protections. Although some agencies test on a random basis, the vast majority restrict testing to those employees who are under suspicion of engaging in drug use.[36] But, even when drug-testing is based on suspicious behavior (such as work performance, physical appearance, or absenteeism), the reasonableness of that suspicion under provisions of the Fourth Amendment may be in question.

The primary issues raised in Fourth Amendment challenges to employee drug tests are whether they constitute an actual "search" and, if so, to what extent they are "reasonable." The first matter has been clearly settled—courts have established that urinalysis falls within the provisions of being a search (of the person) and seizure (of bodily fluids).[37] Legal decisions have not, however, been quite so unambiguous in terms of the reasonableness measure.

The New York City Department of Corrections, for example, encountered conflicting decisions about its random testing policy. Initially, the state supreme court found that the program did not adequately protect employees' rights.[38] But, later, an appellate court upheld the tests, maintaining that the department's compelling interest in employee drug abuse outweighed privacy expectations.[39]

In that regard, other courts have similarly held that the duties of correctional officers in medium- and maximum-security prisons involve a "diminished expectation of privacy," and therefore that drug-testing is a reasonable intrusion, due to the nature of the job.[40] A summary of these and other cases concludes that the courts appear to be permitting random testing of correctional personnel who have:

- regular contact with inmates;

- opportunities to smuggle drugs into a facility;

- access to firearms;

- responsibilities that frequently involve driving vehicles that transport passengers.[41]

These job functions are so significant that the agency's interest in detecting drug use supersedes the employee's right to privacy. But, for all other personnel, testing based on reasonable suspicion is the rule, and future litigation will undoubtedly continue to shape the definition of reasonableness.

CRUEL AND UNUSUAL PUNISHMENT

Under the Eighth Amendment, all persons are protected against the infliction of cruel and unusual punishment. This provision is designed to assure that government's power to punish is limited by civilized standards. Thus it has been the basis of inmate challenges to a wide variety of correctional practices, including disciplinary procedures, use of force, and various conditions of confinement ranging from crowding to smoking.

LEARNING GOALS

Do you know:
15. how the courts have ruled on the constitutionality of overcrowding?
16. how far the right to medical care extends during confinement?
17. the difference between a consent decree and a court injunction?
18. how the Prison Litigation Rights Act has affected correctional litigation?

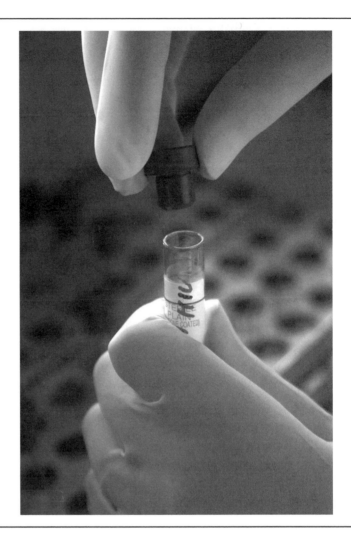

EXHIBIT 14.5
Correctional employees are subject to random drug-testing if they have regular inmate contact, drug-smuggling opportunities, access to firearms, or vehicle operation duties.

Court decisions concerning what does and does not constitute cruel and unusual punishment have also varied over time. During the restrained-hands period, judicial definition of "cruel and unusual" was limited primarily to situations involving extreme barbarity, torture, or excessive cruelty. By the 1980s, however, legal judgments began to reflect "the evolving standards of decency that mark the progress of a maturing society."[42] Yet the pendulum had seemed to shift again somewhat by the mid-1990s, when the current judicial interpretation of cruel and unusual punishment was illustrated by two similar opinions:

- In the first case, an inmate was placed naked in a strip cell without running water for four days, and yet it was found that this action did not violate the Eighth Amendment.

- The second case involved an inmate who was required to sleep on the floor in a poorly heated jail without a mattress or blanket for more than two months. The court said that this "did not deprive the inmate of the minimal civilized measure of life's necessities."[43]

More recently, however, in a 2002 case regarding the use of a hitching post for disciplinary purposes, the Supreme Court made it clear that not only did such practices constitute cruel and unusual punishment but also that the officers involved were not entitled to qualified immunity. (For further details, see the next "Close-up on Corrections.")

CLOSE-UP ON CORRECTIONS
Cruel and Unusual Punishment (*Hope v. Pelzer*, 536 US. 730, 2002)

Mr. Hope was an inmate in the Alabama prison system, which engages in the practice of chaining inmates to a hitching post for disciplinary purposes. He was chained to the post for two hours after getting into a fight with another inmate. His arms were chained above shoulder height, and he experienced pain whenever he tried to move his arms to improve circulation because the handcuffs cut into his wrists. One month later, he was again chained to the post for seven hours with his shirt removed after an altercation with a correctional officer. During the seven hours, he was given water only once or twice, and he was not allowed to go to the bathroom. No clear emergency existed to warrant this treatment, and a correctional officer taunted him about his thirst.

The Supreme Court said there was no justification for this type of punishment and that the correctional officers acted with deliberate indifference to the health or safety of inmates, adding that "the Eighth Amendment violation here is obvious."

Source: Rolando del Carmen, Susan E. Ritter, and Betsy A. Witt, *Briefs of Leading Cases in Corrections* (Cincinnati, OH: Anderson, 2008), pp. 22–23.

Decision-making Guidelines

In making decisions about cases raising Eighth Amendment challenges, courts today are applying certain guidelines that focus on whether the matter being contested:

- shocks the conscience of the court;
- violates the evolving standards of decency in a civilized society;
- imposes punishment that is disproportionate to the offense;
- involves the wanton and unnecessary infliction of pain.[44]

Although these criteria structure judicial decision-making, it is still difficult to predict court rulings in such cases.

Use of Force

Generally, the use of force has been upheld in situations involving self-defense, defense of others, enforcement of institutional regulations, and prevention of escape or a criminal act.[45] This, of course, is assuming that the amount of force used was not excessive under the particular circumstances involved. The U.S. Supreme Court has made it clear that the standard for using force in a prison setting is governed by the Eighth Amendment, ruling that force becomes excessive when it is applied "maliciously and sadistically to cause harm," rather than in a "good faith effort to maintain or restore discipline."[46] In that regard, the outcome of excessive force litigation will primarily depend on:

- whether there was actually a need to use force;[47]

- if so, whether the amount of force used was appropriate and within agency-prescribed policies and procedures;

- what (if any) injuries were inflicted;

- what threat was perceived by responsible correctional officials;

- what efforts were made to temper the use of force.

Upon review by the courts, the answers to these questions will determine whether the use of force in a correctional situation was an operational necessity or a constitutional violation.

Conditions of Confinement

Within the limits of their income, those in free society have the liberty to decide such things as what food they will eat, what clothes they will wear, in what type of residence they will live, with whom they will associate, and when they will visit a doctor or dentist. Needless to say, those incarcerated do not have the freedom to make such choices. As the Supreme Court underscored in one ruling: "An incarcerated person loses more than freedom. The prisoner must depend on the state to make the most basic decisions vital to his or her health and safety."[48]

Everyone, of course, does not agree on how adequately the state makes such decisions. Consequently, inmates have challenged a host of institutional conditions as being in violation of the cruel and unusual punishment provision—particularly when they are confined in an aging, overcrowded facility or subject to inadequate food, clothing, sanitation, or health care. It is obviously beyond the scope of this chapter to consider each of these issues in detail, but when inmates can demonstrate deliberate indifference or intentional mistreatment that creates a substantial risk of serious harm, it is likely that the courts will afford them a remedy. For example, the next "Close-up on Corrections" illustrates some of the gross inadequacies that have brought medical care to the attention of the courts and examines how the Eighth Amendment has been interpreted in this context.

CLOSE-UP ON CORRECTIONS
Inadequate Medical Care

Inmate lawsuits have had a significant effect on the nature of medical care provided in correctional facilities. While truly barbaric issues rarely arise today, consider some of the early cases that "shocked the conscience" of the court:

- An inmate's ear is cut off in a fight. The inmate retrieves the ear, hastens to the prison hospital, and asks the doctor to sew the ear back on. Medical staff, it is alleged, look at the inmate, tell him "You don't need your ear," and toss the ear in the trash. *Williams v. Vincent*, 508 F2d 541 (2d Cir., 1974).

- Medical care for an 1,800-man prison is provided by one doctor and several inmate assistants in a substandard hospital. *Gates v. Collier*, 501 F2d 1291 (5th Cir., 1975).

- Medical services are withheld by prison staff as punishment. Treatments, including minor surgery, are performed by unsupervised inmates. Supplies are limited and few trained medical staff are available in a prison the court terms "barbarous." Twenty days pass before any action is taken for a maggot-infested wound, festering from an unchanged dressing. *Newman v. Alabama*, 503 F2d 1320 (5th Cir., 1974).

Nevertheless, it is almost impossible for a prisoner to succeed on Eighth Amendment grounds if some treatment was provided, even if it was inappropriate or inadequate. To violate the Constitution, the medical care must "shock the conscience," as opposed to being merely negligent. However, simply because a court rules that inadequate care does not rise to the level of an Eighth Amendment violation does not mean that it is an appropriate standard of care. To the contrary, it is simply not so utterly without merit as to fall below the constitutionally established minimum standard [as the following account of an inmate attests].

Source: Adapted from William C. Collins, *Jail Design and Operation and the Constitution: An Overview* (Longmont, CO: National Institute of Corrections, 1998), p. 36.

When I first entered prison, everyone told me how lucky I was to get free medical. I was told I had it made. I even remember a news story I saw on television about a man who had cancer and couldn't afford the treatments. He entered a store, pointed a gun at the clerk, and demanded money. . . . Immediately after, the robber put the gun away and told the clerk to dial 911 and say he was just robbed. He was arrested and went to jail. Then the TV commentator said "and now he will go to prison and get his treatments for cancer." *Yeah right*!

Medical in prison is not what everyone believes it to be. One is given the least costly, least care possible. If you have long-term treatment needs, you will get little and be told to deal with it. You will have to *beg* for all types of care. Medical care in prison is like it is in the third world. . . . If you need long-term medical or dental care, forget it. You might suffer for years, only to be told you will have to have the problem fixed when you get out, if you don't die first.

Source: K.C. Carceral, *Behind a Convict's Eyes: Doing Time in a Modern Prison* (Belmont, CA: Wadsworth/Thomson Learning, 2004), pp. 100–101.

The inadequacy of specific living conditions is often a result of the overall deterioration of services that accompanies institutional crowding. But in and of itself, crowding has not been found to be an Eighth Amendment violation, as was illustrated in two **landmark cases** on this subject:

landmark cases: key legal decisions that have shaped correctional policies and procedures.

- In *Bell v. Wolfish*[49] the court held that there is no constitutional principle requiring "one man, one cell."

- In *Rhodes v. Chapman*[50] no evidence was found that double-celling either "inflicts unnecessary or wanton pain" or is "grossly disproportionate" to the severity of crimes warranting imprisonment.

Double-bunking has not been considered unconstitutional unless it becomes intolerable in combination with other conditions. In such cases, a primary question often has related to whether the **totality of conditions** resulting from a crowded institution meets the test of being cruel and unusual.

totality of conditions: the complete array of living conditions to which offenders are exposed in a correctional facility.

More recently, however, the Supreme Court has signaled that it does not require a culmination of unbearable conditions to rise to the level of a constitutional violation but, rather, that deficiencies involving such basic human needs as food, clothing, shelter, sanitation, safety, and medical care can be considered independently when deciding Eighth Amendment cases.[51] In some situations, this has resulted in an individual action or a particular correctional practice failing to pass the scrutiny of judicial review. But a combination of factors can also produce "deprivation of a single, identifiable human need such as food, warmth, or exercise; for example, a low cell temperature at night combined with a failure to issue blankets."[52] On the other hand, overall conditions of confinement do not constitute cruel and unusual punishment when no deprivation of a specific human need can be verified.

It is one thing to be confined in tight living quarters. The courts seem relatively willing to accept that situation. It is a completely different matter, however, when accommodating too many inmates also jeopardizes some other aspect of their well-being—such as health, safety, or sanitation. That additional complication the courts have been increasingly reluctant to tolerate.

LEGAL AND ADMINISTRATIVE REMEDIES

When it appears futile to contest such allegations, correctional officials can enter a consent decree, essentially agreeing to take remedial action. If, however, the agency elects to contest the issue and the inmate's claim is ultimately successful, the court can issue an **injunction** requiring that specified deficiencies be corrected within an established timeframe. Moreover, injunctions can declare a whole facility to be unconstitutional. In fact, they can even extend to include all of the institutions within the state's entire department of corrections.

injunction: a judicial response to a lawsuit whereby correctional officials are required to rectify specified deficiencies in a given period of time.

Legal actions challenging conditions of confinement have achieved a significant influence in terms of making improvements in the standard of living within correctional institutions. (See the upcoming "Close-up on Corrections" for a list of landmark cases.) Perhaps the most significant contribution of legal action, however, has been the efforts it has generated to avoid lawsuits by more proactively addressing legitimate complaints. Without inmate access to the courts, there might never have been as much incentive to employ **administrative remedies** to reduce litigation, such as formal grievance procedures.

Today, courts will not hear a case until the complainant has exhausted all such internal administrative remedies. For the inmates, this alternative can produce desired results more quickly, without having to go to court. For correctional officials, it can reduce the costly and time-consuming process of becoming entangled in lengthy litigation.

administrative remedies: formal mechanisms used in correctional institutions to reduce potential litigation.

CLOSE-UP ON CORRECTIONS
Landmark Cases Shaping Correctional Law

Conditions of Confinement

Rhodes v. Chapman, 452 U.S. 337 (1981): Double celling of prisoners does not, in itself, constitute cruel and unusual punishment.

Wilson v. Seiter, 501 US. 294 (1991): "Deliberate indifference" is required for liability in conditions of confinement cases.

Woodford et al. v. Ngo, 548 U.S. 81 (2006): Under the Prison Litigation Reform Act, prisoners must first exhaust all administrative remedies, following proper procedure, before they can sue concerning prison conditions in federal court.

Court Access

Johnson v. Avery, 393 U.S. 483 (1969): Prison authorities cannot prohibit prisoners from helping other prisoners prepare legal writs unless they provide reasonable alternatives by which inmates can have access to the courts.

Bounds v. Smith, 430 U.S. 817 (1977): Prison authorities are required to assist inmates by providing meaningful access to the courts.

Disciplinary Hearings

Wolff v. McDonnell, 418 U.S. 539 (1974): Inmates are entitled to due process in prison disciplinary proceedings that can result in the loss of good time credits or in punitive segregation.

Superintendent, Walpole v. Hill, 472 U.S. 445 (1985): Disciplinary board findings that result in the loss of good time credits must be supported by a "modicum" of evidence to satisfy due process requirements.

Use of Force

Hudson v. McMillian, 503 U.S. 1 (1992): Use of excessive physical force against a prisoner may constitute cruel and unusual punishment even though no serious injury results, if that force was used "maliciously and sadistically" to cause harm.

Protection from Injury

Farmer v. Brennan, 511 U.S. 825 (1994): A prison official is not liable for injury inflicted on an inmate by other inmates "unless the official knows of and disregards an excessive risk of harm."

Medical Care

Estelle v. Gamble, 429 U.S. 97 (1976): "Deliberate indifference" to inmate medical needs constitutes cruel and unusual punishment.

Washington v. Harper, 494 U.S. 210 (1990): A prisoner with serious mental illness may be treated with antipsychotic drugs against his will.

Freedom of Religion

Cruz v. Beto, 405 U.S. 319 (1972): Inmates must be given a reasonable opportunity to exercise their religious beliefs.

O'Lone v. Estate of Shabazz, 482 U.S. 342 (1987): Prison policies that in effect prevented inmates from exercising freedom of religion are constitutional because they are reasonably related to legitimate penological interests.

Freedom of the Press

Beard v. Banks, 542 U.S. 40 (2006): A Pennsylvania prison policy that denies dangerous inmates access to newspapers, magazines and photographs does not violate the First Amendment because it is adequately justified by prison officials.

Thornburgh v. Abbott, 490 U.S. 401 (1989): Prison regulations regarding receipt of publications by inmates are valid if reasonably related to a legitimate penological interest.

Visitation

Block v. Rutherford, 468 U.S. 576 (1984): Prisoners have no constitutional right to contact visits or to observe shakedown searches of their cells.

Overton v. Bazzetta, 539 U.S. 126 (2003): Restrictions on prison visitations are reasonable if they bear a rational relation to legitimate penological interests.

Standard for Determining Violation of Constitutional Rights of Inmates

Turner v. Safley, 482 U.S. 78 (1987): A prison regulation that impinges on inmates' constitutional rights is valid if it is reasonably related to legitimate penological interests.

Source: Rolando del Carmen, Susan E. Ritter, and Betsy A. Witt, *Briefs of Leading Cases in Corrections* (Cincinnati, OH: Anderson, 2008), pp. xv–xxvii.

Frivolous Lawsuits

No longer is there any doubt that corrections cannot overlook the legitimate health and safety needs of those entrusted to its care. But not all inmate-initiated litigation has been either fruitful or meaningful. In fact, some maintain that inmate lawsuits have gotten out of control.[53] (In that regard, the next "Close-up on Corrections" features some of the frivolous claims that would be humorous were it not for the time and costs which they consumed.)

CLOSE-UP ON CORRECTIONS
Frivolous Inmate Lawsuits

While the following examples are absurd, keep in mind the fact that many inmate lawsuits are meritorious and have led to significant legal gains against the otherwise unrestrained power of prison officials:

- A Texas inmate filed twenty-two complaints alleging civil rights violations, including violations of his right not to be required to walk barefoot across a cold floor and not to be issued pants that are too small (*Moody v. Miller*);
- A New Jersey inmate claimed he was taken to the Eye, Ear and Speech Clinic, where the state unlawfully injected him in the left eye with a radium electric beam, and that someone now talks to him on the inside of his brain (*Searight v. N.J*);
- A Mississippi inmate sues for not receiving his scheduled parole hearing, although he was out on escape when the hearing was scheduled (*Young v. Murphy*);
- A California inmate says his meal was in poor condition, claiming his sandwich was soggy and his cookie was broken (*Brittaker v. Rowland*);
- A Florida inmate who murdered five people sues after lightning knocks out the prison TV satellite dish and he must watch network programs, which he says contain violence, profanity and other objectionable material (*Jackson v. Barton*).

Source: "Inmates' Frivolous Legal Actions," available at http://www.lectlaw.com/files/fun30.htm (accessed June 10, 2010).

In response, congressional action has been taken to stem the tide of inmate lawsuits through the 1996 **Prison Litigation Reform Act** (PLRA). First and foremost, the PLRA mandates that inmates exhaust all administrative avenues (including every step in prison grievance procedures) before filing a lawsuit. Additionally, this legislation:

- requires inmates to pay a federal court filing fee and limits the award of attorneys' fees in successful lawsuits;

- encourages conducting court proceedings by telephone or video conference (to discourage those filing cases merely to get a trip outside);

- requires judges to screen all inmate complaints against the federal government and immediately dismiss those deemed frivolous or without merit (good-time credits prisoners earn toward early release could be revoked if they file a malicious suit or present false testimony);

- bars prisoners from suing the federal government for mental or emotional injury unless there also was a physical injury.[54]

Prison Litigation Reform Act: federal legislation that, in part, seeks to reduce frivolous inmate lawsuits and curtail court intervention into correctional practices.

Since the PLRA limits the number of suits that can be filed, highly litigious inmates can be prevented from filing any future claims, even those that are potentially legitimate. Overall, this legislation attempts to deter inmate filings, punish those who file frivolous suits, and streamline the litigation process.[55] It has also encouraged states to identify alternatives to litigation through such options as inmate grievance procedures, third-party mediation, and the use of ombudsmen.[56]

Some of the provisions of the PLRA apply only to federal inmates. However, Exhibit 14.6 indicates that this legislation does seem to have had a restraining effect on the filing of petitions by state prisoners as well. The year before the Act was passed (1995), courts throughout the U.S. were burdened with roughly 41,000 prisoner lawsuits, but by 2005 the number had decreased to about 23,000, despite a 45 percent increase in the inmate population during that time.[57] Moreover, the reality is that the vast majority of inmate petitions are actually dismissed, and U.S. district courts very infrequently rule in favor of inmates (in less than 2 percent of their cases).[58] As a result, some inmates complaining about mail service, food quality, and denial of dessert have already lost good-time credits.[59]

National statistics also show that, even though the number of petitions filed by inmates in federal district courts has been increasing, the rate has declined substantially—from 72.7 cases per 1,000 prisoners in 1980 to 19 cases in 2000.[60] Moreover, responding to a survey, nearly three out of four state departments of corrections indicated that the filing of federal civil rights cases had decreased since passage of the PLRA, with some states citing "dramatic reductions."[61] While some

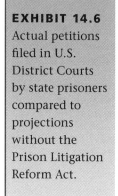

EXHIBIT 14.6

Actual petitions filed in U.S. District Courts by state prisoners compared to projections without the Prison Litigation Reform Act.

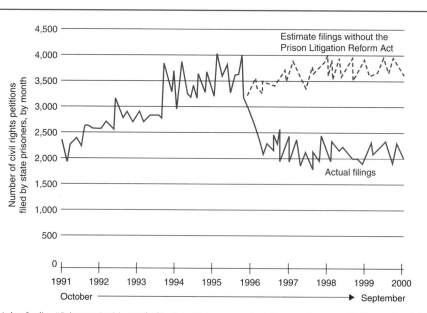

Source: John Scalia, "Prisoner Petitions Filed in U.S. District Courts," *Bureau of Justice Statistics: Special Report* (Washington, DC: U.S. Department of Justice, 2002), p. 6.

applaud this outcome, others take a considerably dimmer view of the PLRA, citing its passage as "the most profound blow to the prisoners' rights movement."[62]

Overall Results of Litigation Reform

The combined impact of such legislation and recent court decisions has been to "set the bar a bit higher for inmates with legitimate complaints and to reduce the number of frivolous complaints that will survive the process."[63] But not everyone views such declining litigation in a positive light. As some lawyers have cautioned, "the benefits of reduced court intervention may carry a heavy price," costing correctional officials one of their major allies in addressing overcrowding and deteriorating facilities.[64] It has also been ruefully observed that a more proactive approach could have curtailed the problem from the onset: "Much of the federal litigation might have been avoided over the past quarter century if state and local governments had met their responsibilities to correctional institutions in the first place."[65]

CAPITAL PUNISHMENT

Thus far, this discussion of inmate litigation has been limited to challenges directed toward some aspect of the restraints or conditions accompanying incarceration. Obviously, inmates also initiate lawsuits in an attempt to overturn their conviction or alter their sentence. These types of cases do not affect the management or operation of correctional facilities. However, because of its Eighth Amendment implications, as well as the widespread controversy it has generated, one particular focus of such appeals requires further consideration—that is, of course, the death penalty.

LEARNING GOALS

Do you know:
19. the arguments for and against capital punishment?
20. to what extent capital punishment has a deterrent effect?
21. how the Supreme Court has ruled on the constitutionality of capital punishment?

The high point of capital punishment occurred during the sixteenth and seventeenth centuries, when tens of thousands of people were put to death—for offenses ranging from murder to failing to remove one's cap in church. Nor were children spared. In Colonial Massachusetts, children could be executed for cursing a parent,[66] in 1801 a 13-year-old child was hanged in England for stealing a spoon,[67] and by 1810 over 200 crimes still remained punishable by death.[68] In the U.S., the youngest person executed during the twentieth century was 14-year-old George Stinney, who was put to death in Texas for murder.[69]

Current Practices

Today, capital punishment is applied much more selectively. Nevertheless, in 2009 there were some 3,173 inmates under sentence of death, ranging from their early twenties to over 65.[70] Although annual executions have yet to reach pre-1950 levels (see Exhibit 14.7), California held the largest number of death row inmates (668), followed by Florida (391), and Texas (356).[71]

Most of those sentenced to death are white (56 percent) males (98 percent), and many have not completed high school (50 percent).[72] While blacks are disproportionately represented, the Supreme Court has been reluctant to address the potential of racial discrimination in sentencing decisions.[73] (In fact, research points toward race of the victim as the most significant factor in terms of racial bias, with those accused of killing a white victim significantly more likely to be sentenced to death.)[74] However, in 2002, the Court did overturn the death penalty for those who are mentally retarded, and in 2005 prohibited capital punishment for juveniles under the age of 18 at the time of their offense.[75]

In order to assure that all possible due process protections have been provided before a human life is taken by the state, a lengthy appellate process is involved in capital cases. Not only do inmates often file appeals on their own behalf, but a sentence of death is subject to automatic review. As a result, death row prisoners have been awaiting their fate for an average of over 14 years,[76] isolated in the closely controlled confinement of what has been described as "a living death."[77]

In recent years (as described in the next "Close-up on Corrections"), federal legislation has toughened standards for review, set strict time limits, and curbed the repeat petitions that often extended the appellate process year after year.[78] Moreover,

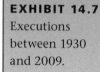

EXHIBIT 14.7
Executions between 1930 and 2009.

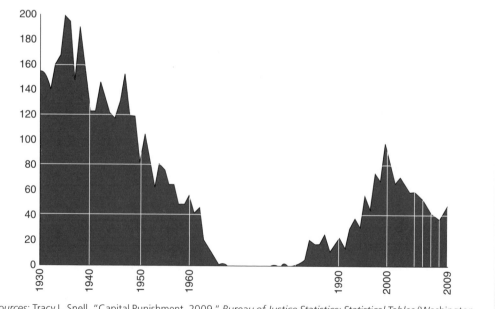

Sources: Tracy L. Snell, "Capital Punishment, 2009," *Bureau of Justice Statistics: Statistical Tables* (Washington, DC: U.S. Department of Justice, December, 2010), p. 1.

all states do not authorize the death penalty. As early as 1847, Michigan became the first state to abolish capital punishment, and by 2010 some 14 states had done likewise.[79] Even in those jurisdictions that have death row inmates, years can go by without an execution. But, when someone is put to death, particularly a high-profile offender, the heated debate over this issue often resurfaces. For example, Karla Faye Tucker's execution in 1998 ignited renewed controversy over the execution of women.

CLOSE-UP ON CORRECTIONS
Expediting Death

Primarily, the Effective Death Penalty Act of 1996 restricts federal court review of a prisoner's challenges to state court decisions. For example, this legislation:

- Presumes that the state court is correct, putting the burden on the prisoner of rebutting the presumption of correctness by "clear and convincing evidence."
- Requires the condemned prisoner to file application for habeas corpus relief no later than 180 days after final state court affirmation of the conviction and sentence, or the expiration of the time for seeking such review.
- Prohibits second or successive appeals.

Thus, the death-sentenced prisoner must file a post-conviction petition with unprecedented speed. . . . Moreover, federal funding for the twenty death penalty resource centers throughout the country was eliminated in 1995, abolishing access to the skilled lawyers who swiftly picked up capital punishment cases after direct appeal was exhausted.

The law prioritizes executing prisoners as quickly as possible, with little regard for constitutional process or innocence. The worst scenario . . . is that condemned prisoners will not be able to find attorneys to handle their cases before the filing period expires. They will then be barred from presenting claims in federal court, regardless of their merit, thus denying them the right to habeas corpus review. Alternatively, at the last minute, the desperate prisoner, crippled by ignorance, may cobble together a poorly researched, poorly argued petition that is doomed to fail. In either case, he or she dies.

Source: Compiled from Lane Nelson, "The Great Writ—Re: The Condemned," in Lane Nelson and Burk Foster, eds., *Death Watch: A Death Penalty Anthology* (Upper Saddle River, NJ: Prentice Hall, 2001), pp. 121–123, 126.

Death Penalty Debates

Capital punishment is a controversial issue that polarizes people on opposite ends of extreme positions. In fact, research over the past 20 years indicates that most of our death penalty attitudes (both pro and con) are based on emotion rather than information or rational argument: "People feel strongly about the death penalty, know little about it, and feel no need to know more."[80] As shown in the next two "Close-up on Corrections," there are staunch advocates for retaining as well as abolishing the death penalty,[81] and evidence does not always support the common myths surrounding this issue.

CLOSE-UP ON CORRECTIONS
Myths and Facts about Capital Punishment

- *Myth 1:* Capital punishment is the only or the best deterrent of capital crimes. *Fact:* There is no scientific evidence that shows that it is a superior deterrent.
- *Myth 2:* Capital punishment has no harmful effects. *Fact:* Scientific evidence shows that capital punishment probably has a counter-deterrent or brutalizing effect. Because capital punishment is so newsworthy, [some] people kill to gain notoriety.
- *Myth 3:* The monetary costs of capital punishment are less than . . . life imprisonment without opportunity for parole. *Fact:* The monetary [legal] costs of capital punishment cases . . . currently average between $2 and $3.5 million more per execution than if the same cases were prosecuted noncapitally. . . .
- *Myth 4:* Innocent people are never executed. *Fact:* In the United States at least 23 people have been legally executed in error during this century.
- *Myth 5:* Capital punishment is no longer administered in a . . . discriminatory [manner]. *Fact:* A massive amount of evidence shows that the death penalty continues to be administered in a discriminatory and illegal way against blacks and the killers of whites.

Source: Robert M. Bohm, "Understanding and Changing Public Support for Capital Punishment," *Corrections Now*, Vol. 1, No. 2 (June, 1996), pp. 1–2. See also Rudolph J. Gerber and John M. Johnson, *The Top Ten Death Penalty Myths: The Politics of Crime Control* (Westport, CT: Praeger, 2007).

CLOSE-UP ON CORRECTIONS
The Death Penalty Debate

	Supporters argue that the death penalty:	Opponents counter that:
Deterrence	Has a deterrent effect—or at least would be a deterrent if it were carried out with greater speed, certainty, and publicity.[82]	This argument raises the question of whether executions can be justified "by the good which their deaths may do the rest of us."[83] More pragmatically, studies do not tend to show significant differences in murder rates between jurisdictions with and without the death penalty, and some research has actually identified a "brutalization" effect that appears to increase homicides after well-publicized executions.[84] In addition, it has been noted that, ironically, support for the death penalty's continued existence depends on its "infrequency, improbability, painlessness, and secrecy."[85]

Crime control	Is needed to protect society from the most serious violent predators, since as long as a murderer is alive "there is always the chance that he or she will murder or harm an innocent person again."[86]	The public could be adequately protected by life without parole and, in any event, murder is a crime with relatively low rates of recidivism.[87]
Retribution	Is fitting retribution or "just deserts"—that is, the most (perhaps the only) appropriate punishment for murder.[88]	Human life is sacred and society does not have the moral right to take it—especially given the potential that an innocent person could be wrongfully executed, or that the death penalty may be applied in a discriminatory manner.[89]
Cost-effectiveness	Saves the taxpayers money in the long run over the cost of lifetime imprisonment.[90]	Research shows that it costs more to put one offender to death than to confine that person at the highest security level for 40 years (with most expenses, surprisingly, incurred at the pretrial phase)[91] and, compared to other inmates, it costs about $90,000 more per year to house someone on death row.[92] Moreover, these expenditures divert funding from other crime prevention initiatives with greater demonstrated ability to effectively protect public safety.
Social utility	Is not completely useless— even if it cannot be defended on other grounds, it may be a legitimate expression of vengeance or aggression by collective society.	If so, the issue becomes one concerning how many people are expendable for this purpose, along with the extent to which such a violent response may be reinforcing further violence rather than strengthening respect for life.

On the basis of empirical evidence, no one has yet argued conclusively that the death penalty is a deterrent to crime. Capital punishment—at least in the manner in which it is presently administered—does not appear to accomplish the purpose of protecting society through general deterrence. When studies have compared homicide rates over the past 50 years between states with the death penalty and adjoining states that have abolished it, "the numbers have in every case been quite similar; the death penalty has had no discernible effect on homicide rates."[93] More recently, statistics indicate that the average homicide rate in death penalty states is actually *higher* (6.6 murders per year per 100,000 people), compared to non-capital states (3.5 murders).[94] In that regard, a former correctional administrator who observed the perpetrators of this act for over half a century concluded that murderers are "often chronic misfits with years of failure behind them," who are "driven by the towering impulse of the moment and incapable of making any fine distinction between [the] consequences of imprisonment versus death."[95]

Constitutional Challenges

Regardless of the public's views supporting or opposing the death penalty, the Supreme Court is ultimately the arbitrator of its constitutionality. Numerous challenges have been filed by death row inmates claiming violation of the cruel and unusual punishment protections of the Eighth Amendment. For many years, these appeals had been largely unsuccessful, until the 1972 *Furman v. Georgia* case.[96] In that ruling, the Supreme Court found that the arbitrary, capricious, and unfair manner in which capital punishment was being applied did represent a constitutional violation.

As illustrated in Exhibit 14.9, this decision had a significant impact on the death row population throughout the country as unconstitutionally imposed death sentences were commuted. Since the Court's action did not ban the death penalty outright, however, a number of states made efforts to rewrite their statutes governing capital punishment in a manner that would be constitutionally acceptable. As a result, in the case of *Gregg v. Georgia*, the Supreme Court subsequently reinstated

EXHIBIT 14.8
Despite numerous legal challenges, the Supreme Court has thus far not ruled against capital punishment on the basis of violating the Eighth Amendment's prohibition against cruel and unusual punishment.

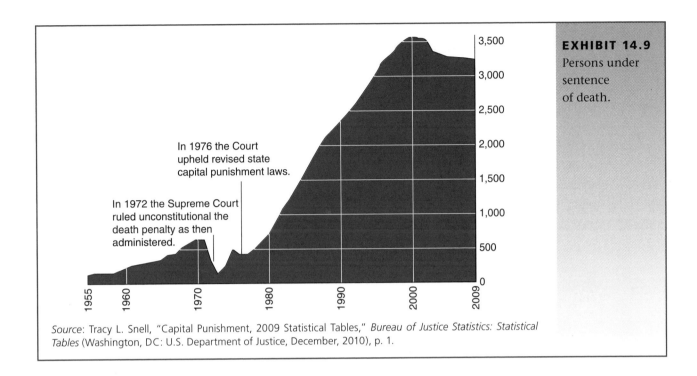

In 1976 the Court upheld revised state capital punishment laws.

In 1972 the Supreme Court ruled unconstitutional the death penalty as then administered.

EXHIBIT 14.9
Persons under sentence of death.

Source: Tracy L. Snell, "Capital Punishment, 2009 Statistical Tables," *Bureau of Justice Statistics: Statistical Tables* (Washington, DC: U.S. Department of Justice, December, 2010), p. 1.

death penalty statutes that contain sufficient safeguards against arbitrary and capricious application.[97] Many of these revised statutes have withstood legal scrutiny and, consequently, the death row population climbed to an all-time high in 2000, as reflected in Exhibit 14.9.

Support for Capital Punishment

In the meantime, public support for the death penalty appears to be waning.[98] At least in part, this may be a result of the high-profile publicity that has accompanied the exoneration of some death row inmates on the basis of DNA analysis. As the next "Close-up on Corrections" explains, such erroneous convictions may occur considerably more often than we realize. The Effective Death Penalty Act is anticipated to have a chilling impact in that regard.

Additionally, it has been suggested that the economy may play a role in reducing support for the death penalty, since it has not gone unnoticed that states could save millions of dollars by abolishing capital punishment. Because of the special housing and security required for death row inmates, along with the extensive appeals process involved in such cases, one state found that substituting life without parole would save $1.3 million per inmate. As one policy analyst put it, "more often than not, the death penalty turns out to be a very expensive form of life imprisonment."[99]

CLOSE-UP ON CORRECTIONS
Righting Wrongful Convictions

In 1994, a congressional judiciary committee researched the possibility of innocent people being executed in this country. Their findings were published in a report titled Innocence and the Death Penalty: Assessing the Danger of Mistaken Executions. It lists 52 death-penalty prisoners from 1975 to 1994 who were released from death row after authorities determined they were innocent. Those were the lucky ones, fortunate enough to have had competent legal counsel and to have been allowed back into court with newly discovered evidence of their innocence. One must wonder how many of the nearly 350 executed since 1975 were innocent and unlucky. . . .

The average length of time between conviction and release was almost seven years for the 52 death row inmates released. Had the Effective Death Penalty Act been passed prior to those 52 people prevailing on their claims of innocence, the majority would have been executed.

Source: Lane Nelson, "The Great Writ—Re: The Condemned," in Lane Nelson and Burk Foster, eds., *Death Watch: A Death Penalty Anthology* (Upper Saddle River, NJ: Prentice Hall, 2001), p. 126.

In the global arena, it has been suggested that international pressure to abolish capital punishment may someday become strong enough to threaten death penalty countries with economic isolation.[100] Internationally, predominant death penalty countries are concentrated in the Middle East, North Africa, and Asia. The U.S. and English-speaking countries of the Caribbean are the only jurisdictions in the Western Hemisphere that retain the death penalty. In fact, the European Union has made the abolition of capital punishment a precondition for membership, and the United Nations Commission on Human Rights has called on all members who have not yet abolished the death penalty to consider suspending executions.[101]

But the U.S. Supreme Court has yet to find capital punishment an Eighth Amendment violation. In that regard, inmates have more successfully invoked the Constitution to challenge the conditions in which they are confined during life than the provisions that constrain their death.

SUMMARY

One of the most prevalent forces shaping correctional policies and procedures in recent years has been the impact of court decisions. Although properly enforced standards may help to protect against litigation, correctional agencies and their employees are subject to civil liability when their actions or inactions result in harm, injury, or death. Beyond direct liability, vicarious liability can occur for failure to train, negligent supervision, or negligent employment/ retention.

The potential for liability has also increased as a result of court rulings. As the Supreme Court began to intervene more actively after a long "hands-off" period, constitutional rights during incarceration were redefined and expanded. Among the First Amendment rights now recognized by the courts are various freedoms related to the practice of religion. However, such protections can be restricted when justified on the basis of institutional order, safety, discipline, or security. Additionally, the freedom to communicate through the mails can be limited. Nor do Fourth Amendment protections against unreasonable search and seizure generally encompass frisk or cell searches. But searches of any kind cannot be employed to abuse or harass inmates. The courts have also recognized personnel drug-testing as falling within the definition of "search and seizure." Although job applicants can routinely be tested, employees enjoy greater safeguards.

Numerous legal challenges have been raised under the Eighth Amendment's prohibition against cruel and unusual punishment. Many of these cases involve institutional crowding. The courts have held that crowding in and of itself does not constitute an Eighth Amendment violation, unless it produces a "totality of conditions" that jeopardizes the inmates' health, safety, or well-being. Some such cases have been settled by voluntary consent decrees. In others, the courts have issued injunctions ordering correctional officials to remedy deficiencies within a given period of time. In an effort to reduce inmate litigation, correctional institutions are initiating more proactive administrative remedies.

In addition to challenging the conditions of confinement, inmate litigation has also sought to overturn the death penalty. Although some states have abolished capital punishment, thousands of prisoners remain on death row. Because of the extreme emotion on both sides of this issue, the death penalty continues to generate considerable controversy. Although the Supreme Court overturned a number of death sentences in 1972 as a result of the manner in which they were implemented, the Court has yet to find capital punishment itself an Eighth Amendment violation. Whether that reluctance will change at some point remains to be seen. In the meantime, the future of the correctional conglomerate will be shaped by the numerous issues, policies, and challenges that are addressed next.

ANSWERS TO LIABILITY CLOSE-UP

1. *Criminal liability.* Since the officer did not intentionally shoot the bystander, it is unlikely that it could be proven that a crime was committed.

2. *Direct civil liability.* Since Johnson raised objections to completing the transportation detail and made it very clear that he was not currently firearms qualified, it is unlikely that he could be held civilly liable. Even if the sergeant later denies remembering

Johnson's verbal objection, the courts could maintain that it is the supervisor's duty to make assignments in a manner consistent with the requisite qualifications (i.e., the supervisor "should have known").

3. *Vicarious liability.* Because the sergeant persisted with assigning Johnson inappropriately despite his protests, grounds potentially exist for holding the sergeant vicariously liable. In other words, the sergeant knew what the situation was, did nothing about it, and that inaction could potentially be construed as the proximate cause of the resulting injury. It is also possible that the agency or other upper-level administrators could be held vicariously liable for "failure to train," since the officer indicated that he had been unable to go to the firearms range when scheduled because the shift was also short-handed at that time. Here, however, it gets somewhat more complicated. If, for instance, the organization had a clear-cut written policy requiring annual firearms requalification and strictly prohibiting the issuance of weapons to anyone without it, liability could be limited to those who actually violated the policy.

FOR FURTHER DISCUSSION

1. Given the current political climate in the U.S., discuss how feasible you think it is that the Supreme Court could revert to the greater judicial activism that characterized the "involved-hands" phase of correctional law. If this were to happen, what implications would it have for corrections, especially in tight economic times?

2. Go online and locate a correctional civil suit that was settled recently. Determine whether the award was nominal, compensatory, or punitive, and, given the facts of the case, argue for and against the court's judgment.

3. Discuss how you would handle the Officer Johnson case if the injured bystander sued and you were the civil court judge handling the case.

4. An inmate has filed a complaint with you, as the warden of a large medium-security prison, about not being able to wear his dreadlocks. He is citing religious discrimination, since Orthodox Jews are allowed to wear their skullcaps, and is threatening to file a First Amendment lawsuit. Determine what additional information you would need to make a decision and, given that information, what your decision would be. Based on past case precedents, do you think your decision would be upheld?

5. An inmate developed a long-standing homosexual relationship with his cellmate, but his partner was transferred to another institution. State regulations prohibit correspondence between inmates, so they are not able to write to each other. They are planning to sue the state, citing

discrimination on the basis of sexual orientation, since married heterosexual couples serving time at different facilities are able to correspond with each other. Use the decision-making standards on page 437 to determine whether or not the state's position is likely to be upheld. Then look up the decision in *Turner v. Safley* (482 U.S. 78, 1987) to see how the Supreme Court ruled in a similar case.

6. In response to security problems and concern about substance abuse among inmates, you have implemented new visiting policies that put a limit of 10 nonfamily members who can be on any one inmate's approved visiting list, prohibited anyone from being on more than one inmate's list, and completely prohibited former prisoners unless they are qualified members of the clergy or attorneys on official business. Inmates are extremely upset about the new regulations and have filed a class action lawsuit. Use the decision-making standards on page 437 to determine whether or not the state's position is likely to be upheld. Then look up the decision in *Overton v. Bazzetta* (539 U.S. 126, 2003) to see how the Supreme Court ruled in a similar case.

7. Put yourself in the position of a strong union leader and argue against random drug-testing for correctional officers. Then play the role of a correctional administrator and refute each of your arguments.

8. In a civil lawsuit, an inmate testifies that he suffered "minor bruises, facial swelling, loosened teeth, and a cracked dental plate" as a result of a beating by correctional officers. He states that the beating took place while he was handcuffed and shackled following an argument with one of the officers, and that a supervisor watched the beating, but merely told the officers "not to have too much fun." Use the decision-making guidelines on pages 428–429 to determine how you would rule in this case. Then look up the decision in *Hudson v. McMillian* (503 U.S. 1, 1992) to see how the Supreme Court actually ruled.

9. Debate the pros and cons of the Prison Litigation Reform Act, from the perspectives of inmates, correctional administrators, and judges.

10. See if you can locate any empirical research that found a deterrent effect associated with capital punishment. In light of the fact that the vast majority of studies have failed to find such an association, discuss why people often think it is a deterrent, and provide reasons to explain why it is not.

11. Argue for and against the death penalty on the basis of both retribution and recidivism.

12. At the age of 13, Stanley "Tookie" Williams co-founded the infamous Crips gang. Subsequently, he was convicted of several robberies and murders and sentenced to death. While in prison, he spoke out against the gang lifestyle, wrote children's books, donated proceeds to community programs, and was nominated for the Nobel Peace Prize. Ultimately, California Governor Arnold Schwarzenegger determined that his rehabilitation was not relevant and refused to grant clemency. Thus Williams was executed on December 13, 2005. Debate whether the governor made the right decision in this case.

13. Given the extremely high price tag for the death penalty, along with the currently weak economy, debate whether that is a valid argument for its repeal or an argument to make it less costly. In terms of the latter, determine what could be done to reduce costs without jeopardizing security, constitutional rights, or the assurance that no one is wrongfully convicted.

CHAPTER 15

Current Trends and Future Issues

Even more important and influential than the rethinking of excessive [punishment] policies has been the severe revenue shortfall confronting virtually all states . . . [which] may offer some hope that U.S. incarceration policy and practice may be moving toward restoring rationality.[1]

Alfred Blumstein

CHAPTER OVERVIEW

With the rapid pace of change in terms of everything from technology to social policy, there has never in the history of corrections been such a need for farsighted, creative, and proactive leadership. The challenges of the twenty-first century demand visionary leaders with farsighted plans for change—leaders who are determined but adaptable.

In an effort to address current challenges, correctional agencies have employed various strategies. Some have turned to greater involvement of the private sector, on the theory that the competitiveness and cost-efficiency characteristic of private industry can be used productively in corrections. Others have sought to reduce litigation by adhering to the administrative and operational standards required for accreditation. Still others have made efforts to enhance the recruitment, retention, and compensation of personnel, to improve physical facilities, work conditions, and administrative practices, or to devote more attention to new initiatives, research, and evaluation.

Some are beginning to take proactive measures to address potential problems before they become pressing crises. But many others are still reacting. When buffeted and confused by the winds of change, it is often tempting to respond with an overreliance on high-tech equipment, short-term fads, or quick-fix solutions. Yet the fundamental issues facing the correctional conglomerate are not amenable to shortcuts. They have not developed, nor will they be resolved, overnight. To the extent that corrections is reluctant to envision the upcoming horizon and plan accordingly, the legacy that is passed on will be of limited improvement over the one that was inherited. Whatever actions are taken or postponed today will shape both the problems and the prospects passed on to our successors. In essence, how we respond to today's difficulties will shape tomorrow's destinies.

CURRENT TRENDS

Court decisions will continue to influence correctional policies and practices as long as differences remain between the rights of free citizens and those of convicted offenders. However, there are also a number of trends beyond changes produced by case law that are shaping the nature of the correctional conglomerate. Some of these have been described in previous chapters—such as trends involving structured sentencing, intermediate sanctions, restorative justice, unit management, objective classification, direct-supervision jailing, and mandatory supervised release.

But, beyond the policy changes and emerging issues discussed previously, corrections is heading in new directions as a result of such catalysts as accountability, accreditation, privatization, and evidence-based practice. Of course, these are not by any means the only current trends that have been unaddressed thus far. But they have been singled out for special attention here as a result of a combination of factors, largely related to either their substantial contribution or the significant controversy that they have generated.

Accountability and the Correctional Mission

During turbulent economic times, it is not surprising to find government agencies being held to a higher level of scrutiny, and the correctional conglomerate is no exception. With revenues declining and voters rebelling against higher taxes in recent years, there has been mounting pressure on all government services, including corrections, to demonstrate greater value and become more accountable for their expenditures.

Among prisons and jails, this means that it is essential to determine on what basis their operations will be assessed. In other words, what standards will be used to identify what is effective or ineffective correctional practice? The answer to that question depends on just what it is that corrections is attempting to accomplish—i.e., what are its goals and objectives?

Going back to previous chapters, it is apparent that corrections can be charged with either (1) the rehabilitative and reintegrative goals of the medical model or (2) the retributive, deterrent, and incapacitative goals of the justice model. Although correctional performance has traditionally been assessed on the basis of recidivism rates, these are criteria for judging the effectiveness of the medical model. Since that public policy paradigm was rejected decades ago, recidivism would no longer seem to be a valid indicator by which to evaluate correctional practice.

Moreover, prison wardens and jails administrators actually have very little influence on the potential for recidivism, which is affected by countless factors beyond what an inmate experiences within correctional institutions. It has therefore been argued that correctional officials should not be held responsible for achieving results on the outside—which are likewise outside of their sphere of influence.[2] But, if not recidivism rates, what are legitimate accountability measures for correctional institutions?

The answer is not what happens to inmates upon release but, rather, how they are treated during confinement. That means establishing reasonable standards of decency during the facility's day-to-day operations. Moreover, that is something over which prison and jail administrators have complete control and, thus, can legitimately be held responsible for. One of the ways that it is assessed is through an accountability process known as accreditation—which moves the standard of measurement from ambiguous recidivism outcomes to standardized institutional measures.

Accountability through Accreditation

Every year, an increasing number of correctional institutions and programs undertake the lengthy process of seeking **accreditation** by the American Correctional Association (ACA) Commission on Accreditation for Corrections. These efforts represent a voluntary desire to upgrade the field of corrections, as well as a proactive means of seeking some protection against litigation. Accreditation is important to corrections, just as it is for hospitals, universities, and other services interested in maintaining appropriate standards and levels of performance.

accreditation: official recognition that a correctional program or facility has met certain national standards following an on-site audit.

ACA has developed more than a dozen manuals that provide standards and guidelines governing correctional administration and operations—for everything from food services to health care, correctional industries, juvenile facilities, adult institutions, small jails, probation, and parole. These guidelines represent minimum requirements that must be met for a facility or program to become accredited. Thus they provide a measure of the quality of service being provided.

Standards regarding correctional administration include such areas as staffing, training, fiscal management, record keeping, and legal rights of offenders. With regard to the direct delivery of services, the guidelines govern basic living conditions, health care, and safety concerns. As such, they cover a wide variety of topics, including:

- the physical plant;
- classification;
- custody and security;
- inmate discipline;
- counseling, education, and recreation;
- health and medical care;
- food services;

- property control;

- library services;

- inmate activities and privileges.

In each of these areas, ACA has established minimum standards with which those pursuing accreditation must be in compliance. The intent is to define fundamental levels of service and operation below which accredited agencies, facilities, or programs must not fall. Because standards are applicable uniformly throughout the country, they are set at a level that is reasonably achievable, rather than a higher level that might ideally be more desirable. Of course, nothing prevents organizations from exceeding the standards, but neither is there any particular incentive to do so.

Although seeking ACA accreditation is voluntary, nearly three out of four adult correctional facilities at the state and federal level are accredited.[3] Yet there are no legislative or legal mandates requiring accreditation. Nor is any additional funding necessarily forthcoming for accredited agencies. The question then becomes why so many have apparently elected to undertake this rather costly and time-consuming process. There are any number of answers, among them:

- *Self-improvement.* By examining its existing practices against nationally accepted minimum standards, an agency can better determine in what areas it is lacking and take appropriate steps to make improvements. Of those involved in accreditation, the vast majority (93 percent) report an improvement in the overall quality of their facilities and programs as a result of this process.[4] As correctional managers themselves have stated: "Accreditation's major benefit to top administration comes from the knowledge that every aspect of operations and administration are now routinely and regularly reviewed. It confirms the organization's strengths, identifies its weaknesses, and enables the organization to develop a systematic resolution to those weaknesses."[5]

- *Pride and morale.* Working toward accreditation is a lengthy process that requires commitment and teamwork on the part of everyone from top management to line staff and even inmates. In an agency that suffers from divisiveness or lack of cooperation, pulling together toward this common goal can generate a team spirit that enhances pride and morale when it is successfully accomplished.

- *Legal defensibility.* By meeting ACA standards, correctional agencies can proactively reduce some of the expensive litigation that could otherwise result from unsafe, unsanitary, or unacceptable conditions. While accreditation will not fully protect an organization from liability, having achieved accredited status can be a strong asset in defending against certain types of claims. For example, a research project that reviewed thousands of pages of court decisions concluded that:

  > Courts often consult ACA standards when attempting to determine appropriate expectations in a correctional setting. . . . [However], while there is no doubt ACA

standards are a primary reference source for courts, they are not considered the only source, nor are they always adopted as the measure of adequacy.... [C]ompliance with ACA standards does not automatically ensure acceptance in court.[6]

In summary, although accreditation is a costly and time-consuming process without economic incentives,[7] it is pursued for a variety of reasons that largely relate to the desire of correctional managers to maintain accountability, reduce litigation, and improve their facilities, practices, and administrative services. Accreditation demonstrates that a basic set of standards has been accepted by an agency, and that it is moving in the direction of developing the types of policies and procedures that are beneficial not only to the inmates but, ultimately, to the entire staff and the public as well. Nevertheless, as an accountability measure, "accreditation has limits, which is why it must complement rather than substitute for other, more independent forms of oversight."[8] See the next "Close-up on Corrections" for a list of what a correctional administrator can do to improve agency performance.

CLOSE-UP ON CORRECTIONS
What Corrections Directors Can Do to Strengthen Performance

Across the country, innovative policy-makers and correctional managers are joining forces to improve transparency, accountability, and performance of the correctional system. The following strategies can be used to further strengthen correctional operations and, ultimately, reduce crime and spiraling prisons costs. . . .

- *Better information leads to better outcomes:*
  - Develop performance measures that matter.
  - Make better use of technology (especially to track performance and adjust management practices).
- *Rethink the money equation:*
  - Seek alternative forms of funding.
  - Develop partnerships to cut down on medical costs.
- *Focus on people and performance:*
  - Hold facility managers accountable for progress toward targeted goals.
  - Pay for security staff on the front end—addressing compensation inequities can save money in the long run.
  - Find nonfinancial ways to improve employee morale and quality of life issues to boost performance and reduce turnover.
  - Develop new leaders to tackle the unique challenges of managing and motivating employees in the high-stress prison environment.

    Source: The PEW Center on the States, *Ten Steps Corrections Directors Can Take to Strengthen Performance* (Washington, DC: The PEW Center on the States, May, 2008), available at http://www.pewcenteronthestates.org/uploadedFiles/GPP.PSPPFinal.pdf.

In that regard, it is notable that, while ACA has been instrumental in promoting facility accreditation and staff certification, there are also a number of other national groups working to stimulate further progress. Among their advancements are the health-related facility standards established by the National Commission on Correctional Health Care, along with initiatives promoted by the American Jail Association, the National Sheriffs' Association, and the American Probation and Parole Association. Likewise, the Bureau of Justice Assistance and the National Institute of Corrections in the U.S. Department of Justice have been instrumental in disseminating information and conducting research to advance correctional practices.

LEARNING GOALS

Do you know:

4. how the private sector has influenced corrections historically?
5. what change the concept of privatization has undergone in recent years?
6. who is liable when a facility is privately managed?
7. the arguments in support of and in opposition to the privatization of corrections?

privatization:
contracting the full operation of a correctional facility to private-sector management.

Privatization in Correctional History

Not everyone would agree that accreditation is being implemented properly or setting standards high enough. Nevertheless, it is difficult to find fault with the basic concept. The same cannot, however, be said of **privatization**. Although privatization is emerging as both a trend and a source of controversy today, private individuals and groups have always played a major role in the field of corrections. See the next "Close-up on Corrections" for a few of the influential efforts that the private sector has demonstrated throughout correctional history. Among the many private organizations still working on behalf of corrections are such national spiritually based groups as Prison Fellowship, the Salvation Army, and Volunteers of America.

CLOSE-UP ON CORRECTIONS
Influence of the Private Sector in Correctional History

- Victims and their families were the early forerunners of the justice system, performing functions now reserved for police and judicial officials.
- The first permanent home for wandering children was built by the Society of St. Vincent de Paul in the seventeenth century.
- John Howard used his own resources to travel throughout Europe examining jail conditions, which resulted in reform of the English penal system.
- The American penitentiary, established in 1790, was based on the philosophy and reform efforts of a private Quaker-affiliated group.
- John Augustus took it upon himself to provide bail, supervise, and redeem petty criminals assigned to him by the courts.
- Today's juvenile court was initiated as a result of pressure on the part of the Chicago Women's Clubs.

Current Developments in Privatization

In addition to the many religious and secular groups that have traditionally been involved in some aspect of correctional work, the privatization of corrections has taken on new meaning today. Publicly funded correctional enterprises are turning with increasing frequency to the private sector in a wide variety of ways.

When government either does not have the specialized expertise necessary to accomplish a particular project or finds that certain services can be provided at less cost by the private sector, it is not uncommon to contract with private industry. In corrections, for example, the preparation of meals and provision of health care are typically contracted out when it is determined that private enterprise is better equipped to offer the service more economically. Particularly for small institutions, it may be cost-prohibitive to hire the personnel and invest in the sophisticated equipment necessary to sustain such services independently, as in the examples described below.

- *Treatment services.* Private sector contracts often fill gaps in treatment services. From boot camps to group therapy programs, there are hundreds of private initiatives operating throughout the country under contract to state and local governments. As long as the demand for drug and alcohol programs continues to outpace supply, it can be expected that such private sector involvement in correctional treatment will expand.

- *Community-based corrections.* Another area where privatization is likely to have continuing impact is in the operation of community-based sanctions. Earlier it was noted that, as attention has been riveted on skyrocketing institutional populations, corresponding caseload increases in community corrections have largely gone unheeded. As a result, private firms are now involved in drug-testing probationers and parolees, administering electronically monitored home confinement, and in some places even supervising community-based offenders. Additionally, as tightened restrictions and closer supervision increase the number of probation and parole violators, needs are expanding for community-based residential facilities.[9] Again, the entrepreneurial spirit of privatization is stepping in to fill gaps in public services.

- *Technical assistance.* Beyond operational contracts, the private sector is often engaged in short-term technical assistance when corrections is faced with undertaking something highly specialized or beyond its existing capabilities. A typical example is the design, construction, or expansion of a facility. From a cost–benefit point of view, the correctional payroll cannot be expected to maintain a permanent staff of the architects, engineers, and other personnel needed for these major, one-time projects.

- *Secure facility operation.* But specific service contracts, short-term consulting, and facility construction represent the privatization of only selected components of the correctional system, much of which has been commonplace for some time. What has changed—and created controversy—in recent years is the movement toward contracting the full operation of secure facilities to the private sector.[10]

The capacity of privately operated correctional institutions has been steadily increasing over the past two decades. In fact, the state legislature in Tennessee seriously considered a proposal that would have privatized nearly the entire prison system,[11] and Texas has long been a leader in the prison privatization movement. By the mid-1990s, the two companies most actively involved in privatization, Corrections Corporation of America (CCA) and Wackenhut Corrections Corporation (now the GEO Group), had reported record levels of business and profits.[12] But then profits took a nosedive. For example, Wackenhut Corrections' stock had dropped from an all-time high of $45 in June, 1996, to less than $8 by mid-April, 2000,[13] and CCA's shares likewise had plunged from a high of $44 in 1998 to 96 cents by April, 2001.[14] While stock prices have rebounded to some extent more recently, some of the reasons for this dramatic decline are highlighted in the dilemmas experienced by these two leaders of prison privatization in the following "Close-up on Corrections."[15]

CLOSE-UP ON CORRECTIONS
Prisons, Profits, and Problems

Six prisoners had escaped in broad daylight from the Northeast Ohio Correctional Center and were still at large. The inmates had cut a four-foot hole in the prison's fence during outdoor recreation, then maneuvered through three rolls of razor ribbon without being detected. No alarm went off, and the officers patrolling the perimeter didn't notice anything amiss. . . .

The company staffed the facility with guards who had little or no experience in corrections—and then imported 1,700 of the most violent inmates from Washington, DC, to fill what was supposed to be a medium-security prison. CCA left metal equipment everywhere, which the prisoners quickly stripped and fashioned into weapons. During the first year alone, 20 prisoners were stabbed and two were murdered.

Source: Michael Wilson, "Steel Town Lockdown," *Mother Jones* (May/June, 2000), pp. 39–40.

A series of scandals in at least four states has hurt Wackenhut where it hurts the most—its bottom line. . . .

- After an August, 1999, riot [in New Mexico] that left an inmate and a guard dead, Wackenhut was faulted for having inadequate and ill-prepared staff earning Wal-Mart wages.
- In Texas, Wackenhut was stripped of a $12 million-a-year contract and fined $625,000. . . . Twelve former officers were indicted for having sex with female inmates. . . .
- In Ft. Lauderdale, five guards at a Wackenhut work-release facility were fired or punished for having sex with inmates. . . .
- In April, 2000, Wackenhut agreed to surrender control of its 15-month-old juvenile prison in Jena, Louisiana. That came a week after the U.S. Justice Department named Wackenhut

in a lawsuit seeking to protect imprisoned boys from harm at the hands of guards and fellow inmates.

Source: James McNair, "Wackenhut Corrections: Prisons, Profits, and Problems,"
The Miami Herald (April 16, 2000), p. E-1.

- *Speculative prisons.* By the turn of the twenty-first century, privatization had taken on yet another dimension—*speculative prisons.* Constructed by private, for-profit companies without a contract with any agency, "spec" prisons market their bedspace to departments of corrections across the country. They have been referred to as a *Field of Dreams* approach—i.e., "If you build it, they will come."[16]

  Much like the residents of hotels and motels who live out of town, inmates in these facilities might come from any number of states, depending upon which agencies buy beds there. And much as the Internet connects travelers with hotel vacancies, there is now a website (jailbedspace.com) for correctional administrators looking for beds available for rent.[17] It could be entirely possible that no inmates housed in a spec prison come from the state in which the facility is located. Nor does the host state's department of corrections have any inherent oversight power over it. As highlighted in the next "Close-up on Corrections," this has raised a number of controversial issues in the ongoing debate over the advantages and disadvantages of privatization—as a result of which some spec prisons are standing empty because there is no interest in using them.[18]

CLOSE-UP ON CORRECTIONS
Speculative Prison Checklist

For-profit speculative prisons raise several troubling issues concerning the three governmental entities involved—the local community, host state, and sending state. For example, how would you answer the following questions?

- *From the perspective of the local community . . .*
  - What are the economic benefits and costs?
  - Should the private provider be required to reimburse the county and/or municipality for governmental costs associated with the prison's development (e.g., new roads, water and sewer systems, etc.)?
  - What regulatory control and oversight will local government exercise (e.g., types of inmates admitted, staffing patterns, perimeter security, release procedures)?
  - Will such regulation (or lack thereof) increase local government's liability exposure?

- *From the perspective of the host state . . .*
  - If the prison is to be regulated, should it be the function of state or local government?
  - Will the private company be charged for regulation costs and oversight?
  - Who mobilizes and pays for emergency support response services?
  - *Should* there be restrictions on where out-of-state offenders can be released?

- *From the perspective of the sending state . . .*
  - Does the department have statutory authority to place inmates out of state?
  - Are there minimum qualifications that the private provider must meet?
  - Is there a mechanism to monitor the contract to ensure that requirements are being met?
  - What is the sending state's liability exposure?
  - How will the effectiveness of privatization be assessed?

Source: Compiled from William C. Collins, *Privately Operated Speculative Prisons and Public Safety: A Discussion of Issues* (Washington, DC: U.S. Department of Justice, n.d.), Appendix A.

The Prison-industrial Complex. Communities that once shunned the construction of a prison in "their backyard" are today actively courting speculative brokers and site planners. As the U.S. has shifted from manufacturing to a service economy, rural areas in particular have felt the brunt of agricultural setbacks, plant closures, layoffs, and unemployment. Many localities therefore not only present no objection to prison construction, but often actively solicit it:

> Prisons are labor-intensive institutions, offering year-round employment. They are recession-proof, usually expanding in size during hard times. And they are nonpolluting—an important consideration in rural areas where other forms of development are often blocked by environmentalists. Prisons have brought a stable, steady income to regions long accustomed to a highly seasonal, uncertain economy.[19]

As a result, some towns now have more inmates than inhabitants. In fact, a new maximum-security prison in one Midwest state was touted as generating 800 jobs and an annual payroll of $40 million—"an important shot in the arm for a poor community badly in need of economic investment."[20] But a recessionary economy is not the only driving force that is fueling the momentum of private interests in corrections.

Each new prison or jail creates a corresponding need for everything from miles of concertina wire to years of telephone services. Just as legislators have determined that being tough on crime is politically popular, private enterprise has discovered that corrections is big business. This combination of political, economic, and bureaucratic interests supporting increased spending on imprisonment has been termed the **prison-industrial complex**.

prison-industrial complex: the multifaceted industrial growth emerging from massive prison expansion, sustaining itself through economic self-interest.

In psychology, a "complex" is "an overreaction to some perceived threat."[21] In corrections, that threat perception now advances the self-interests of prominent architecture and construction firms, along with major Wall Street banks financing prison bonds, not to mention the thousands of private enterprises providing the locking devices, transportation vehicles, security equipment, office furniture, facility plumbing, electrical wiring, health care, food services, and so on that every correctional institution needs to operate. As one observer has noted: "Profits by no means created the machinery of mass incarceration—no more than defense contractors invented war—but the huge profits to be made by incarcerating an ever-growing segment of our population serve the system very well. Profits oil the machinery, keep it humming, and speed its growth."[22]

In this entrepreneurial atmosphere, the higher the occupancy rate, the higher the profit margin, which has led to concern that choices about the denial of personal freedom may be made with an eye toward the bottom line.[23] Essentially, "crime may not pay, but prisons sure do."[24]

Benefits of Privatization.   On the one hand, privatization of correctional facilities has been supported on the grounds of efficiency and cost-effectiveness. This rationale maintains that the private sector has a number of advantages over government, including:

- *Reduced costs.* Because of the competitive nature of private industry and its profit motive, there is more incentive to reduce waste, eliminate duplication, and otherwise streamline activities in a more cost-effective manner. Thus it is maintained that government can obtain more service for less money by opening the management of correctional facilities to a competitive bidding process.

- *Flexibility and creativity.* Bureaucracies are traditionally slow to experiment with new approaches or even respond to immediate needs. In contrast, "[w]hen a need is identified for audiovisual monitors or two-way, portable radios, for example, a corporate decision can be made in minutes and the equipment can

EXHIBIT 15.1
The sprawling growth of prison construction, accompanied by the many related opportunities for industrial profit-making that it supports, have collectively been termed the "prison-industrial complex".

be immediately forthcoming."[25] Advocates of privatization therefore cite additional advantages in terms of greater flexibility, creativity, and responsiveness. As one executive has noted, "when you are looking for innovation, you don't look to government, you look to business."[26]

- *Competitive choice.* When there is dissatisfaction with the manner in which corrections is performing, it may not be easy to do anything about it through the existing system. By bringing in a "clean slate" through privatization, corrections is no longer burdened with "positions remaining from old, out-dated programs . . . or particular management preferences from a long-gone administrator."[27] Moreover, if the performance of a private company is unacceptable, government has the choice of resuming operation of the facility itself or contracting with a competitor. Knowing this presumably generates further incentive to provide high-quality service.

Concerns about Privatization.　In short, proponents of privatization maintain that economy, flexibility, and competition enable private companies to be more innovative and efficient at less cost. Not everyone would agree with that glowing assessment, however.[28] Opponents of the full privatization of correctional facilities cite such concerns as:

- *Quality assurance.* Given the fact that the profit motive is such a strong incentive in the private sector, fear has been expressed that "private operators may be tempted to take shortcuts that could compromise safety" or "reduce the quality and quantity of staff and services."[29] When government contracts with private industry to operate a prison or jail, it is obviously important to specify clearly what minimum standards the contractor must adhere to, as well as to establish procedures for monitoring and enforcing compliance. But, even if care is taken in that regard, there is always the danger that the *minimum required* will become the *maximum provided* in order to lower costs while raising profits. Advocates of privatization counter that "good services and competitive prices are not mutually exclusive."[30] Opponents warn that "the best policy is, buyer beware."[31]

- *Selectivity.* A related argument concerns the types of clients and facilities with which the private sector is willing to become involved. To the extent that low-risk populations and minimum-security institutions are more appealing to private companies, government may find itself in a position of being left with the least desirable correctional workload. As the "last resort," public corrections could ultimately be limited to dealing with the most hard-core clients and managing the highest-security institutions. In Chapter 12, trends in this direction were noted in the juvenile justice system, and Exhibit 15.2 points to a similar pattern in the adult system.

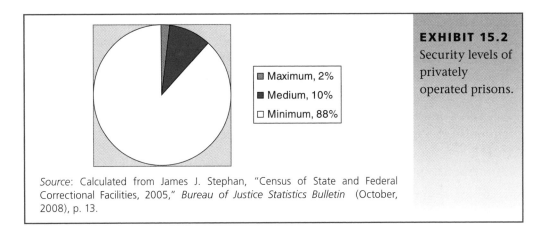

EXHIBIT 15.2
Security levels of privately operated prisons.

Maximum, 2%
Medium, 10%
Minimum, 88%

Source: Calculated from James J. Stephan, "Census of State and Federal Correctional Facilities, 2005," *Bureau of Justice Statistics Bulletin* (October, 2008), p. 13.

- *Liability.* Initially, it might appear that an enticing feature of privatization would be reduced liability for government. However, that attractive potential may occur only to the extent that a privately managed facility is subject to fewer lawsuits than those under public management. In other words, government cannot simply transfer liability to a private corporation through a contractual arrangement. In fact, the Supreme Court dealt with this issue in 1997, holding that the state "cannot transfer its sovereign immunity to a contractor in response to a Section 1983 lawsuit."[32]

  Government is ultimately responsible for its actions, whether they are carried out directly or indirectly through a private company. Nor are private sector employees immune from liability, as determined by another Supreme Court decision.[33] However, several more recent cases have muddied the legal waters, with results sometimes differing on the basis of such technicalities as what jurisdiction the lawsuit is brought against and whether it targets the correctional agency or employees personally.[34] The bottom line is that the state is responsible for every institution operated under its authority—whether private or public.

- *Appropriate roles.* Few would question the involvement of private industry in providing selected services or short-term technical assistance. But whether the entire operation of a correctional facility should be turned over to private enterprise is another issue entirely. Some contend that corrections is essentially a government obligation that should not be divorced from the democratic process in which society formulates public policy through elected officials. As a result of such considerations, an opinion from the attorney general's office in one state maintains that cities cannot contract with a private company to operate local jail facilities, because jails by definition "are to be operated by government."[35]

  Using this line of reasoning, questions have also been raised about the appropriateness of private sector decision-making in such sensitive matters as "[inmate] discipline, use of force, good time forfeiture, and parole recommendations."[36] Especially if compensation is based on a per-inmate fee, there is concern that private sector involvement in such decisions could encourage the overuse of institutions. For example, policies may be adopted that are designed to maintain full occupancy by increasing the frequency of disciplinary actions that, in turn, can lead to less good time and longer sentences. As the John Howard Association has argued, "[s]hort of the death penalty, incarceration is the state's most intrusive control over a citizen's life. It is inappropriate to relinquish this authority to an organization operating with profit as its primary goal."[37]

In response to this concern, many privatization contracts have been written in a manner prohibiting the contractor from making final decisions that "could have an adverse effect on the liberty interests of prisoners."[38] Under such contractual provisions, "private firms have no power to determine who will or who will not be committed to their facilities, to shape determinations of when those who are committed to their facilities will be released, or to control disciplinary processes whose outcome could alter significantly the conditions of confinement."[39]

Research Findings.   As these wide-ranging positions on both sides demonstrate, privatization is neither good nor bad, right nor wrong. Nor is it even clear whether or not privately operated facilities are less expensive. As one correctional administrator has observed: "A well-run correctional facility is a well-run correctional facility—no matter who runs it. A good administrator, whether in the private or public sector, should—and must—be conscious of cost. It is taxpayer money, whether it's being spent by a private contractor or a public sector manager."[40]

Some studies indicate that going private has resulted in "more and better prison services for less money."[41] One review of the research in this area, for example, concludes not only that private management is significantly less expensive, but that the cost savings can be achieved without any sacrifice in terms of the quality of correctional services.[42] On the other hand, findings of the Federal Bureau of Prisons point toward higher numbers of escapes, misconduct reports, and positive drug tests.[43] Reviewing the results of several studies, the U.S. General Accounting Office was unable to document clear evidence of savings and noted that findings in terms of cost and of quality of service in any given year may not hold true for other years.[44]

In that regard, some suspect that private companies may engage in "lowballing" (i.e., purposely underestimating actual costs in order to win a contract), that they have "hidden costs" which are being subsidized by the public sector (e.g., routinely sending serious medical cases to state-operated facilities), and that they may use a smaller and/or less qualified workforce in order to cut labor costs.[45]

Related Issues.   While there is no firm evidence that institutional stability is a direct product of the quality or quantity of staff, questions have been raised about the role that staffing shortcuts may have played in recent disturbances at privately run facilities. In some cases, these concerns are jeopardizing the expansion or renewal of private contracts. For instance, one of the reasons that the Federal Bureau of Prisons put a temporary moratorium on further privatization at one point was the outbreak of riots at two facilities operated under private contract.[46] Moreover, the state with one of the largest number of private prisons—Texas—expressed serious concerns about the need for greater regulation after a "rash of escapes and disturbances."[47]

Such high-profile problems have drawn attention to some of the unresolved issues surrounding the obligations of each party—such as whether government or the private contractor is responsible for paying the costs of recapturing escaped inmates. They have also generated objections to bringing out-of-state inmates into private facilities—a practice that could potentially make the recipient state a "dumping ground" for problem inmates from other jurisdictions.

These and other issues will continue to be debated as more research is conducted, experience is gained, and opinions are voiced.[48] In the meantime, privatization continues to generate contradictory evidence and widely varying points of view, making it somewhat premature to come to definitive conclusions about supporting or opposing it, since neither side has definitively proven its case. While the evidence is mounting on privatization, "the jury is still out."[49]

CONTEMPORARY AND FUTURE ISSUES

Future correctional administrators no doubt will continue to face issues that are as challenging as accreditation and as controversial as privatization. But, beyond some of these obvious ongoing concerns, projecting the future is quite speculative. It is difficult enough to know what the weather will be tomorrow, much less what the horizon holds for such a vast and varied enterprise as corrections. Even today, the multiple goals, diverse practices, and emerging issues facing the correctional conglomerate are neither clearly defined nor easily resolved. But simply because the future cannot be anticipated with complete certainty does not mean that we cannot be alert to the implications of current trends for shaping future issues.

Unfortunately, crisis is frequently the major catalytic agent in stimulating social progress. Yet changes rarely occur overnight in a revolutionary manner. To the contrary, they tend to come about over time through a slower, evolutionary process. Nor are changes in the field of corrections generally extreme diversions from present practices. Rather, they tend to be gradual modifications of what currently exists. To the extent that the past is prologue to the future, we can therefore anticipate much about tomorrow from what is occurring today.

Drugs, Crowding, and Costs

One of the harshest realities that Americans have had to face in recent years has obviously been the drug epidemic. In that regard, consider this stark reality—the United States contains just 5 percent of the world's population, yet its citizens incarcerate 25 percent of the world's prison population and consume two-thirds of the world's illegal drugs.[50] In fact, both of these figures are directly related. The prevalence of drugs throughout all socioeconomic classes is undoubtedly among the major explanations for why high incarceration rates have persisted in the U.S.—with many American states outstripping "any known standard of confinement on earth, even in the Third World."[51]

While Americans with substance abuse problems range from movie stars to truck drivers, it is minority communities that have been most severely affected by this punitive response. Not only have they lost a significant proportion of young men to prisons and jails, leaving struggling women to make ends meet and cope with family responsibilities, but the economic devastation of disproportionate minority incarceration extends well into the future:

> [It] helps to explain why black families are less able to save money and why each successive generation inherits less wealth than their white counterparts. Incarceration acts like a hidden tax . . . and while its costs are most directly felt by the adults closest to the incarcerated family member, the full effect is eventually felt by the next generation as well.[52]

As drugs have begun to affect a broader segment of society, attitudes concerning appropriate responses to the problem are beginning to shift. Yet there remains a heavy emphasis on enforcement, as reflected in Exhibit 15.3, which indicates that

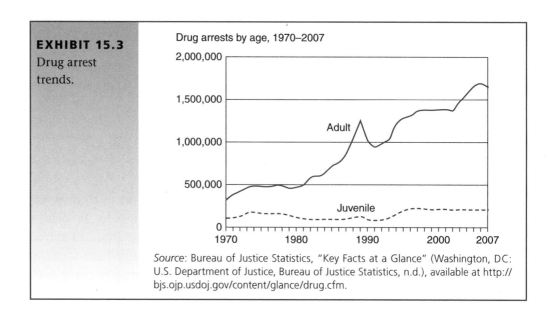

EXHIBIT 15.3
Drug arrest trends.

Drug arrests by age, 1970–2007

Source: Bureau of Justice Statistics, "Key Facts at a Glance" (Washington, DC: U.S. Department of Justice, Bureau of Justice Statistics, n.d.), available at http://bjs.ojp.usdoj.gov/content/glance/drug.cfm.

the number of adult drug-related arrests is climbing at a steady pace, along with its fiscal impact. By the turn of the twenty-first century, it was estimated that the economic damage of substance abuse on the American economy had reached a staggering $160 billion.[53] In response, only $632 million is being spent on treatment and prevention, in contrast to the $74 billion being spent on processing such offenders through the justice system.[54] As Justice Anthony Kennedy starkly observed, "our resources are misspent, our punishments too severe, our sentences too long."[55]

Despite the "war on drugs" (or, more accurately, because of it), drug-related cases have fueled rising probation and parole caseloads and continue to contribute to jail and prison crowding. This dilemma has created a vicious cycle. The burden of accommodating ever-increasing numbers of drug-related offenders has forced corrections into a regression back to the basics—often limiting probation and parole services to monitoring and reporting, and concentrating institutional resources on security and bedspace at the expense of program initiatives. From a cost-effectiveness perspective, this is simply not a sensible approach. For example, comprehensive cost–benefit analysis has found that the return on investing in treatment may well exceed 12:1—that is, every dollar spent on treatment can reduce future costs by $12 or more in terms of substance-related crimes, criminal justice expenditures, and health care costs.[56]

Moreover, on a broader economic scale, disproportionately allocating so much money to correctional institutions produces additional "lost opportunity costs," negating the possibility of directing these funds toward more productive and socially beneficial community endeavors. For example, computer mapping that illustrates where prisoners come from and how much money is spent to imprison them has revealed "million-dollar blocks"—urban neighborhoods where the price tag for incarcerating former residents exceeds $1 million per year.[57]

The question then becomes whether there are better ways to spend those dollars. In other words, "spending exorbitant amounts of money locking people up means there's far less money available for programs that decrease crime—like education, drug treatment, mental health care, and job training."[58] In that regard, statistics in one state reveal that, as funding for higher education dropped 29 percent, funding for prisons increased 76 percent, which is consistent with national trends.[59] During the two decades between 1980 and 2000, for example, correctional spending increased by 104 percent, while spending for education dropped by 21 percent.[60] These misplaced fiscal priorities are reflected in Exhibit 15.4, which illustrates growth of the inmate population in general (and inmate substance abusers in particular), far surpassing that of the general population.

Recognizing such discrepancies, Connecticut has passed legislation designed to shrink its prison population and redirect the savings into such recidivism prevention initiatives as drug treatment and mental health services.[61] Likewise, Rhode Island has embarked on a comprehensive plan to reduce its projected prison growth while promoting risk reduction treatment programming.[62] Hoping to stimulate similar

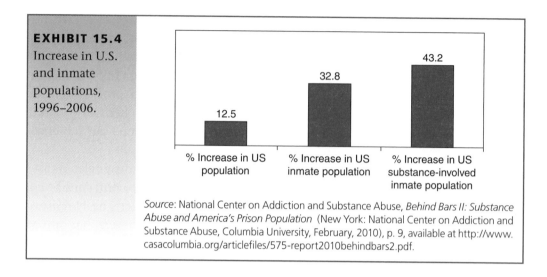

EXHIBIT 15.4
Increase in U.S. and inmate populations, 1996–2006.

12.5   % Increase in US population

32.8   % Increase in US inmate population

43.2   % Increase in US substance-involved inmate population

Source: National Center on Addiction and Substance Abuse, *Behind Bars II: Substance Abuse and America's Prison Population* (New York: National Center on Addiction and Substance Abuse, Columbia University, February, 2010), p. 9, available at http://www. casacolumbia.org/articlefiles/575-report2010behindbars2.pdf.

efforts on a national scale, Congress introduced the Criminal Justice Reinvestment Act of 2009 in order to:

- analyze criminal justice trends to understand what is driving the growth in jail and prison populations;

- develop tailored policy options to reduce correctional expenditures and reinvest in making communities safer;

- measure the impact of these changes and develop accountability measures.[63]

Fiscal Realities and Correctional Priorities

Even before such legislative initiatives had begun to take effect, the growth of institutional populations finally started to level off somewhat by late in the first decade of the twenty-first century. But that encouraging development was more than offset by the discouraging fallout of a declining economy. The national economic recession, along with the accompanying reallocation of fiscal priorities, combined to create massive budgetary shortages throughout the correctional conglomerate. As a result, the budgets of nearly half of the state departments of corrections were cut for fiscal year 2010.[64] Even worse, at the same time that revenues began to decrease, expenses climbed due to escalating populations with chronic illnesses, infectious diseases, mental disorders, and geriatric disabilities.

Correctional administrators have therefore faced making painful fiscal choices between institutional security, health care, and inmate programming. Just as states have shifted funding from education and social services to fund prisons, correctional facilities themselves are increasingly shifting money from programs to pay staff and fund new construction.[65] Given the fundamental necessity of security and health care, many have reduced programming as their only realistic alternative. As a result, "federal, state, and local correctional systems have seen a sharp reduction in programs that provide offenders with the education, vocational, and life skills necessary to prepare for reintegration into society."[66]

But, at the same time, increasing numbers of inmates are entering the correctional system with serious therapeutic needs—ranging from drug treatment to anger management. Likewise, increasing numbers of inmates are preparing for release, many without benefit of institutional programming. As one critic has put it, "Building more prisons to address crime is like building more graveyards to address a fatal disease."[67] Our correctional institutions are undoubtedly costly and arguably counterproductive. Yet fiscally shortsighted public policies continue to respond to the consequences without addressing the underlying causes:

> Many Americans still believe that the answer to the failures of punitive prohibition is more punitive prohibition. This is close to believing that when a medicine is found to fail and have nasty side effects, the patient should be made to take a double dose of it. . . . When arresting half a million Americans . . . did not stop illicit drug use, the fundamentalist response was to arrest a million.[68]

Public Opinion—Fiscal and Policy Implications

As reflected in the drug issue, it is not crime alone that determines the size of correctional caseloads and institutional populations but, rather, prevailing public policy—which reflects the manner in which society responds to criminal behavior. In that regard, we have watched social trends shift from the medical model to the justice model, along with accompanying fluctuations in prison populations. In fact, it has been observed that "the failure of the medical model, in turn, fueled the fears and discontent of those who saw drug use as a moral problem rather than a medical one,"[69] thus justifying harsher penalties.

Yet many of the same conditions that promoted the justice model are equally prevalent today—such as continuing concern over crime rates and a widespread belief that current practices are not working. One major study, for example, concluded that, while California's "get-tough-on-crime" policies have fueled a massive influx of inmates, putting more people behind bars has had little effect on the state's crime rate.[70]

In other states, it appears that "three strikes" provisions are not often being invoked. Despite the political rhetoric surrounding the passage of such legislation, it may be having a greater impact on the courts as a plea bargaining tool than on crime rates. In that regard, if left unchecked, such prosecutorial discretion has the potential to regenerate "the very disparities that sentencing reform was intended to alleviate."[71] Overall, it has been noted that: "Criminal justice policies may be thought of as irrational when their benefits in terms of crime are outweighed by the harms they cause. By most accounts, three-strikes laws meet this definition."[72]

Whether or not the public will continue to support increasingly punitive legislation in the absence of research demonstrating its effectiveness will depend on politics and social attitudes. Although the fiscal crises that states have been experiencing in recent years can provide the stimulus for change, reforms are more likely to be long-term if they are anchored more securely in changing public opinions and policy paradigms. In terms of such attitudes, it is becoming increasingly apparent that the public may not actually be as punitive as policy-makers would have us believe. For example, various studies in recent years have revealed that:

- There is a "strong dissatisfaction" with the current state of criminal justice. While not showing leniency toward crime, polls do indicate support for providing inmates with skills and nonviolent offenders with noninstitutional alternatives such as education, job training, victim compensation, and community service.[73]

- Almost 3 out of 4 Americans (72 percent) believe that the criminal justice system should "try to rehabilitate criminals, not just punish them."[74] Yet 6 out of 10 believe that prisons are largely failing in terms of rehabilitation.[75]

- Even community leaders who are justice policy-makers express views that are "most supportive of rehabilitation and serving the needs of those with mental health and substance abuse problems."[76]

- Overall, citizens advocate a more "balanced, multifaceted" approach to crime[77]— one that "extracts an appropriate measure of just deserts and protects the public from the truly dangerous but that also makes a concerted effort to rehabilitate and restore to the community those who need not be ensnared in a life of crime."[78]

These results suggest an emerging foundation for social policy revision. To the extent that they are truly indicative of prevailing trends, politicians may well be "woefully and persistently misperceiving public views."[79] As one review of the literature concludes, "research on public desires reveals that rather than being confronted with an obstacle to treatment, correctional practitioners and policy-makers have support in their efforts to reduce offending through rehabilitative programming."[80]

If indeed the public is becoming increasingly disenchanted with the existing process, the time is ripe for more creative and less punitive alternatives. In fact, a number of states are already in the process of revising mandatory sentencing laws, reducing prison crowding, and expanding drug treatment. Emboldened by the double impact of a declining economy and a dissatisfied constituency, policy-makers are embarking on reforms that may well outlast the budget crisis.[81] While the exhausting era of "doing more with less" under the justice model has been fiscally and operationally painful for corrections, it may be a cloud with the proverbial "silver lining" if it creates a window of opportunity to consider alternative approaches:

Recession and subsequent revenue declines are having significant effects on corrections. Across the U.S., departments are closing facilities, placing beds in nontraditional space, reducing and/or eliminating programs, cutting operating costs, exploring early offender release options, enacting reduction-in-force policies, and offering employee buyouts. . . . [But] sentencing reform, prevention efforts, and investments in evidence-based treatment will result in greater savings and dividends than internal cost-cutting measures.[82]

Embarking on new, more uplifting approaches is not, however, likely to occur on a widespread basis unless correctional administrators are willing to pursue a more proactive role in influencing public policy choices. In that regard, calls to action have long advocated greater correctional involvement in public policy development,[83] encouraging leaders to become more proactive in "educating and shaping public opinion."[84] A united front has yet to emerge in the form of a determined effort to influence public mandates that guide management practices. Nevertheless, it is clear that correctional administrators can no longer seek refuge in the isolated existence they once enjoyed behind literal and figurative walls.

Learning from Past Mistakes

If there is one lesson that has been learned from the self-defeating impact of the justice model, it is the necessity to plan properly in advance of making significant policy changes. In fact, it is actually impossible to determine whether the justice model might have been more effective if it had not been confronted with the massive institutional crowding that resulted in such widespread early release that its intent was severely compromised. Moreover, that same argument could be made with respect to the medical model. Without funding for treatment programs, its intent was likewise compromised.

As these breakdowns between ambition and actuality illustrate, public policy cannot be fulfilled effectively in the absence of advance planning and resource allocation. It is insufficient simply to change policy in order to appease political constituents. Public opinion and political leadership have too often reacted emotionally to crime, calling for severe and simplistic solutions that have overloaded the correctional conglomerate without commensurate funding. Even the best intentions are doomed to fail in the absence of informed decisions based on projections of expected impact, including the resources required for effective policy implementation.

Policy-making Based on Evaluation Research

Prior to establishing a new policy, serious consideration of fiscal and operational repercussions is critical to achieving success. But, even with careful foresight, plans do not always materialize in practice as they were anticipated in theory. Thus, the need for ongoing study and empirical evaluation cannot be overlooked.

Before conclusions can be drawn about any program, evaluation must be integrated into program planning and practice. Few employers would advocate keeping staff on the payroll without periodic standardized performance evaluations. Yet major criminal justice policies are commonly implemented without giving thought to how their effectiveness will be measured.

Even when outcome assessments have been conducted, the research in this field has generally been haphazard—conducted on an ad hoc basis, often as an afterthought or to meet a funding requirement. Attempts at evaluation in the past have often suffered from inadequate methodology, focused on small populations, and provided disconnected bits of information rather than cumulative knowledge. That uninspiring legacy is showing signs of change as more correctional administrators recognize the value of rigorous empirical research and resulting **evidence-based practices**: "States are [now] using strategic planning, performance reviews, performance measures, outcome evaluations, and cost–benefit analysis. . . . Evidence-based practice is recognized as improving the decision-making process by integrating the best available research [with operational practice]."[85]

evidence-based practices: using the information provided by empirical evidence to guide rational decision-making and operational practices.

Establishing Evidence-based Corrections

Nevertheless, contemporary correctional policy has largely been driven by factors ranging from personal emotion to political grandstanding. As a result, policy shifts and programmatic changes have often occurred with little regard for their effectiveness in terms of reducing recidivism. In the past, this was compounded by the absence of well-designed evaluation studies. As sound research has emerged in more recent years, however, the capability now exists to employ more objective, evidence-based decision-making in program and policy development.[86]

Whether corrections will move forward in this direction or remain trapped in the shifting sands of politically based policy-making remains to be seen. Certainly, there has been considerable momentum urging politicians to embrace more empirically justified correctional policy-making that insulates sentencing from political self-interest and media influence. For, although the public may be righteously outraged by extraordinary offenses, sentencing policy in a democracy must be based on the rationality of substantive analysis and empirical evidence, rather than the emotional reaction to anger and revenge. In recent years, however, that has not often been the case.

Not only have evaluation results been missing from the public policy agenda, but within the correctional conglomerate itself they have also been cited as the "missing link" in organizational decision-making.[87] Moreover, researchers themselves bear some of the responsibility for this state of affairs, insofar as they do not always present findings in a manner that is understandable to practitioners or transferable to the field.[88] In the meantime, solid empirical evidence is accumulating that identifies what does and does not work, which can be used to progressively shape future policy and practice.

As the next "Close-up on Corrections" reveals, the perception that "nothing works" is now woefully outdated. In fact, a recent meta-analysis of nearly 300 evaluation studies found that the majority of treatment programs actually *do* reduce recidivism, prompting the researchers to conclude that, if just one state were to successfully implement a moderate-to-aggressive portfolio of evidence-based options, "A significant level of future prison construction can be avoided, taxpayers can save about two billion dollars, and crime rates can be reduced."[89]

While "nothing works" may be a catchy political sound bite, it reflects uninformed thinking and obsolete research. On the other hand, as the next "Close-up" also reveals, some of the most popular and prevalent correctional initiatives have earned a rather dismal report card on the basis of empirical findings.[90]

Corrections cannot expect to get the funding it deserves without proving its value, which depends on measuring and demonstrating results. Evaluation research and evidence-based decision-making must therefore become essential components in the process of planning policy changes—if for no other reason than because people who are paying the bills have a right to know what is and is not working.

CLOSE-UP ON CORRECTIONS
Identifying What Works

What works?

- Rehabilitation programs that are structured and focused, use multiple treatment components, focus on developing skills, and use behavioral methods.
- Prison-based therapeutic communities for drug-involved offenders.
- Cognitive behavioral therapy that focuses on changing thoughts and attitudes through either moral development or problem-solving.
- Non-prison-based sex offender treatment programs using cognitive behavioral methods.
- Vocational education programs in prison or residential settings.
- Multicomponent correctional industry programs.

What does not work?

- Programs emphasizing specific deterrence, such as shock probation and "scared straight."
- Vague, nondirective, unstructured counseling.
- Programs emphasizing structure, discipline, and challenge, such as old-style military boot camps and juvenile wilderness excursions.
- Initiatives that focus exclusively on increased control and surveillance in the community without accompanying treatment, such as intensive supervised probation or parole, home confinement, and urine testing.

Source: Adapted from Doris Layton MacKenzie, "Evidence-based Corrections: Identifying What Works," *Crime and Delinquency*, Vol. 46, No. 4 (October, 2000), pp. 457–471.

PROJECTING CORRECTIONAL TRENDS

Beyond the issues discussed above, a number of emerging trends have been addressed throughout earlier chapters of this book. Especially in light of their long-term implications, it is useful at this point to briefly recap some of these transitions and consider their implications for the future direction of corrections.

Intermediate Sentencing Alternatives

Initially developed as a "front-door" option for reducing jail and prison crowding, such alternatives as electronic monitoring/ home confinement and intensive supervision probation have become recognized as legitimate approaches in their own right. As a compromise between the lesser restrictions of traditional probation and the severity of incarceration, they provide a reasonable middle ground—addressing the concerns of those who advocate more punitive practices, as well as those who object to the futility of imprisonment.

On a practical level, both crowded facilities and the exorbitant cost of new construction have inspired the growth of intermediate sanctions.[91] Of course, to say that such sanctions are less expensive is not to say that they are cost free—or, as we have seen earlier, that they are necessarily effective. One of the significant drawbacks of many intermediate sanctions is that they have often been implemented "without creating the organizational capacity to ensure compliance with court-ordered conditions."[92] For example, it does no good whatsoever to order a client to get help for an alcohol or drug problem if there is a minimum two-year waiting list for local substance abuse treatment programs.

Research shows that, without the accompanying resources, intensive supervision is unlikely to be any more effective than its traditional predecessor. (See the previous "Close-up.") In the words of one concerned probation administrator, "We need to convince a conflicted public—torn between fear of crime and fear of taxes—that we merit the increased funding needed to make us more effective on their behalf."[93] Currently, community-based alternatives are in a double-bind dilemma, since the public is unwilling to support them without evidence of success, and they are unlikely to be successful without sufficient funding.[94] With appropriate resources, however, intermediate options also provide an opportunity to fulfill two correctional objectives that have been gaining popularity in recent years: *restitution* and *restoration*.

Restorative Justice Concepts

In contemporary society, government assumes full responsibility for apprehending, prosecuting, and punishing criminal behavior. As a result, crime is viewed by the state in almost an abstract manner—as a violation against the interests of society. Such an approach does little to reinforce any sense of either personal responsibility on the part of the offender or personal involvement in the justice process on the part of the victim.

In an effort to address these issues, the concept of *restorative justice* has been gaining momentum. Using various forms of victim–offender mediation and dispute resolution, the restorative focus is centered on bringing together all parties with a stake in a particular offense to deal with the aftermath of the crime, along with its implications for the future. As such, it emphasizes both:

- restoring at least some of the tangible losses experienced by the victim through negotiated restitution arrangements; and

- restoring the offender's sense of personal accountability for the harm caused by his or her actions (and, ultimately, the community's trust in the offender).

For a closer look at how restorative justice differs from the more conventional concept of retributive justice, see the next "Close-up on Corrections." As that comparison shows, sentencing based on restorative justice offers "something for everyone":

- *For victims.* Success is measured by the degree to which damages have been repaired and victims have been involved in, as well as satisfied with, the justice process.

- *For offenders.* Emphasis is on gaining an understanding of the consequences of crime, feelings of remorse, recognition that they have been sanctioned, and (ideally) development of empathy with victims. Positive behavioral outcomes include prompt repayment to victims, completion of community service, and other reparative requirements (e.g., facing the victim in mediation).

- *For the community.* The most important objectives are overall satisfaction that justice has been served, a sense that offenders have been held accountable, and a feeling of community well-being.[95]

Programs based on restorative justice principles can be expected to become increasingly attractive to the extent that social attitudes and values move in a more moderate direction, while still expressing discomfort with absolving offenders of individual responsibility for their conduct.

CLOSE-UP ON CORRECTIONS
Changing Concepts of Justice

TABLE 15.1

Retributive Justice	Restorative Justice
Crime defined as violation of the state.	Crime defined as violation of one person by another.
Focus on establishing blame, on guilt, on past behavior.	Focus on problem-solving, liabilities, obligations, and the future.
Relationships are adversarial.	Relationships involve dialogue and negotiation.
Suffering is imposed to punish, deter, and prevent.	Reconciliation/restoration is the goal.
Interpersonal nature of crime is obscured; conflict seen as individual versus state.	Crime recognized as interpersonal conflict.
Victim is ignored; offender is passive.	Victim rights/needs recognized.
Offender accountability defined as taking punishment.	Offender accountability defined as understanding impact of action, taking responsibility, and making things right.
Response focused on offender's past behavior.	Response focused on harmful consequences of offender's behavior.

Source: Adapted from Howard Zehr, "Restorative Justice," *IARCA (International Association of Residential and Community Alternatives) Journal* (March, 1991), p. 7; see also "Underlying Principles of Restorative Justice," in Michael Braswell, John Fuller, and Bo Lozoff, *Corrections, Peacemaking, and Restorative Justice* (Cincinnati: Anderson, 2001), pp. 142–144.

Changing Nature of Treatment

Even with considerably diminished support for the medical model over past decades, belief in the potential benefits of treatment has not been abandoned. The difference today is that it is more likely to be offered on a voluntary basis rather than as an inducement for early release. As with restorative justice, this reflects a trend toward placing more individual responsibility on the offender, recognizing that rehabilitation is unlikely to be successful in the absence of personal motivation. In that regard, it may be as inappropriate to hold corrections accountable for the behavior of its clients as it would be to hold a hospital accountable for the postrelease behavior of patients who return to bad nutritional habits, smoking, or drinking after release.

Today the nature of "treatment" is also taking on a more pragmatic orientation. In contrast to counseling, group therapy, and other forms of psychological treatment, emphasis today has shifted toward developing productive employment skills (although that is not to imply that such programming is readily available to most offenders).

Society's continuing expression of concern over educational deficits among America's youth may likewise be expected to further strengthen a more pragmatic approach to treatment, with additional emphasis on basic education and vocational training programs. More specifically targeted treatment initiatives can also be anticipated in the future—but only to the extent that treatment itself becomes a greater fiscal priority.

As opposed to the counseling-for-everyone approach, treatment that survives in this era of fiscal austerity will be focused on the needs of alcoholics, drug addicts, sex offenders, and high-risk offenders. In fact, it has been suggested that we "rethink our use of the term 'treatment,' and cast it aside, replacing it with 'risk reduction,' a more realistic objective of correctional programs"[96]—and also one that is more likely to generate public support and accompanying funds.

In many respects, correctional treatment is still coping with fallout from the widely held premise that "nothing works." Yet, as noted earlier, new evidence is emerging that carefully constructed programs *can* work. For a more detailed look at the concepts on which effective programming is based, see the following "Close-up on Corrections."

CLOSE-UP ON CORRECTIONS
What Works?

- Programs that target medium and high risk offenders and focus on criminogenic factors produce more positive results on recidivism than programs that indiscriminately allow any offender to participate.
- Cognitive and behavioral approaches tend to be more successful than other types of treatment (e.g., confrontation or direct deterrence).
- Programs need to be longer and more intense to have a significant impact . . . at least 100 hours in duration, spanning 3–4 months.
- Staff assigned to deliver programs need to be adequately trained and supervised in program delivery.
- Rehabilitative programs offered in community-based settings produce greater reductions in recidivism than programs offered in prisons. . . .
- All prison staff should be involved in the process of changing offender behavior, not just designated treatment staff.
- Prison-based programs are most effective if they are linked to and integrated with community-based services.

Source: Thomas J. Fagan, Shelia M. Brandt, and Andrea L. Kleiver, "Future Directions," in Robert K. Ax and Thomas J. Fagan, eds., *Corrections, Mental Health, and Social Policy* (Springfield, IL: Charles C. Thomas, 2007), p. 364.

Changing Features of Institutions

In addition to the nature of programs offered, indications are already on the horizon that the physical features of correctional institutions are beginning to change as well. These modifications are perhaps most apparent among local jails—where some of the most antiquated facilities are being abolished or modernized, small jails are being consolidated through regionalization, and new architecture and management styles are reflecting the principles of direct-supervision (new-generation) jailing.

Both jails and prisons are also becoming more electronically sophisticated—as keys, locks, and staff monitors are giving way to the technological advancements of computers, video cameras, "smart cards," and even satellite surveillance. In fact, as described in the upcoming "Close-up on Corrections," such technology is already available. One of the dangers of extensive reliance on high-tech hardware, of course, is that it further promotes the dehumanizing effect of incarceration. Direct-supervision and unit management strategies work toward overcoming this drawback, since officers are stationed directly inside housing units, interacting with the inmates on a continual basis.

CLOSE-UP ON CORRECTIONS
Hot New Technologies

Ground Penetrating Radar

Prison administrators in California heard rumors of an impending inmate outbreak. The word was out that a handful of inmates had built a tunnel underneath the . . . institution and were planning to make a break for freedom. A team . . . using a new technology called Ground Penetrating Radar (GPR) was able to locate the elusive tunnel.

Heartbeat Monitoring

The weakest security link in any prison has always been the sallyport, where trucks unload their supplies and trash and laundry are taken out of the facility. Over the years, inmates have hidden in loads of trash, old produce, laundry and any possible container that might be exiting the facility. Today . . . a new technology can detect the heartbeat of a person hidden in a vehicle. The Advanced Vehicle Notification System (AVIAN) . . . works by identifying the shock wave generated by the beating heart, which couples to any surface the body touches.

Smart Cards

Every time an inmate receives an aspirin for a headache, or buys toothpaste from the commissary, a prison clerk must record and file the transaction. Now comes the smart card, a plastic card embedded with a computer chip that will store all types of information about an inmate—movements, medical care, commissary purchases, treatment needs, meals eaten—any information at all.

Drug Detection Devices

Time-consuming physical searches for drugs may become a thing of the past with ion mobility spectrometry. This noninvasive device detects trace amounts of narcotics in people, on clothing, or concealed in packages.

Body Alarms

This electronic alarm enables staff to summon assistance quickly to a particular area. It relies on a pager-sized pendant worn by the employee that, when activated by depressing a button, sends a radio signal to a locator. The central control computer then automatically broadcasts a radio message that an officer in a certain location needs assistance. The time lapse between alarm initiation and broadcast is no more than a few seconds.

Supervision and Management Automated Record Tracking (SMART)

A handheld version of SMART will soon accompany community corrections officers into the field to allow real-time data entry and immediate access to case records. In addition to maintaining an offender's drug test results, treatment referrals, and violation reports, SMART can do anything from tracking offenders' community service to keeping tabs on their participation in vocational, educational, and employment programs.

Hand Geometry

In order to verify exactly who is entering and leaving various points in a correctional facility, hand scanning geometry is now being used for positive identification. The system scans people's hands as they enter and again as they leave certain areas to be sure prisoners are not posing as visitors or employees. For probationers and parolees, it can be used with kiosk video touch screens that allow clients to check in electronically on their reporting dates.

Law Library Terminal

Gone are the days when inmates had to be transported to rooms full of thick legal books in order to meet the requirement of access to a law library. Now, in less than the size of a bulletin board, there is a new wall-mounted computer terminal that delivers required state and federal law data for inmate research at the touch of a finger. Best of all, the system works without need to connect with the Internet, and correctional staff can electronically track each inmate's use, in defense against allegations of restricted access.

Sources: Compiled from Jay Lowe, "Technology Enhances Public Safety in Texas," *Corrections Today* (July, 2004), p. 71; Frank Lu and Lawrence Wolfe, "Technology that Works: An Overview of the Supervision and Management Automated Record Tracking (SMART) Application," *Corrections Today* (July, 2004), p. 80; *Correctional News*, "Product of the Month" (July/August, 2004), p. 50; and Janice Joseph and Rupendra Simlot, "Technocorrections: Biometric Scanning and Corrections," in Roslyn Muraskin, ed., *Key Correctional Issues* (Upper Saddle River, NJ: Prentice Hall, 2010), p. 209.

Economic Shortfalls and Cost-saving Measures

Just as in other components of government, corrections is being expected to do more with less. By the fall of 2002, it was estimated that states throughout the country faced a $40 billion shortfall. (Ironically, that is also precisely what it was costing in 2002 to incarcerate the nearly two million inmates confined in correctional facilities.)[97] Since corrections was the major area of fiscal growth during the previous two decades, it was not surprising that states quickly focused their attention in that direction as they grappled with balanced budget requirements.[98]

In the wake of such massive fiscal shortages, it has become necessary to use both personnel and resources more efficiently.[99] Examples of creative means of doing so exist in both institutional and community-based corrections. Within correctional facilities, for instance, labor-intensive methods of tracking inmate movements and purchases through passes, checklists, and cumbersome paperwork are giving way to the use of electronic scanning devices. In community corrections, electronic monitoring has reduced the need for numerous field visits and home checks, while caseload classification is enabling officers to concentrate their efforts on clients most in need of careful supervision. And everywhere costs are being offset by charging user fees—for services ranging from health care to community supervision, transportation, and even food and lodging.

Despite such efforts, however, corrections continues to struggle with the effects of a declining economy, which creates both an increasing burden and a decreasing ability to pay for it. As a result, some states are even closing prisons and laying off

EXHIBIT 15.5
America's "lock-'em-up" approach to crime-related public policy has recently conflicted with a devastated economy unable to support the high cost of prisons and jails.

correctional staff. As one distraught worker wearily summarized the situation, "We have to do so much with so little for so many."[100]

Privatization

One of the ways that government may seek to save money is through privatization. As described previously in this chapter, it is not at all clear that "for-profit" prisons actually operate at a substantial cost savings—especially when the quality of services and hidden costs are taken into account. But, regardless of the evidence supporting or refuting their costs or capabilities, private providers now have established a firm foothold in corrections. The momentum that they have sparked is expected to continue to grow, and pressure on government to operate more efficiently and engage in more public–private partnerships can be expected to further enhance the prospects for greater private involvement.

In fact, it is perhaps the "threat" more than the reality of privatization that will influence the future of correctional practices. To the extent that public employees believe that their job security is endangered by the potential of privatization, the stimulus may be provided for better services at lower cost in the public sector. As in business and industry, competition can provide a strong incentive for improved performance.

Objectivity in Decision-making

The expanded use of computers has made a substantial impact throughout the field, both directly and indirectly. In a wide variety of capacities, computers are now performing what had previously been very time-consuming and labor-intensive efforts. What is somewhat less apparent is how reliance on computers and other technological innovations has shaped decision-making in a more quantifiable direction.

No longer is the system as willing to accept individual judgments or personal opinions. Rather, we have limited judicial discretion through sentencing guidelines, streamlined parole decision-making through prediction tables, and in many jurisdictions replaced discretionary parole with mandatory supervised release, based on the figures generated by good-time and gain-time schedules. "Hard numbers" are more and more often replacing human judgments in the decision-making process at various points in the justice system. This transition has reduced the potential for abuse, disparity, and favoritism. But it has also contributed to a false sense of security—a belief that data alone can direct human effort, while overlooking the fact that the figures themselves are inherently a product of human values.

Juvenile Justice Transitions

If there is one aspect of the system that still makes an attempt to cling to more personalized, discretionary decision-making, it is juvenile justice. Despite the greater due process protections now afforded young offenders, the juvenile field has yet to abandon its emphasis on *parens patriae* and the medical model. That does not, however, mean that serious juvenile offenders are escaping the wrath of public consternation. Indeed, it appears that responses to juvenile law violators are splitting in opposite directions. On the one hand, hard-core, violent juvenile offenders can increasingly expect to be dealt with in a manner commensurate with the seriousness of their offenses—that is, through adult courts and more punitive sentencing.

At the same time, responses to the least serious status offenders include options ranging from removing them from secure institutions, to diverting them out of the system, to decriminalizing their behavior completely. Again, as in the adult system, it is not simply benevolence that is driving such changes, but also the necessity for efficiency and cost-effectiveness in the face of increasing workloads without accompanying resource allocations. While dealing with status offenders outside of the official juvenile justice system meets such objectives, it will be essential to assure that appropriate services are provided to them through alternative avenues. Otherwise they risk becoming the youthful equivalent of the deinstitutionalization of mental health—in which case the egalitarian objectives of reformers were never fulfilled in practice or provided for in terms of funding.

But, regardless of the nature of their offenses, there is little doubt that the most optimistic approaches for juveniles are those that target early intervention. In that regard, a national panel of experts stated emphatically that in responding to youthful offenders:

- *It is never too early.* Preventive interventions for young children at risk of becoming serious or violent juvenile offenders are effective and should be implemented at an early age.

- *It is never too late.* Interventions and sanctions for known serious or violent juvenile offenders can reduce their risk of reoffending.[101]

Intensifying Needs of Correctional Populations

Society's reaction to the needs of special groups within the larger population can be expected to continue to shape responsiveness to the changing nature of correctional populations. Corrections will be especially challenged to meet the needs of increasing numbers of female offenders, along with those who are HIV infected, physically impaired, mentally ill, or elderly. Nor is there expected to be any decline in the already sizeable numbers of correctional clients suffering from alcohol or drug addictions or other mental disorders. As long as corrections provides an inadequate substitute for everything from teenage pregnancy prevention to domestic abuse intervention, gang interdiction, alcohol and drug treatment, mental health facilities, and geriatric services, it will continue to embrace a conglomerate of unfortunate Americans who were not otherwise diverted from the foreseeable path toward destructive lives.

Whether these populations will receive treatment consideration in concert with their needs will depend primarily on overall fiscal conditions, along with the willingness of taxpayers to support such efforts. To the extent that addressing "special needs" offenders may be considered a luxury in tight economic times, even the limited advancements of recent years may well plateau, or even decline, if the economy does not rebound.

Reentry and Reintegration Challenges

The one thing we know for certain about those behind bars is that, at some point, nearly all of them are coming back into the community. In fact, right now hundreds of thousands of discretionary parolees and mandatory releasees are "doing time" on the streets of neighborhoods throughout the U.S.—under systems that "provide few services and impose conditions that almost guarantee failure."[102] And that is after leaving correctional institutions where few resources were devoted to much beyond occasionally relieving their boredom. With a felony record now added to the social dysfunctions, economic disadvantages, and psychological handicaps that often paved their path to prison in the first place, their future outlook is precarious.[103]

As a result, it is clear why a sizeable proportion of new prison and jail admissions come from the ranks of probation and parole violators. What may not be quite so obvious is that, aside from revamping sentencing policies, there is probably no better way to reduce prison populations than to mobilize the social support needed to enable ex-offenders to make a successful, resource-rich reentry. In that regard, the Second Chance Act funded by Congress in 2009 is targeted toward providing millions of dollars for everything from career training to transitional jobs, mental health services, correctional education, and substance abuse prevention and treatment.[104] But ultimately, whether inmates are phasing out through community-based initiatives or still serving time in secure institutions, it is the correctional staff they interact with whose capabilities and supportive services can make the difference between reintegration and reincarceration.

Personnel Transitions

Like the offenders they work with and supervise, those on the other side of the bars have also been undergoing significant changes in recent years. The white-male-dominated tradition of the correctional labor force is being dismantled by a more diverse and better-educated workforce that is representing new generations of employees—whose values, priorities, attitudes, and work habits differ substantially from those of their predecessors. This "new breed" of workers is both introducing new perspectives on the job and creating new challenges. In contrast to their predecessors, they are demanding a voice in making decisions and establishing policies that affect them.[105]

EXHIBIT 15.6
Today's "new breed" of correctional officers reflects more cultural diversity, demands more organizational participation, and represents tomorrow's leaders.

Source: Courtesy of the Miami-Dade (Florida) County Department of Corrections and Rehabilitation.

Moreover, it is today's operational personnel who represent tomorrow's managers and administrators. In that regard, employees who have never experienced anything but passively responding to orders coming down the chain of command do not make very likely candidates for displaying the visionary leadership skills that will be needed to guide corrections through the twenty-first century. In order to assure continuity and organizational stability during the massive upcoming retirements of the "baby boom" generation, it is essential to effectively recruit, retain, and develop a well-qualified correctional workforce—as well as begin the succession planning that will groom them for the upcoming leadership challenges that they will inevitably face.[106]

Employee Professionalism

From the agency director to the entry-level officer, it is the dedication and commitment of qualified employees that enable corrections to function in the face of inadequate resources, insufficient public support, and involuntary clientele. In fact, a recent national study of correctional practitioners found that "officer quality and morale" ranked first on the list of concerns faced by corrections professionals.[107]

The ability of corrections to recruit and retain the quality of personnel needed in the twenty-first century will largely depend on how well it embraces higher education, encourages broad-based participation, decentralizes decision-making, empowers employees, and promotes ongoing career development—in other words, how much emphasis is placed on professionalizing its most valuable asset.[108] Additionally, if corrections begins to embark on the preservice approach to entry-level training, a significant step will have been taken toward obtaining recognition as a profession (as well as achieving substantial cost reductions). However, the wrong person trained is still the wrong person for the job. Serious attention to valid, job-related, and generationally relevant selection screening will therefore become of even greater importance.[109]

Further strides toward professionalism can also be expected from the national certification initiative being undertaken by the American Correctional Association. In terms of its emphasis on testing, ethics, and continuing education, ACA's correctional certification standards in many ways emulate the credentialing procedures of traditional professions.[110] But it is also essential to note that professionalism is not a "quick fix" for organizational problems, personnel shortcomings, or political impediments:

> Professionalism is not a commodity that can be issued like a uniform, provided like a training program, awarded like a promotion, or decreed like a policy. It is not a weapon to be wielded defensively in response to public apprehensions. It cannot be mandated, forced, or shouted into practice. To the contrary, it is a calling rather than a job . . . not something with which to comply, but rather, to be committed to.[111]

Visionary Leadership

It is difficult to imagine a point in time when there has been a greater need for farsighted, visionary leadership throughout the correctional conglomerate. Late in the twentieth century, national surveys had already begun to identify institutional crowding, staff and funding shortages, and resulting workload increases as the key problems that corrections was anticipated to face in the "near future."[112] Well, the "near future" is now upon us, and overcrowding and understaffing continue to plague the correctional conglomerate. Moreover, while the pressure of institutional numbers may ease somewhat in the coming years, the same is not as likely to be true for probation and parole caseloads.

Maximizing the quality of personnel cannot be expected to miraculously resolve these difficult challenges, but it can contribute considerably toward minimizing their negative impact. Notice that each of these issues represents a *quantifiable* aspect of correctional work. As focus shifts more and more in that direction, it is easy to lose sight of the fact that people are changed by other people. They are not changed for the better by a "program" or a "system," although they can be changed for the worse by being regimented and dehumanized. Overall, the system is much less important than the people who breathe life into it.

As the issue of grooming future leadership illustrates, before it is feasible to deal effectively with the future, it is essential to address the here and now. Yet focusing exclusively on the present also perpetuates a continuously reactive cycle. To use an analogy, the first priority for a drowning person is obviously being rescued. Only by learning how to swim, however, will the potential for further near-misses be avoided. The field of corrections may not yet be "drowning." But it is rowing upstream amid strong currents. In such a situation, there are three choices: give up, row harder, or reduce the strength of the currents.

Shaping the Future

Many of today's correctional administrators are undoubtedly rowing harder. They are, for the most part, making vigorous efforts to cope with limited resources and a constantly changing legal, social, and political environment. But too much time is still spent complaining about how little control they have over their own destiny and not enough time actively planning to shape that destiny.

Only to the extent that vigorous efforts today are combined with a far-reaching vision of tomorrow can we hope to reduce the strength and impact of changing currents for our successors in the twenty-first century. As reflected throughout this text, in many respects efforts are being made by forward-thinking leaders to plant the seeds of change, but:

> Whether they will continue to thrive and grow in the shifting sands of personal emotion, outspoken opinion, and politically-driven policies that have tended to influence the correctional environment remains to be seen. What is not so uncertain is the impact that the correctional conglomerate will continue to exercise on the lives of millions of clients under its care, custody, and control.[113]

In the long run, future generations will judge us not by what obstacles we have or have not faced today but, rather, by what opportunities we have or have not seized today to shape tomorrow's destiny. For destiny is not a result of chance, but a reflection of choice.

SUMMARY

Of the forces that have affected corrections in recent years, accreditation and privatization have been among the most influential. In an effort directed toward voluntary improvement, agencies are increasingly pursuing accreditation by meeting national standards. However, privatization is a much more controversial issue. While private enterprises have long been involved in corrections, the nature of their involvement has changed dramatically in terms of contracting the full operation of entire correctional facilities. Strong sentiments exist on both sides, and reservations have been expressed about whether the administration of correctional institutions is an appropriate role for private industry.

In the future, corrections will continue to be affected by everything from the national economy and prevailing public opinion to drug-related crime and the aging of prison populations. Resulting burdens on both correctional facilities and community caseloads demand doing more with less, as has been the case throughout implementation of the justice model.

In many respects, the justice model does not appear to be functioning much more effectively than its predecessors. However, it must also be acknowledged that, as with earlier models, its implementation was hampered by lack of proper foresight, evaluation research, and resource allocation. With more sophisticated empirical studies being conducted today, the potential exists to fully embrace evidence-based decision-making, but it remains to be seen whether such objectivity will prevail in the politically driven environment which has historically characterized corrections.

Among the trends that are expected to continue to exert an impact are intermediate sentencing alternatives, the concept of restorative justice, more pragmatic treatment approaches, regionalization of jails, and direct-supervision or unit management strategies. Increasingly sophisticated electronic devices, workload classification, and objectivity can also be expected to characterize the future—particularly as pressures continue to mount for greater efficiency, productivity, and cost savings.

The most significant key to the quality of future correctional services, however, will be the quality of future personnel. Much of the capability of tomorrow's leaders will depend on the extent to which today's personnel pursue professionalization through greater involvement with higher education, correctional certification, employee empowerment, and similar advancements toward achieving professional identity.

As in all endeavors, effectively accommodating the future requires both a current commitment toward immediate improvements and the visionary leadership necessary to proactively influence forces on the distant horizon. Shaping the future destiny of the correctional conglomerate is a hefty challenge. It is a lot to expect. It is why corrections is at the same time both fascinating and frustrating.

FOR FURTHER DISCUSSION

1. Discuss why the voluntary accreditation of prisons and jails differs from the mandatory accreditation of hospitals and universities, as well as the pros and cons of making correctional accreditation mandatory.

2. If you were a judge involved in settling inmate lawsuits concerning their confinement, determine in what types of cases your decision would be affected by whether or not the facility was accredited.

3. Go online to see how many examples you can find of the involvement of religious groups in corrections today. Debate to what extent this is (or may

become) a First Amendment issue, especially in terms of the separation of church and state.

4. Identify whether there are any parallels between the Quakers' involvement in the first U.S. penitentiary and the involvement of private enterprise in the operation of correctional facilities today. Particularly in terms of their motives, distinguish between the two.

5. Consider whether we have anyone like John Howard or John Augustus advocating for correctional reform today and, if not, why not (since one could certainly argue that reforms are needed).

6. Compile a list of "unaccounted costs" that are associated with running a private correctional facility, but which are unlikely to be included in their budget (such as the cost of locating and recapturing escapees).

7. Divide into two debate teams—one supporting and one opposing correctional privatization.

8. Go online to find what it costs an inmate in your state to make a long-distance phone call. Compare that to the rate you would pay (without a cell phone), explain why there is a difference, and determine whether you think it is appropriate for the state to "make money" on such services.

9. Divide into two groups—one representing private speculative prisons and one representing government officials in a local community. Consider the following issues for debate:

    - whether local government should assume the costs of infrastructure (roads, water/sewer systems, etc.) associated with building a private prison;

    - if an ambulance or police services are needed at the private prison, who should cover the costs;

    - whether there should be restrictions on where inmates from the private prison can be released.

10. With contributions from participants variously designated to represent political lobbyists, the economic perspective, government, and private industry, determine how this combination of interests has synergistically created the "prison-industrial complex."

11. Put yourself in the position of a government official awarding a prison management contract to a private provider, and identify what provisions you would write into the contract to reduce liability, reflect the public's interest, and assure an acceptable level of service.

12. Determine whether it is appropriate for private industry to "skim off" low-risk correctional populations and minimum-security institutions.

13. Research the *Richardson v. McKnight* Supreme Court case to determine why it was decided that private sector prison employees are not immune from liability.

14. Debate whether there is a valid argument that government is the only legally authorized operator of correctional facilities.

15. Explain why it is so difficult to conduct research studies designed to assess whether public or private correctional facilities are more cost-effective.

16. Go online to find out what the percentage of drug offenders is in your state's correctional institution population. Then use average annual costs of incarceration to calculate what this is costing your state, and compare it to expenditures for higher education.

17. In terms of the logic underlying America's response to crime, explain what is meant by the observation that "Building more prisons to address crime is like building more graveyards to address a fatal disease."

18. Determine what correctional administrators could do to become more proactive in shaping the public policy agenda concerning corrections, but at the same time recognize why they are not more politically active.

19. Outline a plan for establishing evidence-based research as a fundamental basis for both correctional decision-making and public policy-making.

20. Debate the pros and cons of restorative justice versus retributive justice in terms of responding more effectively to violent, property, and drug-related crime.

21. In terms of recruitment, retention, and succession planning, discuss what is needed to advance the professionalism of correctional staff at the operational level.

Notes

Part 1   The Nature, Scope, and Function of Corrections

1 American Correctional Association, ed., *The American Prison: From the Beginning—A Pictorial History* (College Park, MD: American Correctional Association, 1983), p. 253.

1   The Correctional Conglomerate

1 President's Commission on Law Enforcement and Administration of Justice, *Task Force Report: Corrections* (Washington, DC: U.S. Government Printing Office, 1967), p. 1.

2 Kristen A. Hughes, "Justice Expenditure and Employment in the United States, 2003," *Bureau of Justice Statistics Bulletin* (Washington, DC: U.S. Department of Justice, April, 2006), p. 4.

3 Bert Useem and Anne M. Piehl, "Prison Buildup and Disorder," *Punishment and Society*, Vol. 8, No. 1 (2006), p. 95.

4 Christine S. Scott-Hayward, *The Fiscal Crisis in Corrections: Rethinking Policies and Practices* (New York: Vera Institute of Justice, July, 2009), p. 3.

5 The PEW Center on the States, *Ten Steps Corrections Directors Can Take to Strengthen Performance* (Washington, DC: The PEW Center on the States, May, 2008), p. 12.

6 Judith Greene, "Banking on the Prison Boom," in Tara Herivel and Paul Wright, *Prison Profiteers: Who Makes Money from Mass Incarceration* (New York: New Press, 2007), p. 22.

7 "Behind the Numbers: Analyzing Growth in Corrections," *Corrections Alert*, Vol. 3, No. 3 (May 6, 1996), p. 1, quoting Larry Solomon of the National Institute of Corrections.

8 Hughes, "Justice Expenditure and Employment," p. 6.

9 Ibid.

10 "Adult Correctional Populations," available at http://www.ojp.usdoj.gov/bjs/correct.htm.

11 Useem and Piehl, "Prison Buildup and Disorder," p. 88.

12 James J. Stephan, *Census of State and Federal Correctional Facilities, 2005* (Washington, DC: U.S. Department of Justice, October, 2008), p. 4.

13 Ibid., p. 2.

14 Todd D. Minton and William J. Sabol, *Jail Inmates at Midyear 2008—Statistical Tables* (Washington, DC: U.S. Department of Justice, Bureau of Justice Statistics, March, 2009), p. 5.

15 American Jail Association, *Who's Who in Jail Management* (Hagerstown, MD: American Jail Association, 2007).

16 Press Release, "Growth in Prison and Jail Populations Slowing," U.S. Department of Justice, Office of Justice Programs, Bureau of Justice Statistics (March 31, 2009), p. 1.

17 Lauren E. Glaze and Thomas P. Bonczar, "Probation and Parole in the United States, 2008," *Bureau*

of Justice Statistics Bulletin (Washington, DC: U.S. Department of Justice, Bureau of Justice Statistics, December, 2009), p. 3.

18 Ibid., p. 3.

19 Howard Snyder and Melissa Sickmund, *Juvenile Offenders and Victims: 2006 National Report* (Washington, DC: U.S. Department of Justice, Office of Juvenile Justice and Delinquency Prevention, March, 2006), p. 177.

20 Nola M. Joyce, "A View of the Future: The Effect of Policy on Prison Population Growth," *Crime and Delinquency*, Vol. 38, No. 3 (July, 1992), p. 368.

21 Ad Hoc Committee, Criminal Justice Section, American Bar Association, *Responding to the Problem of Drug Abuse: Strategies for the Criminal Justice System* (Washington, DC: American Bar Association, 1992), p. 60. See also Judith Greene, "Controlling Prison Crowding," *Corrections Today*, Vol. 59, No. 1 (February, 1997), pp. 50–65.

22 Dale Parent, Terence Dunworth, Douglas McDonald, and William Rhodes, "Key Legislative Issues in Criminal Justice: Mandatory Sentencing," *National Institute of Justice: Research in Action* (January, 1997), p. 2.

23 Robert Martinson, "What Works? Questions and Answers about Prison Reform," *The Public Interest*, Vol. 35 (Spring, 1975), pp. 22–54.

24 William G. Archambeault and Betty J. Archambeault, *Correctional Supervisory Management: Principles of Organization, Policy, and Law* (Englewood Cliffs, NJ: Prentice Hall, 1982), p. 3.

25 U.S. Department of Justice, *An Analysis of Non-violent Drug Offenders with Minimal Criminal Histories* (Washington, DC: U.S. Department of Justice, 1994).

26 John P. O'Connell, Jr., "Throwing away the Key (and State Money)," *Spectrum* (Winter, 1995). See also the Sentencing Project, *Why "3 Strikes and You're Out" Won't Reduce Crime* (Washington, DC: The Sentencing Project, 1994).

27 Doris Layton MacKenzie, "Corrections and Sentencing in the Twenty-first Century: Evidence-based Corrections and Sentencing," in Richard Tewksbury and Dean Dabney, eds., *Prisons and Jails: A Reader* (New York: McGraw-Hill, 2009), p. 568.

28 John Pratt, *Punishment and Civilization* (Thousand Oaks, CA: Sage Publications, 2002), p. 179.

29 Gordon Bazemore, *Balanced and Restorative Justice: Program Summary* (Washington, DC: U.S. Department of Justice, Office of Juvenile Justice and Delinquency Prevention, 1994), p. 2.

30 Leena Kurki, "Incorporating Restorative and Community Justice into American Sentencing and Corrections," *Sentencing and Corrections: Issues for the 21st Century*, No. 3 (September, 1999).

2 The Impact of Sentencing Policies on Corrections

1 Jeremy Travis, "New Challenges in Evaluating Our Sentencing Policy: Exploring the Public Safety Nexus," *Corrections Compendium*, Vol. 25, No. 10 (October, 2000), p. 26.

2 Federal Bureau of Investigation, *Uniform Crime Reports, 2007*, Table 29, available at http://www.fbi.gov/ucr/cius2007/data/table_29.html.

3 Perry Johnson, addressing the Midwinter Meeting of the American Correctional Association, Miami, FL (January 11, 1993).

4 Jeanne B. Stinchcomb and Daryl Hippensteel, "Presentence Investigation Reports: A Relevant Justice Model Tool or a Medical Model Relic?," *Criminal Justice Policy Review*, Vol. 12, No. 2 (June, 2001), pp. 164–177.

5 Michael Tonry, "Reconsidering Indeterminate and Structured Sentencing," *Sentencing and Corrections: Issues for the 21st Century* (Washington, DC: National Institute of Justice, U.S. Department of Justice, September, 1999), p. 3.

6 Marc L. Miller, "Sentencing Reform through Sentencing Information Systems," in Michael Tonry, ed., *The Future of Imprisonment* (New York: Oxford University Press, 2004), p. 121.

7 "Sentencing Guidelines: A Summary," *Corrections Compendium*, Vol. 24, No. 4 (April, 1999), p. 6.

8 Ibid.

9 "Emphasis on Enforcement Not the Answer to the Drug Crisis, ABA Report Says," *Narcotics Control Digest* (January 29, 1992), p. 4. See also J.P. Caulkins, C.P. Rydell, W.L. Schwabe, and J. Chiesa, *Mandatory Minimum Drug Sentences: Throwing away the Key or the Taxpayers' Money?* (Santa Monica, CA: RAND Corporation, 1997).

10 Marc Mauer, *Race to Incarcerate* (New York: New Press, 2006), p. 75.

11 Stanley E. Adelman, "Supreme Court Invalidates Federal Sentencing Guidelines . . . to an Extent," *On the Line*, Vol. 28, No. 3 (May, 2005), p. 3, citing *U.S. v. Booker*, 125 S. Ct. 738 (2005). A follow-up study by the Sentencing Project found that this easing of sentencing restrictions did, in fact, result in lesser crack cocaine sentences. See Kevin Harris, "Crack Offenders Receive Less Prison Time," *Corrections Today* (April, 2006), p. 15.

12 Mauer, *Race to Incarcerate*, p. 167.

13 Miles D. Harer, "Do Guideline Sentences for Low-risk Traffickers Achieve Their Stated Purpose?," *Federal Sentencing Reporter*, Vol. 7, No. 1 (1994).

14 Caulkins et al., *Mandatory Minimum Drug Sentences*.

15 Peter W. Greenwood, Karyn E. Model, C. Peter Rydell, and James Chiesa, *Diverting Children from a Life of Crime* (Santa Monica, CA: RAND Corporation, 1996).

16 Henry Scott Wallace, "Mandatory Minimums and the Betrayal of Sentencing Reform: A Legislative Dr. Jekyll and Mr. Hyde," *Federal Probation*, Vo. 54, No. 3 (September, 1993), p. 14.

17 Mauer, *Race to Incarcerate*, pp. 124–125.

18 Christopher Wildeman, "Parental Imprisonment, the Prison Boom, and the Concentration of Childhood Disadvantage," *Demography*, Vol. 46, No. 2 (May, 2009), p. 265.

19 Alfred Blumstein and Allen J. Beck, "Factors Contributing to the Growth in U.S. Prison Populations," in Michael Tonry and Joan Petersilia, eds., *Crime and Justice: A Review of Research* (Chicago, IL: University of Chicago Press, 1999).

20 Leonard Pitts, "Drug Sentences Create Racial Caste System," *The Miami Herald* (July 18, 2010), p. 2L.

21 Joey R. Weedon, "Drug War Undergoes Reform," *Corrections Today* (August, 2002), p. 24.

22 "DOJ Says Prison Grant Awards Show Impact of Truth-in-sentencing Laws," *Corrections Digest*, Vol. 28, No. 2 (January 10, 1997), p. 3.

23 "Officials Say Building Grants Have Costly Downside for States," *Corrections Journal* (October 7, 1998), p. 7.

24 Leena Kurki, "Incorporating Restorative and Community Justice into American Sentencing and Corrections," *Sentencing and Corrections: Issues for the 21st Century* (Washington, DC: National Institute of Justice, U.S. Department of Justice, September, 1999), p. 1.

25 Harry Elmer Barnes, *The Story of Punishment: A Record of Man's Inhumanity to Man* (New York: The Stratford Company, 1930), p. 63. Republished by Patterson Smith (Montclair, NJ, 1972). See also G. Abbott, *Tortures of the Tower of London* (London: David & Charles, 1986).

26 Gwynn Nettler, *Responding to Crime* (Cincinnati, OH: Anderson, 1982), p. 11.

27 Tracy Snell, "Capital Punishment 2007: Summary Statistics" (Washington, DC: U.S. Department of Justice, 2008), p. 1, available at http://www.ojp.usdoj.gov/bjs/cp.htm.

28 For a comprehensive review of deterrence literature and an assessment of its effectiveness, see Raymond Paternoster, "The Deterrent Effect of the Perceived Certainty and Severity of Punishment: A Review of the Evidence and Issues," *Justice Quarterly*, Vol. 4, No. 20 (June, 1987), pp. 173–217.

29 Home Office, *Crime, Justice and Protecting the Public* (London: HMSO, 1990), p. 8, cited in John Pratt, *Punishment and Civilization: Penal Tolerance and Intolerance in Modern Society* (London: Sage Publications, 2002), p. 172.

30 Franklin E. Zimring and Gordon J. Hawkins, *Deterrence* (Chicago, IL: University of Chicago Press, 1973), pp. 19–20.

31 Marvin Wolfgang, Robert Figlio, and Thorsten Sellin, *Delinquency in a Birth Cohort* (Chicago, IL: University of Chicago Press, 1972). Peter Greenwood, "Controlling the Crime Rate through Imprisonment," in James Q. Wilson, ed., *Crime and Public Policy* (San Francisco, CA: Institute for Contemporary Studies Press, 1983). Sholomo Shinnar and Reuel Shinnar, "The Effects of the Criminal Justice System on the Control of Crime: A Quantitative Approach," *Law and Society Review*, Vol. 9 (1975), pp. 581–611.

32 Greenwood, "Controlling the Crime Rate," p. 258.

33 Lee S. Pershan, "Selective Imprisonment Should Not Be Used," in Bonnie Szumski, ed., *America's Prisons: Opposing Viewpoints*, Fourth Edition (St. Paul, MN: Greenhaven Press, 1985), p. 100.

34 Mark Mauer, *Americans behind Bars: U.S. and International Use of Incarceration, 1995* (Washington, DC: The Sentencing Project, 1997), p. 11.

35 Andrew Coyle, "The Use and Abuse of Prison around the World," *Corrections Today*, Vol. 66, No. 7 (December, 2004), p. 66.

36 Kevin E. Meehan, "California's Three-Strike Law: The First Six Years," *Corrections Management Quarterly*, Vol. 4, No. 4 (Fall, 2000), pp. 22–33.

37 Cited in Louis P. Carney, *Probation and Parole: Legal and Social Dimensions* (New York: McGraw-Hill, 1977), p. 75.

38 Lawrence F. Travis, Martin D. Schwartz, and Todd R. Clear, *Corrections: An Issues Approach*, Second Edition (Cincinnati, OH: Anderson, 1983), p. 9.

39 Robert Martinson, "What Works? Questions and Answers about Prison Reform," *The Public Interest*, Vol. 35 (Spring, 1975), p. 25. It should, however, be noted that Martinson's report did not specifically conclude that "nothing works," but rather that the methodologies used to evaluate rehabilitative efforts were so inadequate that no effect could be validly measured—which points to the need for implementing more rigorous program evaluation techniques.

40 Ted Palmer, "Martinson Revisited," *Journal of Research in Crime and Delinquency* (July, 1975), pp. 133–152.

41 Francis T. Cullen and Karen E. Gilbert, *Reaffirming Rehabilitation* (New York: Matthew Bender, 1982). See also Paul Gendreau, "The Principles of Effective Intervention with Offenders," in Alan T. Harland, ed., *Choosing Correctional Options that Work* (Thousand Oaks, CA: Sage Publications, 1996), and Francis T. Cullen, "Make Rehabilitation Corrections' Guiding Paradigm," *Criminology and Public Policy*, Vol. 6, No. 4 (November, 2007), pp. 717–728.

42 See, for example, Edward J. Latessa, Francis T. Cullen, and Paul Gendreau, "Beyond Correctional Quackery: Professionalism and the Possibility of Effective Treatment," *Federal Probation* (September, 2002), p. 45.

43 Francis T. Cullen, John B. Cullen, and John F. Wozniak, "Is Rehabilitation Dead? The Myth of the Punitive Public," *Journal of Criminal Justice*, Vol. 16, No. 4 (1988), p. 303.

44 Brandon Applegate and Robin King Davis, "Examining Public Support for 'Correcting' Offenders," *Corrections Today* (June, 2005), p. 94, citing Louis Harris, "Changing Public Attitudes toward Crime and Corrections," *Federal Probation*, Vol. 32, No. 4 (1968), pp. 9–16, and Brandon Applegate, Francis T. Cullen, and Bonnie S. Fisher, "Public Support for Correctional Treatment: The Continuing Appeal of the Rehabilitative Ideal," *Prison Journal*, Vol. 77, No. 3 (1997), pp. 237–258.

45 For a description of "total institutionalization," see Gresham Sykes, *The Society of Captives: A Study of a Maximum Security Prison* (Princeton, NJ: Princeton University Press, 1958).

46 Cullen and Gilbert, *Reaffirming Rehabilitation*, pp. 261–263.

3 The Development of Corrections

1 American Correctional Association (ed.), *The American Prison: From the Beginning—A Pictorial History* (College Park, MD: American Correctional Association, 1983), p. 261.

2 James D. Stinchcomb, *Introduction to Criminal Justice: Instructor's Guide*, six audiovisual presentations (Washington, DC: Robert J. Brady Company, 1972), p. 6.

3 Louis P. Carney, *Probation and Parole: Legal and Social Dimensions* (New York: McGraw-Hill, 1977), p. 76.

4 G. Abbott, *Tortures of the Tower of London* (London: David & Charles, 1986), p. 9.

5 Keith Baker and Robert J. Rubel, *Violence and Crime in the Schools* (Lexington, MA: D.C. Heath, 1980), p. 5.

6 George Ives, *History of Penal Methods* (Montclair, NJ: Patterson Smith, 1970), pp. 104–105.

7 Leslie Fairweather, "The Evolution of the Prison," in Giuseppe de Gennaro and Sergio Lenci, eds., *Prison Architecture* (London: United Nations Social Defence Research Institute, Architectural Press, 1975), pp. 13–14.

8 Robert Johnson, *Hard Time: Understanding and Reforming the Prison* (Belmont, CA: Wadsworth, 2002), p. 34.

9 Ibid., p. 10.

10 Ibid., p. 11.

11 Henry Burns, *Corrections: Organization and Administration* (St. Paul, MN: West, 1975), p. 148.

12 Linda L. Zupan, *Jails: Reform and the New Generation Philosophy* (Cincinnati, OH: Anderson, 1991), pp. 11, 13.

13 William G. Nagel, *The New Red Barn: A Critical Look at the Modern Prison* (New York: Walker, 1973), p. 188.

14 For a description of the emergence of correctional institutions as tools of social control, see John Irwin, *The Jail: Managing the Underclass in American Society* (Berkeley, CA: University of California Press, 1985), p. 4.

15 Leonard P. Liggio, "The Transportation of Criminals: A Brief Political-Economic History," in Randy E. Barnett and John Hagel III, eds., *Assessing the Criminal* (Cambridge, MA: Ballinger, 1977), p. 282, citing the works of Jeremy Bentham.

16 Ives, *Penal Methods*, p. 97.

17 Jay M. Moynahan and V.M. Deitrich, "Prisoners on Ships," *American Jails*, Vol. XIII, No. 3 (July/August, 1999), p. 38.

18 Alexis M. Durham III, "Social Control and Imprisonment during the American Revolution: Newgate of Connecticut," *Justice Quarterly*, Vol. 7, No. 2 (June, 1990), pp. 315–316.

19 Burns, *Corrections*, p. 82.

20 American Correctional Association, *American Prison*, p. 28. See also Cyndi Banks, *Punishment in America* (Santa Barbara, CA: ABC-CLIO, 2005).

21 Burns, *Corrections*, p. 149.

22 Ibid., p. 153.

23 Durham, "Social Control," p. 309, quoting W. Storrs Lee, "Stone Walls Do Not a Prison Make," *American Heritage*, Vol. 18, No. 2 (1967), p. 90.

24 Zupan, *Jails*, p. 14, quoting D.L. Howard, *The English Prisons: Their Past and Their Future* (London: Methuen, 1960).

25 American Correctional Association, *American Prison*, p. 24.

26 Ibid., p. 29.

27 Clemens Bartollas, "The Prison: Disorder Personified," in John W. Murphy and Jack E. Dison, eds., *Are Prisons Any Better? Twenty Years of Correctional Reform* (Newbury Park, CA: Sage Publications, 1990), p. 14.

28 Gordon Crews and Wayne Gillespie, "A Brief History of Corrections in America," in Stephen Stanko, Wayne Gillespie, and Gordon Crews, eds., *Living in Prison: A History of the Correctional System with an Insider's View* (Westport, CT: Greenwood Press, 2004), p. 47.

29 American Correctional Association, *American Prison*, p. 55.

30 Moynahan and Deitrich, "Prisoners on Ships," pp. 37–42.

31 For a documentary on this era, see David Oshinsky, *Worse than Slavery: Parchman Farm and the Ordeal of Jim Crow Justice* (New York: Free Press, 1996).

32 American Correctional Association, *American Prison*, p. 63. For an in-depth look at historical prison development, see John Pratt, *Punishment and Civilization: Penal Tolerance and Intolerance in Modern Society* (London: Sage Publications, 2002).

33 American Correctional Association, *American Prison*, p. 75.

34 John V. Barry, "Captain Alexander Maconochie," *Victorian Historical Magazine*, Vol. 27 (June, 1975), p. 5.

35 For a complete account of Maconochie's efforts, see Norval Morris, *Maconochie's Gentlemen: The Story of Norfolk Island and the Roots of Modern Prison Reform* (New York: Oxford University Press, 2003).

36 Alexander W. Pisciotta, *Benevolent Repression: Social Control and the American Reformatory-Prison Movement* (New York: New York University Press, 1994), p. 42, citing the 1884 *Report and Proceedings* of the New York State Board of Charities. See also Oshinsky, *Worse than Slavery*.

37 Department of Justice, *Annual Report of the Attorney General* (1875), cited in Paul W. Keve, *Prisons and the American Conscience: A History of U.S. Federal Corrections* (Carbondale: Southern Illinois University Press, 1991), p. 18.

38 Keve, *Prisons*, p. 21.

39 Robert Johnson, "American Prisons and the African-American Experience: A History of Social Control and Racial Oppression," *Corrections Compendium*, Vol. 25, No. 9 (September, 2000), p. 28.

40 Jack Greene, *Historical Overview: Chain Gangs in the United States, 1800s–1995* (Lanham, MD: American Correctional Association, 1995), p. 4.

41 American Correctional Association, *American Prison*, p. 95, quoting Louis N. Robinson, *Penology in the United States*, 1921. For a detailed history of prison labor, see Richard C. Brister, "Changing of the Guard: A Case for Privatization of Texas Prisons," *Prison Journal* (September, 1996), pp. 310–330.

42 "Burger Again Calls for More Prison Industries," *Corrections Digest*, Vol. 14, No. 13 (June 15, 1983), p. 1.

43 David M. Reutter, "Florida's Private Prison Industry: Corporation under Siege," in Tara Herivel and Paul Wright, *Prison Profiteers: Who Makes Money from Mass Incarceration* (New York: New Press, 2007), p. 144.

44 *Coleman v. Peyton*, 302 2nd 904 (4th Cir. 1966).

45 *Johnson v. Avery*, 89 S. Ct. 747 (1969).

46 President's Commission on Law Enforcement and Administration of Justice, *Task Force Report: Corrections* (Washington, DC: U.S. Government Printing Office, 1967), p. 93.

47 Ibid., p. 210.

48 Robert Martinson, "What Works? Questions and Answers about Prison Reform," *The Public Interest*, Vol. 35 (Spring, 1975), pp. 22–54.

49 For a more detailed description of changing public perspectives on corrections-related issues, see Timothy J. Flanagan, "Community Corrections in the Public Mind," *Federal Probation*, Vol. 60, No. 3 (September, 1996), pp. 3–9.

50 Adam Nossiter, "Life in Prison Turning into a Real Hard Cell," *Pittsburgh Post-Gazette* (September 18, 1994), p. A-8.

51 Greene, "Historical Overview," p. 5.

52 For a list of the 13 states that partially or fully banned weight lifting as of 1997 (and a discussion of its merits as well as drawbacks), see Susan L. Clayton, "Weight Lifting in Corrections: Luxury or Necessity?," *Corrections Today*, Vol. 20, No. 5 (November, 1997), pp. 1, 3.

53 Peter Finn, "No-Frills Prisons and Jails: A Movement in Flux," *Federal Probation*, Vol. 60, No. 3 (September, 1996), p. 36.

54 Franklin E. Zimring and Gordon Hawkins, "Democracy and the Limits of Punishment: A Preface to Prisoners' Rights," in Michael Tonry, ed., *The Future of Imprisonment* (New York: Oxford University Press, 2004), p. 170.

55 "National Corrections Executive Survey Adds Fuel to 'Frills' Fire," *Corrections Alert*, Vol. 3. No. 1 (April 8, 1996), pp. 1–2.

56 Stephen J. Ingley, "It's the Wave of the Past: Getting Tough (Nasty) on Criminals," *American Jails*, Vol. IX, No. 4 (September/October, 1995), p. 7.

57 Bobbie L. Huskey, "Think Twice before Abolishing Inmate Privileges," *Corrections Today*, Vol. 57, No. 3 (June, 1995), p. 6.

58 "Back on the Chain Gang," *Corrections Digest*, Vol. 26, No. 10 (March 10, 1995), p. 5, quoting Rob Hoelter, director of the National Center on Institutions and Alternatives.

59 "ACA Develops Legislative Priorities for 1995–96," *On the Line*, Vol. 18, No. 4 (September, 1995), p. 1.

60 Robert Johnson, *Hard Time: Understanding and Reforming the Prison* (Belmont, CA: Wadsworth, 2002), p. 7.

Part 2   Correctional Services, Practices, and Institutions

1 Correctional Service of Canada, *Mission of the Correctional Service of Canada* (Ottawa, Ontario: Correctional Service of Canada, 1991), p. 7.

4   Community-based Alternatives

1 Ramsey Clark, *Crime in America* (New York: Simon & Schuster, 1970), p. 220.

2 Ken Kerle, "Jails and Intermediate Punishment," *American Jails*, Vol. 5, No. 1 (March/April, 1991), p. 4.

3 Orville B. Pung, "Let's Abolish 'Probation and Treatment,'" *Overcrowded Times*, Vol. 4, No. 2 (April, 1993), p. 3.

4 Perry Johnson, addressing the Midwinter Meeting of the American Correctional Association, Miami, FL (January 11, 1993).

5 "Community Corrections Survey: Public Indicates Strong Support," *Corrections Today*, Vol. 53, No. 7 (December, 1991), p. 134, citing Neil Tilow, president of the International Association of Residential and Community Alternatives.

6 It should be noted that this chapter is focused exclusively on nonresidential community-based alternatives. Community residential centers are included in the discussion of minimum-security facilities in Chapter 6.

7 National Advisory Commission on Criminal Justice Standards and Goals, *Courts* (Washington, DC: U.S. Government Printing Office, 1973), p. 32.

8 See Richard S. Gebelein, *The Rebirth of Rehabilitation: Promise and Perils of Drug Courts* (Washington, DC: National Institute of Justice, 2000).

9 Gordon Perry and John Walker, "Intermediate Sanctions in Canada," *American Jails*, Vol. 5, No. 1 (March/April, 1991), p. 124.

10 See Jeanne B. Stinchcomb, "Drug Courts: Conceptual Foundation, Empirical Findings, and Policy Implications," *Drugs: Education, Prevention, and Policy*, Vol. 17, No. 2 (April, 2010), pp. 148–167.

11 Bradley Schaffer, "Veterans Courts and Diversion Alternatives," *American Jails*, Vol. XXIII, No. 6 (January/February, 2010), pp. 21–24.

12 For an overview of the nature, functions, and outcomes of such alternatives, see National Association of Pretrial Services Agencies, *Pretrial Diversion in the 21st Century: A National Survey of Pretrial Diversion Programs and Practices* (Washington, DC: National Association of Pretrial Services Agencies, 2009).

13 David E. Duffee, "Community Corrections: Its Presumed Characteristics and an Argument for a New Approach," in David E. Duffee and Edmund F. McGarrell, eds., *Community Corrections: A Community Field Approach* (Cincinnati, OH: Anderson, 1990), p. 4.

14 Benjamin F. Baer, "Good PR Programs Enhance Public Acceptance," in American Correctional Association, *Intermediate Punishment: Community-based Sanctions* (Laurel, MD: American Correctional Association, 1990), p. 16, quoting Barry J. Nidorf, chief probation officer of Los Angeles County, California.

15 Todd R. Clear and George F. Cole, *American Corrections* (Belmont, CA: Wadsworth, 1994), p. 159.

16 Ann H. Crowe, Linda Sydney, Pat Bancroft, and Beverly Lawrence, *Offender Supervision with Electronic Technology* (Lexington, KY: Council of State Governments, 2002), p. 3.

17 Marc Renzema and David Skelton, "Use of Electronic Monitoring in the United States," *National Institute of Justice Reports* (November/December, 1990), p. 11.

18 For a more comprehensive discussion of the negative experiences of offenders on electronic monitoring see Brian K. Payne and Randy R. Gainey, "A Qualitative Assessment of the Pains Experienced on Electronic Monitoring," in Richard Tewksbury and Dean Dabney, eds., *Prisons and Jails: A Reader* (New York: McGraw-Hill, 2009), pp. 533–544.

19 Nancy Marion, "Effectiveness of Community-based Correctional Programs: A Case Study," *Prison Journal*, Vol. 82, No. 4 (December, 2002), pp. 478–497.

20 Gail Townsend, "Kansas Community Corrections Programs," *American Jails*, Vol. 5, No. 1 (March/April, 1991), p. 30. See also Joan Farrall and Dick Whitfield, "Voice Verification and Offender Monitoring," *Journal of Offender Monitoring*, Vol. 12, No. 3 (Summer, 1999), pp. 14–15.

21 Ray Wahl, "Is Electronic Home Monitoring a Viable Option?," in American Correctional Association, *Intermediate Punishment*, p. 27.

22 Lauren E. Glaze and Thomas P. Bonczar, "Probation and Parole in the United States, 2008," *Bureau of Justice Statistics Bulletin* (Washington, DC: U.S. Department of Justice, December, 2009), p. 3.

23 For a more detailed description of the providers of probation services, see American Correctional Association, *Vital Statistics in Corrections* (Lanham, MD: American Correctional Association, 2000), pp. 128–129.

24 See Louis Gesualdi, "The Work of John Augustus: Peacemaking Criminology," *ACJS Today* (September/October, 1999), pp. 1–4.

25 See Thomas P. Bonczar, "Characteristics of State Parole Supervising Agencies, 2006," *Bureau of Justice Statistics Special Report* (Washington, DC: U.S. Department of Justice, August, 2008), p. 1.

26 Although states vary from 33 percent to 100 percent in terms of the percentage of their jurisdictions minimally requiring a bachelor's degree for probation or parole officers, the vast majority of locations in most states maintain this requirement for entry. American Correctional Association, *Vital Statistics in Corrections*, p. 161.

27 Orville B. Pung, "Let's Abolish 'Probation and Treatment,'" *Overcrowded Times*, Vol. 4, No. 2 (April, 1993), p. 3.

28 See Kirsten D. Levingston, "Making the 'Bad Guy' Pay: Growing Use of Cost Shifting as an Economic Sanction," in Tara Herivel and Paul Wright, eds., *Prison Profiteers: Who Makes Money from Mass Incarceration* (New York: New Press, 2007), pp. 52–79.

29 Glaze and Bonczar, "Probation and Parole in the United States, 2008," p. 24.

30 Faye Taxman, E. Shephardson, and J. Byrne, *Tools of the Trade: A Guide to Incorporating Science into Practice* (Washington, DC: National Institute of Corrections, U.S. Department of Justice, Office of Justice Programs, 2004), p. 3.

31 Jeanne B. Stinchcomb and Daryl Hippensteel, "Presentence Investigation Reports: A Relevant Justice Model Tool or Medical Model Relic?," *Criminal Justice Policy Review*, Vol. 12, No. 2 (2001), pp. 164–177.

32 Edward J. Latessa, "Community Supervision: Research, Trends, and Innovations," in Lawrence F. Travis, Martin D. Schwartz, and Todd R. Clear, *Corrections: An Issues Approach*, Second Edition

(Cincinnati, OH: Anderson, 1983), p. 163. See also P.F. Cromwell, G.G. Killinger, H.B. Kerper, and C. Walker, *Probation and Parole in the Criminal Justice System* (St. Paul, MN: West, 1985), pp. 109–110.

33 Patrick A. Langan and Mark A. Cuniff, "Recidivism of Felons on Probation, 1986–1989," *Bureau of Justice Statistics Special Report* (Washington, DC: U.S. Department of Justice, 1992), p. 1.

34 See William D. Burrell, *Trends in Probation and Parole in the States* (Lexington, KY: American Probation and Parole Association, n.d.).

35 "Alternatives to Incarceration Mean Less Recidivism," *Corrections Digest*, Vol. 27, No. 18 (1996), pp. 1–3. Paul Gendreau, Francis T. Cullen, and Donald A. Andrews, "The Effects of Community Sanctions and Incarceration on Recidivism," *Forum on Correctional Research*, Vol. 12, No. 2 (May, 2000), p. 12.

36 P.A. Langan, "Between Prison and Probation: Intermediate Sanctions," *Science* (May 6, 1994), pp. 791–794.

37 *Mempa v. Rhay*, 389 U.S. 128 (1967).

38 *Gagnon v. Scarpelli*, 411 U.S. 778 (1973).

39 National Institute of Justice, "NIJ Survey of Probation and Parole Agency Directors," *National Institute of Justice Update* (Washington, DC: U.S. Department of Justice, 1995), p. 1.

40 William Burrell, *Caseload Standards for Probation and Parole* (Lexington, KY: American Probation and Parole Association, September, 2006), p. 2.

41 Ibid., p. 7.

42 Camille Graham Camp, ed., *The 2002 Corrections Yearbook: Adult Corrections* (Middletown, CT: Criminal Justice Institute, 2003), p. 195.

43 Dan Richard Beto, Ronald P. Corbett, Jr., and John J. DiIulio, Jr., "Getting Serious about Probation and the Crime Problem," *Corrections Management Quarterly*, Vol. 4, No. 2 (Spring, 2000), p. 3.

44 Eric Schlosser, "The Prison-industrial Complex," *Atlantic Monthly* (December, 1998), p. 68.

45 M.G. Neithercutt and D.M. Gottfredson, *Case Load Size Variation and Differences in Probation/Parole Performance* (Pittsburgh, PA: National Center for Juvenile Justice, 1974). See also American Probation and Parole Association, *Results-driven Management: Implementing Performance-based Measures in Community Corrections* (Lexington, KY: American Probation and Parole Association, 1995).

46 Donald Cochrane, "Corrections' Catch 22," *Corrections Today*, Vol. 51, No. 6 (October, 1989), p. 16.

47 Ibid., pp. 17–20. See also Frank S. Pearson, "Evaluation of New Jersey's Intensive Supervision Program," *Crime and Delinquency*, Vol. 34, No. 4 (1988), pp. 437–448.

48 Joan Petersilia and Susan Turner, "Evaluating Intensive Supervision Probation/Parole: Results of a Nationwide Experiment," *National Institute of Justice Research in Brief* (Washington, DC: U.S. Department of Justice, 1993).

49 Betsy Fulton and Susan Stone, "Evaluating the Effectiveness of Intensive Supervision," *Corrections Today*, Vol. 54, No. 8 (December, 1992), p. 82.

50 Ibid., citing Barry Nidorf.

51 Joan Petersilia and Susan Turner, "Objectively Evaluating ISPs," *Corrections Today*, Vol. 53, No. 3 (June, 1991), p. 28.

52 Fulton and Stone, "Evaluating Intensive Supervision," p. 85. See also American Probation and Parole Association, *Restructuring Intensive Supervision Programs: Applying "What Works"* (Lexington, KY: American Probation and Parole Association, 1994).

5   Jails: Pretrial Detention and Short-term Confinement

1 Kenneth E. Kerle, *Exploring Jail Operations* (Hagerstown, MD: American Jail Association, 2003), p. 284.

2 For example, in one 12-month period, jails admitted 13 million inmates, whereas state and federal prisons admitted only about 750,000. William J. Sabol and Todd D. Minton, "Jail Inmates

at Midyear 2007," *Bureau of Justice Statistics Bulletin* (Washington, DC: U.S. Department of Justice, June, 2008), p. 2, and William J. Sabol and Heather Couture, "Prison Inmates at Midyear 2007," *Bureau of Justice Statistics Bulletin* (Washington, DC: U.S. Department of Justice, June, 2008), p. 4.

3 Todd D. Minton, "Jail Inmates at Midyear 2009—Statistical Tables," *Bureau of Justice Statistics: Statistical Tables* (Washington, DC: U.S. Department of Justice, June, 2010), pp. 1–2.

4 James J. Stephan, *Census of Jails, 1999* (Washington, DC: U.S. Department of Justice, August, 2001), p. iii.

5 American Jail Association, *Who's Who in Jail Management* (Hagerstown, MD: American Jail Association, 2007), whose count includes Indian country jails, ICE detention facilities, and metropolitan detention centers administered by the Federal Bureau of Prisons. It should be noted that differing definitions of jails and data collection methodologies may also account for some of this difference.

6 Ibid.

7 Stephan, *Census of Jails, 1999*, p. 3.

8 Sabol and Minton, "Jail Inmates at Midyear 2007," pp. 2–3.

9 See Mark Kellar and Shelley Parker, "Operating a Small Jail in Texas: An Administrative Challenge," *American Jails* (September/October, 2003), pp. 19–23.

10 Morton J. Leibowitz, "Regionalization in Virginia Jails," *American Jails*, Vol. 5, No. 5 (November/December, 1991), pp. 42–43, and Lewis W. Barlow, Sheila Hight, and Marc Hight, "Piedmont Regional Jails as a Community Model," *American Jails* (November/December, 2006), p. 38.

11 American Jail Association, *Who's Who in Jail Management*, pp. 431–433. See also "West Virginia Looks to Cut Jail Fees," *American Jails*, Vol. XXIII, No. 1 (March/April, 2009), p. 86.

12 Brandon K. Applegate, Robin King Davis, Charles W. Otto, Ray Surette, and Bernard J. McCarthy, "The Multifunction Jail: Policy Makers' Views of the Goals of Local Incarceration," *Criminal Justice Policy Review*, Vol. 14, No. 2 (June, 2003), p. 155.

13 Minton, "Jail Inmates at Midyear 2009," p. 10.

14 Allen J. Beck, "Jail Population Growth: National Trends and Predictors of Future Growth," *American Jails* (May/June, 2002), p. 12.

15 Heather C. West and William J. Sabol, "Prisoners in 2007," *Bureau of Justice Statistics Bulletin* (Washington, DC: U.S. Department of Justice, December, 2008), p. 24.

16 "Three VA Sheriffs Sue Department of Corrections," *On the Line*, Vol. 18, No. 2 (March, 1995), p. 2. See also David M. Bogard, "State-ready Inmates in Local Jails: Are You in Jeopardy?," *American Jails* (January/February, 1995), pp. 75–78.

17 Doris J. James, "Profile of Jail Inmates, 2002," *Bureau of Justice Statistics Special Report* (Washington, DC: U.S. Department of Justice, July, 2004), p. 1.

18 Kenneth E. Kerle, "Introduction," in Joel A. Thompson and G. Larry Mays, eds., *American Jails: Public Policy Issues* (Chicago, IL: Nelson-Hall, 1991), p. xiv.

19 Jennifer C. Karberg and Doris J. James, "Substance Dependence, Abuse, and Treatment of Jail Inmates, 2002," *Bureau of Justice Statistics Bulletin* (Washington, DC: U.S. Department of Justice, July, 2005), p. 1.

20 Laura M. Maruschak, "DWI Offenders under Correctional Supervision," *Bureau of Justice Statistics Special Report* (Washington, DC: U.S. Department of Justice, June, 1999), p. 1.

21 Doris J. Wilson, "Drug Use, Testing, and Treatment in Jails," *Bureau of Justice Statistics Special Report* (Washington, DC: U.S. Department of Justice, May, 2000), p. 7.

22 J.P. Caulkins, C.P. Rydell, W.L. Schwabe, and J. Chiesa, *Mandatory Minimum Drug Sentences: Throwing away the Key or the Taxpayers' Money?* (Santa Monica, CA: RAND Corporation, 1997).

23 Joey R. Weedon, "The Role of Jails Is Growing in the Community," *Corrections Today* (April, 2003), p. 18.

24 Stephen H. Gettinger, *New Generation Jails: An Innovative Approach to an Age-old Problem* (Washington, DC: U.S. Department of Justice, 1984), p. 2.

25 Much of the following architectural description is summarized from Lois Spears and Donald Taylor, "Coping with Our Jam-packed Jails," *Corrections Today*, Vol. 52 (June, 1990), p. 20; and W. Raymond Nelson, "Cost Savings in New Generation Jails: The Direct Supervision Approach," *National Institute of Justice Construction Bulletin* (July, 1988), p. 2. See also Richard Wener, "The Invention of Direct Supervision," *Corrections Compendium*, Vol. 30, No. 2 (March/April, 2005), pp. 4–7, 32–34.

26 However, with continually increasing jail crowding in recent years, it should not be surprising that most inmates are no longer confined in single cells. See Christine Tartaro, "Are They Really Direct Supervision Jails? A National Study," *American Jails* (November/December, 2006), pp. 9–17.

27 Brent Swager, "County Jail without Doors," *Corrections Technology and Management*, Vol. 3, No. 2 (March/April, 1999), pp. 46–47, quoting Sgt. Don Kracke.

28 For an alternative to this approach, which encourages inmates to take responsibility for themselves by moving through the facility to obtain services rather than having the services delivered to them, see Sandra Thacker, "A New Principle, a New Generation," *American Jails* (March/April, 2000), pp. 43–52.

29 For more information on the relationship between color schemes and inmate behavior, see I.S.K. Reeves V, "Soothing Shades: Color and Its Effect on Inmate Behavior," *Corrections Today*, Vol. 54, No. 2 (April, 1992), pp. 128–130.

30 Christine Tartaro, "Examining Implementation Issues with New Generation Jails," *Criminal Justice Policy Review*, Vol. 13, No. 3 (September, 2002), pp. 231, 234.

31 David M. Parrish, "The Evolution of Direct Supervision in the Design and Operation of Jails," *Corrections Today*, Vol. 65, No. 6 (October, 2000), p. 127. See also Richard Wener, "Effectiveness of the Direct Supervision System of Correctional Design and Management: A Review of the Literature," *Criminal Justice and Behavior*, Vol. 33, No. 3 (June, 2006), pp. 392–410.

32 Summarized from Nelson, "Cost Savings in New Generation Jails," pp. 4–6. See also Allen R. Beck, "An Evolutionary Step in Direct Supervision Jails: Organizational Culture, Design, and Costs of the Falkenburg Road Jail," *American Jails* (March/April, 2007), pp. 23–30.

33 Gerald J. Bayens, Jimmy J. Williams, and John O. Smykla, "Jail Type and Inmate Behavior: A Longitudinal Analysis," *Federal Probation*, Vol. 61 (September, 1997), pp. 54–62; and Jeffrey D. Senese, "Evaluating Jail Reform: A Comparative Analysis of Podular/Direct and Linear Jail Inmate Infractions," *Journal of Criminal Justice*, Vol. 25, No. 1 (1997), pp. 61–73.

34 Jay Farbstein, Dennis Liebert, and Herbert Sigurdson, *Audits of Podular Direct Supervision Jails* (Washington, DC: U.S. Department of Justice, 1996), p. 2.

35 Jeffery D. Senese, "Evaluating Jail Reform: A Comparative Analysis of Podular/Direct and Linear Jail Inmate Infractions," pp. 61–73; Christine Tartaro and Marissa P. Levy, "The Impact of Jail Environment on Inmate Suicide," *American Jails*, Vol. XXIV, No. 1 (March/April, 2010), pp. 48–55.

36 Senese, "Evaluating Jail Reform: A Comparative Analysis of Podular/Direct and Linear Jail Inmate Infractions," pp. 61–73.

37 James L. Williams, Daniel G. Rodeheaver, and Denise W. Huggins, "A Comparative Evaluation of a New Generation Jail," in Richard Tewksbury and Dean Dabney, eds., *Prisons and Jails: A Reader* (New York: McGraw-Hill, 2009), p. 489.

38 James L. Williams, Daniel G. Rodeheaver, and Denise W. Huggins, "A Comparative Evaluation of a New Generation Jail," *American Journal of Criminal Justice*, Vol. 23, No. 2 (Spring, 1999), pp. 223–246.

39 Richard Werner, William Frazier, and Jay Farbstein, "Building Better Jails," *Psychology Today*, Vol. 21, No. 6 (June, 1987), p. 42. For a more detailed comparison of traditional and direct-supervision jails in terms of rule violations resulting in incident reports, see J.D. Senese, J. Wilson, A.O. Evans, R. Aguirre, and D.B. Kalinich, "Evaluating Jail Reform: Inmate Infractions and Disciplinary Response in a Traditional and a Podular/Direct Supervision Jail," *American Jails* (September/October, 1992), pp. 14–23.

40 Williams, Rodeheaver, and Huggins, "Comparative Evaluation of a New Generation Jail," p. 489.

41 Byron Johnson, "Exploring Direct Supervision: A Research Note," *American Jails* (March/April, 1994), pp. 63–64.

42 Williams, Rodeheaver, and Huggins, "Comparative Evaluation of a New Generation Jail," p. 486.

43 Richard Wener, "Direct Supervision—Evolution and Revolution," *American Jails* (March/April, 2006), p. 24. However, it is noteworthy that, when jails compromise direct-supervision principles and adopt only part of the model, successful outcomes are less likely. See, for example, Christine Tartaro, "Suicide and the Jail Environment: An Evaluation of Three Types of Institutions," *Environment and Behavior*, Vol. 35, No. 5 (September, 2003), pp. 605–620.

44 Wener et al., "Building Better Jails," p. 42.

45 Dillard H. Hughes, "The New Generation Jail: Ten Years After," *American Jails* (May/June, 2003), p. 44.

46 Gettinger, *New Generation Jails*, p. 20. See also Jerry W. Fuqua, "New Generation Jails—Old Generation Management," *American Jails* (March/April, 1991), pp. 80–83.

47 W. Raymond Nelson and Russell M. Davis, "Podular Direct Supervision: The First Twenty Years," *American Jails* (July/August, 1995), pp. 16–22, and Christine Tartaro, "Survey: Direct Supervision Jails," *American Jails* (May/June, 2003), pp. 77–79.

48 James J. Stephan, *Census of Jails, 1991* (Washington, DC: U.S. Department of Justice, Bureau of Justice Statistics, 2001), p. 7.

49 N.E. Schafer, "State Operated Jails: How and Why," *American Jails* (September/October, 1994), pp. 35–44.

50 Robbye Braxton-Mintz and Mike Pinson, "Personnel: Your Most Important Resource," *Corrections Today*, Vol. 62, No. 6 (October, 2000), p. 96. See also Gary E. Christensen, Steven T. Lifrak, and Anthony Callisto, "Twenty-first Century Outcomes: Organizational Assessment and Officer Hiring," *American Jails* (November/December, 2003), pp. 25–31.

51 Braxton-Mintz and Pinson, "Personnel," p. 96.

52 Jeanne B. Stinchcomb and Susan W. McCampbell, "The State of Our Nation's Jails Twenty-five Years Later: Identifying Current Jail Challenges," *American Jails* (January/February, 2008), pp. 15–22.

53 Calvin A. Lightfoot, Linda L. Zupan, and Mary K. Stohr, "Jails and the Community: Modeling the Future in Local Detention Facilities," *American Jails* (September/October, 1991), p. 50. See also Dennis Gilbertson, "Jail Industry Programs and Offender Reentry," *American Jails* (May/June, 2003), pp. 9–13.

54 For example, see Los Angeles County Sheriff's Office, *Education-based Incarceration* (Los Angeles: Los Angeles County Sheriff's Office, 2010).

55 "Reno Announces Grant for New TV Programming in State and Local Jails," *Corrections Digest*, Vol. 26, No. 24 (June 16, 1995), p. 9.

56 Rod Miller, George E. Sexton, and Victor J. Jacobsen, "Making Jails Productive," *National Institute of Justice: Research in Brief* (Washington, DC: U.S. Department of Justice, 1991), p. 1. See also Barbara Auerbach, "Private Sector Jail Industries," *American Jails* (May/June, 2003), pp. 15–18 and "The Right Steps to Expand Use of Inmate Labor," *American Jails* (January/February, 2009), pp. 77–78.

57 See, for example, Ken Kerle, "Jail Health Care" and John Clark, "Correctional Health Care Issues in the Nineties—Forecast and Recommendations," *American Jails* (September/October, 1991), pp. 5, 22–23.

58 Jay M. Pomerantz, "Treatment of Mentally Ill in Prisons and Jails: Follow-up Care Needed," *Drug Benefit Trends*, Vol. 15, No. 6 (2003), pp. 20–21. See also Janet Fraser Hale, Arthur M. Brewer, and Warren Ferguson, "Correctional Health Primary Care: Research and Educational Opportunities," *Journal of Correctional Health Care*, Vol. 14, No. 4 (October, 2008), pp. 278–289.

59 See Jeanne B. Stinchcomb and Susan W. McCampbell, *Jail Leaders Speak: A Summary Report to the Bureau of Justice Assistance* (January 21, 2008), available at http://www.ojp.usdoj.gov/BJA/pdf/Jail_Focus_Group_Report.pdf. (It is notable that workforce-related issues came in second.)

60 Christine Tartaro and Rick Ruddell, "Trouble in Mayberry: A National Analysis of Suicides and Attempts in Small Jails," *American Journal of Criminal Justice*, Vol. 31, No. 1 (2006), pp. 81–91.

61 Christopher J. Mumola, "Suicide and Homicide in State Prisons and Local Jails," *Bureau of Justice Statistics Special Report* (Washington, DC: U.S. Department of Justice, August, 2005), p. 1.

62 Lindsay M. Hayes, *National Study of Jail Suicide: 20 Years Later* (Washington, DC: National Institute of Corrections, April, 2010), pp. 20–21. Additionally, almost half of suicides in holding cells were committed within six hours of confinement.

63 Karberg and James, "Substance Dependence, Abuse, and Treatment of Jail Inmates," pp. 6–7.

64 Hayes, *National Study of Jail Suicide*, p. 16.

65 Paula Marcus and Philip Alcabes, "Characteristics of Suicides by Inmates in an Urban Jail," *Hospital and Community Psychiatry*, Vol. 44, No. 3 (1993), pp. 256–261.

66 E.K. Moscicki, "Epidemiology of Completed and Attempted Suicide: Toward a Framework for Prevention," *Clinical Neuroscience Research*, Vol. 1 (2001), pp. 310–323. See also J.R. Goss, K. Peterson, L.W. Smith, K. Kalb, and B.B. Brodey, "Characteristics of Suicide Attempts in a Large Urban Jail System with an Established Suicide Prevention Program," *Psychiatric Services*, Vol. 53 (May, 2002), pp. 574–579.

67 "Suicide Risk despite Denial (or When Actions Speak Louder than Words)," *Jail Suicide/Mental Health Update*, Vol. 16, No. 1 (Summer, 2007), p. 3.

68 However, the direct-supervision model is unlikely to be successful in reducing suicide vulnerability unless all aspects of it are properly implemented. See Christine Tartaro, "Suicide and New Generation Jails: A National Study," *American Jails* (September/October, 2003), pp. 37–42.

69 Commission on Intergovernmental Relations, *Jails: Intergovernmental Dimensions of a Local Problem* (Washington, DC: Advisory Commission on Intergovernmental Relations, 1984), p. 179. See also Tartaro, "Suicide and New Generation Jails," p. 38.

70 For more information on the screening, supervision, and intervention needed to prevent suicides, see Laura Gater and Lindsay Hayes, "Preventing Inmate Suicide," *Corrections Forum*, Vol. 14, No. 6 (November/December, 2005), pp. 32–37; Ronald L. Bonner, *A Process Approach to Suicide Prevention behind Bars* (Lincoln, NE: iUniverse, 2005); and Gregg W. Etter, "Preventing Jail Inmate Suicides," *American Jails* (November/December, 2008), pp. 29–31, as well as *Jail Suicide/Mental Health Update*, published quarterly by the National Institute of Corrections (at http://www.ncianet.org/ncia/suicide.html).

71 H.J. Steadman, D.W. McCarty, and J.P. Morrisey, *The Mentally Ill in Jail: Planning for Essential Services* (New York: Guilford Press, 1989), p. 34. It is also in a jail's best interest in terms of avoiding potential liability. See Darrell L. Ross, "The Liability Trends of Custodial Suicides," *American Jails*, Vol. XXIV, No. 1 (March/April, 2010), pp. 37–47.

72 Doris J. James and Lauren E. Glaze, "Mental Health Problems of Prison and Jail Inmates," *Bureau of Justice Statistics Special Report* (Washington, DC: U.S. Department of Justice, September, 2006), p. 1. See also Michael P. Maloney, Michael P. Ward, and Charles M. Jackson, "Study Reveals that More Mentally Ill Offenders Are Entering Jail," *American Jails* (April, 2003), pp. 100–103, and Henry J. Steadman, Fred C. Osher, Pamela Clark Robbins, Brian Case, and Steven Samuels, "Prevalence of Serious Mental Illness among Jail Inmates," *Psychiatric Services*, Vol. 60, No. 6 (June, 2009), pp. 761–765.

73 Donna Crawford, "Alternatives to Incarceration for Mentally Ill Offenders," *Community Corrections Report*, Vol. 3, No. 1 (November/December, 1995), p. 1.

74 William M. DiMascio, *Seeking Justice: Crime and Punishment in America* (New York: Edna McConnell Clark Foundation, 1997), p. 22.

75 Thomas N. Faust, "Shift the Responsibility of Untreated Mental Illness out of the Criminal Justice System," *Corrections Today* (April, 2003), p. 6.

76 "Mentally Ill Relegated to Jail Cells," *The Miami Herald* (May 23, 2004), p. 20A, quoting Judge Steve Leifman.

77 Risdon N. Slate, "Seeking Alternatives to the Criminalization of Mental Illness," *American Jails* (March/April, 2009), pp. 20–27; see also Laura Gater, "The Problem of Mental Health in Prison Populations," *Corrections Forum* (March/April, 2004), p. 30.

78 Stinchcomb and McCampbell, *Jail Leaders Speak: Current and Future Challenges to Jail Administration and Operations.*

79 Ken Kerle, "Book Review: Criminalization of Mental Illness—Crisis and Opportunity for the Justice System," *American Jails* (March/April, 2009), p. 81.

80 E. Fuller Torrey, *Out of the Shadows: Confronting America's Mental Illness Crisis* (New York: John Wiley & Sons, 1997), pp. 8–9.

81 Evelyn L. Stratton, Scott Blough, and Kristina Hawk, "Solutions for the Mentally Ill in the Criminal Justice System," *American Jails* (January/February, 2004), p. 15.

82 The Sentencing Project, *Mentally Ill Offenders in the Criminal Justice System: An Analysis and Prescription* (Washington, DC: The Sentencing Project, 2002), p. 5.

83 Thomas J. Fagan, Shelia M. Brandt, and Andrea L. Kleiver, "Future Directions," in Robert K. Ax and Thomas J. Fagan, eds., *Corrections, Mental Health, and Social Policy* (Springfield, IL: Charles C. Thomas, 2007), p. 337.

84 Commission on Intergovernmental Relations, *Jails*, p. 180.

85 Lia Gormsen, "Michigan Coalition Calls for Mental Health Solutions," *Corrections Compendium*, Vol. 33, No. 2 (March/April, 2008), p. 10.

86 See National Alliance for the Mentally Ill and Public Citizen's Health Research Group, *Criminalizing the Seriously Mentally Ill: The Abuse of Jails as Mental Hospitals* (Washington, DC: National Alliance for the Mentally Ill and Public Citizen's Health Research Group, 1992), and Ron Honberg and Darcy Gruttadaro, "Flawed Mental Health Policies and the Tragedy of Criminalization," *Corrections Today* (February, 2005), pp. 22–24.

87 Stratton, Blough, and Hawk, "Solutions for the Mentally Ill in the Criminal Justice System," p. 15.

88 Ibid., p. 17, citing research by the Corporation for Supportive Housing.

89 See Risdon N. Slate and W. Wesley Johnson, *Criminalization of Mental Illness: Crisis and Opportunity for the Justice System* (Durham, NC: Carolina Academic Press, 2008), and Susan W. McCampbell, "Finding Friends in the Right Places—Coalitions to Address the Mentally Ill in Jails," *American Jails* (July/August, 1999), pp. 52–55.

90 National Institute of Justice, "Managing Mentally Ill Offenders in the Community," *National Institute of Justice: Program Focus* (Washington, DC: U.S. Department of Justice, 1994). See also Valerie Hildebeitel, "Addressing the Needs of the Mentally Ill Inmate," *American Jails* (November/December, 1992), pp. 60–61.

91 Edward W. Szostak and Marisa L. Beeble, "Mental Health Jail Diversion," *American Jails* (July/August, 2003), pp. 35–41, and Travis Parker, Gerald T. Foley, Kathleen A. Moore, and Nahama Broner, "Jail Diversion Programs: Finding Common Ground," *American Jails*, Vol. XXIII, No. 4 (September/October, 2009), pp. 25–38.

92 Deborah Linden, "The Mentally Ill Offender: A Comprehensive Community Approach," *American Jails* (January/February, 2000), p. 58. Ronald E. Truss, "Birmingham Municipal Court Mental Health Approach," *American Jails* (November/December, 2003), pp. 32–34.

93 Florida Department of Education, *Curriculum Framework* (April, 2009), available at http://www.fldoe.org/workforce/dwdframe/0910/law/rtf/43010205.rtf. See also James Austin, *Objective Jail Classification Systems: A Guide for Jail Administrators* (Longmont, CO: National Institute of Corrections, 1998).

94 Barbara Krauth, Karin Stayton, and Connie Clem, *Fees Paid by Jail Inmates* (Longmont, CO: National Institute of Corrections, December, 2005), p. 6. See also Karla Crocker, "Inmate Fees for Services," *Corrections Today* (July, 2004), pp. 82–85.

95 Pat Nolan, "Inmate User Fees: Fiscal Fix or Mirage?," *Corrections Today* (August, 2003), p. 23.

96 Ibid. See also Kristen D. Levingston, "Making the 'Bad Guy' Pay: Growing Use of Cost Shifting as an Economic Sanction," in Tara Herivel and Paul Wright, eds., *Prison Profiteers: Who Makes Money from Mass Incarceration* (New York: New Press, 2007), pp. 55–79. For views on the opposite side of this debate (supporting the use of inmate fees), see Michelle M. Sanborn, "The Pay-to-stay Debate: Inmates Must Take Financial Responsibility," *Corrections Today* (August, 2003), p. 22.

97 Todd D. Minton and William J. Sabol, "Jail Inmates at Midyear 2008," *Bureau of Justice Statistics: Statistical Tables* (Washington, DC: U.S. Department of Justice, March, 2009), p. 8. See also David Scharf, "Are Day Reporting and Reentry Programs the Future of Corrections in Our Country?," *American Jails* (July/August, 2008), pp. 25–27.

98 National Institute of Corrections, *Jail Population Reduction Strategies* (Washington, DC: National Institute of Corrections, April, 1995), p. 2. See also Mark A. Cunniff, *Jail Crowding: Understanding Jail Population Dynamics* (Washington, DC: National Institute of Corrections, 2001).

99 Robert C. Cushman, "Jail Crowding: Understanding Jail Population Dynamics—A Practical Guide," *American Jails* (November/December, 2003), pp. 62–67, and Mark A. Cunniff, "Jail Crowding: Understanding Jail Population Dynamics—How Can We Forecast Future Needs?," *American Jails* (May/June, 2003), pp. 55–58.

100 Robert C. Cushman, "Jail Crowding: Understanding Jail Population Dynamics—Understanding the Sources of Jail Crowding," *American Jails* (January/February, 2004), p. 45. See also Applegate et al., "The Multifunction Jail," p. 164.

6 Prisons and Other Correctional Facilities

1 Charles H. Logan, "Criminal Justice Performance Measures for Prisons," in Timothy J. Flanagan, James W. Marquart, and Kenneth G. Adams, *Incarcerating Criminals: Prisons and Jails in Social and Organizational Context* (New York: Oxford University Press, 1998), pp. 262–263.

2 James J. Stephan, *Census of State and Federal Correctional Facilities, 2005* (Washington, DC: U.S. Department of Justice, Bureau of Justice Statistics, October, 2008), p. 2.

3 Ibid.

4 Ibid.

5 Heather C. West and William J. Sabol, "Prisoners in 2007," *Bureau of Justice Statistics Bulletin* (Washington, DC: U.S. Department of Justice, December, 2008), p. 7.

6 Camille Graham Camp, ed., *The 2002 Corrections Yearbook: Adult Corrections* (Middletown, CT: Criminal Justice Institute, 2003), p. 86.

7 James J. Stephan, *State Prison Expenditures, 2001* (Washington, DC: U.S. Department of Justice, Bureau of Justice Statistics, 2004), p. 1.

8 *Sourcebook of Criminal Justice Statistics* (2005), Table 1.2.2005, available at http://www.albany.edu/sourcebook/pdf/t122005.pdf.

9 Stephan, *State Prison Expenditures, 2001*, p. 2.

10 "Study Shows Prison Cheaper than Having Criminals on the Street," *Community Crime Prevention Digest* (January, 1991), p. 4, citing John J. DiIulio's study of prison inmates, conducted for the Wisconsin Policy Research Institute; see also Thomas B. Marvell, "Is Future Prison Expansion Worth the Cost?," *Federal Probation*, Vol. 58 (1994), pp. 59–62, and Michael K. Block, "Supply Side Imprisonment Policy," *National Institute of Justice: Research Report* (Washington, DC: National Institute of Justice, 1997).

11 William Spelman, "The Limited Importance of Prison Expansion," in Alfred Blumstein and Joel Wallman, eds., *The Crime Drop in America* (New York: Cambridge University Press, 2000), p. 125; Jenni Gainsborough and Marc Mauer, *Diminishing Returns: Crime and Incarceration in the 1990s* (Washington, DC: The Sentencing Project, 2000); and Steven Raphael and Michael A. Stoll, eds., *Do Prisons Make Us Safer? The Benefits and Costs of the Prison Boom* (New York: Russell Sage Foundation, 2009).

12 Dale Parent, *Recovering Correctional Costs through Offender Fees* (Washington, DC: U.S. Department of Justice, 1990), p. 1.

13 Ibid., p. 1.

14 "Special Focus: Charging Prisoners for Medical Treatment," *Corrections Alert*, Vol. 1, No. 18 (December 26, 1994), pp. 1–2.

15 Dick Franklin, "Supermax Prisons: More of the Same in the 21st Century? Where Do We Go from Here?," in National Institute of Corrections, *Training Manual: NIC Executive Training for New Wardens* (Longmont, CO: National Institute of Corrections, February, 2000), pp. 2–4.

16 M. Olivero and J. Roberts, "The United States Federal Penitentiary at Marion, IL: Alcatraz Revisited," *New England Journal of Criminal and Civil Confinement*, Vol. 16 (1990), pp. 21–51.

17 Human Rights Watch, *Cold Storage: Super-maximum Security Confinement in Indiana* (New York: Human Rights Watch, 1997), p. 14. See also Daniel P. Mears and William D. Bales, "Supermax Housing: Placement, Duration, and Time to Reentry," *Journal of Criminal Justice*, Vol. 38, No. 4 (July–August, 2010), pp. 545–554.

18 Daniel P. Mears, "A Critical Look at Supermax Prisons," *Corrections Compendium*, Vol. 30, No. 5 (September/October, 2005), p. 7.

19 See, for example, Keith Chen and Jesse Shapiro, "Do Harsher Prison Conditions Reduce Recidivism? A Discontinuity-based Approach," *American Law and Economics Review*, Vol. 9, No. 1 (2007), pp. 1–29.

20 Bernard J. McCarthy, "Community Residential Centers: An Intermediate Sanction for the 1990s," in Peter J. Benekos and Alida V. Merlo, eds., *Corrections: Dilemmas and Directions* (Cincinnati, OH: Anderson, 1992), p. 190.

21 Bobbie L. Huskey, "The Expanding Use of CRCs," *Corrections Today*, Vol. 54, No. 8 (December, 1992), p. 73.

22 Ibid., p. 72.

23 James J. Stephan and Jennifer C. Karberg, *Census of State and Federal Correctional Facilities, 2000* (Washington, DC: U.S. Department of Justice, Bureau of Justice Statistics, 2003), p. 7.

24 Ibid., pp. 6–7.

25 Rodrigo J. Carcedo, Felix Lopez, M. Begona Orgaz, Katalin Toth, and Noelia Fernandez-Rouco, "Men and Women in the Same Prison: Interpersonal Needs and Psychological Health of Prison Inmates," *International Journal of Offender Therapy and Comparative Criminology*, Vol. 52, No. 6 (December, 2008), pp. 641–657.

26 Joycelyn M. Pollock, *Women, Prison and Crime* (Belmont, CA: Wadsworth, 2002), p. 84.

27 Ibid.

28 Barbara Bloom, Barbara Owen, and Stephanie Covington, *Gender-responsive Strategies: Research, Practice, and Guiding Principles for Women Offenders* (Washington, DC: U.S. Department of Justice, National Institute of Corrections, 2003).

29 Jack Alexander and James Austin, *Handbook for Evaluating Objective Prison Classification Systems* (San Francisco, CA: National Council on Crime and Delinquency, 1991).

30 "Prison Statistics: Summary Findings," available at http://www.ojp.usdoj.gov/bjs/prisons.htm#selected.

31 West and Sabol, "Prisoners in 2007," p. 7.

32 Craig Haney, "The Psychological Impact of Incarceration: Implications for Postprison Adjustment," in Jeremy Travis and Michelle Waul, *Prisoners Once Removed: The Impact of Incarceration and Reentry on Children, Families, and Communities* (Washington, DC: The Urban Institute, 2003), p. 35.

33 William DiMascio, *Seeking Justice: Crime and Punishment in America* (New York: Edna McConnell Clark Foundation, 1997), p. 4.

34 Eric Schlosser, "The Prison-industrial Complex," *Atlantic Monthly* (December, 1998), p. 68; Christine Tartaro and Marissa P. Levy, "Density, Inmate Assaults, and Direct Supervision Jails," *Criminal*

Justice Policy Review, Vol. 18, No. 4 (2007), pp. 395–417; Meredith P. Huey and Thomas L. McNulty, "Institutional Conditions and Prison Suicide: Conditional Effects of Deprivation and Overcrowding," *The Prison Journal*, Vol. 85, No. 4 (December, 2005): 490–514.

35 Carol Brooks, Kenneth F. Pompi, and Carl E. Nick, "Correctional Health Care: Barriers, Solutions and Public Policy," *Corrections Today* (October, 2007), pp. 50–52, and Benjamin Steiner, "Comparing State- versus Facility-level Effects on Crowding in U.S. Correctional Facilities," *Crime and Delinquency*, Vol. 54, No. 2 (April, 2008), pp. 259–290.

36 Alfred Blumstein, "Prison Crowding," *National Institute of Justice: Crime File Study Guide* (Washington, DC: U.S. Department of Justice, n.d.), p. 1.

37 Camp, *The 2002 Corrections Yearbook: Adult Corrections*, p. 51.

38 Stephan and Karberg, *Census of State and Federal Correctional Facilities, 2000*, p. v. For an analysis of the predictors of such assaults, see Karen F. Lahm, "Inmate Assaults on Prison Staff: A Multilevel Examination of an Overlooked Form of Prison Violence," *The Prison Journal*, Vol. 89, No. 2 (June, 2009), pp. 131–150.

39 John J. Gibbons and Nicholas de B. Katzenbach, *Confronting Confinement: A Report of the Commission on Safety and Abuse in America's Prisons* (New York: Vera Institute of Justice, June, 2006), pp. 32–33.

40 James B. Jacobs, "Inside Prisons," *National Institute of Justice: Crime File Study Guide* (Washington, DC: U.S. Department of Justice, n.d.), p. 1, quoting historian David Rothman.

41 Ibid.

42 Paraphrased from Dennis Rosenbaum's analogy comparing reactive to proactive policing, in Andrew H. Malcolm, "New Strategies to Fight Crime Go Far beyond Stiffer Terms and More Cells," in John J. Sullivan and Joseph L. Victor, eds., *Annual Editions: Criminal Justice 91/92* (Guilford, CT: Dushkin Publishing Group, 1991), p. 27.

43 The remaining 5 percent had no opinion. Bureau of Justice Statistics, *Sourcebook of Criminal Justice Statistics, 2001* (Washington, DC: U.S. Department of Justice, 2002), p. 128.

44 Bureau of Justice Statistics, *Sourcebook of Criminal Justice Statistics, 2003* (Washington, DC: U.S. Department of Justice, 2004), p. 139, available at http://www.albany.edu/sourcebook/pdf/section2.pdf.

45 Brandon K. Applegate, Robin King Davis, Charles W. Otto, Ray Surette, and Bernard J. McCarthy, "The Multifunction Jail: Policy Makers' Views of the Goals of Local Incarceration," *Criminal Justice Policy Review*, Vol. 14, No. 2 (June, 2003), pp. 155–170.

46 Bureau of Justice Statistics, *Sourcebook, 2001*, p. 112.

47 Robert Johnson, "American Prisons and the African-American Experience: A History of Social Control and Racial Oppression," *Corrections Compendium*, Vol. 25, No. 9 (September, 2000), p. 29.

48 Paul W. Keve, *Prison Life and Human Worth* (Minneapolis: University of Minnesota Press, 1974), pp. 63–64.

49 Camp, *The 2002 Corrections Yearbook: Adult Corrections*, p. 150.

50 Gibbons and Katzenbach, *Confronting Confinement*, p. 75.

51 Joseph Rowan, "Politics and Corrections in America: A Good System Goes Bad in Wisconsin," *CJ: The Americas*, Vol. 5, No. 3 (June/July, 1992), p. 7.

52 American Correctional Association, *Vital Statistics in Corrections* (Lanham, MD: American Correctional Association, 2000), p. 144.

53 See Randy Corcoran, "Changing Prison Culture," *Corrections Today* (April, 2005), pp. 24–27.

54 James D. Stinchcomb, *Opportunities in Law Enforcement and Criminal Justice Careers* (New York: McGraw-Hill, 2003), p. 118.

55 American Correctional Association, *Standards for Adult Institutions*, Fourth Edition (Lanham, MD: American Correctional Association, 2003).

56 John J. DiIulio, Jr., *Governing Prisons* (New York: Free Press, 1987), p. 38.

57 See Paul Hersey, Kenneth H. Blanchard, and Dewey E. Johnson, *Management of Organizational Behavior: Leading Human Resources* (Upper Saddle River, NJ: Prentice Hall, 2007).

7   Dynamics of the Prison Population

1 Bruce Western, Mary Pattillo, and David Weiman, "Introduction," in Mary Pattillo, David Weiman, and Bruce Western, eds., *Imprisoning America: The Social Effects of Mass Incarceration* (New York: Russell Sage Foundation, 2004), p. 3.

2 John Irwin and James Austin, "Who Goes to Prison?," in *It's about Time: America's Imprisonment Binge* (Belmont, CA: Wadsworth, 2001), p. 27.

3 Heather C. West and William J. Sabol, *Prison Inmates at Midyear 2008: Statistical Tables* (Washington, DC: U.S. Department of Justice, March, 2009), p. 3.

4 Bureau of Justice Statistics, *Correctional Populations in the U.S., 1997* (Washington, DC: U.S. Department of Justice, 2000), p. 48.

5 Thomas J. Fagan, Shelia M. Brandt, and Andrea L. Kleiver, "Future Directions," in Robert K. Ax and Thomas J. Fagan, eds., *Corrections, Mental Health, and Social Policy* (Springfield, IL: Charles C. Thomas, 2007), p. 340.

6 U.S. Department of Justice, *Bureau of Justice Statistics, Correctional Populations in the U.S., 1997* (Washington, DC: U.S. Department of Justice, 2000), Table 4.10. For substance abusers, the rate is considerably higher (52 percent) than for others (31 percent). See National Center on Addiction and Substance Abuse, *Behind Bars II: Substance Abuse and America's Prison Population* (New York: National Center on Addiction and Substance Abuse, Columbia University, February, 2010), p. 15, available at http://www.casacolumbia.org/articlefiles/575-report2010behindbars2.pdf.

7 Jeremy Travis, *But They All Come Back: Facing the Challenge of Prisoner Reentry* (Washington, DC: The Urban Institute, 2005), p. 32.

8 West and Sabol, *Prison Inmates at Midyear 2008*, p. 21.

9 Of all arrests for violent crimes in 2008, only 18 percent were of women; of arrests for property-related index offenses, 35 percent were of women. Federal Bureau of Investigation, *Crime in the United States, 2008: Uniform Crime Reports* (Washington, DC: Federal Bureau of Investigation, 2009), Table 42, available at http://www.fbi.gov/ucr/cius2008/data/table_42.html.

10 West and Sabol, *Prison Inmates at Midyear 2008*, p. 2.

11 William J. Sabol and Todd D. Minton, "Jail Inmates at Midyear 2007," *Bureau of Justice Statistics Bulletin* (Washington, DC: U.S. Department of Justice, June, 2008), p. 5.

12 James J. Stephan and Jennifer C. Karberg, *Census of State and Federal Correctional Facilities, 2000* (Washington, DC: U.S. Department of Justice, 2003), p. 8.

13 Barbara Owen and Barbara Bloom, "Profiling Women Prisoners: Findings from National Surveys and a California Sample," *Prison Journal*, Vol. 75, No. 2 (June, 1995), pp. 165–186.

14 Laurence A. Greenfeld and Tracy L. Snell, "Women Offenders," *Bureau of Justice Statistics Special Report* (Washington, DC: U.S. Department of Justice, 2000), pp. 7–8.

15 Key Sun, "Mentally Disordered Offenders in Corrections," in Roslyn Muraskin, ed., *Key Correctional Issues* (Upper Saddle River, NJ: Prentice Hall, 2005), p. 125.

16 Heather C. West and William J. Sabol, "Prisoners in 2007," *Bureau of Justice Statistics Bulletin* (Washington, DC: U.S. Department of Justice, December, 2008), p. 22.

17 Meda Chesney-Lind, "Putting the Brakes on the Building Binge," *Corrections Today*, Vol. 54, No. 6 (August, 1992), p. 30.

18 Elizabeth A. Klug, "Benefits Ban Impacts Women and Children," *Corrections Today* (July, 2002), p. 15.

19 Christopher Mumola, "Incarcerated Parents and Their Children," *Bureau of Justice Statistics Special Report* (Washington, DC: U.S. Department of Justice, 2000), p. 1.

20 Ibid., p. 10.

21 Ibid., p. 1.

22 Sandra Enos, *Mothering from the Inside: Parenting in a Women's Prison* (Albany: State University of New York Press, 2001). See also Terry L. Stawar, *How to Be a Responsible Father: A Workbook for*

Offenders and Diane E. Stawar and Terry L. Stawar, *How to Be a Responsible Mother: A Workbook for Offenders* (Alexandria, VA: American Correctional Association, 2008).

23 Phyllis J. Baunach, *Mothers in Prison* (New Brunswick, NJ: Rutgers University Press, 1985), p. 121. See also Ross D. Parke and K. Alison Clarke-Stewart, "The Effects of Parental Incarceration on Children: Perspectives, Promises, and Policies," in Jeremy Travis and Michelle Waul, *Prisoners Once Removed: The Impact of Incarceration and Reentry on Children, Families, and Communities* (Washington, DC: The Urban Institute, 2003), pp. 189–232.

24 "Female Offenders: Survey Summary," *Corrections Compendium*, Vol. 26, No. 1 (January, 2001), p. 5.

25 Women's Prison Association, *Mothers, Infants and Imprisonment: A National Look at Prison Nurseries and Community-based Alternatives* (New York: Women's Prison Association, 2009), p. 5.

26 Exceptions are South Carolina and Wyoming, where mother–child visitation is prohibited. "Female Offenders: Survey Summary," p. 27.

27 See, for example, Gloria Logan, "Family Ties Take Top Priority in Women's Visiting Program," *Corrections Today* (August, 1992), pp. 160–161, and Kerry Kazura and Kristina Toth, "Playrooms in Prison: Helping Offenders Connect with Their Children," *Corrections Today*, Vol. 66, No. 7 (December, 2004), pp. 128–132.

28 Jackie Crawford, "Alternative Sentencing Necessary for Female Inmates with Children," *Corrections Today* (June, 2003), p. 9, quoting J. Hagan and R. Dinovitzer, "Collateral Consequences of Imprisonment for Children, Communities, and Prisoners," in Michael Tonry and Joan Petersilia, eds., *Prisons, Crime, and Justice* (Chicago, IL: University of Chicago Press, 1999), pp. 125–147.

29 Rini Bartlett, "Helping Inmate Moms Keep in Touch," *Corrections Today* (February, 2001), pp. 102–104. See also "Survey Summary: Computer Use for/by Inmates," *Corrections Compendium* (Summer, 2009), p. 24.

30 Term coined by Kelsey Kauffman, "Mothers in Prison," *Corrections Today* (February, 2001), p. 62.

31 See, for example, Marilyn C. Moses, "Keeping Mothers and Their Daughters Together: Girl Scouts behind Bars," *National Institute of Justice: Program Focus* (October, 1995); Arlene F. Lee, "Children of Inmates: What Happens to These Unintended Victims?," *Corrections Today* (June, 2005), pp. 84–85; Patricia Stoddard Dare, Christopher A. Mallett, and Chiquita Welch, "Parental Substance Use Disorders: Disparate Outcomes for Adjudicated Delinquent Youths," *Corrections Compendium*, Vol. 34, No. 2 (Summer, 2009), pp. 1–8; Jeremy Travis, "Families and Children," in Richard Tewksbury and Dean Dabney, eds., *Prisons and Jails: A Reader* (New York: McGraw-Hill, 2009), pp. 335–350.

32 Michael E. Roettger, "Paternal Incarceration and Adversity in Young Adulthood," *Corrections Today*, Vol. 71, No. 6 (December, 2009), pp. 18–20.

33 Robert B. Greifinger, ed., *Public Health behind Bars: From Prisons to Communities* (New York: Springer, 2007), p. 22.

34 "Public Correctional Policy on Crime Prevention," unanimously ratified by the American Correctional Association Delegate Assembly, January 17, 1996. See also Jeremy Travis, Elizabeth Cincotta McBride, and Amy L. Solomon, *Families Left Behind: The Hidden Costs of Incarceration and Reentry* (Washington, DC: The Urban Institute, June, 2005).

35 Crawford, "Alternative Sentencing Necessary," p. 10.

36 Parke and Clarke-Stewart, "The Effects of Parental Incarceration on Children," p. 197.

37 Mumola, "Incarcerated Parents and Their Children," p. 5.

38 Andrew Coyle, "The Use and Abuse of Prison around the World," *Corrections Today*, Vol. 66, No. 7 (December, 2004), p. 66.

39 Centers for Disease Control and Prevention, "Prevention and Control of Infections with Hepatitis Viruses in Correctional Settings," *Morbidity and Mortality Weekly Report*, Vol. 52, No. RR-1 (2003), pp. 5, 7. See also Wil S. Hylton, "Sick on the Inside: Correctional HMOs and the Coming Prison Plague," in Tara Herivel and Paul Wright, *Prison Profiteers: Who Makes Money from Mass Incarceration* (New York: New Press, 2007), p. 184.

40 Centers for Disease Control and Prevention, "Correctional Facilities and Viral Hepatitis" (May, 2009), available at http://www.cdc.gov/hepatitis/Populations/corrections.htm.

41 Laura M. Maruschak, "HIV in Prisons, 2005," *Bureau of Justice Statistics Bulletin* (Washington, DC: U.S. Department of Justice, September, 2007), p. 3.

42 Ibid.

43 National Commission on Acquired Immune Deficiency Syndrome, *National Commission on AIDS Report: HIV Disease in Correctional Facilities* (Washington, DC: National Commission on Acquired Immune Deficiency Syndrome, 1991), p. 5.

44 There is, however, a vaccine for hepatitis A and hepatitis B, which the Centers for Disease Control and Prevention strongly recommend for all staff members whose duties involve potential exposure to blood or body fluids. See Allen J. Beck and Laura M. Maruschak, "Hepatitis Testing and Treatment in State Prisons," *Bureau of Justice Statistics Special Report* (Washington, DC: U.S. Department of Justice, 2004).

45 See, for example, John R. Miles and Adan Cajina, "The Corrections Initiative: A Collaborative Partnership," *Corrections Today*, Vol. 68, No. 4 (July, 2006), pp. 26–32.

46 Sherwood E. Zimmerman, Randy Martin, and David Vlahov, "AIDS Knowledge and Risk Perceptions among Pennsylvania Prisoners," *Journal of Criminal Justice*, Vol. 19, No. 3 (1991), pp. 239–256.

47 Kim Marie Thorburn, "Health Programs Do Work to Fight AIDS," *Corrections Today*, Vol. 54, No. 8 (December, 1992), p. 127.

48 Laura M. Maruschak, "HIV in Prisons, 2006: Statistical Tables," available at http://www.ojp.usdoj.gov/bjs/pub/html/hivp/2006/hivp06.htm#testing.

49 Barbara A. Belbot and Rolando V. del Carmen, "AIDS in Prison: Legal Issues," *Crime and Delinquency*, Vol. 37, No. 1 (January, 1991), p. 137.

50 Ibid., p. 138.

51 "Court of Appeals 10th, Rejects Fourth Amendment Challenge to Blood Testing of Prison Inmates for AIDS," *Criminal Law Reporter*, Vol. 45, No. 20 (August 23, 1989), p. 2360.

52 "Prisons and Jails—Mandatory AIDS Testing," *Criminal Law Reporter*, Vol. 48, No. 7 (November 14, 1990), pp. 1150–1151.

53 "Inmate HIV Testing," *American Jails*, Vol. 6, No. 5 (November/December, 1992), p. 87.

54 Mark Blumberg and Denny Langston, "Mandatory HIV Testing in Criminal Justice Settings," *Crime and Delinquency*, Vol. 37, No. 1 (January, 1991), pp. 12–13. See also Zimmerman, Martin, and Vlahov, "AIDS Knowledge and Risk Perceptions among Pennsylvania Prisoners," who indicate that "intraprison transmission rates are less than 1%" (p. 249), and "Most HIV-positive Inmates Not Exposed in Prison," *Corrections Today* (June, 2006), p. 12, citing a Centers for Disease Control study.

55 National Commission on Acquired Immune Deficiency Syndrome, *National Commission on AIDS Report*, p. 22.

56 A.F. Anderson, "Aids and Prisoners' Rights Law: Deciphering the Administrative Guideposts," *Prison Journal*, Vol. 69, No. 1 (Spring/Summer, 1989), p. 21.

57 The state's practice is to offer voluntary AIDS tests to all inmates upon entry into the system, along with later testing "if a doctor has reason to think an inmate is infected." See "Inmates' Request for Mandatory Testing Denied," *On the Line*, Vol. 15, No. 2 (March, 1992), p. 2.

58 National Commission on Acquired Immune Deficiency Syndrome, *National Commission on AIDS Report*, p. 22, citing *Smith v. Meachum* (1989).

59 M.J. Olivero, "The Treatment of AIDS behind the Walls of Correctional Facilities," *Social Justice*, Vol. 17, No. 1 (Spring, 1990), p. 114.

60 Belbot and del Carmen, "AIDS in Prison," p. 147.

61 Curtis R. Davis, "AIDS and an Officer's Right to Know," *Corrections Today*, Vol. 53, No. 7 (December, 1991), p. 28.

62 Theodore M. Hammett and Saira Moini, "Update on AIDS in Prisons and Jails," *AIDS Bulletin* (Washington, DC: National Institute of Justice, 1998), p. 7.

63 National Commission on Acquired Immune Deficiency Syndrome, *National Commission on AIDS Report*, p. 3.

64 James E. Lawrence and Van Zwisohn, "AIDS in Jail," in Joel A. Thompson and G. Larry Mays, eds., *American Jails: Public Policy Issues* (Chicago, IL: Nelson-Hall, 1991), pp. 122–124.

65 Christopher J. Mumola and Jennifer C. Karberg, "Drug Use and Dependence, State and Federal Prisoners, 2004," *Bureau of Justice Statistics Special Report* (Washington, DC: U.S. Department of Justice, October, 2006), pp. 3, 6.

66 Howard N. Snyder, "Growth in Minority Detentions Attributed to Drug Law Violators," *Office of Juvenile Justice and Delinquency Prevention: Update on Statistics* (Washington, DC: U.S. Department of Justice, 1990), pp. 1–2, 5. More recently, it has been noted that minority overrepresentation in detention remains greatest for drug offenses—i.e., blacks accounted for 33 percent of all drug cases processed, but 59 percent of drug cases detained. See Shay Bilchik, "Minorities in the Juvenile Justice System," *National Report Series* (Washington, DC: U.S. Department of Justice, Office of Juvenile Justice and Delinquency Prevention, December, 1999), p. 10.

67 Jennifer C. Karberg and Doris J. James, "Substance Dependence, Abuse, and Treatment of Jail Inmates, 2002," *Bureau of Justice Statistics Special Report* (Washington, DC: U.S. Department of Justice, July, 2005), p. 1.

68 Matthew R. Durose and Patrick A. Langan, "Felony Sentences in State Courts, 2004," *Bureau of Justice Statistics Bulletin* (Washington, DC: U.S. Department of Justice, July, 2007), p. 2.

69 Ibid., p. 3.

70 National Institute of Drug Abuse, *Drug Abusing Offenders Not Getting Treatment They Need in Criminal Justice System* (Washington, DC: National Institute of Drug Abuse, July 20, 2009), p. 1, quoting Dr. Redonna K. Chandler.

71 National Center on Addiction and Substance Abuse, *Behind Bars II*, p. 23.

72 "When Ex-cons Come Home to the 'Hood, Will Police Be Ready?," *Law Enforcement News* (February 14, 2001), p. 1.

73 "Survey Summary: Drug Treatment Intervention Summary," *Corrections Compendium* (April, 2001), p. 8.

74 Karen Fein, "Women Prisoners," in Roslyn Muraskin, ed., *Key Correctional Issues* (Upper Saddle River, NJ: Prentice Hall, 2005), p. 266, citing a National Institute of Justice study.

75 *Crime in the United States 2008*, Table 29, available at http://www.fbi.gov/ucr/cius2008/data/table_29.html.

76 U.S. Department of Justice, *Sourcebook of Criminal Justice Statistics, 2001* (Washington, DC: U.S. Department of Justice, 2002), p. 248.

77 Christopher J. Mumola, "Substance Abuse and Treatment, State and Federal Prisoners, 1997," *Bureau of Justice Statistics Special Report* (Washington, DC: U.S. Department of Justice, 1999), p. 1.

78 Barbara Gordon, *I'm Dancing as Fast as I Can* (New York: Bantam Books, 1979), p. 98. For a more recent analysis, see Chris Sigurdson, "The Mad, the Bad, and the Abandoned: The Mentally Ill in Prisons and Jails," in Richard Tewksbury and Dean Dabney, eds., *Prisons and Jails: A Reader* (New York: McGraw-Hill, 2009), pp. 95–107.

79 Mark Nichols, Lawrence L. Bench, Erica Morlok, and Karen Liston, "Analysis of Mentally Retarded and Lower-functioning Offender Correctional Programs," *Corrections Today* (April, 2003), p. 119.

80 Ibid. Although early studies found that approximately 9 percent of offenders suffer from mental retardation, more recent research indicates that its prevalence is considerably lower (between 1 percent and 4 percent).

81 Ibid., p. 120.

82 Thomas Tiberia, "Helping Correction Officers Recognize and Interact with Handicapped Offenders," *American Jails*, Vol. 6, No. 2 (May/June, 1992), p. 32.

83 For examples of how various states are addressing the special needs of developmentally disabled offenders, see "Policy Statement 18: Development of Treatment Plans, Assignment to Programs,

and Classification/Housing Decisions" (New York: Council of State Governments, Justice Center, n.d.), available at http://consensusproject.org/the_report/ch-IV/ps18-development-treatment/ recommendation18-I. See also Mary F. Farkas, "Teamwork in the Social Skills Development Unit Helps Adaptively Impaired Inmates," *Corrections Today* (December, 2000), pp. 118–120.

84 Daniel Kagen, "Landmark Chicago Study Documents Rate of Mental Illness among Jail Inmates," *Corrections Today* (December, 1990), p. 166, quoting John Monahan.

85 Doris J. James and Lauren E. Glaze, "Mental Health Problems of Prison and Jail Inmates," *Bureau of Justice Statistics Special Report* (Washington, DC: U.S. Department of Justice, September, 2006), p. 1.

86 Ibid., p. 3. See also Dean H. Aufderheide and Patrick H. Brown, "Crisis in Corrections: The Mentally Ill in America's Prisons," *Corrections Today*, Vol. 67, No. 1 (February, 2005), pp. 30–33.

87 Chris Sigurdson, "The Mad, the Bad, and the Abandoned: The Mentally Ill in Prisons and Jails," *Corrections Today* (December, 2000), p. 70. See also Human Rights Watch, *Ill-equipped: U.S. Prisons and Offenders with Mental Illness* (New York: Human Rights Watch, 2003).

88 James and Glaze, "Mental Health Problems of Prison and Jail Inmates," p. 1.

89 Sigurdson, "The Mad, the Bad, and the Abandoned," *Corrections Today*, p. 72.

90 Lance Couturier, Frederick Maue, and Catherine McVey, "Releasing Inmates with Mental Illness and Co-occurring Disorders into the Community," *Corrections Today* (April, 2005), p. 82. See also Heather Barr, "Transinstitutionalization in the Courts: *Brad H. v. City of New York*, and the Fight for Discharge Planning for People with Psychiatric Disabilities Leaving Rikers Island," *Crime and Delinquency*, Vol. 49, No. 1 (January, 2003), pp. 97–123.

91 "Treatment Plan Sought after Inmates Are Released," *Correctional News* (November/December, 1999), p. 22. For example, one of the plaintiffs was a 44-year-old homeless man with schizophrenia who had been jailed 26 times, but never received postrelease psychiatric care or help with obtaining housing, Medicaid benefits, or Social Security disability payments. Subsequently, the city agreed to provide access to treatment needed to maintain psychiatric stability upon release. Susan Saulny, "City Agrees to Help Care for Mentally Ill Inmates after Release," *New York Times*, January 9, 2003, available at http://www.urbanjustice.org/pdf/press/ nytimes_09jan03.pdf.

92 David Kalinich, Paul Embert, and Jeffrey Senese, "Mental Health Services for Jail Inmates: Imprecise Standards, Traditional Philosophies, and the Need for Change," in Joel A. Thompson and G. Larry Mays, eds., *American Jails: Public Policy Issues* (Chicago, IL: Nelson-Hall, 1991), p. 81. See also H. Richard Lamb and Leona L. Bachrach, "Some Perspectives on Deinstitutionalization," *Psychiatric Services*, Vol. 52, No. 8 (2001), pp. 1039–1045.

93 Laura Tahir, "Supervision of Special Needs Inmates by Custody Staff," *Corrections Today* (October, 2003), p. 108.

94 See Fagan, Brandt, and Kleiver, "Future Directions," p. 371.

95 Irina R. Soderstrom, "Mental Illness in Offender Populations: Prevalence, Duty and Implications," *Mental Health Issues in the Criminal Justice System* (January, 2008), pp. 1–17.

96 "Agencies and Facilities Must Comply with New Federal Law on Disabled," *Corrections Today*, Vol. 54, No. 6 (August, 1992), p. 143.

97 Paula N. Rubin and Susan McCampbell, "The Americans with Disabilities Act and Criminal Justice: Mental Disabilities and Corrections," *National Institute of Justice: Research in Action* (Washington, DC: U.S. Department of Justice, 1995), pp. 1–2.

98 "8th Circuit Strikes down ADA for State-run Facilities," *Correctional Education Bulletin*, Vol. 3, No. 3 (1999), p. 7.

99 Ericia Kempker, "The Graying of American Prisons: Addressing the Continued Increase in Geriatric Inmates," *Corrections Compendium*, Vol. 28, No. 6 (June, 2003), p. 1.

100 See J.W. Marquart, D.E. Merianos, J.L. Hebert, and L. Carroll, "Health Condition and Prisoners: A Review of Research and Emerging Areas of Inquiry," in Richard Tewksbury and Dean Dabney, eds., *Prisons and Jails: A Reader* (New York: McGraw-Hill, 2009), pp. 277–290.

101 Elizabeth Anderson and Theresa Hilliard, "Managing Offenders with Special Health Needs: Highest and Best Use Strategies," *Corrections Today*, Vol. 67, No. 1 (February, 2005), pp. 58–61.

102 Elaine Crawley, "Institutional Thoughtlessness in Prisons and Its Impacts on the Day-to-Day Prison Lives of Elderly Men," *Journal of Contemporary Criminal Justice*, Vol. 21, No. 4 (November, 2005), pp. 350–363.

103 "Elderly Inmates: Survey Summary," *Corrections Compendium*, Vol. 26, No. 5 (May, 2001), p. 7.

104 Kempker, "The Graying of American Prisons," p. 22.

105 Philip A. Zimbardo, *Transforming California's Prisons into Expensive Old-age Homes for Felons: Enormous Hidden Costs and Consequences for California's Taxpayers* (San Francisco, CA: Center on Juvenile and Criminal Justice, 1994). See also Ryan S. King and Marc Mauer, "Aging behind Bars: 'Three Strikes' Seven Years Later," White Paper (Washington, DC: The Sentencing Project, 2001).

106 Kempker, "The Graying of American Prisons," p. 22.

107 Hava Leisner, "Nationwide, More Elderly Inmates Are in Prison: States Battle Increasing Health Care Costs by Building Geriatric Prisons," *Correctional News* (July/August, 2000), p. 46.

108 Lia Gormsen, "North Carolina and Alabama Join States that Release Dying Inmates," *Corrections Compendium*, Vol. 33, No. 5 (September/October, 2008), p. 35.

109 John Dawes, "Dying with Dignity: Prisoners and Terminal Illness," *Illness, Crisis and Loss*, Vol. 10 (2002), p. 192.

110 John M. Glionna, "At 92, Freed Inmate Ends His Life All Alone," *The Miami Herald* (July 12, 2002), p. 4A.

Part 3 Correctional Institutions: Custody, Treatment, Confinement, and Release

1 Roy King, "The Rise and Rise of Supermax: A Solution in Search of a Problem," *Punishment and Society*, Vol. 1, No. 2 (1999), pp. 163–186.

8 Custodial Procedures

1 Grace L. Wojda, Raymond G. Wojda, Norman Erik Smith, and Richard K. Jones, *Behind Bars* (Alexandria, VA: American Correctional Association, 1991), p. 3.

2 John J. DiIulio, *Governing Prisons: A Comparative Study of Correctional Management* (New York: Free Press, 1987), p. 92.

3 Lucien X. Lombardo, *Guards Imprisoned: Correctional Officers at Work*, Second Edition (Cincinnati, OH: Anderson, 1989), p. 64.

4 Paraphrased from DiIulio, *Governing Prisons*, p. 41.

5 Scarlett V. Carp and Joyce A. Davis, "Planning and Designing a Facility for a Special Needs Population," *Corrections Today*, Vol. 53, No. 2 (April, 1991), p. 102. For a description of how the structure of prisons has changed over time, see Courtney A. Waid and Carl B. Clements, "Correctional Facility Design: Past, Present, and Future," *Corrections Compendium*, Vol. 26, No. 11 (November, 2001), pp. 1–5, 25–29.

6 James B. Jacobs and Harold G. Retsky, "Prison Guard," *Urban Life*, Vol. 4, No. 1 (April, 1975), p. 19.

7 Wil S. Hylton, "Sick on the Inside: Correctional HMOs and the Coming Prison Plague," in Tara Herivel and Paul Wright, eds., *Prison Profiteers: Who Makes Money from Mass Incarceration* (New York: New Press, 2007), p. 180.

8 Jack Harne and Frances Scott, "NIJ Tests New Technologies," *Corrections Today* (August, 2009), pp. 88–89.

9 Bill Scism, "Correctional Security Technology: Catch the Wave," *Corrections Today* (August, 2009), pp. 8, 12.

10 Janice Joseph and Rupendra Simlot, "Technocorrections: Biometric Scanning and Corrections," in Roslyn Muraskin, ed., *Key Correctional Issues* (Upper Saddle River, NJ: Prentice Hall, 2005), pp. 128–148.

11 John S. Shaffer, "Vulnerability Analysis in the Correctional Environment," *Corrections Today* (December, 2003), p. 120.

12 Warren Rohn and Trish Ostroski, "Advances in Technology Make It Easier to Monitor Inmates," *Corrections Today*, Vol. 53, No. 4 (July, 1991), p. 144.

13 Ibid.

14 Laura Gater, "The Problem of Mental Health in Prison Populations," *Corrections Forum* (March/April, 2004), p. 31.

15 J. Scott Orr and Lyric Wallwork Winik, "Unescorted Prisoners Take the Bus," *Parade* (May 31, 2009), p. 6.

16 Philip J. Boyle and James G. Ricketts, "Using Technology to Achieve Higher Efficiency in Correctional Facilities," *Corrections Today*, Vol. 54, No. 5 (July, 1992), pp. 78–80.

17 Camille Graham Camp, ed., *The 2002 Corrections Yearbook: Adult Corrections* (Middletown, CT: Criminal Justice Institute, 2003), pp. 48–49.

18 Cecil Angel and Dan Shine, "Fugitive of '57 Can Stay a Free Man," *The Miami Herald* (April 1, 2001), p. 26A.

19 "Cell Phones Proliferate as Inmate Contraband," *Correctional News* (July/August, 2004), p. 25. See also William Scism and Sterling Bryan, "Can Technology Address the Contraband Cell Phone Problem?," *Corrections Today*, Vol. 70, No. 5 (October, 2008), pp. 48–49.

20 Jay Lowe, "Technology Enhances Public Safety in Texas," *Corrections Today* (July, 2004), p. 69.

21 Heath C. Hoffmann, George E. Dickinson, and Chelsea L. Dunn, "Communication Policy Changes in State Adult Correctional Facilities from 1971 to 2005," *Criminal Justice Review*, Vol. 32, No. 1 (March, 2007), pp. 47–64.

22 "Two New Jails Hold World's Largest Video Visitation System," *Correctional News* (May/June, 2004), p. 35. See also "News Briefs: More States Turn to Videoconferencing," *Corrections Today* (June, 2009), p. 14.

23 Christopher Hensley, Sandra Rutland, and Phyllis Gray-Ray, "The Effects of Conjugal Visits on Mississippi Inmates," *Corrections Compendium*, Vol. 25, No. 4 (April, 2000), p. 1. The five states are California, Mississippi, New Mexico, New York, and Washington.

24 Ibid., p. 20.

25 "Family Visitation," *Corrections Compendium*, Vol. 4, No. 7 (January, 1980), pp. 2–5.

26 Camp, *The 2002 Corrections Yearbook*, p. 148.

27 In fact, as late as 1992 (by which time Willie Horton was confined in a Maryland prison), he was still being widely referred to in conjunction with presidential campaigning, prompting a *Wall Street Journal* editorial which called for "a furlough" of the Willie Horton issue. See Paul A. Gigot, "Willie Horton: The Mother of All Diversions," *The Wall Street Journal* (April 17, 1992), p. A-10.

28 "Number of Prison Furloughs Increases," *On the Line*, Vol. 15, No. 2 (March, 1992), p. 5.

29 Lombardo, *Guards Imprisoned*, p. 100.

30 *Wolff v. McDonnell*, 418 U.S. 539 (1974).

31 *Sandin v. Conner*, 2293 U.S. S. Ct. (1995).

32 "Double Jeopardy for Prison Rioting," *Corrections Alert*, Vol. 2, No. 8 (July 24, 1995), p. 7, citing *U.S. v. Brown*, 9th Circuit.

33 Adria Lynn Libolt, "Technology Cannot Be a Replacement for Creative Planning and Programming," *Corrections Today*, Vol. 53, No. 4 (July, 1991), p. 21.

34 Anthony L. Guenther and Mary Quinn Guenther, "Screws vs. Thugs," in Ben M. Crouch, ed., *The Keepers: Prison Guards and Contemporary Corrections* (Springfield, IL: Charles C. Thomas, 1980), p. 171.

35 Gresham M. Sykes, *Society of Captives: A Study of a Maximum Security Prison* (Princeton, NJ: Princeton University Press, 1958), p. 58. The following discussion of the "corrupt alliance" between inmates and officers is based on Chapter 3, "The Defects of Total Power," of this reference.

36 Ibid., p. 47.

37 Ibid., p. 51.

38 Ibid., pp. 56–57.

39 Robert Blair and Peter C. Kratcoski, "Professionalism among Correctional Officers: A Longitudinal Analysis of Individual and Structural Determinants," in Peter J. Benekos and Alida V. Merlo, *Corrections: Dilemmas and Directions* (Cincinnati, OH: Anderson, 1992), p. 117.

40 Robert B. Levinson, *Unit Management in Prisons and Jails* (Lanham, MD: American Correctional Association, 1999), p. 10.

41 James Houston, *Correctional Management* (Chicago, IL: Nelson-Hall, 1999), pp. 326–327.

42 James H. Webster, "Designing Facilities for Effective Unit Management," *Corrections Today*, Vol. 53, No. 2 (April, 1991), p. 38.

43 Houston, *Correctional Management*, p. 329.

44 "Survey Summary: Special Housing," *Corrections Compendium*, Vol. 26, No. 7 (July, 2001), p. 6.

45 Robert B. Levinson, "The Future of Unit Management," *Corrections Today*, Vol. 53, No. 1 (April, 1991), p. 46.

9   Treatment and Related Programs

1 Quoted in J.M. Taylor, "Pell Grants for Prisoners," *The Nation* (January 25, 1993), p. 90.

2 Richard G. Kiekbusch, "Leadership Roles: How Are We Doing?," *American Jails* (November/December, 1992), p. 6.

3 W. Wesley Johnson, Katherine Bennett, and Timothy J. Flanagan, "Getting Tough on Prisoners: Results from the National Corrections Executive Survey, 1995," *Crime and Delinquency*, Vol. 43, No. 1 (January, 1997), p. 31.

4 Francis T. Cullen, Edward J. Latessa, Velmer S. Burton, and Lucien X. Lombardo, "The Correctional Orientation of Prison Wardens: Is the Rehabilitative Ideal Supported?," *Criminology*, Vol. 31, No. 1 (1993), pp. 84–85.

5 John Pratt, *Punishment and Civilization* (Thousand Oaks, CA: Sage Publications, 2002), p. 179.

6 W. Ray Nelson, "The First International Symposium on the Future of Law Enforcement," *Direct Supervision Network*, Vol. 1 (April/June, 1991), p. 4.

7 Simon Dinitz, "The Transformation of Corrections: 50 Years of Silent Revolutions," *Training Manual: Executive Training for New Wardens* (Longmont, CO: National Institute of Corrections, February, 2000), p. 15.

8 Hans Toch, "The Care and Feeding of Typologies and Labels," *Federal Probation*, Vol. 34, No. 3 (September, 1970), pp. 15–19.

9 In one alcohol/drug treatment program, for example, it was found that court-ordered referrals had better success rates than did voluntary entrants. Marie Ragghianti and Toni Glenn, *Reducing Recidivism: Treating the Addicted Inmate* (Center City, MN: Hazelden, 1991), p. 12.

10 President's Commission on Law Enforcement and Administration of Justice, *Task Force Report: Corrections* (Washington, DC: U.S. Government Printing Office, 1967), p. 20.

11 Stephen D. Gottfredson and Laura J. Moriarty, "Statistical Risk Assessment: Old Problems and New Applications," *Crime and Delinquency*, Vol. 52, No. 1 (2006), pp. 178–200.

12 Christopher Baird, "A Question of Evidence: A Critique of Risk Assessment Models Used in the Justice System," *Special Report* (Madison, WI: National Council on Crime and Delinquency, February, 2009), p. 4.

13 Kevin Whiteacre, "Case Manager Experiences with the LSI-R at a Federal Community Corrections Center," *Corrections Compendium* (November/December, 2004), pp. 1–5, 32–35. For a comprehensive

overview of this topic, see Patricia Van Voorhis, "An Overview of Offender Classification Systems," in Patricia Van Voorhis, Michael Braswell, and David Lester, eds., *Correctional Counseling and Rehabilitation* (New Providence, NJ: Matthew Bender, 2009), pp. 133–161.

14 Jack Alexander and James Austin, *Handbook for Evaluating Objective Prison Classification Systems* (Washington, DC: National Institute of Corrections, 1992), p. 1.

15 Summarized in Patricia Van Voorhis, "An Overview of Offender Classification Systems," p. 141.

16 Robert A. Buchanan and Karen L. Whitlow, *Guidelines for Developing, Implementing, and Revising an Objective Prison Classification System* (Washington, DC: National Institute of Justice, 1987), p. 1. See also National Institute of Corrections, *Jail Classification System Development: A Review of the Literature* (Longmont, CO: National Institute of Corrections, 1992), pp. 12–13.

17 Hans Toch, "Inmate Classification as a Transaction," *Criminal Justice and Behavior*, Vol. 8, No. 1 (March, 1981), p. 4.

18 Michael W. Forcier, "The Development of the Modern Classification System," in Bruce I. Wolford and Pam Lawrenz, eds., *Classification: Innovative Correctional Programs* (Richmond, KY: Department of Correctional Services, 1988), p. 2, citing James Austin, "Assessing the New Generation of Prison Classification Models," *Crime and Delinquency*, Vol. 29, No. 4 (October, 1983), pp. 561–576.

19 Kathryn Ann Farr, "Classification for Female Inmates: Moving Forward," *Crime and Delinquency*, Vol. 46, No. 1 (January, 2000), pp. 3–17.

20 Lawrence L. Bench and Terry D. Allen, "Investigating the Stigma of Prison Classification: An Experimental Design," *Prison Journal*, Vol. 38, No. 4 (2003), pp. 367–371.

21 James Austin, "Objective Offender Classification Is Key to Proper Housing Decisions," *Corrections Today*, Vol. 56, No. 4 (July, 1994), pp. 94–96.

22 Carl B. Clements, "Offender Classification: Two Decades of Progress," *Criminal Justice and Behavior*, Vol. 23, No. 1 (March, 1996), p. 139.

23 "Survey Summary: Faith-based Programming," *Corrections Compendium*, Vol. 28, No. 8 (August, 2003), p. 8.

24 Todd R. Clear, Bruce D. Stout, Harry S. Dammer, Linda L. Kelly, Patricia L. Hardyman, and Carol A. Shapiro, *Prisoners, Prisons, and Religion: Final Report* (Newark, NJ: School of Criminal Justice, Rutgers University, 1992).

25 Judith Coleman, "Chaplains: God's Partners in Prison," *Corrections Today* (December, 2003), p. 122.

26 For additional suggestions, see Robert Toll, "How a Multifaith Chaplaincy Program Operates in a County Detention Facility," *American Jails* (January/February, 2004), pp. 19–24.

27 Phil Danna, "Lights, Camera, Religion," *American Jails* (July/August, 1992), pp. 60–62.

28 Melvina T. Sumter and Todd R. Clear, "Religion in the Correctional Setting," in Roslyn Muraskin, ed., *Key Correctional Issues* (Upper Saddle River, NJ: Prentice Hall, 2005), p. 113.

29 Byron R. Johnson and David B. Larson, "Linking Religion to the Mental and Physical Health of Inmates: A Literature Review and Research Note," *American Jails* (September/October, 1997), pp. 29–30.

30 Pat Nolan, "Prison Fellowship and Faith-based Initiatives," *On the Line*, Vol. 25, No. 5 (November, 2002), p. 1.

31 Stephen T. Hall, "Faith-based Cognitive Programs in Corrections," *Corrections Today* (December, 2003), p. 113. See also Rebecca L. Propst, *Psychotherapy in a Religious Framework: Spirituality in the Emotional Healing Process* (New York: Human Science Press, 1988).

32 See Samantha M. Shapiro, "Jail for Jesus," in Tara Herivel and Paul Wright, *Prison Profiteers: Who Makes Money from Mass Incarceration* (New York: New Press, 2007), pp. 128–140.

33 Caroline Wolf Harlow, "Education and Correctional Populations," *Bureau of Justice Statistics Special Report* (Washington, DC: U.S. Department of Justice, 2003), p. 2.

34 Elizabeth Greenberg, Eric Dunleavy, and Mark Kutner, *Literacy behind Bars: Results from the 2003 Assessment of Adult Literacy Prison Survey* (Washington, DC: U.S. Department of Education, May, 2007), p. 29, available at http://nces.ed.gov/pubs2007/2007473.

35 "High-Tech Tutors: Wisconsin Uses Literacy Program Statewide," *Corrections Today*, Vol. 52, No. 7 (December, 1990), p. 142.

36 Dennis J. Stevens, "Educational Programming for Offenders," *Forum on Correctional Research*, Vol. 12, No. 2 (May, 2000), p. 30.

37 Michelle Tolbert, *State Correctional Education Programs: State Policy Update* (Washington, DC: National Institute for Literacy, 2002).

38 For a description of a reading program that is designed to strengthen bonds between incarcerated parents and their children, see Sara Urrutia, "Words Travel: A Model Family-strengthening and Literacy Program," *Corrections Today* (April, 2004), pp. 80–83.

39 See Carl Nick, Rob Olding, Jo Jorgenson, and Melisa Gilbert, "Expanding Distance Learning Access in Prisons: A Growing Need," *Corrections Today* (August, 2009), pp. 40–43.

40 Sylvia G. McCollum, "Prison College Programs," *Prison Journal*, Vol. 73, No. 1 (March, 1994), p. 51. See also Stevens, "Educational Programming," p. 30, where "solid support for a positive relationship between correctional education and reduced recidivism" is noted.

41 Cathryn A. Chappell, "Post-secondary Correctional Education and Recidivism: A Meta-analysis of Research Conducted 1990–1999," *Journal of Correctional Education*, Vol. 55, No. 2 (2004), pp. 148–169.

42 Johnson, Bennett, and Flanagan, "Getting Tough on Prisoners," p. 33.

43 James J. Stephan and Jennifer C. Karberg, *Census of State and Federal Correctional Facilities, 2000* (Washington, DC: U.S. Department of Justice, Bureau of Justice Statistics, 2003), p. 11.

44 Wendy Erisman and Jeanne Bayer Contardo, *Learning to Reduce Recidivism: A Fifty-state Analysis of Postsecondary Correctional Education Policy* (Washington, DC: Institute for Higher Education Policy, November, 2005), p. 13, available at http://www.inpathways.net/recidivism.pdf.

45 Daniel Hanneken and Anne Dannerbeck, "Practical Solutions: Addressing Offenders' Educational Opportunities and Challenges," *Corrections Compendium*, Vol. 32, No. 2 (March/April, 2007), pp. 1–4, 37.

46 Barbara J. Auerback, George E. Sexton, Franklin C. Farrow, and Robert H. Lawson, *Work in American Prisons: The Private Sector Gets Involved* (Washington, DC: U.S. Department of Justice, 1988), p. 9.

47 Stephan and Karberg, *Census*, p. 11.

48 Elizabeth Greenberg, Eric Dunleavy, and Mark Kutner, *Literacy behind Bars: Results from the 2003 Assessment of Adult Literacy Prison Survey* (Washington, DC: U.S. Department of Education, May, 2007), p. 51, available at http://nces.ed.gov/pubs2007/2007473.

49 Jeffrey Ian Ross and Stephen C. Richards, *Behind Bars: Surviving Prison* (Indianapolis, IN: Alpha Books, 2002), p. 105.

50 Allen Beck et al., *Survey of State Prison Inmates, 1991* (Washington, DC: U.S. Department of Justice, 1993), p. 27.

51 Ross and Richards, *Behind Bars*, p. 105.

52 Simon Dinitz, "The Transformation of Corrections: 50 Years of Silent Revolutions," *Training Manual: Executive Training for New Wardens* (Longmont, CO: National Institute of Corrections, February, 2000), p. 15.

53 Joan Petersilia, *When Prisoners Come Home: Parole and Prisoner Reentry* (New York: Oxford University Press, 2003), p. 17.

54 Barbara Auerbach, "Private Sector Jail Industries," *American Jails* (May/June, 2003), pp. 15–18.

55 Merry Morash, Timothy S. Bynum, and Barbara A. Koons, "Women Offenders: Programming Needs and Promising Approaches," *National Institute of Justice: Research in Brief* (Washington, DC: U.S. Department of Justice, National Institute of Justice, 1998), p. 4.

56 Barbara Bloom, Barbara Owen, and Stephanie Covington, *Gender-responsive Strategies: Research, Practice, and Guiding Principles for Women Offenders* (Washington, DC: U.S. Department of Justice, National Institute of Corrections, 2003), p. 23.

57 Stephan and Karberg, *Census*, p. 13.

58 *Klinger v. Department of Corrections*, 1994, 31 F. 3d. 727 (8th Cir.).

59 Karen Fein, "Women Prisoners," in Roslyn Muraskin, ed., *Key Correctional Issues* (Upper Saddle River, NJ: Prentice Hall, 2005), p. 264, citing *Jeldness v. Pearce*, 30 F3d 1220, 1229, 9th Cir. 1994.

60 Peter Finn, "No-Frills Prisons and Jails: A Movement in Flux," *Federal Probation* (September, 1996), pp. 35–43.

61 "TV or Not TV? Programming for Inmates to Get Educational Spin," *Law Enforcement News* (October 15, 1996), p. 1.

62 Marcia J. Carter and Kelly J. Russell, "What Is the Perceived Worth of Recreation? Results from a County Jail Study," *Corrections Today* (June, 2005), pp. 80–91.

63 Alfred C. Schnur, "The New Penology: Fact or Fiction?," *Journal of Criminal Law, Criminology and Police Science*, Vol. 49 (November/December, 1958), pp. 331–334.

64 President's Commission on Law Enforcement and Administration of Justice, *Task Force Report*, p. 97.

65 Michael S. Serrill, "Is Rehabilitation Dead?," *Corrections Magazine*, Vol. 1, No. 5 (May/June, 1975), pp. 3–7, 10–12, 21–32.

66 Charles W. Thomas and David M. Petersen, *Prison Organization and Inmate Subcultures* (Indianapolis, IN: Bobbs-Merrill, 1977), p. 36.

67 Jerome Miller, "Sentencing: What Lies between Sentiment and Ignorance?," *Justice Quarterly*, No. 3 (1986), p. 231.

68 For a look at how one system has established such a custody–treatment partnership, see Sherry Macpherson, "Collaboration between Clinicians and Custody Staff Benefits the Entire Prison," *Corrections Today* (April, 2004), pp. 116–119.

69 Depending on whether the estimate of one-fourth or one-third of offenders with a severe mental disorder is used, these psychologists would statistically be responsible for treating 188–248 inmates. See Jennifer L. Boothby, "Contemporary U.S. Corrections, Mental Health, and Social Policy," in Robert K. Ax and Thomas J. Fagan, eds., *Corrections, Mental Health, and Social Policy* (Springfield, IL: Charles C. Thomas, 2007), p. 47.

70 The Sentencing Project, *Mentally Ill Offenders in the Criminal Justice System: An Analysis and Prescription* (Washington, DC: The Sentencing Project, 2002), p. 3.

71 Steven Raphael and Michael A. Stoll, "Why Are So Many Americans in Prison?," in Steven Raphael and Michael A. Stoll, eds., *Do Prisons Make Us Safer? The Benefits and Costs of the Prison Boom* (New York: Russell Sage Foundation, 2009), pp. 27–72.

72 *Estelle v. Gamble*, 97 S. Ct. 285 (1976). In this case, an inmate sued on the grounds that he was denied parole because of a psychological evaluation indicating that he would not complete the parole period successfully, yet the institution had not offered psychiatric services to deal with his problems.

73 Daniel Pollak, "Legal Briefs: *Bailey v. Gardebring*, U.S. Court of Appeals, 8th Circuit, 1991," *Corrections Today*, Vol. 54, No. 2 (April, 1991), pp. 26–28.

74 Kenneth Adams, Timothy J. Flanagan, and James W. Marquart, "The Future of the Penitentiary," in Timothy J. Flanagan, James W. Marquart, and Kenneth G. Adams, eds., *Incarcerating Criminals: Prisons and Jails in Social and Organizational Context* (New York: Oxford University Press, 1998), p. 326.

75 Ruth E. Masters, *Counseling Criminal Justice Offenders* (Thousand Oaks, CA: Sage Publications, 2004), pp. 7–8.

76 Michael Braswell, "The Purpose of Correctional Counseling," in David Lester, Michael Braswell, and Patricia Van Voorhis, *Correctional Counseling* (Cincinnati, OH: Anderson, 1992), p. 25.

77 Masters, *Counseling Criminal Justice Offenders*, p. 243.

78 "Budget Cuts Affect Drug Treatment," *Correctional News*, Vol. 8, No. 3 (May/June, 2002), p. 1. The state referred to is Florida.

79 Wayne Sage, "Crime and Clockwork Lemon," *Human Behavior*, Vol. 3, No. 9 (September, 1974), pp. 16–25. See also "Behavior Modification Program Report Released by GAO," *Corrections Digest*, Vol. 6, No. 17 (August 30, 1975), pp. 1–2.

80 By 1975, sufficient national attention had been brought to behavior modification to promote a symposium on the topic. See "Symposium—The Control of Behavior: Legal, Scientific, and Moral Dilemmas, Part I," *Criminal Law Bulletin*, Vol. 2, No. 5 (September/October, 1975), pp. 598–636. In addition, court cases have supported the right of an individual to freedom or privacy of the mind (*Stanley v. Georgia*, 394 U.S. 559 [1968]) and raised serious questions regarding "tinkering" with mental processes through the use of drugs (*Mackey v. Procunier*, 477 F. 2d 877 [1973]).

81 Allen J. Beck and Laura M. Maruschak, "Mental Health Treatment in State Prisons, 2000," *Bureau of Justice Statistics Special Report* (Washington, DC: U.S. Department of Justice, 2001), pp. 1, 4.

82 See, for example, Barbara H. Zaitzow and Kathryn Brooks, "Psychotropic Control of Women Prisoners: The Perpetual Abuse of Imprisoned Women," Paper presented at the annual meeting of the American Society of Criminology, Atlanta, GA, November 14, 2007.

83 *Washington v. Harper* case (110 S. Ct. 1028); see Fred Cohen, "A Closer Look at Mentally Disordered Inmates and Forcible Medication," *Correctional Law Reporter*, Vol. 2, No. 2 (May, 1990), p. 20. More recently, the Louisiana Supreme Court held in 1992 that "an incompetent inmate cannot be forced to take drugs that might make him sane enough to be executed." See "National News Briefs," *Corrections Today*, Vol. 54, No. 8 (December, 1992), p. 16.

84 See William Glasser, *Reality Therapy* (New York: Harper & Row, 1965).

85 Boyd D. Sharp, *Changing Criminal Thinking: A Treatment Program* (Alexandria, VA: American Correctional Association, 2000), p. 2. For a comprehensive overview, see Patricia Van Voorhis and David Lester, "Cognitive Therapies," in Patricia Van Voorhis, Michael Braswell, and David Lester, eds., *Correctional Counseling and Rehabilitation* (New Providence, NJ: Matthew Bender, 2009), pp. 185–211.

86 Richard A. Wells, *Planned Short-term Treatment* (New York: Free Press, 1994), pp. 214–215. See also Jessica B. Konopa, Emil Chiauzzi, David Portnoy, and Thomas M. Litwicki, "Recovery from the Inside Out: A Cognitive Approach to Rehabilitation," *Corrections Today* (August, 2002), pp. 56–58.

87 Miriam Haworth, "Program to Improve Inmate Behavior Also Helps Boost Staff Relations," *Corrections Today* (December, 1993), p. 120.

88 Paul Gendreau, "The Principles of Effective Intervention with Offenders," in Alan T. Harland, ed., *Choosing Correctional Options that Work: Defining the Demand and Evaluating the Supply* (Thousand Oaks, CA: Sage Publications, 1996), p. 121.

89 Pamela K. Withrow, "Cognitive Restructuring: An Approach to Dealing with Violent Inmates," *Corrections Today* (August, 1994), pp. 112–115.

90 Jeanette Germain, "Addictions Recovery, Cognitive Restructuring, and a Team Effort," *Corrections Today* (February, 1996), p. 70.

91 Howard Abadinsky, *Probation and Parole*, Seventh Edition (Englewood Cliffs, NJ: Prentice Hall, 2000), pp. 286–287.

92 See, for example, Shannon J. Osborne and Renee Bair, "Healing Inmates' Hearts and Spirits with Man's Best Friend," *Corrections Today* (April, 2003), pp. 122–123, 146; Todd Harkrader, Tod W. Burke, and Stephen S. Owen, "Pound Puppies: The Rehabilitative Uses of Dogs in Correctional Facilities," *Corrections Today* (April, 2004), pp. 74–79, and Charles N. Alexander, Kenneth G. Walton, David Orme-Johnson, Rachel S. Goodman, and Nathaniel J. Pallone, eds., *Transcendental Meditation in Criminal Rehabilitation and Crime Prevention* (Binghamton, NY: Haworth Press, 2003).

93 Correctional Service of Canada, *Principles of Effective Correctional Programming* (Toronto: Correctional Service of Canada, 2003).

94 See Faye S. Taxman and Jeffrey A. Bouffard, "Assessing Therapeutic Integrity in Modified Therapeutic Communities for Drug-involved Offenders," *Prison Journal*, Vol. 82, No. 2 (June, 2002), pp. 189–212.

95 James A. Inciardi et al., "Therapeutic Communities and Work Release: Effective Modalities for Drug-involved Offenders," *NIJ Research Review*, Vol. 1, No. 3 (September, 2000), p. 2.

96 James Austin, "The Limits of Prison Drug Treatment," *Corrections Management Quarterly*, Vol. 2, No. 4 (1998), p. 73.

97 Brian Shapiro, "The Therapeutic Community Movement in Corrections," *Corrections Today*, Vol. 63, No. 1 (February, 2001), pp. 26, 32, citing research conducted by Douglas Lipton. See also the similar findings of M.L. Hiller, K. Knight and D.D. Simpson, "Prison-based Substance Treatment, Residential Aftercare, and Recidivism," *Addiction*, Vol. 94, No. 6 (1999), pp. 833–842.

98 Daniel P. Mears, Sarah Lawrence, Amy L. Solomon, and Michelle Waul, "Prison-based Programming: What It Can Do and Why It Is Needed," *Corrections Today*, Vol. 64, No. 2 (April, 2002), pp. 66–67.

99 Christine S. Scott-Hayward, *The Fiscal Crisis in Corrections: Rethinking Policies and Practices* (New York: Vera Institute of Justice, 2009), pp. 3, 5.

100 U.S. Department of Health and Human Services, *Substance Abuse Treatment for Women Offenders: Guide to Promising Practices* (Rockville, MD: U.S. Department of Health and Human Services, 2002), p. 12.

101 *For Our Health and Safety: Joining Forces to Beat Addiction* (Sacramento, CA: Little Hoover Commission on California State Government Organization and Economy, 2003).

102 Austin, "The Limits of Prison Drug Treatment," p. 73.

103 Jeremy Travis, "Reentry and Reintegration: New Perspectives on the Challenges of Mass Incarceration," in Mary Pattillo, David Weiman, and Bruce Western, eds., *Imprisoning America: The Social Effects of Mass Incarceration* (New York: Russell Sage Foundation, 2004), p. 254.

104 Ibid.

10 The Effects of Institutional Life

1 Michael G. Santos, *About Prison* (Belmont, CA: Wadsworth, 2004), p. 218.

2 Chad Trulson, "The Social World of the Prisoner," in Joycelyn M. Pollock, ed., *Prisons: Today and Tomorrow* (Sudbury, MA: Jones & Bartlett, 2006), p. 89.

3 Victor Hassine, *Life without Parole: Living in Prison Today* (Los Angeles: Roxbury Publishing, 1999), p. 47.

4 In fact, these same reactions were reported among students confined to a room in their home for just 48 hours as an assignment for a college course. See Jeanne B. Stinchcomb, "Prisons of the Mind: Lessons Learned from Home Confinement," *Journal of Criminal Justice Education*, Vol. 13, No. 2 (2002), pp. 463–478.

5 See Nicolett Parisi, "The Prisoner's Pressures and Responses," in Nicolett Parisi, ed., *Coping with Imprisonment* (Beverly Hills, CA: Sage Publications, 1982), pp. 9–11, who maintains that both *internal* and *external* stimuli contribute to pressures and strategies of coping in prison.

6 Wayne Gillespie, "The Context of Imprisonment," in Stephen Stanko, Wayne Gillespie, and Gordon A. Crews, eds., *Living in Prison: A History of the Correctional System with an Insider's View* (Westport, CT: Greenwood Press, 2004), p. 67.

7 Jim Thomas, Harry Mike, Jerome Blakemore, and Anmarie Aylward, "Exacting Control through Disciplinary Hearings: 'Making Do' with Prison Rules," *Justice Quarterly*, Vol. 8, No. 1 (March, 1991), p. 41. On the other hand, it has been argued that neither of these two models adequately accounts for adaptations to confinement. See Thomas J. Schmid and Richard S. Jones, "Ambivalent Actions: Prison Adaptation Strategies of First-time, Short-term Inmates," in Richard Tewksbury, ed., *Behind Bars: Readings on Prison Culture* (Upper Saddle River, NJ: Pearson Prentice Hall, 2006), pp. 3–16. For a comprehensive discussion of the research on both, see Chad Trulson, "The Social World of the Prisoner," in Pollock, ed., *Prisons*, pp. 91–92.

8 Philip G. Zimbardo, "Pathology of Imprisonment," in Lawrence F. Travis, Martin D. Schwartz, and Todd R. Clear, eds., *Corrections: An Issues Approach*, Second Edition (Cincinnati, OH: Anderson, 1983), pp. 99–104. (The remainder of the discussion of what has become known as the "Zimbardo experiment" is summarized from this source.)

9 Ibid., p. 101.

10 Craig Haney, "The Psychological Impact of Incarceration: Implications for Postprison Adjustment," in Jeremy Travis and Michelle Waul, *Prisoners Once Removed: The Impact of Incarceration and Reentry on Children, Families, and Communities* (Washington, DC: The Urban Institute, 2003), p. 39.

11 Meg Laughlin, "Ex-convicts Learn How to Embrace Freedom," *The Miami Herald* (February 15, 2004), p. 3B, quoting Bernie DeCastro.

12 Jeffrey Ian Ross and Stephen C. Richards, *Behind Bars: Surviving Prison* (Indianapolis, IN: Alpha Books, 2002), p. 150.

13 Hassine, *Life without Parole*, p. 35.

14 Peter O. Peretti, "Desocialization–Resocialization Process within the Prison Walls," *Canadian Journal of Corrections*, Vol. 12, No. 1 (January, 1970), pp. 59–66.

15 Donald Clemmer, *The Prison Community* (New York: Rinehart and Winston, 1958).

16 John J. Vollmann, "Imposed Socialization: A Functional Control in a Total Institution," *Sociological Research Symposium VIII* (Richmond, VA: Virginia Commonwealth University, 1978).

17 Erving Goffman, *Asylums: Essays on the Social Situation of Mental Patients and Other Inmates* (Garden City, NY: Anchor Books, 1961) describes a "total institution" as a "place of residence and work where large numbers of like-situated individuals, cut off from the wider society for an appreciable period of time, together lead an enclosed, formally-administered round of life" (p. xiii).

18 Gresham M. Sykes, *The Society of Captives: A Study of a Maximum Security Prison* (Princeton, NJ: Princeton University Press, 1958).

19 John Irwin and Rick Mockler, "Prison Comforts Make Little Difference," in Bonnie Szumski, *America's Prisons: Opposing Viewpoints* (St. Paul, MN: Greenhaven Press, 1985), p. 86.

20 Stephen Stanko, "Surviving in Prison," in Stanko, Gillespie, and Crews, eds., *Living in Prison*, p. 177.

21 Haney, "The Psychological Impact of Incarceration," p. 42.

22 Charles Campbell, *Serving Time Together: Men and Women in Prison* (Fort Worth: Texas Christian University Press, 1980), p. 229.

23 Haney, "The Psychological Impact of Incarceration," p. 39.

24 Glenn D. Walters, "Changes in Criminal Thinking and Identity in Novice and Experienced Inmates," *Criminal Justice and Behavior*, Vol. 30, No. 4 (August, 2003), p. 401.

25 Haney, "The Psychological Impact of Incarceration," p. 41.

26 Ibid.

27 Boyd D. Sharp, *Changing Criminal Thinking: A Treatment Program* (Alexandria, VA: American Correctional Association, 2000), pp. 2, 48.

28 Ibid., p. 53.

29 Hassine, *Life without Parole*, p. 39.

30 Recent research confirms that core components of the code have remained remarkably consistent over time; see Paula L. Faulkner and William R. Faulkner, "Effects of Organizational Change on Inmate Status and the Inmate Code of Conduct," in Tewksbury, ed., *Behind Bars: Readings on Prison Culture*, pp. 75–96.

31 See Barbara Owens and Doris L. MacKenzie, "The Mix: The Culture of Imprisoned Women," in Mary Stohr and Craig Hemmens, eds., *The Inmate Prison Experience* (Upper Saddle River, NJ: Pearson Prentice Hall, 2004), pp. 152–172.

32 John Irwin, "The Prison Experience: The Convict World," in George G. Killinger and Paul F. Cromwell, Jr., eds., *Penology: The Evolution of Corrections in America* (St. Paul, MN: West, 1973), p. 202, quoting an interview with a Soledad inmate.

33 Haney, "The Psychological Impact of Incarceration," p. 41.

34 Craig Hemmens and James W. Marquart, "Race, Age, and Inmate Perceptions of Violence in Prisons," *Corrections Compendium*, Vol. 24, No. 2 (February, 1999), p. 4.

35 John J. Gibbons and Nicholas de B. Katzenbach, *Confronting Confinement: A Report of the Commission on Safety and Abuse in America's Prisons* (Washington, DC: Vera Institute of Justice, 2006), p. 29.

36 Jarvis Masters, "Scars," in Don Sabor, Terry Kupers, and Willie London, eds., *Prison Masculinities* (Philadelphia, PA: Temple University Press, 2001), p. 205.

37 For more information on these initiatives, see Andrew L. Goldberg and Doris Wells, "NIJ's Response to the Prison Rape Elimination Act," *Corrections Today* (June, 2009), pp. 91–92, 94.

38 Tim McGlone, "Virginia Inmates File Suits to Stop Prison Violence," *The Virginian Pilot* (June 24, 2010).

39 Joycelyn M. Pollock-Byrne, "Women in Prison: Why Are Their Numbers Increasing?," in Peter J. Benekos and Alida V. Merlo, *Corrections: Dilemmas and Directions* (Cincinnati, OH: Anderson, 1992), p. 91.

40 Mary Dodge and Mark R. Pogrebin, "Collateral Costs of Imprisonment for Women: Complications of Reintegration," *Prison Journal*, Vol. 81, No. 1 (March, 2001), p. 43.

41 Kathryn Watterson Burkhart, *Women in Prison* (New York: Doubleday, 1973), pp. 365–366. More recent research indicates that, while the structure of their social relationships may be changing, sexual relations are still a significant part of life in women's prisons. In fact, because of greater acceptance of same-sex relationships, there now appears to be less regulation of the personal lives of female inmates. See Candace Kruttschnitt and Rosemary Gartner, *Marking Time in the Golden State: Women's Imprisonment in California* (Cambridge, England: Cambridge University Press, 2005).

42 Barbara Bloom, Barbara Owen, and Stephanie Covington, "A Theoretical Basis for Gender-responsive Strategies in Criminal Justice," Paper presented at the American Society of Criminology Annual Meeting (Chicago, IL, November, 2002), p. 12.

43 Wayne Gillespie, "Women and Prison," in Stanko, Gillespie, and Crews, eds., *Living in Prison*, p. 95.

44 Trulson, "The Social World of the Prisoner," p. 106.

45 See, for example, Candace Kruttschnitt and Sharon Krompotich, "Aggressive Behavior among Female Inmates: An Exploratory Study," *Justice Quarterly*, Vol. 7, No. 2 (June, 1990), p. 384, and Nancy Wolff et al., "Physical Violence inside Prisons: Rates of Victimization," *Criminal Justice and Behavior*, Vol. 34, No. 5 (May, 2007), pp. 588–599.

46 Christine E. Rasche, *Special Needs of the Female Offender: Curriculum Guide for Correctional Officers* (Tallahassee, FL: Florida Department of Education, n.d.), p. 68. See also John DeBell, "The Female Offender: Different . . . Not Difficult," *Corrections Today*, Vol. 63, No. 1 (February, 2001), p. 89.

47 Joycelyn M. Pollock, *Women, Prison and Crime* (Belmont, CA: Wadsworth, 2002), p. 80.

48 John M. Vanyur and Barbara Owen, "Managing Female Offenders in Mixed-gender Facilities: The Case of a Federal Jail," *American Jails* (May/June, 2003), p. 68.

49 Barbara Bloom, Barbara Owen, and Stephanie Covington, *Gender-responsive Strategies: Research, Practice, and Guiding Principles for Women Offenders* (Washington, DC: U.S. Department of Justice, National Institute of Corrections, 2003), p. 58.

50 Merry Morash, Timothy S. Bynum, and Barbara A. Koons, "Women Offenders: Programming Needs and Promising Approaches," *National Institute of Justice: Research in Brief* (Washington, DC: U.S. Department of Justice, National Institute of Justice, 1998), p. 4.

51 Human Rights Watch Women's Rights Project, *All Too Familiar: Sexual Abuse of Women in U.S. State Prisons* (New York: The Ford Foundation, 1996).

52 Bloom, Owen, and Covington, *Gender-responsive Strategies*, p. 26.

53 Lawrence A. Greenfeld, *Prisons and Prisoners in the United States* (Washington, DC: U.S. Department of Justice, 1992), p. 2.

54 Pollock, *Women, Prison and Crime*, p. 105.

55 Barbara Bloom, Joan Johnson, and Elizabeth Belzer, "Effective Management of Female Offenders: Applying Research on Gender-responsive Correctional Strategies to Local Jails," *American Jails* (September/October, 2003), p. 33.

56 Santos, *About Prison*, p. 92.

57 National Institute of Corrections, *Management Strategies in Disturbances and with Gangs/Disruptive Groups* (Washington, DC: U.S. Government Printing Office, 1992), p. 2.

58 Marie Griffin and John Hepburn, "The Effect of Gang Affiliation on Violent Misconduct among Inmates during the Early Years of Confinement," *Criminal Justice and Behavior*, Vol. 33, No. 4 (2006), pp. 419–448.

59 Ed Tromanhauser et al., "Gangs and Guns: A Task Force Report," *American Jails* (May/June, 1995), p. 63.

60 Dan Eckhart, "Civil Actions Related to Prison Gangs: A Survey of Federal Cases," *Corrections Management Quarterly*, Vol. 5, No. 1 (2001), pp. 59–64.

61 See Alfonso J. Valdez, "Prison Gangs 101," *Corrections Today*, Vol. 71, No. 1 (February, 2009), pp. 40–43.

62 Irving Spergel et al., *Gang Suppression and Intervention* (Washington, DC: Office of Juvenile Justice and Delinquency Prevention, 1994), p. 15.

63 William J. Morgan, Jr., "The Major Causes of Institutional Violence," *American Jails* (November/December, 2009), p. 69.

64 Salvador Buentello, "Combating Gangs in Texas," *Corrections Today*, Vol. 54, No. 5 (July, 1992), p. 58. Nationwide, about one-third of the inmate-on-inmate violence in prisons is attributed to gangs; see George W. Know, "A National Assessment of Gangs and Security Threat Groups in Adult Correctional Institutions," *Journal of Gang Research*, Vol. 7, No. 3 (2000), pp. 1–45.

65 William Toller and Basil Tsagaris, "Managing Institutional Gangs: A Practical Approach Combining Security and Human Services," *Corrections Today*, Vol. 58, No. 6 (October, 1996), p. 111.

66 Paul Keve, *Prison Life and Human Worth* (Minneapolis: University of Minnesota Press, 1974), p. 6.

67 "Violence on the Rise at Federal Prisons," *Corrections Digest*, Vol. 26, No. 4 (January 27, 1995), p. 5.

68 Gibbons and Katzenbach, *Confronting Confinement*, p. 22, quoting Donald Spector.

69 Keve, *Prison Life*, p. 67.

70 Bert Useem and Anne M. Piehl, "Prison Buildup and Disorder," *Punishment and Society*, Vol. 8, No. 1 (2006), p. 95.

71 Steven D. Dillingham and Reid H. Montgomery, Jr., "Prison Riots: A Corrections' Nightmare since 1774," in Michael Braswell, Steven Dillingham, and Reid Montgomery, Jr., eds., *Prison Violence in America* (Cincinnati, OH: Anderson, 1985), p. 19.

72 James B. Jacobs, "Prison Reform and the Ruins of Prisoners' Rights," in Michal Tonry, ed., *The Future of Imprisonment* (New York: Oxford University Press, 2004), p. 188. See also Useem and Piehl, "Prison Buildup and Disorder," p. 95.

73 Dillingham and Montgomery, "Prison Riots," pp. 23–24, citing a study of collective violence between 1900 and 1970.

74 Keve, *Prison Life*, p.15.

75 Bert Useem, Camille Graham Camp, George M. Camp, and Renie Dugan, "Resolution of Prison Riots," *National Institute of Justice: Research in Brief* (Washington, DC: U.S. Department of Justice, October, 1995), p. 7.

76 Summarized from American Correctional Association, *Causes, Preventive Measures, and Methods of Controlling Riots and Disturbances in Correctional Institutions* (Upper Marlboro, MD: Graphic Communications, 1998), pp. 8–11. See also Richard C. McCorkle, Terance D. Miethe, and Kriss A. Drass, "The Roots of Prison Violence: A Test of the Deprivation, Management, and 'Not-So-Total' Institution Models," *Crime and Delinquency*, Vol. 41, No. 3 (July, 1995), pp. 317–331.

77 Bert Useem and Jack A. Goldstone, "Forging Social Order and Its Breakdown: Riot and Reform in U.S. Prisons," *American Sociological Review*, Vol. 67 (August, 2002), pp. 499–525.

78 Sue Mahan, "An 'Orgy of Brutality' at Attica and the 'Killing Ground' at Santa Fe: A Comparison of Prison Riots," in Parisi, *Coping with Imprisonment*, p. 76.

79 Dick Franklin, "Contemporary Issues in Prison Management," *Training Manual, NIC Executive Training for New Wardens* (Longmont, CO: National Institute of Corrections, February, 2000), p. 8.

80 D.M. Rothman, "Attica System: You Can't Reform the Bastille," *Nation* (March 19, 1973), p. 366.

81 R. Arjen Boin and Menno J. Van Duin, "Prison Riots as Organizational Failures: A Managerial Perspective," in Tewksbury, ed., *Behind Bars: Readings on Prison Culture*, p. 445.

82 Ellis MacDougall and Reid H. Montgomery, Jr., "American Prison Riots, 1971–1983," Unpublished paper, College of Criminal Justice, University of South Carolina, Columbia, p. 26.

83 Useem et al., "Resolution of Prison Riots," p. 13.

84 Clinton Van Zandt and G. Dwayne Fuselier, "Nine Days of Crisis Negotiations: The Oakdale Siege," *Corrections Today*, Vol. 51, No. 4 (July, 1989), p. 24.

85 American Correctional Association, *Causes, Preventive Measures*, p. 23.

86 Quoted by Scott Minerbrook, "A Different Reality for Us," *Newsweek* (May 11, 1992), p. 36.

87 See Phillip R. Magaletta, John M. Vanyur, and Kimberly Digre, "On the Consequences of Listening: Hostage Incidents in the Federal Bureau of Prisons," *Corrections Today* (August, 2005), pp. 90–92.

88 National Institute of Corrections, *Management Strategies in Disturbances*, p. 47.

89 Mahan, "Orgy of Brutality," p. 68.

90 John J. DiIulio, Jr., *Governing Prisons: A Comparative Study of Correctional Management* (New York: Free Press, 1987), p. 33, quoting an anonymous prison manager.

91 Hassine, *Life without Parole*, p. 78.

92 Steve Lerner, "Prisons Are Violent and Dehumanizing," in Bonnie Szumski, ed., *America's Prisons: Opposing Viewpoints*, Fourth Edition (St. Paul, MN: Greenhaven Press, 1985), p. 72.

11 Transition from Confinement to Community

1 Joan Petersilia, *When Prisoners Come Home: Parole and Prisoner Reentry* (New York: Oxford University Press, 2003), p. 139.

2 Eric Schlosser, "The Prison-industrial Complex," *Atlantic Monthly* (December, 1998), p. 70.

3 Petersilia, *When Prisoners Come Home*, p. 247.

4 "Prison without Walls: Summary Report on New York Parole; Citizens' Inquiry on Parole and Criminal justice, Inc.," in Calvert R. Dodge, ed., *A Nation without Prisons* (Lexington, MA: D.C. Heath, 1975), p. 83, quoting the New York State Special Commission on Attica.

5 Timothy A. Hughes, Doris James Wilson, and Allen J. Beck, "Trends in State Parole, 1990–2000," *Bureau of Justice Statistics Special Report* (Washington, DC: U.S. Department of Justice, 2001), p. 2. Four additional states have abolished discretionary parole for certain violent offenders.

6 *Online Etymology Dictionary*, available at http://www.etymonline.com (accessed November 3, 2009). The original seventeenth-century reference was to a promise by a prisoner of war not to escape.

7 Edward Lindsey, "Historical Sketch of the Indeterminate Sentence and Parole System," *Journal of the American Institute of Criminal Law and Criminology*, Vol. 16 (1925), p. 9.

8 Michael Tonry, "Reconsidering Indeterminate and Structured Sentencing," *Sentencing and Corrections: Issues for the 21st Century* (September, 1999), p. 3.

9 Petersilia, *When Prisoners Come Home*, p. 73. The state cited is Massachusetts.

10 Katharine Bradley and Michael Oliver, *The Role of Parole* (Boston, MA: Community Resources for Justice, 2001), pp. 4–5.

11 Approximately 100 more serve on a part-time basis. See Peggy B. Burke, ed., *A Handbook for New Parole Board Members* (Washington, DC: National Institute of Corrections, April, 2003), p. vii.

12 President's Commission on Law Enforcement and Administration of Justice, *Task Force Report: Corrections* (Washington, DC: U.S. Government Printing Office, 1967), p. 67.

13 Howard Abadinsky, *Probation and Parole: Theory and Practice* (Upper Saddle River, NJ: Pearson Prentice Hall, 2006), p. 225.

14 Edward E. Rhine, William R. Smith, and Ronald W. Jackson, *Paroling Authorities: Recent History and Current Practice* (Lanham, MD: American Correctional Association, 1991), p. 37.

15 Ibid.

16 Kevin R. Reitz, "Questioning the Conventional Wisdom of Parole Release Authority," in Michael Tonry, ed., *The Future of Imprisonment* (New York: Oxford University Press, 2004), p. 228.

17 Mario A. Paparozzi and Roger Guy, "The Giant that Never Woke: Parole Authorities as the Lynchpin to Evidence-based Practices and Prisoner Reentry," *Journal of Contemporary Criminal Justice*, Vol. 25, No. 4 (2009), pp. 397–411.

18 Since the mid-1970s, an increasing volume of cases has significantly expanded the workload of parole boards. In response, the U.S. Parole Commission and many of the larger states have adopted the use of *hearing examiners*, who are not members of the parole board. Under this system, the board acts in executive session on the recommendations of the hearing examiner.

19 *Menechino v. Oswald*, 430 F.2d 402, 407 (2d Cir. 1970).

20 *Greenholtz v. Inmates*, 442, U.S. 1 (1979).

21 See American Correctional Association, *Standards for Adult Parole Authorities* (Alexandria, VA: American Correctional Association, current edition).

22 Victor Hassine, *Life without Parole: Living in Prison Today* (Los Angeles: Roxbury Publishing, 1999), p. 11.

23 Jessica Mitford, "Kind and Usual Punishment in California," in Jerome H. Skolnick and Elliott Currie, eds., *Crisis in American Institutions*, Second Edition (Boston, MA: Little, Brown, 1973), p. 512.

24 "Citizens' Study Calls for End to Parole," *LEAA Newsletter*, Vol. 4, No. 2 (July, 1974), p. 23.

25 Herman Schwartz, "Let's Abolish Parole," *Reader's Digest* (August, 1973), pp. 185–190.

26 Ibid.

27 Paula M. Ditton and Doris James Wilson, "Truth in Sentencing in State Prisons," *Bureau of Justice Statistics Special Report* (Washington, DC: U.S. Department of Justice, 1999), p. 1.

28 Lauren E. Glaze and Thomas P. Bonczar, "Probation and Parole in the United States, 2007: Statistical Tables," *Bureau of Justice Statistics Bulletin* (Washington, DC: U.S. Department of Justice, August, 2009), p. 4.

29 Joan Petersilia, "Prisoner Reentry: Public Safety and Reintegration Challenges," *Prison Journal*, Vol. 81, No. 3 (2001), p. 471.

30 Orville B. Pung, "Introduction," in American Correctional Association, *Correctional Issues: Probation and Parole* (Lanham, MD: American Correctional Association, 1990), p. vi.

31 U.S. Department of Justice, *Correctional Populations in the United States, 1995* (Washington, DC: U.S. Department of Justice, 1997), p. 126.

32 Lauren E. Glaze and Thomas P. Bonczar, "Probation and Parole in the United States, 2006," *Bureau of Justice Statistics Bulletin* (Washington, DC: U.S. Department of Justice, December, 2007), p. 6. Although 2008 data indicate a slight increase in discretionary releases (to 43 percent), it is unclear whether this is a deviation in recent trends or a reflection of changing data-reporting methodology. See Lauren E. Glaze and Thomas P. Bonczar, "Probation and Parole in the United States, 2008," *Bureau of Justice Statistics Bulletin* (Washington, DC: U.S. Department of Justice, December, 2009), p. 53.

33 William K. Smith, Edward E. Rhine, and Ronald W. Jackson, "Parole Practices: Survey Finds U.S. Agencies Undergoing Changes," in American Correctional Association, *Correctional Issues*, p. 37.

34 "Hitting the Boards," *Corrections Compendium*, Vol. 5, No. 5 (November, 1980), p. 1. However, using a more rigorous definition, it was found a decade later that only 23 states were using "formal, structured guidelines" in making parole release decisions. See Rhine et al., *Paroling Authorities*, p. 67.

35 Petersilia, *When Prisoners Come Home*, pp. 72, 150.

36 Don A. Andrews and James Bonta, *The Level of Service Inventory—Revised* (Toronto: Multi-Health Systems, 1995).

37 Jeremy Travis, "But They All Come Back: Rethinking Prisoner Reentry," *Sentencing and Corrections: Issues for the 21st Century* (Washington, DC: U.S. Department of Justice, 2000), p. 1.

38 Petersilia, *When Prisoners Come Home*, p. 53.

39 Kim Wozencraft, "The Scarlet Letter," *Prison Life* (June, 1994), p. 22.

40 Michael G. Santos, *About Prison* (Belmont, CA: Wadsworth, 2004), p. 220.

41 K.C. Carceral, *Behind a Convict's Eyes: Doing Time in a Modern Prison* (Belmont, CA: Wadsworth/ Thomson Learning, 2004), p. 58.

42 For a list of prerelease services and programs offered by correctional agencies throughout the country, see "Survey Summary: Parole," *Corrections Compendium* (June, 2001), pp. 15–16.

43 See Christopher T. Lowenkamp and Edward J. Latessa, "Developing Successful Reentry Programs: Lessons Learned from the 'What Works' Research," *Corrections Today*, Vol. 67, No. 2 (April, 2005), pp. 72–77.

44 Calculated from Camille Graham Camp, ed., *The 2002 Corrections Yearbook: Adult Corrections* (Middletown, CT: Criminal Justice Institute, 2003), pp. 1, 146.

45 Gerald G. Gaes and Newton Kendig, "The Skill Sets and Health Care Needs of Released Offenders," in Jeremy Travis and Michelle Waul, *Prisoners Once Removed: The Impact of Incarceration and Reentry on Children, Families, and Communities* (Washington, DC: The Urban Institute, 2003), p. 132.

46 Donald Braman and Jenifer Wood, "From One Generation to the Next: How Criminal Sanctions Are Reshaping Family Life in Urban America," in Travis and Waul, *Prisoners Once Removed*, p. 181.

47 Petersilia, *When Prisoners Come Home*, pp. 21, 53.

48 Jeremy Travis, "Prisoner Reentry: The Iron Law of Imprisonment," in Roslyn Muraskin, ed., *Key Correctional Issues* (Upper Saddle River, NJ: Prentice Hall, 2005), pp. 65–66.

49 For an overview of how some states are coping, see Len Engel, John Larivee, and Richard Luedeman, "Reentry and the Economic Crisis: An Examination of Four States and their Budget Efforts," *Corrections Today* (December, 2009), pp. 42–45.

50 Serious and Violent Offender Re-entry Initiative website, Office of Justice Programs, U.S. Department of Justice, http://www.ojp.usdoj.gov/reentry/learn.html.

51 Theodore M. Hammett, "Health-related Issues in Prisoner Reentry to the Community," Paper presented at the Reentry Roundtable on Public Health Dimensions of Prisoner Reentry of the Urban Institute, Washington, DC, October, 2000.

52 Joey R. Weedon, "The Foundation of Re-entry," *Corrections Today* (April, 2004), p. 6.

53 Craig Haney, "The Psychological Impact of Incarceration: Implications for Postprison Adjustment," in Travis and Waul, *Prisoners Once Removed*, p. 37.

54 Rhine et al., *Paroling Authorities*, pp. 102–103.

55 Barry J. Nidorf, "Probation and Parole Officers: Police Officers or Social Workers?," in American Correctional Association, *Correctional Issues*, p. 73.

56 Jeffrey Spelman, "An Initial Comparison of Graduates and Terminated Clients in America's Largest Re-entry Court," *Corrections Today* (August, 2003), pp. 74–77, 83.

57 Jeremy Travis, *But They All Come Back: Facing the Challenges of Prisoner Reentry* (Washington, DC: The Urban Institute, 2005), pp. 67–68.

58 See Marc Mauer and Meda Chesney-Lind, eds., *Invisible Punishment: The Collateral Consequences of Mass Imprisonment* (Washington, DC: The Sentencing Project, 2002).

59 John J. Larivee, "Returning Inmates: Closing the Public Safety Gap," *Corrections Compendium* (June, 2001), pp. 4, 10.

60 In fact, one person has been there so long that "Julia Tuttle Causeway Bridge" is listed as the legal residence on his driver's license. See Fred Grimm, "Woman Joins Sex Offender Group Living under Julia Tuttle Causeway," *The Miami Herald* (March 24, 2009).

61 Marilyn D. McShane and Wesley Krouse, *Community Corrections* (New York: Macmillan, 1993), p. 238.

62 Schlosser, "The Prison-industrial Complex," p. 69. The state referred to is California.

63 "Rules for Restoration of Civil Rights for Felons and Impacts on Obtaining Occupational Licenses and Other Opportunities," *The Florida Senate: Interim Project Report* (December, 2007), p. 2. See also Jeremy Travis, "Reentry and Reintegration: New Perspectives on the Challenges of Mass

Incarceration," in Mary Pattillo, David Weiman, and Bruce Western, eds., *Imprisoning America: The Social Effects of Mass Incarceration* (New York: Russell Sage Foundation, 2004), p. 259.

64 Joan Petersilia, "Hard Time: Ex-offenders Returning Home after Prison," *Corrections Today* (April, 2005), pp. 66–71. The state referred to is California.

65 Sesha Kethineni and David Falcone, "Employment and Ex-offenders in the U.S.," *Probation Journal*, Vol. 54, No. 1 (2007), p. 42.

66 Travis, "Reentry and Reintegration," p. 259.

67 "Denial of Federal Benefits Program and Clearinghouse," *Bureau of Justice Assistance: Program Brief* (July, 2002), pp. 2–3.

68 Vanessa St. Gerard, "Study Cites Legislation Too Tough on Ex-inmates," *Corrections Today* (August, 2003), p. 18.

69 *Felony Disenfranchisement Laws in the United States*, White Paper prepared by the Sentencing Project, Washington, DC (September, 2008), p. 1. See also Christopher Uggen and Jeff Manza, "Lost Voices: The Civic and Political Views of Disenfranchised Felons," in Pattillo, Weiman, and Western, eds., *Imprisoning America*, p. 254; Jeffrey Reiman, "Liberal and Republican Arguments against the Disenfranchisement of Felons," *Criminal Justice Ethics* (Winter/Spring, 2005), pp. 3–18; and Katherine Irene Pettus, *Felony Disenfranchisement in America: Historical Origins, Institutional Racism, and Modern Consequences* (New York: LFB Scholarly Publishing, 2005).

70 Harry Holzer, Steven Raphael, and Michael Stoll, "How Do Employer Perceptions of Crime and Incarceration Affect the Employment Prospects of Less-educated Young Black Men?," in Ronald B. Mincy, ed., *Black Males Left Behind* (Washington, DC: The Urban Institute, March, 2006), p. 73.

71 Petersilia, "Hard Time," p. 67.

72 Holzer, Raphael, and Stoll, "How Do Employer Perceptions of Crime and Incarceration Affect the Employment Prospects of Less-educated Young Black Men?," p. 81.

73 Helen Lam and Mark Harcourt, "The Use of Criminal Record in Employment Decisions: The Rights of Ex-offenders, Employers and the Public," *Journal of Business Ethics*, Vol. 47, No. 3 (October, 2003), p. 242.

74 American Bar Association, *Standards for Criminal Justice: Collateral Sanctions and Discretionary Disqualification of Convicted Persons* (Chicago, IL: American Bar Association, 2004).

75 Bruce Western, Mary Pattillo, and David Weiman, "Introduction," in Pattillo, Weiman, and Western, *Imprisoning America*, p. 5. See also Michael Tonry, "Has the Prison a Future?," in Tonry, ed., *The Future of Imprisonment*, p. 23.

76 Ed Rhine, John R. Matthews, Lee A. Sampson, and Hugh Daley, "Citizens' Circles: Community Collaboration in Re-entry," *Corrections Today* (August, 2003), pp. 53–54.

77 Gordon Bazemore and Jeanne Stinchcomb, "Promoting Successful Re-entry through Service and Restorative Justice: Theory and Practice for a Civic Engagement Model of Community Reintegration," *Federal Probation*, Vol. 68, No. 2 (September, 2004), pp. 14–24.

78 For additional information on re-entry initiatives, see Donald G. Evans, "New Ideas and Evidence-based Practices: The Case for Inmate Reentry," *Corrections Today* (June, 2005), pp. 28–29; Elizabeth C. McBride, Christy Visher, and Nancy LaVigne, "Informing Policy and Practice: Prisoner Reentry Research at the Urban Institute," *Corrections Today* (April, 2005), pp. 90–93; Ralph Fretz, "Step Down Programs: The Missing Link in Successful Inmate Reentry," *Corrections Today* (April, 2005), pp. 102–107; Lowenkamp and Latessa, "Developing Successful Reentry Programs," pp. 72–77; Jesse Jannetta, "Assembling the Jail Reentry Puzzle," *American Jails*, Vol. XXIII, No. 4 (September/October, 2009), pp. 9–18; DonaLee Brezzano, "The Federal Bureau of Prisons Shifts Reentry Focus to a Skills-based Model," *Corrections Today*, Vol. 71, No. 6 (December, 2009), pp. 50–57.

79 Petersilia, *When Prisoners Come Home*, p. 77.

80 Cheryl L. Ringel, Ernest L. Cowles, and Thomas C. Castellano, "Changing Patterns and Trends in Parole Supervision," in *Critical Issues in Crime and Justice* (Newbury Park, CA: Sage Publications, 1997), p. 299.

81 Nidorf, "Probation and Parole Officers," p. 70.

82 Ibid., p. 74.

83 Shadd Maruna and Thomas P. LeBel, "Welcome Home? Examining the 'Reentry Court' Concept from a Strengths-based Perspective," *Western Criminology Review*, Vol. 4, No. 2 (2003), p. 91.

84 *Greenholtz v. Inmates of the Nebraska Penal and Correctional Complex*, 442 U.S. 1 (1979).

85 *Morrisey v. Brewer*, 408 U.S. 471 (1972).

86 *Gagnon v. Scarpelli*, 411 U.S. 778 (1973). As was discussed in Chapter 4, in this case the Supreme Court extended many of the same due process procedures to probationers.

87 Smith et al., "Parole Practices," p. 42.

88 Heather C. West and William J. Sabol, "Prisoners in 2007," *Bureau of Justice Statistics Bulletin* (Washington, DC: U.S. Department of Justice, December, 2008), p. 3.

89 Vanessa St. Gerard, "Connecticut Focuses on Breaking Recidivism Cycle," *Corrections Compendium*, Vol. 28, No. 10 (October, 2003), p. 26.

90 Thomas Watkins, "Amid Budget Crisis, Parole Made Easier," *The Miami Herald* (April 4, 2010), p. 19A.

91 Patrick A. Langan and David J. Levin, "Recidivism of Prisoners Released in 1994," *Bureau of Justice Statistics Special Report* (Washington, DC: U.S. Department of Justice, 2002), p. 1.

92 Timothy A. Hughes, Doris J. Wilson, and Allen J. Beck, "Trends in State Parole, 1990–2000," *Bureau of Justice Statistics Special Report* (Washington, DC: U.S. Department of Justice, 2001), p. 11.

93 Dale J. Ardovini-Brooker, "Correctional Education: The History, the Research, and the Future," in Muraskin, ed., *Key Correctional Issues*, p. 216.

94 Reitz, "Questioning the Conventional Wisdom of Parole Release Authority," p. 215.

95 Petersilia, *When Prisoners Come Home*, p. 17. See also Jeremy Travis, Anna Crayton, and Debbie A. Muklamal, "A New Era In Inmate Reentry," *Corrections Today* (December, 2009), pp. 38–41.

96 George Ives, *A History of Penal Methods* (Montclair, NJ: Patterson Smith, 1970), pp. 382–383.

Part 4 Juvenile Corrections, Staff Concerns, Legal Issues, and the Future

1 Jeanne B. Stinchcomb, Susan W. McCampbell, and Leslie Leip, *The Future Is Now: Recruiting, Retaining, and Developing the 21st Century Jail Workforce* (Washington, DC: U.S. Department of Justice, Bureau of Justice Assistance, March, 2009), p. 125, available at http://www.ojp.usdoj.gov/newsroom/pressreleases/2010/BJA10045.htm.

2 Jeanne B. Stinchcomb, Susan W. McCampbell, and Elizabeth P. Layman, *FutureForce: A Guide to Building the 21st Century Community Corrections Workforce* (Washington, DC: U.S. Department of Justice, Bureau of Justice Assistance, September, 2006), p. ix.

12 Juvenile Corrections

1 President's Commission on Law Enforcement and Administration of Justice, *Task Force Report: Juvenile Delinquency and Youth Crime* (Washington, DC: U.S. Government Printing Office, 1967), p. 7.

2 See, for example, Steven L. Schlossman, *Love and the American Delinquent* (Chicago, IL: University of Chicago Press, 1977), pp. 113–123.

3 Anthony M. Platt, *The Child Savers: The Invention of Delinquency* (Chicago, IL: University of Chicago Press, 1969), pp. 36–43.

4 Ibid.

5 Helen Rankin Jeter, *The Chicago Juvenile Court* (Washington, DC: U.S. Government Printing Office, 1922), p. 5.

6 In fact, it has been argued that the legislation establishing a separate juvenile court represented no significant innovations. See Sanford J. Fox, "Juvenile Justice Reform: An Historical Perspective," *Stanford Law Review*, Vol. 22 (June, 1970), p. 1187.

7 Anthony M. Platt, "The Rise of the Child-saving Movement," in Paul Lerman, ed., *Delinquency and Social Policy* (New York: Praeger, 1970), p. 18.

8 Lawrence Schultz, "The Cycle of Juvenile Court History," *Crime and Delinquency*, Vol. 19, No. 4 (October, 1973), p. 460.

9 Platt, *The Child Savers*, p. 107, quoting from the Illinois Board of Public Charities, *Sixth Biennial Reports* (Springfield, IL: H.W. Rokker, 1880), p. 104.

10 Julian Mack, "The Juvenile Court," *Harvard Law Review*, Vol. 23 (1909), p. 104.

11 Bernard Flexner, Reuben Oppenheimer, and Katharine F. Lenroot, *The Child, the Family, and the Court: A Study of the Administration of Justice in the Field of Domestic Relations* (Washington, DC: U.S. Government Printing Office, 1939), p. 66, citing the Children's Bureau of the U.S. Department of Labor.

12 National Commission on Criminal Justice Standards and Goals, *Courts* (Washington, DC: U.S. Government Printing Office, 1973), p. 289.

13 *Kent v. United States*, 383 U.S. 541, 86 S. Ct. 1045, 16 L.Ed.2d 84 (1966).

14 Barry Krisberg, "The Evolution of the Juvenile Justice System," in John J. Sullivan and Joseph L. Victor, *Criminal Justice 92/93* (Guilford, CT: Dushkin Publishing Group, 1992), p. 154.

15 Jennie L. Shufelt and Joseph J. Cocozza, "Youth with Mental Health Disorders in the Juvenile Justice System: Results from a Multi-state Prevalence Study," *National Center for Mental Health and Juvenile Justice: Research and Program Brief* (June, 2006), p. 2.

16 *Schall v. Martin*, 104 S. Ct. 2403 (1984).

17 U.S. House of Representatives, *Incarceration of Youth Who Are Waiting for Community Mental Health Services in the United States* (Washington, DC: U.S. House of Representatives, Committee on Government Reform, July, 2004).

18 Ibid., p. 7.

19 Christopher J. Mumola, "Suicide and Homicide in State Prisons and Adult Jails," *Bureau of Justice Statistics Special Report* (Washington, DC: U.S. Department of Justice, August, 2005), p. 5.

20 Campaign for Youth Justice, *Jailing Juveniles: The Dangers of Incarcerating Youth in Adult Jails in America*, Campaign for Youth Justice Report (November, 2007), p. 10, available at http://www.campaignforyouthjustice.org/Downloads/NationalReportsArticles/CFYJ-Jailing_Juveniles_Report_2007-11-15.pdf.

21 Ibid., p. 17.

22 Matt Olsen, "Kids in the Hole—Juvenile Offenders," *The Progressive* (August, 2003), citing Craig Haney, available at http://findarticles.com/p/articles/mi_m1295/is_8_67/ai_106225215/.

23 Ira M. Schwartz, *Justice for Juveniles* (Lexington, MA: Lexington Books, 1989), p. 82.

24 Campaign for Youth Justice, *Jailing Juveniles: The Dangers of Incarcerating Youth in Adult Jails in America*.

25 Melissa Sickmund, Howard N. Snyder, and Eileen Poe-Yamagata, *Juvenile Offenders and Victims: 1997 Update on Violence* (Pittsburgh, PA: National Center for Juvenile Justice, 1997), p. 43.

26 Michael J. Dale, "Children in Adult Jails: A Look at Liability Issues," *American Jails*, Vol. 4, No. 5 (January/February, 1991), p. 31, citing *Hendrickson v. Griggs*, 672 F. Supp. 1126 (N.D. Iowa 1987).

27 Office of Juvenile Justice and Delinquency Prevention, *Annual Report: How OJJDP Is Serving Children, Families, and Communities* (Washington, DC: Office of Juvenile Justice and Delinquency Prevention, 2008), p. 90. The two states remaining in noncompliance were Mississippi and South Carolina.

28 Howard N. Snyder and Melissa Sickmund, *Juvenile Offenders and Victims: A National Report* (Pittsburgh, PA: National Center for Juvenile Justice, 1995), p. 146.

29 Ibid., p. 202.

30 Ibid., p. 200.

31 Office of Juvenile Justice and Delinquency Prevention, *Annual Report*, p. 89. The two states are Mississippi and Washington.

32 See, for example, Bart Lubow, "Safely Reducing Reliance on Juvenile Detention: A Report from the Field," *Corrections Today* (August, 2005), pp. 66–72.

33 Snyder and Sickmund, *Juvenile Offenders and Victims: A National Report*, p. 146.

34 The teenager died at the Miami-Dade Juvenile Detention Center after no response to his pleas for help; see "Controversy Follows Death at Detention Center," June 17, 2003, details at http://www.local10.com/news/2276210/detail.html.

35 Greg Bolt, "Other States Mimicking Juvenile System," *Oregon Corrections Association Reports* (Fall, 1991), p. 17, quoting Dennis Maloney.

36 See Jeffrey A. Butts and Daniel P. Mears, "Reviving Juvenile Justice in a Get-tough Era," *Youth and Society*, Vol. 33, No. 2 (December, 2001): 169–198.

37 Larry W. Callicutt, "Placement of State-committed Juveniles," *Corrections Today* (February, 2004), pp. 37–38.

38 Howard N. Snyder and Melissa Sickmund, *Juvenile Offenders and Victims: 2006 National Report* (Pittsburgh, PA: National Center for Juvenile Justice, March, 2006), p. 197.

39 For a summary of state compliance with this initiative, see Office of Juvenile Justice and Delinquency Prevention, *Disproportionate Minority Confinement: 2002 Update* (Washington, DC: Office of Juvenile Justice and Delinquency Prevention, 2003). By 2002, this mandate had been expanded to encompass disproportionate minority contact at any point in the juvenile justice system.

40 Snyder and Sickmund, *Juvenile Offenders and Victims: 2006 National Report*, p. 209.

41 Ibid., pp. 206, 209.

42 Anne M. Nurse, "The Structure of the Juvenile Prison," *Youth and Society*, Vol. 23, No. 3 (March, 2001), p. 360.

43 Snyder and Sickmund, *Juvenile Offenders and Victims: 2006 National Report*, p. 195.

44 Sarah Livsey, Melissa Sickmund, and Anthony Sladky, "Juvenile Residential Facility Census, 2004: Selected Findings," *Juvenile Offenders and Victims: National Report Series Bulletin* (January, 2009), p. 7. Only 1 percent of private facilities are over their standard bed capacity, compared to 11 percent of public facilities.

45 Ibid., p. 4.

46 Randall G. Shelden and Michelle Hussong, "Juvenile Crime, Adult Adjudication, and the Death Penalty: Draconian Policies Revisited," *Justice Policy Journal*, Vol. 1, No. 2 (Spring, 2003), p. 13.

47 Livsey, Sickmund, and Sladky, "Juvenile Residential Facility Census, 2004," p. 7.

48 David Roush and Michael McMillen, "Construction, Operations, and Staff Training for Juvenile Confinement Facilities," *JAIBG Bulletin* (January, 2000), p. 3.

49 David Shichor and Clemens Bartollas, "Private and Public Juvenile Placements: Is There a Difference?," *Crime and Delinquency*, Vol. 36, No. 2 (April, 1990), p. 297.

50 Dale G. Parent, "Conditions of Confinement," *Juvenile Justice*, Vol. 1, No. 1 (Spring/Summer, 1993), pp. 2–7.

51 Allen J. Beck, Paige M. Harrison, and Paul Guerino, "Sexual Victimization in Juvenile Facilities Reported by Youth, 2008–09," *Bureau of Justice Statistics Special Report* (January, 2010), p. 1.

52 Parent, "Conditions of Confinement," p. 3.

53 Melissa Sickmund, "Juveniles in Corrections," *Juvenile Offenders and Victims: National Report Series Bulletin* (June, 2004), pp. 9, 14.

54 Glen E. McKenzie, "ACA Accreditation for Juvenile Corrections," *Corrections Today* (February, 2004), p. 53.

55 Camille Graham Camp, ed., *The 2002 Corrections Yearbook: Adult Corrections* (Middletown, CT: Criminal Justice Institute, 2003), p. 90.

56 Ibid.

57 See *Nelson v. Heyne*, 491 F.2d 352 (7th Cir.1974) and *Morales v. Turman*, 383 E Supp. 53 (Ed. Texas 1974).

58 Hunter Hurst, "Turn of the Century: Rediscovering the Value of Juvenile Treatment," *Corrections Today*, Vol. 52, No. 1 (February, 1990), p. 49.

59 Barry C. Feld, "The Punitive Juvenile Court and the Quality of Procedural Justice: Disjunctions between Rhetoric and Reality," *Crime and Delinquency*, Vol. 36, No. 4 (October, 1990), p. 453.

60 J. Steven Smith, "Detention Is an Invaluable Part of the System, But It's Not the Solution to All Youths' Problems," *Corrections Today*, Vol. 53, No. 1 (February, 1991), p. 59.

61 Snyder and Sickmund, *Juvenile Offenders and Victims: 2006 National Report*, p. 234.

62 Jeanne B. Stinchcomb, "Recovering from the Shocking Reality of Shock Incarceration—What Correctional Administrators Can Learn from Boot Camp Failures," *Corrections Management Quarterly*, Vol. 3, No. 4 (1999), p. 43.

63 Doris Layton MacKenzie and Claire Souryal, *Multisite Evaluation of Shock Incarceration* (Washington, DC: U.S. Department of Justice, 1994), p. 28.

64 U.S. General Accounting Office, *Prison Boot Camps* (Washington, DC: U.S. General Accounting Office, April, 1993), cited in Campaign for an Effective Crime Policy, *Public Policy Reports: Evaluating Boot Camp Prisons* (Washington, DC: Campaign for an Effective Crime Policy, 1994), p. 4.

65 Michael Peters, David Thomas, and Christopher Zamberlan, *Boot Camps for Juvenile Offenders: Program Summary* (Washington, DC: U.S. Department of Justice, 1997), p. 23.

66 "Researchers Evaluate Eight Shock Incarceration Programs," *National Institute of Justice Update* (Washington, DC: U.S. Department of Justice, 1994), p. 1.

67 For an analysis of where the breakdown has occurred between the intent and reality of boot camps, see Jeanne B. Stinchcomb, "From Optimistic Policies to Pessimistic Outcomes: Why Won't Boot Camps either Succeed Pragmatically or Succumb Politically?," *Journal of Offender Rehabilitation* (Spring, 2004).

68 "Boot Camp May Not Be Best Method to Help Delinquents," *Corrections Digest* (June 29, 1994), p. 8, quoting Kathleen Heidi.

69 Merry Morash and Lila Rucker, "A Critical Look at the Idea of Boot Camp as a Correctional Reform," *Crime and Delinquency*, Vol. 36, No. 2 (April, 1990).

70 Donald J. Hengesh, "Think of Boot Camps as a Foundation for Change, Not an Instant Cure," *Corrections Today*, Vol. 53, No. 6 (October, 1991), pp. 106–108.

71 Thomas C. Castellano and Susan M. Plant, "Boot Camp Aftercare Programming: Current Limits and Suggested Remedies," in American Correctional Association, *Juvenile and Adult Boot Camps* (Lanham, MD: American Correctional Association, 1996), pp. 233–256.

72 Jeanne B. Stinchcomb and W. Clinton Terry, "Predicting the Likelihood of Rearrest among Shock Incarceration Graduates: Moving beyond Another Nail in the Boot Camp Coffin," *Crime and Delinquency*, Vol. 47 (2001), p. 240.

73 See also John P. Sullivan, Melonie B. Sullivan, and Edward Hopkins, "Family Centered Treatment: A Unique Alternative," *Corrections Today* (June, 2006), pp. 78–80.

74 Shelden and Hussong, "Juvenile Crime, Adult Adjudication, and the Death Penalty," p. 6. (It should be noted that the authors are not advocating this approach but, rather, are using metaphorical language here.)

75 Cindy S. Lederman, "The Juvenile Court: Putting Research to Work for Prevention," *Juvenile Justice*, Vol. VI, No. 2 (December, 1999), p. 24. See also W. Jeff Hinton, Patricia L. Sims, Mary Ann Adams, and Charles West, "Juvenile Justice: A System Divided," *Criminal Justice Policy Review*, Vol. 18, No. 4 (December, 2007), pp. 466–483.

76 Benjamin Adams and Sean Addie, "Delinquency Cases Waived to Criminal Court, 2005," *OJJDP Fact Sheet* (June, 2009), p. 1.

77 David L. Myers, *Excluding Violent Youths from Juvenile Court: The Effectiveness of Legislative Waiver* (New York: LFB Scholarly Publishing, 2001).

78 Snyder and Sickmund, *Juvenile Offenders and Victims: A National Report*, p. 156. See also Jeffrey A. Butts and Daniel P. Mears, "Reviving Juvenile Justice in a Get-tough Era," *Youth and Society*, Vol. 33, No. 2 (December, 2001): 169–198.

79 D.M. Altschuler, "Trends and Issues in the Adultification of Juvenile Justice," in Patricia Harris, *Research to Results: Effective Community Correction* (Alexandria, VA: American Correctional Association, 1999).

80 Shelden and Hussong, "Juvenile Crime, Adult Adjudication, and the Death Penalty," p. 10.

81 Kevin J. Strom, "Profile of State Prisoners under Age 18, 1985–97," *Bureau of Justice Statistics Special Report* (February, 2000), p. 1.

82 Ibid., p. 3.

83 Robert B. Levinson and John J. Greene, *New "Boys" on the Block: Under-18-year-olds in Adult Prisons—Final Report* (Alexandria, VA: American Correctional Association, June, 1998), p. vi.

84 David W. Roush and Earl L. Dunlap, "Juveniles in Adult Prisons: A Very Bad Idea," *Corrections Today* (June, 1997), p. 21. See also Richard E. Redding, "Conditions and Programming for Juveniles in Correctional Facilities," Unpublished paper, University of Virginia, Juvenile Forensic Evaluation Resource Center, Charlottesville, VA, 2000.

85 Levinson and Greene, *New "Boys" on the Block*, p. vii.

86 James Austin, Kelly Dedel Johnson, and Maria Gregoriou, *Juveniles in Adult Prisons and Jails: A National Assessment* (Washington, DC: Institute on Crime, Justice, and Corrections, George Washington University, and National Council on Crime and Delinquency, 1996), p. xi. For a discussion of the pros and cons of sentencing youthful offenders to adult facilities, see Lamar Smith, "Sentencing Youths to Adult Correctional Facilities Increases Public Safety," and Shay Bilchik, "Sentencing Juveniles to Adult Facilities Fails Youths and Society," *Corrections Today* (April, 2003), pp. 20–21.

87 Quoted in Levinson and Greene, *New "Boys" on the Block*, p. vi.

88 Krisberg, "Evolution of the Juvenile Justice System," p. 158.

89 National Council on Crime and Delinquency, "Jurisdiction over Status Offenses Should Be Removed from the Juvenile Court," *Crime and Delinquency*, Vol. 21, No. 2 (April, 1975), p. 97.

90 Ibid., p. 98, quoting Judge David Bazelon, U.S. District Court of Appeals.

91 National Advisory Commission on Criminal Justice Standards and Goals, *A National Strategy to Reduce Crime* (Washington, DC: U.S. Government Printing Office, 1973), p. 121.

92 Office of Juvenile Justice and Delinquency Prevention, *Annual Report*, p. 89. The two states are Mississippi and Washington.

93 Roush and McMillen, "Construction, Operations, and Staff Training for Juvenile Confinement Facilities," p. 3.

94 Anne L. Schneider, *Reports of the National Juvenile Justice Assessment Centers: The Impact of Deinstitutionalization on Recidivism and Secure Confinement of Status Offenders* (Washington, DC: U.S. Department of Justice, 1985), p. 1.

95 Heidi M. Hsia and Marty Beyer, "System Change through State Challenge Activities: Approaches and Products," *Juvenile Justice Bulletin* (March, 2000), pp. 1–2.

96 Roush and McMillen, "Construction, Operations, and Staff Training for Juvenile Confinement Facilities," p. 3.

97 Alden D. Miller, Lloyd E. Ohlin, and Robert B. Coates, "The Aftermath of Extreme Tactics in Juvenile Justice Reform: A Crisis Four Years Later," in David F. Greenberg, ed., *Corrections and Punishment* (Beverly Hills, CA: Sage Publications, 1977), p. 230.

98 Ira M. Schwartz, "Correcting Juvenile Corrections," *Criminal Justice 92/93* (Guilford, CT: Dushkin Publishing Group, 1992), p. 179, citing Barry Krisberg, James Austin, and P.A. Steele, *Unlocking Juvenile Corrections: Evaluating the Massachusetts Department of Youth Services* (San Francisco, CA: National Council on Crime and Delinquency, 1989).

99 John T. Whitehead and Steven P. Lab, *Juvenile Justice: An Introduction* (Cincinnati, OH: Anderson, 1990), pp. 348–349, citing a study conducted by Ira M. Schwartz, J. Jackson-Beeck, and R. Anderson, "The 'Hidden' System of Juvenile Control," *Crime and Delinquency*, Vol. 30 (1984), pp. 371–385.

100 Allen F. Breed and Barry Krisberg, "Juvenile Corrections: Is There a Future?," *Corrections Today*, Vol. 48, No. 8 (December, 1986), p. 17.

101 Schneider, *Reports of the National Juvenile Justice Assessment Centers*, p. vi.

102 Paul H. Hahn, *The Juvenile Offender and the Law* (Cincinnati, OH: Anderson, 1984), p. 220, quoting Don M. Gottfredson.

13 Staff—The Key Ingredient

1 John J. Gibbons and Nicholas de B. Katzenbach, *Confronting Confinement: A Report of the Commission on Safety and Abuse in America's Prisons* (New York: Vera Institute of Justice, 2006), p. 63.

2 Jeanne B. Stinchcomb, "Introduction," in American Correctional Association, *Correctional Issues: Correctional Management* (Alexandria, VA: American Correctional Association, 1990), p. vi.

3 James J. Stephan, *State Prison Expenditures, 2001* (Washington, DC: U.S. Department of Justice, Bureau of Justice Statistics, June, 2004), p. 4. More recent estimates put the percentage even higher, at 75–80 percent. See Christine S. Scott-Hayward, *The Fiscal Crisis in Corrections: Rethinking Policies and Practices* (New York: Vera Institute of Justice, July, 2009), p. 2.

4 Tod Kembel, "Cultivating Our People: The Art of Leadership," *American Jails*, Vol. 5, No. 1 (March/April, 1991), p. 90.

5 Compiled from Camille Graham Camp, ed., *The 2002 Corrections Yearbook* (Middletown, CT: Criminal Justice Institute, 2003), pp. 154, 219.

6 James J. Stephan, *Census of State and Federal Correctional Facilities, 2000* (Washington, DC: U.S. Department of Justice, Bureau of Justice Statistics, August, 2003), p. 14, and James J. Stephan, *Census of Jails, 1999* (Washington, DC: U.S. Department of Justice, Bureau of Justice Statistics, 2001), p. 9.

7 Camp, ed., *The 2002 Corrections Yearbook*, p. 219.

8 For a detailed account of the difficulties faced by women in correctional management positions, see Susan C. Craig, "Management within a Correctional Institution," in Roslyn Muraskin, ed., *Key Correctional Issues* (Upper Saddle River, NJ: Prentice Hall, 2010), pp. 55–69.

9 Camp, ed., *The 2002 Corrections Yearbook*, p. 155.

10 Jeanne B. Stinchcomb, "Developing Correctional Officer Professionalism: A Work in Progress," *Corrections Compendium*, Vol. 25, No. 5 (May, 2000), p. 2, citing data gathered by *Corrections Compendium* (May, 2000), pp. 10–11.

11 Linda E. Zimmer, *Women Guarding Men* (Chicago, IL: University of Chicago Press, 1986), p. 6. See also Joann B. Morton, "The 'Agency of Women': Women and ACA," *Corrections Today*, Vol. 57, No. 5 (August, 1995), p. 82.

12 Barbara W. Jones, "Relevant Rulings: Examining the Case for Women in Corrections," *Corrections Today*, Vol. 54, No. 6 (August, 1992), p. 104.

13 Linda L. Zupan, "Men Guarding Women: An Analysis of the Employment of Male Correction Officers in Prisons for Women," *Journal of Criminal Justice*, Vol. 20, No. 4 (1992), p. 297.

14 Joseph R. Carlson, Richard H. Anson, and George Thomas, "Correctional Officer Burnout and Stress: Does Gender Matter?," *Prison Journal*, Vol. 83, No. 3 (September, 2003), p. 278.

15 Zimmer, *Women Guarding Men*, p. 57.

16 The following information is summarized from ibid., pp. 65–69.

17 National Institute of Justice, *Women in Criminal Justice: A Twenty-year Update* (Washington, DC: National Institute of Justice, U.S. Department of Justice, 1998).

18 Camp, ed., *The 2002 Corrections Yearbook*, p. 163.

19 Summarized from Zimmer, *Women Guarding Men*, pp. 60–65.

20 Kelly Cheeseman, Janet Mullings, and James Marquart, "Inmate Perceptions of Staff across Various Custody Levels of Security," *Corrections Management Quarterly*, Vol. 5 (Spring, 2001), pp. 41–48.

21 Men were assaulted 3.6 times more often. Joseph R. Rowan, "Who Is Safer in Male Maximum Security Prisons?," *Corrections Today*, Vol. 58, No. 2 (1996), pp. 186–189.

22 National Institute of Corrections, *Sexual Misconduct in Prisons: Law, Agency Response, and Prevention* (Longmont, CO: National Institute of Corrections, May, 2000). See also Office of the Inspector General, *Deterring Staff Sexual Abuse of Federal Inmates* (Washington, DC: U.S. Department of Justice, Office of the Inspector General, 2005).

23 Susan W. McCampbell and Elizabeth P. Layman, *Training Curriculum for Investigating Allegations of Staff Sexual Misconduct with Inmates* (Naples, FL: Center for Innovative Public Policies, October, 2000), Section 1, pp. 4–5.

24 U.S. General Accounting Office, *Women in Prison: Sexual Misconduct by Correctional Staff*, Report to the Honorable Eleanor Holmes Norton, House of Representatives (Washington, DC: U.S. General Accounting Office, June, 1999).

25 Barbara Bloom, Barbara Owen, and Stephanie Covington, *Gender-responsive Strategies: Research, Practice, and Guiding Principles for Women Offenders* (Washington, DC: U.S. Department of Justice, National Institute of Corrections, 2003), p. 25.

26 Jeanne B. Stinchcomb, "Police Stress: Could Organizational Culture Be the Culprit?," *Law Enforcement Executive Forum* (Spring, 2004).

27 Lynne C. Lancaster and David Stillman, *When Generations Collide: Who They Are. Why They Clash. How to Solve the Generational Puzzle at Work* (New York: HarperCollins, 2000), pp. 30–31.

28 Jeanne B. Stinchcomb, Susan W. McCampbell, and Leslie Leip, *The Future Is Now: Recruiting, Retaining, and Developing the 21st Century Jail Workforce* (March, 2009), Final report submitted to the U.S. Department of Justice, Bureau of Justice Assistance, Washington, DC, p. 56, available at http://www.cipp.org/pdf/Developingthe21stCenturyJailWorkforceCopysenttoBJA.pdf.

29 American Correctional Association, *2003 Directory of Adult and Juvenile Correctional Departments, Institutions, Agencies, and Probation and Parole Authorities* (Alexandria, VA: American Correctional Association, 2003). See also Eric G. Lambert, "To Stay or Quit: A Review of the Literature on Correctional Staff Turnover," *American Journal of Criminal Justice*, Vol. 26, No. 1 (Fall, 2001), p. 61, where even higher turnover rates are cited.

30 Leigh Branham, *Keeping the People Who Keep You in Business* (New York: AMACOM Division, American Management Association, 2001).

31 Barbara Sims, "Surveying the Correctional Environment: A Review of the Literature," *Corrections Management Quarterly*, Vol. 5, No. 2 (Spring, 2001), p. 4; Risdon N. Slate, Ronald E. Vogel, and W. Wesley Johnson, "To Quit or Not to Quit: Perceptions of Participation in Correctional Decision-making and the Impact of Organizational Stress," *Corrections Management Quarterly*, Vol. 5, No. 2 (Spring, 2001), pp. 74–75; and Mary K. Stohr, Ruth L. Self, and Nicholas P. Lovrich, "Staff Turnover in New Generation Jails: An Investigation of Its Causes and Prevention," *Journal of Criminal Justice*, Vol. 20 (1992), p. 457.

32 Jeff Maahs and Travis Pratt, "Uncovering the Predictors of Correctional Officers' Attitudes and Behaviors: A Meta-analysis," *Corrections Management Quarterly*, Vol. 5, No. 2 (Spring, 2001), p. 17.

33 Stohr, Self, and Lovrich, "Staff Turnover in New Generation Jails," p. 457.

34 Allan L. Patenaude, "Analysis of Issues Affecting Correctional Officer Retention within the Arkansas Department of Correction," *Corrections Management Quarterly*, Vol. 5, No. 2 (Spring, 2001), p. 59. See also William H. Price, Richard Kiekbusch, and John Theis, "Causes of Employee Turnover in Sheriff Operated Jails," *Public Personnel Management*, Vol. 36, No. 1 (Spring, 2007), pp. 51–63.

35 Patenaude, "Analysis of Issues Affecting Correctional Officer Retention," p. 64.

36 Gary L. Dennis, "Here Today, Gone Tomorrow: How Management Style Affects Job Satisfaction and, in Turn, Employee Turnover," *Corrections Today* (June, 1998), pp. 96–101.

37 Stinchcomb, McCampbell, and Leip, *The Future Is Now*.

38 Jane Lommel, "Turning around Turnover," *Corrections Today*, Vol. 66, No. 5 (August, 2004), p. 56.

39 Jeanne B. Stinchcomb "Correctional Officer Stress: Is Training Missing the Target?," *Issues in Correctional Training and Casework* (October, 1986), pp. 19–23. For a current overview, see William J. Morgan, "Correctional Officer Stress: A Review of the Literature 1977–2007," *American Jails* (May/June, 2009), pp. 33–43.

40 Kevin N. Wright, William G. Saylor, Evan Gilman, and Scott Camp, "Job Control and Occupational Outcomes among Prison Workers," *Justice Quarterly*, Vol. 14, No. 3 (September, 1997), p. 525; and Slate, Vogel, and Johnson, "To Quit or Not to Quit," p. 74.

41 Dennis, "Here Today, Gone Tomorrow," p. 97. See also Eric G. Lambert and Eugene A. Paoline, "The Influence of Individual, Job, and Organizational Characteristics on Correctional Staff Job Stress, Job Satisfaction, and Organizational Commitment," *Criminal Justice Review*, Vol. 33, No. 4 (2008), pp. 541–564.

42 Julie A. Honnold and Jeanne B. Stinchcomb, "Officer Stress: Costs, Causes, and Cures," *Corrections Today*, Vol. 47, No. 7 (December, 1985), pp. 49–50. More recently, research has determined that both supervisory trust and management trust relate significantly to lower job stress and higher job satisfaction. See Eric G. Lambert, Shanhe Jiang, and Nancy L. Hogan, "The Issue of Trust in Shaping the Job Stress, Job Satisfaction, and Organizational Commitment of Correctional Staff," *Professional Issues in Criminal Justice*, Vol. 3, No. 4 (2008), pp. 37–63.

43 Doris T. Wells, "Reducing Stress for Officers and Their Families," *Corrections Today* (April, 2003), pp. 24–25. See also Mark J. Strickland, "Causations of Stress among Correctional Officers," *American Jails*, Vol. XX, No. 3 (July/August, 2006), pp. 69–77.

44 Gerald W. McEntee and William Lucy, *Prisoners of Life: A Study of Occupational Stress among State Corrections Officers* (Washington, DC: American Federation of State, County and Municipal Employees, n.d.), p. 22 and Table 25. (The three states included in this study were Pennsylvania, Illinois, and Washington.) For a similar review of the current status of stress research, see Robert G. Huckabee, "Stress in Corrections: An Overview of the Issues," *Journal of Criminal Justice*, Vol. 20, No. 5 (1992), pp. 479–486.

45 Sarah J. Tracy, "Correctional Contradictions: A Structural Approach to Addressing Officer Burnout," *Corrections Today* (April, 2003), p. 94.

46 Marilyn D. McShane, Frank P. Williams, and David Shichor, *Correctional Management in the 1990's: A National Survey of Correctional Managers*, Vol. II (San Bernardino, CA: California State University, Department of Criminal Justice, 1990), p. 10.

47 Stinchcomb, McCampbell, and Leip, *The Future Is Now*, Appendix A.

48 See, for example, Douglas L. Yearwood, "Recruitment and Retention Issues in North Carolina," *American Jails* (September/October, 2003), pp. 9–14.

49 Moreover, one agency discovered that reduced hiring standards did not even attract an increased number of applicants. See Ray Bynum, "Corrections as a Profession: Parity Issues in Corrections," *American Jails*, Vol. 20, No. 3 (2006), pp. 81–86.

50 Jeanne B. Stinchcomb, "Making the Grade: Professionalizing the 21st Century Workforce through Higher Education Partnerships," *Corrections Today*, Vol. 66, No. 5 (August, 2004), pp. 90–98.

51 Jeanne B. Stinchcomb, Susan W. McCampbell, and Elizabeth P. Layman, *FutureForce: A Guide to Building the 21st Century Community Corrections Workforce* (Washington, DC: U.S. Department of Justice, National Institute of Corrections, 2006).

52 Yearwood, "Recruitment and Retention Issues," p. 14.

53 American Correctional Association, *Vital Statistics in Corrections* (Alexandria, VA: American Correctional Association, 2000), p. 161.

54 American Correctional Association, *Performance-based Standards for Adult Local Detention Facilities* (Alexandria, VA: American Correctional Association, 2004), p. 115.

55 "Survey Summary: Correctional Budgets," *Corrections Compendium*, Vol. 25, No. 12 (December, 2000), p. 8.

56 June Damanti and Jeanne B. Stinchcomb, "Moving toward Professionalism: The Preservice

Approach to Entry-level Training," *Journal of Correctional Training* (Summer, 1990), pp. 9–10. See also Jeanne B. Stinchcomb, "Jails and Academe: A Partnership Made on Wall Street," *American Jails* (May/June, 1999), pp. 85–86.

57 Robert B. Levinson, Jeanne B. Stinchcomb, and John J. Greene, "Corrections Certification: First Steps toward Professionalism," *Corrections Today*, Vol. 63, No. 5 (August, 2001), pp. 125–138.

58 Jeanne B. Stinchcomb, "Correctional Certification: Getting down from the Bandwagon and Leading the Band," *Corrections Now* (February, 2004), p. 4.

59 Stinchcomb, McCampbell, and Leip, *The Future Is Now*, p. 71.

60 Stan Stojkovic, David Kalinich, and John Klofas, *Criminal Justice Organizations: Administration and Management* (Belmont, CA: Wadsworth, 2003), p. 7.

61 See Jeanne B. Stinchcomb and Susan W. McCampbell, "A Leader's Most Lasting Legacy," *American Jails*, Vol. XXIV, No. 2 (May/June, 2010), pp. 9–12.

62 John P. Kotter, *What Leaders Really Do* (Boston, MA: Harvard Business Review, 1999), p. 51 (referring to U.S. corporations).

63 Jeanne B. Stinchcomb and Susan W. McCampbell, "From Organizational Management to Inspirational Leadership: Changing Roles and Training Implications for Newly Elected Sheriffs," *Sheriff* (January–February, 2004), pp. 18–21, 42–44.

64 Susan C. Craig, "Management within a Correctional Institution," in Roslyn Muraskin, ed., *Key Correctional Issues* (Upper Saddle River, NJ: Prentice Hall, 2010), p. 67.

65 James B. Jacobs, "Prison Reform and the Ruins of Prisoners' Rights," in Michael Tonry, ed., *The Future of Imprisonment* (New York: Oxford University Press, 2004), p. 180. See also Randy Corcoran, "Changing Prison Culture," *Corrections Today* (April, 2005), pp. 24–25.

66 Stinchcomb, "Police Stress."

14 Legal Issues and Liability

1 *Farmer v. Brennan*, 511 U.S. 825, 114 S. Ct. 1970 (1994).

2 Terms used to describe these three phases of correctional law development are from William G. Archambeault and Betty J. Archambeault, *Correctional Supervisory Management: Principles of Organization, Policy, and Law* (Englewood Cliffs, NJ: Prentice Hall, 1982), p. 195; see also Kate King, "Prisoners' Constitutional Rights," in Roslyn Muraskin, ed., *Key Correctional Issues* (Upper Saddle River, NJ: Prentice Hall, 2005), pp. 151–152.

3 *Ruffin v. Virginia*, 62 Va. 790 (1871). However, it has also been argued that "the Ruffin case itself does not particularly support the restrictive view attributed to it" and that other cases decided in the same time period "do not indicate that the judiciary had no interest in the welfare of prisoners." See Donald H. Wallace, "Ruffin v. Virginia and Slaves of the State: A Nonexistent Baseline of Prisoners' Rights Jurisprudence," *Journal of Criminal Justice*, Vol. 20, No. 4 (1992), pp. 334, 340.

4 See William C. Collins, *Correctional Law for the Correctional Officer* (Alexandria, VA: American Correctional Association, 2004), pp. 7–15.

5 Chadwick L. Shook and Robert T. Sigler, *Constitutional Issues in Correctional Administration* (Durham, NC: Carolina Academic Press, 2000), p. 40, citing *Turner v. Safley*, 482 U.S. 78 (1987).

6 *Rhodes v. Chapman*, 452 U.S. 337 (1981), p. 349.

7 For an analysis of recent inmate-related decisions, see Christopher E. Smith, "Prisoners' Rights and the Rehnquist Court Era," in Richard Tewksbury and Dean Dabney, eds., *Prisons and Jails: A Reader* (New York: McGraw-Hill, 2009), pp. 41–57.

8 Linda Greenhouse, "High Court Makes It Harder for Prisoners to Sue," *New York Times* (June 20, 1995), p. A11.

9 W. Wesley Johnson, Katherine Bennett, and Timothy J. Flanagan, "Getting Tough on Prisoners: Results from the National Corrections Executive Survey, 1995," *Crime and Delinquency*, Vol. 43, No. 1 (January, 1997), p. 26.

10 However, it is noteworthy that in one case the Supreme Court held that what an official "should have known" cannot be used to prove "deliberate indifference." See William C. Collins and John Hagar, "Jails and the Courts . . . Issues for Today, Issues for Tomorrow," *American Jails* (May/June, 1995), p. 22, citing *Farmer v. Brennan*, 114 S. Ct. 1970 (1994).

11 Darrell L. Ross, "A 20-year Analysis of Section 1983 Litigation in Corrections," *American Jails* (May/June, 1995), p. 14.

12 Alvin W. Cohn, "Reducing Opportunities for Litigation," *American Jails* (May/June, 1998), p. 36.

13 Collins, *Correctional Law for the Correctional Officer*, p. 71.

14 Barbara B. Knight and Stephen T. Early, Jr., *Prisoners' Rights in America* (Chicago, IL: Nelson-Hall, 1986), pp. 188–189.

15 Collins, *Correctional Law for the Correctional Officer*, p. 70.

16 Knight and Early, *Prisoners' Rights in America*, p. 188.

17 Collins, *Correctional Law for the Correctional Officer*, p. 72.

18 "Handling Problems in the Face of Ambiguous RFRA," *The Corrections Professional*, Vol. 1, No. 1 (August 25, 1995), p. 8.

19 King, "Prisoners' Constitutional Rights," p. 155.

20 Ibid., citing *Banks v. Havener*, 234 F. Supp. 27 (E.D. Va. 1964).

21 Knight and Early, *Prisoners' Rights in America*, p. 207, citing *Gallahan v. Hollyfield*, 670 F.2d 1345 (4th Cir. 1982).

22 Daniel Pollack, "Legal Briefs," *Corrections Today*, Vol. 54, No. 8 (December, 1992), p. 156, citing *Scott v. Mississippi Department of Corrections*, 961 F.2d 77 (5th Cir. 1992).

23 *Mayweathers v. Terhune*, 328 F.Supp.2d 1086 (E.D.Cal. 2004).

24 John W. Palmer, *Constitutional Rights of Prisoners* (New Providence, NJ: Matthew Bender, 2010), pp. 124–125.

25 "Faith-based Programming—Table 3: Accommodations," *Corrections Compendium*, Vol. 28, No. 8 (August, 2003), pp. 16–18.

26 "Court's Invalidation of RFRA Should Ease, but Not Remove, Burden on Correctional Facilities," *Corrections Alert*, Vol. 4, No. 8 (July 28, 1997), pp. 1–5.

27 See *Cutter v. Wilkinson*, 544 U.S. 709 (2005). For additional information, see Christopher Mitchell and Joan Kennedy, "How RLUIPA Affects Your Agency," *Corrections Today*, Vol. 71, No. 6 (December, 2009), pp. 96–97.

28 Collins, *Correctional Law for the Correctional Officer*, p. 77, citing *Procunier v. Martinez*, 94 S. Ct. 1800 (1974).

29 *Brandenburg v. Ohio*, 395 U.S. 444, 48 Ohio Op.2d 320 (1969).

30 Palmer, *Constitutional Rights of Prisoners*, p. 87.

31 John McLaren, "Prisoners' Rights: The Pendulum Swings," in Joycelyn M. Pollock, ed., *Prisons: Today and Tomorrow* (Sudbury, MA: Jones & Bartlett, 2006), p. 357.

32 Collins, *Correctional Law for the Correctional Officer*, p. 92.

33 Daniel Pollack, "Legal Briefs," *Corrections Today*, Vol. 54, No. 2 (April, 1992), p. 28.

34 Ibid., p. 76, citing *Blackburn v. Snow*, 771 F.2d 556 (1st Cir. 1985). See also *Spear v. Sowders*, 33 F.3d 576 (6th Cir., 1994).

35 Camille Graham Camp, ed., *The 2002 Corrections Yearbook: Adult Corrections* (Middletown, CT: Criminal Justice Institute, 2003), p. 175.

36 "Drug Testing: Survey Summary," *Corrections Compendium*, Vol. 25, No. 9 (September, 2000), p. 12.

37 *Allen v. City of Marietta*, 601 F. Supp. 482 (N.D. Ga. 1985).

38 "NY Judge Bans Drug Tests for Corrections Officers," *Corrections Digest* (July 13, 1988), p. 2.

39 "NY Appeals Court Upholds Drug Testing for Jail Officers," *Corrections Digest* (November 15, 1988), p. 9.

40 Randall Guynes and Osa Coffey, "Employee Drug-testing Policies in Prison Systems," *National Institute of Justice: Research in Action* (Washington, DC: U.S. Department of Justice, 1988), p. 6.

41 J. Devereux Weeks, "Jail Employee Drug Testing under Fourth Amendment Limitations," *American Jails*, Vol. 4, No. 3 (September/October, 1990), p. 30.

42 *Rhodes v. Chapman*, 452 U.S. 337 (1981).

43 Allen F. Breed, "Corrections: A Victim of Situational Ethics," *Crime and Delinquency*, Vol. 44, No. 1 (January, 1998), p. 14., citing respectively *Williams v. Delo*, 49 F. 3d. 442 (8th Cir., 1995) and Summers v. Sheahan, 883 F. Supp. 1163 (N.D., Ill., 1995).

44 Collins, *Correctional Law for the Correctional Officer*, p. 106.

45 Palmer, *Constitutional Rights of Prisoners*, p. 34.

46 *Hudson v. McMillian*, 112 S. Ct. 995 (1992).

47 Paraphrased from Collins, *Correctional Law for the Correctional Officer*, pp. 144–145.

48 Daniel Pollack, "Legal Briefs," *Corrections Today*, Vol. 53, No. 4 (July, 1991), p. 27, citing *Hutto v. Finney*, 437 U.S. 678 (1978).

49 *Bell v. Wolfish*, 441 U.S. 520, 542 (1979).

50 *Rhodes v. Chapman*, 452 U.S. 337, 348 (1981).

51 *Wilson v. Seiter*, 502 U.S. 294 (1991).

52 Ibid.

53 See, for example, Rick M. Steinmann, "Are Inmate Lawsuits Out of Control?," in Charles B. Fields, ed., *Controversial Issues in Corrections* (Needham Heights, MA: Allyn & Bacon, 1999), pp. 239–246.

54 "New Law Curbs Lawsuits," *Corrections Digest*, Vol. 27, No. 22 (May 31, 1996), pp. 1–2. For an analysis of the Prison Litigation Reform Act, see James B. Jacobs, "Prison Reform and the Ruins of Prisoners' Rights," in Michael Tonry, ed., *The Future of Imprisonment* (New York: Oxford University Press, 2004), pp. 179–196.

55 Jeffery R. Maahs and Craig Hemmens, "The Prison Litigation Reform Act and Frivolous Section 1983 Suits," *Corrections Management Quarterly*, Vol. 2, No. 3 (Summer, 1998), p. 93.

56 Shook and Sigler, *Constitutional Issues in Correctional Administration*, p. 51.

57 Robert B. Greifinger, Joseph Bick, and Joe Goldenson, *Public Health behind Bars: From Prisons to Communities* (New York: Springer, 2007), p. 32.

58 "Inmate Claims Burdening Courts, but Rate per Prisoner Is Down," *Criminal Justice Newsletter*, Vol. 28, No. 19 (October 1, 1997), p. 2.

59 "Texas Prisoners Penalized for Frivolous Lawsuits," *Corrections Digest* (November 8, 1996), p. 6.

60 John Scalia, "Prisoner Petitions Filed in U.S. District Courts, 2000," *Bureau of Justice Statistics Special Report* (Washington, DC: U.S. Department of Justice, 2002), p. 1.

61 "The Prison Litigation Reform Act: Survey Summary," *Corrections Compendium*, Vol. 25, No. 7 (July, 2000), pp. 7–15. A follow-up study in 2003 likewise found a 69 percent decrease. See "Inmate Lawsuits and Grievances: Survey Summary," *Corrections Compendium*, Vol. 28, No. 6 (June, 2003), p. 8.

62 James B. Jacobs, "Prison Reform amid the Ruins of Prisoners' Rights," in Tonry, ed., *The Future of Imprisonment*, p. 185.

63 Shook and Sigler, *Constitutional Issues in Correctional Administration*, p. 42.

64 Collins and Hagar, "Jails and the Courts," p. 19.

65 Ken Kerle, "Editorial: *Jones v. Wittenburg*," *American Jails* (May–June, 1995), p. 5.

66 James R. Eisenberg, *Law, Psychology, and Death Penalty Litigation* (Sarasota, FL: Professional Resources Press, 2004), p. 7.

67 L. Kay Gillespie, *Inside the Death Chamber: Exploring Executions* (Boston, MA: Pearson Education, 2003), p. 111.

68 *The Handbook Guide to Murder* (London: Handbook Publishing, 1998), p. 17.

69 Gillespie, *Inside the Death Chamber*, p. 112.

70 Tracy L. Snell, "Capital Punishment, 2009: Statistical Tables," *Bureau of Justice Statistics: Statistical Tables* (Washington, DC: U.S. Department of Justice, December, 2010), p. 1 and Table 5.

71 Ibid., Table 4.

72 Ibid., Table 5.

73 Michael J. Sniffen, "No Reversal of Fortune for Blacks on Death Row," in John J. Sullivan and Joseph L. Victor, eds., *Criminal Justice 92/93*, Sixteenth Edition (Guilford, CT: Dushkin Publishing Group, 1992), p. 227.

74 Paige H. Ralph, Jonathan R. Sorensen, and James W. Marquart, "A Comparison of Death-sentenced and Incarcerated Murderers in Pre-Furman Texas," *Justice Quarterly*, Vol. 9, No. 2 (June, 1992), pp. 185–209, whose study concludes that it was not the defendant's race but the victim's race that was the primary extralegal variable affecting sentencing decisions. Likewise, David C. Baldus, C.A. Pulaski, Jr., and George Woodworth, "Comparative Review of Death Sentences: An Empirical Study of the Georgia Experience, *Journal of Criminal Law and Criminology*, Vol. 74 (1983), pp. 661–753, found that a person accused of killing a white victim was 4.3 times more likely to be sentenced to death than a person accused of killing a black victim, and Amnesty International, *United States of America: Death by Discrimination—The Continuing Role of Race in Capital Cases* (2003), available at http://web.amnesty.org/library/index/engamr510462003, notes that, although the victims of murder are nearly evenly split between black and white, 80 percent of those executed since reinstatement of the death penalty have murdered a white victim.

75 See *Atkins v. Virginia*, 536 U.S. 304 (2002), and *Roper v. Simmons*, 543 U.S. 551 (2005).

76 Snell, "Capital Punishment, 2009: Statistical Tables," Table 12. However, the three offenders executed in Alabama in 2007 had spent an average of 23 years on death row. Lia Gormsen, "Death Row Wait Doubles," *Corrections Compendium*, Vol. 33, No. 5 (September/October, 2008), p. 35.

77 Robert Johnson, *Death Work: A Study of the Modern Execution Process* (Pacific Grove, CA: Brooks/Cole Publishing Company, 1990), p. 35.

78 See, for example, "Death Penalty Appeals Centers Winding Down as Federal Funding Ends Nationwide," *Corrections Digest* (February 23, 1996), p. 8.

79 Snell, "Capital Punishment, 2009: Statistical Tables," p. 2.

80 Phoebe C. Ellsworth and Samuel L. Gross, "Hardening of the Attitudes: Americans' Views on the Death Penalty," *Journal of Social Issues*, Vol. 1 (1994), pp. 19–52.

81 For a more complete discussion of both sides of this issue, see Ernest van den Haag and John P. Conrad, *The Death Penalty: A Debate* (New York: Plenum Press, 1983), along with Alan S. Bruce and Theresa A. Severance, "The Death Penalty," in Muraskin, ed., *Key Correctional Issues*, pp. 322–324.

82 Iain Murray, "Studies Show that the Death Penalty Deters Crime," in Diane Andrews Henningfeld, ed., *The Death Penalty: Opposing Views* (Farmington Hills, MI: Greenhaven Press, 2006), pp. 93–98.

83 David Hoekema, "Capital Punishment: The Question of Justification," in John B. Williamson, Linda Evans, and Anne Munley, eds., *Social Problems: The Contemporary Debates* (Boston, MA: Little, Brown, 1981), p. 318.

84 Rudolph J. Gerber and John M. Johnson, *The Top Ten Death Penalty Myths: The Politics of Crime Control* (Westport, CT: Praeger, 2007), p. 65.

85 Ibid., p. 80.

86 Wesley Lowe, "Capital Punishment Protects Public Safety More Effectively than Does Life Imprisonment," in Roman Espejo, ed., *Does Capital Punishment Deter Crime?* (Farmington Hills, MI: Greenhaven Press, 2003), pp. 47–52.

87 Gennaro F. Vito and Deborah G. Wilson, "Back from the Dead: Tracking the Progress of Kentucky's Furman-commuted Death Row Population," *Justice Quarterly*, Vol. 5, No. 1 (1988), pp. 101–111; and Gary W. Potter, "Capital Punishment Is an Ineffective Crime Control Policy," in Espejo, ed., *Does Capital Punishment Deter Crime?*, pp. 53–62.

88 Bob Goodlatte, "Executions Deliver Reasonable Retribution," in Henningfeld, ed., *The Death Penalty*, pp. 51–54.

89 Kenneth R. Overberg, "The Death Penalty Is Not Consistent with Religious Ethics," in Henningfeld, ed., *The Death Penalty*, pp. 71–79. See also "The Myth of Retribution," Chapter 7 in Gerber and Johnson, *The Top Ten Death Penalty Myths*, pp. 139–164; and Carl M. Cannon, "The Possibility of

Wrongful Executions Justifies Abolishing the Death Penalty," in Mary E. Williams, ed., *Is the Death Penalty Fair?* (Farmington Hills, MI: Greenhaven Press, 2003), pp. 41–51. Although it is difficult to document the extent of racism in capital punishment, research indicates that those who murder whites are more likely to receive the death penalty than the killers of blacks. Among the many studies in this area, see, for instance, U.S. General Accounting Office, *Death Penalty Sentencing: Research Indicates Pattern of Racial Disparities* (Gaithersburg, MD: U.S. General Accounting Office, 1990), along with the arguments of Jeffery L. Johnson and Colleen F. Johnson, "The Death Penalty Is Unfair to Minorities and the Poor," in Williams, ed., *Is the Death Penalty Fair?*, pp. 7–13.

90 For example, a 2003 Gallup poll found 11 percent of respondents citing monetary savings as a primary reason for supporting the death penalty (although this was down from 20 percent in 2001). See Goodlatte, "Executions Deliver Reasonable Retribution," p. 53.

91 Gerber and Johnson, *The Top Ten Death Penalty Myths*, p. 165.

92 Lia Gormsen, "Death Row Wait Doubles," *Corrections Compendium*, Vol. 33, No. 5 (September/October, 2008), p. 35.

93 David Hoekema, "Capital Punishment: The Question of Justification," in John B. Williamson, Linda Evans, and Anne Munley, eds., *Social Problems: The Contemporary Debates*, Third Edition (Boston, MA: Little, Brown, 1981), p. 318.

94 Rudolph J. Gerber and John M. Johnson, *The Top Ten Death Penalty Myths: The Politics of Crime Control* (Westport, CT: Praeger, 2007), p. 65.

95 Paul W. Keve, "The Costliest Punishment—A Corrections Administrator Contemplates the Death Penalty," *Federal Probation*, Vol. 56, No. 1 (March, 1992), p. 13.

96 *Furman v. Georgia*, 408 U.S. 238 (1972).

97 *Gregg v. Georgia*, 428 U.S. 153 (1976).

98 Robert M. Bohm, "The Future of Capital Punishment in the U.S.," *ACJS Today* (November/December, 2000), p. 1.

99 "Debating the Cost of Capital Punishment," *Parade* (January 31, 2010), p. 6.

100 Ibid., p. 5.

101 Gary Hill, "Capital Punishment—A World Update," *Corrections Compendium*, Vol. 26, No. 7 (July, 2001), p. 16.

15 Current Trends and Future Issues

1 Alfred Blumstein, "Restoring Rationality in Punishment Policy," in Michael Tonry, ed., *The Future of Imprisonment* (New York: Oxford University Press, 2004), p. 62.

2 Charles H. Logan, "Criminal Justice Performance Measures for Prisons," in Timothy J. Flanagan, James W. Marquart, and Kenneth G. Adams, *Incarcerating Criminals: Prisons and Jails in Social and Organizational Context* (New York: Oxford University Press, 1998), pp. 260–268.

3 Camille Graham Camp, ed., *The 2002 Corrections Yearbook: Adult Corrections* (Middletown, CT: Criminal Justice Institute, 2003), p. 90.

4 American Correctional Association, *Directory of Adult and Juvenile Correctional Departments, Institutions, Agencies, and Probation and Parole Authorities* (Lanham, MD: American Correctional Association, 1990), p. 596.

5 M. Wayne Huggins and Charles J. Kehoe, "Accreditation Benefits Nation's Jails, Juvenile Detention Centers," *Corrections Today*, Vol. 54, No. 3 (May, 1992), p. 42.

6 Rod Miller, "Standards and the Courts: An Evolving Relationship," *Corrections Today*, Vol. 54, No. 3 (May, 1992), p. 60.

7 Because the accreditation process can become quite expensive, in an era when the resources to pay for it are increasingly limited, some jurisdictions have adopted state standards in an effort to demonstrate accountability without the requisite resources to achieve accreditation on a national level.

8 John J. Gibbons and Nicholas de B. Katzenbach, *Confronting Confinement: A Report of the Commission on Safety and Abuse in America's Prisons* (New York: Vera Institute of Justice, June, 2006), p. 89.

9 Kenneth McGinnis, "Impact of 'Get Tough' Policies on Community Corrections," *Corrections Management Quarterly*, Vol. 2, No. 3 (Summer, 1998), pp. 70–78.

10 For a discussion of historical developments in this regard, see Anne Larason Schneider, "Public–Private Partnerships in the U.S. Prison System," in Richard Tewksbury and Dean Dabney, *Prisons and Jails: A Reader* (New York: McGraw-Hill, 2009), pp. 583–598.

11 However, the measure was defeated in 1998. James Turpin and Donna Lyons, "Criminal Justice Legislation," *Corrections Compendium*, Vol. 24, No. 2 (February, 1999), p. 3.

12 Prison Reform Trust, "Top Two's Revenues Grow," *Prison Privatisation Report International* (London: Prison Reform Trust, November, 1996), p. 3.

13 James McNair, "Wackenhut Corrections: Prisons, Profits, and Problems," *The Miami Herald* (April 16, 2000), p. E-1.

14 "Private Prisons Feel the Financial Crunch," *American Police Beat* (May, 2001), p. 53.

15 By 2004, however, their performance had rebounded somewhat, as reflected in stock prices that were once again on the rise. For example, Corrections Corporation of America was trading for $39.13 on July 13, 2004, and Wackenhut Corrections was bought out at $33 a share in May, 2002, by GEO Corporation Group.

16 William C. Collins, *Privately Operated Speculative Prisons and Public Safety: A Discussion of Issues* (Washington, DC: U.S. Department of Justice, n.d.), p. 3.

17 "Web Site Connects Jail-bed Renters with Sellers," *Correctional News* (July/August, 2004), p. 45.

18 "Private Prisons Feel the Financial Crunch," p. 53.

19 Eric Schlosser, "The Prison-industrial Complex," *Atlantic Monthly* (December, 1998), p. 57.

20 Ed Marciniak, "Standing Room Only: What to Do about Prison Overcrowding," *Commonweal* (September 30, 2009), quoting Illinois Governor George Ryan.

21 Ibid., p. 54.

22 Judith Greene, "Banking on the Prison Boom," in Tara Herivel and Paul Wright, *Prison Profiteers: Who Makes Money from Mass Incarceration* (New York: New Press, 2007), p. 26.

23 Schlosser, "The Prison-industrial Complex," p. 60; see also "CCA Wants More People in Prison," *Correctional News* (March/April, 2001), p. 8.

24 Greene, "Banking on the Prison Boom," p. 127, quoting Bill Deener of the *Dallas Morning News*.

25 T. Don Hutto, "Corrections Partnership: The Public and Private Sectors Work Together," *Corrections Today*, Vol. 50, No. 6 (October, 1988), p. 20.

26 Michael A. Kroll, "Prisons Cannot Rehabilitate," in Bonnie Szumski, ed., *America's Prisons*, Fourth Edition (St. Paul, MN: Greenhaven Press, 1985), p. 26.

27 James D. Henderson, "Private Sector Management: Promoting Efficiency and Cost-effectiveness," *Corrections Today*, Vol. 50, No. 6 (October, 1988), p. 100.

28 For a thorough examination of both sides of this issue, see Kenneth A. Ray and Kathy O'Meara-Wyman, "Privatizing and Regionalizing Local Corrections: Some Issues for Local Jurisdictions to Consider," *Corrections Today* (October, 2000), pp. 116–120.

29 Allen L. Patrick, "Private Sector: Profit Motive vs. Quality," *Corrections Today*, Vol. 48, No. 2 (April, 1986), p. 68.

30 Hutto, "Corrections Partnership," p. 22.

31 Patrick, "Private Sector," p. 74.

32 James Turpin, "1997 Supreme Court Decisions," *Corrections Today*, Vol. 59, No. 6 (October, 1997), p. 19.

33 Chadwick L. Shook and Robert T. Sigler, *Constitutional Issues in Correctional Administration* (Durham, NC: Carolina Academic Press, 2000), p. 102, citing *Richardson v. McKnight*, 521 U.S. 399 (1997).

34 Stanley E. Adelman, "Supreme Court Rules on Potential Liabilities of Private Corrections," *Corrections Today* (July, 2002), p. 28. See also Alexander M. Holsinger and Tom "Tad" Hughes,

"*Correctional Services Corporation v. Malesko*: Boss, 'They Can't Hurt You Now,'" *Criminal Justice Policy Review*, Vol. 14, No. 4 (December, 2003), pp. 451–463.

35 "Private Jail Controversy in Washington State Causes Problems," *Correctional News* (March/April, 2001), p. 1.

36 Michael J. Mahoney, "Prisons for Profit: Should Corrections Make a Buck?," *Corrections Today*, Vol. 50, No. 6 (October, 1988), p. 107.

37 Ibid.

38 Charles W. Thomas and Charles H. Logan, "The Development, Present Status, and Future Potential of Correctional Privatization in America," in Gary W. Bowman, Simon Hakim, and Paul Seidenstat, eds., *Privatizing Correctional Institutions* (New Brunswick, NJ: Transaction Publishers, 1993), p. 223.

39 Ibid.

40 Samuel F. Saxton, "Contracting for Services: Different Facilities, Different Needs," *Corrections Today*, Vol. 50, No. 6 (October, 1988), p. 17. See also B.E. Price, *Merchandizing Prisoners: Who Really Pays for Prison Privatization?* (Westport, CT: Praeger, 2006).

41 Charles H. Logan and Bill W. McGriff, *Comparing Costs of Public and Private Prisons: A Case Study* (Washington, DC: U.S. Department of Justice, 1989), p. 7. See also Robert W. Poole, Jr., "Privately Operated Prisons Are Economical," in Szumski, *America's Prisons*, pp. 123–126.

42 Thomas and Logan, "The Development, Present Status, and Future Potential of Correctional Privatization in America," p. 231. See also Geoffrey F. Segal and Adrian T. Moore of the Reason Foundation, *Weighing the Watchmen: Evaluating the Costs and Benefits of Outsourcing Correctional Services* (January, 2002), available at http://www.reason.org/ps289.pdf.

43 Paul Kepos, ed., *Crime, Prisons, and Jails* (Farmington Hills, MI: The Gale Group, 2008), p. 96.

44 U.S. General Accounting Office, *Private and Public Prisons: Studies Comparing Operational Costs and/ or Quality of Service* (Washington, DC: U.S. General Accounting Office, 1996), p. 13.

45 Dale K. Sechrest and David Shichor, "Private Jails: Locking Down the Issues," *American Jails* (March/ April, 1997), p. 12.

46 Ibid., p. 14.

47 "TDCJ Board Chairman Says He's Fed Up with Private Prisons after Escapes, Riots," *Corrections Digest*, Vol. 27, No. 36 (September 6, 1996), p. 1. See also "Laws Lag Behind Booming Private Prison Industry," *Corrections Digest*, Vol. 27, No. 46 (November 15, 1996), pp. 1–2.

48 See, for example, Scott Camp and Gerald Gaes, *Private Prisons in the U.S., 1999: An Assessment of Growth, Performance, Custody Standards, and Training Requirements* (Washington, DC: U.S. Bureau of Prisons, 2000).

49 James B. Jacobs, "Prison Reform amid the Ruins of Prisoners' Rights," in Tonry, ed., *The Future of Imprisonment*, p. 190.

50 Joseph A. Califano, Jr., "Forward," in National Center on Addiction and Substance Abuse, *Behind Bars II: Substance Abuse and America's Prison Population* (New York: National Center on Addiction and Substance Abuse, Columbia University, February, 2010), p. i, available at http://www.casacolumbia.org/articlefiles/575-report2010behindbars2.pdf.

51 Kevin R. Reitz, "Questioning the Conventional Wisdom of Parole Release Authority," in Tonry, ed., *The Future of Imprisonment*, p. 219.

52 Donald Braman, "Families and Incarceration," in Marc Mauer and Meda Chesney-Lind, eds., *Invisible Punishment: The Collateral Consequences of Mass Imprisonment* (New York: New Press, 2002), p. 156.

53 Office of National Drug Control Policy, *The Economic Costs of Drug Abuse in the U.S.* (Washington, DC: U.S. Department of Justice, Office of National Drug Control Policy, 2001).

54 National Center on Addiction and Substance Abuse, *Behind Bars II*, p. ii.

55 Supreme Court Associate Justice Anthony M. Kennedy, August 9, 2003, cited in Jeremy Travis, *But They All Come Back: Facing the Challenges of Prisoner Reentry* (Washington, DC: The Urban Institute, 2005), p. 3.

56 Ibid., p. 6, citing research by the National Institute on Drug Abuse.

57 Jennifer Gonnerman, "Million-dollar Blocks: The Neighborhood Costs of America's Prison Boom," in Tara Herivel and Paul Wright, *Prison Profiteers: Who Makes Money from Mass Incarceration* (New York: New Press, 2007), p. 34. For additional discussion of race and class disparities reflected in the nation's prisons, see Glenn C. Loury, *Race, Incarceration, and American Values* (Cambridge, MA: MIT Press, 2008).

58 Gonnerman, "Million-dollar Blocks," pp. 27–35.

59 James Austin, Marino Bruce, Leo Carroll, Patricia L. McCall, and Stephen C. Richards, "The Use of Incarceration in the United States," *Critical Criminology: An International Journal*, Vol. 10, No. 1 (2001), p. 20.

60 Vincent Schiraldi and Jason Zeidenberg, *Cellblocks or Classrooms? The Funding of Higher Education and Its Impact on African American Men* (Washington, DC: Justice Policy Institute, 2002), p. 4.

61 Gonnerman, "Million-dollar Blocks," pp. 33–34. Under a program called Justice Reinvestment, other states (such as Kansas, Vermont, and Texas) have also implemented early release initiatives, redirecting some of the money saved to high-risk neighborhoods from which many inmates come; see David Cole, "Can Our Shameful Prisons Be Reformed?," *The New York Review of Books*, Vol. 56, No. 18 (November 19, 2009).

62 A.T. Wall, "Rhode Island Halts Growth in the Inmate Population while Increasing Public Safety," *Corrections Today*, Vol. 72, No. 1 (February, 2010), pp. 40–44.

63 Gwyn Smith-Ingley, "The Introduction of the Justice Reinvestment Bill," *American Jails*, Vol. XXIV, No. 1 (March/April, 2010), p. 7.

64 Christine S. Scott-Hayward, *The Fiscal Crisis in Corrections: Rethinking Policies and Practices* (New York: Vera Institute of Justice, July, 2009), p. 3.

65 Joan Petersilia, *When Prisoners Come Home: Parole and Prisoner Reentry* (New York: Oxford University Press, 2003), p. 243.

66 Joey R. Weedon, "The Foundation of Re-entry," *Corrections Today* (April, 2004), p. 6.

67 Robert Gangi, Jr., cited in "The Crime of Black Imprisonment," *Los Angeles Times* (April 22, 1990).

68 Craig Reinarman and Harry G. Levine, *Crack in America: Demon Drugs in America* (Berkeley, CA: University of California Press, 1997), p. 334.

69 Andrew D. Leipold, "The War on Drugs and the Puzzle of Deterrence," *Journal of Gender, Race, and Justice* (Spring/Summer, 2002), retrieved from http://web.lexis-nexis, p. 12.

70 Leonard A. Marowitz, *Why Did the Crime Rate Decrease through 1999? (And Why Might It Decrease or Increase in 2000 and Beyond?): A Literature Review and Critical Analysis* (Sacramento: California Department of Justice, 2000). See also Bruce Western, *Punishment and Inequality in America* (New York: Russell Sage Foundation, 2006).

71 Kirby D. Behre and A. Jeff Ifrah, "You Be the Judge: The Success of Fifteen Years of Sentencing under the United States Sentencing Guidelines," *American Criminal Law Review*, Vol. 40, No. 1 (Winter, 2003), p. 6.

72 Matthew B. Robinson, "The Mouse Who Would Rule the World: How American Criminal Justice Reflects the Themes of Disneyization," *Journal of Criminal Justice and Popular Culture*, Vol. 10, No. 1 (2003), p. 70.

73 "New Poll Shows Surprisingly Forgiving Attitude toward Crime and Punishment: Most Americans Don't Want to Throw Away the Key" (July 19, 2001), available at www.aclu.org/features/f071901a.html.

74 Bureau of Justice Statistics, *Sourcebook of Criminal Justice Statistics* (2005), available at www.albany.edu/sourcebook, reflecting a 2003 poll conducted by the Pew Research Center.

75 Ibid.

76 Brandon K. Applegate, Robin King Davis, Charles W. Otto, Ray Surette, and Bernard J. McCarthy, "The Multifunction Jail: Policy Makers' Views of the Goals of Local Incarceration," *Criminal Justice Policy Review*, Vol. 14, No. 2 (June, 2003), p. 155.

77 Hart Research Associates, "Changing Public Attitudes toward the Criminal Justice System" (New York: Soros Foundation, February, 2002), available at http://www.soros.org/initiatives/usprograms/focus/justice/articles_publications/publications/hartpoll_20020201.

78 Francis T. Cullen, Jennifer A. Pealer, Bonnie S. Fisher, Brandon K. Applegate, and Shannon A. Santana, "Public Support for Correctional Rehabilitation in America: Change or Consistency?," in Julian V. Roberts and Mike Hough, eds., *Changing Attitudes to Punishment: Public Opinion, Crime and Justice* (Devon, England: Willan Publishing, 2002), p. 143.

79 Ibid.

80 Brandon Applegate and Robin King Davis, "Examining Public Support for 'Correcting' Offenders," *Corrections Today* (June, 2005), p. 102.

81 Jon Wool and Don Stemen, "Changing Fortunes or Changing Attitudes? Sentencing and Corrections Reforms in 2003," *Federal Sentencing Reporter*, Vol. 16, No. 4 (April, 2004), p. 305.

82 Justin Jones, "Guest Editorial: Driving Our Business," *Corrections Today* (June, 2009), p. 6. See also Christopher A. Innes, "The Simple Solution for Reducing Correctional Costs," *Corrections Today*, Vol. 72, No. 1 (February, 2010), pp. 32–34.

83 Richard P. Seiter, "Managing within Political Comfort Zones: An Interview with Allen Ault," *Corrections Management Quarterly*, Vol. 1, No. 1 (Winter, 1997), p. 74.

84 Mike DeWine, "Public Opinion and Corrections: A Need to Be Proactive," *Corrections Management Quarterly*, Vol. 1, No. 3 (Summer, 1997), p. 6.

85 Christopher A. Innes and Sherry Carroll, "Researchers Discuss Budgets and Best Practices at Annual Meeting," *Corrections Today* (June, 2009), p. 87. See also Roberto Hugh Potter and Ron D. McCuan, "One More Component for Moving Evidence-based Research into Practice," *Corrections Today* (October, 2009), p. 118, and Donald P. Moynihan, "The Impact of Managing for Results Mandates in Corrections: Lessons from Three States," *Criminal Justice Policy Review*, Vol. 16, No. 1 (March, 2005), pp. 18–37.

86 See, for example, Lorraine R. Reitzel, "Best Practices in Corrections: Using Literature to Guide Intervention," *Corrections Today*, Vol. 67, No. 1 (February, 2005), pp. 42–45, and Doris Layton MacKenzie, "Corrections and Sentencing in the Twenty-first Century: Evidence-based Corrections and Sentencing," in Tewksbury and Dabney, *Prisons and Jails*, pp. 561–571.

87 Doris Layton MacKenzie, "Evidence-based Corrections: Identifying What Works," *Crime and Delinquency*, Vol. 46, No. 4 (October, 2000), p. 463.

88 Edward J. Latessa, "The Challenge of Change: Correctional Programs and Evidence-based Practices," *Criminology and Public Policy*, Vol. 3, No. 4 (November, 2004), p. 552.

89 Steve Aos, Marna Miller, and Elizabeth Drake, *Evidence-based Public Policy Options to Reduce Future Prison Construction, Criminal Justice Costs, and Crime Rates* (Olympia: Washington State Institute for Public Policy, October, 2006), p. 1, available at http://www.wsipp.wa.gov/rptfiles/06-10-1201.pdf. (The state they are referring to is Washington.) Additionally, an analysis of dozens of reviews that included about 1,000 studies concluded that nearly two out of three reduced recidivism, by an average of 10 percent. See Paula Smith, Paul Gendreau, and Claire Goggin, "Correctional Treatment: Accomplishments and Realities," in Patricia Van Voorhis, Michael Braswell, and David Lester, eds., *Correctional Counseling and Rehabilitation* (Cincinnati, OH: Anderson, 2009), p. 316.

90 Merely because a program does not appear on the "what works" list does not necessarily mean that it is ineffective. Nor does absence from the "what does not work" list necessarily indicate the reverse, since the researcher who compiled these lists used relatively high standards of methodological rigor before incorporating studies. Moreover, these results reflect only the specific initiatives listed and do not, for instance, reflect whether they might be more effective when combined with various forms of treatment.

91 Charles B. DeWitt, "Assessing Criminal Justice Needs," *National Institute of Justice: Research in Brief* (Washington, DC: U.S. Department of Justice, 1992), p. 3.

92 Joan Petersilia, "Probation in the United States: Practices and Challenges," *NIJ Journal* (September, 1997), p. 5.

93 Barry J. Nidorf, "Surviving in a 'Lock Them Up' Era," *Federal Probation*, Vol. 60, No. 3 (March, 1996), p. 8.

94 Joan Petersilia, "Prisoner Reentry: Public Safety and Reintegration Challenges," *Prison Journal*, Vol. 81, No. 3 (2001), p. 374.

95 Gordon Bazemore and Mark Umbreit, "Rethinking the Sanctioning Function in Juvenile Court: Retributive or Restorative Responses to Youth Crime," *Crime and Delinquency*, Vol. 41, No. 3 (July, 1995), p. 305. See also Gordon Bazemore and Jeanne B. Stinchcomb, "Promoting Successful Reentry through Service and Restorative Justice: Theory and Practice for a Civic Engagement Model of Community Reintegration," *Federal Probation*, Vol. 68, No. 2 (2004), pp. 14–24.

96 Orville B. Pung, "Let's Abolish 'Probation' and 'Treatment,'" *Overcrowded Times* (April, 1993), p. 3.

97 Vincent Schirldi and Judith Greene, "Public Opinion Shifts as States Re-examine Prison Policies in Face of Tightening Budgets," *On the Line* (May, 2002), p. 1.

98 Blumstein, "Restoring Rationality in Punishment Policy," p. 62.

99 See, for example, "Tough Economy Can Mean New Opportunities," *American Jails*, Vol. XXIII, No. 2 (May/June, 2009), pp. 71–73.

100 "Soaring Probation Caseloads Leave Agents, Experts Fearing a Breakdown," *Crime Control Digest* (March 28, 1997), p. 1, quoting Diego Cruz.

101 "Expert Panel Issues Report on Serious and Violent Juvenile Offenders," *OJJDP Fact Sheet* (Washington, DC: U.S. Department of Justice, 1997), p. 2.

102 Petersilia, "Prisoner Reentry," p. 374.

103 See Anthony C. Thompson, *Releasing Prisoners, Redeeming Communities: Reentry, Race, and Politics* (New York: New York University Press, 2008).

104 See the National Reentry Resource Center website at http://nationalreentryresourcecenter.org/.

105 Jeanne B. Stinchcomb, Susan W. McCampbell, and Elizabeth P. Layman, *FutureForce: A Guide to Building the 21st Century Community Corrections Workforce* (Washington, DC: National Institute of Corrections, 2006), pp. 37–38, 82–83.

106 See ibid. and Jeanne B. Stinchcomb, Susan W. McCampbell, and Leslie Leip, *The Future Is Now: Recruiting, Retaining, and Developing the 21st Century Jail Workforce* (March, 2009), Final report submitted to the U.S. Department of Justice, Bureau of Justice Assistance, Washington, DC, available at http://www.cipp.org/pdf/Developingthe21stCenturyJailWorkforceCopysenttoBJA.pdf.

107 American Correctional Association and Aramark Correctional Services, *Effective Partnership: A Reorientation of Managed Services to Focus on Corrections Outcomes*, White Paper (Alexandria, VA: American Correctional Association and Aramark Correctional Services, 2008), available at http://www.aramark.com/ServicesandIndustries/CaseStudies/CorrectionsOutcomes.aspx.

108 See Jeanne B. Stinchcomb, "Making the Grade: Professionalizing the 21st Century Workforce through Higher Education Partnerships," *Corrections Today* (August, 2004), and Jeanne B. Stinchcomb, "Bridging the Great Divide: Educational Partnerships for Promising Practices in Community Corrections," *Topics in Community Corrections—Annual Issue 2005: Developing Tomorrow's Community Corrections Leadership and Managers* (Washington, DC: National Institute of Corrections, U.S. Department of Justice, 2005), pp. 18–25.

109 Jeanne B. Stinchcomb and Leslie Leip, "When the Applicant Surplus Subsides: Evidence-based Recruitment Strategies to Meet Tomorrow's Workforce Needs," *Sheriff*, Vol. 62, No. 3 (June, 2010).

110 Jeanne B. Stinchcomb, "Correctional Certification: Getting down from the Bandwagon and Leading the Band," *Corrections Now* (February, 2004), p. 4.

111 Jeanne B. Stinchcomb, "Developing Correctional Officer Professionalism: A Work in Progress," *Corrections Compendium*, Vol. 25, No. 5 (May, 2000), pp. 4, 18.

112 "NIJ Survey of Police Chiefs and Sheriffs," *NIJ Update* (Washington, DC: U.S. Department of Justice, 1995), pp. 1–2, and DeWitt, "Assessing Criminal Justice Needs," p. 8.

113 Stinchcomb, "Correctional Certification," p. 4.

Glossary/Index

Note: page numbers ending in *e* refer to exhibits. Page numbers ending in *t* refer to tables.

accreditation: The status achieved by a correctional program or facility when it is recognized as having met certain national standards following an on-site audit by the Commission on Accreditation for Corrections of the American Correctional Association

active, nonevaluative listening: Energetically participating in the listening process without passing judgment in terms of what is being said

adaptive behaviors: Various responses through which inmates adjust to the institutional setting, including such psychological defense mechanisms as rejecting authority, projecting blame, or rationalization

addict: Someone who has a physical and psychological dependence on one or more drug(s), who has built up a physical tolerance that results in taking increasingly larger doses, and who has an overpowering desire to continue taking the drug(s). One can become addicted to illegal as well as legal drugs (such as alcohol)
   see also drug users

adjudication: The stage that would be considered "trial" in the criminal justice system, which in juvenile court refers to a hearing to establish the facts of the case

and respect for authority are developed through a regimen of strenuous physical training and strict discipline   23*e*, 381–382, 483

correctional officer: The position title accepted throughout the field of corrections when referring to uniformed, operational personnel working in custodial institutions (in contrast to the outdated term "guard")   261*e*, 357–358, 396–423